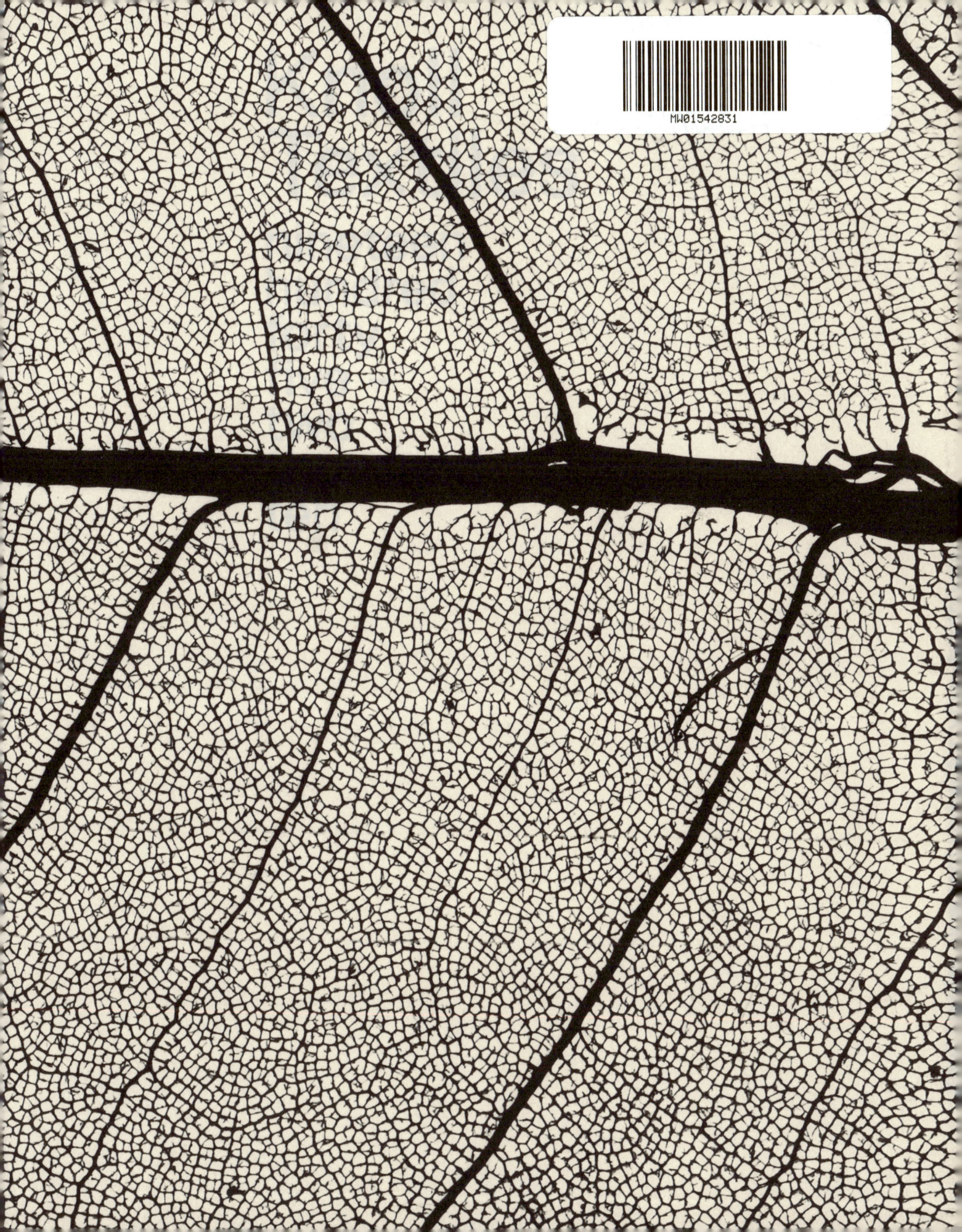

Wolf Bauer. *Delta* ("Gold/Copper" colorway), ca. 1970. Made by Pausa AG for Knoll Textiles. Used for drapery; cotton velvet; screen-printed. KnollTextiles Archive. Cat. 184.

Earl Martin, Editor
Paul Makovsky
Bobbye Tigerman
Angela Völker
Susan Ward

Knoll Textiles

Published for Bard Graduate Center: Decorative Arts, Design History, Material Culture, New York by Yale University Press, New Haven and London

This catalogue is published in conjunction with the exhibition *Knoll Textiles, 1945–2010*, held at the Bard Graduate Center: Decorative Arts, Design History, Material Culture from May 18, 2011 through July 31, 2011.

Project director: Earl Martin
Curatorial team: Paul Makovsky, Earl Martin, Angela Völker, and Susan Ward
Project and research associate:
Ann Marguerite Tartsinis
Project photography coordinator: Alexis Mucha
Catalogue production: Laura Grey, New York, and Sally Salvesen, London
Copy editors: Martina D'Alton with Ron Broadhurst and Barbara Burn
German translator: Abigail Ryan Prohaska

Catalogue design: Irma Boom

Chief Curator and Executive Editor of Exhibition Publications, Bard Graduate Center:
Nina Stritzler-Levine

Library of Congress Cataloging-in-Publication Data
Knoll Textiles, 1945–2010 / Earl Martin, editor.
p. cm.
Issued in connection with an exhibition held May 18, 2011-July 31, 2011, Bard Graduate Center, New York.
Includes bibliographical references and index.
ISBN 978-0-300-17069-6 (alk. paper)
1. KnollTextiles (Firm)--Exhibitions.
2. Textile design--United States--History--20th century--Exhibitions.
3. Textile design--United States--History--21st century--Exhibitions.
I. Martin, Earl (Earl James), 1974-
II. Bard Graduate Center: Decorative Arts, Design History, Material Culture.
TS1425.K59K59 2011
677'.022--dc22
2011004833

Copyright © 2011 Bard Graduate Center: Decorative Arts, Design History, Material Culture. Copyright for individual essays are held by the authors and the Bard Graduate Center: Decorative Arts, Design History, Material Culture. All rights reserved. This book may not be reproduced in whole or in part, in any form (beyond that copying permitted in Sections 107 and 108 of the U.S. Copyright Law and except by reviewers for the public press), without written permission from the publisher.

ISBN 978-0-300-17069-6

Printed and bound in Italy

Cover: Antoinette Lackner Webster (Toni Prestini). *Prestini*, introduced 1948. Made by Louisville Textiles for Knoll Textiles. Used for upholstery; cotton; plain weave. KnollTextiles Archive. Cat. 23.
Endpapers: Herbert Matter (attributed). Leaf, ca. 1951, see fig. 3.34.

Knoll Textiles, 1945–2010 has been generously supported by Knoll, Inc.

Additional funding provided by the National Endowment for the Arts, the New York State Council on the Arts, a state agency, and the Graham Foundation for Advanced Studies in the Fine Arts.

KnollTextiles

Eszter Haraszty. *Knoll Stripes* sample folder, ca. 1951. Made for Knoll Associates, Inc.
Textile samples: cotton; plain weave, screen-printed; mounted on paper.
KnollTextiles Archive. Cat. 43.

Contents

9 **Foreword**
Susan Weber

15 **Introduction**
Earl Martin

25 **Editor's Note**

26 **Chronology**
Compiled by Ann Marguerite Tartsinis

1
36 **The Design, Promotion, and Production of Modern Textiles in the USA, 1940–60**
Susan Ward

2
74 **Knoll Before Knoll Textiles, 1940–46**
Paul Makovsky

3
102 **Making Knoll Textiles: Integrated Fabrics for Modern Interiors, 1945–65**
Susan Ward

4
178 **The Heart and Soul of the Company: The Knoll Planning Unit, 1944–65**
Bobbye Tigerman

5
228 **Knoll without the Knolls: Change and Transformation, 1963–78**
Angela Völker

6
268 **Tradition and Reinvention: Knoll Textiles, 1978–2010**
Angela Völker

306 **Designer Biographies**
Earl Martin and Ann Marguerite Tartsinis, editors

414 **Checklist of the Exhibition**
430 **Bibliography**
432 **Photographic Credits**

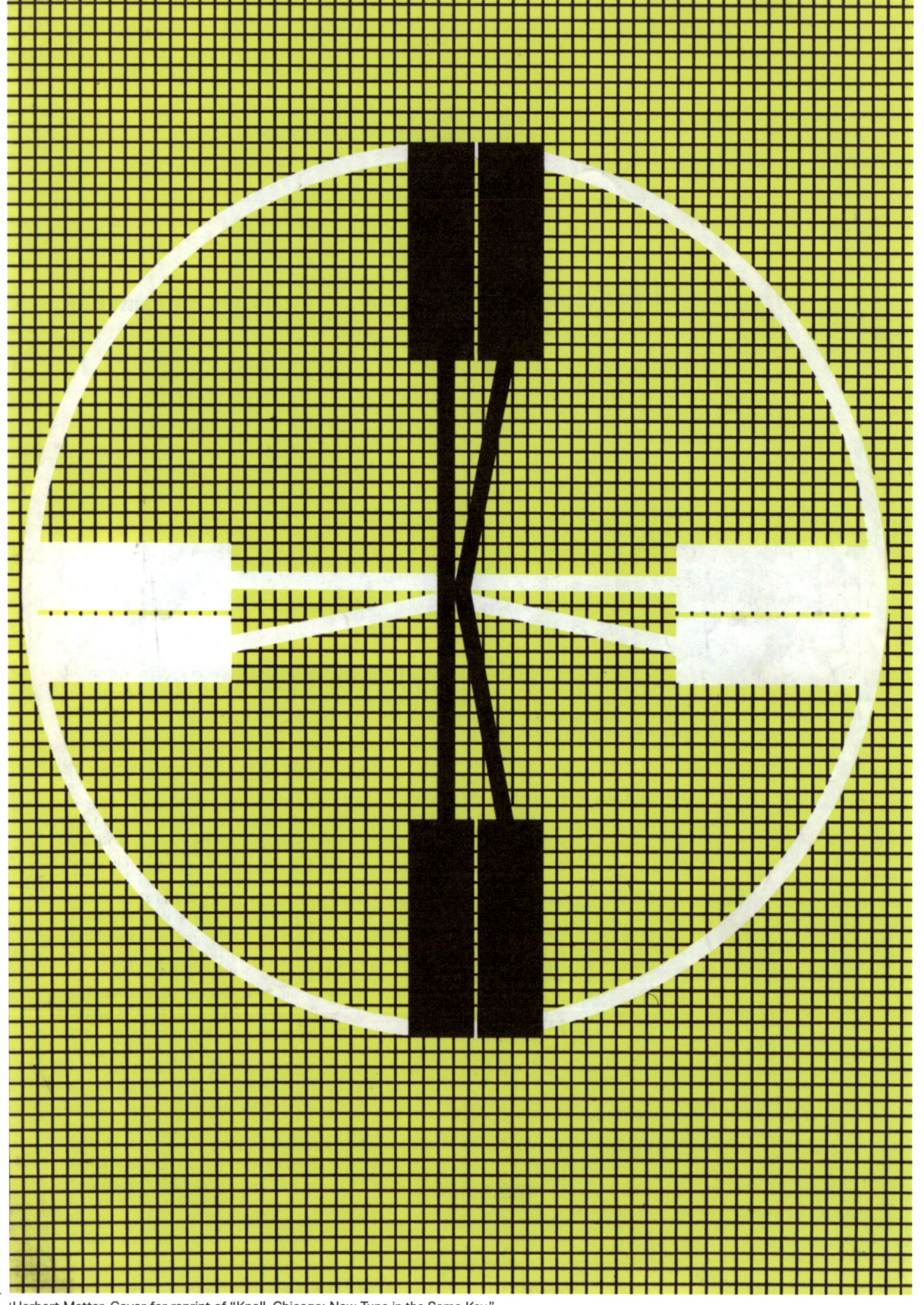

Herbert Matter. Cover for reprint of "Knoll, Chicago: New Tune in the Same Key," *Interiors*, February 1954. Knoll Archives.

Foreword

In 1940 Hans Knoll established a small furniture company in New York City that became one of the best-known design companies in the world, supplying furniture, textiles, and office planning to a wide clientele. Initially the focus on textiles was to provide upholstery for furniture. When Florence Schust began working for Knoll in 1942 (Schust and Knoll married in 1946), she brought a focused artistic vision and penchant for experimentation with new materials. Many innovations followed as Knoll hired more designers and became immersed in creating textiles for modern corporate interiors. By the 1950s Knoll was an industry leader in the textile field. Decades later the forward thinking mentality and commitment to quality that originated with the founders continues. Yet until now Knoll textiles have not been the focus of serious concentrated study.

Among the many challenges historians face when researching individual design companies is the lack of adequate archives. All the traces of the past, assorted materials and documents historians relish, frequently disappear with changes in owners whose priorities tend to be on the present and the future. Knoll, however, is an exception. Archives—at their factory in Pennsylvania and their showroom and headquarters in New York—preserve extensive records of the company's development, including their textile division. These repositories are in regular use by Knoll as a resource, mined for vintage designs that can be reinterpreted for today's market or can provide inspiration for new creations. Thanks to the existence of such rich archives, we are now able to present the first comprehensive examination of a largely overlooked, underestimated aspect of design history.

In 2006, while preparing for another exhibition, *Sheila Hicks Miniatures*, the Bard Graduate Center first became aware of the KnollTextile Archive. Shortly after that exhibition, David Schutte and David Bright, executives at Knoll, approached me about organizing a small archival-based exhibition, which eventually opened at the Park Avenue Armory in October 2008. That project revealed why the role of textiles in the illustrious Knoll product line would be an important area to examine more fully. To organize a larger exhibition the Bard Graduate Center (BGC) assembled a curatorial team under the direction of Earl Martin, associate curator at the BGC. He was joined by Paul Makovsky (editorial director of *Metropolis* and Florence Knoll's biographer), Angela Völker (former head of the textile department at the MAK, Vienna), and Susan Ward (an independent curator and textile historian). I am grateful to each member of the team for sharing their expertise and expanding our knowledge of Knoll textiles. Because many Knoll textiles function primarily as upholstery fabrics, finding vintage examples was a formidable task. I want to thank the curators, especially Earl Martin, for the outstanding work undertaken to uncover this material, often found in obscure locations.

I am grateful to our sponsors: Knoll, Inc., The National Endowment for the Arts, the New York State Council on the Arts, a state agency, the Graham Foundation for Advanced Studies in the Fine Arts, and the Lily Auchincloss Foundation. They recognized the potential for this project to enhance our knowledge of textiles and design history and perhaps to help inspire the next generation of textile designers.

I am especially grateful for the extensive assistance we received from the staff of Knoll including: David Bright, Carol Connell, Dorothy Cosonas, Kathryn Gray Gluibizzi, Colleen James, Linda Kasper, Sheri Kline, Andrea Loukin, David Schutte, Deborah Stoudt, Kevin Thornton, and Celeste Wells. Florence Knoll Bassett was a major source of inspiration for this project. Knoll Textiles would not have happened without her unique vision. A number of former Knoll employees shared their memories and provided valuable information about the company. The history of Knoll Textiles is better known because of information we received from: Kristl Andrus, J. Christoph Bünzli, Robert and Laura Cadwallader, Vincent Cafiero, Allan Denenberg, Mae Festa, Martha Kaihatsu, Candace Key, Merle Lindby-Young, Brian Lutz, Carl Magnusson, Takaaki Matsumoto, Jeffrey Osborne, Al Pfeiffer, Jens Risom, Toby Rodes, Arthur Sager, Annette Schaich, Trudy and Richard Schultz, Doreen Rose Stempien, Richard Wagner, and Haru Yoshida.

Many of Knoll's textile designers, past and present, and their family members, graciously responded to research inquiries and also agreed to lend work to the exhibition: Sarah Baker, Jan-Paul Barnard, Jhane Barnes, Harry and Brenda Bassett, Anne Beetz, Lois Bryant, Nicole Casey, Klaus Dombrowski, Ruben Eshkanian, Anne Garber, Jean Pierre Garrault, Ulrike Greiner-Rhomberg, Kathrin Hagge, Christa Häusler-Goltz, Sheila Hicks, Bernd Hielle, Katrin Hielle-Dahm, Steffi Kiessling-Plewa, Christina Laubi, Paul Lewis, David Littell, Bo Markelius, Oskar Maute, Paul Maute, Parry Merkley, Roger Meyers, the Estate of Frances Breese Miller, Sarah Nestel, Shirley F. Nickerson, Clarissa Notley, Elisha Prouty, Adrian Pulfer, Dana Romeis, Lisa Ruddick, Margie Ruddick, Peter Seipelt, Hazel Siegel, Georgianna Stout, Suzanne Tick, Nob and Non Utsumi, Tim Van Campen, Francisca Reichardt Vietsch, Karin Vogelsang, Margarete Warth, Hollis Webster, Margaret Webster, Tina Wendler, Elizabeth Whelan, and Robin Whitten.

I want to thank our institutional and individual lenders for their generous support and assistance: The Architectural Archives, University of Pennsylvania, Philadelphia: Nancy Thorne, William Whitaker; Archives of American Art, Smithsonian Institution: Marisa Bourgoin, Susan M. Cary, Wendy Hurlock, Liza Kirwin; John H. and David E. Bright; Brooklyn Museum: Elisa Flynn, Barry Harwood, Rima Ibrahim; Carol S. Connell; Cooper-Hewitt, National Design Museum, Smithsonian Institution: Susan Brown, Gregory Herringshaw, Steve Langehough, Matilda McQuaid, Kimberly Randall, Sarah Scaturro; Cora Ginsburg LLC: Titi Halle, Michele Majer, Leigh Wishner; Cranbrook Art Museum, Bloomfield Hills, Michigan: Roberta Frey Gilboe, Reed Kroloff, Gregory Wittkopp, Emily Zilber; Dallas Museum of Art: Hillary Bober, Brent Mitchell, Bonnie Pitman, Kevin W. Tucker; Ruben Eshkanian; Mae Festa; KnollTextiles Archive, New York, and Knoll Museum, East Greenville, Pennsylvania; the family and friends of Ross Littell; The Metropolitan Museum of Art, New York: Jane Adlin, Nancy Britton, Emily Foss, Cynthia Iavarone; Milliken & Company: Kaye Gosline Dowling; Minneapolis Institute of Art: Tanya Morrison, Jennifer Komar Olivarez, Eike D. Schmidt; The Montreal Museum of Fine Arts: Danièle Archambault, Nathalie Bondil, Diane Charbonneau, Simon Labrie, Rosalind Pepall, Natalie Vanier; Museum of Modern Art, New York: Barry Bergdoll, Paul Galloway, Roger Griffith, Pamela Popeson, Whitney Snyder; Shirley F. Nickerson and Terry A. Larson; Philadelphia Museum of Art: Dilys Blum, Laura Camerlengo, Kristina Haugland, Katherine Hiesinger, Joseph McDermott, Sara Reiter, Shannon N. Schuler; Cindia Reyes; Dana Romeis; The Estate of Dorothy Cole Ruddick; Trudy and Richard Schultz; University of Alberta: Janine Andrews, Anne Bissonnette, Vlada Blinova, Erin McDonald; Andy Lin and Larry Weinberg; Elizabeth Whelan; Yale University Art Gallery:

L. Lynne Addison, Katherine Chabla, Melissa Durkee, Patricia Kane; and two private collectors who wish to remain anonymous. Margo Delidow, Roger Griffith, Sarah Scaturro, and Tae Smith participated in the challenging conservation effort for this project, I thank them for their dedicated work.

The production of this exhibition catalogue also required the consolidated effort of the excellent curatorial team. Earl Martin did an exceptional job as general editor. The chapters cover a range of issues related to Knoll textiles, thoughtfully presented by the curatorial team as authors, as well as Bobbye Tigerman, assistant curator of decorative arts and design at the Los Angeles County Museum of Art. In undertaking research, it became clear that some of the designers, especially the early ones, were little known, if not all but forgotten. A major contribution of this volume, therefore, is the section of "Designer Biographies," eighty-four in all, published together for the first time. Earl Martin and Ann Marguerite Tartsinis, assistant curator at the Gallery, led this research effort and wrote many of the individual texts. I am grateful to them and the other contributors: Caroline M. Hannah, Hedvig Hedqvist, Christian A. Larsen, Alexis Mucha, Catherine Brooke Penaloza-Patzak, Elizabeth St. George, Sonya A. Topolnisky, Angela Völker, and Susan Ward. With such a large group of authors, the editoral challenges were considerable. Martina D'Alton did a superb job as copyeditor, assisted by Ron Broadhurst and Barbara Burn. Essential proofreading was undertaken by Charmain Devereaux and Roberta Fineman. For non-English texts, Richard J. Littell and Abigail Prohaska provided critical translations. It was a pleasure working with Irma Boom whose marvelous design of this volume continues the long tradition of innovative graphic design associated with Knoll. Laura Grey, director of graphic design at the BGC, and Sally Salvesen, at Yale University Press in London, contributed greatly to the production of this volume. Bruce White's magnificent new photographs have made it possible to publish many of the Knoll textiles for the first time in color. Alexis Mucha, coordinator of photography, secured photographs and arranged for much of the photography, as well as helping to prepare the picture captions. Han Vu, digital technology designer, provided critical assistance with image databases and distribution of images to the publisher.

Ian Sullivan designed the magnificent exhibition and assisted with numerous tasks related to the preparation and mounting of the textiles for installation. Eric Edler, registrar at the BGC, and Olga Valle Tetkowski, manager of curatorial projects, attended to the complex task of requesting and administering the loans. I would also like to thank the installation crew at the Bard Graduate Center for their professionalism and diligence.

We received invaluable research assistance from: Chris Abbate; American Textile History Museum: Karen Herbaugh, Clara Sheridan; David Anthone; Arkitekturmuseet, Stockholm: Frida Melin; Art Institute of Chicago: Judith Barter, Odile Joassin, Christopher Monkhouse, Zoe Ryan; Artek: Beth Dickstein, Mirkku Kullberg, Simone Vingerhoets-Ziesmann; The Baltimore Museum of Art: Emily Rafferty; The Cleveland Museum of Art: Louise Mackie, Deirdre L. Vodanoff; Cooper-Hewitt, National Design Museum Library, Smithsonian Institution: Elizabeth Broman, Stephan Van Dyk; The Cooper Union: Claire Gunning; Cranbrook Archives: Leslie Edwards, Robbie Terman; Denver Art Museum: Donna Kerwin; Deutsches Textilmuseum, Krefeld: Brigitte Tietzel, Claudia Wisniewsky; Die Neue Sammlung, Munich: Josef Strasser; John Flack; Frances Loeb Library, Harvard University, Graduate School of Design: Mary Daniels, Inés Zalduendo; Helfried Kodré; Michael Gotkin; Hamon Arts Library, Southern Methodist University: Ellen Buie Niewyk; David Hanks; Ruth Hartmann; Helena Hernmark; Heriot-Watt University: Helen Taylor; Historic New England: Adrienne Donohue, Wendy Hubbard, Julie Solz; Indianapolis Museum of Art: R. Craig Miller; The Josef and Anni Albers Foundation: Oliver Barker, Brenda Danilowitz, Andrés Garces, Nicholas Fox Weber; Giles Kotcher; Landesmuseum Württemberg, Stuttgart: Rainer Y; Belinda Lanks; Jack Lenor Larsen; Tom Latone; John Leavitt; Ljungbergs Textiltryck, Rydboholm: Bibbi Nilsson; Los Angeles County Museum of Art: Wendy Kaplan, Sharon Takeda; Machine Age, Boston: Normand Mainville; Magnum Photos: Michael Shulman; Margaret Maile; Jane Merkel; Tomoko Miho; Catherine Murray; The Museum at FIT:

Lynn Felsher; Museum für Kunst und Gewerbe, Hamburg: Rüdiger Joppien, Angelika Riley; Museum of Art, Rhode Island School of Design: Joanne Dolan Ingersoll; Museum of the City of New York: Donald Albrecht, Barbara Livenstein; Museum of Fine Arts, Boston: Pamela Parmal, Heather Porter, Lauren Whitley; Museum of Modern Art Archives: Michelle Harvey; Nationalmuseum, Stockholm: Micael Ernstell, Gertrud Nord, Cilla Robach; Majel Chance Obata; Esther Perman; Ron Pietersma; Paula Poorman; Dungjai Pungauthaikan; Regierungspräsidium Stuttgart: Dieter Büchner; Melanie Ryan; Gro Aga Sache; Peter Schultz; Bill Shea; Thousand Islands Arts Center: Amber Meyers; Kirsten Toftegaard; Tony Vaccaro; Virginia Museum of Art: Howell Perkins, Barry Shifman, Courtney Yevich; Walker Art Center: Jill Vuchetich; Winterthur Museum: Joelle Wickens; The Wolfsonian–Florida International University: Cathy Leff, Marianne Lamonaca.

In the extensive photographic research for this volume, we were assisted by many individuals and institutions: American Textile History Museum, Massachusetts: Clare Sheridan; The Architectural Archives of the University of Pennsylvania: William Whitaker; Archives of American Art, Smithsonian Institution: Wendy Hurlock Baker; Art Resource, New York: Jennifer Belt, Robin Stolfi; Arts & Architecture: David Travers; Roberta Bayley; Brooklyn Museum: Ruth Janson; The Cleveland Museum of Art: Mary Suzor; Cooper-Hewitt, National Design Museum, Smithsonian Institution: Kimberly Randall; Cora Ginsburg, LLC, New York: Leigh Wishner; Cranbrook Archives, Bloomfield Hills, Michigan: Robbie Terman; Cranbrook Museum of Art, Bloomfield Hills, Michigan: Roberta Frey Gilboe, R. H. Hensleigh; Dallas Museum of Art: Jeff Zilm; Estate of Robert Damora: Matthew and Sirkka Damora; Esto: Christine Cordazzo; The Josef and Anni Albers Foundation, Bethany, Connecticut: Oliver Barker, Brenda Danilowitz; KnollTextiles, New York: Katherine Gray Gluibizzi, Colleen James; The Library of Congress, Washington, D.C.; Brian Lutz; The Metropolitan Museum of Art, New York: Neal Stimler; Minneapolis Institute of Art: Heidi Raatz; The Montreal Museum of Fine Arts: Christine Guest, Marie-Claude Saia; Museum of Arts and Design, New York: Brian MacElhose; Nationalmuseum, Stockholm: Eva Karlsson; New York Public Library: Stephan Saks; Philadelphia Museum of Art: Giema Tsakuginow; Ronald C. Pietersma; Jens Risom; Rockefeller Archive Center, New York: Michele Hiltzik; University of Alberta, Clothing and Textiles Collection, Edmonton, Canada: Anne Bissonette; Walker Art Center, Minnesota: Jill Vuchetich; Yale University Art Gallery, New Haven.

The remarkable staff of our Development, Education, External Affairs, Finance and Administration offices, and the faculty and staff of Academic Programs also made a substantial contribution to this landmark project. To all of them I would like to express my appreciation.

Susan Weber
Director and Founder, Bard Graduate Center

Foreword

Gretl and Leo Wollner. *Rivers* ("Purple/Brown" colorway), ca. 1972.
Made by Pausa AG for Knoll Textiles. Used for drapery, wall hanging; cotton velvet;
screen-printed. Courtesy Cindia Reyes. Cat. 194.

Introduction
Earl Martin

Knoll Textiles, 1945–2010 celebrates the extraordinary accomplishments in the field of textiles by one of the world's leading design companies. Most historians of design or decorative arts inevitably know of Knoll, or perhaps more pointedly, Knoll furniture. The company's furniture designers in the postwar period included leaders in the field: Ludwig Mies van der Rohe, Eero Saarinen, Harry Bertoia, and Florence Knoll Bassett herself, to name just a few. Textiles, however, have also been an essential part of Knoll almost since the company's founding, and *Knoll Textiles, 1945–2010* sheds light on the largely untold story of the Knoll textile division, and in so doing also broadens our understanding of modern design history.

Since its founding in 1993, the Bard Graduate Center (BGC) has been committed to exploring and documenting the history of decorative arts and design as well as bringing neglected areas of these fields of study to light. The *Knoll Textiles* project provided especially fertile ground for new research. Knoll played a leading role in producing iconic pieces of modern furniture during the postwar period, and this part of its history has been closely examined by design historians and museums since the 1980s, when developments in post–World War II interiors and furnishings began to be of scholarly interest. The textile arm of the company, however, although equally prominent and integral to the firm, has not been extensively studied. *Knoll Textiles* examines the development of textiles and their deployment by one of the world's leading design companies over more than sixty years.

Assessing the Literature

Until now, only a small number of publications have touched upon aspects of Knoll textile production or have profiled a few of its textile designers. For the most part textiles have been folded into larger histories. Beginning in the early 1980s, seminal exhibitions and their accompanying catalogues first considered modernism in architecture and design of the mid-twentieth century. *Design in America: The Cranbrook Vision* (1983), for example, organized by the Detroit Institute of Arts and the Metropolitan Museum of Art, chronicled the impact of the Cranbrook Academy of Art and leading designers and educators associated with this institution, from its founding in the early twentieth century through midcentury.[1] *Design in America* considered key figures in the textile history of Knoll, notably Florence Knoll Bassett, who trained at the Michigan design school, and Finnish-born Marianne Strengell, who was head of Cranbrook's textile department. Through her teaching, Strengell had a profound influence on the generation of textile designers who led the field in the second half of the twentieth century. She also contributed significantly to the early Knoll textile collections. Another 1983 exhibition, *Design Since 1945*, organized by Kathryn B. Hiesinger of the Philadelphia Museum of Art, presented the first extensive survey of midcentury design.[2] Jack Lenor Larsen, a leading figure in the postwar textile community, wrote the eloquent introduction to the section on textiles in the exhibition catalogue, highlighting the pioneering work of the Knoll textile division in the late 1940s through the 1950s, emphasizing Florence Knoll's contributions and the work of Eszter Haraszty, Evelyn Hill Anselevicius, and Suzanne Huguenin. This exhibition inspired Anselevicius to donate a selection of the textiles she designed for Knoll to the Philadelphia Museum of Art, many of which are included in *Knoll Textiles*.

In the 1990s several notable histories of modern design briefly discussed Knoll textiles. *Design 1935–1965, What Modern Was* (1991) focused on the Liliane and David M. Stewart collection, then at the Musée des Arts Décoratifs de Montréal, and now part of the Montreal Museum of Fine Arts.[3] Several important figures at Knoll Textiles in this period—Florence Knoll, Eszter Haraszty, and Ross Littell, among others—were featured in this publication. David Hanks, curator of the Stewart Program for Modern Design at the Montreal Museum, generously offered the BGC access to original research material related to these and other individuals for the *Knoll Textiles* project. The BGC's exhibition catalogue, *Women Designers in the USA, 1900–2000*, also considered the design work of Florence Knoll, as well as Knoll textile designers Marianne Strengell, Eszter Haraszty, Anni Albers, Jhane Barnes, and Dorothy Cosonas.[4] In 2002, *US Design 1975–2000* at the Denver Art Museum briefly mentioned a selection of textiles Suzanne Tick and Kathrin Hagge designed for Knoll from 1999 to 2001.[5]

The literature devoted specifically to twentieth-century textile history can be divided primarily into surveys outlining changes that occurred in fabric design and more focused examinations of certain aspects or individuals. The surveys—such as *Twentieth-Century Pattern Design* (Lesley Jackson's invaluable book) and *Von Morris bis Memphis* (a catalogue of the textile collection of the Neue Sammlung, Munich)—are good introductions, but lack in-depth analysis of Knoll textiles.[6] Monographs and articles on the work of the leading designers, such as Anni Albers and Marianne Strengell, have provided insight into their association with Knoll, but the vast majority of the designers who contributed to the Knoll Textiles collection over the last seventy years have been excluded from design history literature.

Since the 1970s, several corporate histories of Knoll have been published. These outline the story of Knoll Textiles in only the broadest of strokes. In *Knoll au Louvre*, the catalogue of the 1972 exhibition held at the Musée des arts décoratifs in Paris, textiles were given half a page of text and two pages of photographs, while the remaining sixty-eight pages of the book were devoted to furniture and furniture designers.[7] The most widely consulted history of the company, *Knoll Design* (1981), also has a brief summary of the textile division—what amounts to only fifteen of the book's more than three hundred pages.[8] The most recent history of the company, *Knoll: A Modernist Universe* (2010), opens with an image of Hans and Florence Knoll standing in front of the fabric wall in the New York showroom in the early 1950s, but again provides only an overview of the textile history of the company.[9] In conjunction with the sixtieth anniversary of the division in 2007, KnollTextiles published its own celebratory, but brief history, *KnollTextiles: 60 Years of Modern Design*.[10] Moreover, our own extensive research over the last four years has revealed that all of these various accounts of Knoll Textiles contain inaccuracies that further complicate the understanding of this leading contributor of modern textiles.

The Catalogue

The primary aim of *Knoll Textiles* is to provide an accurate and in-depth account of the firm's textiles and to emphasize their importance in the overall history of the company. Extensive archival research at KnollTextiles and in Knoll's general archive, was the basis for this project.

In addition, a comprehensive survey of the interior design and architectural literature was undertaken to ascertain the actual context for textile production at a decisive moment in the history of modernism in the United States and to a lesser degree in Europe. Whenever possible, the authors and curators working on this project contacted the individuals, past and present, who provided direction and leadership at Knoll and Knoll Textiles, as well as the many designers who created textile patterns for the company over the last seventy years. Research was also undertaken in the institutional archives of the Cranbrook Academy of Art and the Museum of Modern Art (MoMA) in New York City. This catalogue reflects the countless hours of research and dozens of interviews undertaken in the course of this project.

Knoll Textiles begins with the context for modern textiles in the United States from the late 1930s through the early 1960s, the period during which Knoll and the Knoll textile division were founded and expanded exponentially into a thriving company with a global reach. As Susan Ward explains in chapter one, modern textiles in the United States experienced a dynamic transformation between 1940 and 1960. Before 1940 textiles suited for use in modern interiors were largely unavailable in America. Focusing primarily on exhibitions and competitions, Ward chronicles the astounding transformation in textile design and discusses the influence of, among others, designer/weavers teaching at key institutions, such as Marianne Strengell at Cranbrook, Marli Ehrman at the Institute of Design in Chicago, and Anni Albers at Black Mountain College in North Carolina. These individuals not only forged a path for the acceptance of modern textiles in America with their own designs, but also trained many of the designers who would shape textile design in the postwar period. Ward also shows how the textile industry's initial reluctance to accept modern textiles eventually gave way to a growing commercial interest in this sector of the market. Out of this interest came a much closer engagement between handweaver/designers and textile manufacturers and wholesalers than ever seen before or since.

In chapter two Paul Makovsky examines the formation of the company's two founders, Hans Knoll and Florence Schust (later Knoll Bassett), and the early history of the firm before the founding of the textile division in 1947. Through extensive archival research and close perusal of period documents, Makovsky dates the founding of Hans Knoll's furniture company to 1940. During the early years, the focus was on expanding a line of modern furniture, but Hans Knoll soon came to consider textiles an important part of his emerging business. The first Knoll catalogue published in 1942 advertised printed drapery textiles by Frances Breese Miller, who can be considered the first textile designer to work for Knoll. That year, Hans Knoll began working with Florence Schust, a young architect and graduate of the Cranbrook Academy and student of Mies van der Rohe, who would further ensure the central place of textiles within the world of Knoll. Schust began to design interiors for the firm on a freelance basis but within a few years her role at the company became much more central, overseeing design-related matters in all aspects of the business. One of her most innovative decisions was to use men's suiting fabrics as upholsteries on Knoll furniture in 1945, after deciding that the available interior textiles were not suitable for Knoll's unconventional furniture. Schust sought tweeds and flannels for their simple nondirectional weaves and subtle textures, which were more in keeping with the unornamented lines of the company's furniture. Knoll's first direct engagement with textile manufacturers documented by this project was also in 1945, when Bridgeport Fabrics of Bridgeport, Connecticut, developed a "salt & pepper" webbing for Knoll to use as upholstery. The occurance of these two milestones in the same year marked the growing importance of textiles at the firm and thus we have used 1945 as a starting point in the title of this catalogue and exhibition.

Knoll formally launched a separate textile division in 1947. Renamed Knoll Textiles in the early 1950s, it almost immediately became a leading purveyor of textiles appropriate for modern interiors, a field that was small but growing. For a short time Knoll was a unique entity in the furniture and textile fields—it was the first furniture company to open a textile division and to sell both furniture and textiles to the architecture and design trade. Other companies would soon follow Knoll's lead, realizing the advantages to developing textiles specifically for their furniture lines and generally expanding their market share by offering comprehensive services to the design community.

In chapter three Susan Ward focuses on the formative years between World War II and the early 1960s, beginning with the varied designs that Florence and Hans Knoll selected for their first textile collection, which debuted in February 1947 in a small showroom on East Sixty-fifth Street in New York City (fig. 1). The first collection revealed Knoll's interest in new and unconventional materials such as Saran-fiber upholsteries (a plastic fiber used by the military during World War II) and a number of highly textural natural-fiber weaves imported from the Phillipines. Florence Knoll used lengths of these textiles as room dividers and applied them to cabinet doors—a precursor to the panel fabrics of today.

Fig. 1 Florence Knoll. Knoll textile division showroom, 31 1/2 East Sixty-fifth Street, New York, N.Y., 1947. Photographed by Phyllis A. Dearborn, Dearborn-Massar. Knoll Archives.

This first Knoll textile collection also established the practice of giving prominence and credit to designers. Knoll was among the first to consistently recognize and promote textile designers, frequently associating the phrase "designed by" with a new fabric. Among the most notable designers featured in the first collection were former Bauhaus weaving master Gunta Stölzl, Swedish textile designer Astrid Sampe, and Marianne Strengell, whom Florence Knoll had known at Cranbrook. The diversity of printed drapery fabrics was also characteristic of the early Knoll collections, which included examples by leaders in modern printed-textile design, such as Noémi Raymond and Angelo Testa. In 1949 Knoll hired the Hungarian designer Eszter Haraszty, initially to create pattern designs, promoting her a year later to head the overall operations of the textile division. Haraszty's innovative and unconventional color sense and her skill as a designer of printed fabric would soon bring Knoll Textiles greater acclaim. As Knoll's furniture sales and interior design commissions expanded in the first half of the 1950s so did the need for new upholsteries designed specifically to withstand heavy use, such as *Transportation Cloth* (1950), which was first developed for use in the General Motors Technical Center in Warren, Michigan. Also during the 1950s Knoll introduced innovative handwoven fabrics designed by Evelyn Hill that featured a wide variety of unconventional fibers and colors. These fabrics were intended for a specific category of clients, notably occupants of corporate executive suites, interiors that became increasingly important for the company.

After Hans Knoll's death in 1955, Florence Knoll assumed directorship of the company and led it to even greater renown worldwide. With the departure of Eszter Haraszty that same year, Suzanne Huguenin, her Swiss assistant, became the new head of Knoll Textiles. Huguenin worked closely with Florence Knoll and the Planning Unit to develop textiles appropriate for corporate office installations. These included a large variety of open-weave casements, such as those contributed by Anni Albers beginning in 1957, to cover the window walls and air-conditioning units of modern office buildings. Huguenin also oversaw the addition of highly durable fabrics made with synthetic fibers, an area in which Knoll became an industry leader. Among these, Huguenin's own *Knoll Nylon Homespun*, introduced in 1958, sold in the millions of yards as part of Knoll's offerings over the next thirty years.

Fig. 2 Florence Knoll Bassett/Knoll Planning Unit. Paste-up plan for Cowles Magazines' executive office, ca. 1961. *Cato* and other textile samples, wood samples on paper. Knoll Archives. Cat. 158.

Fig. 3 Florence Knoll Bassett/Knoll Planning Unit. Lounge area, Cowles Magazines' executive office, ca. 1962. Photographed by Robert Damora. Courtesy Estate of Robert Damora.

The Knoll Planning Unit is the focus of chapter four by Bobbye Tigerman. She describes the central role this division played in establishing the reputation of the company in the postwar period and how Planning Unit projects led to the development of many Knoll products, including textiles. Florence Knoll's distinctive approach to design and planning, which became known as "the Knoll look," was predicated on the full integration of both furniture and fabrics to create a cohesive interior. The success of this approach allowed the Planning Unit to move rapidly from small and diverse installations in hospitality, office, and educational settings in the second half of the 1940s and early 1950s, to much more ambitious and extensive installations for entire corporate campuses and office buildings in the mid-1950s through the 1960s. Tigerman also discusses the Planning Unit's design process, how Florence Knoll and her staff included textiles as an integral design element and created "paste-ups," models or plans that included textile swatches and wood veneer chips to represent the placement of furniture within a proposed interior (fig. 2). These paste-ups enabled clients to see the actual colors and tactile qualities of the interior schemes, often ensuring their approval for the eventual installation (fig. 3). This chapter also considers the importance of the showrooms, where innovative installations demonstrated the cutting-edge interior design solutions offered by Florence Knoll and the Planning Unit, while also providing a stimulus for textile and furniture sales. The early showrooms in New York played a crucial part in establishing Knoll's design leadership. They included the 1947 textile division showroom (Florence Knoll's first showroom design); the main showroom at 601 Madison Avenue, redesigned in 1948 to include the textile division (fig. 4); and a new showroom at 575 Madison Avenue, opened in 1951 and arguably Florence Knoll's most celebrated showroom design.

Fig. 4 Florence Knoll. Knoll showroom, 601 Madison Avenue, New York, N.Y., 1948. View from entrance, with textile display in the background, left. Photographed by Ezra Stoller. Ezra Stoller © ESTO, 69J.002c.

When Florence Knoll married Harry Hood Bassett in 1958 she began to remove herself from the day-to-day operations of the company, and a year later, while retaining the directorship, she sold Knoll to the office furniture manufacturer Art Metal. The many business and creative changes that Knoll experienced during the 1960s are discussed by Angela Völker in chapter five. In the late 1950s the textile industry in the United States experienced a decline, and during this time Knoll Textiles began to source more of its offerings from European manufacturers. Huguenin made a major contribution to the textile product line at this time by introducing handwoven upholstery and drapery fabrics designed and produced by Paul Maute in Germany. One of these, the highly popular *Cato* upholstery fabric, enjoys the distinction of being the oldest Knoll textile still in production in 2011. At the end of 1963, Huguenin left Knoll, and with Florence Knoll Bassett's retirement two years later, Knoll Textiles experienced a period of stagnation. In 1965, Robert Cadwallader, a new director of marketing, began to lead Knoll on new path. While he first focused on the furniture side in his role as marketing head and, after 1971, as president of the firm, he called on Barbara Rodes to revitalize Knoll Textiles. Rodes worked closely with a number of designers and manufacturers in her native Germany, developing new products for the Knoll collection.

The sale of Knoll to the finance company Walter Heller International in 1968 had little impact on the company at first. In 1969 the company changed its name to Knoll International and the following year opened a new showroom in New York, the first one not designed by Florence Knoll Bassett and the Knoll Planning Unit. Knoll Textiles embarked on a decidedly new direction in 1969, introducing a collection of large-repeat printed fabrics on cotton velvet by the German designer Wolf Bauer. This paved the way for wider offerings in the 1970s of innovative print fabrics, handwoven textiles by Paul Maute, and Jacquard-woven upholsteries designed by Marga Hielle-Vatter and manufactured in Germany. In this decade Knoll also introduced new categories of textiles to its line, including velvets and other pile fabrics, as well as fabrics designed to be used on the vertical surfaces of the office systems that were beginning to dominate Knoll's contract furniture line. These partition or panel fabrics were first introduced by the company in the mid-1970s.

In chapter six Völker explores the sweeping changes and design innovations at Knoll Textiles from 1977 to the present. In 1977, Heller International sold Knoll to General Felt Industries, a company headed by Marshall Cogan and Stephen Swid, the first of several changes in corporate ownership since that time. Knoll Textiles soon had new management under the leadership of vice president and general manager Arthur Sager and was reorganized as an independent division with a separate sales force along with new directives to greatly expand sales to clients beyond the furniture side of the company. During the 1980s under the creative directors Richard Wagner and Merle Lindby-Young, Knoll Textiles entered the market for wallcoverings, and designs for vertical fabrics expanded. Wagner and Lindby-Young brought a renewed focus to working with leading weaver/designers and textile artists, and before long Knoll was again in the forefront of the interior textiles sector. Restyled as KnollTextiles (one word) in 1988, the division also began to explore collaborations with designers active in the fashion industry, such as Jhane Barnes, who regularly contributed new and innovative textiles from 1983 until 1998.

In 1990 the company had another new owner, Westinghouse Electric Corporation, and there were significant changes in the leadership and direction of KnollTextiles. In 1990 under Hazel Siegel (director of design, 1989–92) the division released the largest new collection of fabrics in Knoll's history. The first half of the decade, however, saw a rapid turnover of design directors at KnollTextiles, reflecting general company turmoil, and in 1995 Knoll was sold again, to Warburg Pincus Ventures. KnollTextiles appointed Suzanne Tick design director late in 1996 and a new era began. Tick made important administrative changes and renewed the focus on innovation and the use of new materials. She designed and developed fabrics that served as benchmarks for the contract textile industry in the areas of environmentally friendly products and technical textiles, helping to assure Knoll's position as a leader in the industry.

In 2005 Dorothy Cosonas became Tick's successor. Heavily inspired by the world of fashion in her design work, she brought a sartorial focus to the Knoll collection, most notably through the introduction of Knoll Luxe in 2008, a separate brand of high-quality upholstery and drapery fabrics. Cosonas created the first Luxe collection and subsequently engaged innovative fashion designers such as Proenza Schouler and Rodarte. Fittingly, in 2010 Knoll opened a small showroom dedicated to Knoll Luxe in the Decoration & Design Building on Third Avenue in New York City, only blocks away from the site of its first textiles showroom of 1947 (fig. 5).

Fig. 5 Knoll Luxe showroom, Decoration & Design Building, 979 Third Avenue, New York, N.Y., 2010. Photographed 2011.

The catalogue concludes with biographies of more than eighty designers who have contributed textiles to Knoll over the last seventy years, giving overdue recognition to this large and diverse group. One of the Gallery's most extensive research projects, this resource fills a gap in design history and hopefully opens new paths for study of the history of commercial textile design in the second half of the twentieth century.

The Exhibition

The curatorial process we engaged in while planning this exhibition is indicative of the unique challenges of focusing on twentieth-century commercial textiles. For the most part this segment of the textile field has been dismissed or undervalued by both the design community and museums. We began with a comprehensive survey of American museum collections which unearthed a number of Knoll textiles, primarily printed drapery fabrics. These are perhaps the most easily recognizable Knoll Textiles products; they frequently identify the company name, the name of the print, and the designer's name on the selvedge of the textiles. Although important in the Knoll Textiles collection, prints were overshadowed in terms of quantity of production and design innovation by upholstery fabrics. Most museums, however, did not consider commercial upholstery fabrics worthy of inclusion in design collections or as objects in their own right until after 1980, and since then, only a small number have been added to important collections. Very few examples of Knoll upholstery textiles are in major museums across the United States, or so it appeared after our initial investigation. Since Knoll has been a leader in the introduction of iconic modern upholstered furniture since the late 1940s, however, we were able to locate a number of original fabrics on furniture in museum collections around the United States. In almost every case, these objects were catalogued by museums solely as furniture, and the upholstery, even when it was a central aspect of the design, was largely ignored. Textile designers were not identified. Our task became a formidable one—to identify the weave structures and appearances of the upholstery textiles made by Knoll through examination of original samples preserved in KnollTextiles Archive, and to match these to the upholsteries on the furniture in museums. Susan Ward, a co-curator on this project, spearheaded this initiative, and we are pleased to include a few examples of early Knoll upholsteries on furniture drawn from museum collections.

Many times, however, original upholsteries had either been replaced before the furniture entered a museum collection, or even later, at the behest of curators who felt that the furniture form was the important aspect of the design, ignoring the significance of the textile that covered it. This practice of replacing worn upholstery is even more widespread in the world of private collectors. The destruction of these textiles, however, was not always due to their poor condition, but to the deterioration of the materials that support them. One example is the foam cushioning that Knoll frequently employed since the late 1940s to create the distinctive rounded curves and precise angles specified by many of its designers, not knowing that this material has a limited lifespan before becoming calcified and brittle. Vintage upholstery has often been replaced for no other reason than to resolve the problem of the disintegrating foam. Despite this common practice, in the course of this project, we located important examples of early upholsteries on furniture in private collections. Since the beauty of both the textiles and the precise forms of the furniture was sometimes compromised by the deterioration of the underlying foam, we decided to undertake our own conservation project. Our initial consultation with Joelle. Wickens at Winterthur and Nancy Britton at the Metropolitan Museum of Art revealed that conservation of modern furniture is in its infancy. Knowing that we had assembled furniture with the potential to reveal critical aspects of this largely forgotten field, we engaged Roger Griffith, associate conservator at the Museum of Modern Art, and Margo Delidow, Andrew W. Mellon Fellow in Conservation Education at the Institute of Fine Arts, to restore the upholstered furniture. The five chairs that constitute this unprecedented work on twentieth-century furniture conservation have become outstanding additions to the exhibition. They convey the beauty of upholstery textiles created by several leading Knoll designers as they were originally intended to be used.

We also discoverd Knoll textile samples and sample kits in leading museums. In several cases, these historically critical yet seemingly ephemeral documents had not been formally accessioned, reflecting the secondary place of textiles in the hierarchy of museum collection practices. Our interest in examining and borrowing these objects instigated their reevaluation by curators and earned them a formal place in these collections—conferring a new level of respect to both the textiles and related promotional objects as being worthy of preservation and study.

Many of the objects included in this exhibition do not call traditional museum collections home. Loans have been assembled from the KnollTextiles Archive in New York, often the sole repository of some of these fabrics, even if it is only as small swatches. Knoll's corporate collection of furniture and other objects, located at the Knoll Museum in East Greenville, Pennsylvania, was another resource for original Knoll upholsteries on furniture. Knoll textile designers and former Knoll employees have also provided loans, including many textiles that were stored in attics and basements, sometimes for more than fifty years. Private collectors have been a major source of loans for the exhibition. I personally discovered a number of outstanding examples of Knoll textiles dating to the 1970s and 1980s, including the one shown in the opening illustration for this introduction, through a family friend who mentioned to my mother that she had "a few Knoll fabrics" in her Wisconsin basement.

The weave structures identified for the textiles illustrated in this volume were compiled by Sarah Scaturro, textiles conservator, Cooper Hewitt, National Design Museum, Smithsonian Institution, and her colleague Julia Carlson. They have based these designations on Irene Emery's *The Primary Structure of Fabrics* (1966) and *Watson's Advanced Textile Design* (1977), as well as suggestions from Desiree Koslin of the Fashion Institute of Technology, New York.[11] We thank them for their diligence in studying more than one hundred different textile weave structures used at Knoll. In a few cases, however, samples of textiles were unavailable for examination, and structures for these fabrics have not been provided.

Editor's Acknowledgments

First I want to join Susan Weber in thanking the many lenders and lending institutions, designers, former Knoll employees, and the individuals at diverse libraries, museums, and archives, as well as myriad experts in the field who have provided invaluable assistance in making this exhibition and catalogue a success. Without them *Knoll Textiles* would not be possible. I wish to offer a more personal thanks to a few individuals. My deepest gratitude is to Susan Weber, founding director of the BGC, and Nina Stritzler-Levine, chief curator and executive editor of gallery publications, for their confidence in my abilities, for encouraging me to take on this important project, and for their strong ongoing support to make it a reality. I thank the curatorial team, Paul Makovsky, Angela Völker, and Susan Ward, for joining me in this multiyear journey to uncover the story of Knoll Textiles. Kathryn Gray Gluibizzi, design studio coordinator at KnollTextiles and manager of the KnollTextiles Archive, gave at times almost daily assistance and was willing to accommodate even the most mundane requests. I also thank my colleagues at the Bard Graduate Center for supporting the final realization of this project over the past year: Eric Edler, Laura Grey, Alexis Mucha, Ian Sullivan, Olga Valle Tetkowski, and Han Vu. While not formally on staff, Martina D'Alton has once again extended her deft editorial hand to the BGC in her work on this volume—I am truly thankful for it. I extend a special note of gratitude to Ann Marguerite Tartsinis, assistant curator at the BGC, who joined our staff less than a year ago but has played an invaluable role in making *Knoll Textiles* a reality. Without her, this project would not have happened. Finally, I thank my parents, Mary and Jim Martin, my sister Kathryn, and my friends in New York and elsewhere, who provided their ongoing encouragement and supported me in incalculable ways over the past few years during my exploration of all things Knoll.

1   See Joan Marter et al., eds., *Design in America: The Cranbrook Vision 1925–1950*, exh. cat. (New York: Harry N. Abrams, 1983).
2   Kathryn B. Hiesinger and George H. Marcus, eds., *Design Since 1945*, exh. cat. (Philadelphia: Philadelphia Museum of Art, 1983).
3   Martin Eidelberg, ed., *Design 1935–1965: What Modern Was* (Montreal: Musée des Arts Décoratifs de Montréal; New York: Harry N. Abrams, 1991).
4   Pat Kirkham, ed., *Women Designers in the USA, 1900–2000: Diversity and Difference*, exh. cat. (New York: Bard Graduate Center; New Haven and London: Yale University Press, 2000).
5   R. Craig Miller, ed., *USDesign, 1975-2000*, exh. cat. (Munich and New York: Prestel Verlag, in association with the Denver Art Museum, 2002).
6   Lesley Jackson, *Twentieth-Century Pattern Design: Textile and Wallpaper Pioneers* (New York: Princeton Architectural Press, 2002); Hans Wichmann, *Von Morris bis Memphis: Textilien der Neuen Sammlung Ende 19. bis Ende 20. Jahrhundert* (Basel: Birkhäuser, 1990).
7   Christine Rae and Massimo Vignelli, *Knoll au Louvre*, exh. cat. (Milan: Amilcare Pizzi S.p.A. for Knoll International, 1971). The exhibition was held at the Pavillon de Marsan, part of the Palais du Louvre.
8   Eric Larabee and Massimo Vignelli, *Knoll Design* (New York: Harry N. Abrams, 1981). The contributions of Knoll furniture designers are weighed much more heavily, Ludwig Mies van der Rohe, for example, is given the same amount of space in the book as the entire history of Knoll Textiles.
9   Brian Lutz, *Knoll: A Modernist Universe* (New York: Rizzoli, 2010).
10 Nurit Einik, *KnollTextiles: 60 Years of Modern Design* (New York: Knoll Inc., 2007).
11 Irene Emery, *The Primary Structure of Fabrics* (Washington: Textile Museum, 1966); Z.J. Grosicki, *Watson's Advanced Textile Design: Compound Woven Structures* (London, Boston: Newnes-Butterworths, 1977).

Editor's Note

Editor's Note

The Knoll company name has changed several times over the last seventy plus years. We use the contemporary corporate name in the sections of this catalogue that discuss those periods: Hans Knoll Furniture (1940–43), H. G. Knoll Associates (1943–46), Knoll Associates, Inc. (1946–69), Knoll International (1969–90), Knoll Group (1990–95), Knoll, Inc. (1995–2011). We employ a similar approach to reflect changes in the name of the textile division. In the early years it was simply referred to as the "textile division of Knoll Associates" (1947–ca. 1950). After this it was formally named Knoll Textiles (ca. 1950–88) and beginning in 1988 KnollTextiles (one word), the name it carries today.

In addition, Knoll, though an American company, opened showrooms in Europe as early as 1951 and established international divisions that sold Knoll Textiles from the early 1950s through 1991. Very few records of these textiles have been preserved in the Knoll Archives or KnollTextiles Archive. While we have provided what information we have located on the international divisions, in large part this catalogue refers to KnollTextiles in the United States.

Many of the key designers and leaders discussed in this book are women, whose names reflect changes in their marital status over the course of their lives. We have identified them by the name appropriate to the periods of their lives we consider. For example, the co-founder of Knoll was "Florence Schust" (her birth name) from 1917 to 1946, when she became "Florence Knoll," and since 1958 she has been "Florence Knoll Bassett."

The language of the textile discipline can be arcane to those not in the field. For good general references, especially concerning textiles for interiors, please see Jack Lenor Larsen and Jeanne Weeks, *Fabrics for Interiors: A Guide for Architects, Designers, and Consumers* (New York: Van Nostrand Reinhold, 1975), and Helen Anstey and Terry Weston, *The Anstey Weston Guide to Textile Terms* (London: Weston Publishing Ltd., 1997).

Colorway names (designated by quotation marks) preserve the original wording and style from the price lists in the KnollTextiles Archive. Names of colorways are not provided for patterns not found in existing Knoll price lists. A checklist of objects in the exhibition begins on page 414. In the object dimensions given there, height precedes width and depth. For textiles in current KnollTextiles production only the width is given.

Chronology
Compiled by Ann Marguerite Tartsinis

From our large collection of fine upholstery fabrics.

Advertisement for Knoll Associates, Inc., designed by Herbert Matter, 1965. Knoll Archives.

1940
- Hans G. Knoll Furniture Company is established in New York City by Hans Knoll at 444 Madison Avenue.

1941
- Hans G. Knoll Furniture Company leases offices and opens a showroom at 601 Madison Avenue.
- Hans Knoll hires designer Jens Risom.
- Hans Knoll and Risom furnish reception lobby of Johnson & Johnson Ligature Laboratories, in New Brunswick, New Jersey.
- *Organic Design Exhibition* at The Museum of Modern Art, New York (MoMA). Printed textile designs by Noémi Raymond are awarded first prize in the Printed Fabrics category, and several are later adapted for commercial production by Knoll.

1942
- First Knoll catalogue features a group of printed sheer drapery fabrics by Frances Breese Miller, as well as furniture designs by Risom and Ernst Schwadron.
- Florence Schust starts working on a freelance basis for Hans Knoll designing interiors for the company. Her first project is the design of the Pentagon offices for Henry Stimson, Secretary of War (1940–45).

Fig. C.1
Advertisement for Hans Knoll Furniture. From *Interiors*, August 1942.

1943
- Name of company is changed to H. G. Knoll Associates.
- Introduction of *650* line of furniture designed by Risom. Chairs and sofas in this line are offered with cotton webbing as a standard upholstery option; initially this webbing comes from supplies rejected by the United States government.
- Knoll furnishes lounges in the Calvert Houses, apartments for military and factory workers in suburban Washington, D.C., for the United States government.

1944
- Knoll Planning Unit (KPU) is established. It becomes a main source of design development for Knoll and serves as the interior design branch of the company.
- Knoll begins exhibiting and selling furniture through Bloomingdale's department store in New York City.
- Hans Knoll writes to Ralph Rapson regarding the company's plans to establish a textile division.

Fig. C.2
Advertisement for Knoll Associates, Inc., designed by Herbert Matter, featuring Knoll planning services. From *Interiors*, February 1954.

1945
- KPU designs and furnishes interiors of the Air Transport Command airport terminal in Washington, D.C.
- A new line of furniture at Bloomingdale's is introduced with designs by Ralph Rapson, Abel Sorensen, and Jens Risom.
- Florence Schust begins using men's suiting fabrics on Knoll furniture as upholstery.
- Bridgeport Fabrics of Bridgeport, Connecticut, develops "salt & pepper" webbing exclusively for Knoll.

1946
- H. G. Knoll Associates becomes Knoll Associates, Inc.
- Hans Knoll and Florence Schust marry on August 1.
- Florence Knoll and KPU design and furnish the Rockefeller family offices in the RCA Building, Rockefeller Center, New York City. A printed drapery fabric—*Isles*, designed by Shirley Fletcher Rapson—is used in the office conference room; it will be part of Knoll's first textile collection the following spring.
- Florence and Hans Knoll travel to Sweden and form a partnership with Nordiska Kompaniet (NK), the leading Swedish department store, to import Swedish furniture into the United States. The Knolls meet with Astrid Sampe, head of NK's Textilkammare (textile design studio), and make initial arrangements to import Swedish fabrics. NK will later become Knoll's licensee in Sweden.

1947
- Knoll presents the "Authentic Swedish Room" installation at the 601 Madison Avenue showroom featuring imported NK furniture and textiles designed by Astrid Sampe and Sven Markelius.
- Knoll Associates establishes a textile division with a separate showroom that opens in February at 31 1/2 East 65th Street in New York City.
- Upholstery fabrics introduced in the first collection include *Cartree*, *Devil*, and handwovens by Marianne Strengell, as well as *Vallis*, a Swiss handwoven probably designed by Gunta Stadler-Stölzl.
- Printed drapery fabrics introduced in the first collection include *Shooting Stars* and *Propellers* by Marianne

Strengell, *Isles* by Shirley Fletcher Rapson, *Manhattan* by Josef Frank, *Honeycomb* and *Rings* by Astrid Sampe, and *Campagna* by Angelo Testa. *Campagna* remains in the line until 1964.
- Herbert Matter becomes Knoll's graphic designer until 1966.
- KPU furnishes the Madison Room for Harry S. Manchester, Inc. Department Store, Madison, Wisconsin.

Fig. C.3
Advertisement for Textile Division, Knoll Associates, Inc., designed by Herbert Matter, 1948. Herbert Matter papers, M1446, Dept. of Special Collections, Stanford University Libraries, Stanford, Calif.

1948
- Florence Knoll redesigns the main showroom at 601 Madison Avenue and incorporates the textile division; the separate textile showroom is closed.
- *Prestini* upholstery designed by Antoinette Lackner Webster (Toni Prestini) is introduced; it remains in the line until 1982.
- Owens-Corning Fiberglas Corporation showroom and office interiors in New York, designed and furnished by KPU, feature fiberglass draperies and upholsteries designed by Marianne Strengell.
- KPU designs and furnishes complete office interiors for North American Life and Casualty Company, Minneapolis, Minnesota.
- Exhibition held in the Knoll showroom features textiles by Swedish designer Astrid Sampe; her upholstery design *Sampe Stripe* enters the Knoll collection.
- *Womb* chair by Eero Saarinen introduced.
- Knoll introduces in the United States printed fabric designs by Swedish designers, including *Markelius* by Sven Markelius and *Apples* by Stig Lindberg.
- Noémi Raymond's *Chinese Coins* and *Reeds and Bars* are introduced.
- Knoll distributes printed fabrics designed by Alexander Girard.

1949
- KPU project: Alice Crocker Lloyd Residence Hall at the University of Michigan.
- *An Exhibition for Modern Living* at the Detroit Institute of Arts features Knoll furniture and fabrics in a room installation created by Florence Knoll.
- *House in the Museum Garden*, an exhibition house by Marcel Breuer at MoMA features fabrics and furniture by Knoll.
- Knoll opens first showroom outside of New York at 160 East Superior Street, Chicago, Illinois.
- Eszter Haraszty is hired as a part-time textile designer.

1950
- Eszter Haraszty becomes head of the textile division.
- *Cinders*, the first print designed by Haraszty, is introduced.
- *Mosaic* by Noémi Raymond is introduced.
- Showrooms in Dallas, Boston, and Atlanta are opened.
- *Good Design* exhibition series organized by MoMA in New York and the Merchandise Mart in Chicago opens and continues until January 1955.
- First sections of General Motors Technical Center in Warren, Michigan, open, designed by Eero Saarinen and featuring furnishings by Knoll.
- *Transportation Cloth* by Eszter Haraszty is developed for use in the General Motors Technical Center and becomes part of the collection in 1951, remaining in the line until 1978.

Fig. C.4
Advertisement for Knoll Associates, Inc., designed by Herbert Matter, featuring Eszter Haraszty's *Transportation Cloth* and Franz Lorenz's *Scotch Linen*, 1952. From page in a portfolio compiled by Eszter Haraszty. The Montreal Museum of Fine Arts, Liliane and David M. Stewart Collection, Gift of the American Friends of Canada through the generosity of Eszter Haraszty, D88.178.2.8v.

- *Knoll Index of Contemporary Design* is published.
- *Knoll Color Fabric Guides* designed by Eszter Haraszty and Herbert Matter are published, featuring coordinated groups of Knoll draperies and upholsteries.
- *Scotch Linen* upholstery designed by Franz Lorenz is introduced.

Fig. C.5
Advertisement for Textile Division, Knoll Associates, Inc., designed by Herbert Matter, featuring *Knoll Fabric Color Guides*, 1950. Private collection.

1951
- Headquarters and New York showroom move to 575 Madison Avenue, interiors designed by Florence Knoll and KPU.
- *Puli* by Marianne Strengell is introduced.
- Knoll opens Stuttgart showroom.
- *Living-Up-to-Date* exhibition at the Baltimore Art Museum features Knoll furniture and textiles in a room installation by Florence Knoll.
- *Knoll Stripes* by Eszter Haraszty is introduced.

1952
- Harry Bertoia wire furniture is introduced. *Prestini* becomes standard upholstery fabric for Bertoia chair covers.
- Showroom opens in Washington, D.C.
- Chicago showroom moves to the Merchandise Mart.
- *Knoll Furniture and Textiles* exhibition is held at the Dallas Museum of Fine Arts.
- *Tracy* by Eszter Haraszty is introduced.
- Suzanne Huguenin is hired as Haraszty's assistant.
- Evelyn Hill designs a group of handwoven upholsteries and draperies for Knoll.

Fig. C.6
Advertisement for Knoll Associates, Inc., designed by Herbert Matter, featuring Eszter Haraszty's *Tracy*. From *Interiors*, August 1952.

1953
- KPU project: ALCOA building interiors, Pittsburgh, Pennsylvania.
- KPU project: International Center of the Carnegie Endowment for International Peace, New York City.
- KPU project: United States Embassy, Havana, Cuba.

Fig. C.7
Advertisement for Knoll Associates, Inc., designed by Herbert Matter, featuring the ALCOA building. From *Interiors*, November 1953.

- Printed fabrics *Fibra* designed by Eszter Haraszty, *Lazy Lines* by Astrid Sampe, and *Pythagoras* by Sven Markelius are introduced.
- *Kerry Linen* by Evelyn Hill is introduced.

1954
- KPU project: CBS executive floor, New York City.
- KPU project: Center for Advanced Study in the Behavioral Sciences, Palo Alto, California.
- KPU project: United States Embassy, Stockholm, Sweden.
- *Rugby* by Astrid Sampe is introduced.
- *Triad* by Eszter Haraszty is introduced.
- *Naugahyde* is introduced into the fabric collection.

Fig. C.8
Advertisement for Knoll Textiles, Inc., designed by Herbert Matter, featuring Eszter Haraszty's *Triad*. From *Interiors*, May 1955.

1955
- Knoll-Drake furniture designed by Ladislav Rado is introduced.
- Second group of *Handwovens* by Evelyn Hill is introduced.
- Hans Knoll dies in a car accident in Cuba on October 8. Florence Knoll becomes president of Knoll Associates, and Cornell Dechert is named general manager.
- Eszter Haraszty leaves Knoll; Suzanne Huguenin becomes head of Knoll Textiles.
- Robert Cadwallader joins Knoll as a sales associate in the Dallas showroom.
- *Parallel Bar* furniture designed by Florence Knoll is introduced.

1956
- *Textiles USA* exhibition is mounted at MoMA.
- San Francisco and Milan showrooms open.
- *Prisma* by Sven Markelius is introduced.
- *Lana* upholstery by Eszter Haraszty is introduced.
- *Shades* by Emily Belding, the first Knoll casement fabric to use ramie yarn, is introduced.

1957
- *Fiberglas Casement* by Anni Albers is introduced.
- *Furrows* by Suzanne Huguenin is introduced.
- *Trellis* by Reuben Eshkanian is introduced.
- *Pedestal* furniture collection by Eero Saarinen is introduced.
- KPU project: Connecticut General Life Insurance Company, Bloomfield, Connecticut.

1958
- *Nylon Homespun* by Suzanne Huguenin is introduced, is later renamed *Knoll Nylon Homespun*, and remains in production until 1988.
- Florence Knoll marries Miami-based banker Harry Hood Bassett.
- KPU project: Deering Milliken headquarters and sales office, New York City.
- *Mira* by Ross Littell is introduced.

Fig. C.9
Advertisement for Knoll Textiles, Inc., designed by Herbert Matter, featuring *Nylon Homespun* and other textiles, 1958. Bard Graduate Center: Decorative Arts, Design History, Material Culture; New York.

1959
- Florence Knoll sells Knoll to Art Metal Incorporated. She continues to oversee design and to head the Knoll Planning Unit.
- Barbara Rodes (later Rodes-Segerer) joins Knoll Germany.
- *Chess*, *Criss Cross*, *Spheres*, and *Discs* by Ross Littell are introduced.
- *Domus* and *Polo* by Suzanne Huguenin are introduced.
- *Skol* by Vibeke Bruun de Neergaard is introduced.
- KPU project: H.J. Heinz Company offices, Pittsburgh, Pennsylvania.
- *Lattice* by Anni Albers is introduced.
- *Peru* and *Polystripes* by Suzanne Huguenin are introduced.

1960
- Los Angeles showroom opens.
- Rome showroom opens.
- *Brigadoon* by Suzanne Huguenin is introduced.

1961
- Headquarters and New York showroom move to 320 Park Avenue.
- *Arno* and *Cato* by Paul Maute are introduced; *Cato* remains in production in 2011.
- *Bangkok* by Henning Watterston is introduced.

1962
- *Tracey* by Suzanne Huguenin is introduced.
- *Rail* by Anni Albers is introduced.
- KPU project: Offices of Cowles Magazines (publishers of *Look*), New York City.
- *Scotch Mist* by Peter Simpson is introduced.
- *Ebro* by Paul Maute is introduced.

1963
- *Linea*, and *Quartet* by Suzanne Huguenin are introduced; *Quartet* is discontinued in 1978 but reintroduced in the *Archival Collection* 2009.
- Suzanne Huguenin leaves Knoll.

1964
- *Heather*, *Bourette Silk*, and *Horizons* by Paul Maute are introduced.
- Sheila Hicks is contracted to design fabrics and to act as a color and materials consultant.

1965
- Florence Knoll Bassett retires.
- Robert Cadwallader is named director (later vice president) of marketing.
- *Track* by Anni Albers is introduced.
- *York* upholstery is introduced.
- KPU project: CBS Building, New York City.

Fig. C.10
Advertisement for Knoll Associates, Inc., designed by Herbert Matter, featuring *York*, 1965. Knoll Archives.

1966
- Wire-based furniture designed by Warren Platner is introduced.
- *Morocco* by Paul Maute is introduced.
- *Inca* by Sheila Hicks is introduced.
- *Harrow* by Julia Keiner-Forchheimer is introduced.
- Massimo Vignelli replaces Herbert Matter as Knoll's graphic designer.

1967
- New graphic formats and program designed by Vignelli debut.
- *Jupiter* and *Stratton* by Julia Keiner-Forchheimer are introduced.

Fig. C.11
Advertisement for Knoll International, designed by Massimo Vignelli, ca. 1970. Knoll Archives.

1968
- Knoll purchases Gavina SpA and in 1969 introduces Gavina furniture, including the *Malitte* seating system by Roberto Sebastian Matta.
- Walter E. Heller International Corporation of Chicago acquires Art Metal and its subsidiaries, including Knoll.
- *Lumière* and *Mosaic* by Wolf Bauer are introduced.
- Gae Aulenti redesigns Boston showroom.

Fig. C.12
Advertisement for Knoll International introducing the Gavina Group furniture featuring *Malitte* modular seating, ca. 1969. Bard Graduate Center: Decorative Arts, Design History, Material Culture, New York.

1969
- *Delta*, *Stones*, *Fragment*, and *Collage* by Wolf Bauer are introduced in the United States.
- Knoll Associates is renamed Knoll International.

1970
- Robert Cadwallader is named executive vice president of Knoll International.
- New York showroom, moves from 320 Park Avenue to 745 Fifth Avenue. The new showroom is designed by Gae Aulenti.
- *Dynamic* by Marga Hielle-Vatter is introduced.
- *Tiber* by Paul Maute is introduced.

Fig. C.13
Knoll Textiles, Textiles Price List, 1970. Designed by Massimo Vignelli. KnollTextiles Archive.

1971
- Barbara Rodes (after 1976, Rodes-Segerer) is named director of textile development worldwide.
- Robert Cadwallader becomes president of Knoll after Cornell Dechert becomes chairman of the board.
- Printed fabrics *Slant* by Ulrike Rhomberg-Greiner, *Omahar* by Francisca Reichardt, *Lines* by François Dallegret, *Yves* and *Wheels* by Wolf Bauer, and *Sling* by Gretl and Leo Wollner are introduced.
- *Tacoma* by Marga Hielle-Vatter is introduced.
- *Stephens Office Landscape System* by Williams Stephens is introduced.

1972
- *Knoll au Louvre* exhibition held at Musée des Arts décoratifs, Paris.
- *Three Meter Print Collection* by Gretl and Leo Wollner, including *Rivers*, *Roads*, *Sails*, and *Trails*, is introduced.
- Knoll sponsors "Transparent," a casement fabric design competition at the Staatliche Akademie der Bildenden Künste (State Academy of Art and Design) in Stuttgart.
- *Atoll*, *Almanach*, *Brabant*, *Serenade*, and *Marabu* by Paul Maute are introduced.
- *Knoll Velvet* is introduced and remains in production in 2011.
- *Durban* by Jan-Paul Barnard is introduced.

1973
- Barbara Rodes (after 1976, Rodes-Segerer) appointed vice president and director of Knoll Textiles worldwide.
- *Loop* and *Nebula* by Paul Maute are introduced.
- *The Collection*, an exhibition devoted to Knoll Textiles, is held at the Knoll showroom in New York.
- Three student designs from the "Transparent" competition are selected for inclusion in the Knoll collection: *Puzzle* by Margarete Warth, *Comet* by Friedrich Goth, and *Meton* by Sybille Dobringer.
- Print fabrics by Lynne Crosbee are introduced.

1974
- *Sequoia* by Suzanne Huguenin is introduced.
- *Cornaro* by Paul Maute is introduced.
- *Lasar* by McNutt Weaving is introduced.

1975
- *Jhet* by Anni Albers is introduced.
- *Zapf System* by Otto Zapf is introduced.

1976
- *Partition Fabric*, Knoll's first fabric exclusively for use on office panel systems, is introduced.
- *Eclat*, *Eclat-S*, *Eclat-T*, and *Epos-T* by Anni Albers are introduced.
- *Tournee* by Marga Hielle-Vatter is introduced.
- *Chord*, *Knoll Bouclé*, *Kamee*, *Parsifal*, and *Atlantis* by Paul Maute are introduced.

1977
- Marshall Cogan and Stephen Swid of General Felt Industries purchase Knoll International. Robert Cadwallader resigns.
- *Regency* panel fabric is introduced and remains part of the collection until 2010.
- Arthur Sager is hired as vice president and general manager of Knoll Textiles.
- Printed textiles *Grille*, *Triad*, *Crossroads*, *Ribbon*, *Interplay*, *Benday*, *Aquarelle*, and *Pyramid* by Christa Häusler are introduced.
- *Cocoon* by Paul Maute is introduced.
- *Knoll Cotton Velvet* is introduced.
- *Nylon Homespun Pinstripe* and *Check* are introduced.

Fig. C.14
Advertisement for Knoll International, designed by Massimo Vignelli, featuring *Knoll Cotton Velvet*, 1977. Knoll Archives.

1978
- Barbara Rodes-Segerer resigns.
- Richard Wagner is named creative director of Knoll Textiles.
- Many fabrics are dropped from the collection, including all prints.
- Knoll Textiles becomes a separate operating division of Knoll International.

Fig. C.15
Advertisement for Knoll International, designed by Massimo Vignelli, featuring *Nylon Homespun Pinstripe* and *Check*, 1978. Knoll Archive.

1979
- Peter Seipelt is hired as design director for Knoll Textiles in Europe.
- *Collection 1* of printed fabrics by Nob and Non Utsumi is introduced.
- *Desna* upholstery is introduced for use on *Diffrient* chair collection.

1980
- Arthur Sager resigns, and Richard Wagner is appointed vice president and general manager of Knoll Textiles.
- New York showroom opens at 655 Madison Avenue, designed by the architecture firm Venturi and Rauch.

1981
- Merle Lindby-Young is hired as creative director of Knoll Textiles.
- Arthur Sager returns to Knoll in an executive position overseeing Knoll Textiles and other divisions.
- Printed fabrics by Peter Seipelt are introduced.
- *Furrows Wallcarpeting* is introduced.

1982
- *Adrian Parry Collection* of printed fabrics by Adrian Pulfer and Parry Merkley is introduced.
- Knoll Design Center showroom and offices open at 105 Wooster Street in New York's Soho district.

1983
- First upholstery collection by Jhane Barnes is introduced, including *Nuance*, which remains in the line until 2010.

1984
- Knoll Textiles introduces a group of wallcoverings under the name Knoll Wall.
- New graphic program by Knoll Graphics designers, including Harold Matoussian and Takaaki Matsumoto, is introduced.

1985
- First upholstery collection by Dana Romeis is introduced.

Fig. C.16
Knoll Textiles envelope, designed by Takaaki Matsumoto, 1985. Knoll Archives.

1986
- Stephen Swid leaves Knoll.
- *Knoll Window Collection* is introduced, including five designs by Jhane Barnes.

1987
- The Signature Series, a group of coordinated panel fabrics, wallcoverings, and drapery fabrics, is introduced.
- Robin Whitten's *American Craftsman Collection* of upholstery fabrics is introduced.
- Merle Lindby-Young leaves Knoll Textiles.

1988
- Knoll is reorganized into four new divisions: KnollOffice, KnollTextiles, KnollAccents (eventually renamed KnollExtra), and KnollStudio.
- Second upholstery collection by Dana Romeis is introduced.
- Vertical Variations, a program of customized panel fabrics, wallcoverings, and draperies, is introduced.

1989
- *Anne Beetz Collection* is introduced.
- Richard Wagner and Arthur Sager leave Knoll.
- Hazel Siegel is named managing director of design for KnollTextiles.
- Knoll introduces a group of upholsteries by Jhane Barnes, including the innovative knit textiles *Waves*, *Pinwheels*, *Strata*, and *Luna*.

Fig. C.17
Advertisement for KnollTextiles, featuring Jhane Barnes's *Pinwheels*, 1989. Knoll Archives.

1990
- *Hazel Siegel Collection* is introduced, the largest introduction in KnollTextiles history.
- Knoll International is purchased by Westinghouse Electric Company. Westinghouse combines Knoll International, Shaw-Walker Company, and Reff Inc. into a new entity, the Knoll Group.

1991
- KnollTextiles operations in Europe are suspended, and Knoll's European print collection is purchased by Alato.
- Peter Eisenman's *Snakes and Ladders Collection* of upholsteries is introduced.

1992
- Hazel Siegel resigns from KnollTextiles. Staff designer Suzin Steerman is named senior designer for all product developments at KnollTextiles.
- *Constructions Collection* by Jhane Barnes, Knoll's first group of non-woven, non-textile wallcoverings, is introduced.
- *Chronology Collection* by Jhane Barnes is introduced, including *Transition*, which remains in production in 2011.

1993
- Suzin Steerman's *Urban Geometry Collection*, *Hemisphere Collection*, and *Kabuki Collection* are introduced.
- *American Mosaic Collection* by Tim Van Campen is introduced.
- Knoll introduces its first healthcare textile collection, the *Horizon Collection*, which is made up of eight drapery fabrics by Jhane Barnes.

1994
- Suzin Steerman contributes four new designs to the *Horizon Collection* of healthcare fabrics.

1995
- Deborah Steele is named vice president of marketing and design for KnollTextiles.
- Suzanne Tick's *A New Day Collection* is introduced.
- The Knoll Group is sold to Warburg Pincus Ventures and renamed Knoll, Inc.

1996
- *Screenplay Collection* by Claudine Piaget is introduced.
- The environmentally friendly panel fabrics *Resolution* and *Clarity*, designed by Suzanne Tick, are introduced and remain part of the collection in 2011.
- Deborah Steele leaves KnollTextiles.

1997
- Suzanne Tick is named creative director of KnollTextiles.
- KnollTextiles celebrates the fiftieth anniversary of its founding and introduces the *Decades Collection*, new versions of patterns from the company's archive.
- Knoll Museum opens at the Knoll complex in East Greenville, Pennsylvania.

1998
- The final Jhane Barnes designs for Knoll are introduced.
- KnollTextiles debuts the "Integrated Interior," a program that will regularly introduce wallcoverings, panel fabrics, draperies, and upholstery fabrics that work together in a cohesive way in an interior.
- *Silver Screen* drapery by Suzanne Tick is introduced and remains in production in 2011.

2000
- *Imago*, a hard-surface material composed of textiles encapsulated in high-performance resin, is introduced.

2001
- Andrew Cogan becomes CEO of Knoll.
- Suzanne Tick's panel fabrics *Foil Rap* and *Hard Rock* are introduced and remain in production in 2011.

2003
- *Stephen Sprouse Collection* is introduced.

2004
- *Field Theory Collection* and *Chatter Collection* by 2x4, Inc. are introduced.
- *Woodland Collection* by Elizabeth Whelan is introduced.
- Suzanne Tick resigns as creative director for KnollTextiles but continues to regularly contribute designs to the collection.

Fig. C.18
Brochure for KnollTextiles entitled *Field Theory Collection* and *Chatter Collection*, designed by 2x4, Inc., 2004. Courtesy 2x4, Inc.

2005
- Dorothy Cosonas is named creative director of KnollTextiles.

2006
- First collection of upholstery fabrics by Dorothy Cosonas is introduced.
- Wallcovering collections by LTL and Abbott Miller are introduced.

2007
- KnollTextiles celebrates the sixtieth anniversary of its founding and introduces the *Archival Collection*, which revives patterns from the company's historic catalogue of designs.
- *Rivington* by Dorothy Cosonas is introduced.

2008
- Knoll Luxe brand introduced in March with a collection of designs by Dorothy Cosonas.
- *Proenza Schouler Collection* for Knoll Luxe is introduced.

Fig. C.19
Brochure for Knoll Luxe, designed by The Moderns, 2008. KnollTextiles Archive.

2010
- *Rodarte Collection* for Knoll Luxe is introduced.

Fig. C.20 Advertisement for KnollTextiles, introducing Jhane Barnes's *Pella*, 1997. Knoll Archive.

1 The Design, Promotion, and Production of Modern Textiles in the USA, 1940–60

Susan Ward

Knoll Textiles came into being against a broad canvas of changes in the American textile industry in the mid-twentieth century. These changes can be charted through the records of the design exhibitions and competitions that flourished at this time. They provide a fascinating glimpse of major trends and new developments in textile design from the early 1940s to the late 1950s, a period roughly bracketed by two exhibitions: *Organic Design in Home Furnishings* (1941) and *Textiles USA* (1956). In between there were scores of others, and thanks to the careful preservation of documents by institutions such as the Museum of Modern Art in New York and the Cranbrook Academy of Art in Bloomfield Hills, Michigan, this moment in design history can be examined in some detail.

This period was also marked by the arrival of many prominent designers and artists from Europe, who had fled the political climate of the 1930s. They found positions at key educational institutions, and their students, ideas of modernism and new attitudes toward textile design and technology fanned out across the country. Several European handweaver/designers brought new life to the field of woven textiles, inspiring a generation of American weavers and broadening the outlook of American manufacturers. The screen-printing technique, still relatively new at the time, was also embraced by this generation of designers and used on both a craft level and an industrial scale. Designers started their own companies and began to team with manufacturers, establishing celebrity status in the burgeoning design world.

In the decade after World War II, perhaps more than at any time before or since, the importance of good design was a theme that pervaded American culture. Jack Lenor Larsen later wrote of this period, "it is difficult to explain the velocity with which design exploded out of the dim war years."[1] With the acute postwar housing shortage, new developments in the design of homes and home furnishings were considered news—the subject of articles in art and design periodicals, but also in major newspapers and in mass-circulation magazines such as *Life*. This was a heady time for designers starting their own textile companies, and working with industrial partners, but it was not to last. The conditions that had fostered the postwar American design boom began to change in the mid-1950s, and the old separations between textile artists and industry began to reemerge. By the end of the period, the American textile industry was falling into a difficult decline, forcing American companies such as Knoll to rely more and more on European designers and manufacturers.

Organic Design and the Foundations of Postwar Textile Design

In 1941 the Museum of Modern Art (MoMA) in New York staged *Organic Design in Home Furnishings,* an exhibition that distilled ongoing changes and recent developments in contemporary furniture and fabrics (figs. 1.1, 1.2).[2] Although its textile component has been largely overlooked by design historians, it was a seminal event with long-lasting repercussions. Even a decade later, the designer Alvin Lustig described it as "perhaps the most important single event shaping the direction of modern American fabric design."[3] It not only focused attention on the requisite textiles for modern furniture and interiors, but also helped introduce new ideas about textile design to a wider audience, including the conservative American textile industry. While looking ahead, *Organic Design* also provided a kind of record of changes

Fig. 1.1 Noémi Raymond. Printed textile length, ca. 1941. Cotton; plain weave, screen-printed. Raymond Collection, The Architectural Archives, University of Pennsylvania. Cat. 1.

that were underway in American textiles even before the war.

Museum competitions and exhibitions—in concert with design-conscious manufacturers and entrepreneurs—would play an important role in the postwar years, and *Organic Design* heralded this development. It was announced in 1940 as the first major undertaking of MoMA's recently formed Department of Industrial Design, under the direction of architect and designer Eliot Noyes. The competition, which included furniture, lighting, and textile designs and was cosponsored by a group of twelve major American department stores, set out "to select a group of designers capable of creating a useful and beautiful environment for today's living, in terms of furniture, fabrics and lighting."[4] The winning designers would be given the opportunity to work with manufacturers to bring their designs to the marketplace, and the results would go on display in the *Organic Design* exhibition a year later.

The exhibition committee coined "organic design" to describe the qualities that they felt distinguished the winning furniture designs—meaning that the designs "began with today's living problems and grew out of their needs" and that the design and function were "an organic whole."[5] Noyes further defined this as "an harmonious organization of the parts within the whole, according to structure, material, and purpose. Within this definition there can be no vain ornamentation or superfluity, but the part of beauty is none the less great—in ideal choice of material, in visual refinement, and in the rational elegance of things intended for use."[6]

While a definition of "organic" textiles was not similarly spelled out, the design community would have understood the winning textiles on display as demonstrating "organic," materials-based, functionally integrated approaches to woven and printed textile design—approaches that were relatively new on the American scene. In the early 1930s, American weavers and textile designers had begun to shift their focus from surface imagery to texture, fibers, and construction, a shift that reflected the influence of European modernism and the Bauhaus.[7] One of the first weavers to produce furnishing fabrics in this "structural" idiom in the United States was a German-born artist, Maria Kipp, who had been the first female graduate of the Staatliche Textilberufsschule (State Academy for Textile Industries) in Muenchberg, Bavaria, a prominent German textile center. She immigrated to the United States in 1924 at the age of twenty-four and established a successful handweaving studio in Los Angeles in 1926, thereafter producing custom fabrics for many modernist California architects and designers (fig. 1.3).[8]

Kipp was but one of the many prominent European artists and designers to immigrate to the United States in the early twentieth century. Their numbers increased during the 1930s, as the world moved toward war, and among the new arrivals were several important textile designers who would have a significant and long-lasting impact on American textile design. In 1933 Anni Albers, who had been on the Bauhaus faculty, arrived from Germany to teach at Black Mountain College in North Carolina, where she remained until 1949. Marli Ehrman, a Bauhaus graduate, was at the School of Design (later Institute of Design) in Chicago from 1939 to 1946.[9] As educators Albers and Ehrman followed many Bauhaus practices, emphasizing direct experimentation with materials and weave structures.[10] Another new arrival, and perhaps ultimately the most influential, was Marianne Strengell, who emigrated from Finland in 1936 and taught at the Cranbrook Academy of Art (hereafter referred to as Cranbrook) from 1937 to 1961. Strengell had been trained in the Scandinavian tradition, but she largely abandoned the decorative patterning common in Scandinavian weaving in favor of color and texture effects and emphasized working directly with materials in her teaching.[11]

By the early 1940s, the approach to textile design that these women championed and taught, which was referred to as "contemporary handweaving," had spread to American handweavers in general.[12] During this period "the style pendulum began to swing violently away from pattern and toward color and texture. It was then that handweavers really made more progress in the designing of fabrics and in creative weaving than in all the preceding years of this century."[13] As weaver and educator Ed Rossbach (who studied weaving at Cranbrook in the mid-1940s) later wrote: "Woven structure, like architectural structure, was being exposed. Patterning arose from this structure."[14]

A few pioneering American designers also advanced the cause of contemporary handweaving and modern textile design before the war. Californian Dorothy Liebes had a European connection, having studied textile design with Paul Rodier in Paris for a year before opening her own weaving studio in San Francisco in 1930.[15] A savvy businesswoman with a gift for promotion, Liebes became known for her use of unusual materials such as wood, bamboo, and leather, and for "vibrating" color combinations. As director of the decorative arts exhibition for the Golden Gate International Exposition (1939–40) in San Francisco, she made many professional connections, and in 1940 she secured a contract to design upholstery and drapery fabrics for a leading manufacturer, Goodall Fabrics of Sanford, Maine.[16] The Liebes–Goodall collaboration helped make her a nationally known figure (fig. 1.4), America's "first lady of the loom."[17]

In New York, another early leader in modern textiles emerged in the late 1930s. Boris Kroll established his own firm, Cromwell Designs, in 1938, renaming it Boris Kroll Fabrics in 1946. He was one of the first designers to concentrate on modern upholstery fabrics for the contract market and to use both hand and power looms.[18] Although he did not participate in as many competitions and exhibitions as some of his contemporaries, he was prominent within the trade and by the early 1950s had established a reputation "for pioneering in textured fabrics notable for advanced design and hardy quality."[19]

MoMA's *Organic Design* exhibition of 1941 prominently showcased the new structural strain of contemporary weaving and was one of the first American installations to demonstrate its use in modern interiors. Marli Ehrman's simple plain weaves and twills won first prize for woven fabrics. Their surface patterns (stripes, checks, or streaks of contrasting colors) resulted from the choice and order of warp and weft yarns in colors ranging from neutral earth tones to deep reds and blues (figs. 1.5, 1.6). Six of her handwoven patterns were selected for production (each in several colorways) by the Moss Rose Manufacturing Company of Philadelphia.[20] Moss Rose, which at the time specialized in Jacquard-woven furnishing fabrics, was one of the first American mills to recognize the value of working with outside designers and continued to participate in MoMA exhibitions over the next decade.[21] The firm's adaptations of Ehrman's fabrics were woven on Jacquard looms and therefore had a more complex weave structure, but they nonetheless retained the simple surface textures of her handwoven samples (figs 1.7, 1.8). Many of the furniture designs in *Organic Design*, including winning chair designs by Charles Eames and Eero Saarinen (fig. 1.9), were upholstered in Ehrman/Moss Rose upholstery fabrics, providing designers and manufacturers with a model of the kind of fabrics that the sleek forms and unbroken surfaces of modern upholstered furniture designs would require.[22]

The winning designs in the printed fabrics category of *Organic Design*, while attributed to architect Antonin Raymond for reasons unknown, were actually the work of his wife and collaborator, Noémi Raymond (fig. 1.10).[23] After spending much of the preceding two decades working on architectural projects in Japan, the Raymonds had returned to the United States in 1938.[24] Their work reflects a modernist aesthetic strongly influenced by traditional Japanese design and craftsmanship, as can be seen in the textiles and rugs that Noémi Raymond created for the interiors they planned. Noémi Raymond's submissions to *Organic Design* used multiple single-screen patterns that could be layered and combined in different ways—including printing the motif that would later become Knoll's *Mosaic* (1950) over what became Knoll's *Chinese Coins* (1948)—thereby demonstrating the variety of effects that could be achieved with the screen-printing process (fig. 1.1). The Raymond textile designs submitted to *Organic Design* largely included Japanese motifs or made reference to the Japanese textile techniques of *shibori* (tie-dye) and *katazome* (stencil-dyeing). As with the upholstery fabrics, many of them were displayed in the exhibition to suggest appropriate use as floor-to-ceiling draperies in modern interiors—where they would, as Alvin Lustig later wrote, "function as [a] plane of color or texture rather than as panels to hang on either side of a hole in the wall."[25]

As a group, the printed textiles in *Organic Design* (figs. 1.2, 1.11) demonstrated the expressive possibilities and versatility of the screen-printing technique.[26] A number of American artists and designers, including textile designer Ruth Reeves, had already worked with this technique. Reeves, who had studied painting in Paris with Fernand Léger during the 1920s, designed a groundbreaking collection of modern block- and screen-printed fabrics for the New York retailer W. & J. Sloane in 1930.[27] Screen printing was still relatively new, however, and used primarily for custom designs or small-scale production. Innovative American designer Dan Cooper, for one, regularly used abstract block- and screen-printed textiles (often printed on rough-textured linen) for drapery and upholstery beginning in the late 1930s.[28]

Like Ehrman, the Raymonds were paired with a textile manufacturer, Cyrus Clark Company, a New York firm primarily known for chintzes and traditional floral prints, who was to produce and promote the winning MoMA designs. The collaboration, however, was not successful, perhaps reflecting the limited understanding of modern fabrics in America at the time. After Noémi Raymond met with Clark in February 1941, Antonin Raymond reported to Noyes at MoMA that the company "took a decidedly negative attitude toward the problem, as though they had been dragged, [in] spite of themselves, into this affair." He also enclosed an open letter to the competition committee, stressing the importance of marketing modern textiles by demonstrating their use with modern furniture and interiors, insisting that "it is very evident that these designs cannot be popularized by being sold with the old stock across the counter."[29] Five of Noémi Raymond's print designs, plus one by honorable-mention–winner Virginia Nepodal, who would come to prominence as design director for Greeff Fabrics during the 1950s, were produced in limited quantities by Clark and shown in use as both draperies and upholstery in the exhibition (fig. 1.11). Most of the Raymond textiles on view in the exhibition were printed, however, possibly on the Raymonds' own initiative, by Cold Spring Bleachery in Yardley, Pennsylvania.[30]

The story of Noémi Raymond's *Organic Design* textiles between the close of the exhibition in 1941 and 1948, when more of her 1941 designs were finally put into production, reflects the dramatic changes that took place in the textile marketplace during and after World War II. Raymond exhibited some of the panels at other venues, including the first annual International Textile Exhibition at the Woman's College of the University of North Carolina in 1944 and the First Biennial Exhibition of Contemporary Textiles and Ceramics at Cranbrook in 1946.[31] She remained wary of dealing with commercial manufacturers, however, telling Marianne Strengell before the First Biennial, "I have not worked out any more textiles of late—not since the beginning of

Fig. 1.2 Installation view, *Organic Design in Home Furnishings* exhibition, MoMA, New York, September 24–November 9, 1941. Hanging textiles are by Noémi Raymond and include the panel in fig. 1.1 (fifth from the left). Photographed by Samuel H. Gottscho. Photographic Archive, The Museum of Modern Art, New York, IN148.3.

Fig. 1.3 Maria Kipp. Hand loomed gauze textile, 1949. Cotton, rayon, mohair and metallic thread. Collection of Cranbrook Art Museum, Bloomfield Hills, Michigan. Museum purchase, Founders Fund.

Fig. 1.4 Detail of Dorothy Liebes in her Sutter Street Studio, San Francisco, California, 1947. Photographed by Charles E. Steinheimer. Time & Life Pictures/Getty Images.

Fig. 1.5 Top left Marli Ehrman. Detail, handwoven upholstery fabric sample (no.13308), ca. 1940. Cotton and wool. The Museum of Modern Art, New York, Gift of the designer, 884.1942.
Fig. 1.6 Top right Marli Ehrman. Detail, machine woven upholstery fabric (no. 13308), ca. 1940. Manufactured by Moss Rose Manufacturing Co., Philadelphia, Penn. Cotton. The Museum of Modern Art, New York, Gift of the designer, 892.1942.

Fig. 1.7 Bottom left Marli Ehrman. Detail, handwoven upholstery fabric sample (no. 13309), ca. 1940. Cotton. The Museum of Modern Art, New York, Gift of the designer, 885.1942.
Fig. 1.8 Bottom right Marli Ehrman. Detail, machine woven upholstery fabric (no. 13309), ca. 1940. Manufactured by Moss Rose Manufacturing Co., Philadelphia, Penn. Cotton. The Museum of Modern Art, New York, Gift of the designer, 895.1942.

Fig. 1.9 Top Installation view, *Organic Design in Home Furnishings* exhibition, MoMA, New York, September 24–November 9, 1941. Chairs upholstered in Marli Ehrman's fabrics (Moss Rose Manufacturing Co.); settee (left) in Noémi Raymond's *Speckles* (Cyrus Clark). Furniture designed by Charles Eames and Eero Saarinen. Photographic Archive, The Museum of Modern Art, New York, IN148.11.

Fig. 1.10 Bottom Detail of Noémi Raymond in her Tokyo studio, ca. 1953. Raymond Collection, The Architectural Archives, University of Pennsylvania.

Fig. 1.11 Bottom Installation view, *Organic Design in Home Furnishings* exhibition, MoMA, New York, September 24–November 9, 1941. Fabrics designed by Noémi Raymond including *Strip Fields* pattern (center left) and by Virginia Nepodal (textile far right); printed by Cyrus Clark and Cold Spring Bleachery. Photographed by Samuel H. Gottscho. Photographic Archive, The Museum of Modern Art, New York, IN148.9.

Fig. 1.12 Top left Installation view, *Second National Biennial Exhibition of Contemporary Textiles and Ceramics*, 1949. *Reeds and Bars* by Noémi Raymond for Knoll is at center right. Photographed by Harvey Croze. Cranbrook Archives, Bloomfield Hills, Mich., AA2385-15.

Fig. 1.13 Top right Marianne Strengell, ca. 1943. Cranbrook Archives, Marianne Strengell Papers, 1991-07.

Fig. 1.14 Angelo Testa. *Filo*, ca. 1948. Made for Knoll Associates, Inc. Used for drapery; cotton; plain weave, screen-printed. Cooper-Hewitt, National Design Museum, Smithsonian Institution, Gift of Mae Festa, 1991-157-8. Cat. 16.

the war. The lack of materials— and the fact that, after the Museum of Modern Art experiment, I realized that one could meet with no satisfaction unless one *manufactured* and *sold* oneself—decided me to wait until I could do so."[32]

In 1947 Raymond submitted her *Strip Fields* pattern (another of the *Organic Design* panels) to a competition org-anized by the Philadelphia Print Club.[33] By 1948, Knoll had put two of Raymond's designs into production (*Reeds and Bars* and *Chinese Coins*), and F. Schumacher and Company had printed two others, proudly submitting one of them (*Strip Fields*) to the *American Textiles,'48* exhibition at the Metropolitan Museum of Art (see fig. 1.20).[34] Raymond was invited by Strengell to exhibit in the Second Biennial at Cranbrook in 1949; this time she arranged to have her fabrics shipped directly from the manufacturers (fig. 1.12).[35] After Knoll introduced another of Raymond's designs, *Mosaic*, in 1950, her work was again shown in MoMA's galleries, in one of the *Good Design* exhibitions organized by Edgar Kaufmann Jr.[36] In little under a decade, the textile world had caught up to Raymond's modern aesthetic; once considered non-commercial, she now found herself at the center of a thriving midcentury textile revolution.

**A Fresh and Unbiased Start:
Raising the Quality of Textile Design**

MoMA's *Organic Design* exhibition opened in September 1941, just a few months before the United States entered World War II. By then modern design had taken on a new association with broader notions of freedom and democracy. At the exhibition opening, the architect Wallace K. Harrison, chairman of the museum's Trustee Committee on Industrial Design, contrasted the artistic freedom enjoyed in the United States with the suppression of modern art and the Aryan-ization of culture in Nazi Germany. He linked the *Organic Design* exhibition to the nation's overarching goals, saying that "we Americans . . . are engaged in building our culture for the future with the knowledge and strength that we are fighting to live in a better world, not die for the preservation of a past culture."[37] The United States' entry into the war in December placed almost immediate restrictions on materials and required the conversion of textile factories to meet defense needs. Any momentum in the marketplace generated by the *Organic Design* exhibition was therefore short-lived.

Some designers and commentators, however, saw the restrictive conditions of wartime as an opportunity for a new start in design. In 1942 Marianne Strengell (fig. 1.13) called on those involved in creating textiles to use the next few years to improve the products of the textile industry at all levels:

It is of the greatest future importance to use this enforced breathing spell to the best advantage. Every ounce of willpower, ingenuity, and talent should be turned in the right direction—to prepare for [the] post-war world to come. . . . Many big concerns have already devoted one department to nothing but work for the post-war period, experimenting ceaselessly, utilizing new ideas, planning and probing. It is of the utmost importance that the textile industry should do the same. . . . There are great hopes for the future . . . Hopes for more interesting processes in materials, for new discoveries in fibers, and for greater freedom in design. Hopes for a fresh and unbiased start.[38]

The curriculum for Cranbrook weaving students that Strengell wrote in 1942 reflected these aspirations. She included two topics of particular importance at this time: study of and experimentation with new materials and study of a wider range of techniques, such as designing for the power loom.[39] Ehrman, at the Institute of Design in Chicago, likewise encouraged her students to make samples for both hand and power looms and to experiment with new materials, especially plastics.[40] At Black Mountain College, Albers taught weaving as "a preparatory step to machine production," and throughout her own career, she experimented with synthetic and industrial materials.[41]

In reflecting on her work for Goodall Fabrics, Dorothy Liebes expressed the idea "that hand-weaving at its best could and should be used as experimental laboratory material for mechanical reproduction."[42] Like Strengell, Liebes believed that wartime material shortages must lead to more creative use of available materials. In October 1942 the New York furniture retailer W. & J. Sloane held an exhibition of her fabrics (both hand- and machine-woven), "made entirely of non-priority materials."[43] Though Strengell, Ehrman, and Albers continued to believe that handwoven textiles had a place in modern interiors, they all placed a high priority on preparing their students to improve the design of machine-woven textiles after the war.

Screen printing and printed-textile design also developed considerably during the war. Some larger manufacturers began using screens after a 1942 government requirement that all copper printing rollers not used within the last year be surrendered as scrap metal for the war effort.[44] Block and screen printing were part of the new Cranbrook curriculum, and at about this time Strengell began to design her own printed patterns.[45] Through this and similar initiatives at other schools, many new artists were attracted to the textile field at this time. Since small screen-printing operations could be set up at a relatively low cost, and designs could be printed on the fabrics available during the war, students and young designers, some of whom would later found their own companies, began to experiment with the technique. Chicago-based designer Angelo Testa, for example, who became a leading designer of printed textiles, created some of his most famous patterns, including *Filo*, (fig. 1.14) while he was still a student at the School of Design, in 1942.[46] His print designs and design philosophy—emphasizing abstract form, line, color, and texture over representational pattern—were prominently featured in the October 1945 and July 1946 issues of *Arts & Architecture*.[47] Another Chicago designer, Ben Rose, made his first textile prints as table mats that he printed in his kitchen to give away as Christmas gifts in 1945.[48]

With materials scarce, institutions planned new competitions and exhibitions to emphasize the importance of design. The first International Textile Exhibition was held at the Woman's College of the University of North Carolina in November 1944, with the goal of bringing "the finest textiles in the world to a central place where they can be seen by interested persons" and providing a venue for designers, manufacturers, and retailers to see new and innovative work.[49] An enthusiastic review in *Upholstering* magazine praised the quality of the work on view and the effort to encourage creative textile design "at a time when this major industry faces a post-war period of gigantic readjustment to unprecedented demands."[50] The winners received purchase awards (meaning that their designs were purchased for production) contributed by the exhibition's sponsors, which included such firms as Burlington Mills, American Enka Corporation, Celanese Corporation of America, and the Marshall Field and Company department stores.[51]

The University of North Carolina's competitive exhibitions were held annually until 1954 and attracted entries from a wide range of established designers, students, university faculty, and hobbyists (fig. 1.15).[52] By 1946 a category for woven synthetic fabrics had been added (possibly at the request of the sponsors, who offered technical advice), and it was announced that the "designs and textures of materials may be studied by leading manufacturers in the field with the idea of producing them by machine."[53] The participating designers recognized the significance of these events. Weaver Robert Sailors, a regular participant who received several awards over the years, viewed them as providing an opportunity to see a wide range of contemporary work and generally elevating the quality of design over the years.[54]

Soon after the end of the war, Cranbrook began preparations for a series of biennial exhibitions featuring modern ceramic and textile design. The first of these opened in 1946 and three others followed, the last in 1953. Like the International Textile Exhibitions, these invitational exhibitions set out to bring together the best contemporary work for the benefit of Cranbrook students and the general public. Each installment aimed "to seek out new directions and new designers" and brought together work by most of the leading weavers and textile designers of the day.[55] Regular participants included Anni Albers, Marli Ehrman, Maria Kipp, Lillian Garrett, Angelo Testa, Alexander Girard, Ruth Adler Schnee, and Henning Watterston.[56]

In addition to educational institutions, American manufacturers also sponsored competitions for woven textiles. La France Industries, a large mill headquartered in La France, South Carolina, held three competitions in the 1940s, the first of which, in 1944, focused on "modern upholstery and drapery designs adaptable to power loom weaving" and awarded a first prize ($100 for a "modern leaf design") to Marianne Strengell. The company was unable to put the winning designs into production, however, because of wartime yarn shortages.[57] In their next two competitions (1945 and 1947), they gave separate prizes to professional and amateur designers. Antoinette Lackner Prestini (later Webster), who designed the upholstery *Prestini* (1948) for Knoll, won the fifth amateur prize in 1947.[58] The Moss Rose company in Philadelphia also hosted annual competitions from 1946 until 1952. These were restricted to students in American textile and design schools and to designs (modern or traditional) suitable for weaving on Jacquard looms, like those used in the Moss Rose factory.[59] Competitions such as these helped manufacturers identify promising designers and kept textile design (as well as the sponsoring companies' names) in the public eye.

MoMA's advocacy for contemporary textiles appropriate to modern interiors continued after the war. In 1945 the museum mounted *Modern Textile Design,* a small circulating exhibition curated by Susanne Wasson-Tucker of the Department of Industrial Design. On display were textiles by leading designers—Albers, Liebes (designs for Goodall Fabrics), Testa, and Cooper—"chosen to emphasize the value of well-designed textiles in the modern interior."[60] After closing at MoMA, the show traveled to colleges, universities, and art museums around the country.[61]

In February 1946, a few months after *Modern Textile Design* left the museum for its national tour, MoMA announced a competition for printed fabric design, sponsored by a group of leading department stores. The leading textile firm Brunschwig & Fils would put several of the winning designs into production.[62] The goal was to stimulate "progressive activity in this field by encouraging a fresh approach among designers and by promoting an understanding and appreciation on the part of the public and trade groups," in the hope of overcoming the shortage of modern prints on the market.[63] *Printed Textiles for the Home*, an exhibition of selected submissions, opened at MoMA in March 1947.[64] There had been an astonishing 2,443 designs submitted by 1,149 entrants.[65] The jury of five consisted of Marcel Breuer, René d'Harnoncourt, James Johnson Sweeney, Zelina Brunschwig (the company's director of design), and Aline Louchheim of *Art News* magazine.[66] Four of the prize-winning fabrics—by Yvonne Delattre, Milton Weiner (two prizes), and Frederic Károly (fig. 1.16)—were put into production and widely publicized. These featured overall patterns of repeated small motifs, which may have seemed more practical to the manufacturer—several larger-scale and more fanciful designs received prizes, but were not put

Fig. 1.15 Top Cover (based on printed fabric designed by Henriette W. Mueller), *International Textile Exhibition* catalogue, Department of Art, Woman's College of the University of North Carolina, Greensboro, November 1–30, 1948. Courtesy Susan Ward.

Fig. 1.16 Bottom Installation view, *Printed Textiles for the Home* exhibition, MoMA, New York. March 11–June 15, 1947. Photographed by Soichi Sunami. Photographic Archive, The Museum of Modern Art, New York, IN345.1.

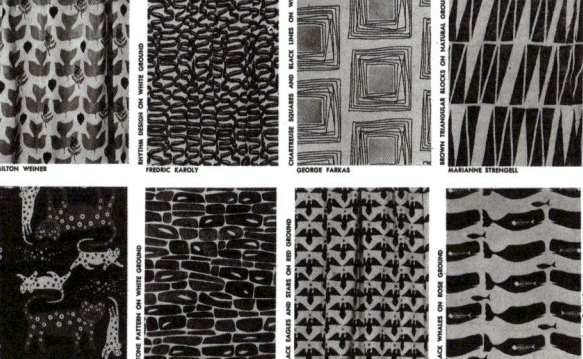
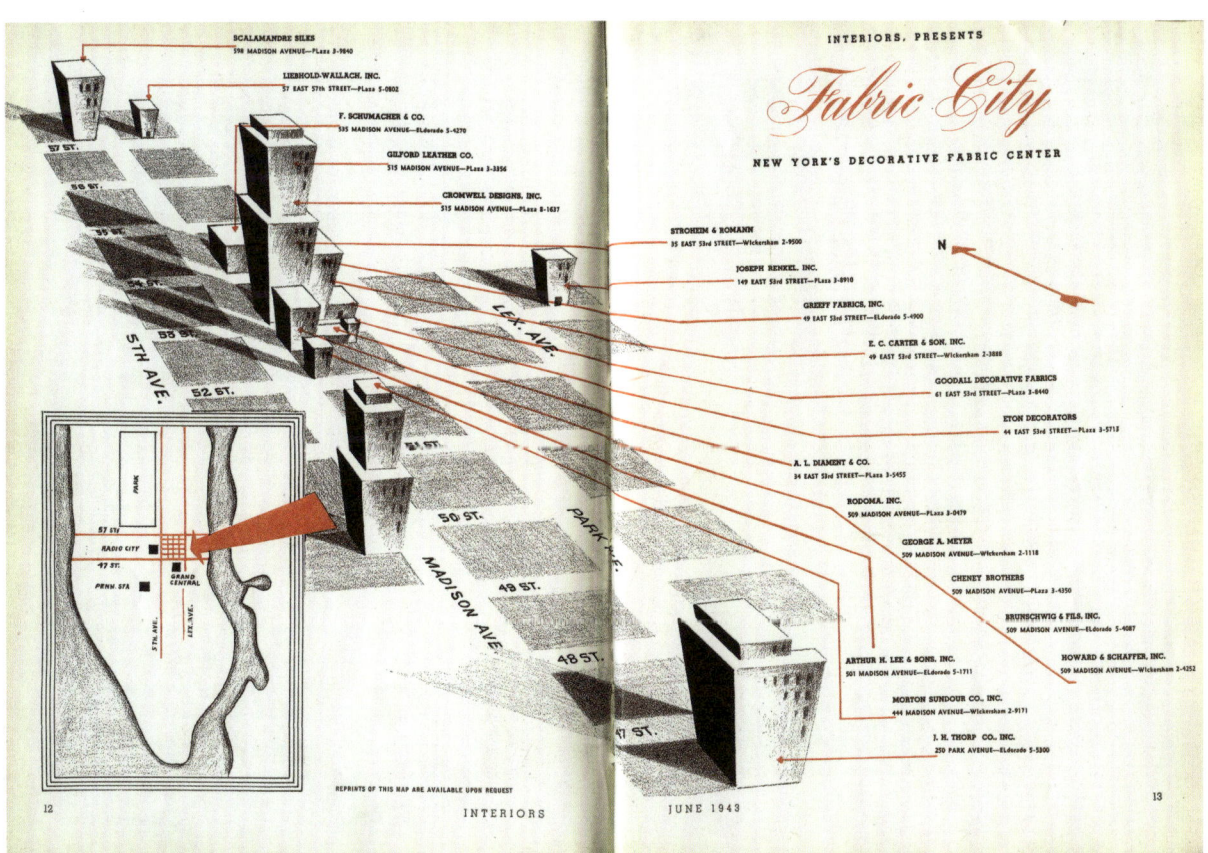

Fig. 1.17 Top "Textures" article featuring prizewinners from *Printed Textiles for the Home* exhibition, MoMA, New York, including designs by Marianne Strengell (right page, top row, far right) Alexander Girard and Eero Saarinen (bottom row, second from left). From *Arts & Architecture*, April 1947.

Fig. 1.18 Bottom Map of the Manhattan area designated "Fabric City," with textile wholesalers identified and located. From *Interiors*, June 1943.

Fig. 1.19 Top left Advertisement for Louisville Textiles (tearsheet), designed by Parson, Huff & Northlich, 1961. From Advertising scrapbooks, MS 71, Business records, 1888–1967, Louisville Textiles archive, American Textile History Museum, Lowell, Mass.

Fig. 1.20 Bottom Installation view, *American Textiles, '48* exhibition, The Metropolitan Museum of Art, November 24, 1948–January 2, 1949. The rayons and cottons displayed include Noémi Raymond's *Strip Fields* for Schumacher (far right). The Metropolitan Museum of Art, New York, L22885.

Fig. 1.21 Top right Upholstery fabrics designed by Lillian Garrett for Louisville Textiles. From "Textiles and Designers," *Everyday Art Quarterly*, Summer 1949. Photographed by John Szarkowski. Walker Art Center, Minneapolis.

Fig. 1.22 Owens-Corning Fiberglas Corporation interior, New York, featuring Fiberglas curtains and upholstery designed by Marianne Strengell, 1948. Interior by Gordon Bunshaft, architect, Skidmore, Owings & Merrill; and the Knoll Planning Unit. Photographed by Ezra Stoller. © Ezra Stoller/Esto, 8J10.

into production. Designs by some of the fifteen honorable-mention winners, who included such proponents of modern design as June Groff, Marianne Strengell, Alexander Girard, Ray Eames, and Juliet Kepes, were also widely published (fig. 1.17).[67] With museum and media attention at such a high level, textile design was becoming a dynamic and increasingly attractive field for many designers and artists.

Since the *Organic Design* exhibition of 1941, competitions and exhibitions had helped to spur and had charted the rise of modern textile design in the United States. The cumulative effect of these initiatives was reflected in a 1947 *Interiors* review of the spring textile collections. According to the reviewer, an "unprecedented fanfare" accompanied new designs and "more than ever before, manufacturers are publicizing their designers, and placing emphasis on the new and unusual or on the fine and rare. The trend is signaled by four nearly simultaneous competitions. . . . all are being closely watched by manufacturers waiting to sign up design talent as fast as they can find it."[68] Some of the newly released fabrics featured in the review included simple, textured upholstery fabrics from La France Industries, along with modern fabrics from Boris Kroll and two relative newcomers, Ben Rose and Knoll Textiles—established as a division of Knoll the same year.

The Decorative Textiles Industry — Old and New Paradigms

In the early 1940s, the New York showrooms of major distributors of upholstery, drapery, and other fabrics used in interiors, such as F. Schumacher & Co., Brunschwig & Fils, and Stroheim & Romann, were concentrated between Forty-seventh and Fifty-seventh streets, and Fifth and Lexington avenues, an area *Interiors* dubbed "Fabric City" in 1943 (fig. 1.18).[69] The majority of these firms, usually referred to as decorative fabric houses, were not manufacturers, but rather what are known in the trade as *converters*, or *jobbers*. They each had a reputation for particular styles or types of fabrics and acted as intermediaries between the interior design trade on one hand and networks of specialized mills, importers, and other suppliers on the other. Most of their showrooms, then as now, were open to the "trade" only—mainly architects, interior designers, and retailers. Broadly defined, jobbers buy larger quantities of fabric from mills and other suppliers and sell them in smaller quantities to decorators and retail customers. Converters purchase unfinished fabrics (called "gray goods") and arrange for them to be finished (bleached, dyed, printed, and so on) to a buyer's specifications.[70] In practice, however, the role of these decorative fabric houses was more active and complex. In some cases, firms commissioned designs and then found mills to manufacture them; in others, they purchased exclusive rights to designs that had been developed by a mill, perhaps suggesting slight changes in the fiber content or color. Others might purchase a base fabric (Belgian linen, for example) from an importer, have it dyed or bleached by one mill, and printed with a custom design by another. The finished fabric would then be sold under the name of the converter.[71]

Within the mills, new patterns were generally the work of in-house design departments whose designers worked anonymously. The usual working method was described by a representative of the Original Textile Company in 1953, in response to an inquiry regarding the designer of a textile submitted to an exhibition at Cranbrook: "This design as well as the majority of [our] designs [was] . . . created by our staff of designers and we do not as a matter of principle designate the name of the creator. Since in most cases it is not one but several persons who carry through the sampling in its various stages, we prefer . . . that the designer be listed as the Original Textile Company."[72] Designs were also purchased from freelancers, either outright or on a royalty basis, but even then mills only occasionally marketed fabrics as the work of a particular designer, especially before World War II. A mill would generally develop designs for a particular market and might supply similar fabrics to a wide range of companies in that market, including those directly in competition with each other. For example, in the 1950s and 1960s a number of mills were simultaneously weaving or printing fabrics for the textile divisions of competitors Herman Miller and Knoll.[73] In the early 1960s, advertisements in trade publications for Louisville Textiles listed over sixty of the mill's current customers, including Herman Miller, Jens Risom Design, Heywood-Wakefield Co., Dunbar, F. Schumacher & Co., and Jofa (fig. 1.19).[74]

After the war, a number of developments combined to create opportunities for new kinds of textile companies and new roles for designers within existing firms. At the end of the war, as the textile industry faced the challenge of returning to civilian production, some companies played it safe and produced conservative lines, while others actively sought out new directions. One such direction was offered by recent advances in man-made (synthetic) fibers. Wartime needs for goods such as nylon parachutes and rot-resistant Saran mosquito netting led to considerable research and development. New fibers brought new opportunities and challenges to existing mills, and the fiber manufacturers, such as DuPont (nylon, Orlon acrylic, Dacron polyester), Dow Chemical (Saran), and Owens-Corning Fiberglas, became important players in the postwar textile industry. Another important factor was the postwar building boom, as new glass-sheathed office buildings and modern homes created a demand for new kinds of furnishing fabrics, such as sheer, fireproof casements and upholsteries that could be easily cleaned.

Industry views of this changing postwar textile landscape were reflected in the pages of *American Fabrics*, a quarterly magazine founded in 1946 to help manufacturers of clothing and interiors fabrics understand the latest technological advances and anticipate market trends.[75] It also helped those who designed, worked with, or sold textiles to keep up with advances in the industry. Much of its coverage during its first decade was devoted to developments in fiber science, dying, printing, and finishing, issues that were of particular interest to the trade.[76] In 1948 the magazine teamed with the Metropolitan Museum of Art in organizing the exhibition *American Textiles, '48* (November 24, 1948–January 2, 1949), (figure 1.20).[77] The museum's aim was to promote its collections as a resource for American designers, as well as to celebrate achievements in the contemporary American textile industry.[78] It emphasized the independence of American design (which no longer turned to Europe for leadership) and the "Fiber Revolution" brought about by new man-made materials.[79] The exhibition included modern prints such as Laverne Originals' *Fun to Run* and Noémi Raymond's *Strip Fields* for Schumacher alongside traditional patterns such as *Cris de Paris*, a Brunschwig & Fils design based on an eighteenth-century French print.[80]

After the war, as the textile industry began to embrace modernist ideas about pattern, color, and composition, emphasizing the fact that fabrics had been "designed" and identifying designers by name became useful marketing tools, part of a new branding strategy. In 1946 Marianne Strengell noted, "Designing fabrics today is an extremely exciting and joyous experience. There is an open mind and ever present interest in experimental work on the part of the manufacturer."[81] Following the lead of Goodall Fabrics, whose decision to hire and promote Dorothy Liebes had been very successful, several other weaving mills at this time employed known designers to supplement their in-house design teams. In the fall of 1946, Louisville Textiles hired weaver Lillian Garrett as chief designer (fig. 1.21) and a few years later produced at least one design by Russel Wright, who was mostly known for his work in ceramics.[82] Henning Watterston, who maintained a custom handweaving studio in New York, worked as a freelance designer (including designing handwoven fabrics for the small Menlo Textiles mill in the late 1940s) and in 1952 joined the design staff of Craftex Mills in Philadelphia, an industry leader.[83] Emily Belding also designed for both hand and power looms as a freelancer, selling designs to Arundell Clarke, Habitat, and Knoll Associates before joining the staff of another Philadelphia mill, William Whitaker & Sons, in 1956.[84] Marli Ehrman followed up her earlier work for Moss Rose by creating drapery and upholstery fabrics for the Edwin Raphael Company and Marie Nichols in the early 1950s.[85]

Manufacturers of synthetic fibers also hired well-known weavers to demonstrate the possibilities of their products, and given modern handweavers' enthusiasm for experimentation with new materials, these were particularly apt collaborations. In 1946, for example, Dobeckmun Company had Dorothy Liebes create colors for Lurex, its new metallic yarn.[86] The same year, Owens-Corning Fiberglas began work on its new offices on East Fifty-sixth street in New York City and commissioned Marianne Strengell to incorporate fiberglass into fabrics to be used throughout the building. Fabrics combining plastic-covered fiberglass yarns (Tensolite) with wool, cotton, mohair, and metallic yarns, along with resin-coated all-fiberglass fabrics, were used not only for draperies and upholstery, but also for wall and ceiling surfaces (fig. 1.22). Some of Strengell's designs were produced by Owens-Corning's textile division, and one of them may later have been adapted for Knoll (see chapter 3).[87] Fiberglass, being fireproof and well-suited for use in drapery fabrics, became an important material for postwar textiles and was the object of many collaborations between well-known designers and industry over the next decade. To cite just one example, in 1957, when Owens-Corning developed a new textured fiberglass yarn called Aerocor, it worked with leading firms including Isabel Scott, Jack Lenor Larsen, Marie Nichols, and Knoll to create designs for casement fabrics (sheer or open-weave, light-filtering fabrics suited to large windows) incorporating the yarn.[88]

One mill that combined experimental approaches to new materials and to design was the Original Textile Company of Paterson, New Jersey (fig. 1.23). A 1950 article in *Mademoiselle* on opportunities for handweavers noted that "Henry Fleischman of Original Textile welcomes new weaves, [and] is sympathetic to contemporary design."[89] The company worked with several important designers and companies. They wove fabrics for Knoll—Marianne Strengell's *Devil* (1947), Anni Albers's *Fiberglas Casement* (1957), and the upholstery fabrics *Afro* (1958) and *Domus* (1959)—as well as at least one upholstery fabric for Herman Miller in the early 1950s.[90] Strengell was also commissioned directly by the company to create fabrics, such as the 1950 design *Cactus*.[91] Despite its relatively small size, the mill worked with a variety of old and new materials, some of them so new that they were still in the development phase.[92] Original Textile even experimented (as would some other mills) with asbestos fiber, a material, along with Saran and nylon, used in several surviving samples of about 1950 designed by Albers (fig. 1.24). It is not clear if these textiles were ever produced commercially.[93]

Several of the larger converters, while continuing to carry more traditional patterns, were proactive in adding modern designs to their collections soon after the war. F. Schumacher & Co., for example, produced prints by Noémi Raymond, Angelo Testa, and Vera Neumann.[94] Greeff Fabrics printed designs by Testa, and Konwiser featured modern designs by Joe Bascom, Matt Kahn, and Sara Provan.[95] Very few converters specialized in modern fabrics or carried both woven and printed fabrics, but those that did so included

Fig. 1.23 Advertisement for Original Textile Company. From *Upholstering*, June 1950. Art & Architecture Collection, Miriam and Ira D. Wallach Division of Art, Prints and Photographs, The New York Public Library, Astor, Lenox and Tilden Foundations.

Fig. 1.24 Anni Albers. Sample, ca. 1950. Manufactured by Original Textile Company. Saran, nylon, asbestos. The Josef and Anni Albers Foundation, Bethany, Conn., 1994.15.177a.

Fig. 1.25 Alexander Girard. *Feathers*, samples of four colorways, 1957. Manufactured for Herman Miller Textiles. Cotton and polyester; silk; cotton and polyester; cotton and linen; plain weave, screen-printed. Cooper-Hewitt, National Design Museum, Smithsonian Institution / Art Resource, NY.

Knoll, Arundell Clarke, and Jud Williams.[96] For some time Knoll was the only furniture company to market textiles under its own name (see chapter 3), although the Herman Miller Furniture Company (before the founding of its own textile division in 1952) worked with the textile converter Marie Nichols, who for a time sold textiles through Herman Miller showrooms.[97]

In 1952 architect and designer Alexander Girard was hired to direct the new division, Herman Miller Textiles, and over the next twenty years he designed all of the company's textiles, both printed and woven. Girard's approach to assembling the Herman Miller collection was similar to the approach taken at Knoll. Both firms focused on how textiles would coordinate with each other, the firm's furniture, and the overall interior, to provide texture and added visual interest.[98] Girard's bold, playful style and distinctive color palette, influenced by folk art (of which he was an enthusiastic collector), harmonized well with the furniture designs and whimsical sensibility of two other famous Herman Miller designers, Charles and Ray Eames (fig. 1.25).

In the postwar period a large number of newly established, small, independent firms met the growing demand for modern screen-printed textiles, many of them founded by people outside the textile industry, such as architects, graphic designers, and painters printing their own designs. These fabrics tended to be sold outside of the traditional fabric markets, either directly to architects and interior designers or through the network of small contemporary design stores that opened around the country after the war, such as New Design in New York and Richmond Bradshaw in Washington, D.C.[99] Designers such as Ben Rose (in 1946) and Ruth Adler Schnee (in 1947), for example, found themselves in business almost by accident and subsequently set up more sophisticated screen-printing operations in order to complete early commissions.[100] Angelo Testa likewise began by printing his own designs but also sold designs to converters such as Greeff, Cohn-Hall-Marx, and Knoll.[101] From 1946 to around 1950, before heading Herman Miller Textiles, Alexander Girard designed and printed his own fabrics and sold them through his design store in Grosse Pointe, Michigan (several were also distributed by Knoll for a short time; see chapter 3).[102] Architect and interior designer Ben Baldwin and abstract painter William Machado formed a successful fabric design partnership in the late 1940s. They retailed Baldwin-Machado fabrics through such outlets as Baldwin Kingrey, the Chicago design store co-owned by Baldwin's sister, Kitty (Baldwin) Weese, wife of the architect Harry Weese.[103]

More technically sophisticated textile-printing operations were founded by Vera and George Neumann (Printex, see chapter 3), and another influential husband-and-wife team, Leslie and D. D. (Doris) Tillett. Leslie Tillett (like George Neumann) had a thorough knowledge of color chemistry and textile-printing technology, and together the Tilletts became known for their unorthodox methods of designing directly with dyes on fabric (rather than working from preparatory drawings) and printing on fiberglass fabrics using innovative techniques.[104]

Another strategy adopted by new textile-printing firms after the war was to assemble a collection by known designers in other fields—what Alvin Lustig called "personalities with *names*."[105] One of the most successful of these was Laverne Originals, founded in 1942 by Estelle and Erwine Laverne who had begun by printing their own designs for textiles and wallpapers in the 1930s.[106] In 1948 they introduced the first "name" collection called the *Contempora* series, and thereafter produced printed designs by a range of well-known artists, architects, and designers, including Lustig, Alexander Calder, Ray Komai, György Kepes, and Ross Littell.[107] The *Stimulus* collection that Schiffer Prints (a division of the Mil-Art Company, Inc.) introduced in 1949 was the most prominent of the "name" collections, with designs by Salvador Dalí, George Nelson, Ray Eames, Paul McCobb, Abel Sorensen, and Bernard Rudofsky (fig. 1.26). The collection was developed for Schiffer by Lawrence Anton Maix, a former Knoll sales manager who was also an early sales agent for fabrics by Ben Rose.[108]

Shortly after the introduction of the *Stimulus* collection, Maix founded L. Anton Maix, his own textile company, and commissioned designs from Serge Chermayeff, Paul Rand, Jens Risom, and Alvin Lustig, to form the *Campagna* collection in April 1950.[109] Maix continued to produce high-quality modern printed textiles through the 1950s.[110] Two other "name collections" intended primarily as dress fabrics were the *Modern Master Print* series by Fuller Fabrics and *Signature Fabrics* by Associated American Artists.[111] Knoll Textiles followed a similar strategy, and although it did not assemble designs into named collections or series, it was perhaps the first company to promote a group of "names" that included designers of both printed and woven textiles. This marketing approach had had great success with Knoll's furniture collections.

Although founding a company to produce woven fabrics was a more complex and expensive undertaking than starting a printing operation, a number of influential handweavers were able to establish small but successful firms in the 1940s and 1950s. Else Regensteiner and Julia McVicker founded their studio, reg/wick, in Chicago in 1945 and produced custom handwoven textiles along with prototypes for power-loom weaving to be executed by Forster Textile Mills, in Chicago Heights.[112] In 1947 Robert Sailors, who had been Marianne Strengell's assistant and the power-loom instructor at Cranbrook, founded Contemporary Textiles, in Bitely, Michigan, and built a successful business weaving custom fabrics on both hand and power looms.[113] Although comparatively little-known today, Isabel Scott Fabrics was one of the most successful weaver-run companies in the early 1950s. Scott, who first learned to weave in her native Scotland, founded a handweaving studio in New York in 1948, added a line of power-loomed fabrics in 1950, and by 1953 opened a second, larger weaving studio in Philadelphia, where her machine-woven textiles were made.[114] Her fabrics received considerable acclaim and were used in prominent installations like the United Nations and the executive offices of the U.S. Steel Corporation.[115] In 1947 designer and businessman Norman Loring founded Rancocas Fabrics, a handweaving mill specializing in custom fabrics for architects, interior designers, and converters such as Knoll (see chapter 3).[116]

Perhaps the most innovative of the designer/weavers to start companies after the war was Jack Lenor Larsen, whose eponymous firm was incorporated in 1952. Trained at Cranbrook with Strengell, Larsen began by handweaving custom fabrics, but in 1951 also started to experiment with methods of achieving a distinctive handwoven look on power looms.[117] Throughout his career, Larsen has experimented with new materials as well as new and unusual ways of using existing materials. He has worked with companies such as Thaibok (for which he designed fabrics in the early 1950s) and weavers from around the globe to develop new fabrics, introducing to the United States and later to European markets handspun yarns and handwoven fabrics from Haiti, Mexico, Columbia, and North Africa (fig. 1.27).[118] Larsen's mix of hand- and power-loom production and new and conventional fibers, as well as his collaborations with weavers worldwide, exemplified the collaborative spirit of the time—a time when designing, manufacturing, and marketing textiles were all seen as integral to the creative process.

Good Design is Your Business: Design Consciousness in the Marketplace

In 1947 an exhibition titled *Good Design is Your Business* opened at the Albright Art Gallery in Buffalo, New York. It was intended primarily to encourage the American public to support good design, but its title message also held significance for American manufacturers—good design would be good for business.[119] Museums, curators, designers, and industry groups consistently preached this message to manufacturers and the general public throughout the decade after the war. Though museums continued to sponsor design competitions (such as MoMA's 1949 International Competition for Low-Cost Furniture Design), the focus of many curators shifted from generating new ideas to a focus on actual objects that were already being manufactured, "not dreams, but things actually available today," as expressed in one exhibition catalogue, and from the cultivation of new designers to the cultivation of informed consumers and enlightened manufacturers.[120] Although some commentators expressed concern about the display of commercial products in museum settings, such reservations were temporarily set aside amid the optimism of the postwar years, and exhibitions of well-designed products, organized by museums, universities, and galleries throughout the country, were popular with curators, manufacturers, and museum visitors alike.[121]

One of the important new venues for such exhibitions, the Everyday Art Gallery at the Walker Art Center in Minneapolis, opened its inaugural exhibition, *Ideas for Better Living*, in January 1946. *Arts & Architecture* hailed this new venture, a gallery entirely devoted to educating the public about good design, as "the first gun in what may well become a nationwide movement for 'better living' through active consumer participation and education in modern design."[122] The same year, the Walker began publishing *Everyday Art Quarterly: A Guide to Well Designed Products*, a journal that helped to greatly extend the gallery's influence and educational reach (fig. 1.28). The art center further promoted modern design and architecture with ambitious projects such as the 1947 "Idea House II" (a model house built on the center grounds).[123] In 1949 another Walker exhibition, *Modern Textiles*, included 130 drapery and upholstery fabrics from designers and mills around the country, and many of these were illustrated in a special issue of *Everyday Art Quarterly* (fig. 1.29). This exhibition, the largest and most comprehensive to date to focus exclusively on modern design in textiles, included fabrics by small, designer-run companies such as Adler-Schnee and Robert Sailors, as well as machine-woven fabrics by large manufacturers such as Dan River Mills. One whole wall in the gallery was devoted to printed textiles by Knoll, including *Apples*, *Isles*, and *Shooting Stars*.[124]

Design awards helped to underscore the value now placed on good design. Beginning in 1947 the American Institute of Decorators (AID) presented annual awards "to make known to the consumer what the market offers in good design, and to commend those who have created the best each year in furniture, fabrics, wall coverings and floor coverings."[125] Designs introduced within the previous year were submitted for consideration by manufacturers and judged worthy of citation by a guest jury of notable "museum officials and other design authorities," such as Edgar Kaufmann Jr. (MoMA curator), Meyric R. Rogers (Art Institute of Chicago curator), and Edward Durell Stone (dean of the Yale School of Architecture).[126] An exhibition of twenty-five of the designs, including fabrics by Dorothy Liebes for Goodall (first-prize winner), Alexander Girard, and Ben Rose, was held at the Art Institute of Chicago and later circulated nationally by the American Federation of Arts.[127]

An Exhibition For Modern Living, organized by Alexander Girard for the Detroit Institute of Arts in 1949, also attracted national attention (fig. 1.30). More than 150,000 people visited the exhibition, making it one of the museum's most successful to date.[128] Over two thousand objects were divided

TREES *by Edward Wormley*

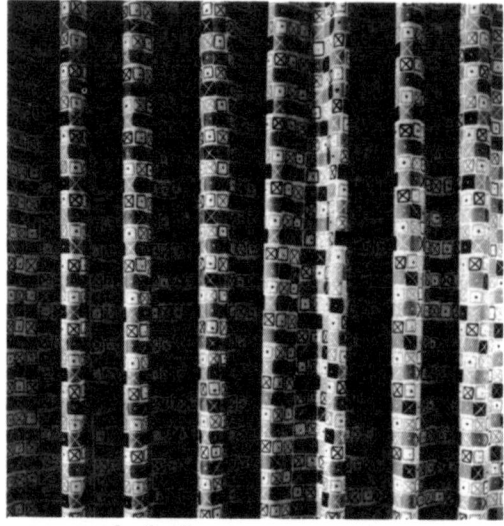
CROSSPATCH *by Ray Eames*

CHAIN *by Paul McCobb*

SI AND NO *by Bernard Rudofsky*

SONATA D'ETE *by Salvador Dali*

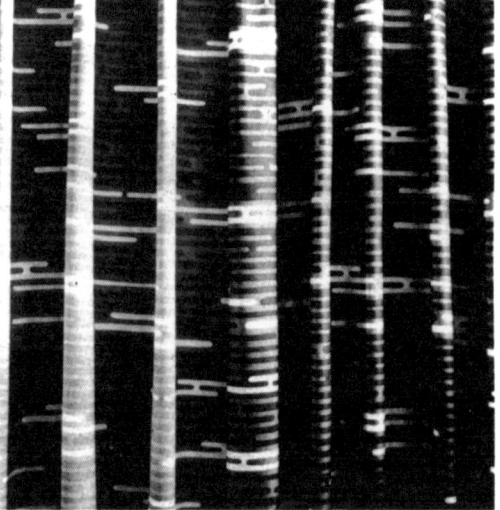
DETOUR *by Abel Sorenson*

Fig. 1.26 *Schiffer Prints'* Stimulus Fabric Collection. From "Modern Printed Fabrics," *American Fabrics*, Winter 1951-52.

Fig. 1.27 Jack Lenor Larsen. Detail of *Jason*, 1956. Manufactured for Jack Lenor Larsen Inc. Egyptian cotton, goat hair, metallic gimp; leno-weave. Museum of Art and Design, Gift of the artist, 2001, 2001.87.

Fig. 1.28 Top Cover, with printed fabrics designed by Angelo Testa, *Everyday Art Quarterly*, no. 1, Summer 1946. Photographed by Rolphe Dauphin. Walker Art Center, Minneapolis.

Fig. 1.29 Bottom Entrance to *Modern Textiles* exhibition, Everyday Art Gallery, Walker Art Center, 1949. Behind chair, from left: handwoven plaid by Marianne Strengell; "cotton bouclé" (probably *Prestini*) by Knoll; *Little Men with Bird* print by Ruth Adler Schnee. Photographed by John Szarkowski. Courtesy Walker Art Center, Minneapolis.

Fig. 1.30 Top left Cover of *An Exhibition for Modern Living* catalogue, 1949. Color lithograph. Detroit Institute of Arts, USA/The Bridgeman Art Library, DTR397497.
Fig 1.31 Bottom Installation view, *An Exhibition for Modern Living*, 1949. Installation designed by Florence Knoll. Photographed by Elmer L. Astleford. Detroit Institute of Arts, USA/The Bridgeman Art Library.

Fig. 1.32 Top right Installation view, "Hall of Objects," *An Exhibition for Modern Living*, 1949. Photograph. Detroit Institute of Arts, USA/The Bridgeman Art Library.

between a series of installations created by prominent designers such as Charles Eames, George Nelson, and Florence Knoll (fig. 1.31) and a large "Hall of Objects" (fig 1.32). Kaufmann of MoMA served on the Committee of Advisors for the exhibition. In his contribution to the catalogue he praised the exhibition as "the most comprehensive statement yet made in favor of modern design" in America, and articulated his hope that exhibitions such as this would inspire "manufacturers, designers, retailers, shopmen, technicians, salesmen – [to] look and think about what they see"—a goal he would continue to pursue in MoMA's *Good Design* exhibitions.[129]

Jointly sponsored by MoMA and the Merchandise Mart of Chicago, the *Good Design* series brought Kaufmann's mission of "stimulating the appreciation and creation of the best design among manufacturers, designers and retailers" directly into the marketplace (fig. 1.33).[130] The program ran from 1950 to 1955 and consisted of three exhibitions per year. The first two exhibitions displayed the museum's selections of the best-designed objects to have come on the market in the previous six months and were held at the Merchandise Mart, the huge wholesale showroom building in Chicago, in conjunction with the January and June home furnishings markets. The third installment, in November, consisted of a selection of the best objects from the January and June shows and opened simultaneously at MoMA and the Merchandise Mart. The exhibition objects (chosen primarily from items submitted for consideration by manufacturers and distributors) were selected by a committee consisting of Kaufmann and two rotating "outside authorities in the field" (such as museum directors, designers, and retailers). Their choices were based on "design intended for present-day life, in regard to usefulness, to production methods and materials and to the progressive taste of the day."[131]

The idea of mounting a museum exhibition in the heart of the commercial furnishings market was controversial. In January 1950 *Interiors* reported, "There were undoubtedly a good many in the trade who were prepared to scold the Merchandise Mart for collaborating with the Museum of Modern Art," but noted that "the exhibition was greeted with pleasure and praise," and that it was stimulating "a sudden new faith in good design" and inspiring "a remarkable number of staid sources to come out with modern lines."[132] Betty Pepis of the *New York Times* praised the museum for bringing the exhibition to the trade on its home ground and for supplying "the missing link between art and the home-furnishings industry."[133] Kaufmann was pleased with the success of the inaugural exhibition in January 1950. Before the opening of the June 1950 exhibition at the Merchandise Mart, he thanked the trade for their cooperation and for offering museum officials the chance to discuss design problems with manufacturers, retailers, and salesmen—"to test the Museum's standards in the active world of business . . . to relate its standards and influences to every day life, and to develop them accordingly."[134] The exhibitions also attracted a large general audience to the Merchandise Mart, which was usually open only to the trade.

Though the selections were subjective and sometimes controversial, over the next five years the *Good Design* series provided regular overviews of what was in development and on the market, and newspapers, design magazines, and more specialized publications such as *Handweaver & Craftsman* published lengthy features on each exhibition. Even negative reviews of particular selections as not representative of the best on the market were useful in providing a starting point for further discussion. For the general public, the exhibitions offered access to objects that were usually confined to wholesale showrooms. For manufacturers, designers, and converters, *Good Design* became a badge of innovation and, arguably, a powerful incentive to strive for excellence. For the small and newly formed companies specializing in modern textiles, being chosen for inclusion in a *Good Design* exhibition meant valuable publicity. It also provided a useful marketing tool—a *Good Design* logo or tag was a mark of prestige, and could be featured in a firm's own publicity efforts and advertisements. Knoll, for example, included the logo in the selvedge markings of several of the printed fabrics selected for *Good Design*, such as *Triad* (fig. 1.34).

Good Design and other exhibitions, through catalogues and press releases, publicized the names of manufacturers and designers. This in turn encouraged textile mills (who ordinarily would remain anonymous along with their design staff) to release fabrics under their own names and to credit individual designers. Louisville Textiles (Russel Wright and Lillian Garrett) and Original Textile (Anni Albers and Marianne Strengell) were two prominent examples. This practice was not universally adopted; Moss Rose fabrics, for example, were regularly submitted to exhibitions without designer credits, a paradox given the company's previous sponsorship of design competitions. *Good Design* exhibitions also commended companies for innovation in manufacturing and importing. The textile section, for example, often included imported fabrics that were not designer fabrics in the usual sense, but rather represented important introductions onto the American market, such as Knoll's handwoven *Jhuri Silk* from India (see chapter 3) and Thaibok's silk fabrics developed in Thailand.

To mark the five-year anniversary of the *Good Design* exhibitions, the June 1954 edition (also shown that fall in New York) took the form of a celebratory retrospective, or "a balanced program of retrospect and forecast," with one hundred "best products" chosen by a committee of MoMA staff members, as well as one hundred "best-selling products" (based on manufacturer and distributor records) that had been included in *Good Design* exhibitions since 1950 (fig. 1.35).[135] In January 1955, *Good Design* opened as usual in Chicago, but this was to be its last installment; despite intentions to keep the series running, MoMA and the Merchandise Mart decided to suspend it indefinitely.[136] The mid-1950s also saw the end of the Cranbrook Biennials and the International Textile Exhibitions in North Carolina—two series that had done so much to promote modern textile design since the war.[137]

There were undoubtedly many reasons behind the termination of these exhibitions, but perhaps foremost was a remarkably sudden shift in the mood and direction of the market. In the textile industry in particular, the focus turned more and more from the residential to the contract market, as American corporations built themselves expansive new glass-walled skyscrapers and suburban campuses. Jack Lenor Larsen recalled this dramatic change as occurring around 1955, when "contract became big, overnight. The postwar period was over, residential modern was over.... By the end of the '50s, a lot of salesmen didn't want to bother with selling [just] a chair or two," when with the same effort they could sell an entire building.[138] At the same time, the design pendulum at the high end of the residential market swung back toward more traditional furniture and textiles, and historically inspired styles and patterns began to win awards from the American Institute of Decorators—good design and modern design were no longer synonymous.

Interiors observed on the occasion of the penultimate *Good Design* exhibition that the "exhibitions provided a place, without commercial bias, where the consumer could see and evaluate new designs that he might never discover in stores or magazines."[139] One effect of the end of the *Good Design* program and the new corporate climate was that the general public was again denied access to the wholesale textile market. Designs were still widely published in the press, but they became less accessible to those not in the trade, and it became more difficult for unknown designers to have their work seen by the public. Another effect was to reduce the general visibility of modern design in the marketplace. In a review of the January 1956 Midwest furniture market, Lazette Van Houten wrote in *Arts & Architecture* that attendance and sales were high, but "design of any importance... was almost non-existent." Possibly, she suggested, without the *Good Design* shows to prod them in the right direction, American manufacturers and retail buyers (except for those dedicated to the modern movement, such as Knoll) preferred to update or "modernize" more familiar styles, such as "the style hit of the session... 'modernized' Italian provincial."[140]

Textiles USA and Beyond

Just as MoMA's *Organic Design in Home Furnishings* in 1941 seemed to herald a new era in modern design by synthesizing the previous decade of change, the 1956 exhibition *Textiles USA* (figs. 1.36, 1.37) put a period to the postwar era. Presented as a continuation of the *Good Design* program, in reality it was quite a different event, reflecting the changes then taking place in the textile industry much as the *Organic Design* exhibition had done sixteen years earlier. Similar in format to *American Textiles, '48*, which had been held at the Metropolitan Museum, *Textiles USA* was a joint venture with *American Fabrics* magazine, sponsored by a group of fifty American textile firms and restricted to work produced in the United States within the previous decade.[141] Curated by Greta Daniel, it surveyed achievements in American textile design and production for home furnishings, clothing, and industrial and institutional uses. The home furnishings fabrics selected were modern, reflecting general trends in design over the previous ten years—many had previously appeared in *Good Design* exhibitions. The exhibition catalogue, however, noted changes in direction within the industry as a whole, such as the important trend toward synthetic, easy-to-maintain fabrics designed to be inexpensive and readily replaced. In the catalogue's introduction, Arthur Drexler, director of MoMA's Department of Architecture and Design, wrote: "If American textiles differ from those of other countries they do so, first of all, because of the sheer quantity in which they are produced and distributed. Daily our advertising celebrates in prose and song the advantages of maximum production and consumption.... the cheapness, availability, variety, and controlled improvement of our artifacts are indeed remarkable. Spurred by competition, these developments do more than give us an abundance of material goods; they are changing our ideas of cheapness, availability, variety, and improvement. Quantity can and does create a new conception of quality."[142] While Drexler may not have viewed such developments as an unreserved good, attitudes had clearly changed dramatically since the idealistic days of *Organic Design*, with low cost and quantity now triumphing over "the rational elegance of things intended for use."[143]

Perceptions about the relationship between hand- and power-loom weaving were also changing. In *Textiles USA*, unlike earlier exhibitions, handwoven pieces were displayed in a separate room (fig. 1.38). Drexler noted that since machines could now imitate the distinctive imperfections of handweaving, craftsmen could be "free to explore what now might properly be called 'pure' textile design" and that "perhaps the most interesting example in the exhibition is the utterly useless reed and Velon fabric by Thelma Becherer. Fragile and curiously poetic, this work deserves to be admired in itself, like an ornamental vase."[144] These subtle shifts in perceptions were indicative of the more substantial changes to come in the 1960s, when what Drexler called "pure" textile design, now known as "fiber art," would assume pride of place over functional handweaving.

Not surprisingly, a reviewer for *Handweaver & Craftsman*

Fig. 1.33 Top Installation view, *Good Design* exhibition, MoMA, New York, November 27, 1951-January 27, 1952. Installation designed by Finn Juhl. Photographed by Soichi Sunami. Photographic Archive, The Museum of Modern Art, New York, IN494.1.

Fig. 1.35 Bottom Installation view, *Good Design: Fifth Anniversary* exhibition, MoMA, New York, February 8–March 20, 1955. Center front: *Belding Blocks* by Emily Belding for Habitat; rear wall: Pythagoras by Sven Markelius for Knoll. Photographed by Tom Yee. Photographic Archive, The Museum of Modern Art, New York, IN570.4B.

Fig. 1.34 Eszter Haraszty. *Triad* ("Black, Red, Pink, Persimmon on White" colorway), introduced ca. 1954, this example ca. 1955. Made by Printex for Knoll Textiles. Used for drapery; cotton; plain weave, screen-printed. The Museum of Modern Art, New York, Gift of Knoll Associates, SC25.1975.1.

Fig. 1.36 Installation view, *Textiles U.S.A.* exhibition, MoMA, New York, August 29-November 4, 1956. Installation designed by Bernard Rudofsky. Photographed by George Barrows. Photographic Archive, The Museum of Modern Art, New York, IN606.9.

Fig. 1.37 Installation view, *Textiles U.S.A.* exhibition, MoMA, New York, August 29-November 4, 1956. Installation designed by Bernard Rudofsky. Photographed by George Barrows. Photographic Archive, The Museum of Modern Art, New York, IN606.3.

objected to the description of such textiles as "useless," pointing out that the fabrics were designed for specific functions (such as draperies or room dividers) and were representative of the work that handweavers were doing for architects and interior decorators. The reviewer also took issue with curator Daniels's statement elsewhere in the catalogue that the handweaver's chief contribution now appeared to be in the design of fabrics for mass production, arguing that there was still a place in the market for functional handwoven textiles.[145]

Textiles USA was promoted by its organizers as a celebration of the progress made in textile design and production since the war. Its upbeat message was also an attempt to boost the fortunes of the domestic textile industry, which was struggling to adapt to changing conditions while undergoing a long-term overall decline. In 1958 a U.S. Senate investigation of the problems besetting the industry found that while total production for all United States industries had increased 45 percent between 1947 and 1957, overall textile production had declined 2 percent. The most dramatic declines were in the production of woolen fabrics (down 44.2 percent) and rayon and acetate fabrics (down 26.3 percent). While production of fabrics made of the newer man-made fibers (such as nylon and fiberglass) had increased 1,500 percent, this segment of the industry was not large enough to offset the declines in other areas.[146] In addition, the textile mill closures that had begun in New England in the 1920s had continued after the war, with 717 mill liquidations reported in the press between 1946 and 1957.[147] Another report prepared in 1957 pointed to another significant shift: American firms were now increasingly importing or commissioning fabrics from overseas manufacturers. It estimated that between 1947 and 1957, American textile exports had declined by 41.4 percent, while imports had risen by 650 percent.[148]

Just as the textile market turned more and more to contract work, American textile manufacturers increasingly emphasized artificial fibers, and were able to satisfy demands for hard-wearing synthetic fabrics for use in office interiors. However, a concurrent trend toward more luxurious fabrics and natural fibers, particularly at the higher end of the market, was increasingly being satisfied by European designers and mills, as American woolen mills disappeared. Knoll, which had always emphasized the international character of its designs, signaled this shift in an advertisement (fig. 1.39) placed (paradoxically) in the *American Fabrics* issue devoted to *Textiles USA*, with copy reading, "Knoll textiles, international in scope, represent exclusive developments by the leading designers of Europe and America."[149] The advertisement featured two textiles woven in the United States and two made in Scotland.[150] Knoll would become even more active internationally in the 1960s, in both its choice of designers and textile manufacturers and the markets to which it catered (see chapter 5). Many of Knoll's competitors would follow a similar strategy—other innovative companies, such as Jack Lenor Larsen, also expanded their international operations during this period, opening European showrooms and subsidiaries to reach the European market and working more and more with European mills.

In the decade after World War II, a singular confluence of factors—social, ideological, economic, technological, and artistic—combined to foster a spirit of innovation and cooperation in textile design and throughout the decorative textile industry. Perhaps more than at any time before or since, American museums, educators, designers, mills, and manufacturers thought of themselves as working toward a common goal—the creation of better textiles for the modern world—and all seemed to be moving in this direction. On one hand, new synthetic fibers and industrial finishes were the subject of intense research and experimentation and were quickly embraced by American textile manufacturers. On the other, designers working in the craft techniques of hand silk-screen printing and handweaving founded new companies to produce their own modern textiles. For a time these two strands were not seen to be in opposition, as handweavers experimented with synthetic materials and designed for machine production, and textile mills and chemical corporations hired them to do so. Some of the mills facing the difficulties of readjusting to peacetime production after the war or confronting the economic challenges of the postwar period chose a progressive approach to design and materials as both a social good and a sound business strategy.

The many textile design competitions and exhibitions in the postwar years played a vital role in promoting the ideals of cooperation between art and industry, and in helping to build a consensus (albeit temporary) about what constituted "good design." Their success, however, was likewise made possible by the unique economic and artistic conditions that gave birth to the postwar design boom. In the mid-1950s, when those conditions began to change, the role of such exhibitions was no longer clear, and they began to disappear. Innovation in fibers, technology, design, and production certainly continued, much of it geared to the ever-expanding contract market, but it continued in the context of an industry and market that was becoming ever more specialized, international, and complex.

Fig. 1.38 Handwoven fabrics display, *Textiles USA* exhibition, MoMA, New York, August 29–November 4, 1956. Installation designed by Bernard Rudofsky.
Photographed by George Barrows.
Photographic Archive, The Museum of Modern Art, New York, IN606.16.

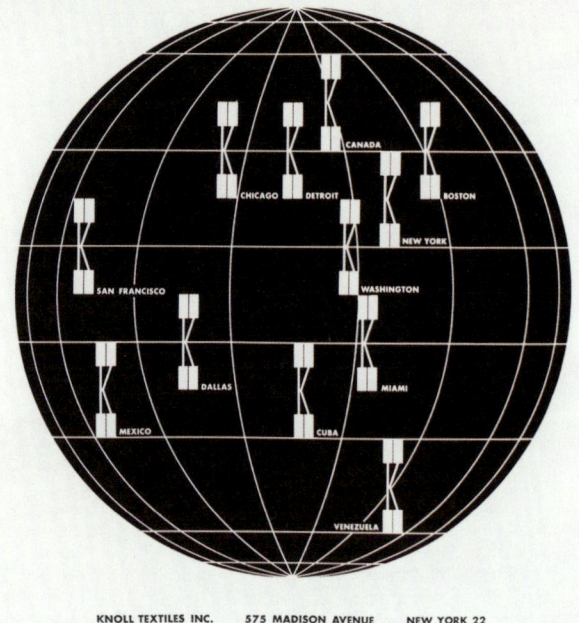

Fig. 1.39 Advertisement for Knoll Textiles, designed by Herbert Matter.
From *American Fabrics*, Fall 1956.

1   Jack Lenor Larsen, "Textiles," in *Design Since 1945*, ed. Kathryn B. Hiesinger and George H. Marcus (Philadelphia: Philadelphia Museum of Art, 1983), 174.
2   The exhibition, on view from September 24 to November 9, 1941, is best remembered for displaying revolutionary chair designs by Charles Eames and Eero Saarinen which presaged postwar developments; see R. Craig Miller, "Interior Design and Furniture," in *Design in America: The Cranbrook Vision 1925–1950*, eds. Joan Marter et al. (New York: Harry N. Abrams, 1983), 109–12.
3   Alvin Lustig, "Modern Printed Fabrics," *American Fabrics*, no. 20 (Winter 1951–52): 62.
4   MoMA press release 40916-54, September 30, 1940, online Press Release Archive, www.moma.org. The competition was originally called the "Industrial Design Competition for Home Furnishings"; see ibid.
5   Ira A. Hirschman, vice president of Bloomingdale's, quoted in MoMA press release 41614-46, June 14, 1941, online Press Release Archive, www.moma.org.
6   Eliot F. Noyes, *Organic Design in Home Furnishings* (New York: Museum of Modern Art, 1941), 1.
7   See Mary Schoeser, "Textiles: Surface, Structure, and Serial Production," in *Craft in the Machine Age: The History of Twentieth-Century American Craft 1920–1945*, ed. Janet Kardon (New York: Harry N. Abrams with the American Craft Museum, 1995), 110–21; and Mary Schoeser and Whitney Blausen, "'Wellpaying Self Support': Women Textile Designers," in *Women Designers in the USA, 1900–2000: Diversity and Difference*, ed. Pat Kirkham (New York and New Haven: Bard Graduate Center and Yale University Press, 2000), 145–83.
8   For Kipp see Marlyn R. Musicant, "Maria Kipp: Autobiography of a Hand Weaver," *Studies in the Decorative Arts* 8, no. 1 (Fall–Winter 2000–2001): 92–107; and Dorothy Bryan, "Maria Kipp—Her Career as a Weaver," *Handweaver and Craftsman* 3, no. 1 (Winter 1951–52): 15–17, 59.
9   The School of Design was renamed the Institute of Design in 1944.
10   Ehrman had her students start with simple structures, but vary the fibers, colors, and density of threads, emphasizing the importance of learning to design "an interesting warp [which] lends itself to a great variety of textile designs"; quoted in Laszlo Moholy-Nagy, *Vision in Motion*, 8th ed. (Chicago: Paul Theobold and Company, 1969), 87; see also Anni Albers, "Handweaving Today – Textile Work at Black Mountain College," *The Weaver* 6, no. 1 (Janurary–February 1941): 4).
11   Ed Rossbach, "Marianne Strengell," *American Craft* 44, no. 2 (April/May 1984): 9. Strengell forbade her students to visit the library for the first half year of their studies, forcing them to form their own design ideas. Like Ehrman, she had them weave small samples to see how many designs they could get out of a single warp. Marianne Strengell, Oral history interview by Mark Coir, pp. 54–55, December 17, 1990, Oral History Collection, Cranbrook Archives, Bloomfield Hills, Michigan. Online (oral histories, archival collections): www.cranbrook.edu/archives.
12   See Rossbach, "Marianne Strengell," 10.
13   Berta Frey, "American Handweaving—A Mid-Century Viewpoint," *Handweaver and Craftsman* 1, no. 1 (April 1950): 6.

14   Rossbach contrasts this kind of weaving with the concurrent revival of traditional American weaving and its characteristic weaves such as overshot, in which patterns are formed by floats independent of the basic structure; see Ed Rossbach, "Fiber in the Forties," *American Craft* 42, no. 5 (October/November 1982): 15. As a Cranbrook student Rossbach participated in the International Textile Exhibitions at the Woman's College of the University of North Carolina; see Christa C. Mayer Thurman, "Textiles," *Design in America: The Cranbrook Vision 1925–1950*, ed. Joan Marter et al. (New York: Harry N. Abrams, 1983), 205, 320 n. 132.
15   Ed Rossbach, "The Glitter and Glamour of Dorothy Liebes," *American Craft* 42, no. 4 (December 1982/January 1983): 9.
16   Liebes's first collection for Goodall was released in 1941. See Regina Lee Blaszczyk, "Designing Synthetics, Promoting Brands: Dorothy Liebes, DuPont Fibres and Post-war American Interiors," *Journal of Design History* 21, no. 1 (Spring 2008): 81; and *Dorothy Liebes: Retrospective Exhibition* (New York: Museum of Contemporary Crafts of the American Crafts Council, 1970), 34.
17   Liebes was first given this sobriquet in an advertisement for Goodall Fabrics, *Interiors* (June 1941): 4–5; see also "Dorothy Wright Liebes, First Lady of the Loom," *Interiors* (July 1947): 86–91, 134–36; "Top Weaver," *Life* (November 24, 1947): 93–95; Blaszczyk, "Designing Synthetics, Promoting Brands," 82–84.
18   "Kroll, Boris," in Mel Byars, *The Design Encyclopedia* (New York: John Wiley & Sons, 1994), 307. The firm changed names most likely in the latter half of 1946. See Advertisement for Boris Kroll Fabrics/Cromwell Designs, Inc., *Interiors* (July 1946): 127. By December, Kroll's advertising no longer included any references to Cromwell Designs; see Advertisement for Boris Kroll Fabrics, *Interiors* (December 1946): 45.
19   "A New Home for Boris Kroll," *Interiors* (December 1951): 115–18, 180–81.
20   Noyes, *Organic Design*, 38. Strengell won Honorable Mention in Woven Fabrics; ibid., 2.
21   The company's president, Berthold Strauss, served on the selection committee for *Good Design*, Merchandise Mart, June 1950; see MoMA press release, "Large New Group of 'Good Design,'" [June 1950], online Press Release Archive, www.moma.org. Moss Rose was also the first manufacturer for Knoll's *Nylon Homespun* in 1958.
22   Noyes, *Organic Design*, 13, 15, 38.
23   It is not clear why the textile designs were submitted under Antonin's name, although the Raymonds may have submitted this and another entry (in the "Furniture for a One-room Apartment" category for which they received an honorable mention) under their architectural firm ("Antonin Raymond, Architect"), using the company letterhead; Antonin's later correspondence with MoMA was sent on this letterhead.
24   The Raymonds worked for Frank Lloyd Wright in 1919 on the Imperial Hotel in Tokyo, and Antonin established an independent firm there in 1921; see Kurt G. F. Helfrich and William Whitaker, eds., *Crafting a Modern World: The Architecture and Design of Antonin and Noémi Raymond* (New York: Princeton Architectural Press, 2006), 267–69.
25   Lustig, "Modern Printed Fabrics," 66.

26   Screen printing, a variation of stencil printing, uses lightweight screens of sheer silk or synthetic fabric stretched on a frame, with parts of the screen (corresponding to the negative space of the design) blocked out with film, varnish, photo-sensitive emulsion, or another masking medium. Unlike printing blocks, which must be laboriously carved and small enough for easy handling, fabric screens are relatively simple to create, correct, and reuse, and make it easy to print large-scale motifs and large repeats. See Terence Conran, *Printed Textile Design* (London: Studio Limited, 1957), 13–14, 85–90.
27   Lesley Jackson, *Twentieth-Century Pattern Design: Textile and Wallpaper Pioneers* (New York: Princeton Architectural Press, 2002), 87–88.
28   See Thurman, "Textiles," in *Design in America*, 197; Schoeser, "Textiles," in *Craft in the Machine Age*, 120–21; "Sticks and Rags," *Interiors* (December 1943): 106–7. See also chapter 2, in this volume. Cooper continued to be a prominent textile designer and wholesaler through the early 1960s.
29   Antonin Raymond to Eliot Noyes, February 10, 1941, Curatorial Exhibition Files, Exh. 148, Museum of Modern Art Archives, New York (hereafter, CUR, Exh. [number], MoMA Archives). Antonin Raymond also later recalled in his autobiography that Clark found Noémi's designs "odd" and thought they would not sell; see Antonin Raymond, *An Autobiography* (Rutland, VT: Charles E. Tuttle Co., Inc., 1973), 322. While Clark may have dismissed the Raymond designs, a few years earlier they had printed a modern design by Ruth Reeves and exhibited it in the Golden Gate Exposition in 1939; see *Decorative Arts: Official Catalog* (San Francisco: Department of Fine Arts Division of Decorative Arts, Golden Gate International Exposition, 1939), 98. Later, in 1948, they imported and printed floral patterns designed by Arne Jacobsen for the Danish company Grautex; see "Fabrics Designed in Denmark Here," *New York Times*, November 20, 1948, 8. In 1949 Clark was an exhibitor at the Detroit Institute of Arts; see A. H. Girard and W. D. Laurie, Jr., eds., *An Exhibition For Modern Living* (Detroit: Detroit Institute of Arts, 1949), 95.
30   Cold Spring Bleachery was credited as a printer on some of the exhibition labels, and officers of the company were apparently invited to see the exhibition; see Marshall Cole (Cold Spring Bleachery) to Eliot Noyes, October 29, 1941, CUR, Exh. 148, MoMA Archives. Noémi Raymond may have worked on her own with Cold Spring after the exhibition; see Noémi Raymond to Antonin Raymond, October 11, 1949, October 20, 1950. November 12–14, 1950, Raymond Collection, Architectural Archives, University of Pennsylvania.
31   *Annual International Textile Exhibition 1944* (Greensboro, N.C.: Weatherspoon Art Gallery, Woman's College of the University of North Carolina), n.p. (Raymond won second place in printed textiles); First Biennial Exhibition of Contemporary Textiles and Ceramics, February 3–28, 1946, curatorial exhibition files, Cranbrook Academy of Art Museum. Several printed lengths from the *Organic Design* exhibition were acquired by MoMA; others remained with the designer and are now in the Raymond Collection, Architectural Archives, University of Pennsylvania (see figs. 1.1 and 3.17).

32   Noemi Raymond to Marianne Strengell, January 15, 1946, First Biennial Exhibition of Contemporary Textiles and Ceramics, February 3–28, 1946, curatorial exhibition files, Cranbrook Academy of Art Museum.
33   See "Come the New Fabrics," *Interiors* (March 1947): 83. Raymond's design won an award.
34   *Strip Fields* and *Mesh and Starfish* were printed by Schumacher in 1948 and *Chinese Coins*, *Reeds*, and *Reeds and Bars* by Knoll the same year. Knoll released *Mosaic* in 1950. For a chronology of the Raymonds' lives and careers, see Helfrich and Whitaker, *Crafting a Modern World*, 265–75.
35   *Mesh and Starfish* and *Strip Fields* were lent by Schumacher, and *Chinese Coins* and two colorways of *Reeds and Bars* by Knoll (Second National Biennial Exhibition of Contemporary Textiles and Ceramics, February 1–27, 1949, curatorial exhibition files, Cranbrook Academy of Art Museum).
36   *Mosaic* was shown in *Good Design*, Merchandise Mart, January 1951 and MoMA, Fall 1951.
37   Quoted in MoMA press release 41924-73, September 25, 1941, online Press Release Archive, www.moma.org.
38   Marianne Strengell Dusenbury, "Texture, Color and Quality," *California Arts & Architecture* (November 1942): 32–33. The title of the article referred to what Strengell felt was most needed in contemporary textiles.
39   Thurman, "Textiles," 196–97. Strengell arranged to have a power loom installed at Cranbrook for student use in 1945, see "Art Academy Has Power Loom," *Interiors* (December 1945): 122.
40   Moholy-Nagy, *Vision in Motion*, 86–87. A student sample from 1940 incorporating cellophane and several from 1942 incorporating Saran threads are illustrated.
41   Anni Albers, quoted in Mary Emma Harris, *The Arts at Black Mountain College* (Cambridge, Mass.: MIT Press, 1987), 24.
42   "Dorothy Liebes: California Craftsman Restates the Vocabulary of the Hand Loom in Terms of Modern Technique," *California Arts & Architecture* (February 1942): 20.
43   Advertisement for W. & J. Sloane, *New York Times*, October 18, 1942, 52.
44   "Fabrics from the New Spring Lines," *Interiors* (February 1943): 45. Unlike roller printing, the screen-printing process did not require the use of priority materials—screen frames were generally made of wood, and a variety of fabrics could be used in place of the traditional (and restricted) silk mesh.
45   See Thurman, "Textiles," 197. Although *Shooting Stars* and *Propellers*, printed by Knoll in 1947, were the first of Strengell's print designs to be put into production, four of her earlier print designs appear in photographs taken in 1944 and 1945; photographs dated January 19, 1944 (6521) and December 28, 1945 (AA-808-1-3), Marianne Strengell Papers (1991-07), Cranbrook Archives. Another print design was submitted to MoMA's 1946 Competition for Printed Fabrics, winning an honorable mention (List of prize winners, Printed Fabrics Competition, June 1946, CUR, Exh. 345, MoMA Archives; see fig. 1.17).
46   June O. Goldberg, "The Brief Commercial Career of Angelo Testa," MA thesis, Fashion Institute of Technology–State University of New York, 2003, 92–93;

Christa C. Mayer Thurman, "Angelo Testa," in *Rooted in Chicago: Fifty Years of Textile Traditions* (Chicago: Art Institute of Chicago Museum Studies, 1997), 12–13. Three of Testa's print designs were on the cover of the first issue of *Everyday Art Quarterly* with a caption reading, "These fabrics are scheduled to go into production this year and will be available at moderate prices"; see "Furniture and Fabrics," *Everyday Art Quarterly,* no. 1 (Summer 1946): 10.

47 "Textiles," *Arts & Architecture* (October 1945): 42–43; "Angelo Testa," *Arts & Architecture* (July 1946): 42–43.

48 Thurman, "Ben Rose, Inc.," in *Rooted in Chicago*, 24–25.

49 W. (Walter) C. Jackson [dean of the college], foreword to *Annual International Textile Exhibition 1944* (Greensboro, N.C.: [Witherspoon Art Gallery], 1944), n.p.

50 "International Textile Exhibition," *Upholstering* (April 1944), 17. The reviewer praised woven work from Cranbrook, including that of Marianne Strengell (second-place award winner) and her assistant and former student, Robert Sailors (first-place award winner).

51 *Annual International Textile Exhibition 1944*, n.p.

52 See ibid. and *International Textile Exhibition*, November 1–30, 1948 (Greensboro, N.C.: [Witherspoon Art Gallery], 1948), n.p. See also Thurman, "Textiles," 204–5, 320 n. 131.

53 "For Your Information," *Interiors* (December 1946): 14.

54 Robert Sailors to Norma Hardin, January 5, 1947, quoted in Thurman, "Textiles," 204.

55 Eva Ingersoll Gatling, foreword to *Fourth Biennial Exhibition of Textiles and Ceramics* (Bloomfield Hills, Mich.: Cranbrook Academy of Art Museum, 1953), n.p. The Museum also acquired a number of important works from these exhibitions, including the Maria Kipp textile shown in fig. 1.3 (purchased in 1951) and two lengths of the 1953 Knoll pattern *Tracy* (see chapter 3).

56 For complete lists of the participating artists in each of these exhibitions, see Thurman, "Textiles," 319 nn. 112–14.

57 "La France Fabric Design Contest," *Upholstering* (August 1947): 18–19. The 1944 competition was open to students and former students of art schools.

58 "Fabric Design Contest Planned," *New York Times*, March 21, 1947, 36; "$650 in Prizes Won by Fabric Designers," *New York Times*, June 12, 1947, 28.

59 The winning designers received a cash prize (which was apparently a purchase award), with "utilization [to] be announced later"; see "Moss Rose Rewards Design Students," *Upholstering* (June 1947): 80–81, 102. The sixth Moss Rose competition, held in 1952, is the latest for which evidence has been found thus far; "Cranbrook Academy of Art Student News Letter," 1953, Cranbrook Archives (1998-05c), 2:4.

60 MoMA press release 45801-23, August 1, 1945 [August 23, 1945], online Press Release Archive, www.moma.org.

61 Exhibition Check Lists, 1945-46 and 1947-48, CE II.1.83.1, MoMA Archives. At the end of its first two-year national tour, the exhibition was revised and circulated for an additional two years.

62 MoMA press release 46211-12, February 11, 1946, online Press Release Archive, www.moma.org.

63 Exhibition program, "The Museum of Modern Art Competition for Printed Fabrics," CUR, Exh. 345, MoMA Archives.

64 The competition program had been sent to a long list of painters, sculptors, and artists in other media, in addition to art schools and textile designers; "Printed Fabric Competition (1946) Program List," Registrar Exhibition Files, Exh. 345, Museum of Modern Art Archives, New York (hereafter REG, Exh. [number], MoMA Archives).

65 MoMA press release 46624-32, June 24, 1946, online Press Release Archive, www.moma.org; CUR, Exh. 345, MoMA Archives. The *Organic Design* exhibition received 648 entries in all media; see MoMA press release 41130-7, January 30, 1941, online Press Release Archive, www.moma.org.

66 MoMA press release 47307-9, March 7, 1947, MoMA Press Release Archives.

67 "Textures," *Arts & Architecture* (April 1947): 22–23; "Prize-Winning Design for Decoration Fabric in U.S.A.," *International Textiles-Amsterdam* (clipping, REG, Exh. 345, MoMA Archives).

68 "Come the New Fabrics," *Interiors* (March 1947): 82. The "simultaneous competitions" were *Printed Textiles for the Home* (MoMA); first annual awards given by the American Institute of Decorators in January 1947; printed fabric competition sponsored by the Philadelphia Print Club (award winners included an Angelo Testa design for Cohn-Hall-Marx and Noémi Raymond's *Strip Fields*), and the Moss Rose competition which had begun in 1946.

69 "Fabric City," *Interiors* (June 1943): 11–14+.

70 See Jack Lenor Larsen and Jeanne Weeks, *Fabrics for Interiors: A Guide for Architects, Designers, and Consumers* (New York: Van Nostrand Reinhold, 1975), 128–30.

71 The name of the mill or mills that manufactured it would be known only to the mill's own customers (usually other converters, or manufacturers of upholstered furniture).

72 Stephen I. Fleischman to Eva Ingersoll Gatling, January 30, 1953, Fourth Biennial Exhibition of Contemporary Textiles and Ceramics, February 14–March 15, 1953, curatorial exhibition files, Cranbrook Academy of Art Museum.

73 These mills included American Art Textile Printing, Craftex, Original Textile, Orinoka Mills, and Printex, along with suppliers U.S. Rubber and Joynel; see Leslie Piña, *Alexander Girard Designs for Herman Miller* (Atglen, PA: Schiffer Publishing Ltd., 1998), 20–22.

74 Louisville Textiles advertisements, advertising scrapbook, Louisville Textile Co. Records, Osborne Library, American Textile History Museum. Knoll, for whom Louisville was still weaving *Prestini*, is not listed in these advertisements, indicating that perhaps some of the mill's customers preferred to keep their suppliers confidential.

75 Its promotional mission was clearly stated on a title page in the front of each issue: "dedicated to the belief that Fashion begins with the Fabric . . . that the American textile industry casts a major influence on the economic and social aspects of the world in which we live . . . that American textiledom has deservedly attained the world's pinnacle from which it can never be dislodged."

76 By the early 1950s, new trademarked fibers and finishes were appearing on the market so rapidly that *American Fabrics* published reference guides for its readers; see e.g. "Progress Report on the New Fibers," *American Fabrics,* no. 24 (Winter 1952–53): 57–70; "American Fabrics Presents a Key to the Man-Made Fibers," *American Fabrics,* no. 26 (Spring 1953): 70–74; "Guide to Some Well Known Finishes and Finishing Terms," *American Fabrics,* no. 28 (Spring 1954): 80–83.

77 The Department of Industrial Coordination later reported that over 100 exhibiting firms had applied for information on research, design, and other services at the museum; see "Reports of the Departments," *Metropolitan Museum of Art Bulletin,* n.s. 8, no. 1 (Summer 1949): 20. Making museum collections available to designers cut off from Europe assumed new currency during World War II; e.g., the Metropolitan Museum invited American fashion designers and textile manufacturers to study European Renaissance objects in the collection and then mounted the *Renaissance in Fashion 1942* exhibition; see "Renaissance in Fashion 1942," *Metropolitan Museum of Art Bulletin* 37, no. 5 (May 1942): 121, 123–25. *American Fabrics* regularly featured historic textiles and design styles intended as design inspiration for its readers.

78 The American Textiles '48 was reminiscent of the Metropolitan Museum's exhibitions of American industrial art in the 1920s and 1930s, in which the museum represented "neutral ground"; see Richard F. Bach, "American Industrial Art: An Exhibition of Contemporary Design," *Metropolitan Museum of Art Bulletin* 24, no. 2 (February 1929): 39–42.

79 The exhibition was labeled "a progress report" on "an industry that has reached maturity and is able to function in the postwar world without the stimulus of foreign inspiration"; the introduction of man-made fibers was described as "one of the most revolutionary developments in the long history of weaving"; see *American Textiles, '48*, exh. brochure, 1948, n.p., Thomas J. Watson Library, Metropolitan Museum of Art, New York.

80 Industrial textiles, including a Saran insect-screen cloth developed during the war by the Lumite Corp., were also included. See "Treasury of Textiles—Part II. . . The Present," *American Fabrics,* no. 8 (Winter 1948): 87–89; "American Textiles, '48" official exhibition entry cards, 1948, Thomas J. Watson Library, Metropolitan Museum of Art, New York. The cards have small fabric samples attached.

81 Marianne Strengell, "Marianne Strengell Writes About Designing Tomorrow's Fabrics," *Upholstering* (March 1946): 58. Strengell's optimistic assessment likely suggested a more pervasive interest among manufacturers in experimentation than probably existed.

82 For Garrett see "Designers Cannot be Isolationists," *Upholstering* (October 1947): 32, 34. Garrett's first collection for Louisville included a large-scale abstract Jacquard pattern (see fig. 1.21). Garrett had participated in biennial exhibitions at Cranbrook in 1946 and 1949 and may have recommended Louisville Textiles to Marianne Strengell—the mill later wove several of Knoll's early upholsteries, including Strengell's designs *Buster* and *Cartree* (see chapter 3). A design by Russel Wright for Louisville Textiles was exhibited in *Good Design,* MoMA, Fall 1951; it is not clear if this design was submitted for the exhibition by Louisville or by the designer (REG, Exh. 494, MoMA Archives).

83 For Watterston designs for Menlo, see Advertisement for Menlo Textiles, *Interiors* (November 1947): 161; "The Good Word on Fabrics," *Interiors* (November 1947): 114, 164, 166; "A Review of the Fabric Market," *Interiors* (April 1948): 89. For Watterston at Craftex, see "Craftex Mills adds Watterston to Design Staff," *Upholstering* (September 1952): 164. In 1962 one of his Craftex fabrics, *Bangkok*, became part of the Knoll collection.

84 For Belding designs for Arundell Clarke see Polly Weaver, "Jobs Looming," *Mademoiselle* (July 1950): 117; one of her designs for Habitat (*Shades and Tints*) appeared in *Good Design,* Merchandise Mart, January, 1955, and was subsequently put into production by Knoll. See also "Emily Belding: Textile Designer," *Handweaver & Craftsman* 7, no. 1 (Winter 1955–56): 26.

85 For Ehrman fabrics for Marie Nichols see "Merchandise Cues," *Interiors* (August 1949): 134 and "The New Fabrics," *Interiors* (September 1949): 129. Her upholstery fabric also appeared in *Good Design*, Merchandise Mart, January and June, 1950, and MoMA, Fall 1950. For her designs for the Edwin Raphael Company, see "Fabrics," *Everyday Art Quarterly,* no. 25 (1953): 14–15; drapery and upholstery fabrics for Edwin Raphael were exhibited in *Good Design*, Merchandise Mart, January 1953, and MoMA, Fall 1953.

86 In the late 1940s, Liebes's other consulting clients included United Wallpaper (wallpapers with the look of "hand-loomed fabrics") and Jantzen Knitting Mills (colors and fabrics for swimwear and sweaters); she later worked with a wide range of synthetic fibers as a consultant for DuPont from 1955 to 1971. See Blaszczyk, "Designing Synthetics, Promoting Brands," 75, 81, 75.

87 "The House that Fiberglas Built," *Upholstering* (March 1948): 62–64, 116. According to this article, the upholstery fabrics were manufactured by Hess, Goldsmith, and Co., and "should be on the market in a few months," and the hand-woven drapery fabrics "are expected to be mass-produced shortly." The Owens-Corning Fiberglas Building, designed by Skidmore, Owings & Merrill, was an interiors project for the Knoll Planning Unit; see "Eight Solutions to Merchandise Display: Fiberglas House," *Interiors* (October 1948): 112–17; and chap. 4. Strengell participated in a similar project in 1956, when she was commissioned by Alcoa to create an "all-aluminum" rug using experimental yarns; see Leslie S. Edwards, "Structure and Surface: Marianne Strengell and Woven Texture," *Modernism* 10, no. 4 (Winter 2007–8): 76–77, 84.

88 "Glass Fiber Made to Look Natural," *New York Times*, December 10, 1957, 58; "Aerocor: New Potential for Owens-Corning's Fiberglas," *Interiors* (February 1958): 126. Aerocor yarn was used by Knoll for Anni Albers's *Fiberglas Casement* (1958) and for *Knoll Fiberglas* (1957), a basic sheer that Knoll sold as casement fabric and as a base fabric for printing.

89 Weaver, "Jobs Looming," 117. No archival records for Original Textile have yet surfaced, but its name appears repeatedly in accounts of exhibitions such as *Good Design* and the Cranbrook biennials.

90 For Knoll see *Devil*, *Fiberglas Casement*, *Afro*, and *Domus* files, KnollTextiles Archive,

New York; for Herman Miller see "Nelson and Eames Design New Pieces for Herman Miller," *Upholstering* (February 1951): 132. In addition to *Fiberglas Casement,* they wove a number of other designs by Anni Albers, one of which (for Patterson Fabrics) was in *Good Design,* MoMA, Fall 1950.

91 This drapery fabric, priced at $21 per yard, was shown in *Good Design,* Merchandise Mart, January 1951, and MoMA, Fall 1951.

92 In 1949 the company operated twenty-four automatic looms and produced cotton, rayon, linen, wool, and "glassfibre" drapery and upholstery fabrics; see *Davison's Textile Blue Book* (Ridgewood, N.J.: Davison Publishing Co., 1949), 471. By comparison, the same year, the Moss Rose manufacturing company operated 30 plain and 180 Jacquard looms, and worked with cotton, wool, worsted, mohair, and rayon yarns (ibid., 340).

93 Three samples incorporating Saran, nylon, and asbestos, marked with "Original Textile Company" tags, survive in the Josef and Anni Albers Foundation, Bethany, Conn. (inv. nos. 1994.15.75a, 1994.15.77a, 1994.15.78a); a related group of Saran and nylon samples in the same collection (inv. nos. 1994.15.67–.73 and 1994.15.76) were probably also designed for Original Textile. Several samples at MoMA (acc. nos. 450.1970.12–.17) appear to belong to this same group. Suzanne Huguenin (see chap. 3) also described experimenting with asbestos during her career at Knoll (Huguenin, interview by Kate Carmel, October 30, 1987, Stewart Collection Archive, Museum of Fine Arts, Montreal, courtesy David Hanks).

94 A Testa design for Schumacher (*Square Deal*) was shown in *Good Design,* Merchandise Mart, June 1953, and MoMA, Fall 1953. Schumacher was an important early client for Vera Neumann and Printex; see Isadore Barmash, "Vera Neumann: I Start Everything as a Painting," in *The Self-Made Man* (New York: MacMillan, 1969), 301. Neumann worked regularly with them through the 1970s.

95 Thurman, "Angelo Testa," in *Rooted in Chicago,* 14; *Furniture Forum* 2, no. 3 (April 1951): 13, section 3, illus.; *Furniture Forum* 2, no. 4 (June 1951): 15, section 3, illus. For a Konwiser design by Sara Provan see Lesley Jackson, *Twentieth-Century Pattern Design: Textile & Wallpaper Pioneers* (New York: Princeton Architectural Press, 2002), 117, illus.

96 Weaver, "Jobs Looming," 117. Judson Williams apparently worked for Goodall before starting his own business in the mid-1940s; Marianne Strengell designed textiles for him in 1949 (Mary Roche, "The Hand-Loomed Look," *New York Times,* September 4, 1949, 106). Another Strengell design for Williams was shown in *Good Design,* MoMA, Fall 1953.

97 Nichols was offering a collection of fabrics through Herman Miller showrooms in 1949; the collection included Angelo Testa prints and handwoven fabrics from the Philippines; see "Merchandise Cues," *Interiors* (August 1949): 134. In addition, upholstery fabrics designed by Marli Ehrman and Gloria Wasserman were available on Herman Miller furniture or by the yard (Roche, "Hand-Loomed Look").

98 See "Fabrics," *Everyday Art Quarterly,* no. 25 (1953): 10.

99 Lustig, "Modern Printed Fabrics," 66.

100 Christa C. Mayer Thurman, "Ben Rose, Inc.," in *Rooted in Chicago,* 26–27. Ruth Adler had only read about screen printing before she began printing textiles; Ruth Adler Schnee, Oral history interview by Anita Schnee, November 24–30, 2002, Archives of American Art, Smithsonian Institution; Jackson, *Twentieth-Century Pattern Design,* 109.

101 See Goldberg, "Brief Commercial Career of Angelo Testa"; Thurman, "Angelo Testa," in *Rooted in Chicago,* 12–17.

102 In 1948 Girard's store sold (in addition to his own designs) fabrics by Goodall, Angelo Testa, Knoll, Schulke, June Groff, and Antoinette Webster; see "Where to Buy Well Designed Objects," *Everyday Art Quarterly,* no. 7 (Spring 1948): 3. Girard designs were shown in a January 1947 exhibition at the Art Institute of Chicago, in connection with the first AID design awards; in the Second Biennial Exhibition at Cranbrook in 1949; and in the exhibition *Modern Textiles* at the Everyday Art Gallery, Walker Art Center, also in 1949. See Mary Roche, "3 Receive Awards for New Designs," *New York Times,* January 4, 1947, 12; *Second National Biennial Exhibition of Contemporary Textiles and Ceramics* (Bloomfield Hills, Mich.: Cranbrook Academy of Art Museum, 1949); "Textiles," *Everyday Art Quarterly,* no. 11 (Summer 1949): 7. It is not clear if Girard continued to print and retail his own textiles after 1950.

103 John Brunetti, *Baldwin Kingrey: Mid-century Modern in Chicago, 1947–1957* (Chicago: Wright, 2004), 99–100. Baldwin-Machado fabrics were included in numerous exhibitions, such as *Modern Art in Your Life* (MoMA, 1949), the Third Biennial Exhibition at Cranbrook (1951), and *Textiles USA* (MoMA, 1956). Baldwin and Machado called their partnership Design Unit New York, and their fabrics are sometimes identified with this name.

104 See Don Wallance, *Shaping America's Products* (New York: Van Nostrand Reinhold, 1956), 99–101; "Pilot Printing Plant," *Interiors* (June 1949): 104–11; and "The Tilletts Are at It Again," *Upholstering* (September 1949): 43–45.

105 Lustig, "Modern Printed Fabrics," 68. The development of "name" collections of modern textiles in America was roughly contemporary with similar projects initiated by Astrid Sampe at NK's Textilkammare in Sweden, which culminated in the *Signerad Textile* (Signed Textile) collection released in 1954; see Anne-Marie Ericsson, "Modernismens Genombrott," in Jan Brunius et al., *Svenska Textilier 1890–1990* (Trelleborg: Signum/Lund, 1994), 197–229; see also chap. 3 in this volume.

106 "The Levities of Laverne," *Interiors* (March 1952): 113–14.

107 Jackson, *Twentieth-Century Pattern Design,* 113.

108 See "Schiffer's Superlative Stimulus," *Interiors* (July 1949): 134–36; "Hand-Screened Moderns," *Interior Design and Decoration* (September 1949): 58. Maix was listed as the New York agent for Ben Rose textiles in 1948, see "Newsreel," *Interiors* (July 1948): 124. It is not clear how long Maix worked for Knoll after the war (see chapter 3), but in late 1947 he was described as "former sales manger of Hans Knoll, Inc."; see "'Non-Objectionable' Modern," *Upholstering* (September 1947): 60.

109 "New Patterns Shown by Fabric Designers," *New York Times,* April 22, 1950, 12. Some of the *Campagna* group designs may have been printed in 1949 (Giles Kotcher, research article, ca. 1995, n.p., Courtesy of Giles Kotcher).

110 L. Anton Maix added woven textiles to his line in the early 1950s, but apparently did not credit them to specific designers during this period. Much later, in 1966, he imported a collection designed by Peter Simpson for Bute Fabrics; see *Home Furnishings Daily* (November 23, 1966), quoted in Kotcher, research article.

111 See Jackson, *Twentieth-Century Pattern Design,* 116; and Alice Zrebiec, "Joan Miró," in *Design 1935–1965: What Modern Was,* ed. Martin Eidelberg (New York: Harry N. Abrams, 1991), 240–41.

112 Thurman, "Else Regensteiner and Julia McVicker," in *Rooted in Chicago,* 22.

113 Thurman, "Robert Sailors," in *Rooted in Chicago,* 35–41.

114 Walter Rendell Storey, "Isabel Scott, Handweaver and Designer," *Handweaver & Craftsman* (Spring 1953): 14; Weaver, "Jobs Looming," 117.

115 Storey, "Isabel Scott." One of Scott's fabrics received an AID award in 1949 (ibid.), and two of her designs were selected for *Good Design,* MoMA, January 1951; see *Furniture Forum* 2, no. 3 (April 1951): 12, section 3.

116 "Rancocas Fabrics," *Handweaver & Craftsman* 8, no. 2 (Spring 1957): 41–43.

117 Larsen collaborated with weaver Dick Bolan in these experiments; see Jack Lenor Larsen, *A Weaver's Memoir* (New York: Harry N. Abrams: 1998), 29–30; David Revere McFadden et al., *Jack Lenor Larsen: Creator and Collector* (London and New York: Merrell Publishers Limited, 2004), 176.

118 Larsen, *Weaver's Memoir,* 32.

119 "By exercising careful design judgment in buying, we consumers should be able to effect a gradual increase in the number of good designs available. For this reason, good design is *our* business." Charles P. Parkhurst Jr., "A Consumer Looks for Good Designs," from *Good Design is Your Business* (Buffalo, N.Y.: Buffalo Fine Arts Academy, 1947), quoted in *Everyday Art Quarterly,* no. 4 (Summer, 1947): 5.

120 E. P. Richardson, introduction to *Exhibition for Modern Living,* 7.

121 For a discussion of these exhibitions, see Arthur J. Pulos, *The American Design Adventure* (Cambridge, MA: MIT Press, 1988), 68–77.

122 Elizabeth McCausland, "Gallery of Everyday Art," *Arts & Architecture* (March 1946): 39.

123 See *Everyday Art Quarterly,* no. 5 (Fall 1947); the issue is devoted to the Idea House. In 1948, *Life* magazine arranged for "an average U.S. family, living in an average home," to move for a week into the Idea House and published a feature on their experiences; see "How Livable is a Modern House?", *Life* (October 18, 1948): 105–8.

124 *Everyday Art Quarterly,* no. 11 (Summer 1949).

125 Roche, "3 Receive Awards for New Designs." They were first awarded at the AID's annual meeting in January 1947.

126 Kaufmann, Rogers, and Stone served on the first jury along with William Wurster (dean of the MIT School of Architecture) and department store executives from Gump's, San Francisco, and B. Altman and Company, New York. "Awards to be Made in Home Furnishings," *New York Times,* October 16, 1946, 32.

127 Roche, "3 Receive Awards for New Designs."

128 *Bulletin of the Detroit Institute of Arts* 29, no. 2 (1949–50): 39, online at www.dalnet.lib.mi.us/greenstone/dia/diaBulletins/29-2.pdf.

129 Kaufmann further described how the growth of design could be fostered by the way it is "commissioned, produced, advertised, and sold" (Edgar Kaufmann Jr., "Modern Design in America Now," in *Exhibition For Modern Living,* 27). Kaufmann's essay was also published in *Arts & Architecture* (November 1949): 29.

130 MoMA press release 491109-78, November 9, 1949, online Press Release Archive, www.moma.org.

131 MoMA press release, "Large New Group of 'Good Design'," [June 1950], online Press Release Archive, www.moma.org.

132 "For Your Information," *Interiors* (February 1950): 142.

133 Betty Pepis, "Art and Industry Linked on Homes," *New York Times,* January 17, 1950, 31.

134 MoMA press release, "Large New Group of 'Good Design'," [June 1950], online Press Release Archive, www.moma.org.

135 Introduction to *Good Design* (June 1954): n.p.

136 Greta Daniel to Vera Neumann, April 11, 1955, CUR, Exh. 570, MoMA Archives.

137 The last Cranbrook Biennial was held in 1953 and the last International Textile Exhibition in 1956.

138 Jack Lenor Larsen, interviewed by author, February 2, 2010.

139 Lois Wagner, "Good Design: The Fifth Anniversary," *Interiors* (August 1954): 82.

140 Lazette Van Houten, "Furniture—January 1956," *Arts & Architecture* (March 1956): 34.

141 "Fabrics must be woven, knitted, printed and dyed in the United States. They should be contemporary in feeling and manufactured during the last ten years"; from the program for the *American Fabrics* exhibition, CUR, Exh. 606, MoMA Archives.

142 Arthur Drexler, introduction to *Textiles USA* (New York: MoMA, 1956), 3.

143 Noyes, *Organic Design,* 1.

144 Arthur Drexler, introduction to *Textiles USA* (New York: MoMA, 1956), 3.

145 "Textiles USA," *Handweaver & Craftsman* 7, no. 1 (Fall 1956): 25.

146 U.S. Senate Committee on Interstate and Foreign Commerce, *Problems of the Domestic Textile Industry,* 86th Cong., 1st Sess., Senate Report No. 42 (Washington, D.C.: Government Printing Office, 1959), 2. According to this report, broadwoven fabric production between 1947 and 1957 declined: overall, 12.4 billion to 12.1 billion linear yards; cotton, 9.8 billion to 9.5 billion; wool, 516 million to 288 million; rayon and acetate, 1.9 billion to 1.46 billion; newer man-made fibers (increase), 51 million to 778 million linear yards (ibid., 4).

147 Ibid., 4.

148 William H. Miernyk, "A Projection of Textile Production in the United States to 1970," 1957, typescript, American Textile History Museum Library, Lowell, Mass.

149 Advertisement for Knoll Associates, *American Fabrics,* special issue, no. 38 (Fall 1956): xvi–xvii.

150 These were *Kerry Linen* and *Minor* woven by Donald Brothers of Dundee, Scotland as well as *Rugby* and *Prestini* woven by the American mills Orinoka and Louisville Textiles, respectively.

2 Knoll Before Knoll Textiles, 1940–46

Paul Makovsky

The beginnings were very tough. Not only was it difficult to get contemporary work, but it was extremely difficult to get the furniture produced once we had the client and the job. Everything was difficult. Fabrics were difficult. Even the glues were inferior glues. The only material available at the time was wood. Everything was on a wartime basis. We had to use ingenuity to get anything produced at all.
—Florence Knoll Bassett[1]

Knoll, which would become one of the premiere design firms of the postwar period, came into being at an inauspicious moment—World War II was sweeping through Europe and would soon engulf much of the globe. This meant wartime restrictions on materials for the furnishings industry, but it was these same wartime shortages that forced the fledgling company founded by Hans G. Knoll to search out new materials and to find new uses for old ones, a practice of innovation and experimentation that remained a hallmark of the company in the postwar years. During this time Hans Knoll also made valuable connections in the United States and abroad with manufacturers, suppliers, and designers, one of whom, Florence Schust (later Florence Knoll Bassett), brought a creative vision that transformed the company's product line and its design philosophy. Among her innovations was Knoll's textile division, which was established in 1947. However, its development is interwoven with the early history of the company and must be understood in that context.

Hans Knoll and the Founding of the Knoll Furniture Company

Little is known of the early career of Hans Knoll (1914–1955) (fig. 2.1). Eszter Haraszty, the head of Knoll Textiles in the first half of the 1950s, later recalled, "Hans had lots of stories, but nobody could confirm them, and really, nobody cared."[2] He was the son of Walter Knoll, a leading furniture manufacturer in Feuerbach, Germany, just outside Stuttgart. Founded in 1925, Walter Knoll & Co. quickly gained much success and acclaim for manufacturing innovative modernist furniture.[3] In 1928 the company developed the popular *Prodomo* seating system, which featured a new patented design of flat steel web springing—an elastic steel suspension for the seat and back—making it possible to use lightweight upholstered cushions or to affix the upholstery directly to the frame with tacks. *Prodomo* was more economical to manufacture than traditional furniture, and customers could choose from a wide variety of colorful upholstery fabrics. During the early 1930s, the line was extended to include sofas, lounge chairs, and cantilevered tubular steel furniture. In World War II, however, Walter Knoll & Co. was pressed into war production, until bomb damage in 1942 forced the factory to close, not to reopen until after the war.[4]

Hans Knoll's first job was in the textile business, working in London from 1933 to 1935 for the British branch of Jantzen Knitting Mills, an American manufacturer of knitted products, such as sweaters, hosiery, and jackets, and, later, swimsuits.[5] Based in Portland, Oregon, Jantzen was a forward-looking company, working with new materials such as Lastex, a rubberized yarn, and with synthetics such as rayon blended with cotton or silk.[6] Knoll, whose exact role at Jantzen is unclear, was thus exposed early on to the profitability of working with new materials and the importance of branding.

In London, Knoll also worked from 1935 to 1937 with Plan, Ltd., a furniture and interiors company founded by architect Serge Chermayeff in 1932.[7] The company sold modern wood and tubular steel furniture, hand-knotted rugs, and lighting. A licensing agreement also allowed it to retail British-made

Abel Sorensen. *Model 50S* stool, ca. 1947. Webbing made by Bridgeport Fabrics for Knoll Associates, stool made by Knoll Associates Inc. Birch, cotton webbing; plain weave. Knoll Museum, East Greenville, Penn. Cat. 6.

versions of Walter Knoll's *Prodomo* lounge chairs and occasional furniture, and Hans Knoll had joined the company to introduce his family firm's *Elbo* range of low-slung lounge chairs with the same spring mechanism.[8] Plan, Ltd.'s upholstery fabrics were woven by Donald Brothers, a company based in Dundee, Scotland, that gained prominence in the 1930s for its high-quality linen and textured upholstery textiles and which would later supply some Knoll Textiles patterns.[9] In 1937 Hans Knoll returned to Nazi Germany, and by June 1938 Plan, Ltd. had gone into liquidation. Despite its brief history, Plan, Ltd. has been characterized as "one of the more significant modernist experiments in the manufacture and retail of contemporary furniture and furnishings in Britain during the interwar years."[10]

By the late 1930s the political and economic situation in Germany had worsened, and there were strong rumblings of the coming European conflict. In 1937, at the age of twenty-three, Hans Knoll immigrated to the United States, assisted by the family that owned the Jantzen Knitting Mills.[11] Knoll arrived in New York on the SS *American Farmer* on September 21, 1937, his passage paid by the prominent American lawyer Bronson Winthrop, for reasons unknown.[12] Winthrop, a partner at the Manhattan law firm of Winthrop, Stimson, Putnam & Roberts, had strong political and social ties to the upper echelons of New York society and a few years later helped Knoll secure an important government commission to design the interiors for the offices of Henry Stimson, the secretary of war (1940–45). Knoll initially planned to stay in the United States for only a year and listed both Winthrop and the New York office of Jantzen in the Empire State Building as contacts.[13] By January 1939, however, he had put down roots in his new home, marrying Barbara Southwick, a native of Long Island, and settling in Brookville, New York.[14]

According to Knoll corporate histories, Hans Knoll started his company in 1938, when "in a single second-story room on 72nd Street, he constituted himself the Hans G. Knoll Furniture Company, bravely nailing up a sign which read: Factory No. 1."[15] Despite this romantic account, it seems more likely that the company was founded in 1940.[16] In his 1943 naturalization papers, Knoll stated that between 1938 and 1940 he worked as a salesman for George Ditmar, a furniture retailer and wholesaler with a showroom on Madison Avenue.[17] Through Ditmar, Knoll began to establish connections in the American furniture business, first focusing on building a network of sales contacts, then developing a product line. The two must have struggled—in March 1940, Ditmar filed for bankruptcy, and Knoll leased space in the same building under his own name and a year later, in December 1941, moved to 601 Madison Avenue, which would be the company's home for nearly a decade.[18]

Knoll's first initiative was to sell his father's *Prodomo* chair to architects and designers. In 1938 he most likely brokered an agreement between his father's company and the Mueller Furniture Company of Grand Rapids, Michigan, to produce and sell "a line of Swedish modern furniture for both living room and office." Marketed under the *Prodomo* name, the line included chairs featuring Walter Knoll's patented spring system.[19] In 1940, at the second season of the New York World's Fair, Hans Knoll supplied the *Prodomo* chairs displayed in architect Allmon Fordyce's "Living Kitchen" installation in the *America at Home* exhibition (fig. 2.2).[20] They featured a single cushion covering back and seat in a bold blue, green, and white striped fabric, rather than a traditional heavy upholstery, giving them a functional and contemporary look. The cushion could easily be removed for cleaning, and the design was lauded as "a new type of chair construction" that was "both comfortable and sanitary."[21]

In May 1941 Hans Knoll became the wholesale sales representative in the metropolitan New York area for Artek-Pascoe, Inc., a joint venture between Clifford Pascoe and Artek, the Finnish company that manufactured, distributed, and promoted architect Alvar Aalto's plywood furniture.[22] The market for modern design in the United States was small but growing, and Artek was perhaps the favorite manufacturer among American modernist architects and designers at the time—from Harwell Hamilton Harris and William Wurster in California to Edward Durell Stone, G. Holme Perkins, and Carl Koch on the East Coast, among others.[23] Hans Knoll's business arrangement with Artek, however, was short-lived. Only two known commissions specified Artek furniture through Knoll in 1941, and the following year Knoll's first product catalogue makes no mention of Artek-Pascoe.[24]

Collaboration with Jens Risom

In 1941 Knoll hired Jens Risom, a twenty-five-year-old Danish designer. Risom had worked in the design department at Nordiska Kompaniet (NK), Sweden's largest department store. This was followed by a position in a small design studio and retail outlet in Stockholm that specialized in residential furniture which Risom has described as "Funkis"—the term used at the time to describe modern Scandinavian functionalist design.[25] From 1936 to 1938 he studied furniture design with Ole Wanscher at the Kunsthåndvaerkerskolen (School for Arts and Crafts) in Copenhagen, Denmark, where his classmates included Hans Wegner and Børge Morgensen.[26] In 1939 he immigrated to the United States, later acknowledging that "by and large it was a gamble."[27]

Risom found work in New York with the respected textile and interior designer Dan Cooper, who had a showroom in the Fuller Building (Madison Avenue and Fifty-seventh Street), and sold his own textile designs as well as imported Scottish linens and wool fabrics.[28] Cooper hired Risom to create contemporary printed fabrics which Risom later described as simple patterns with dots and curves and no overlapping designs. According to Risom, "I don't think they sold well, but I don't think anything sold well in those days."[29] Risom eventually convinced Cooper to let him design furniture, and he created a small collection of four or five pieces.

The Cooper office was a meeting place for young designers and architects such as George Nelson and Edward Durell Stone. In 1940 Stone commissioned Risom to make furniture for Stone's "House of Ideas," a model house sponsored by *Collier's* magazine, built on a terrace at Rockefeller Center, overlooking Fifth Avenue, and including "a marvelous exhibition of furniture, fabrics and colors."[30] Risom also recalled, however, that "Dan Cooper was getting all the credit, but I was doing all the work, so it was one of the reasons why I felt I should go out on my own."[31] In 1941 he did just that.

By this time, Risom had met Hans Knoll, who was selling what Risom remembers as "furniture of no importance." Knoll needed a designer and someone to oversee manufacturing, while Risom was looking for someone with a showroom, sales ability, and connections. "We needed each other," Risom explained. They worked out an arrangement whereby Risom provided Knoll with sketches for furniture and oversaw their production, while Knoll secured the clients. One of their first commissions was to design and fabricate pickled and bleached walnut furniture for architects Robert I. Powell and Alexander Perry Morgan for the reception foyer of the Johnson & Johnson Ligature Laboratory in New Brunswick, New Jersey (1941), (fig. 2.3).[32] Risom described these as a "majestic group of pieces for a very large reception room with tables and chairs" and recalled that "we just went out and bought the fabrics. It was just really the basic design of the pieces and then getting them made. Hans didn't know anything about fabricating. He knew people in Grand Rapids but didn't want to have anything to do with that. We farmed it out to several of the top, expensive cabinetmakers in town and they were happy to have the work."[33]

A larger commission was for Glen King, who owned the Ford dealership and the U-Tote-Em grocery chain in McKenzie, Tennessee.[34] Risom designed the interior furnishings for a new house for King's son, Chandler, and his new bride, Sybil West, and remembers the furniture as "plain and modern; not great; it filled a couple of big vans and the furnishings were basically one-offs, because at that time, we had nothing else."[35] Intrigued by the scope of the commission, Risom and Knoll decided to travel to Tennessee and personally oversee the installation. They also used the opportunity to travel around the country, visiting architects and designers, making important contacts, and studying the potential market for a new line of modern furniture that would be designed by Risom and sold by Knoll. Armed with a list of the leading architects and contemporary furniture stores, given to them by Howard Myers, the publisher and editor of *Architectural Forum*, they visited Dallas, Los Angeles, San Francisco, Chicago, and other cities from May to September 1941.[36] While traveling, Risom worked at night and on weekends, making scale drawings of designs for orders from salesman running the Knoll office back in New York. The trip cemented their resolve: "We were convinced after that if we did things right, did it well, and fast enough, we would succeed," recalls Risom.[37] The move from fabricating furniture for others to offering design services and eventually a standard furniture line began to resonate with Knoll and Risom. As their client base grew, more and more upholstered furniture was specified, and, as a result, more textiles were needed.

By the spring of 1942, Knoll assembled the furniture Risom had designed into a collection that was offered to architects and interior designers via Knoll's first catalogue.[38] This initial product line was indicative of the direction the company was hoping to take at the time—wood home furnishings and some upholstered pieces in a modern idiom. Risom designed fifteen pieces, mostly to be fabricated from cherry wood. One pair of chairs had interlaced leather strips forming the seat and back (see fig. 2.3), while an upholstered studio couch featured built-in storage space. There were two easy chairs, one upholstered in a houndstooth pattern with a recessed wooden base (*Model 620*), the other in a large-scale plaid pattern with sides in a solid weave and a wooden sled base (*Model 621*) (fig. 2.4). The catalogue also featured a collection of upholstered seating from a Grand Rapids manufacturer as well as five upholstered pieces with splayed legs by the Austrian-born designer Ernst Schwadron, then head designer for Rena Rosenthal, Inc.[39] The soft curves of these pieces were covered in a range of fabrics—a leaf pattern overlaying a dotted ground, a chenille-like solid, and a nubby texture—that are difficult to identify from period black-and-white photographs (fig. 2.5).

The catalogue specified sizes and choice of woods but did not offer a choice of upholstery textiles, suggesting that these were selected on an ad hoc basis and were not then considered an important part of the business. Risom later recalled that the upholstery textiles were simply purchased from local suppliers in a few basic colors and plaids.[40] A page at the end of the catalogue, however, showcased the sheer drapery fabrics designed by Frances Breese Miller, Knoll's first textile designer. These were printed on "ninon and marquisette, for practical and unique window treatments" and were available in any color or as "special orders on your own material" (fig. 2.6).

Miller may be best remembered today for The Sandbox (1933), her modernist house in Bridgehampton, New York, but she was well known during the 1930s and 1940s for rug and textile designs.[41] She adapted traditional techniques to create handmade hooked rugs with discreet abstract

Fig. 2.1 Left Hans Knoll on a *Model 652W3* settee, ca. 1945. Photographed by Roy Stevens. Knoll Archives.

Fig. 2.3 Right Reception foyer, Johnson & Johnson Ligature Laboratory, New Brunswick, N.J., 1941. Knoll Archives.

Fig. 2.2 Two *Prodomo* chairs in the "Living Kitchen" installation, *America at Home* exhibition, New York World's Fair, 1940. Photographed by Richard Averill Smith. Knoll Archives.

Fig. 2.4 Left Page from first Knoll catalogue, featuring *Model 621* chair designed by Jens Risom, 1942. Courtesy Jens Risom.

Fig. 2.5 Right Page from first Knoll catalogue, featuring *Model 202* and *Model 203* chairs designed by Ernst Schwadron, 1942. Courtesy Jens Risom.

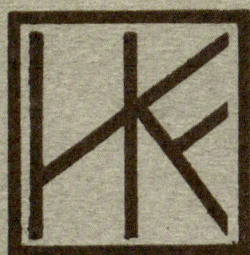

Printed Sheers

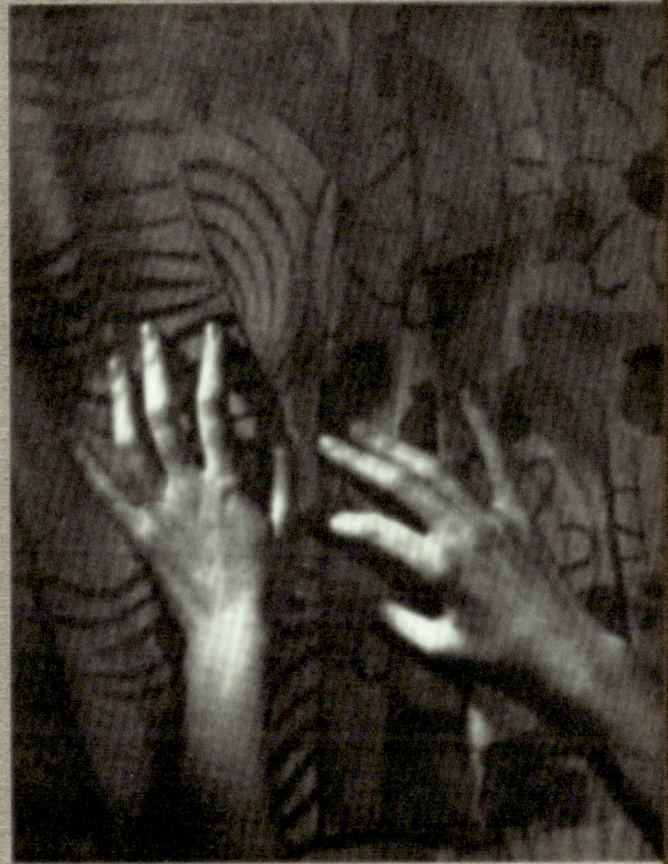

A new and important addition to our line is printed sheers created by Frances Miller, well-known textile designer.

On ninon and marquisette, for practical and unique window treatments.

Available in any color.

Special orders on your own material.

Samples upon request.

HANS KNOLL FURNITURE • 601 MADISON AVENUE • NEW YORK, N.Y.

Fig. 2.6 Page from first Knoll catalogue, featuring "Printed Sheers" designed by Frances Breese Miller, 1942. Courtesy Jens Risom.

patterns that relied largely on texture and were precursors to today's machine-made "carved" carpets.[42] Experimenting with a variety of textiles, she created abstract airbrush patterns on woven cellophane, prints on fishnet, and stencils on satins. Many of these motifs were marine based—inspired by shells and the motion and reflection of water—which is evident in the examples offered in Knoll's 1942 catalogue.[43]

By the early 1940s, Miller had received rug and textile commissions from many of the top New York architects, designers, and decorators including Skidmore, Owings & Merrill, Frances Elkins, Henry Dreyfuss, and McMillan, Inc. Her printed textiles received an honorary mention in the Museum of Modern Art's influential 1941 *Organic Design* exhibition (see chapter 1).[44] Miller's prominence in New York society and her increasing stature in the design circles undoubtedly appealed to an ambitious entrepreneur like Knoll, but just how they met is not known. Her innovative textiles matched the aesthetic of the company's fledgling line, but they were probably not in the line for very long, since her work is only included in the first catalogue. The ever-increasing restrictions on raw materials and manufacturing for civilian use brought about by World War II seem to have led Knoll to concentrate on developing a furniture line first. In any event it would be five years before another textile designer would enter the company's line.

Wartime Shortages—Furniture, Textiles, and Material Innovations

The United States entry into the war meant restrictions on the civilian use of many raw materials and manufactured products as well as the conversion of many factories to wartime production. Furniture and textile production were among the industries affected. Limited quantities of metals, for example, forced designers to develop wood replacements for steel springs or to eliminate springs altogether by substituting foam rubber and bent plywood, until these materials also became unavailable.[45] Upholstery textiles became scarce as the war went on, with textile mills concentrating on military contracts.[46] By 1945, under government orders, furniture manufacturers had reduced the number of designs to 35 percent of those made in September 1941.[47] Moreover, the shortage of skilled textile workers, government limitations on dyes, and number of plants doing war work severely limited manufacturing output, or as one writer put it, "Sateen and glazed chintzes have gone to war. Even cotton fabrics are scarcer. Printed goods are at a premium."[48] Upholstered furniture was also limited during the war because down and other feather fillings were being used for flight suits and sleeping bags for service personnel rather than home furnishings. Knoll began to rethink the way it manufactured its products and by 1943 had developed a system for prefabricating furniture using standardized parts that could be assembled by the consumer without screws or nails. First came the *Model 666* side chair, a Risom design that contained "no metal, no plywood, no springs, and no accessories."[49] It was soon followed by the *650* line, a group of five chairs and two settees, also designed by Risom (fig. 2.7), which allowed for "the use of non-essential materials without sacrifice to comfort, design, or durability."[50] The pieces consisted of seat and back components that could be upholstered in the traditional manner or with interlaced webbing and that were cradled in a structural frame of blond, natural-finished birch. A Knoll brochure for the line highlighted its "flexibility, economy, and comfort" as well as its production based on "minimum labor in manufacture and assembly."[51]

The chairs and settees in the *650* line required only two yards of fabric to cover a seat and back component, but the brochure did not offer specific upholstery options for the line. The company most likely was still accommodating upholstery orders on an ad hoc basis. Of the two *650* line chairs illustrated in a *New York Times* review of the collection, one was covered in striped canvas and another in cotton tweed, while the article noted that "rough-textured upholstery fabrics, canvas and even occasionally non-priority leather" were used on this "beautiful, well-designed, easily shipped furniture, at pleasant prices."[52]

Knoll's use of interlaced cotton webbing to replace traditional upholstery was another wartime accommodation. Webbing as a furniture material was certainly not new—Shaker furniture makers had used it in the nineteenth century as had Scandinavian modernist designers such as Bruno Mathsson and Alvar Aalto in the 1930s and these predecessors were almost certainly well known to Knoll and Risom.[53] The stripped-down and utilitarian look of Knoll's webbed furniture in the 1940s offered a fresh, contemporary choice in the American market of the time.

Risom recalled that Knoll first acquired webbing from prewar supplies until the government requisitioned it.[54] Made of cotton or jute, it came in a natural color and was sold by upholstery supply stores as stretchers for underneath cushions or to reinforce springs but was not meant to be seen. As these supplies dried up, Risom discovered quantities of cotton parachute belting that had not met government specifications, and Knoll was able to purchase these defective materials. "We didn't care if it was strong enough to swing a man in the air in a parachute," he recalled.[55] Initially Knoll's standard webbing was "olive drab" dictated by its military origins or could be dyed green or brown at a slightly higher price.[56]

In September 1944 Walter Baermann, a designer then heading Knoll's Planning Unit, wrote about the challenges facing manufacturers of upholstered furniture, a field that was still essentially craft-based and resistant to mass industrial production.[57] Perhaps reflecting on Knoll's success during the war years, he argued that "war-time restrictions have fostered engineering ingenuity, and war-time technology has produced many new materials and production methods. The upholstered furniture industry must and will use all these advantages. It will grow up into a real industry; it will mass produce and pre-fabricate."[58]

By 1945 Knoll was collaborating with Bridgeport Fabrics, a Connecticut-based supplier of webbing for the government as well as furniture manufacturers, to develop webbing in a variety of colors, textures, and eventually with subtle patterns (fig. 2.8).[59] With postwar furnishing requirements in mind, Bridgeport set about expanding the range of webbing options in addition to trying to improve colorfastness, tensile strength, elasticity, and weave construction.[60] The results included "salt & pepper," which had been "designed expressly for H. G. Knoll" (fig. 2.9).[61] Knoll's success with the *666* and *650* lines of chairs and settees led to further experiments with webbing after the war, including webbing manufactured with plastic fibers.[62]

The use of webbing had allowed Knoll to produce lightweight chairs with stripped-down forms and simple construction and to turn a profit during difficult economic times. Knoll's reputation grew, and for at least the next two decades, it was heralded as a leading manufacturer of modern furniture in the United States, a position maintained in large part through the design leadership of Florence Knoll Bassett.[63]

Florence Knoll and the Making of Knoll Associates

Florence Knoll Bassett was born Florence Margaret Schust on May 24, 1917, in Saginaw, Michigan. Orphaned in 1931, she was sent a year later to Kingswood School, a boarding school in Bloomfield Hills, Michigan.[64] The school was part of the Cranbrook educational complex that included the Cranbrook Academy of Art, which opened in 1932 and would soon become a celebrated breeding ground for modernist designers in America.[65] Cranbrook's buildings and furnishings were largely designed by members of the Finnish Saarinen family—Eliel, a leading architect, his wife, Loja, a weaver and textile designer who directed Cranbrook's weaving studio, and their son Eero, an architecture student and budding designer—who had come to Cranbrook by invitation in 1925. The campus and its furnishings had a profound impact on Florence Schust, who recalled, "It was a visual heaven for me to see all these wonderful objects and materials and everything which was entirely new to me. . . . Everything was handmade which was really extraordinary. It was such a stunning event for me that there was no question that that was where I wanted to be."[66]

In this environment Schust gravitated toward architecture as a career, and her earliest mentor was Rachel de Wolfe Raseman, a Cornell-trained architect and the art director of Kingswood. When Raseman asked her student if she wanted "to go into fabric or dress design," Schust replied, "I think I'd like to design a house."[67] Schust concentrated on this first design assignment, taking "as much time as I could spare away from my other studies to draw the plans and elevations and make a model."[68] The interiors of the house were an important part of the plan, and integration of textiles was a significant lesson for the young designer. In the model Schust drew furniture and added swatches of fabrics to represent those to be used—a working method she would use throughout her time at Knoll.[69]

She also became close to the Saarinen family at Cranbrook, including their children, Eero and Pipsan, traveling through Europe with them and staying at their summer home, Hvitträsk (built 1901–3), not far from Helsinki, Finland. Like Cranbrook, the house featured fully integrated interiors. Textiles were particularly prominent. Largely done by Loja Saarinen, they included carpets and *ryijy* (handwoven textiles designed to be attached to a wall and draped over a bench to provide warmth). The artful combination of color, pattern, and texture of textiles integrated with furniture, lighting, and art in these interiors had a profound impact on Schust (fig. 2.10).[70]

Schust graduated from Kingswood in 1934 and then studied design at Cranbrook from September 1934 to June 1935, and intermittently after that until 1939.[71] In her first year she engaged in a seminal project for her development as a designer: space planning and designing furniture for her dorm room.[72] She also designed and fabricated textiles for the project—striped carpet, upholstery, and a wall hanging with a geometric motif influenced by the work of Loja Saarinen (fig. 2.11).[73] As she recalled, "It was a very important event, and gave me the direction for the rest of my life."[74]

After leaving Cranbrook in 1935, Schust went on to study briefly at Columbia University and the University of Munich, and then the Architectural Association in London. She had been encouraged by Alvar Aalto, a friend of the Saarinen family, to attend the Architectural Association, where she enrolled in the advanced studies course, only leaving in 1939, when the outbreak of the World War II required all American students to return home.[75] In late 1939 she interned in the offices of architects Walter Gropius and Marcel Breuer in Cambridge, Massachusetts, and then continued her architecture studies at the Armour Institute (later Illinois Institute of Technology) in Chicago under Mies van der Rohe, who, she later wrote, "had a profound effect on my design approach."[76] After graduating in 1941, she moved to New York and began freelancing with different designers and architectural firms such as Herbert Bayer, Raymond Loewy, Richard Marsh Bennett, and the partnership of Wallace K. Harrison, Max Abramovitz, and Jacques-André Fouilhoux.[77]

THESE COMPONENTS

650 LINE

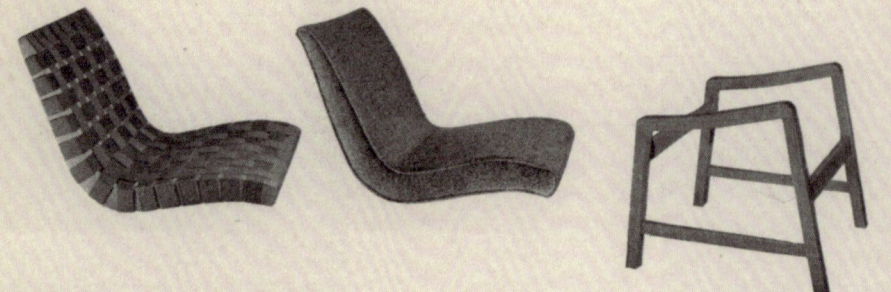

MAKE THESE UNITS

652U $42.90

652W $30.00

652U $39.00

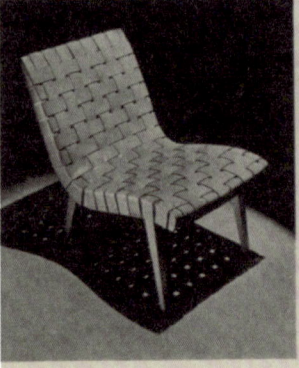
654L $64.00   654W $27.00   652U2 $70.00   ALSO THREE SEATER $94.00

652U ARM CHAIR
H 31" D 31" W 23½"
Upholstered in canvas, lacquered frame

652W ARM CHAIR
Same dimensions as above
Webbed in olive drab webbing, also brown or green

652U ARM CHAIR
Same dimensions as above
2 yds. 50" material required

654L CHAIR
H 31" D 31" W 20"
Saddle leather lacing, brown or red

654W CHAIR
Same dimensions as above
Olive drab webbing, also brown or green

652U2 TWO SEATER
H 31" D 31" L 44"
4 yds. 50" material required

652U3 THREE SEATER, not shown
H 31" D 31" L 64"

COMPLETE PRICE LIST ON LAST PAGE
ALL DESIGN PATENTS PENDING

Fig. 2.7 H. G. Knoll Associates brochure, ca. 1943. Knoll Archives.

Fig. 2.8 Top Advertisement for Bridgeport Fabrics Inc. From *Upholstering*, October 1946. Art & Architecture Collection, Miriam and Ira D. Wallach Division of Art, Prints and Photographs, The New York Public Library, Astor, Lenox and Tilden Foundations.

Fig. 2.9 Bottom Detail of "Salt & Pepper" webbing on *Model 50S* stool designed by Abel Sorensen, ca. 1946. Webbing made by Bridgeport Fabrics for Knoll Associates, stool made by Knoll Associates. Birch, cotton webbing; plain weave. Knoll Museum, East Greenville, Penn. Cat. 6.

Fig. 2.10 Bottom Herman Gesellius, Armas Lindgren, and Eliel Saarinen, architects. Dining room at Hvitträsk in Kirkkonummi, Finland. Built 1901–3. Photographed ca. 2010. The National Board of Antiquities, Finland.

Fig 2.11 Top Florence Schust. Sketch of dormitory room at the Cranbrook Academy of Art, 1934. Florence Knoll Bassett papers, 1932–2000, Archives of American Art, Smithsonian Institution.

Fig. 2.12 Florence Knoll, ca. 1957. Photographed by Margaret Bourke-White. Knoll Archives.

During this time, Florence Schust met Hans Knoll. She remembered him visiting Harrison, Abramovitz, and Fouilhoux, trying to sell chairs, and Ann Hatfield, another designer who was working as a consultant to the office, introduced them.[78] He asked Schust if she would be interested in designing interiors for a project he had secured. She later recalled that "he didn't know how to do them since he wasn't a designer. He asked me to do them for him on a freelance basis."[79] Her first freelance job for Knoll, turned out to be Secretary of War Henry Stimson's office in the newly built Pentagon building.[80] Completed in late 1942, the space had an ornate nineteenth-century desk and heavy club chairs that *Architectural Forum* described as "quiet, conservative, and completely in the manner of Government's executive offices from time immemorial."[81] In its traditionalism it was unlike Florence Knoll's later work for the company but led to more contracts from the government which increasingly involved integrated interiors.[82]

The Knoll Planning Unit and H. G. Knoll Associates

Florence Schust's early success at designing interiors for Hans Knoll ultimately led to her heading the Knoll Planning Unit. Soon the roles of the company's two main figures became defined—Hans Knoll would take care of the business end of things—making sales and securing contracts as he always had—while architect-designer Schust would act as design director for the company, eventually overseeing the entire product line, clarifying the firm's graphic identity, and serving as head of the Planning Unit (fig. 2.12). In 1944 Hans Knoll established the Planning Unit, which was first led by industrial designer Walter Baermann. This entity was initially dedicated to product design development and working with other manufacturers to help them enter the home furnishings market (see chapter 4). However, by late 1945 Baermann had departed and Florence Knoll came to head the Planning Unit, transforming it into the interior design division of the firm, where all aspects of a project—textiles, furniture, and space planning—would be systematically and carefully coordinated. A Knoll brochure published during the mid-1950s explained that the Planning Unit "grew out of a demand by private clients to provide interiors in which the concept embodied in the Knoll line of furniture and fabrics is carried to its logical conclusion: fusion of its architectural space and its contents."[83] The careful coordination of design meant that there would be a growing need for specific textiles and furniture. As the Planning Unit projects grew in size and scope, the furnishings line expanded, along with the need for textiles.

One of Schust's earliest interiors projects for H. G. Knoll Associates was a recreation lounge for defense workers at an unnamed aircraft plant published in *Interiors* magazine in 1943 (fig. 2.13).[84] The low-cost, flexible space, which included a dispensary for equipment and soft drinks, a stage, and gaming areas, clearly reflected Schust's skill at creating complex and original interiors by selecting different materials and using varied textures and color combinations. While it is unclear if this project was actual or prospective, it also points to the financial benefit brought to the young firm by interior design commissions—rather than selling one or two chairs to a residential consumer, they would be able to specify large quantities of Knoll furniture for the interiors of a governmental or corporate customer. Significantly, government contracts became an important avenue of growth for the company during the war.[85]

The Calvert Houses, located in Maryland about seven miles from central Washington, D.C., and built to house government workers and employees of a local factory, was another early Knoll commission that demonstrated the potential profitability of working on large-scale government projects.[86] Completed in 1943, the complex consisted of forty apartment buildings designed by Skidmore, Owings & Merrill under the authority of the National Capital Housing Authority, a government agency. Apartments were arranged in a variety of configurations including eight one-bedroom "minimum apartments" in buildings that also featured a "club room"—a communal living and recreational space. Knoll was commissioned to furnish these club rooms. They employed varied combinations of Risom-designed chairs, settees, and tables, which, in turn, meant specifying significant quantities of webbing and upholstery fabrics for each room (fig. 2.14).[87]

The new company name, H. G. Knoll Associates, had begun to be used in the summer of 1943.[88] By that fall, according to Hans Knoll, there were five employees in the offices and showrooms at 601 Madison Avenue and nine in an upholstery factory on East Forty-ninth Street.[89] In 1944 Knoll began to exhibit and sell its furniture through Bloomingdale's, the leading New York department store.[90] The arrangement was not without its problems: Florence Knoll Bassett recalled having to cover Hans's obligations to Bloomingdale's with $50,000 from her trust fund.[91] Such a commitment to the company effectively made her co-owner of the firm.

Florence Knoll and Early Textiles

As the interior design projects grew in number, the need for fabrics coordinated to Knoll's modern interiors became more apparent. Florence Knoll searched for suitable alternatives to what she later characterized as the "brocade and chintz with cabbage roses" that were "the current vogue in the textile showrooms."[92] She found viable options in men's suiting fabrics in "ranges of grey and beige flannels and tweeds from Scotland," which she thought looked elegant on a chair and could be readily purchased in quantity from

New York tailors.[93] She later recalled that the idea of using this type of fabric originated in a "very handsome Scottish linen of heavy weight" which she had used in her student days at the Architectural Association in London.[94] Two surviving samples, supplied by W. Bill Ltd. of London (fig. 2.15), give an indication of the kind of British suiting fabrics purchased by Knoll.[95] Their plain weave, textural quality, and subtle colors are typical of suiting fabrics favored by Florence Knoll which made Knoll's upholstery textiles as fresh and interesting as its furniture. The company used such fabrics as upholstery for a fairly short time, most likely between 1944 and 1946.[96]

In early 1945 Knoll introduced a new collection of furniture with designs by Ralph Rapson, Abel Sorensen, and Jens Risom, including several chairs that expanded on Knoll's use of webbing and upholstery. Marketed under the slogan "Equipment for Living," the collection was launched in a series of room settings at Bloomingdale's.[97] The group included several Risom-designed chairs that had been introduced in 1943 as well as new side chairs by Sorensen which were first used in the Planning Unit's project for the interiors of the Air Transport Command at Washington National Airport (1945), (figure 2.16).[98] In addition, there were striking new designs by Ralph Rapson—a series of chairs and a rocker (with and without arms), all of which were offered in webbed or upholstered versions.[99]

Florence Knoll embraced the use of textiles as a crucial element in the company's design of interiors, not only in meeting the client's need for upholstered furnishings, draperies, and wallcoverings, but also in spurring the creation of new designs to fullfill that need. The *New York Times* wrote of the collection that "even more striking, possibly, than the design details of these chairs are the unusual fabrics used for coverings—not one of which in normal times would have been called an orthodox upholstery material. But they reflect not only today's textile troubles but also a possible trend for the future, since the Knoll designers say they adopted them as much from choice as from necessity and will probably use similar weaves after the war."[100] Several pieces were upholstered in "soft wool suitings such as a gray flannel-like fabric with a woven green stripe or a deep wine basket weave with a bright blue fleck," reported to be the first used on "ready-made" furniture (fig. 2.17).[101] Other upholsteries in the collection included a "brightly dyed sturdy cotton" that was originally intended for military use and government surplus "creamy tan cowhide." At a time when quality fabrics were still scarce, the company was taking upholstery fabrics in a refreshingly new direction and setting the stage for further growth.

Knoll Associates and the Postwar

One of the few times Hans Knoll revealed his business strategies was in a 1945 article for *Upholstering* magazine, when he expressed his concerns about the direction the home furnishings industry might take after the war.[102] Knoll saw a danger in rapid conversion of factories from wartime to civilian postwar production and feared that a quest for quick profits might damage the home furnishings industry.[103] He described his concern as related less to increased competition than to having the market flooded with "ill-considered products" that he claimed would lower consumer confidence in the industry. His own company, however, would create "the best of all possible furniture in terms of design, of structure and of economy"—a tagline featured in Knoll's advertising campaign in early 1945 (fig. 2.18). Knoll argued that wartime shortages had proved a valuable education for the company as a manufacturer of upholstered furniture, forcing it to become resourceful and innovative. The company's use of old materials in a new way—such as government-surplus webbing and cotton and men's suiting fabrics—paved the way for postwar experimentation with new processes and materials such as molded fiberglass, plastics, and synthetic textiles. Knoll outlined the key role that the company's Planning Unit would play—by conducting market research on consumer needs and new materials, by determining the sales potential of new designs, and by working with new designers to develop original products.[104] A miniature model of an interior by Florence Schust—complete with her designs for a modular storage system and prototype Ralph Rapson chairs of aluminum and foam rubber—demonstrated the experimental nature of the Planning Unit at the time. It was not only a space for creating interior solutions, but also a laboratory in which products were developed (fig. 2.19).

Knoll wasted no time in bringing newly developed products to the peacetime market. In 1946 the company launched a new Jens Risom–designed line of upholstered furniture that was again featured at Bloomingdale's as well as at Abraham & Straus in New York. The *New York Times* highlighted one of the chairs, a modern interpretation of the classic wing chair which was upholstered in a "tweed fabric," and described it as "roomy but not too overpowering" and "made for comfort but not for napping."[105] Men's suiting fabrics, selected by Florence Knoll, were beginning to provide a "signature" look for the company: "Texture and coloring of the tweeds, many in dark brown and tans, have evidently appealed on their own merits rather than on a basis of availability."[106] The *Times* review also noted other Risom-designed upholstered furniture in the new collection, ranging from individual chairs to settees for three and featuring a new type of spring construction that prevented

Fig. 2.13 Top Florence Schust. View looking into lounge. Illustration from "Rest Between Riveting," *Interiors*, July 1943.

Fig. 2.14 Bottom "Club room," Calvert Houses, Maryland, ca. 1943. From Walter Baermann, "Post-War Upholstered Furniture," *Upholstering*, September 1944. Art & Architecture Collection, Miriam and Ira D. Wallach Division of Art, Prints and Photographs, The New York Public Library, Astor, Lenox and Tilden Foundations.

Fig. 2.15 Two samples, ca. 1945. Manufactured for W. Bill Ltd. Wool with paper tags. Courtesy of Paul Makovsky.

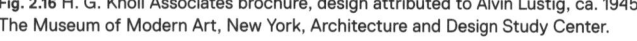

Fig. 2.16 H. G. Knoll Associates brochure, design attributed to Alvin Lustig, ca. 1945. The Museum of Modern Art, New York, Architecture and Design Study Center.

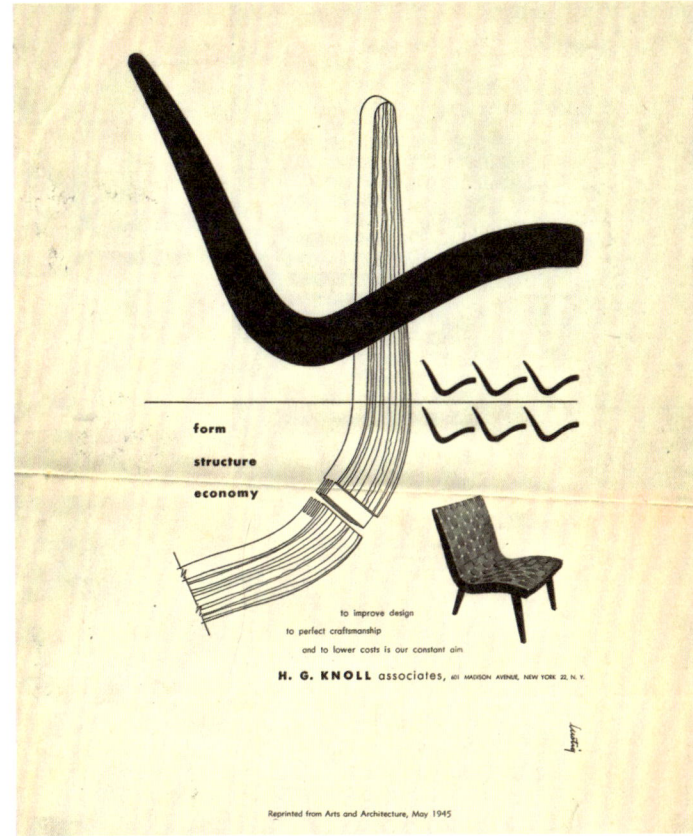

Fig. 2.17 Top left Living room with *Model 658U* sectional sofa. From H. G. Knoll Associates brochure, design attributed to Alvin Lustig, ca. 1945. The Museum of Modern Art, New York, Architecture and Design Study Center.
Fig. 2.18 Top right Advertisement for H. G. Knoll Associates, designed by Alvin Lustig. From *Arts & Architecture*, July 1945. Knoll Archives.
Fig. 2.19 Bottom left Florence Schust. Model of a room featuring modular storage system designed by Schust and chairs designed by Ralph Rapson. From Hans Knoll, "Reconversion Responsibility," *Upholstering*, July 1945. Art & Architecture Collection, Miriam and Ira D. Wallach Division of Art, Prints and Photographs, The New York Public Library, Astor, Lenox and Tilden Foundations.
Fig. 2.20 Bottom right Page from H. G. Knoll Associates catalogue, featuring *Model 21* chair and *Model 22* settee designed by Jens Risom, ca. 1946. The Museum of Modern Art Library, New York.

edges from sagging. Highly textured weaves— a "rough cotton mixture woven like burlap"—were available in multiple colorways (fig. 2.20).[107]

Hans Knoll and Florence Schust had been de facto partners at least since 1945 when she covered his debt to Bloomingdale's. On August 1, 1946, they were married, two months after the business had incorporated under a new name, Knoll Associates, Inc.—better reflecting the equal status of the partners.[108] As president and general manager of the small company, Hans continued to handle the finances, administration, and sales with a charisma and entrepreneurial spirit that helped position Knoll as a leader in the field especially in the postwar years. Florence's creative talents provided a more focused design direction.[109] Early on there were differences between the two partners. Looking back at the early years of the company, Knoll Bassett would be somewhat critical of the design direction: "Many of the designs Hans had at that time were too romantic and they didn't quite fit in with my ideas. They were Scandinavian. I suggested to him that he try to find other designers to work with him."[110]

After their marriage, Hans and Florence Knoll traveled to Sweden, where they visited architect Elias Svedberg, head of furniture design at the Nordiska Kompaniet (NK) store in Stockholm (fig. 2.21).[111] The Knolls quickly formed a partnership with this venerable Swedish company to import Swedish design into the United States. In a company newsletter Svedberg endorsed Hans Knoll as the only person who had succeeded in making modern furniture a successful business in the United States.[112] Sweden was a logical choice for the Knolls as a source for contemporary design. From 1930 to 1950, the country had the highest growth rate in the world, and Swedish functionalism enjoyed a golden age during this period.[113] Sweden, which had been neutral during World War II, had been an incubator for designs that were launched into production soon after the war.

The Knolls also visited many of NK's suppliers, choosing examples of furniture, textiles, and accessories by some of the best-known designers in Sweden—Svedberg, Bruno Mathsson, Fritz Hansen, and Erik Wörtz (furniture); Astrid Sampe and Sven Markelius (textiles); and Lisbet Jobs-Söderlundh (ceramics). In January 1947 Knoll Associates presented what was said to be the first postwar shipment of Swedish furniture and textiles installed as an "Authentic Swedish Room" in the firm's New York showroom.[114] The installation, which was aimed at buyers from department stores, was divided into living and dining areas intended to represent a middle-class Swedish home or apartment. (fig. 2.22).[115] Along with NK's affordable and easy-to-assemble *Triva* furniture designed by Svedberg, which shipped flat-packed (thereby avoiding higher duty tariffs), the installation featured furniture from Dux and Bruno Mathsson.[116]

The textiles in the display were products of NK's Textilkammare (textile design studio), headed since 1936 by Astrid Sampe, and were much admired by the media. *Upholstering* magazine commented on the bright colors, natural wood tones, and small-patterned textiles that would "dispel some of this country's current ideas about Swedish home furnishings."[117] The magazine featured a sofa with tufted back that was covered in a bright raspberry-colored woven texture, as well as a deep butter-toned printed drapery fabric called *Markelius*, after its designer, Sven Markelius (fig. 2.23).[118] Most of the upholsteries, however, as well as the handwoven rugs, were designed by Sampe and featured only texture or small-scale motifs in colors ranging from clear delicate blues, browns, red-and-gray, or green-and-gray combinations.

The "Authentic Swedish Room" project marked the beginning of an ongoing relationship that Knoll would have with NK. Knoll imported NK furniture for a few years, and NK became Knoll's licensee in Sweden when the company began expanding overseas in the 1950s. Swedish fabric designs remained part of Knoll's offerings through the 1960s.

Planning Unit projects also continued to provide impetus for the development of new designs. One important early commission, completed in 1946, was an office suite for the Rockefeller family located on the fifty-sixth floor of the RCA Building at Rockefeller Center, which featured Florence Knoll's inspired planning and use of materials. In thanking the Knolls for their work, Nelson Rockefeller wrote, "One rarely finds such an effective blending of good taste, originality and administrative ability."[119] Among the new designs featured in the office was a boat-shaped conference table that would later become a signature product in the Knoll line as well as upholstered desk and side chairs, designed by Florence Knoll. The chairs cradled the sitter in a continuous curve for an added "sense of luxury."[120] While it is unclear exactly which upholstery fabrics Florence Knoll used in this commission, one of the firm's first printed drapery fabrics, *Isles*, was used as curtains in the conference room, probably for the first time (fig. 2.24). The pattern had been developed by Cranbrook-educated designer Shirley Fletcher Rapson (later Nickerson) and was presented to the Knolls by her husband, designer Ralph Rapson (fig. 2.25).[121] Knoll Associates introduced *Isles* commercially as part of the new textile division's first collection in early 1947.

During the second half of the 1940s, textiles assumed a more prominent place in the company, especially as Knoll's product line expanded, its interiors commissions increased, and company showrooms opened around the country. The foundations that Hans Knoll had built and the design direction that Florence Knoll had given the company resulted in a thriving textile division that became an industry leader in the postwar period.

Fig. 2.21 From left: Lars Eriksson, chief manager, furniture production, Nordiska Kompaniet (NK); Florence Knoll; Hans Knoll; Tom Björklund, NK executive; Elias Svedberg, head of furniture design, NK. Photographed in Sweden in 1946. Carl Magnusson Collection, Cranbrook Archives, Bloomfield Hills, Mich.

Fig. 2.22 Dining area of the "Authentic Swedish Room" installation, 1947. Photographed by Phyllis A. Dearborn, Dearborn-Massey. Knoll Archives.

Fig. 2.23 Sven Markelius. *Markelius*, designed ca. 1942, this example ca. 1948. Manufactured for Knoll Associates. Cotton, jute, linen; plain weave, screen-printed. The Cleveland Museum of Art, Purchase from the J.H. Wade Fund, 1948.493.

Fig 2.24 From left: Winthrop, Laurance, John, David, and Nelson Rockefeller in the library of their New York office, February 28, 1949. Photographed by Philippe Halsman. Rockefeller Archive Center, New York.

Fig. 2.25 Shirley Fletcher Rapson (later Nickerson.) Prototype for Knoll pattern *Isles*, ca. 1945. Cotton; plain weave, screen-printed. Courtesy Shirley Fletcher Nickerson. Cat. 3.

Research on Florence Knoll Bassett and Knoll's early years has been supported by a grant from the Graham Foundation for Advanced Studies in the Fine Arts. I am grateful to Horace Havemeyer III, publisher of Metropolis magazine, for his support in publishing several articles on Florence Knoll which laid the foundation for this essay's research. Florence Knoll Bassett generously shared her memories and this essay is dedicated to her.

1 Florence Knoll Bassett (hereafter FKB), interview, draft 3, ca. 1977, p. 3, FKB designer file, Knoll Archive, Knoll Inc.
2 Estzer Haraszty, interview, ca. 1977, p. 12, Estzer Haraszty designer file, KnollTextiles Archives.
3 The information in this section is drawn from "Courage for the Modern Age," *Walter Knoll: Design Reloaded* (Herrenberg: Neunplus 1, 2006), 58–65. One of Walter Knoll's early triumphs was manufacturing many of the furniture designs shown in 1927 at *Die Wohnung* (The Dwelling) at the Weissenhof Estate in Stuttgart. This seminal exhibition is best known for showcasing the work of modernist architects and designers such as Mies van der Rohe, Walter Gropius, Le Corbusier, and Mart Stam, see ibid., 60.
4 By then the company had moved its headquarters from Feuerbach to Herrenberg, about twenty-five miles south of Stuttgart. Ibid., 62–63.
5 "Hans G Knoll," *Current Biography Yearbook* (New York: H. W. Wilson Co., 1955), 334–36.
6 Timeline, Jantzen web site, www.jantzenswim.com/timeline.asp.
7 Hans Knoll, naturalization statement, DSS Form 304, Alien Personal History and Statement, Order No. 2401A, October 8, 1943, File NYS, RG 147, Box 59, National Archives Northeast Region, New York (hereafter referred to as Knoll Alien Personal History and Statement). The entry for "Hans G Knoll" in *Current Biography Yearbook* (p. 335) described Hans as being president of Plan, Ltd. between 1935 and 1937, although this has not been confirmed.
8 Barbara Tilson, "Plan Furniture 1932–1938: The German Connection," *Journal of Design History* 3, nos. 2/3 (1990): 145–55. The information in this paragraph largely derives from this article.
9 Donald Brothers later produced Knoll Textiles's *Scotch Linen, Kerry Linen, Highland Tweed,* and *Highland Stripe*. For Donald Brothers early history see Helen Douglas, "The Feel for Rugged Texture," in *Dissentangling Textiles*, ed. Mary Schoeser and Christine Boydell (London: Middlesex University Press, 2002), 177–84.
10 Tilson, "Plan Furniture 1932–1938," 145.
11 The mill was owned by the Zehntbauer family. Robert Knoll, Hans's brother, recalled being in the U.S. in the 1930s: "I was connected with the textile industry in Portland, Oregon, where we had friends. . . . [In] 1936, my father called me back, and I had to obey, of course. . . . Hans, he was working in England at the time, came back to Germany too. And he decided, 'Now I have a chance to go to the States,'" interview, ca. 1977, Knoll Archives. For family history, see *Walter Knoll: Design Reloaded*, 63.
12 New York Passenger Lists, 1820–1957 [database on-line], http://www.ancestry.com.
13 Ibid.
14 "Barbara Southwick Wed," *New York Times*, January 19, 1939, 26. They had two children, but the marriage did not last, and by 1943, they were separated; see Knoll, Supplement (October 16, 1943) to Alien Personal History and Statement.
15 Eric Larrabee, *Knoll Design* (New York: Abrams, 1981), 19. See also Brian Lutz, *Knoll: A Modernist Universe* (New York: Rizzoli, 2010), 11, 17. The New York City telephone directory, Manhattan White Pages (Summer 1933–Summer 1934, microfilm reel 34) lists "H. G. Knoll & Company" at 511 East 72nd Street during the 1930s and early 1940s. However, this listing was for Henry G. Knoll, a chemist. Henry Knoll is listed in the New York City telephone directory, Manhattan White Pages (1943–44, microfilm reel 57) at 503 East 72nd Street, and the Manhattan Yellow Pages (Fall 1943–Summer 1944, microfilm reel 12) lists the Knoll Chemical Co. at that address. It is not known whether Henry Knoll was any relation to Hans Knoll.
16 This date is borne out by articles published in the early 1950s, when the company began to gain widespread recognition: e.g., Olga Gueft, "Outpost in Dallas: Knoll Opens a Lone Star Branch," *Interiors* (June 1950): 90; Gueft, "Knoll Associates Move Into The Big Time," *Interiors* (May 1951): 75; and John D. Morse, "The Story of Knoll Associates," *American Artist* (September 1951): 46.
17 See Knoll Alien Personal History and Statement. The summer 1938 New York City telephone directory lists George Ditmar and Co. at 35 East 50th Street. Ditmar moved his company to 444 Madison Avenue (the Newsweek building) in June 1939; see "Stores Featured in Lease Reports," *New York Times*, June 14, 1939, 47. The summer 1940 edition of the New York City telephone directory, Manhattan White Pages (microfilm reel 53), lists both Hans Knoll and George Ditmar and Co. at 444 Madison Avenue, with a shared phone number. The December 1940 edition of the Manhattan White Pages (microfilm reel 54) lists George P. Ditmar at 366 Madison while Hans Knoll remains at 444 Madison Avenue, but with a new telephone number. The fall–winter 1940 edition of the Manhattan Yellow Pages (1940–41) (microfilm reel 10) again lists the Hans G. Knoll Company at 444 Madison Avenue and then in the December 1942 edition of the Manhattan Yellow Pages (1941–42, microfilm reel 11) the company is listed at 601 Madison Avenue.
18 At the time of his bankruptcy, Ditmar had assets of just $685 and liabilities of $19,650; see "Business Records," *New York Times*, March 26, 1940, 34. For Knoll's lease at 444 Madison Avenue see "Bickford's Rents 505 5th Ave. Unit," *New York Times*, March 21, 1940, 50. For Knoll's lease at 601 Madison Avenue see "Old Shoe Concern Makes Short Move," *New York Times*, December 4, 1941, 46.
19 "News and Notes of the Advertising World," *New York Times*, June 1, 1938, 40.
20 James Ford and Katherine Morrow Ford, *Design of Modern Interiors* (New York: Architectural Publishing Co., 1942), 66.
21 Ibid., 66. Knoll's *Prodomo* chair (along with the company's *Model 652W* armchair [1943] designed by Jens Risom) was included in *Art in Progress*, the Museum of

Modern Art's fifteenth-anniversary exhibition; see *Art in Progress*, exh. cat. (New York: Museum of Modern Art, 1944), 237.
22 See "Forum of Events," *Architectural Forum* (May 1941): 76; and "Forum of Events," *Architectural Forum* (July 1941): 56.
23 See Ford and Ford, *Design of Modern Interiors*. See also Nina Stritzler-Levine, "'Out of the Archive': Thoughts on Artek in America," in *Essays on Finnish Modernism*, ed. Marianne Aav and Jukka Savolinen (Helsinki: Designmuseo, 2010), 58-73. Other manufacturers and designers that sold modern furniture during the early 1940s included Dan Cooper, Rena Rosenthal, T.H. Robsjohn-Gibbings, and Charak on the East Coast; Herman Miller and Dunbar in the Midwest; and Hendrik Van Keppel and Barker Brothers Furniture on the West Coast; see "Modern Furniture," *California Arts and Architecture* (January 1942): 21–23. Artek dominated the London market for modern furniture in the late 1930s and would not have escaped Hans Knoll's attention; see Eeva-Liisa Pelkonen, *Alvar Aalto: Architecture, Modernity, and Geopolitics* (New Haven: Yale University Press, 2009), 114.
24 Artek furniture was specified in a General Motors project, 1941 (according to a letter in Jens Risom's personal archive), and in the Johnson & Johnson Ligature reception room by Powell and Morgan, 1941; see "Building for Defense: A Trio of Modern Plants," *Architectural Forum* (November 1941): 331–34; "Interiors for Interiors, or, A Stitch in Time," *Interiors* (September 1942): 20–23.
25 Jens Risom, telephone conversation with author, November 9, 2009. Risom graduated in 1934 from the Niels Brock Copenhagen Business College in Denmark.
26 Jens Risom, telephone conversation with author, December 12, 2010; Mel Byars, "Jens Risom," in *The Design Encyclopedia* (London: Laurence King, 2004), 629.
27 Jens Risom, telephone conversation with author, August 3, 2010.
28 Ibid. Risom recalled that the job with Cooper came through a connection with a curator at the Museum of Modern Art.
29 Ibid. Among the offerings at Dan Cooper was: "A line pattern designed by Jens Risom is printed on cotton crash"; see Walter Rendell Storey, "Home Decoration: Modernity In a More Gracious Pattern," *New York Times*, December 29, 1940, D9.
30 Jens Risom, telephone conversation with author, November 9, 2009. For more on the installation, see "Terrace House for Collier's," *Architectural Forum* (August 1940): 107–10.
31 Jens Risom, telephone conversation with author, November 9, 2009.
32 "Building for Defense," 331-34 and "Interiors for Interiors," 20–23. *Architectural Forum* initially incorrectly credited Alvar Aalto with the furniture design, but later noting that "This furniture, with the exception of two [Aalto] chairs, was designed by Powell & Morgan, and executed by Hans Knoll"; "Forum of Events," *Architectural Forum* (December 1941): 78.
33 Jens Risom, telephone conversation with author, August 3, 2010.
34 The commission came through an interior decorator. According to Risom "These people wanted a very modern house and the decorator said we could get into magazines and newspapers because their son was going to get married in front of the double window as soon as the house was finished"; ibid.
35 Ibid.
36 Jens Risom, telephone conversation with author, November 9, 2009. Risom noted that in most cases, architects' wives owned the furniture shops and bought the fabrics or imported furniture—mostly Scandinavian, especially the work of Alvar Aalto.
37 Jens Risom, telephone conversation with author, August 3, 2010. Risom also recalled, "Of course, the way Hans was, he wanted to run the whole thing, and I was going to be his draftsman and designer."
38 The catalogue was hand-assembled by Risom and Knoll, by gluing photographs of the products to printed cardstock; Jens Risom, personal archive. The collection was noted in the period press; see "Interiors Selection of 1942 Furniture," *Interiors* (February 1942): 38, 67; "Newsreel," *Interiors* (February 1942): 56; "Modern Cherry Furniture Danish Designed," *Art News* 41 (April 1 1942): 35; Charlotte Hughes, "Things for the Household," *New York Times*, May 10, 1942, D5.
39 Rosenthal ran a retail shop in New York, wholesaled modern home designs she featured there, and hired many designers from Austria and Germany in the 1930s and 1940s, like Schwadron (1896–1979). For examples of his other work at the time see "Park Avenue Modern," *Interiors* (May 1942): 20–23.
40 "It was not a very important part of the business, nor was it a very attractive one—most of that went out quickly." Jens Risom, telephone conversation with author, November 9, 2009.
41 For The Sandbox see Alistair Gordon, *Weekend Utopia: Modern Living in the Hamptons* (New York: Princeton Architectural Press, 2001), 35–36. For more on Miller (1893–1985) see her three-part autobiography: *Tanty: Encounters with the Past* (Sag Harbor, N.Y.: Sandbox Press, 1979); *More About Tanty* (Sag Harbor, N.Y.: Sandbox Press, 1980); and *Tanty: The Daring Decades* (Sag Harbor, N.Y.: Sandbox Press, 1981).
42 Her rugs and textiles were included in numerous exhibitions: the Century of Progress exposition in Chicago (1933); the International Exposition in Paris (1937), where she was awarded a gold medal for Decorative Textiles; the Metropolitan Museum of Art in New York (1937); the Golden Gate Exposition in San Francisco (1939); the Heinz Building at the New York World's Fair (1939), among others.
43 "Frances Miller Features Simplicity in Fabrics: Pioneer in the Field Unusual Designs," *Christian Science Monitor*, March 12, 1941, 9.
44 Eliot Noyes, *Organic Design in Home Furnishings* (New York: Museum of Modern Art, 1941), ii. The exhibition showcased several other designers who would later work with Knoll in both the textile and furniture divisions: Henning Watterston (1916–2009), Noémi Raymond (1889–1980), Eero Saarinen (1910–1961), Oscar Stonorov (1905–1970), and Marianne Strengell (1909–1998).
45 For wartime innovations by designers and design students see László Moholy-Nagy, "New Trends in Furniture," *Upholstering* (March 1943): 8–10, 28; Gilbert Rohde, "Modern as Applied to the Design of Upholstered Furniture," *Upholstering* (April 1943): 10–11; Norman Bel Geddes "Springless Furniture Suggests Design for Furniture of the Future," *Upholstering* (May 1943): 6–9.
46 "Price Easing Held, Upholstery Need," *New York Times*, October 2, 1945, 35.
47 "What is the Home Furnishing Situation?," *Upholstering* (August 1945): 18.
48 Ibid.
49 "This First-Rate Medium Priced Modern Furniture Is a Wartime Product," *Architectural Forum* (June 1943): 2. See also Martin Eidelberg, ed., *Design 1935–1965: What Modern Was* (Montréal: Musée des arts decoratifs de Montréal; New York: Abrams, 1991), 51 and "Newsreel," *Interiors* (June 1943): 62–63.
50 H. G. Knoll Associates brochure, ca. 1943, Knoll Archives.
51 Ibid.
52 Mary Madison, "The Home in Wartime," *New York Times*, July 18, 1943, SM24.
53 For Shaker chairs and American examples by the Ficks-Reed Company see J.R. Carleton, "Furniture Webbing for Webbed Furniture," *Upholstering* (September 1945): 28–29; for Swedish designs from the 1930s see Lis Hogdal, ed., *Bruno Mathsson: Architect and Designer* (Malmö: Bökforlaget; New York: Bard Graduate Center for Studies in the Decorative Arts, Design, and Culture; London: Yale University Press, 2006), 14–26. For Aalto see Göran Schildt, *Aalto: The Mature Years* (New York: Rizzoli, 1991); and Ásdís Ólafsdóttir, *Le mobilier d'Alvar Aalto dans l'espace et dans le temps: la diffusion internationale du design 1920–1940* (Paris: Publications de la Sorbonne, 1998). Risom recalled that Aalto "was way ahead of us, because he was the one who brought all that webbed furniture." Jens Risom, telephone conversation with author, November 9, 2009.
54 Jens Risom, telephone conversation with author, August 3, 2010.
55 Ibid.
56 H. G. Knoll Associates brochure, ca. 1943, Knoll Archives.
57 Walter Baermann, "Post-War Upholstered Furniture," *Upholstering* (September 1944): 13–15, 42–43.
58 Ibid., 15.
59 Carleton, "Furniture Webbing," 28–29, 60–62. By 1946 Bridgeport Fabrics was advertising woven webbing made of cotton or plastic yarns especially for both indoor and outdoor furniture; see Advertisement for Bridgeport Fabrics, *Upholstering* (July 1946): 3; Advertisement for Bridgeport Fabrics, with Knoll *Model 654W*, *Upholstering* (October 1946): 9.
60 Carlton, "Furniture Webbing," 61.
61 Ibid., 28.
62 The Concordia Gallia Corporation, for example, made plastic webbing woven from Saran, an extruded monofilament developed by Dow Chemical, in a wide range of colors, weaves, widths, and weights. Its high tensile strength meant that it was stain- and water-resistant and resistant to abrasion; see "New Patterns Feature in Plastic Webbing," *Upholstering* (January 1947): 50, 60, 74; Advertisement for Cogon, with Knoll *Model 652L*, *Upholstering* (January 1947): 17; Advertisement for Cogon, with Knoll chair, *Upholstering* (August 1947): 23.
63 Jens Risom was drafted into the army during the summer of 1943; he returned to Knoll in December 1945, but the company had changed and he did not stay long: "As director of design, Shu [Florence Schust] was about metal, plastics, and the Bauhaus, and I was about Scandinavia and wood, so I knew that I wasn't going to have much of a role there." Jens Risom, telephone conversation with author, August 3, 2010. Knoll kept Risom designs, especially for seating, in the line, but his departure symbolized the direction the company would take in the postwar years.
64 Her parents were Mina M. Schust (née Haist) and Frederick E. Schust, a well-to-do businessman who was president of the Schust Baking Company. Her father died in 1923, her mother in 1931. Her legal guardian, Emil Tessin, vice-president of the Second National Bank and Trust Company of Saginaw, agreed to send her to Kingswood; see FKB papers, Portfolio, Box 1, Folder 1, p. 9, Archives of American Art, Washington, D.C.
65 The complex also included the Cranbrook School for Boys. For Cranbrook history see Cranbrook Schools Historic Timeline, http://www.schools.cranbrook.edu/timeline.htm. See also Robert Judson Clark et al., *Design in America: The Cranbrook Vision, 1925–1950* (New York: Abrams, in association with the Detroit Institute of Arts and the Metropolitan Museum of Art, 1983), 35–46.
66 FKB, interview, n.d., p. 1, Knoll Archives, courtesy FKB.
67 FKB, interview by Bill Ferehawk for the Eero Saarinen Project, March 28, 2004, p. 1, Knoll Archive.
68 FKB papers, Portfolio, Box 1, Folder 1, p. 6, Archives of American Art, Washington, D.C.
69 FKB, interview, n.d., p. 2, Knoll Archives, p. 2, courtesy FKB.
70 FKB, telephone conversation with author, October 31, 2004.
71 Schust attended the School of Architecture at Columbia University during fall 1935 and returned to Cranbrook between fall 1936 and August 1937 and again in August, September, and December 1939. See "Florence Margaret Schust Knoll Bassett," in *Design in America*, 270.
72 The room included a chair designed by Eero Saarinen. Schust would later draw parallels between designing this room and her work at Knoll: "The metal arm chair in the sketch was previously designed for Kingswood by Eero—it is interesting to reflect the same relation happened at Knoll when Eero designed chairs and I designed what I referred to as the 'fill-in' pieces—mostly cabinetry." FKB papers, Portfolio, Box 1, Folder 1, p. 9, Archives of American Art, Washington, D.C.
73 Ibid. The textiles and rugs were put in storage and are now missing; see H. Deno, Second National Bank & Trust Company to Mrs. Anders Nissen, January 2, 1936, FKB papers, Box 4, Folder 2, Archives of American Art, Washington, D.C.
74 FKB, interview, n.d., p. 2, Knoll Archives, courtesy FKB.
75 "Florence Margaret Schust Knoll Bassett," in *Design in America*, 270.
76 FKB Papers, Portfolio, Box 1, Folder 1, p. 13, Archives of American Art, Washington, D.C.

77 Harrison, Abramovitz, and Fouilhoux were a leading architectural firm responsible for several large commissions in New York, including Rockefeller Center, the United Nations buildings, and Lincoln Center. The firm gave the Knoll Planning Unit several important commissions, including the interiors of the Alcoa Building in Pittsburgh, Pennsylvania, see chapter 4 in this volume.
78 Knoll Bassett later recalled that Hatfield "had an interest in modern design and she was a friend of Hans Knoll. And so through Ann Hatfield, I met Hans, then I saw him at other functions around New York with other young designers and architects"; FKB, interview, n.d., p. 14, Knoll Archives, courtesy FKB. For Hatfield, see Noyes, *Organic Design*, 46; "Ann H. Rothschild, 86, Interior Designer, Dies," *New York Times*, November 14, 1989.
79 FKB, telephone conversation with author, November 5, 2001.
80 FKB, interview, n.d., p. 14, Knoll Archives, courtesy FKB. Apparently Stimson moved into his offices November 14, 1942; see Steve Vogel, *The Pentagon: A History* (New York: Random House, 2009), 555.
81 "Pentagon Building," *Architectural Forum* (January 1943): 51. See also "Stimson's New Offices," *Life* (December 21, 1942): 83–84. Knoll Bassett said she never saw the completed interiors, and at the time she thought that Stimson was from the Navy and so specified a navy blue carpet. FKB, interview, n.d., pp. 14–15, Knoll Archives, courtesy FKB.
82 Knoll Bassett later recalled that "from that, we got other government jobs. It was a time when there was nothing much else going on"; FKB, interview, n.d., p. 15, Knoll Archives, courtesy FKB.
83 Knoll Planning Unit brochure, ca. 1957, author's collection.
84 The project was executed with Peter Hardnen, another Knoll associate. See "Rest Between Riveting," *Interiors* (July 1943): 23–24, 65–66.
85 In addition to USO lounges, the company had contracts with the Navy between 1942 and 1946. See Hans Knoll Furniture Company—U.S. Navy Contracts, 1942–1946, Series C, Box 13, Folder 6, Fanny E. Holtzmann papers, American Jewish Archives, Cincinnati, Ohio.
86 "Washington Housing," *Architectural Forum* (January 1944): 53–58.
87 Ibid., 58. The rooms also featured printed draperies by Dan Cooper, most likely because Knoll did not have curtain fabrics in the line at the time.
88 For the first recorded use see "Newsreel," *Interiors* (June 1943): 62–63; Mary Madison, "The Home in Wartime," *New York Times*, July 18, 1943. The new name may have been Hans Knoll's way of making his enterprise appear to have a large staff of designers at work, but as FKB later recalled: "I was the 'Associate.'" FKB, telephone conversation with author, November 5, 2001.
89 Knoll Supplement to Alien Personal History and Statement.
90 For an early reference to the relationship with Bloomingdale's see "Furnishings for the Country Cabin," *New York Times*, January 18, 1944, 24.
91 This translates to more than $600,000 in 2011 terms. "Chronology of Florence Knoll Bassett's Life and Work," manuscript, courtesy FKB. The capital provided by Florence Schust to Hans Knoll is mentioned in Maeve Slavin's proposed prologue to an unpublished biography of Florence Knoll Bassett, see FKB Papers, Letters, 1960–1968, Box 4, Folder 4, p. 3, Archives of American Art, Washington, D.C. Risom also recalled Knoll's financial difficulties in the early years: "I don't know if they over extended themselves but they never did well"; Jens Risom, telephone conversation with author, August 3, 2010.
92 FKB, "History of Knoll Textiles," manuscript, 1996, KnollTextiles Archive.
93 Ibid.; and FKB, telephone conversation with the author, January 10, 2006.
94 FKB, telephone conversation with the author, January 10, 2006.
95 These samples, once belonging to FKB, are now in the author's collection.
96 FKB, telephone conversation with the author, January 10, 2006.
97 Mary Roche, "Rocking Chair Forms Headliner in New Collection of Furniture," *New York Times*, March 16, 1945, 18. See also "Equipment for Living," *Arts and Architecture* (May 1945): 36–38. It seems likely that Knoll was referring to the rhetoric of leading European modernists such as Le Corbusier with the "Equipment for Living" slogan.
98 Ibid.; and H. G. Knoll Associates, "Equipment for Living" brochure, ca. 1945, Knoll Associates/International research file, Department of Architecture and Design, Museum of Modern Art, New York. For the Air Transport Command installation, see also "ATC International Air Terminal," *Architectural Forum* (March 1945): 97–105.
99 Schust introduced Rapson to Knoll in 1944 and Knoll asked him to submit studies for a coordinated line of furniture. See Jane King Hession, Rip Rapson, and Bruce N. Wright, *Ralph Rapson: Sixty Years of Modern Design* (Afton, Minn.: Afton Historical Society Press, 1999), 79–84. Rapson became the first of many Cranbrook-trained designers to work for Knoll. The list eventually included Harry Bertoia, Antoinette Lackner Webster (Toni Prestini), Shirley Fletcher Nickerson (Shirley Rapson), Eero Saarinen, and Marianne Strengell. When Rapson opened a store in Boston in 1950 with contemporary furniture and textiles, Knoll Associates was a major supplier, and Florence Knoll was a consultant; ibid., 88.
100 Roche, "Rocking Chair Forms Headliner," 18.
101 Ibid.
102 Hans Knoll, "Reconversion Responsibility," *Upholstering* (July 1945): 28–30, 57.
103 Ibid., 28.
104 Ibid., 57.
105 "Designer Offers Chair to Sleep In," *New York Times*, August 9, 1946, 12.
106 Ibid.
107 Ibid.
108 "Hans G Knoll," *Current Biography Yearbook*, 334–36. According to a 1962 court case, Knoll and Schust had founded Knoll Associates, Inc., in 1943 as a partnership, three years before it was incorporated (June 1946) and they married; see "'Knoll Associates Inc. . . . in regard to the Alleged Violation of Sec. 2(a) of the Clayton Act,' Complaint, December 27, 1962–Decision, August 2, 1966," in Federal Trade Commission Decisions, vol. 70 (July–December 1966), 331.
109 In 1947 the company purchased a woodworking plant in Pennsburg, Penn., for $28,000, and installed machinery for the manufacture of furniture. That same year, it opened a factory at 1554 Third Avenue in Manhattan; see New York City telephone directory, Manhattan White Pages (Winter 1946–September 1947, microfilm reel 60). The January 1950 (microfilm reel 63) and November 1950 (microfilm reel 64) editions of the New York City telephone directory, Manhattan White Pages, then list the Manhattan factory at 503 East 72nd Street (the same address given for "Henry Knoll" in 1943), after which there is no phone listing for a Knoll factory in Manhattan.
110 FKB, interview, n.d., draft 2, p. 1–2, Knoll Archive.
111 The trip was so productive that Hans Knoll planned to visit Sweden annually. Earlier that year, Svedberg traveled to the United States and Canada to study the launching of NK products in the American market. See "Arkitekt Svedbergs Amerikaresa och några av dess resultat," *Rullan* [NK newsletter] (September–October 1946): 10–11, 13+.
112 Ibid. Svedberg was also assured of the new relationship by the fact that Hans's father, Walter Knoll, had had steady business relations with NK for several years.
113 Helena Mattsson, "Designing the Reasonable Consumer," in Mattsson and Sven-Olov Wallenstein, *Swedish Modernism* (London: Black Dog, 2010), 76.
114 Mary Roche, "New Ideas and Inventions," *New York Times*, February 16, 1947, SM40. The collection was called "Authentic Swedish" to distinguish it from "Swedish Modern," which was generally considered cheap and vaguely Scandinavian-looking furniture that had been on the market since before the war.
115 See "Available Now: The Best Furniture in Years," *Interiors* (March 1947): 78; Mary Roche, "New Ideas and Inventions," *New York Times*, February 16, 1947, SM40.
116 For Mathsson's part in the Knoll venture see Hogdal, *Bruno Mathsson*, 206–8.
117 One of Svedberg's chairs was covered in a "red and white machine woven material" designed by Astrid Sampe. "Swedish Design Creates 'Knock-down' Furniture," *Upholstering* (April 1946): 20–23, 62, 72.
118 "Swedish Knockdown Furniture to Be Promoted Here," *Upholstering* (February 1947): 66.
119 Nelson A. Rockefeller to Mr. and Mrs. Hans Knoll, December 14, 1946, FKB papers, Box 4, Folder 2, Archives of American Art, Washington, D.C. The building, located at 30 Rockefeller Plaza, is now known as the GE Building.
120 FKB quoted in Lutz, *Knoll*, 33. One of the chairs from the Rockefeller installation is now in the collection of the Cranbrook Art Museum, Bloomfield Hills, Mich. The textured yellow upholstery now on the chair may not be original; see Ruth T. Kuhlman (secretary to Laurance Rockefeller) to Susan Waller (curator, Cranbrook Art Museum), September 23, 1986, CAM 1986.35 object file, Cranbrook Art Museum.
121 Shirley Fletcher studied for a short time at Cranbrook in the early 1940s before marrying Ralph Rapson.

3 Making Knoll Textiles: Integrated Fabrics for Modern Interiors, 1945–65

Susan Ward

While many of the characteristics that would come to define Knoll Textiles were apparent from its founding in 1947, it took several years of experimentation to fully define the division's role within the company and for Knoll Textiles to develop as a distinctive brand. This experimentation had begun in the early 1940s, as Hans Knoll sought to expand the product line of his young company and forge connections with manufacturers, and as Florence Knoll sought out appropriate upholstery fabrics from the limited options available at the time. Knoll's first forays into the unfamiliar textile market included a wide range of designs and materials, perhaps seeking to appeal to a broader audience. Between 1947 and the early 1950s, however, as Florence Knoll and the Knoll Planning Unit developed their distinctive approach to interiors, the textile division began to concentrate on the kinds of patterns and textures favored by the Planning Unit (see chapter 4), becoming an integral part of the company. The division continued to build on this foundation with the continuing rise of the contract market through the early 1960s, seeking out innovation in both design and technology while remaining true to Florence Knoll's vision of interior textiles as an integral part of modern interiors.

Before 1947: Experimentation and Collaboration

Relatively little is known about the fabrics used to upholster Knoll furniture before the founding of the textile division in 1947.[1] A Knoll brochure from about 1943 included upholstered versions of Jens Risom seating designs covered in an unidentified textured fabric (see fig. 2.7), and although the yardage needed was specified, no fabrics were offered or described. If an order was not "C.O.M." (customer's own material), Knoll would presumably select and obtain a suitable fabric, an increasingly difficult task during World War II when upholstery fabrics were in short supply.[2] By 1945 Knoll's unconventional use of apparel fabrics as upholstery materials (see chapter 2) was receiving a favorable response in the industry and among critics.[3] Florence Knoll Bassett later reflected that the wool suiting fabrics she used on Knoll furniture at the time provided the simple textural weaves and subtle colors she was seeking. The few additional upholstery fabrics that can be identified from published accounts just after the war were quite plain. A "red cotton fabric" was shown on a Ralph Rapson rocking chair in *Furniture and Fabrics*, a 1946 exhibition at the Walker Art Center. Materials like these probably came from one of the few suppliers, such as Moss Rose and Angelo Testa, who were beginning to make textiles appropriate for the modern furniture Knoll was producing.[4]

Knoll's experiments with selling printed fabrics by the yard began as early as 1942. The first Knoll catalogue advertised printed sheer curtain fabrics designed by Frances Breese Miller (see chapter 2 and fig. 2.6).[5] This experiment did not last long—Miller's fabrics were not part of any later Knoll collections. By 1944, however, Hans Knoll had revived the idea and was planning to introduce a complete textile line. In October of that year, Knoll wrote to architect Ralph Rapson, who was then designing furniture for the company: "At a meeting the other day which we held among ourselves, we decided that we should add a textile division to our post-war plans. We have a very good opportunity of selling contemporary fabrics with our furniture and also of selling fabrics to the stores by the yard. . . . I have a person in mind who would be willing to coordinate the designers' work with a small mill which is available for the production of these textiles."[6]

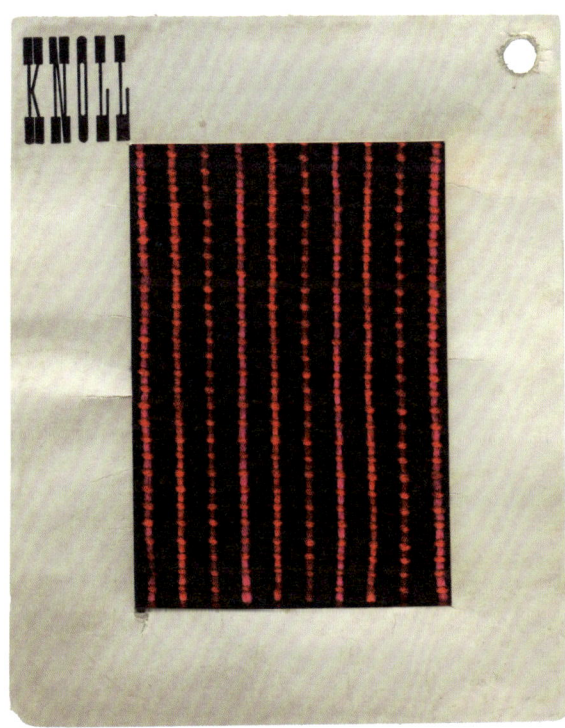

Evelyn Hill Anselevicius. Handwoven samples, ca. 1952–60. Made for Knoll Textiles. Used for upholstery; various materials including wool, nylon, gimp and plastic. Philadelphia Museum of Art, CTK 11a, 12, 13, 69-1983-15. Cats. 93, 78, 79, 82.

The correspondence between Knoll and Rapson in 1944 and 1945 also sheds light on the origins of the Knoll Textiles print *Isles*, designed by Shirley Fletcher Rapson (see figs. 2.25 and B.39), and on the frustrations of conducting a business of this type during and just after the war. In the same 1944 letter, Knoll wrote: "We would like to work out various designs and Shirley's name was mentioned as having done some designing in the textile field."[7] By the fall of 1945, Knoll was anxious to put Shirley Rapson's fabric designs into production, but progress was slow—owing to wartime material shortages of basic cloths.[8] This early initiative was still on hold in December when Knoll wrote that "although we have the materials, we haven't as yet gotten the screen for Shirle's prints. I shall let you both know as soon as we have made further progress. Everything seems to take a very long time."[9] Although it is not known if *Isles* was sold by Knoll before 1947, it was printed for use as curtains in a 1946 Planning Unit project—the offices at Rockefeller Center that Florence Knoll designed for the Rockefeller family (see chapter 2 and fig. 2.24).

Although wartime shortages hampered Knoll's early efforts to have fabrics printed, they also spurred experimentation. A notable example was Knoll's use of webbing in place of traditional upholstery on its chairs (see chapter 2). During the war, surplus cotton webbing (such as that used for parachute straps) which had failed to meet government standards was one of the few materials readily available.[10] Toward the end of the war, webbing (although never officially part of Knoll's textile collection) became the first product that the firm developed in direct collaboration with textile manufacturers. These collaborations provided attractive materials that could be sold by the yard, independent of their use on Knoll furniture. The success of these products may have convinced Hans and Florence Knoll to work with other textile manufacturers in a similar way, leading Knoll to become a textile converter, commissioning and developing fabrics to be sold under its own name (for a discussion of the textile trade and converters, see chapter 1).

By the summer of 1945, as manufacturers made plans to return their factories to civilian production, Hans Knoll offered to share with prospective home-furnishings manufacturers the "valuable schooling in resourcefulness and ingenuity" Knoll had acquired during the war.[11] He announced that the Knoll Planning Unit was already working collaboratively with manufacturers to help them enter the home-furnishings field. Bridgeport Fabrics of Bridgeport, Connecticut, for example, a maker of automotive and aircraft fabrics that had supplied webbing to the government (and probably to Knoll) during the war, was among the first companies to benefit from such a collaboration with Knoll.[12] In a September 1945 article in *Upholstering* magazine, a designer for Bridgeport discussed the problems of returning to civilian production from the manufacturer's point of view. He stressed the importance of collaboration and designing to meet the requirements of modern furniture and used as an example a new "'salt & pepper' webbing designed expressly for H. G. Knoll" (see fig. 2.9).[13] Knoll had similar arrangements with a number of other manufacturers in the immediate postwar period, including the Anchor Plastics Company, which made Aeroflex, an extruded plastic webbing (fig. 3.1); the Concordia-Gallia Corporation, makers of Cogon woven plastic webbing; and the Chicopee Manufacturing Corporation, makers of a plastic upholstery fabric woven from Saran fiber and marketed under the trade name Lumite.[14] Knoll furniture appeared in advertisements for all of these companies, not only reinforcing Knoll's image as an innovative company interested in using modern materials, but also underlining the suitability of such materials for modern furniture (fig. 3.2). One of the Lumite fabrics developed with the Chicopee Manufacturing Corporation was included in the Knoll textile division collection from about 1948 to 1950. Variously called *Saran* or simply *P1-P7* "plastic upholstery," it was available in both solid colors and stripes and offered as standard upholstery on some Knoll chairs (fig. 3.3).[15]

"Introducing Textiles": Assembling the Knoll Collection

The Knoll textile division formally debuted in February 1947 with the opening of a new showroom at 31 ½ East 65th Street, about seven blocks from the main Knoll showroom at 601 Madison Avenue, in New York City (fig. 3.4). Designed by Florence Knoll, this small showroom (see figs. 4.32 and Introduction fig. 1) was under the direction of Arundell Clarke, a British designer and decorator who had immigrated to New York in the 1930s. By the 1940s Clarke was himself a successful textile converter and had developed a reputation for seeking out talented but lesser-known designers and using "existing and otherwise ignored industrial fabrics in new and fresh ways."[16] His role in assembling the first Knoll textile collections is unclear; in advertisements and press reports he was described variously as head of the new division and showroom or as a sales agent.[17] Certainly Clarke would have been in a position to advise Florence and Hans Knoll on the workings of the textile market and to assist them in establishing relationships with designers, mills, and suppliers. Clarke's formal association with Knoll seems to have ended by May 1948, when the Knoll textile division was integrated into the redesigned 601 Madison Avenue showroom (see figs. 4.33, 4.34).[18]

Clarke can be credited with introducing a group of handwoven plant-fiber fabrics, which were highlights of the first Knoll collection and among the first Philippine textiles to be imported into the United States after the war.[19] These fabrics included *Moonlight*, an iridescent sheer curtain fabric of pineapple fiber, and *Abaca*, a hemp cloth resembling handkerchief linen.[20] Another of the Philippine imports, an irregular matting of woven pandanus-leaf fiber, named *Pandanus* (fig. 3.5), went on to become a standard fabric for Knoll, remaining in the line until 1963.[21] *Pandanus* was used extensively by the Planning Unit as a wall covering, to front the sliding doors of the cabinets Florence Knoll designed, and for some upholstery applications, such as the backrests of the *Model 700* daybeds designed by Richard Stein (1948). The firm's sales bulletins reveal the difficulties Knoll had in maintaining a reliable supply of *Pandanus*, not only because of weather (typhoons destroyed an entire season's output in 1957), but also due to changes in the organization of cottage industries in the Philippines. Despite these difficulties, it remained a very popular material. An April 1957 sales bulletin reported that a shipment of 900 yards of *Pandanus* had been sold out within the previous six weeks.[22]

Clarke probably played a part in sourcing some of the more unconventional fabrics available in the early collections, including *Fishnet* (cat. 9), a knotted linen netting supplied to Knoll by W. Auger, a provider of commercial fishing nets. Used as a casement fabric in windows and as room dividers, *Fishnet* became another Knoll "trademark" textile and was used in many of the firm's early showrooms (fig. 3.6). In 1956 Knoll introduced a smaller-scale cotton version called *Minnow* that was described as "an ideal solution to hide window air conditioners."[23] Other unconventional fabrics that Knoll stocked in the early years included plain cotton duck (a tightly woven canvas), used for upholstery and as a base fabric for printing, and, more surprisingly, "old-fashioned horsehair," also for upholstery.[24]

Swedish Imports and American Translations

A number of the leading Swedish designers working in a modern idiom after the war helped to enhance the early Knoll textile collections. The key contributor was Astrid Sampe, director of the Textilkammare (textile design studio) of the Stockholm department store Nordiska Kompaniet (NK). A talented designer in her own right, Sampe was also a leader in commissioning textiles from designers working in other areas of the applied arts and architecture. The most notable of those represented in the early Knoll textile collections were the ceramic artist Stig Lindberg and the architect Sven Markelius. The exact nature of the arrangement between Knoll and NK is not clear, but it seems that Knoll sought exclusive rights to import or print specific NK patterns in the United States.[25] The first of these, for both the textile collection and the "Authentic Swedish Room" presented in early 1947, included three small-motif prints by Sampe—*Raindrops*, *Honeycomb* (fig. 3.7), and *Ciphers*— and *Markelius*, a pattern Sven Markelius had designed in the early 1940s (see figs. 2.23 and B.88).[26]

By 1948 new NK fabric patterns were added to the collection, and Knoll also began manufacturing some NK designs in the United States. These included *Apples* by Stig Lindberg, a new addition to the textile collection the same year (introduced first in Sweden as *Fruktlada* in 1947; fig. 3.8).[27] In July 1948, when Sampe visited New York, Knoll presented an exhibition of a new collection of Swedish fabrics, both imports and "American translations" of Swedish designs. Among several upholstery fabrics that were being woven on machine looms in the United States was a striped design incorporating Tensolite, a yarn of fiberglass coated with plastic.[28] The addition of fiberglass yarn in the weft (fig. 3.9) was intended to make the fabric more durable and gave the white stripes a glossy finish.[29] *Sampe Stripe*, a version of the same design with the fiberglass replaced by rayon, was carried by Knoll beginning in 1948 and remained in the collection for several years.[30]

A number of additional Swedish prints were introduced between 1948 and 1950. *Waves* (see fig. B.72), by the Danish architect Arne Jacobsen (who went to Sweden during World War II), and *Plantsoon*, a design of stylized flower beds (fig. 3.10), are recorded in Knoll price lists and photographs, but there is no record of where they were printed. Other Swedish prints that seem to have been available for a relatively short time in 1948 and 1949 included *Paving Stones* as well as the Astrid Sampe designs *Crossbars* and *Rings* (fig. 3.11).[31]

Early Print Collections

The majority of the early Knoll prints were small in scale, with geometric patterns that were intended to create overall textured effects when pleated into drapery or used as upholstery. As one reviewer of the first collection aptly explained, "no pattern is so busy, so pictorial, or so insistent that it becomes obtrusive."[32] This notwithstanding, the early Knoll collections also included some surprisingly pictorial and large-scale designs, such as *Manhattan*, designed by Josef Frank, the Austrian-born architect working in Sweden.[33] Before 1950, when Knoll was new to both the textile market and the field of pattern design, the company experimented with a variety of "looks." This was easier to do with prints than with woven fabrics—since new yardage could be quickly printed to order on a standard base cloth, there was no need to invest in a large inventory.

Marianne Strengell, who had become interested in printed textile design in the early 1940s (see chapter 1), provided two prints, *Shooting Stars* (fig. 3.12 and cat. 14) and *Propellers* (see fig. B.126), for the first Knoll collection in 1947.[36] She may also have contributed to bringing *Isles* (see fig. B.39) to the attention of Knoll. She included it in a group of "textile studies" by former Cranbrook students that she published in 1945.[37] In the version of *Isles* produced by Knoll,

Fig. 3.1 Left Plastic webbing on *Model 703WAC* armchair designed by Abel Sorensen, ca. 1947. Webbing attributed to Anchor Plastics Company; chair made by Knoll Associates, Inc. Plastic webbing; chair: birch or maple. Knoll Museum, East Greenville, Penn.

Fig. 3.2 Right Advertisement for Lumite Division, Chicopee Manufacturing Corporation. From *Upholstering*, March 1948. Art & Architecture Collection, Miriam and Ira D. Wallach Division of Art, Prints and Photographs, The New York Public Library, Astor, Lenox and Tilden Foundations.

Fig. 3.3 *Saran* ("Red and White stripe" colorway, *P2*), on *Model 666UAC* armchair designed by Jens Risom, ca. 1948. Upholstery made by Chicopee Manufacturing Corporation, chair made by Knoll Associates, Inc. Upholstery: *Saran*; twill variation; chair: maple, steel springs, cotton batting. Private collection. Cat. 10.

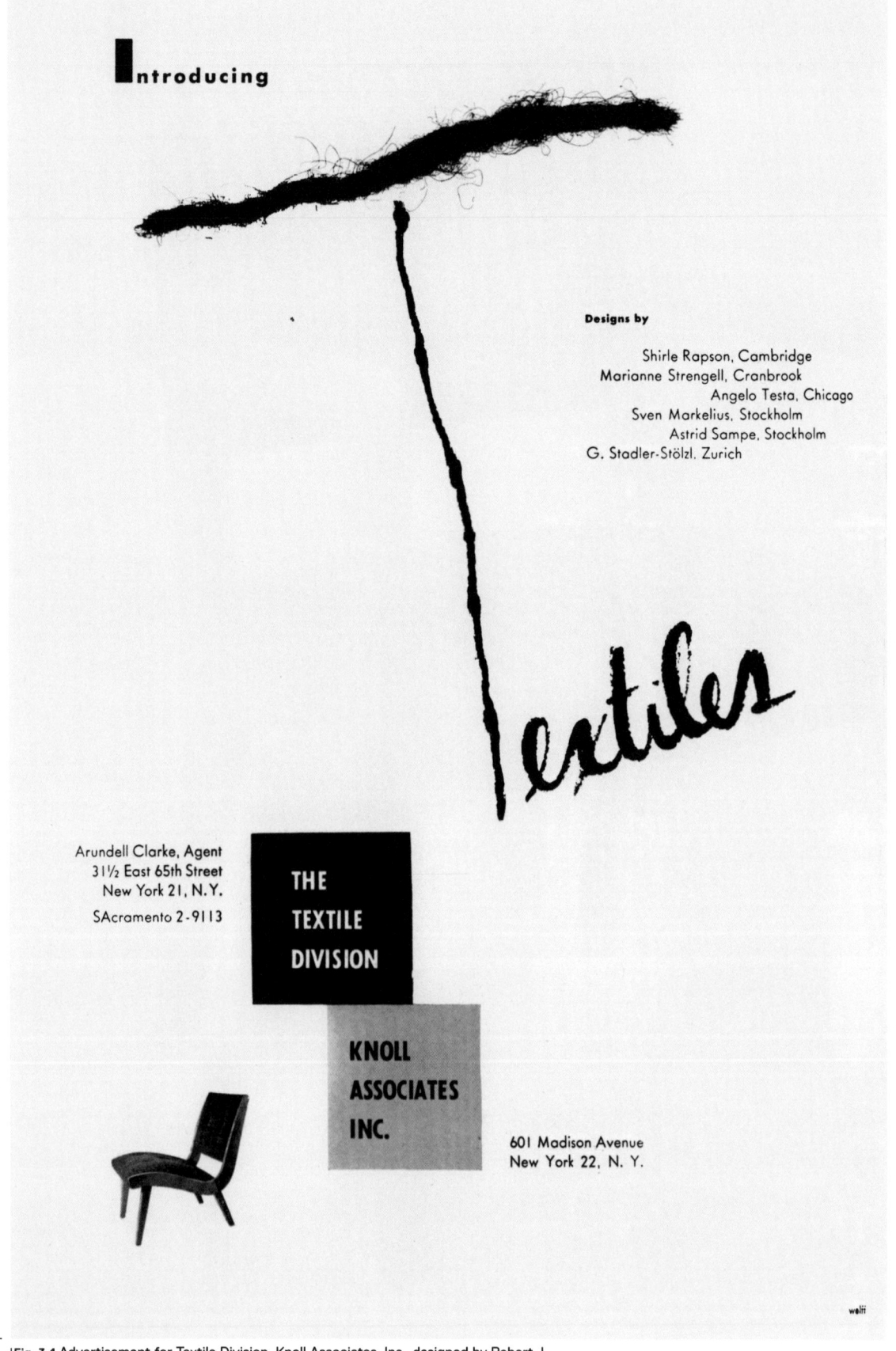

Fig. 3.4 Advertisement for Textile Division, Knoll Associates, Inc., designed by Robert J. Wolff. From *Interiors*, March 1947.

Fig. 3.5 *Pandanus* ("Red Plaid" colorway), introduced 1947, this example ca. 1948. Made in the Philippines for Knoll Associates, Inc. Wall covering, upholstery, and other uses; Pandanus leaf fiber; plain weave. The Museum of Modern Art, New York, P384. Cat. 8.

Fig. 3.6 Left *Fishnet* in use at Knoll showroom, Dallas, Tex., 1950. Photographed by Arthur S. Siegel. Knoll Archives.

Fig. 3.7 Right Selected fabrics from the first Knoll Textile collection including, from left: Angelo Testa's *Campagna*, a Marianne Strengell handwoven (possibly *Silvertone*), Astrid Sampe's *Honeycomb*, and Strengell's *Shooting Stars*, 1947. Photographed by Phyllis A. Dearborn, Dearborn-Massar. Knoll Archives.

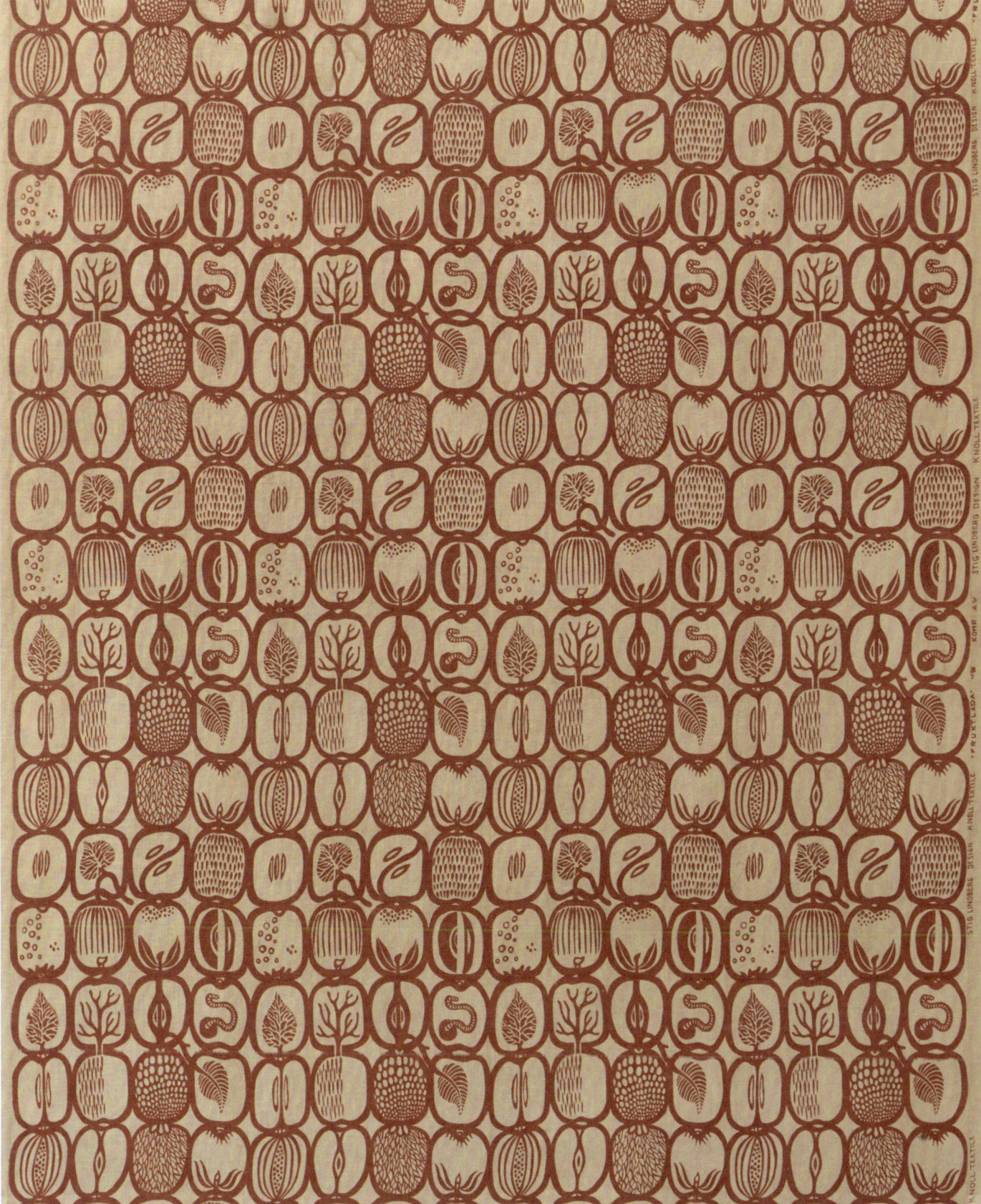

Fig. 3.8 Stig Lindberg. *Apples* ("Red on Natural" colorway), ca. 1948. Made for Knoll Associates, Inc. Used for drapery; linen, jute, and cotton; plain weave, screen-printed. Private collection. Cat. 20.

Fig. 3.9 Astrid Sampe. Detail of textile related to Knoll's *Sampe Stripe*, ca. 1948. Made for Nordiska Kompaniet's Textilkammare, Stockholm. Used for upholstery; cotton, fiberglass, wool; simple weave with twill variation. The Museum of Modern Art, New York, Given anonymously, SC36.1975. Cat. 19.

Fig. 3.10 Top *Plantsoon*, introduced ca. 1950. Photographed by Herbert Matter, ca. 1950. KnollTextiles Archive.

Fig. 3.12 Bottom Marianne Strengell Hamerström. *Shooting Stars* (in two colorways), introduced 1947. Photographed by Herbert Matter, ca. 1950. KnollTextiles Archive.

Fig. 3.11 Right Advertisement for Knoll Associates, Textile Division, designed by Herbert Matter, featuring Knoll patterns including Astrid Sampe's *Rings* and *Crossbars*. From *House & Garden*, October 1949. Library, Bard Graduate Center: Decorative Arts, Design History, Material Culture; New York.

Fig. 3.13 Alexander Girard. *Spines*, ca. 1948. Made for Alexander Girard. Used for drapery; linen; plain weave, screen-printed. Cooper-Hewitt, National Design Museum, Smithsonian Institution, 1969-165-15. Cat. 17.

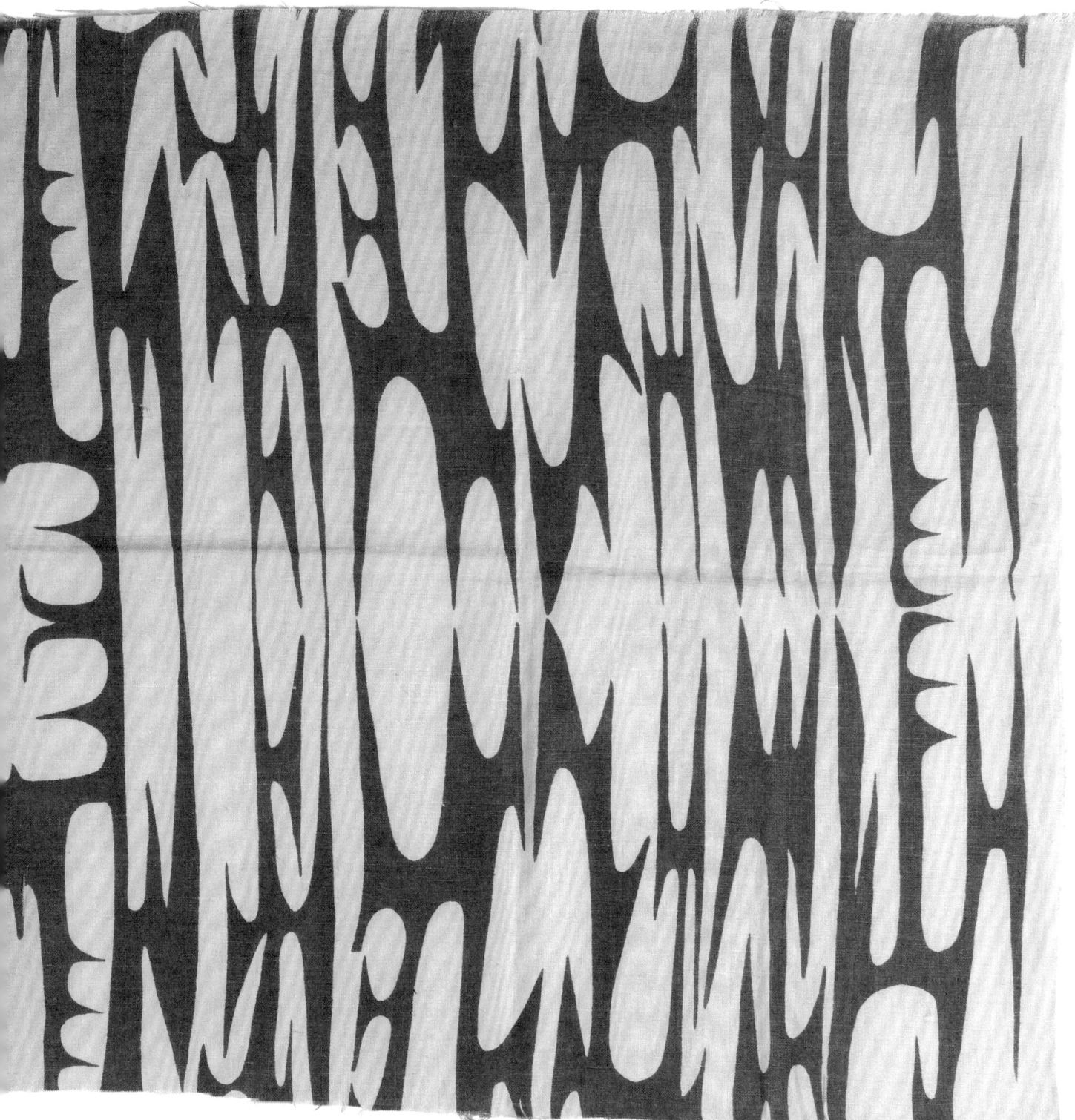

Shirley Rapson's original design (see fig. 2.25) was turned 90 degrees, perhaps with the thought that vertical rectangles would be more suited to use as pleated draperies.

During 1947–49 Knoll also distributed fabrics designed by Alexander Girard, best known for his later textile work with Herman Miller, who at the time was printing and selling his own designs at his retail shop in Grosse Pointe, Michigan. Girard's patterns *Spines* (fig. 3.13), *Links*, and *Wires* (see figs. B.41 and 42) were published during this period both with and without a Knoll credit, indicating Girard's arrangement with Knoll was not exclusive.[34] The same is true of three prints by Angelo Testa that were briefly available through Knoll during this period—*Animal Forms*, *Filo* (see fig. 1.14), and *Indian Heads* (see fig. B.132).[35]

Knoll's approach to creating a collection of fabrics by "name" designers differed from that of contemporary companies such as Laverne Originals, which frequently added new designs and included many kinds of patterns (see chapter 1). Knoll tended to select one or two designs from each designer and to keep them in the line a long time, thereby establishing each pattern as part of the company's standard design vocabulary while still achieving variety by producing them in new colorways and on new base fabrics. For example, in 1947 Knoll introduced *Campagna*, by Angelo Testa (fig. 3.14), a pattern of delicate concentric rectangles based on a stylized aerial view of farm fields, and it remained in the collection until 1964. Instead of adding other patterns by the prolific Testa, Knoll printed *Campagna* in many colors and various base fabrics over the years. A 1958 sales bulletin, announcing the sheer version of *Campagna* (fig. B.131), shows this strategy at work: "We have tried out Campagna on our K90 cloth and although the design is by now admittedly old and well known, it looks so beautiful on the sheer Linen/Dacron gauze that we have decided to add it to our line."[38]

Noémi Raymond was among the most important of the early Knoll print designers and one of the few to be represented by multiple print designs. Raymond had won first prize for printed fabrics in the *Organic Design in Home Furnishings* competition at MoMA in 1941 (see chapter 1), having entered some of the designs that Knoll printed almost ten years later. In the spring of 1948 Knoll introduced *Reeds and Bars* (see fig. B.100), which had been shown in the *Organic Design* exhibition. Knoll also printed it without the horizontal lines, as *Reeds*. Another Raymond print introduced in 1948, *Chinese Coins* (fig. 3.15) was a simplified version of *Speckles*, which had been in *Organic Design* and was probably based on a type of Japanese tie-dye patterning known as *kanoko shibori* ("fawn spot" tie-dying; below).[39] Printed on a heavyweight cotton appropriate for either drapery or upholstery, *Chinese Coins* appears to have sold quite well.[40] In December 1948 Raymond wrote to her husband that Hans Knoll wanted her to make another pattern "as practical and as popular as the Chinese Coins"—a request that probably served as the impetus for the creation of *Mosaic* the following year.[41] Raymond's final design for Knoll was *Mosaic* (fig. 3.16). In 1949, while it was in development, Raymond's husband was in Japan, and the two traded letters that reveal some details of the creation and production of Knoll's early prints. In October 1949, Raymond, who lived in New Hope, Pennsylvania, wrote that she was planning a day trip to New York City to "work with the Knolls on their fabrics," and the following week, she reported that the trip had been discouraging: "The last screen I made had either been poorly printed or was a bad design. We shall experiment with other colors and better cloth."[42] On October 28, she noted, "This morning I met Knoll's man at the printers and got them started on some new colors." Then on November 7 she wrote of going to "the factory where I must work on some changes on the screen for Knoll. I shall stop at the office too."[43] Although these letters do not identify the textile printer, they suggest that the development of the design was a hands-on, cooperative process, involving the designer, Hans and Florence Knoll, and the unnamed printer.[44]

Power-loomed Fabrics for Modern Interiors

From 1947 through the early 1950s, Marianne Strengell (see fig. 1.13) was a major contributor to Knoll's collection of upholstery fabrics, and her work and design philosophy strongly influenced how textiles were perceived at Knoll. Strengell believed that upholstery fabric "should be a part of architecture as a whole and of furniture in particular, rather than attempting to live an independent life of its own in disregard of the atmosphere of its surroundings."[45] By this Strengell meant that upholstery fabric should play an equal, essential, and fully integrated role with architectural details or furniture in the look of the modern interior, and that textiles, like architecture, must be functional as well as beautiful. Instead of pattern or complex structure, she favored color and texture effects, which she achieved through innovative and subtle combinations of varied fibers.[46]

Since Strengell was a well-known weaver and designer by 1947, the two machine-woven upholstery fabrics (*Devil* and *Cartree*) she contributed to the first Knoll collection—"the first of Miss Strengell's designs to be produced in mass quantity"—were generally considered to be highlights of the collection.[47] The more successful of the two was *Devil* (fig. 3.17). Woven for Knoll by the Original Textile Company, it was made with a warp of cotton dyed in clear colors against a weft of alternating black wool and textured (*ratiné*) cotton yarns. Using these simple contrasts of color and texture, and varying the plain-weave structure with floats to keep the eye from moving in straight lines, Strengell created a surface

Opposite Japanese textile fragment belonging to Noémi Raymond, ca. 1925. Silk, plain weave, tie-dyed (*shibori*). Raymond Collection, The Architectural Archives, University of Pennsylvania.

Fig. 3.14 Angelo Testa. *Campagna* ("Green" colorway), introduced 1947, this example before 1950. Made for Knoll Associates, Inc. Used for drapery; linen; plain weave, screen-printed. Cooper-Hewitt, National Design Museum, Smithsonian Institution, Gift of Nicholas A. Pappas, FAIA, 2002-14-3. Cat. 15.

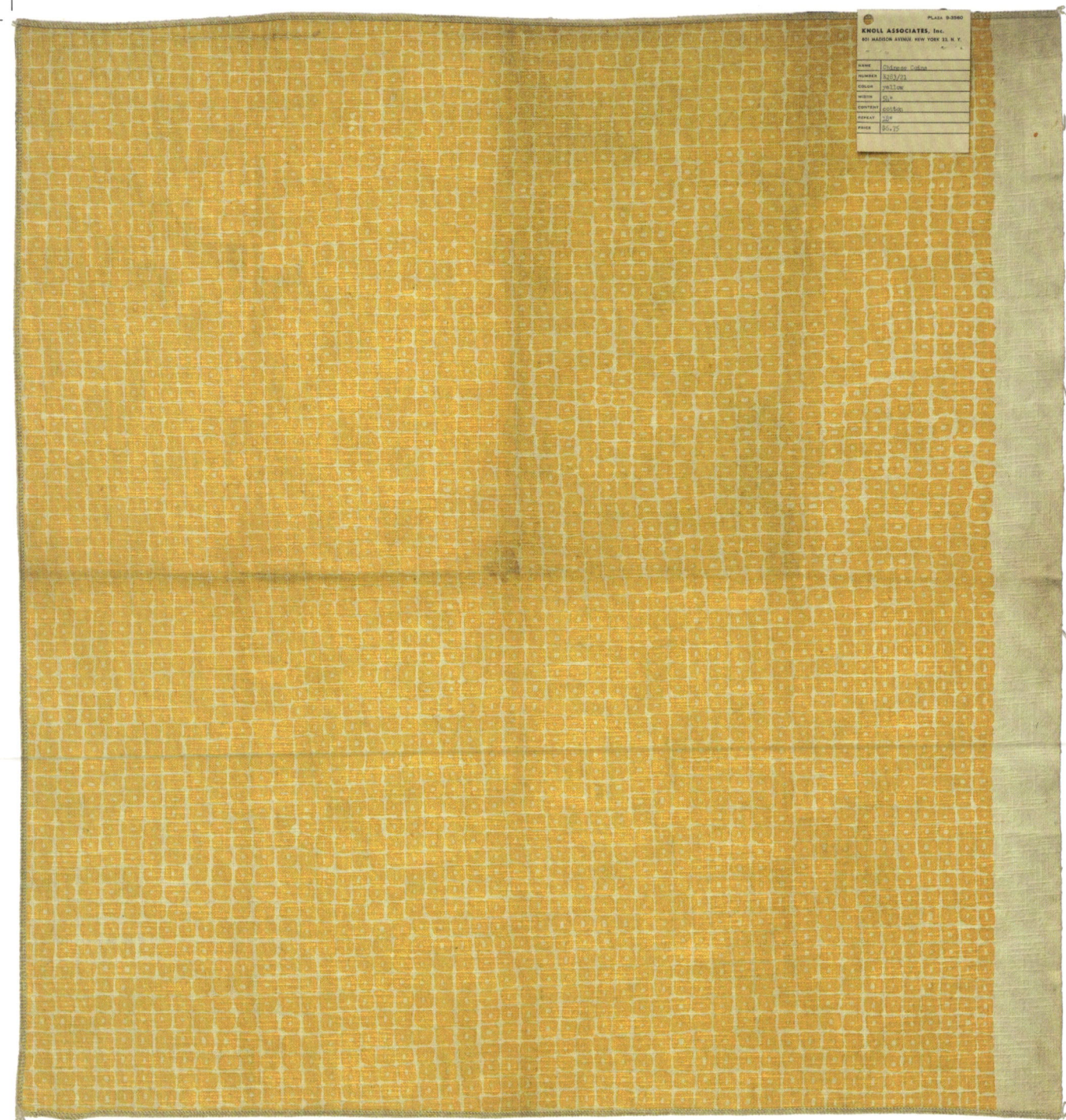

Fig. 3.15 Noémi Raymond. *Chinese Coins* sample ("Yellow" colorway), ca. 1948. Made for Knoll Associates, Inc. Used for upholstery, drapery; cotton; plain weave, screen-printed. The Museum of Modern Art, New York, P383. Cat. 11.

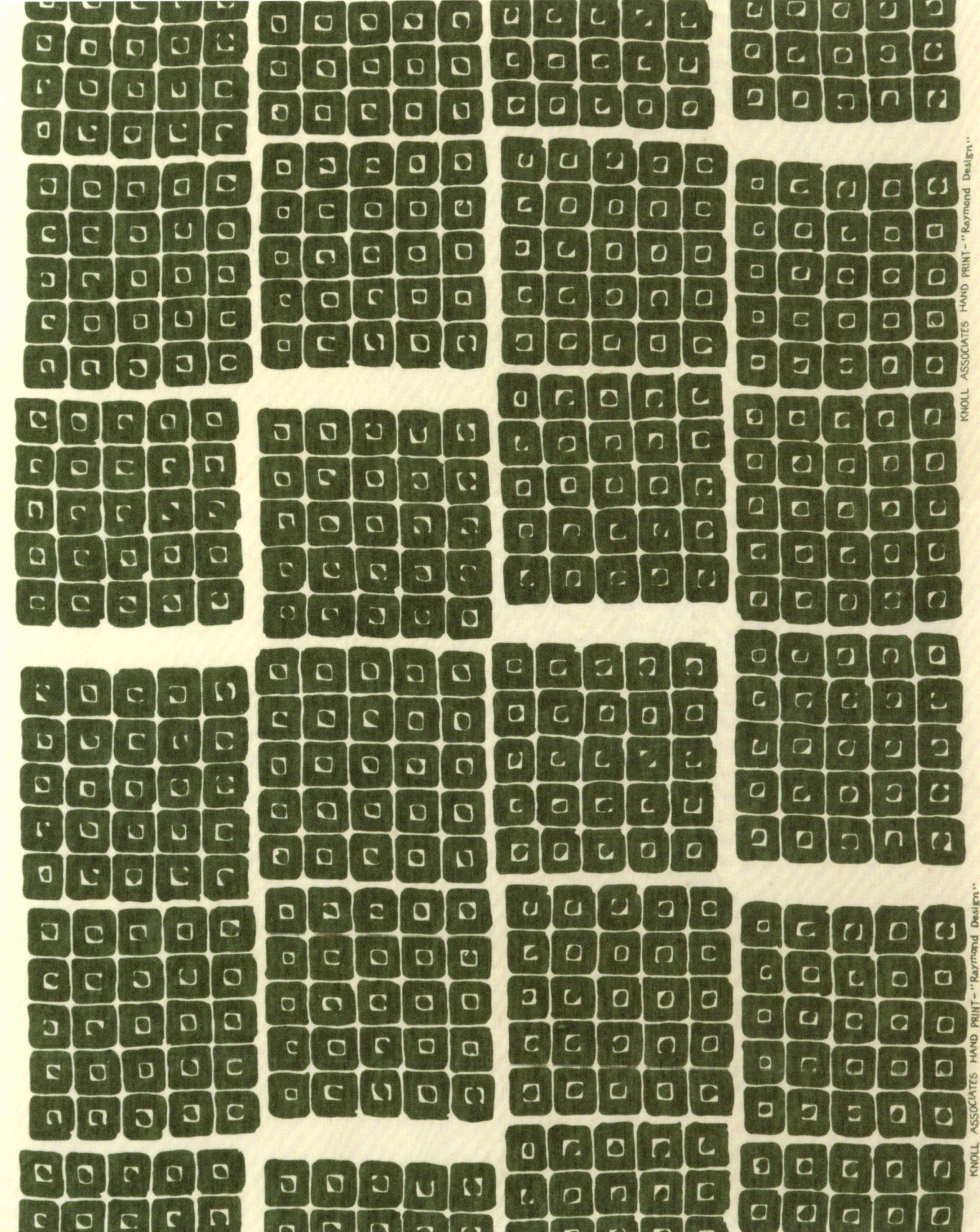

Fig. 3.16 Noémi Raymond. *Mosaic* ("Green on White" colorway), ca. 1950.
Made for Knoll Associates, Inc. Used for drapery; rayon; plain weave, screen-printed.
Private collection. Cat. 13.

Fig 3.17 Marianne Strengell Hammarström. *Devil* samples, introduced 1947, these examples ca. 1950. Made by Original Textile Company for Knoll Associates, Inc. Used for upholstery; wool, cotton; plain-weave–derived compound weave with supplemental wefts. KnollTextiles Archive. Cat. 27.

Fig. 3.18 Marianne Strengell Hammarström. *Cartree* samples, ca. 1947.
Made by Louisville Textiles for Knoll Associates, Inc. Used for upholstery; cotton;
plain weave with alternating single and paired wefts. KnollTextiles Archive.

that is complex but not distracting. Even the few small surviving swatches of *Devil* make it possible to imagine its effectiveness as upholstery, particularly on sculptural furniture such as the Saarinen *Womb* chair.[48]

Her other contribution to the first collection, *Cartree* (fig. 3.18), was named after Florence Knoll's English sheepdog. An all-cotton variation of *Devil*, it had a similar structure and dark/light contrast (thick weft yarns in dark colors set against a warp and alternating wefts in white) to create a ribbed effect. Both *Cartree* and *Buster* (see fig. B.128), a related cotton upholstery fabric also designed by Strengell and introduced in 1949, have a higher-relief, more patterned appearance than is typical for Strengell's fabrics. This kind of pattern, however, appears several times in a group of samples from the early 1940s preserved in the archive of Louisville Textiles, the mill that wove *Cartree* and *Buster* for Knoll.[49] Since Strengell's approach when working with a mill was to become familiar with their equipment and to work "with their own yarns and within their limitations," it is possible that she had been partly inspired by the textiles already being woven by the mill.[50]

Puli (1951) was the final machine-woven upholstery fabric that Strengell designed for Knoll (fig. 3.19). The name, which refers to a breed of long-haired Hungarian herding dog, may have been suggested by Eszter Haraszty (the Hungarian-born designer then heading the textile division) to complement *Cartree*. More characteristic of Strengell's designs, with its unusual combination of materials (a warp of cotton, linen, and glossy rayon gimp, with a heavy weft of jute), *Puli* created a rich and subtle effect. Although the gimp used in the warp is rayon, the darker warp yarns placed next to it make it appear almost metallic. It was introduced in a range of tones including persimmon and "Parma violet" in 1951 and was selected for the 1952 *Good Design* exhibition at MoMA.[51]

Strengell made several other contributions to the Knoll textile line during the early years. One, known only from written sources, was a drapery fabric of fiberglass and wool designed around 1949 and described in Knoll advertisements as "a revolutionary Fiberglas weave."[52] This fabric may have been an adaptation of one of those Strengell designed for Owens-Corning Fiberglas's new building on East Fifty-sixth Street in New York. Another Strengell design was a new textured cotton furniture webbing called *Pebble Weave* (fig. 3.20). Knoll featured it as part of the fabric display wall in the redesigned 601 Madison Avenue showroom that opened in May 1948 (see fig. 4.34). By 1949 Webcraft, its manufacturer, was marketing it directly to the interior design trade.[54] The irregular vertical streaks of "pebbled" texture, created by varying the spacing and twist of the warp threads, were a practical translation of the kinds of textural effects that Strengell explored in her handwoven textiles, such as the nubby, high-relief lines formed by thick, irregular warps in the samples in figure 3.21. Strengell was evidently pleased with the *Pebble Weave* design, as she included a sample (or samples) in a 1950 solo exhibition of her work at Cranbrook.[55]

Antoinette Lackner Prestini was a weaving student at Cranbrook between 1945 and 1947 and taught weaving there during the summer 1947 session. In the spring of 1948, Knoll introduced her design, *Prestini*, a cotton upholstery fabric woven for Knoll by Louisville Textiles (fig. 3.22).[56] *Prestini* had studied with Strengell at Cranbrook, but this design surpassed even her mentor's textiles for Knoll in demonstrating the design principles she had learned from Strengell. *Prestini* has a rich color effect and interesting texture achieved by extremely simple means. The weft and half of the warp is a novelty *ratiné* yarn of cotton and rayon, given a nubby, zigzag texture by tightly twisting thick and thin elements together (fig. 3.23). The twist of the yarn gives the fabric its high-relief effect and elasticity. Alternating with the *ratiné* warp yarns are warps of a plain, two-ply yarn, in the same or a contrasting color, which show through on both sides of the fabric, forming a background pattern of tiny dots.

The dimensional stability and balanced quality of *Prestini*, with the same amount of stretch in both warp and weft directions, also made it a good choice for upholstering unusual shapes such as Harry Bertoia's *Diamond* chairs (introduced by Knoll in 1952), for which it became one of the standard fabrics (fig. 3.24). Richard Schultz, who developed the upholstered seat covers for the Bertoia chairs, recalls that it was a challenge to find a fabric that would stay smooth against the foam in the cover with only a light layer of glue and neither ties nor tufting. In a recent interview he explained that "the technique was highly dependent on the ability of the fabric to take the shape—there was nothing holding it in that shape except the glue. *Prestini* was perfect for that."[57]

Florence Knoll Bassett later described *Prestini* as "the sort of simple and direct design we were looking for."[58] The fabric remained a staple of the the Knoll line until 1982, long after the other early cotton upholsteries had been discontinued. Although the fiber content was shifted to all-cotton from the early 1950s on, and there were slight adjustments in color and finishing over the years, *Prestini* remained essentially unchanged, and by 1962 over 100,000 yards had been sold.[59]

Early Handwovens

As a counterpart to the inexpensive machine-woven upholsteries like *Devil* and *Prestini*, handwoven upholstery and drapery fabrics designed by Strengell were offered by the textile division from its beginning in 1947 through the early 1950s, but little is known about these fabrics. Publicity photographs taken of the first textile collection (see fig. 3.7) give some idea of the appearance of two of the designs,

Fig. 3.19 Marianne Strengell Hammarström. *Puli* swatches, ca. 1951. Made for Knoll Textiles. Used for upholstery; linen, jute, wool, rayon; plain-weave–derived simple weave. KnollTextiles Archive. Cat. 105.

Fig. 3.20 Left Marianne Strengell Hammarström (attributed). *Pebble Weave* webbing samples, ca. 1945. Made for Knoll Associates, Inc. Used for upholstery; cotton; plain weave. KnollTextiles Archive. Cat. 5.
Fig. 3.21 Right Marianne Strengell Hammarström. Samples of handwoven fabrics. Photographed ca. 1941. Cranbrook Archives, 5650-2, folder 15-8.

Fig. 3.22 Bottom left Antoinette Lackner Prestini (later Webster). *Prestini*, ca. 1948. Made by Louisville Textiles for Knoll Associates, Inc. Used for upholstery; cotton, rayon; plain weave. Private collection.

Fig. 3.23 Top left Crimp *ratiné* yarn samples, ca. 1960–68. Louisville Textiles archive, American Textile History Museum, Lowell, Mass., 1968.10.6.1.

Fig. 3.24 Top right Antoinette Lackner Prestini (later Webster). Detail of *Prestini* ("Yellow" colorway) on *Small Diamond* chair designed by Harry Bertoia, this example ca. 1957. Upholstery made by Louisville Textiles for Knoll Textiles; chair made by Knoll Associates. Upholstery: cotton; plain weave; chair: plastic-coated wire frame, foam rubber. Private collection. Cat. 111.

but press descriptions simply mention that a range of Strengell designs could be ordered.⁶⁰ A 1950 price list offered two groups of "Strengell Handwovens"—seven upholstery fabrics and five drapery fabrics—listed by number and color.⁶¹ The upholstery fabrics included *K820*, or *Silvertone*, of wool and rayon, and *K811*, a green fabric of wool, mohair, cotton, and rayon, which appears to have been similar to *Puli*, Strengell's power-loomed design.⁶² Less is known about the drapery fabrics, though some of them may have corresponded to the striped fabrics shown in several black-and-white photographs from this period.⁶³

It is likely that the majority of the handwovens Strengell designed for Knoll, as with most of her custom handwoven fabrics for projects such as Eero Saarinen's General Motors Technical Center, were woven by Gerda Nyberg, a skilled Swedish-born handweaver who worked from her home in Pontiac, Michigan, not far from Cranbrook. Nyberg, who worked for Strengell full-time between 1945 and the 1960s, recorded her weaving assignments, including orders woven for Knoll between January 1949 and March 1951, thus shedding some light on the production of these textiles.⁶⁴ In 1949, for example, she noted three deliveries of *Silvertone* adding up to a total of 73 yards.⁶⁵ In the following year, she wove four orders of upholstery fabric for Knoll, totaling 201 yards. Two orders, for "gray upholstery" (49 yards) and "white upholstery" (40 ½ yards), were woven concurrently between August and September 1950. Apparently the white upholstery was a rush order, as the entry reads: "Was finished Sept. 16, was packed and delivered 1 o'clock in the middle of the night, to Knoll's Studio, New York."⁶⁶ Although there is no way to know if the entries specifically mentioning Knoll are the only fabrics Nyberg wove for the company, her records provide evidence that these expensive fabrics ($19.50 per yard in 1950) were included in the Knoll line not merely for prestige but because Knoll was able to communicate to its customers the distinctive qualities that such textiles could contribute to particular modern interior schemes. Knoll was among the first firms in the postwar period to explore the idea of luxury in modern textiles, and over the following decades, luxurious handwoven textiles would continue to be a mainstay of the Knoll line.

International Designers of Knoll Textiles

The presentation of the first Knoll Textiles collection, as revealed in the extensive press coverage, emphasized both the number of designers involved and its international scope. According to the *New York Times*, the collection represented the work of "half a dozen of the most talented textile designers of this country and Europe."⁶⁷ Over the next decade, Knoll continued to cultivate and promote the international character of both the collection and the designers, an approach that set it apart from other companies producing collections of textiles by "name" designers (primarily American), such as Schiffer Prints and L. Anton Maix (see chapter 1). In addition to licensing prints from European designers and working with Astrid Sampe and NK through the 1950s, Knoll Textiles, in its early years, brought in a number of unusual imports.

Among these was *Vallis*, a textile from the 1947 collection that was described, again in the *New York Times*, as "a handweave of homespun wool from a special breed of Swiss mountain sheep" and in *Upholstering* as "a heavy handwoven fabric of homespun wool . . . from Switzerland, in dark earthbrown with fine lines in natural tones, or with colors reversed."⁶⁸ While extant samples of this textile have not been located, a few surviving photographs may show *Vallis* in the darker colorway. Another photograph (ca. 1948) of a Florence Knoll armchair upholstered in "Swiss hand-spun, handwoven, natural with beige markings" (fig. 3.25) seems to correspond with the second description.⁶⁹ The mention of hand-spun yarn suggests that one or both of these textiles may have been designed by Gunta Stadler-Stölzl, who was listed as one of the designers of the first Knoll collection. Stadler-Stölzl, who had taught at the Bauhaus, was then running her own handweaving workshop in Zurich, Switzerland, and is known to have used much hand-spun wool during the postwar years.⁷⁰ From France, Knoll imported *Bauret Stripes* (1950), a cotton twill with woven stripes, reminiscent of awning canvas (see fig. B.22). Jean Bauret, who is credited with the design, was a textile manufacturer and art collector who commissioned textile designs from several avant-garde artists in the late 1940s.⁷¹ His specific connection to Knoll is not known.

Imported textiles incorporating distinctive fibers and yarns, such as *Pandanus* and the other Philippine fabrics mentioned above, also contributed to the international scope of the Knoll textile collections. In 1950 Knoll introduced two new types of imported woven silk, reflecting a growing trend for luxurious materials in the modern textiles market, especially in the Knoll offerings. A collection of Italian silks in solid colors and stripes (see fig. B.25), handwoven in Venice by the workshop of Michela Bronzini, were described by *Interior Design and Decoration* as "unlike anything else on the market," and when they were included in the June 1950 *Good Design* exhibition, they were noted as part of "a striking enrichment of the fabric market."⁷² A handwoven fabric of heavy tussah (wild) silk from India, initially called simply "handwoven silk from India" and later named *Jhuri Silk*, represented a kind of textile new to the American market.⁷³ In a review of the 1951 *Good Design* exhibition in *Handweaver and Craftsman*, it was described as "the most beautiful and exciting piece of all" in the drapery division, with "an absolutely indescribable lusciousness."⁷⁴ Richard Schultz, who had begun working in the Planning Unit in

Fig. 3.25 Top Gunta Stadler-Stölzl (attributed). "Swiss handspun, handwoven" upholstery, possibly *Vallis*, on *Model 25* armchair designed by Florence Knoll, ca. 1948. Photograph. The Museum of Modern Art, New York, Architecture and Design Study Center, AD543.

Fig. 3.26 Bottom Detail of jacket made of *Jhuri Silk* textile, ca. 1955. Textile handwoven in India by Sarabhal Agencies for Knoll Associates, Inc. Used for drapery and upholstery; silk; twill weave. Courtesy Richard and Trudy Schultz. Cat. 68.

Fig. 3.27 Top right Eszter Haraszty. Photograph attributed to Herbert Matter. Courtesy Ronald C. Pictersma.

Fig. 3.28 Bottom right Noémi Raymond. *Chinese Coins* sample ("Black on Red" colorway), ca. 1950. Made for Knoll Associates, Inc. Used for drapery; cotton; plain weave, screen-printed. Private collection. Cat. 39.

Fig. 3.29 Bottom left Advertisement for Knoll Associates, designed by Herbert Matter, featuring *Knoll Fabric Color Guide* for *Cinders* and *Handwovens K65/H-K68/H*. From *Interior Design*, April 1952.

1950, recalls that Florence Knoll had a *Womb* chair upholstered in this silk in her Sutton Place apartment. Schultz later was able to salvage enough scraps from the Knoll factory for his wife Trudy to make a jacket for herself (figs. 3.26).[75]

Eszter Haraszty: Color and Coordination

Eszter Haraszty (fig. 3.27) began her productive career at Knoll in 1949, first working part-time as a textile designer, but as her distinct talent for color became apparent, she was soon made a color consultant for Knoll Associates and head of Knoll Textiles, a position she held from about 1950 until 1955.[76] Trained as an artist in Budapest, Haraszty came to the United States in 1947 and arrived at Knoll at a pivotal moment for the textile division, just as new furniture designs and Planning Unit projects were creating a need for new kinds of fabrics and larger quantities of textiles, requiring a capable person to coordinate the department. Knoll Associates was also defining its image as a comprehensive purveyor of good design to a much wider audience through new showrooms, exhibitions, and publications, such as the *Knoll Index of Contemporary Design*. Haraszty, who had a flamboyant personality, had a penchant for bold unconventional colors, and the work she did in collaboration with Herbert Matter (Knoll's graphic designer at the time) on catalogues and sample kits, along with her prize-winning textile designs, made key contributions to the image-making process.

One of her first projects at Knoll, in late 1949 or early 1950, was to create a coordinated color palette across the entire textile line. Although it is difficult to judge from the mostly black-and-white photographs that survive, the previous color range appears to have been a mix of clear primary colors and more subdued tones. After the war many architects and designers, such as Angelo Testa and Alexander Girard, began producing their own textiles in part because they were unable to obtain fabrics in primary colors. As Girard later recalled, these colors were then so out of favor that one of the few places they could be found was in discount outlets, such as the bargain basement of Macy's department store in New York City.[77] Along with noting "flat bright primary colors" in Knoll's 601 Madison Avenue showroom,[78] commentaries about the company's early textile collections described subdued tones, including Swedish-inspired "muted earth colors," from an orangey copper and an olive green to a medium blue and "earth yellow."[79] Samples dating to about 1948 (see fig. 3.18), along with several surviving color photographs of the Knoll showrooms in New York and Boston, taken in 1948 and 1950 (fig. 4.35), give a sense of this palette, which also included a warm gray.

While revising the color offerings for textiles, Haraszty (probably with Matter) began working on a new promotional brochure, titled the *Knoll Color Guide*. It had an innovative format comprised of nine folders, each featuring a large swatch of a Knoll print on the left, opposite smaller ones of additional colorways of the same print and woven fabrics that could be coordinated with it. These quick visual guides showed how curtain and upholstery textiles could be combined in interior schemes. They functioned as reference guides for interior decorators, cross-promoted the print and woven collections, and, above all, demonstrated the company's wider emphasis on careful planning and integration. Haraszty's new palette seems to have retained most of the "old" colors, though the primary colors, particularly the reds, became noticeably brighter and more saturated. Several prints, including *Chinese Coins* and *Apples*, now appeared in unusual combinations of darker colors, such as black on red, dark blue, or brown on rust grounds (fig. 3.28 and cat. 40).[80]

The new colors and the coordinated approach were praised in the press. *Interior Design* reported that "Knoll Associates have devoted practically their whole attention to a complete color revision of some of their best numbers, such as 'Apples,' 'Chinese Coins,' and 'Shooting Stars,' which are appearing in some sharp, clear, paint-box colors, with never a greyed one among them."[81] The *Knoll Color Guide*, "coordinated by Eszter Haraszty," was described as "an amazing collection of key designs . . . offered to the trade at three dollars the set—a smart for-planning buy."[82] When Knoll issued a revised edition of the *Knoll Color Guide* in the spring of 1952 (fig. 3.29), the magazine commented: "As with most ventures by this dynamic firm, this just-off-the-press volume hits the spot when it comes to convenience, trim efficiency, and plain, old-fashioned usefulness."[83]

Haraszty increasingly added brighter and more intense colors—canary and saffron yellow, shocking pink, bright persimmon, and a wide range of saturated blues and greens—to the textile palette. She also experimented with unusual combinations of colors, including orange with shocking pink; her assistant, Suzanne Huguenin, later recalled that Haraszty was the first to use these colors together.[84] She also combined bright primary colors with olive or charcoal, as in *Knoll Stripes*, and vibrating two-tones of the same primary color, as in the print *Ringles* (fig. 3.30). *Triad* (1954), described in a Knoll press release as "a chord of three tones" translated into color with "three harmonious color tones and one accent note," was another demonstration of Haraszty's skill as a colorist; the colorways printed on dark grounds were particularly striking (fig. 3.31).[85] These innovations in color were unlike anything else then on the American market. Haraszty's more unusual creations may not always have been financially successful, but the colors consistently received favorable notice in the press and played an important role in establishing the "look" for which Knoll became known in the early 1950s.

Fig. 3.33 Top Printing room, Printex Corporation, Ossining, N.Y., May 2, 1951. Photographed by Gottscho-Schleisner, Inc., Library of Congress, Prints & Photographs Division, Gottscho-Schleisner Collection, LC-G612-T01-59136.

Fig 3.31 Bottom Eszter Haraszty. *Triad* ("Red, Royal, Orange, and White on Persimmon" colorway), introduced ca. 1954, this example ca. 1955. Made by Printex for Knoll Textiles. Used for drapery; cotton; plain weave, screen-printed. The Museum of Modern Art, New York, Gift of Knoll Associates, SC25.1975.3.

Fig. 3.30 Left Carol Summers. *Ringles* swatch ("Geranium Red" colorway), ca. 1954. Made for Knoll Textiles. Used for drapery; cotton; plain weave, screen-printed. Private collection. Cat. 41.

Fig. 3.32 Right Eszter Haraszty. *Knoll Stripes* swatch ("Olive, Black, and Red" colorway), ca. 1951. Made for Knoll Associates, Inc. Used for drapery; cotton; plain weave, screen-printed. Private collection. Cat. 44.

New Prints

Haraszty had actually designed her first pattern for Knoll before she was hired by the company. The horizontal stripe pattern was used in 1949 as a drapery fabric in the "House in the Museum Garden" at MoMA, designed by her compatriot Marcel Breuer.[86] The subsequent version that Knoll presented in 1951 and marketed as *Knoll Stripes* (fig. 3.32) became a signature Knoll textile, in part because of Haraszty's distinctive color choices. The press release described these colors as groups of "clear sunlight tones . . . mixed spontaneously with . . . deep rustic tones of olive, charcoal and rust," choices that were appropriate for "multiple color situations, picking up hesitant tones in a room, recalling tired accents."[87] *Cinders* (1950), the first of her designs to be created after Knoll hired her, was based on a drawing she had made of rain on a windowpane and added another practical, small-motif pattern to Knoll's range (see fig. 3.29).[88]

Haraszty frequently worked with the screen-printing firm Printex on her printed fabric designs. This company was described at the time as "the only large commercial plant of its scope combining complete designing, screen making, and printing operations under one roof."[89] Owned by Vera Neumann (who designed under the name "Vera") and her husband, George, it was located in Ossining, New York.[90] George Neumann was from an old Hungarian textile-printing family, giving him an understanding of the textile industry in general and the technology of textile printing. He was also a "sensitive colorist" with a thorough understanding of dye chemistry.[91] Printex's hand-printing room (fig. 3.33) had eight 40-yard printing tables, where 600 yards of fabric could be printed at one time. Working with Printex, "one of the most up-to-date and efficient units of its kind in the world," made it possible for Haraszty to experiment and to achieve colors and effects that might not have been possible elsewhere.[92]

The majority of Knoll's patterns in the 1940s and 1950s cannot be linked to a particular printer, as records have been lost. Other than Printex, Knoll frequently used American Art Textile Printing of New York, which also printed the majority of Alexander Girard's designs for Herman Miller in the 1950s and 1960s.[93] Others included Stonehenge Processing Co., Cedar Grove, New Jersey; New London Textile Print Works, New London, Connecticut; and Winston Prints, Lebanon, Pennsylvania (which also printed for Jack Lenor Larsen).[94]

Two of Haraszty's most successful prints, introduced in 1952 and 1953, were abstract patterns based on photographic images. *Tracy* (1952) was adapted from a Matter photograph showing the vein pattern or "skeleton" of a leaf (fig. 3.34). In making the pattern, Haraszty isolated parts of the photograph (by selectively tracing it or cutting it apart) making two separate screen motifs, which were arranged in rows to form a repeat pattern. One screen included the main structure of the leaf, which became a treelike shape, and the other included only the delicate background pattern. These two screens were then combined in a variety of ways. On a cotton and rayon drapery fabric, there were one-color versions, with both screens printed in the same color (fig. 3.35), and three-color versions, with the "trunk" printed in white, and the veins in black, on a colored ground (fig. 3.36). There were also versions printed on sheers, white silk gauze and cotton batiste, some with only the trunk screen, in black (fig. 3.37); on others only the vein screen, in white, was printed (fig. 3.38). There was also a version printed on *Dobby*, one of Knoll's heavier-weight textured woven cottons that could be used for both drapery and upholstery applications (see cat. 50).

Haraszty is most famous today for the 1953 design *Fibra*. Perhaps inspired by the photomurals of antique looms that Herbert Matter created for the 575 Madison Avenue showroom, Haraszty asked the photographer Erich Hartmann to take a series of photographs of the wire heddles of the loom in Evelyn Hill's weaving studio (fig. 3.39).[95] She then edited the photographs to create the large-scale repeat design as a single screen across the width of the fabric. For the color variations, she further edited the design to arrive at two-color (fig. 3.40) and four-color versions (fig. 3.41), giving an effect of vertical stripes. Over the years *Fibra* was in production (1953–72), the design was printed on Belgian linen and as a sheer on linen scrim, cotton batiste, and fiberglass. It won a First Award for Printed Fabrics from the American Institute of Decorators (AID, 1953), was selected for a *Good Design* exhibition (1953), and was widely published. Haraszty also adapted the pattern for a collection of clothes she designed for the sportswear manufacturer B. H. Wragge.[96]

The archive records for *Fibra* provide some idea of the trial and error process that went into developing many of Knoll's prints, both before and after the fabric's introduction. The most unusual versions of *Fibra*, and the ones that caused the most problems, were those printed on dark backgrounds (black, blue, and orange). The method originally used to apply the dark background colors—coating the fabric with pigment dye (a powdered coloring agent, with a liquid binder)—produced a dramatic color effect but made the fabric so stiff that it was difficult to sell (see fig. B.47). Some versions were even printed with an experimental technique that coated both sides of the fabric, which proved more problematic still. Nonetheless, throughout 1954 and 1955, Knoll and Printex gradually worked out some satisfactory methods of dyeing and printing each of the colorways.[97]

In the early 1950s, Knoll introduced a series of single-print designs by a wide range of designers. Very little is known about some of these designers or how they were hired by Knoll. In the case of *Filigree* (1950), for example, designer Dorothy Cole was an illustrator in New York when

Fig. 3.34 Herbert Matter (attributed). Leaf, ca. 1951. Photograph. From page featuring *Tracy* in a portfolio compiled by Eszter Haraszty. The Montreal Museum of Fine Arts, Liliane and David M. Stewart Collection, Gift of the American Friends of Canada through the generosity of Eszter Haraszty, D88.178.2.4v.

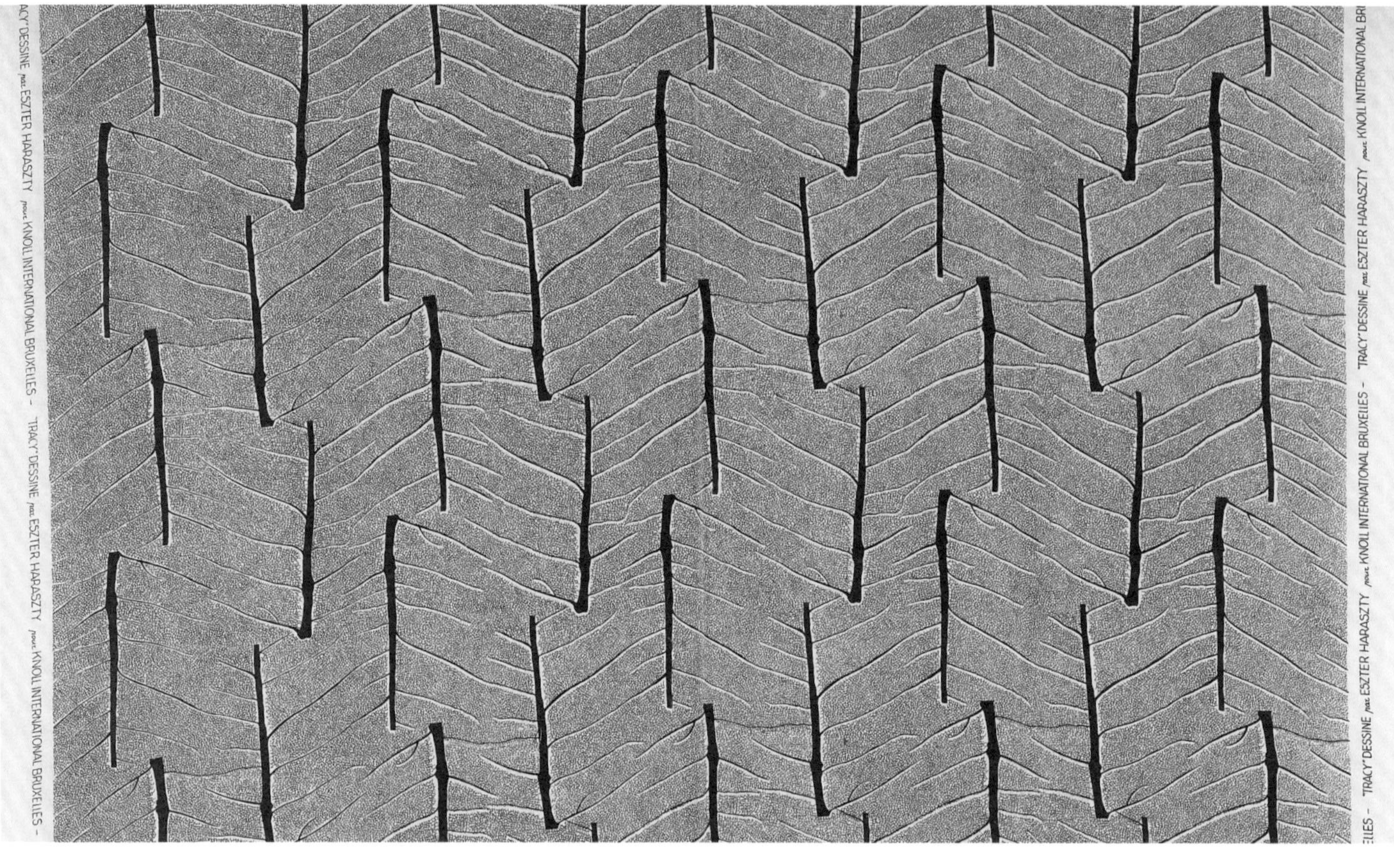

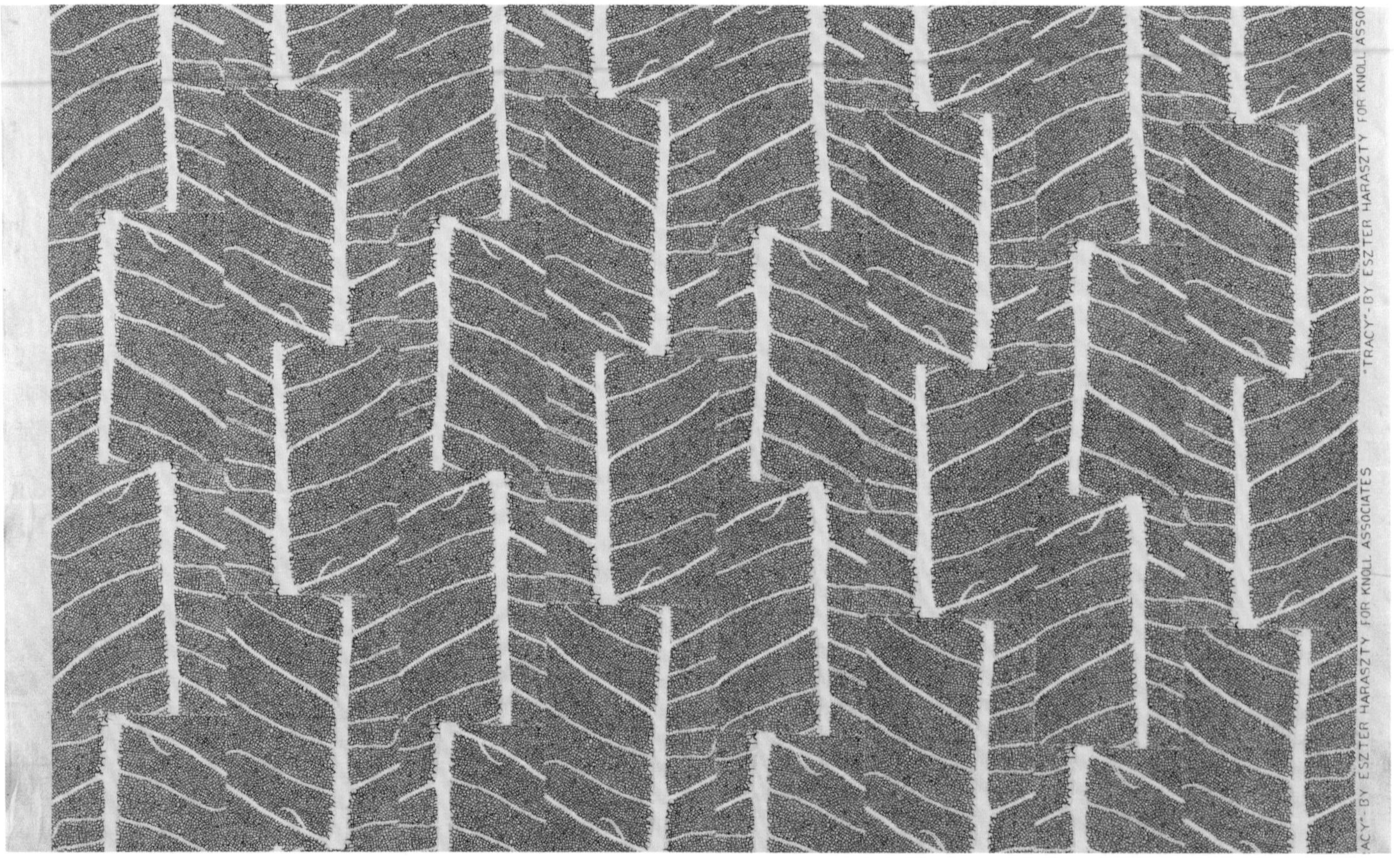

Fig. 3.35 Top Eszter Haraszty. *Tracy* ("Blue on White" colorway), introduced 1952, this example ca. 1960. Made for Knoll International Bruxelles. Used for drapery; cotton; plain weave, screen-printed. Minneapolis Institute of Arts, Gift of funds from Richard L. Simmons, 2004.65.1. Cat. 49.

Fig. 3.36 Bottom Eszter Haraszty. *Tracy* ("Black and White on Yellow colorway), 1952. Made for Knoll Textiles. Used for drapery; cotton, rayon; plain weave, screen-printed. Cranbrook Art Museum, Bloomfield Hills, Mich., Museum purchase, CAM 1953.4. Cat. 48.

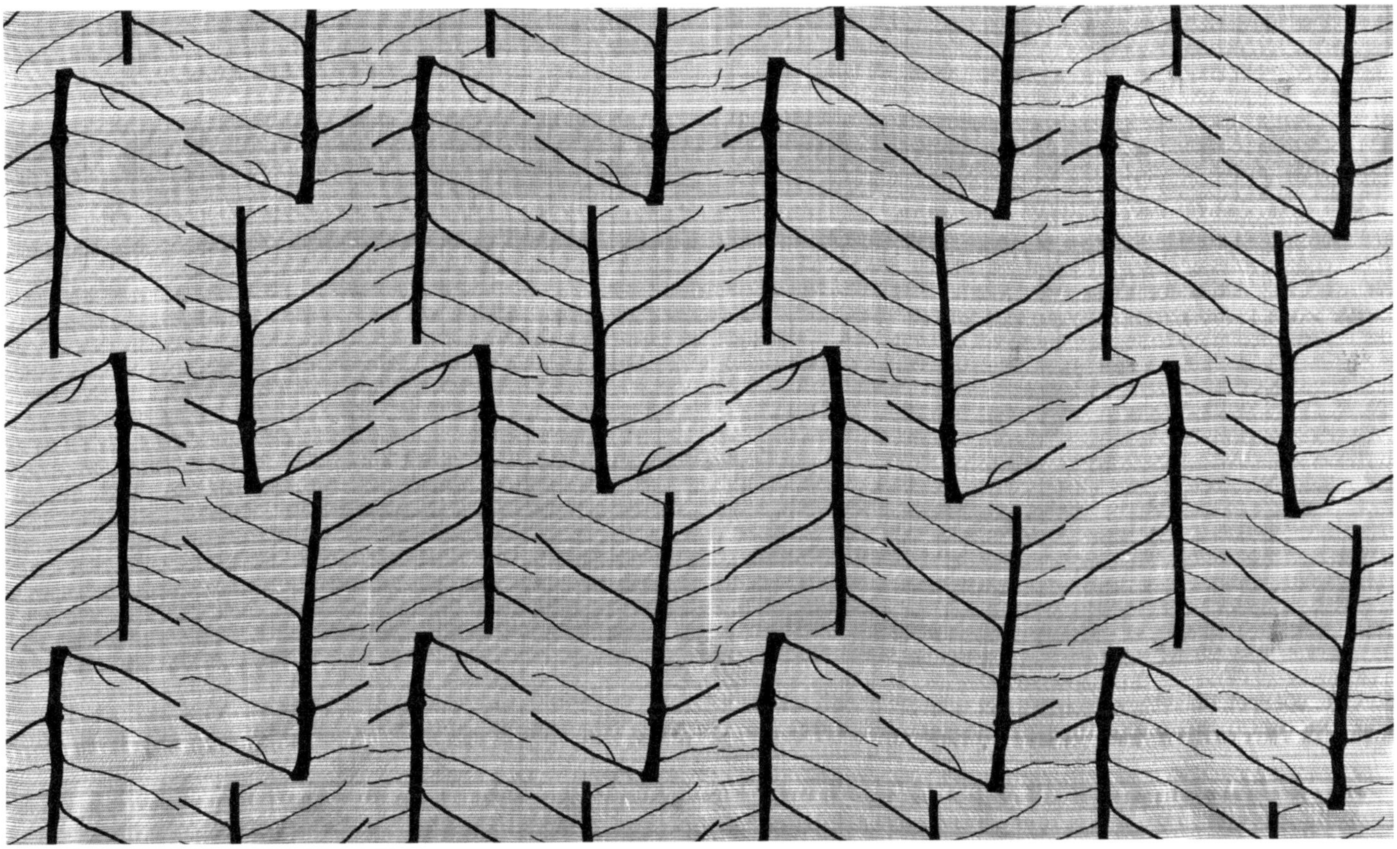

Fig. 3.37 Top Eszter Haraszty. *Tracy* ("Black on White" colorway), 1952. Made for Knoll Textiles. Used for drapery; silk gauze; plain weave, screen-printed. Cranbrook Art Museum, Bloomfield Hills, Mich., Museum purchase, CAM 1953.3. Cat. 47.

Fig. 3.38 Bottom Eszter Haraszty. *Tracy* ("White on White" sheer), introduced 1952, this example ca. 1955. Made for Knoll Textiles. Used for drapery; silk gauze; plain weave, screen-printed. The Museum of Modern Art, New York, Gift of Knoll Associates, SC30.1975. Cat. 46.

Fig. 3.39 The heddles of Evelyn Hill's loom, 1952. Contact sheet.
Photographed by Erich Hartmann. Magnum Photos.

Fig. 3.40 Eszter Haraszty. *Fibra* sample ("Black and White on Natural" colorway), introduced 1953, this example ca. 1965. Made by Printex for Knoll Textiles. Used for drapery; linen; plain weave, screen-printed. Courtesy Susan Ward.

Fig. 3.41 Eszter Haraszty. *Fibra* sample ("White, Orange, Blue, Black on Natural" colorway, with small colorway swatches attached), 1953. Made by Printex for Knoll Textiles. Used for drapery; linen; plain weave, screen-printed. KnollTextiles Archive, donated by Doreen Rose Stempien.

Fig. 3.42 Top left Albert Herbert. *Diamonds* ("Yellow and Citron" colorway), with small colorway swatches attached, introduced 1951, this example ca. 1954. Made for Knoll Textiles. Used for drapery; linen; plain weave, screen-printed. Cooper-Hewitt, National Design Museum, Smithsonian Institution, Gift of Mae Festa, 1991-157-3-a. Cat. 56.
Fig. 3.44 Top right Inge Toft. *Kon-Tiki* sample ("White on Bachelor Blue" colorway), with small colorway swatches attached, ca. 1954. Made by L. F. Foght for Knoll Textiles. Used for drapery; cotton; plain weave, screen-printed. Cooper-Hewitt, National Design Museum, Smithsonian Institution, Gift of Mae Festa, 1991-157-2-a. Cat. 63.
Fig. 3.43 Bottom Paule Vézelay. *Sequence* sample ("Yellow & Black" colorway), with small colorway samples attached, introduced 1950, this example ca. 1951–55. Made for Knoll Textiles. Used for drapery; cotton; plain weave, screen-printed. Private collection. Cat. 55.

Hans Knoll asked her to develop a design; it was then turned over to Haraszty in the textile division to put into production (see fig. B.29).[98] Albert Herbert, who was a member of the Knoll Planning Unit and later designed a number of geometric prints for other manufacturers, created *Diamonds*, introduced in 1951 (fig. 3.42). In keeping with Knoll's widely promoted "International Designer" collection, press releases usually noted the home country of each designer along with his or her name. International designers for its print collection included Paule Vézelay, an Englishwoman working in Paris, who designed *Sequence* (1950) (see figs. 3.43 and 4.46) and later did similar textiles for Heals in London. Inge Toft, the Danish designer of *Kon Tiki* (1954), printed her own textiles under the name Ingetoft and worked for the manufacturer L. F. Foght of Denmark (fig. 3.44).[99] Colcombet, listed as the creator of *Sparklers* (1953), was actually a French textile manufacturer specializing in fashion fabrics (see fig. B.28 and cat. 60).

In 1953 two important new patterns by Swedish designers were added to the print collection: Astrid Sampe's *Lazy Lines* (fig. 3.45) and Sven Markelius's *Pythagoras* (fig. 3.46).[100] *Lazy Lines* was printed by Knoll in the United States, but *Pythagoras* was always printed in Sweden for NK (Knoll's supplier) by Ljungbergs, probably because of the complexity of the pattern.[101] *Pythagoras* was originally designed in 1952 as a theater curtain for the Trade Union Center in Linköping, Sweden (see fig. B.89), and was used in the Economic and Social Chamber (ECOSOC) at the United Nations before Knoll put it into the line. Both patterns were selected by MoMA for *Good Design* exhibitions. *Prisma* (fig. 3.47), another pattern by Markelius, was introduced by Knoll in 1956, winning the First Award for Printed Fabrics in the AID Home Furnishings Design Competition in 1957.[102] It was initially available on linen, imported from Sweden, but in late 1957 Knoll began to print it in the United States on fiberglass and in two new colors, orange and turquoise. The fiberglass version was discontinued in 1959 because on this base fabric it was difficult to achieve the exact registration the pattern required. The printing of the linen version was apparently taken over at this time by the American printer Winston Prints.[103]

New Upholsteries

Eszter Haraszty had no experience in making or designing woven textiles when she began at Knoll. Nevertheless, her design skills and color sense were immediately put to use in developing new upholstery fabrics. Her lack of experience may even have been an asset, as Suzanne Huguenin, who was hired as Haraszty's assistant in 1952, later recalled: "In the beginning we were in many ways ignorant about how to run a department, or what to do about certain fabrics. Particularly in the textile department, we were almost amateurs, but that was probably the charm. It was probably also the reason why it became an exciting line, because we were not burdened by technicalities."[104] Many former employees have cited the unusual level of freedom that Hans Knoll gave to designers—both to learn on the job and to develop designs on their own terms and schedules. He placed priority on the quality of the final product, trusting his designers, and this was a key factor in the company's early success.[105]

A new line of heavyweight linen upholstery fabric, called *Scotch Linen* (1950), was one of the first fabrics developed at Knoll after Haraszty became head of the textile division (fig. 3.48).[106] The manufacturer was Donald Brothers Ltd. of Dundee, Scotland, a small firm that had long specialized in high-quality linen furnishing fabrics.[107] Haraszty's lack of technical knowledge required working with mills such as Donald Brothers that understood Knoll's priorities and collaborating closely with these mills. She later remembered that most of her work on woven fabrics was done on-site at the mills because Hans Knoll believed in sending designers to work with manufacturers and "was willing to spend the money and my time" in developing new fabrics. She "spent a lot of time in Scotland developing fabrics" at one mill in particular, probably Donald Brothers.[108]

The Swiss weaver Franz Lorenz is credited with the design of *Scotch Linen*, which came in a wide range of two- and three-tone checks and plaids in clear, coordinated colors.[109] Featured in the 1951 *Good Design* exhibition, its crisp appearance was especially suited to Florence Knoll's clean-lined seating designs, and it was used in many of her Planning Unit interiors. During the early 1950s, it was one of Knoll's most popular fabrics and remained in the line until 1966, even though the demand for linen upholstery fabrics had declined in the late 1950s.[110]

Another of Haraszty's early projects, which she later called her "greatest design success," was *Transportation Cloth* (fig. 3.49).[111] It was developed in 1949 and 1950, to be used as upholstery in Saarinen's General Motors Technical Center office installations, and was officially introduced into the Knoll collection in 1951 when the firm opened the showroom at 575 Madison Avenue.[112] *Transportation Cloth* was made with a new Avisco rayon yarn made by the American Viscose Company and was woven for Knoll by Louisville Textiles. The combination of the yarn's strength with the weave structure (paired warps tightly covering a slightly thicker weft) made this fabric highly resistant to abrasion and therefore eminently suited to withstand heavy-duty wear. Haraszty recalled it as "the first industrial fabric—the first one that stood all the tests."[113] Even the fabric's name, thought to have been suggested by Hans Knoll, evoked the strong, durable nature of the upholsteries used in railroad cars or airplanes (see fig. C.4) and became a generic term for this kind of upholstery fabric.[114] In its two-color version, the impression of strength conveyed by the

Fig. 3.45 Astrid Sampe. *Lazy Lines* ("Orange, Ochre, Yellow on White" colorway), introduced 1953, this example ca. 1955. Made by Stonehenge Processing for Knoll Textiles. Used for drapery; linen; plain weave, screen-printed. The Museum of Modern Art, New York, Gift of Knoll Associates, SC18.1975. Cat. 57.

Fig. 3.46 Sven Markelius. *Pythagoras* ("Spectrum Red" colorway), introduced in the United States 1953, this example ca. 1956. Made by Ljungbergs Textiltryck for Knoll Textiles. Used for drapery; linen, cotton; plain weave, screen-printed. Cooper-Hewitt, National Design Museum, Smithsonian Institution, 1956-123-1. Cat. 58.

Fig. 3.47 Sven Markelius. *Prisma* ("Blue" colorway), ca. 1956. Made by Ljungbergs Textiltryck for Knoll Textiles. Used for drapery; linen; plain weave, screen-printed. Cooper-Hewitt, National Design Museum, Smithsonian Institution, Gift of Mae Festa, 1991-157-1-b. Cat. 121.

Fig. 3.48 Franz Lorenz. *Scotch Linen* samples, introduced 1950, these examples 1955–60. Made by Donald Brothers for Knoll Textiles. Used for upholstery; linen; plain weave. KnollTextiles Archive.

Fig. 3.49 Top Eszter Haraszty. *Transportation Cloth* samples, introduced 1950, these examples ca. 1955. Made by Louisville Textiles for Knoll Textiles. Used for upholstery; Avisco rayon; plain weave. From page featuring *Transportation Cloth* in a portfolio compiled by Eszter Haraszty; the samples in the top row were mounted with the warps running horizontally. The Montreal Museum of Fine Arts, Liliane and David M. Stewart Collection, Gift of the American Friends of Canada through the generosity of Eszter Haraszty, D88.178.2.8v.

Fig. 3.50 Bottom Eszter Haraszty. *Nylon Transportation Cloth*, on *Womb* chair and ottoman designed by Eero Saarinen, ca. 1965. Made by Orinoka Mills for Knoll Textiles, chair and ottoman made by Knoll Associates. Upholstery: rayon, nylon; plain weave; chair and ottoman: tubular steel, foam rubber over molded fiberglass platform. Cranbrook Art Museum, Bloomfield Hills, Mich., Gift of Glen Paulsen, CAM 1998.12. Cat. 45.

tightly packed warps is accentuated by the addition of irregularly spaced warps in a contrasting color, creating subtle vertical streaks.

Featured in the 1951 *Good Design* exhibition, *Transportation Cloth* sold very well. Despite its reputation for durability, the original Avisco rayon was highly susceptible to soiling and sun damage, which could cause the fabric to weaken and split. In response to complaints from Knoll and its customers, American Viscose developed an improved yarn in 1956.[115] In 1959 Knoll introduced an enhanced version with a nylon warp and a name to reflect this change (*Nylon Transportation Cloth*, fig. 3.50), which remained in production until 1979.

Evelyn Hill Handwovens

By about 1951 Marianne Strengell was no longer involved in designing handwovens for Knoll, possibly because she had received a major new commission to create textiles for Saarinen's General Motors Technical Center.[116] Perhaps with the idea of finding a replacement for Strengell's contributions, Haraszty hired the designer and weaver Evelyn Hill (fig. 3.51) to create a new series of handwoven fabrics for Knoll. The firm had been commissioned to provide special luxury fabrics for a house that Edward Larrabee Barnes was designing for the Weiner family in Fort Worth, Texas, and Hill's initial assignment was probably to work on them.[117] Knoll established a weaving studio for Hill (which Haraszty later called the "weaving department") in their Long Island City warehouse. There Hill (and possibly other weavers) made the textiles for the Barnes house and worked on developing ideas for new designs.[118] By March 1952 Hill had developed a line of over fifty handwoven designs available by special order, in brilliant colors coordinated by Haraszty (fig. 3.52).[119] The line was presented at the AID national conference in New York in a dramatic display (fig. 3.53) designed by Haraszty and Herbert Matter. Featuring a continuous ribbon of fabric moving through a stark, white-walled space, it was described in the *New York Times* as a "modern maze of handwoven textiles . . . brilliantly exciting in color and depth, with orange, purple, chartreuse and deep blue-greens clashing in a heady fashion."[120] Working with Rancocas Fabrics of Burlington, New Jersey, Knoll put a coordinated group of these handwovens into production in larger quantities, under the shared name *Handwoven*, with each design further identified by its pattern number (*H900–H950*). A second, all-wool series, *H960–H978*, was added in 1955; these were relatively simple in structure and available in a range of carefully coordinated solids and stripes (fig. 3.54). A final addition to the line, in 1957, was *H980*, a wool and rayon design similar to *H930*.

Hill had studied design and weaving in Texas and New Mexico, as well as at Black Mountain College in North Carolina; she had also studied architecture at the Institute of Design in Chicago. While in Chicago she worked for the weaver Majel Chance and became interested in textiles and their relationship to architecture.[121] Her designs for Knoll are remarkable for the unusual combinations of materials and the assured manner with which she juxtaposed different textures, colors, and scales. A single fabric might include plastic, rayon, silk, mohair, fiberglass, and horsehair, as in *K28-H*, and thick colored wool wefts might be contrasted with shiny black plastic warps, as in *H920* (fig. 3.55). Her juxtapositions of different yarns recalled the work of Strengell, although Hill sometimes created such extreme contrasts between warp and weft that the finished fabric had a tendency to fall apart when cut.[122] Her designs were also remarkable for their use of color, which she developed with Haraszty, ranging from brilliant colors juxtaposed with black to subtle compositions of tans and grays.[123] Some Hill *Handwovens*, such as *H910* (fig. 3.56), appear surprisingly complex and "busy," but Florence Knoll seems to have appreciated the presence and texture they could bring to upholstered furniture such as her *Parallel Bar* seating, and the Knoll Planning Unit regularly specified their use.[124]

Rancocas Fabrics, the mill that wove the two series of Hill *Handwovens*, likely also played an active role in their development. The owner Norman Loring had an excellent color sense and often combined colors to achieve "most unusual results"—which would have made him an ideal collaborator for Hill and Haraszty.[125] Jack Lenor Larsen, whose company later purchased Rancocas Fabrics, recalled that the mill had a "curious device" for combining two bobbins in a shuttle, which made it easier to run two weft yarns together in a shed (the opening created on a loom when some warps are raised) without twisting, as in *H930* (see cats. 100-102).[126] Hill used this technique in her designs in a variety of ways, sometimes running together two tones of the same color to produce a subtle shading effect, and sometimes creating striated patterns by twisting the yarns around each other. Using the latter technique—loosely twisting together one black and two colored yarns in one shed—Hill created the flamelike pattern of *Kerry Linen* (1953) (fig. 3.57). This fabric was adapted from a handwoven sample by Hill (possibly an upholstery fabric designed for the Barnes house) and was woven by Donald Brothers in Scotland. *Highland Tweed* and *Highland Stripes* (both 1956) (see fig. B.120), while not credited to Hill, were variations developed with Donald Brothers using the same yarns and construction as *Kerry Linen*.[127] Hill (under her married name, Evelyn Hill Anselevicius) later designed two other machine-woven upholsteries for Knoll, *Rover* and *Tara* (1963), which were likely adapted from her previous handwoven work.[128] Another Hill design incorporating Saran fiber, called *Synthesis* (1953), is known only from printed sources.[129]

Making Knoll Textiles: Integrated Fabrics for Modern Interiors, 1945–65

Fig. 3.51 Evelyn Hill in her weaving studio, Knoll warehouse, Long Island City, N.Y., 1952. Photographed by Erich Hartmann. Magnum Photos.

Fig. 3.52 Evelyn Hill Anselevicius. *Handwoven* samples, ca. 1952. Used for upholstery; various materials including wool, rayon gimp, plastic, nylon, and chenille. Philadelphia Museum of Art, CTK 23. Cat. 75.

Fig. 3.53 Herbert Matter and Eszter Haraszty. Knoll installation, national conference of the American Institute of Decorators, Waldorf-Astoria Hotel, New York, 1952. Herbert Matter papers, M1446. Dept. of Special Collections, Stanford University Libraries, Stanford, Calif.

Fig. 3.54 Evelyn Hill Anselevicius. *Handwoven H971* ("Chinese Red, Persimmon, and Shocking Pink Stripes" colorway), ca. 1955. Made by Rancocas Fabrics for Knoll Textiles. Used for upholstery; wool; basket weave. Courtesy Richard and Trudy Schultz. Cat. 88.

Fig. 3.55 Evelyn Hill Anselevicius. Detail of *Handwoven H920* ("Black with Yellow" colorway), ca. 1952. Made by Rancocas Fabrics for Knoll Textiles. Used for upholstery; wool, plastic; basket weave. Courtesy Richard and Trudy Schultz. Cat. 84.

Fig. 3.56 Evelyn Hill Anselevicius. *Handwoven H910/1* ("Natural, White with Black" colorway) and *H910/2* ("Natural, Black with White" colorway), ca. 1952. Made by Rancocas Fabrics for Knoll Textiles. Used for upholstery; wool, jute, plastic; plain weave with alternating single and paired wefts. Courtesy Richard and Trudy Schultz. Cats. 85, 86.

Fig. 3.57 Evelyn Hill Anselevicius. *Kerry Linen* ("Persimmon and Black" colorway), ca. 1953. Made by Donald Brothers for Knoll Textiles. Used for upholstery; linen, cotton; plain weave. Philadelphia Museum of Art, CTK5.

A Complete Textile Line

Through the 1950s, the number of Planning Unit commissions and large contract orders increased, requiring Knoll to diversify its textile collection to meet the needs of a variety of customers and budgets. There was also a marked increase in the company's emphasis on performance testing, quality control, and finishing processes that were meant to protect fabrics and make them easier to care for, reflecting a growing trend within the textile industry. These processes included latex backing for upholstery, Mitin (a moth-proofing agent added to wool fibers), and protective finishes such as Scotchgard (introduced in 1956). Several options for flame proofing, mildew proofing, and making fabrics water-repellent were available for an additional cost by the early 1950s, and, from 1954 to 1958, Knoll promoted K-Plus, a Dow Corning silicone finish (sylmerizing), which offered greater spot and stain resistance.[130] Two fabrics insulated with Milium, a heat-reflecting aluminum coating developed by Deering Milliken Company, were introduced in 1954. *Fresco Milium*, a cotton percale in bright colors, was intended as an inexpensive drapery fabric or an insulated lining for more expensive drapery fabrics, and a version of *Triad* was printed on a Milium-insulated base fabric (see fig. C.8 and cat. 66) and described as "a print with its own lining."[131]

In the mid-1950s, with the increased demand for elegant upholstery and seating and as advances in fiber-blending technology made wool more durable, Knoll launched *Rugby* (fig. 3.58 and see fig. B.113). Its design came of necessity. The Knoll Planning Unit was working on the furnishings for the American Embassy in Stockholm and had intended to use *Transportation Cloth*, but the Swedish mill that was to weave it was unable to obtain the special rayon yarn required. Searching for a substitute, Florence Knoll and Astrid Sampe adapted a Swedish railroad upholstery which became *Rugby*. With its rich appearance and two-tone coloring, *Rugby* became a signature fabric for Knoll, the first to bridge the gap between luxury and high performance. The American version introduced in 1954, woven by Orinoka Mills and intended to be a more elegant and higher-priced *Transportation Cloth*, was made from wool and nylon with a double warp for increased durability.[132]

Also woven by Orinoka was *Lana* (1956), an all-wool fabric originally intended for use on Bertoia chairs—it was essentially a more luxurious version of *Prestini* (fig. 3.59).[133] As with *Prestini*, the pattern was formed by using two colors in the warp and one in the weft, but the worsted yarn gave *Lana* a smooth surface and an even, gridded appearance, especially when the second warp color (the "dots" of the pattern) was darker than the other yarns. *Lana* quickly became a popular fabric. Because it was too soft for some applications, a stronger and slightly heavier version in a wool/nylon blend was introduced in 1959. Although Knoll raised the price by $2.00 per yard, the new *Lana* was more popular than its predecessor and remained in the collection until 1978.[134]

Knoll also continued to work with manufacturers on the development of new materials, introducing an all-Saran upholstery fabric, *Sarano* (see cat. 142), developed with Dow Chemical in 1956, and sheer drapery fabrics made of a variety of synthetic yarns, including Fortisan—a yarn developed by the American Viscose Company, with strong resistance to sun damage—and various combinations of Dacron (polyester), Saran, and nylon. Prints on fiberglass, which was both durable and fireproof, were so popular in the late 1950s that a separate section of the textile price lists was devoted to them in 1957. In the same year Knoll announced the introduction of fiberglass dyed in a range of exclusive brilliant colors.[135] Knoll kept up with the latest industrial developments and was frequently one of the first companies to adopt a new fiber as it became available. This gave Knoll a reputation for innovation but could also cause problems when untested materials were used. *Sarano*, for example, was one of the first all-plastic fabrics to achieve a "homespun" look. Popular at first, it also had recurring problems with unevenly spun yarns that caused frequent and lengthy production delays.[136] When such problems occurred, Suzanne Huguenin was always "very candid" with Knoll's sales staff and customers. She recalled a speech she gave to a group of architects about a promising Saran casement that had developed unexpected problems: "I told the architects, 'Things like this do happen if you work with new fibers. It does not mean that Knoll has supplied you with a bad product. This is all in the experimental stage.' This the architects got interested in, and didn't forget."[137]

Naugahyde, a vinyl-coated fabric originally added to the collection in 1954, was not exclusive to Knoll, but Knoll worked with the manufacturer, U.S. Rubber, to improve its looks and performance and to develop exclusive colors and qualities. Together they originated brightly colored Naugahyde (initially to match the plastic backs of Saarinen *Model 72* side chairs) as well as Naugahyde with plain embossing, introduced in 1955, as an alternative to the conventional faux leather texture.[138] They called this *Elastic Naugahyde*, and two years later presented *Breathing Naugahyde*, a coordinated variation featuring colored vinyl stripes on a white cotton twill ground (fig. 3.60) that had the added advantage of "breathability," meaning that it was less hot to sit on.[139] A 1958 variation, *Knoll Vinyl Cord* (1958), was a German import with fine ribs resembling corduroy. Knoll was also first to introduce a special "extra dull" finish in 1960, the same year they introduced their last vinyl fabric during this period, *Brigadoon* (fig. 3.61), designed by Huguenin and developed for Knoll by DuPont in 1960. It had an unusual texture, made by first printing with the base color, then embossing with a pattern of vinyl dots (meant to reproduce

Fig. 3.59 Eszter Haraszty. *Lana* ("Persimmon" colorway) on *Model 31* chair designed by Florence Knoll, ca. 1956. Upholstery made by Orinoka Mills for Knoll Textiles, chair made by Knoll Associates. Upholstery: wool, nylon; basket weave; chair: chrome-plated steel, foam rubber. Brooklyn Museum, Gift of Liliane M. Stewart, 2002.70.1. Cat. 118.

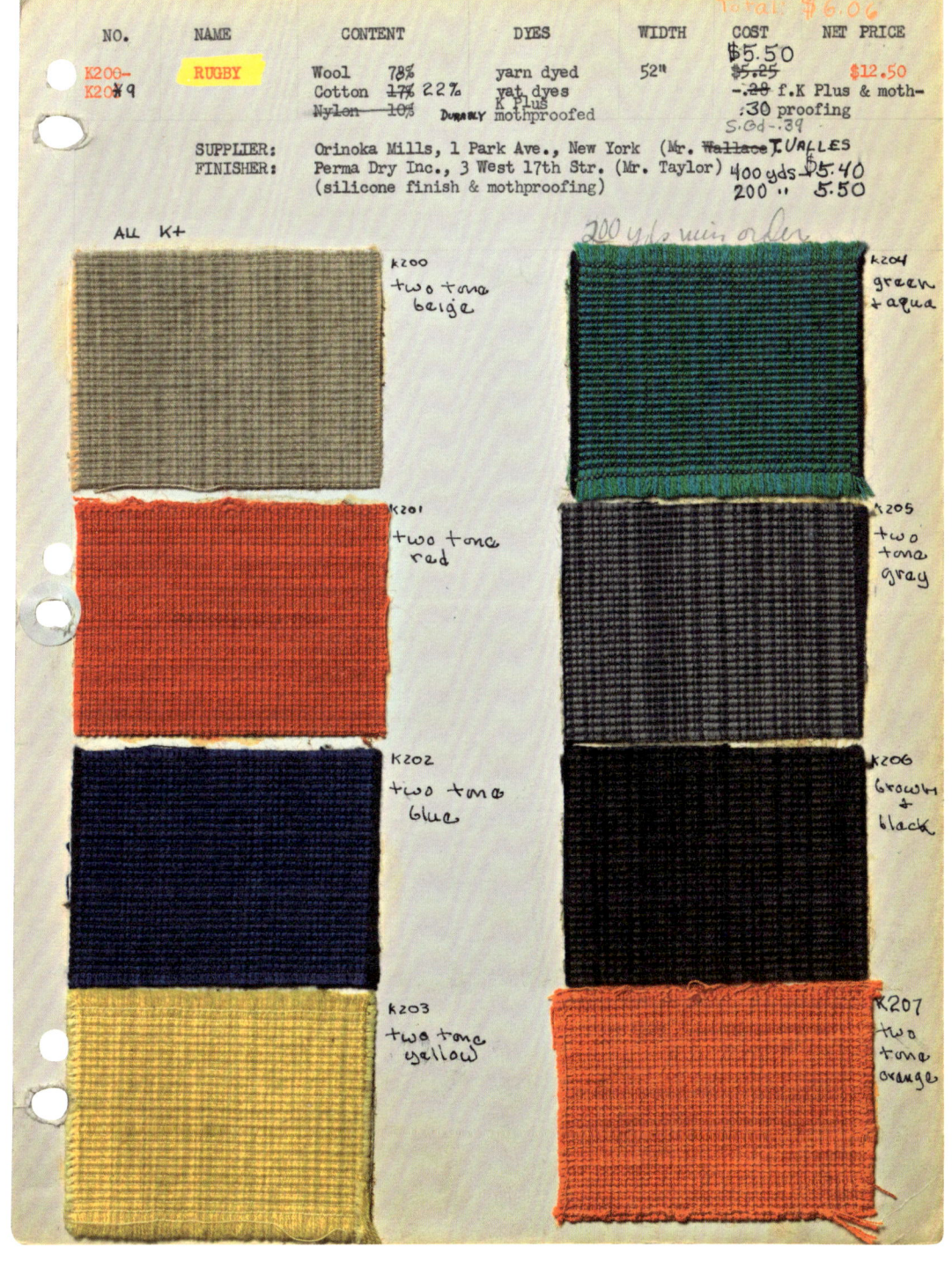

Fig. 3.58 Astrid Sampe. *Rugby* data page with 8 colorways attached, ca. 1955. Samples made by Orinoka Mills for Knoll Textiles. Textile samples: cotton, wool, nylon; basket weave; mounted on paper. KnollTextiles Archive. Cat. 107.

Fig. 3.60 Advertisement for Knoll Associates and Knoll Textiles showing *Elastic Naugahyde* and *Breathing Naugahyde*, designed by Herbert Matter. From *Interiors*, June 1957.

Fig. 3.61 Suzanne Huguenin. *Brigadoon* ("Black and White" colorway), on *Model 72P* side chair designed by Eero Saarinen, ca. 1965. Made by E. I. Du Pont de Nemours & Co. for Knoll Textiles, chair made by Knoll Associates. Upholstery: vinyl on cotton knit backing; chair: fiberglass shell, metal legs, foam rubber. Knoll Museum, East Greenville, Penn. Cat. 153.

the surface texture of Knoll's *Scotch Linen*) and running the material twice through a perforating machine to add tiny air holes.[140] All of these vinyl fabrics were popular choices for the Saarinen side chairs, and *Elastic Naugahyde* and *Brigadoon* became standard for the seat pads and seat covers of Bertoia chairs.

The mid-1950s also saw the introduction of the first of the Knoll "budget" fabrics.[141] The rationale for offering less-expensive options within the Knoll line was to reduce the number of budget-minded customers specifying another company's fabric ("C.O.M."—customer's own material) for a piece of Knoll furniture.[142] The first two budget fabrics were *Chico* (1953) and *Merit* (1955), both woven by Louisville Textiles. *Merit*, the more successful of the two, was designed by Eszter Haraszty and had a slightly patterned weave, but was changed to a plain-weave fabric in December 1957, partly because the fabric had been copied by several other mills at a lower price (fig. 3.62).[143] A third, slightly more durable budget fabric, *Domus*, was issued in 1958, designated "for those jobs where Merit (woven with a black warp and colored weft) is not colorful enough."[144]

During this period Knoll developed lighter-weight, inexpensive, multipurpose fabrics appropriate for a range of uses—as upholstery, draperies, slipcovers, or bedspreads. Like the budget fabrics, these designs met the needs of the Planning Unit and helped discourage customers from specifying other suppliers' textiles. Imported from Holland and introduced in 1953, *Dobby* (see fig. B.50) was a warp-faced cotton plain weave—with a "shot" effect (warps and wefts of contrasting colors) in some colorways—and *Ombré* (1955), a blend of wool, cotton, jute, and viscose (a kind of rayon), had a similar shot effect and irregular surface texture, but it sold poorly, mainly because many customers found it too scratchy.[145]

Spectra and *Spectra Magna* (both 1955) were among the few Knoll textiles from this period with woven patterns (fig. 3.63 and cats. 114 and 115). Unlike Herman Miller, for which Alexander Girard regularly designed small woven patterns for upholstery fabrics, Knoll continued to favor texture over pattern. Both fabrics were designed by Haraszty as a checkerboard of three closely related tones and two alternating woven surfaces, giving the effect of six colors. They were woven by Orinoka Mills, the same mill responsible for *Lana* and *Rugby* as well as a number of Girard's woven patterns for Herman Miller.[146]

Transitions

The death of Hans Knoll in October 1955 followed by the departure of Eszter Haraszty shortly thereafter occurred just as the furnishing and textile industries were shifting their focus more and more to the contract market. With Florence Knoll, head of the Planning Unit (which had been partly responsible for stimulating the growth of the contract market), now sole head of the company, Knoll was ideally positioned for further growth. Knoll Textiles increasingly featured fabrics appropriate for large modernist office and institutional installations—designs that would function well as part of an overall coordinated Planning Unit scheme. They fit the somewhat conservative taste of many contract clients, while also offering sufficient variations of color, texture, and pattern (stripes and plaids) to avoid monotony when used on a grand scale.

After Hans's death, Knoll needed to reassure the market that the company would continue, even stronger than before, under Florence Knoll's leadership.[147] In 1956 *American Fabrics* magazine devoted a special issue to the *Textiles USA* exhibition at MoMA, profiling leading designers and companies, focusing on their philosophies when choosing or designing textiles. In writing about Knoll, however, they concentrated on Florence Knoll and the Planning Unit, describing the company as one that had pioneered collaboration with designers and had sought to use the newest materials and methods. There was no specific discussion of the design of the textile featured, *Sarano*, which was shown as part of the Knoll Planning Unit's design for Dow Chemical's executive offices (see fig. 4.13).[148] This kind of coverage perhaps reflected the firm's new market strategy, one directed primarily to contract clients.

Suzanne Huguenin (fig. 3.64) succeeded Haraszty as the head of Knoll Textiles in 1955 and led the division through the changing market conditions of the late 1950s and early 1960s. She had joined Knoll as Haraszty's assistant in 1952 and learned the textile business on the job, seeing to the practical details of running the department while studying textiles at night at New York University. As she later said, "I think the fact that I came from no background at all directly to Knoll, and was only exposed to good design in furniture and to excellence in fabric, could have been much better than any schooling. I never had to make any mistakes, style-wise."[149] Huguenin was an exceptionally capable administrator who paid great attention to detail—important qualifications as the development of new fabrics became more and more reliant on scientific and industrial processes.

As head of Knoll Textiles, Huguenin worked directly with mills to develop new fabrics and to improve the performance characteristics of existing designs. She also spent much of her time visiting Knoll showrooms around the country and the world—promoting the collection, training sales staff, and listening to the comments and complaints of sales staff and customers.[150] By the late 1950s, she had developed a thorough understanding of the textile industry and market and Knoll's place in it. Under her direction, Knoll textiles truly were "planned for specific roles to meet specific needs," both within particular interior projects and in the textile market in general.[151]

Fig. 3.62 Top Eszter Haraszty. *Merit* (original weave, "Blue and Black" colorway) with two *Merit* swatches (revised weave), ca. 1955 and 1960. Used for upholstery; rayon, cotton; original: plain weave with alternating paired and grouped (6 yarn) warps; revised: plain weave. Made by Louisville Textiles for Knoll Textiles. Courtesy Richard and Trudy Schultz.

Fig. 3.63 Bottom Eszter Haraszty. *Spectra* sample ("Turquoise and Green" colorway, with small colorway swatches attached), introduced 1956, this example ca. 1958. Made by Orinoka Mills for Knoll Textiles. Used for upholstery; linen, cotton; twill variation. KnollTextiles Archive, donated by Doreen Rose Stempien. Cat. 113.

Fig. 3.64 Left Suzanne Huguenin in her Greenwich Village apartment and studio, ca. 1960. Courtesy of Christine Laubi.

Fig. 3.65 Right Emily Belding. Detail of *Shades and Tints* ("Brown" colorway), ca. 1954. Made for Habitat Associates. Used for drapery; ramie; plain weave. The Museum of Modern Art, New York, Gift of Habitat Associates, SC52.1975.1. Cat. 123.

New Fabrics for New Requirements

During the mid-1950s, Knoll's collection of curtain and casement fabrics—lighter-weight fabrics that could form a second layer behind heavier "draperies"—expanded considerably. Casement fabrics (open-weave, sheer, or semisheer fabrics that filtered light without blocking it) had grown in importance as glass-walled office buildings proliferated. In 1954 there were only five plain curtain fabrics, including casements, in the Knoll collection, but by 1957 there were sixteen, and "Sheers and Casements" had their own section in the Knoll price list. Most of the new casement fabrics added during this time were plain weaves, with little variation in structure but considerable variation in materials. In addition to synthetics, new natural-fiber fabrics were added, including an imported *Linen Casement* from Belgium and a new handwoven Indian silk.

Toward the end of the decade, Knoll also began to widen the choice of casement fabrics to include some with bolder texture and structural interest appropriate for use along large window walls. As part of this effort, and perhaps to revive the idea of the "designer collection," Florence Knoll and Huguenin brought in some well-known freelance handweavers and designers, and by the early 1960s they had greatly expanded the range of the casement collection. The first casement fabric from a freelance designer was the 1956 introduction *Shades* (fig. 3.65), a black-and-white striped design by Emily Belding that had been a *Good Design* exhibition selection in 1955 (originally produced for another New York firm, Habitat). The first casement on the market made entirely of ramie (a vegetable fiber), *Shades* was strong and resistant to sunlight but sold very poorly, largely because clients were hesitant to specify such an unfamiliar material.[152] More successful additions were a loosely woven *Wool Casement* (1957), designed by Evelyn Hill and originally developed for the Planning Unit,[153] and *Trellis* (1957), an open-weave linen casement, designed by Ruben Eshkanian and developed for installations where window air conditioners required an open fabric and where *Fishnet* was not sufficiently elegant (fig. 3.66).[154]

In 1957 weaver and designer Anni Albers agreed to consult with Knoll on the development of new textiles on a royalty basis, the first of which, *Fiberglas Casement*, was launched in December 1957 (fig. 3.67).[155] This fabric was a leno weave (a weave in which warps cross over each other diagonally and lock in wefts) in the new textured fiberglass Aerocor yarn and was included in a publicity campaign by Owens-Corning, the manufacturer of the yarn.[156] Aerocor turned out to have very low resistance to abrasion, however, with the result that the movement of draperies back and forth across a windowsill caused the yarn to break.[157] After considerable experimentation with Owens Corning and Original Textile (the manufacturer of the fabric), Knoll introduced an improved version in July 1959, but continuing problems with quality control led them to discontinue the fabric six months later.[158] Three linen casements that Albers designed for Knoll, *Lattice* introduced in 1959 (fig. 3.68), *Rail* introduced in 1962 (fig. 3.69), and *Track* introduced in 1965 (see fig. B.5), were much more successful, and all remained in the collection until 1978, earning regular royalties for Albers.[159] *Lattice* and *Track* were similar in structure to *Fiberglas Casement* but with different spacing and yarn thicknesses; *Rail* was made of a heavier linen yarn and given added strength and visual interest by spacing the twisted warp pairs close together in groups of three.

The new natural fiber casements Knoll added in the late 1950s and early 1960s were mostly imported from European mills. Several of the linen casements, including *Trellis*, *Lattice*, and two 1959 introductions, *Breeze* (a plain cotton and linen sheer) and *Goatshair Casement* (goat hair and linen), came from Belgium.[160] Albers's *Rail* and *Track* were manufactured in Italy, and *Nimbus* (1960) and *Kinna* (1961), both of wool and viscose, in Sweden. Peter Simpson, then the design director for Donald Brothers (the weavers of *Scotch Linen* and *Kerry Linen*), contributed *Scotch Mist*, a loosely woven casement of slub wool and linen yarns (fig. 3.70), in 1962 (a slub yarn has an uneven thickness). Donald Brothers was also the source for *Tracey* (1961) and possibly *Cirrus* (1963).[161] These casements introduced more texture and variety in fiber into the Knoll collection, but their structures—all variations on a rectilinear grid, in the same manner as Knoll's classic *Fishnet*—remained fairly homogenous. Although many other designers and firms, such as Jack Lenor Larsen and Isabel Scott, had introduced casements with unusual structures beginning in the early 1950s, Knoll's collection did not include this kind of "architectural" casement until 1964.[162]

In early 1958, just after issuing the first Anni Albers casement at the end of 1957, Knoll also launched *Mira* (see fig. B.83), the first of a series of new drapery prints by Ross Littell, a furniture and textile designer who had created prints for Laverne Originals. A year later he contributed four more designs to the Knoll line: *Chess* (see fig. B.85), *Discs* (see fig. B.84), *Spheres* (fig. 3.71), and *Criss-Cross* (fig. 3.72), the last of which won a citation of merit from AID in 1960.[163] Littell's prints were bolder than what Knoll had sold previously, with strong positive-negative contrasts and pronounced geometric patterns that could be read from a distance. As with the casement fabrics, they worked well with long window walls, on which smaller and more delicate patterns might be "lost." Knoll may also have been reacting to the success of Girard's bold designs for Herman Miller, such as *Quatrefoil* (1954) and *Feathers* (1957; see fig. 1.25). While the colorways for the Littell prints were coordinated with the existing Knoll palette, they also reflected

Fig. 3.66 **Top left** Ruben Eshkanian. Detail of *Trellis* ("White" colorway), introduced 1957, this example ca. 1960. Made in Belgium, supplied through Joynel, for Knoll Textiles. Used for drapery; linen; plain-weave–derived simple weave. Courtesy Ruben Eshkanian. Cat.124.
Fig. 3.67 **Top right** Anni Albers. Detail of *Fiberglas Casement* sample ("White" colorway), ca. 1958. Made by Original Textile Company for Knoll Textiles. Used for drapery; fiberglass; plain gauze (leno) weave. The Museum of Modern Art, New York, Gift of Josef Albers, 450.1970.90. Cat. 126.

Fig. 3.68 **Bottom left** Anni Albers. Detail of *Lattice* swatch ("Oatmeal" colorway), ca. 1975. Made in Belgium, supplied through Joynel, for Knoll Textiles. Used for drapery; linen; plain gauze (leno) weave. KnollTextiles Archive. Cat. 130.
Fig. 3.70 **Bottom right** Peter Simpson. Detail of *Scotch Mist* ("Off-White" colorway), introduced 1962, this example ca. 1970. Made by Donald Brothers for Knoll Textiles. Used for drapery; wool, linen; plain weave. University of Alberta Clothing and Textiles Collection, 1990.65.23. Cat. 125.

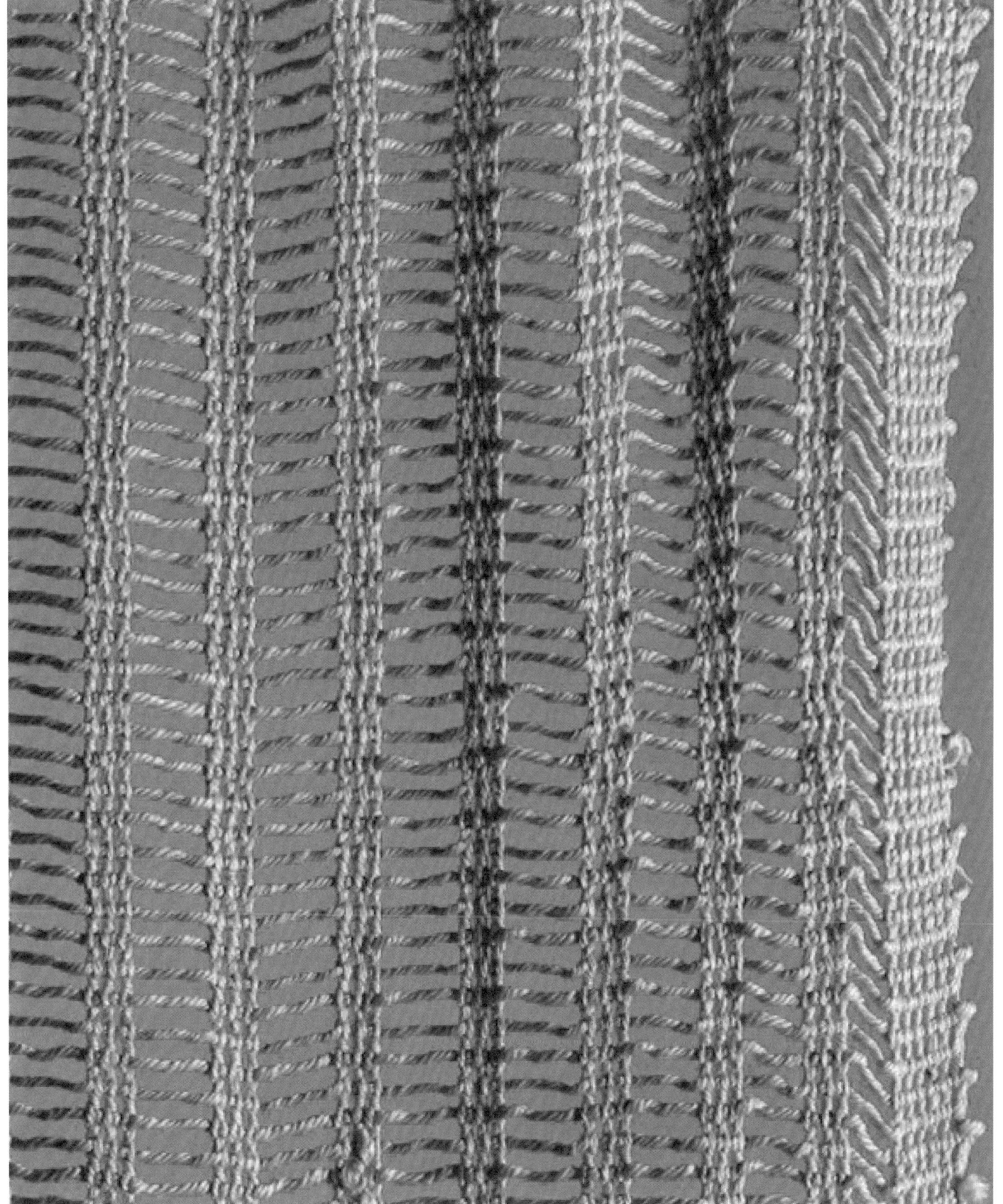

Fig. 3.69 Anni Albers. Detail of *Rail* ("Natural" colorway), ca. 1962.
Made by Testori for Knoll Textiles. Used for drapery; linen; plain gauze (leno) weave.
Courtesy Richard and Trudy Schultz. Cat. 128.

Fig. 3.71 Ross Littell. *Spheres* ("Black on Natural" and "Red and Orange on Persimmon" colorways), introduced 1959. Made by Winston Prints for Knoll Textiles. Used for drapery; linen, cotton; plain weave, screen-printed. The Montreal Museum of Fine Arts, Liliane and David M. Stewart Collection, Gift of the American Friends of Canada through the generosity of Ben Short, D87.236.1. Cat. 133.

Fig. 3.72 Ross Littell. *Criss-Cross* ("Tan on White" colorway), ca. 1959. Made for Knoll Textiles. Used for drapery; linen; plain weave, screen-printed. The Montreal Museum of Fine Arts, Liliane and David M. Stewart Collection, Gift of the American Friends of Canada through the generosity of Ben Short, D87.121.1.

Fig. 3.73 Suzanne Huguenin. *Peru* curtain with a *Womb* sofa, ca. 1959. Knoll Archives.

Fig. 3.74 Suzanne Huguenin. *Quartet* curtain ("Royal/Sapphire/Sky/Ice Blue" colorway), 1963–78. Made by Winston Prints for Knoll Textiles. Dacron polyester; plain weave, screen-printed. Private collection. Cat. 141.

the new earth tones that had entered into the line in 1958–59, most notably through the introduction of *Nylon Homespun*.[164]

Huguenin also designed several popular geometric and striped prints. *Peru* (1959), a large-scale pattern of alternating stripes and chevrons, was based on an Andean weaving motif and printed by Winston Prints on a heavy, slub linen imported from Belgium (fig. 3.73). *Polystripes* (1959) and *Linea* and *Quartet* (both 1963) were bold but relatively simple patterns of wide vertical stripes (sixteen inches wide for *Polystripes*, and twelve inches for *Quartet*). They depended on color and scale for effect. Printed on Zephyr, a Dacron polyester batiste, *Quartet* (fig. 3.74) became a perennial favorite, remaining in the collection until 1978 and being reissued as part of the *Archival Collection* in 2009. *Linea* (see fig. B.68), with its irregular arrangement of wide earth-toned stripes, offered an updated interpretation of earlier striped prints, such as *Knoll Stripes* and *Triad*. Meanwhile, many of Knoll's older prints—including *Campagna* from the first collection—remained in production, printed on linen, fiberglass, and a variety of new synthetic sheers.

New Upholsteries— Performance and Luxury

When she became head of Knoll Textiles, Suzanne Huguenin made developing new upholstery fabrics one of her main priorities. These fabrics fell largely into two groups, each reflecting general trends in the textile industry (see chapter 1): hard-wearing synthetics, developed by American mills and corporations and cross-promoted with the corporations involved; and new wool upholsteries, sourced and developed in Europe. Rather than introducing large numbers of new designs, Knoll focused on a few particularly promising patterns, refined them through extensive testing, and when they became successful, continued to promote them year after year in a greatly expanded range of colors. This approach yielded high-quality textiles that were soon dubbed "classics" by Knoll while also giving the collection as a whole a fairly conservative air.

Huguenin's greatest success, *Nylon Homespun* (1958), was discovered almost by accident (fig. 3.75). The Moss Rose Manufacturing Company, a Philadelphia mill (see chapter 1), was interested in working with Knoll, but when Huguenin visited them she found nothing of interest, until one of their designers showed her an experimental sample woven with a heavy nylon carpet yarn developed by DuPont (fig. 3.76). She asked the mill not to show it to any of Knoll's competitors and brought the sample to Florence Knoll, who also thought it was "fabulous."[165] The "homespun" look of the fabric came from the yarn, which had a slub texture achieved by spinning new and waste nylon fibers together. Even though *Nylon Homespun* was expensive, owing to the complexity of the spinning process and the cost of newly developed dyes, it was an immediate success, selling over 5,000 yards in its first year.[166] *Nylon Homespun Two-Tone* (fig. 3.77) was added to the collection in 1960, followed by *Nylon Homespun Stripe* (1963) as well as a pinstriped version (1976). In 1964 the name of the fabric was changed to *Knoll Nylon Homespun*, and some time later the yarn was changed to a less slubbed one, resulting in a more uniform appearance.[167] It continued to be one of Knoll's most popular fabrics through the 1980s. Its durability also makes it one of the few upholstery fabrics from this period to have survived in relatively large quantities.

Another important nylon upholstery introduced by Huguenin in 1961 was *Bangkok* (see fig. B.144), designed by Henning Watterston and manufactured by Craftex. It was woven with a warp of Taslan (a textured nylon yarn developed by DuPont in 1957) and a weft of slub spun nylon yarn, giving it an appearance reminiscent of Thai silk shantung.[168] The color palette, with brilliant jewel tones and iridescent "shot" effects, was also borrowed from Thai silks. A coordinating *Bangkok Stripe* was introduced in 1962, and both fabrics were very successful, staying in the line until the 1970s. Another upholstery woven with Taslan yarn was *Polo* (1959), with fine nylon warps on the face, a second "back" warp, and a weft of cotton. It was featured in a DuPont advertising campaign but was not quite as successful as *Bangkok*.[169] *Sahara* (1959) was machine-woven from wool and cotton to imitate the irregularities of a handwoven, hand-spun fabric (fig. 3.78). The apparently irregular surface texture was actually a complex and barely perceptible repeat pattern woven on a Jacquard loom, yielding a durable fabric with the look of handwoven fabrics from Morocco that were popular at the time.[170] It was woven by Orinoka Mills, the same mill that wove *Polo*, *Rugby*, and *Lana*.

When the wool industry in the United States fell into decline in the late 1950s (see chapter 1), Knoll increasingly turned to European mills and designers for other new wool upholsteries, as they did for new linen casements. In 1957 and 1959 they introduced two highly successful European-made upholstery fabrics. *Furrows* (1957) was a reversible fabric of blended wool, cotton, and rayon, made in Belgium (fig. B.67).[171] Like *Rugby*, it combined the look and attractive texture of wool with a high resistance to abrasion, and by 1962 it was already being described as "a Knoll standard fabric [for] such institutions as IBM and General Motors" and was frequently specified for the seats of Saarinen *Model 71* armchairs, combined with leather or Naugahyde for the back.[172] *Skol* (1959), developed in Denmark for Knoll by the C. Olesen company and designed by Vibeke Bruun de Neergaard, was a twill weave with a cotton warp and a wool weft of two closely related colors twisted together, producing a shaded two-tone effect (fig. 3.79).[173] Also an

Fig. 3.76 Advertisement for DuPont promoting *Nylon Homespun*. From *Interior Design*, April 1958.

Fig. 3.77 Suzanne Huguenin. *Knoll Nylon Homespun* ("Two-Tone Black and White" colorway), on *Model 46* chair designed by Max Pearson, ca. 1965. Upholstery made by Moss Rose Manufacturing Co. for Knoll Textiles, chair made by Knoll Associates. Upholstery: nylon; plain weave; chair: cast aluminum, steel, plywood, plastic shell, latex foam rubber. Private collection. Cat. 145.

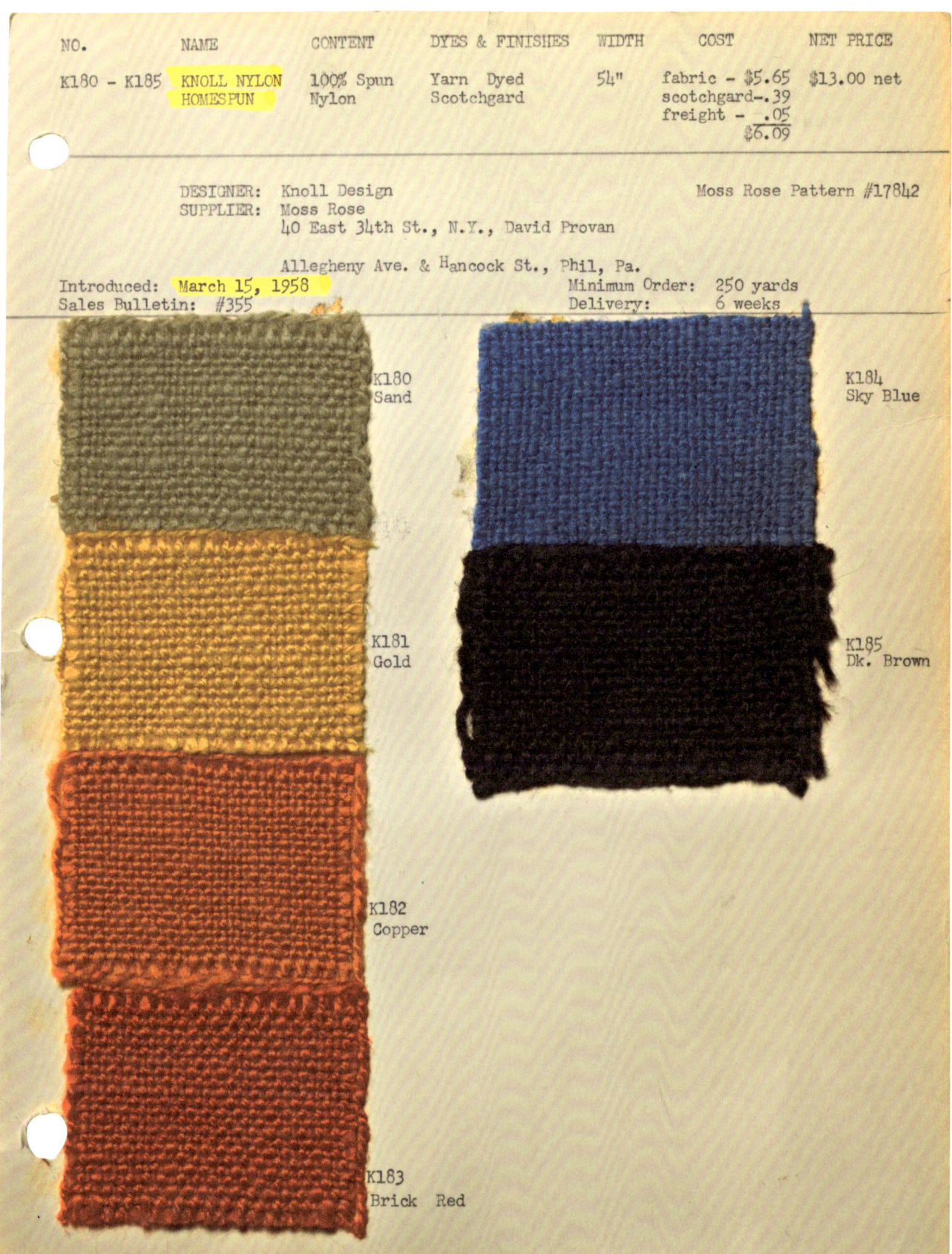

Fig. 3.75 Suzanne Huguenin. *Nylon Homespun* data page with six colorways attached, ca. 1958. Samples made by Moss Rose Manufacturing Co. for Knoll Textiles. Textile sample; nylon; plain weave, mounted on paper. KnollTextiles Archive. Cat. 143.

Fig. 3.78 Top Detail of *Sahara* ("Orange" colorway), introduced 1959, this example ca. 1965. Made by Orinoka Mills for Knoll Textiles. Used for upholstery; wool, cotton; plain-weave–derived compound weave with paired warps. Private collection.

Fig. 3.79 Bottom Vibeke Bruun de Neergaard. Detail of *Skol* ("Cerise" colorway), introduced 1960. Made by C. Olesen for Knoll Textiles. Used for upholstery; wool, cotton; 3/1 twill weave. Courtesy Mae Festa. Cat. 154.

Fig. 3.80 Bottom Paul Maute. Detail of *Arno* sample ("White/Black" colorway), introduced 1961, this example ca. 1968. Made by Paul Maute for Knoll Textiles. Used for upholstery; wool; plain weave. Courtesy Paul Makovsky.

Fig. 3.81 Top left Paul Maute. Detail of *Ebro* sample ("Royal/Aqua" colorway), introduced 1963, this example ca. 1968. Made by Paul Maute for Knoll Textiles. Used for upholstery; wool; plain weave. Courtesy Paul Makovsky.

Fig. 3.82 Top right Paul Maute. Detail of *Heather* sample ("Green/Gold" colorway), introduced 1964, this example ca. 1968. Made by Paul Maute for Knoll Textiles. Used for upholstery; wool; plain weave. Courtesy Paul Makovsky.

Fig. 3.83 Paul Maute. *Cato* swatches, ca. 1965. Made by Paul Maute for Knoll Textiles. Used for upholstery; wool, rayon; plain weave with grouped warps and supplemental wefts. Private collection.

immediate success, *Skol* was made available in a wide range of bright colors as well as heathered neutrals (eighteen by 1965). By 1962, *Furrows* and *Skol* had each sold "well over 30,000 yards."[174]

The final important group of upholsteries introduced by Huguenin—handwoven by Paul Maute's mill in Germany— were discovered through Wohnbedarf, Knoll's licensee in Switzerland, where Huguenin saw *Arno* (fig. 3.80) being used on a Knoll chair.[175] Maute had been weaving some of the Evelyn Hill *Handwoven* designs for Knoll Germany and was (like Rancocas Fabrics) a production handweaving factory, of a type that was becoming unsustainable in the United States by the 1960s. Maute, whom Huguenin described as "an extremely gifted designer and ingenious technician," also had his own wool carding, spinning, and dyeing operations on-site, which contributed to the quality of his yarns.[176] The Maute handwovens became signature Knoll fabrics and were woven in a wide range of colors through the 1960s and 1970s. *Arno* (1961) was a simple, plain-weave fabric, but the interaction of the thin black warps (grouped in pairs) and the slightly irregular colored wefts created an interesting surface texture. Knoll later introduced two variations with the same weave structure but slightly different yarns: *Ebro* (1962) had warps and wefts in contrasting colors (fig. 3.81), and *Heather* (1964) featured heathered yarns and warps and wefts in closely related colors (fig. 3.82). A more luxurious handwoven upholstery, *Cato* (1961), was also an immediate success, selling over 1,600 yards in the first six months, and is still in production in 2011 (although now it is machine-woven in Scotland).[177] *Cato*'s structure at first appears to be complex, but it is essentially a plain or basket weave. As with several of Evelyn Hill's *Handwovens*, the high-relief effect is created through subtle variations in color and by varying the size and spacing of the yarns (fig. 3.83).

A Well-Established Line

By the early 1960s, the Knoll Textiles collection had been carefully refined to meet the needs of the Planning Unit and large contract clients. While the company continued to introduce new textiles and fibers to the line and work with new designers, the collection was becoming more homogenous and self-referential, emphasizing Knoll's tradition and reputation. The company's internal documents and marketing used phrases such as "one of the oldest fabrics in our line," or "a classic in the line"— even for relatively new fabrics, such as *Cato* (1961).[178]

Knoll Textiles, like many of the textiles the division produced during its first thirty years, was created to fill a specific demand—to provide textiles appropriate for modern interiors and modern living. From the textile division's improvisatory beginnings through the creative flowering of the 1950s to its position as an innovative and globally significant purveyor of high-quality contract textiles in the early 1960s, the strength of Knoll Textiles had been based upon collaboration and experimentation. The character of the textile collections was also shaped by the preferences and business savvy of its founders, Hans and Florence Knoll, and by the model of integrated design that they established to define the Knoll identity. Hans Knoll's entrepreneurial pursuit of collaboration with manufacturers, and his and Florence's ability to recognize and nurture talent, established the company's creative culture, while Florence Knoll's high standards for design and quality and her skill as design director shaped Knoll's visual identity and demonstrated the importance of textiles for contemporary interior design.

1 No archival records identifying these early fabrics have been located; they were shown only in black and white in published accounts and rarely identified.

2 H. G. Knoll Associates brochure, ca. 1943, Knoll Archives. During the war many weaving mills were converted from civilian to military production, meaning shortages and delays for civilian orders; see "Fabrics from the New Spring Lines," *Interiors* (February 1943): 45.

3 See Mary Roche, "Rocking Chair Forms Headliner In New Collection of Furniture," *New York Times*, March 16, 1945: 18; "Designer Offers Chair to Sleep in," *New York Times*, August 9, 1946: 12.

4 For the Rapson rocker with "red cotton fabric" see "Furniture and Fabrics: Highlights from an Exhibition," *Everyday Art Quarterly*, no. 1 (Summer 1946): 9. For another Rapson rocker upholstered in "a nubby woolen covering by Moss-Rose" see Hans Knoll, "Reconversion Responsibility," *Upholstering* (July 1945): 30. For a Risom chair upholstered in an Angelo Testa print (*Little Elephant*) see "New Chairs," *Life* (May 20, 1946): 47.

5 Hans Knoll Furniture Company sale cat. [ca. 1942], photocopy, Knoll Archives.

6 Hans G. Knoll to Ralph Rapson, October 12, 1944, Knoll Archives. Although there is no direct evidence about the identity of the mill or individual Knoll had in mind, Lawrence ("Larry") Anton Maix, who worked as a sales manager for Knoll from the early 1940s to 1947, may have been involved. I am grateful to Giles Kotcher for this information from an unpublished research article. It is also possible that Knoll was referring to Arundell Clarke, who became coordinator for the textile division in 1947.

7 Hans G. Knoll to Ralph Rapson, October 12, 1944. Shirley Fletcher had been a weaving student at Cranbrook in 1941–42, before she married Rapson. See Jane King Hession et al., *Ralph Rapson: Sixty Years of Modern Design* (Afton, Minn.: Afton Historical Society Press, 1999), 46; Shirley Fletcher, student file, Cranbrook Academy of Art Office of the Registrar (1990-19), Cranbrook Archives. *Isles* was released with "Shirle Rapson" credited as designer.

8 Hans G. Knoll to Ralph Rapson, October 11, 1945, Knoll Archives. Knoll spelled the designer's first name "Shirley" in his October 12, 1944 letter, and "Shirle" in subsequent letters.

9 Hans G. Knoll to Ralph Rapson, December 20, 1945, Knoll Archives.

10 See H. G. Knoll Associates brochure, ca. 1943, Knoll Archives. The chairs in this brochure were offered with "Olive drab" webbing, the same webbing dyed green or brown, or with more costly leather strapping.

11 Hans Knoll, "Reconversion Responsibility," *Upholstering* (July 1945): 28–30, 57.

12 Bridgeport Fabrics was awarded a government contract to supply "cotton webbing, O.D. [Olive Drab]" in 1941; see "Defense Contracts in Day $54,725,775," *New York Times*, May 15, 1941, 40. Bridgeport may have manufactured some of the surplus olive drab cotton webbing used by Knoll during the war.

13 J. R. Carleton, "Furniture Webbing for Webbed Furniture," *Upholstering* (September 1945): 28–29, 60–61. Bridgeport Fabrics may also have later manufactured Knoll's plain cotton webbing; "Webbing" file, n.d., KnollTextiles Archive.

14 "Plastics Come to Town," *Upholstering* (May 1946): 45; Advertisement for Anchor Plastics, *Upholstering* (June 1946): 67; "Greater Beauty, Longer Service with Plastic Woven Fabrics," *Upholstering* (September 1948): 44–45. A Jens Risom chair webbed with "woven strips of translucent nylon sheeting" was shown in the DuPont display in the first national plastics exposition, held by the Society of the Plastics Industry at Grand Central Palace; see "The Way is Clear for Plastic Furnishings," *New York Times*, April 24, 1946, 30.

15 *P1-P3*, described as "striped plastic" in brown with white, red with white and yellow with white, is listed in Knoll Associates, Inc., "Textile Price List," November 1, 1948, Brooklyn Museum Library; *Saran*, in the three stripe colors mentioned plus four solid colors, is listed in a partial "Textile Price List," ca. 1950–51, KnollTextiles Archive.

16 Alvin Lustig, "Modern Printed Fabrics," *American Fabrics*, no. 20 (Winter 1951–52): 72. For Clarke see "Arundell Clarke Textile Showroom," *Interiors* (October 1948): 150. Clarke's fabrics appeared in most of the major exhibitions and publications over the next decade. Weaver and designer Jack Lenor Larsen also worked for the firm in the early 1950s; see Jack Lenor Larsen, Oral history interview by Arline M. Fisch, February 6–8, 2004, Archives of American Art, Smithsonian Institution.

17 Mary Roche, "Work of Noted Textile Designers Put on View at New Showroom," *New York Times*, February 27, 1947, 24; Advertisement for Knoll Associates ("Introducing Textiles"), *Interiors* (March 1947): 26; and *Everyday Art Quarterly*, no. 4 (Summer 1947): 13. See also "Weaves and Prints at Knoll's," *Interiors* (April 1947): 128–32.

18 Clarke's name does not appear in Knoll publications, advertisements, or accounts of the company in period press after the initial introduction of the textile division in 1947. In 1948, he presented a textile collection of his own (including fabrics designed by Angelo Testa and Emily Belding) in his showroom (Mary Roche, "Decorators' Work is Displayed Here," *New York Times*, September 2, 1948, 26) and submitted textiles to the Metropolitan Museum's *American Textiles, '48* exhibition under his own name; see *American Textiles '48* exhibition entry cards, Thomas J. Watson Library, Metropolitan Museum of Art, New York. There were no entries submitted by Knoll.

19 Florence Knoll Bassett later recalled these were brought in for Knoll by Arundell Clarke, "from his travels in the Far East." See Florence Knoll Bassett, "History of Knoll Textiles," typescript, 1996, KnollTextiles Archive.

20 Roche, "Work of Noted Textile Designers." No samples of *Moonlight* or *Abaca* are known to survive.

21 *Pandanus* was also available in a "plasticized" version by the next year (and later with vinyl backing). The "plasticized" version is listed in Knoll Associates, Inc., "Textile Price List," November 1, 1948, Brooklyn Museum Library.

22 Knoll sales bulletin no. 298, April 5, 1957, *Pandanus* file, KnollTextiles Archive.

23 Knoll sales bulletin no. 183, February 24, 1956, *Fishnet* file, KnollTextiles Archive. *Minnow* (also sourced from commercial fishing net manufacturers) was originally imported from Japan, but in March 1957 a finer, knotless version was found in West Germany, manufactured by Itzehoer Netzfabrik.

24 The cotton duck (used as a base fabric for the print *Apples*) was manufactured by Wellington Sears Co., a large-scale supplier of industrial textiles; see handwritten notation, *Apples* file, KnollTextiles Archive. For *Horsehair*, see "The Market," *Interior Design and Decoration* (April 1949): 11; it was also included in the 1950 Knoll "Textile Price List" and *Knoll Color Guides*. A 1949 article described Knoll's horsehair upholstery as "not the same as the horsehair of the 1880s, for it is mixed with other fibers and has a somewhat different look"; see "Designers Put Touch of Home into Showroom," *Chicago Tribune*, June 12, 1949, SW–A3.

25 Other NK printed fabrics were imported into the United States by a variety of American and Swedish firms between the 1940s and 1960s. For Bonniers see "Textile Imports Offered," *New York Times*, November 26, 1949, 53. For Wolfin Associates see "The Market: In the Swedish Idiom," *Interior Design* (May 1954): 42. For Brown-Hunsaker, Los Angeles, see "Fabrics," *Arts & Architecture* (November 1954): 28; and Advertisement for NK's Textilkammare, *Kontur* 5 (1955): 44.

26 According to author Eva Rudberg, the *Markelius* design, also known as *Markelius Ruta* (Markelius's square), was made "one or two years into the forties" for the Stockholm Building Society building in Stockholm; see Rudberg, *Sven Markelius* (Stockholm: Arkitektur Förlag, 1989): 123); a chronology of the architect's projects in the same book dates the pattern to 1943 (ibid., 187).

27 Examples examined by the author of Knoll's version of *Apples*, on both linen (Cora Ginsburg LLC; private collection) and cotton duck (Cleveland Museum of Art, CMA 1952.402; author's collection) are marked with the title in Swedish (from the original Swedish screen) and Lindberg's "hand" mark (the cipher used to mark his ceramic designs for Gustavsberg), with "Knoll Textile" and "Stig Lindberg Design" added in slightly different lettering. "Stig Lindberg Design" was incorrectly applied to a surviving length of *Markelius* now in the collection of the Cleveland Museum of Art (fig. 2.23); these are the only markings appearing on it, suggesting that the two patterns were printed by the same (probably American) printer. Unlike the later NK prints *Prisma* and *Pythagoras*, there are no known examples of *Apples* or *Markelius* marked both "Knoll Textile" and "Made in Sweden."

28 "Swedish Fabrics Go on Exhibition," *New York Times*, July 9, 1948, 12. A photograph accompanying the article showed a Jens Risom chair upholstered with this striped textile.

29 A striped fabric designed by Sampe (see fig. 3.9) and dated 1948 is in MoMA (SC36.1975), and seems to match period photos of the striped textile with fiberglass and *Sampe Stripe*, but no further information on its history or place of manufacture has so far been discovered.

30 Knoll Associates, Inc., "Textile Price List," November 1, 1948, Brooklyn Museum Library.

31 "Swedish Fabrics Go on Exhibition," *New York Times*, July 9, 1948, 12. *Crossbars*, *Paving Stones*, and *Rings* appear in Advertisement for Knoll Associates designed by Herbert Matter, *House & Garden* (October 1949): 212. *Paving Stones* was also published as "Stockholm import, #K189," in *Interior Design and Decoration* (October 1949): 55. A sample of *Buttons* (NMK 96/1971) in the NK Textilkammare Archive, Nationalmuseum in Stockholm is marked on the selvedge "NK Sweden Knoll Textile Division."

32 "Integrated Fabrics," *Art News* (May 1947): 60.

33 Roche, "Work of Noted Textile Designers." Frank is listed as a designer of Knoll textiles in Advertisement for Knoll Associates ("Introducing Textiles"), *Interiors* (March 1947): 26. *Manhattan* does not appear in any surviving photographs of the Sixty-fifth Street showroom, and there is no documentation suggesting it was carried by Knoll after 1947. It was produced in Sweden for Svenskt Tenn, where Frank was chief designer; see Nina Stritzler-Levine, ed., *Josef Frank, Architect and Designer* (New Haven and London: Yale University Press for the Bard Graduate Center, 1996), 258.

34 The Cooper-Hewitt National Design Museum has samples of *Links* (1969-165-16) and *Wires* (1969-165-18) with attached paper tags from Girard's own company and pattern and colorway numbers indicated; no Girard textiles with Knoll tags or markings have thus far been found. It not clear how or by whom the textiles in Girard's own line were printed.

35 "Fabrics," *Arts & Architecture* (March 1948): 32–36, illustrates Testa's *Indian Head* as "Angelo Testa for Knoll Associates," as well as Girard's *Spines* and *Wires* with no Knoll credit; "The Good Word on Fabrics," *Interiors* (November 1947): 106–8, credits Girard's *Spines* and *Links* as well as Testa's *Indian Heads* to Knoll. *Filo*, *Animal Forms*, and *Indian Heads*, on heavy cotton and credited to Knoll, appeared in Mary Roche, "Home: New Ideas and Inventions," *New York Times*, October 12, 1947, SM38. *Filo* by Knoll was honored as one the "Best of 1947" by AID; see Mary Roche, "Honors for Design," *New York Times*, February 15, 1948, SM38. *Wires* was published as a Knoll fabric in connection with the 1949 MoMA exhibition *Modern Art in Your Life*; see *Museum of Modern Art Bulletin* 27, no. 1 (1949): 32. Girard was listed among the "International Designers of Knoll Textiles" on a folder containing the 1948 Knoll catalogue and price lists (Brooklyn Museum Library), but his textiles do not appear in the Knoll "Textile Price List," November 1, 1948, therein nor on any other price lists found so far. An example of *Filo* (see fig. 1.14) was donated to the Cooper-Hewitt National Design Museum by Mae Festa who worked for Knoll between 1948 and 1952 and obtained the fabric during this time. By 1951 *Indian Heads* was distributed by Knoll competitor Richards Morgenthau; see "High on a Mountain," *Interior Design and Decoration* (September 1951): 94.

36 Strengell seems to have been particularly fond of *Shooting Stars* and later identified it as the first fabric she designed for Knoll. Marianne Strengell, Oral history interview by Robert F. Brown, January 8–

December 16, 1982, Archives of American Art, Smithsonian Institution.

37 Marianne Strengell, "Textile Studies," *Arts & Architecture* (July 1945): 28–29. The other designers were Ray Eames, Harry Bertoia, and Jill Mills Mitchell. Another former Cranbrook student, designer Ruth Adler Schnee, recalled that Hans Knoll came to visit her in Detroit in 1947, shortly after she had begun to print her own designs, to ask about including her design *Fancy Free* in the Knoll line, but that her father and their lawyer, whom she had asked to help with the negotiations, could not agree with Knoll on the terms of a contract. Ruth Adler Schnee, Oral history interview by Anita Schnee, November 24–30, 2002, Archives of American Art, Smithsonian Institution.

38 Knoll sales bulletin no. 357, March 10, 1958, *Campagna* file, KnollTextiles Archive.

39 A fragment of Japanese red silk with *kanoko shibori*, (see fig. 3.16) owned by Raymond, is in the Raymond Collection, The Architectural Archives, University of Pennsylvania.

40 See advertisement for Knoll Associates (with *Chinese Coins*), *Interiors* (May 1948): 33. For *Chinese Coins* on the seat cushion of a prize-winning Donald Knorr chair manufactured by Knoll in MoMA's International Competition for Low-Cost Furniture, see Olga Gueft, "Three Judgements, Manufacturing the Prize Winners," *Interiors* (March 1950): 97. In the 1950s, *Chinese Coins* was printed by New London Textile Print Works and later by Stonehenge Processing, and Testa's *Campagna* was printed by American Art Textile Prints (KnollTextiles Archive), but these may not have been the original printers.

41 Noémi Pernessin Raymond to Antonin Raymond (N. P. Rayond to A. Raymond), December 10, 1948, Raymond Collection, The Architectural Archives, University of Pennsylvania.

42 N. P. Raymond to A. Raymond, October 11, 1949 and October 20, 1949.

43 N. P. Raymond to A. Raymond, October 28, 1949 and November 7–8, 1949.

44 Herbert Matter may also have been involved; see this pattern (not yet named) in Advertisement for Knoll Associates, designed by Herbert Matter, *House & Garden* (October 1949): 212. The other patterns in the advertisement are identified, but *Mosaic* is identified as *Raymond Design*.

45 Marianne Strengell, quoted in "Marianne Strengell Writes about Designing Tomorrow's Fabrics," *Upholstering* (March 1946): 14.

46 Her student Ed Rossbach later noted, "Her effects derive from warp and weft in the simplest constructions. Everything is straightforward and clear ... her fabrics do not appear to strive to be interesting, or avant-garde ... or to carry statements. They are architectural materials"; see Rossbach, "Marianne Strengell," *American Craft* 44, no. 2 (April/May 1984): 8.

47 Roche, "Work of Noted Designers"; Eugenia Sheppard, "International Textile Exhibit Held at Knoll's," *New York Herald Tribune*, February 27, 1947, 18.

48 For a *Womb* chair upholstered in *Devil* see *Marianne Strengell*, exh. cat. (Bloomfield Hills, Mich.: Cranbrook Academy of Art Museum, 1950), checklist no. 94. The chair had been loaned by the Saarinen family; see loan paperwork, curatorial exhibition files, *Marianne Strengell*, September 14–October 8, 1950, Cranbrook Academy of Art Museum. Remnants of *Devil* fabric (in the yellow colorway) were recently discovered on the chair, which is still in the collection of the family, underneath later replacement upholstery (Leslie Edwards, Head Archivist, Cranbrook Archives, conversation with author, December 2009). A length of *Devil* was acquired by MoMA (SC159.1948), but its current location within the collection is unknown.

49 Unbound sample book pages, Louisville Textiles, n.d., American Textile History Museum, Lowell, Mass. (Louisville Textiles fabric and yarn samples, 68.10.12). The range of pattern numbers and designs suggests a date of the late 1930s to early 1940s.

50 Marianne Strengell, Oral history interview by Robert F. Brown , January 8–December 16, 1982, Archives of American Art, Smithsonian Institution. The only known surviving examples of furniture upholstered in these two Strengell fabrics are a Saarinen *Grasshopper* chair upholstered in *Cartree*, Yale University Art Gallery (1976.11.1), and a Jens Risom armchair upholstered in *Buster*, Knoll Museum, East Greenville, Penn. The upholstery on both chairs is in poor condition.

51 Five colorways of *Puli* were shown in the January *Good Design* exhibition at the Merchandise Mart in Chicago, and three in the fall 1952 MoMA installation. *Good Design*, Merchandise Mart (January) and MoMA, 1952.

52 Advertisement for Knoll Associates, designed by Herbert Matter, *House & Garden* (October 1949): 212. Strengell included this fabric in her 1950 Cranbrook exhibition; see *Marianne Strengell*, exh. cat., checklist no. 94. The packing list from Knoll identified it as *K900 Fiberglas*; curatorial exhibition files, *Marianne Strengell*, September 14–October 8, 1950, Cranbrook Academy of Art Museum.

53 Strengell worked with Owens-Corning; Skidmore, Owings & Merrill; and the Knoll Planning Unit on this project between 1946 and 1949. (Leslie S. Edwards, "Structure and Surface: Marianne Strengell and Woven Texture," *Modernism* 10, no. 4 (Winter 2007–8): 82-83.) See also chaps. 1 and 4.

54 For "Chair webbings in rich-textured constructions by Marianne Strengell" see "Eight Solutions to Merchandise Display," *Interiors* (October 1948): 111 (illus.). A year later Webcraft was offering "Pebble-weave (originally handloomed by Marianne Strengell)" as well as Saran webbing, plastic webbing, and a two-color design called "Textone"; see "Knoll Webbings By-the-yard," *Interiors* (October 1949): 142.

55 *Marianne Strengell*, exh. cat., checklist no. 96.

56 Advertisement for Knoll (with *Prestini*), *Interiors* (May 1948): 33; "Down with the Overstuffed Chair," *Upholstering* (July 1948): 122. Originally, the same fabric was available in a piece-dyed (dyed after weaving), solid-color version called *Oslo* (discontinued June 1951); see *Prestini* file, KnollTextiles Archive.

57 Richard and Trudy Schultz, interview by the author, April 27, 2010.

58 Knoll Bassett, "History of Knoll Textiles," KnollTextiles Archive. Knoll Bassett recalled discovering the fabric during a visit the Knolls made to Lackner Prestini's (then) husband, the sculptor and teacher James Prestini, in Chicago. However, the fabric was most likely designed when Lackner Prestini was a student at Cranbrook (1945–47) or shortly thereafter; her daughters, Margaret and Hollis Webster, believe that the Prestinis were divorced or in the process of divorcing when she started at Cranbrook (Margaret Webster and Hollis Webster, conversations with author, May 8, 11, and 24, 2010). Antoinette Lackner Prestini was enrolled at Cranbrook from Summer 1945 to Spring 1947 (Cranbrook student rosters, 1943–49, Cranbrook Archives [1981–09] 14:5-7, 14:11).

59 "Prestini," from Suzanne Huguenin, *Knoll Textiles Sales Guide* (1962), courtesy Daniel Kroger.

60 Roche, "Work of Noted Designers."

61 Partial "Textile Price List," ca. 1950–51, KnollTextile Archive. The only known price list to predate this one, published in November 1948, does not list the Strengell handwovens.

62 Ibid.; for a black-and-white photograph of K811 see *Knoll Index of Contemporary Design* (New York: Knoll Associates, 1950), 77.

63 Partial "Textile Price List," ca. 1950–51, KnollTextiles Archive. The fabrics (*K800–804*) were a blend of wool, mohair, cotton, and rayon, available in natural, green, gray, blue, and yellow, or dyed to order (15 yard minimum order). For a photograph of the striped fabrics, see Brian Lutz, *Knoll: A Modernist Universe* (New York: Rizzoli, 2010): 107.

64 Christa C. Mayer Thurman, "Textiles," in *Design in America: The Cranbrook Vision 1925–1950*, ed. Joan Marter et al. (New York: Harry N. Abrams, 1983), 197, 319 n. 102.

65 Gerda Nyberg's notebook (scanned copy of original in possession of Nyberg family), Cranbrook Archives. One delivery was made of 23 yards on September 24 and an additional 25 yards on September 30, and on December 11 of that year she "put up 28 varparmar [25 yards] of Silverton (2/9 Reed)." In her entries, Nyberg gives the length of the warp "put up" on the loom in *varparmar* (meaning the amount of yarn wound onto the warping reel [*varpa*]), and the finished amount in yards; e.g., in the December 11 entry she added "28 varparmar makes 25 yards fin'd."

66 Ibid. Nyberg wove 124 more yards of "white upholstery" for Knoll in February and March 1951, and 42 yards of *Silvertone* in September 1951.

67 Roche, "Work of Noted Designers."

68 Ibid.; "Knoll Associates Introduces Textiles," *Upholstering* (April 1947): 92.

69 The darker colorway is shown in a number of photographs in the Herbert Matter papers, M1446. Dept. of Special Collections, Stanford University Libraries, Stanford, Calif.. For the armchair photo see Knoll Associates research file, Architecture & Design Study Center, MoMA. A typed caption on the reverse gives the description of the upohlstery and the design date of the chair as 1948 and indicates that the photograph was received by MoMA's Department of Industrial Design in January 1949.

70 "G. Stadler-Stölzl, Zurich" is mentioned in the first advertisement for Knoll's textiles division (see fig. 3.4) and in press coverage of the first collection; see "Weaves and Prints at Knoll's," *Interiors* (April 1947): 128. However, there is no indication of what she designed. Her workshop in Zurich was called Handweberei Flora (Flora Handweaving Mill); see www.guntastolzl.org/. According to Stadler-Stölzl's daughter Monica Stadler, she used "a lot of hand-spun wool" after the war, when materials were difficult to get, and had it dyed to order or dyed it herself (quoted in Matthew Bourne, "Form and Function," *Modern Carpets & Textiles* 1 [Autumn 2005]: 61).

71 Cora Ginsburg, *A Catalogue of Exquisite and Rare Works of Art Including 15th to 20th Century Costume Textiles and Needlework* (2003), 22–23; Cora Ginsburg, *A Catalogue of Exquisite and Rare Works of Art Including 17th to 20th Century Costume Textiles and Needlework* (Winter 2004), 26. The artists included Serge Poliakoff and André Lanskoy.

72 MoMA press release, "Large New Group of 'Good Design'," [June 1950], online Press Release Archive, www.moma.org; "Spring Fabrics 1951," *Interior Design and Decoration* (April 1951): 112.

73 Jack Lenor Larsen recalls this fabric as "very glamorous—we hadn't seen any silk for a long time, and this was a new kind of silk"; Jack Lenor Larsen, interview by the author, February 2, 2010. Knoll gave the textile the name *Jhuri Silk* in 1954.

74 Gladys Rogers Brophyl, "More Textiles Shown in 'Good Design' 1951," *Handweaver & Craftsman* 2, no. 2 (Spring 1951): 39.

75 Richard and Trudy Schultz, interview by the author, April 27, 2010.

76 Eszter Haraszty, interview by Kate Carmel, May 1989 (notes by Christine Laidlaw), Stewart Collection Archives, Montreal Museum of Fine Arts, courtesy David A. Hanks & Associates.

77 Ralph Caplan, *The Design of Herman Miller* (New York: Whitney Library of Design, 1977), 60; quoted in Leslie Piña, *Alexander Girard Designs for Herman Miller* (Atglen, Penn.: Schiffer Publishing, 1998), 17.

78 "Showroom for Knoll Associates, Inc., New York," *Architectural Record* (November 1948): 93.

79 Roche, "Work of Noted Designers."

80 "Chicago First Stop on This Fabric Tour," *Chicago Daily Tribune*, November 5, 1950, SW_AA.

81 "Fall Fabrics 1950," *Interior Design* (October 1950): 60.

82 "New Knoll Showroom: A Study in Space and Texture," *Interior Design and Decoration* (April 1951): 30.

83 "Fabrics From Knoll ... Swatches And All," *Interior Design* (April 1952): 19.

84 Suzanne Huguenin, interview, ca. 1977, p. 2, Huguenin Designer Biography file, Knoll Archives. This color combination was also used in the early 1950s in Thai silks imported by Thaibok, by Alexander Girard in his fabrics for Herman Miller, and in the designs of Vuokko Eskolin-Nurmesniemi for Printex in Finland.

85 Knoll press release, [ca. 1955], *Triad* file, KnollTextiles Archive. *Triad* won a First Award from AID and was chosen for the *Good Design* exhibition in January 1955.

86 *The House in the Museum Garden (Museum of Modern Art Bulletin)* 16, no. 1 (1949): 5. The fabric is listed as by "Eszter," and available through Arundell Clarke. This was one of several screen prints Haraszty designed for Drago Studio, a small textile printing and painting workshop on East Fifteenth Street. Another pattern is illustrated in "The New Fabrics," *Interiors* (March 1950): 106. Some of these were carried by Arundell Clarke; see "Hand-Screen Fabrics," *Interior Design and Decoration* (July 1949): 8.

87 Knoll press release, n.d. (ca. 1951), *Knoll Stripes* file, KnollTextiles Archive.

88 The drawing was made at Marcel Breuer's house in New Canaan, Conn. Eszter Haraszty, interview by Kate Carmel.

89 "Fabrics and Papers Mix Happily with Nature in the Ossining Studio and Home of Designer Vera Neumann," *Interiors* (November 1951): 103.

90 According to Haraszty, Printex printed all of her designs. Eszter Haraszty, interview, January 25, 1977, p. 10, Haraszty Designer Biography file, Knoll Archives. In the KnollTextiles Archive, Printex is only identified as the printer for *Fibra* and *Triad*. Haraszty may have met the Neumanns through (fellow Hungarian) Marcel Breuer, or vice versa. Haraszty stayed with Breuer's family when she first came to the U.S., and Breuer later designed a house for the Neumanns as well as the New York showroom for Scarves by Vera. For the Neumanns' house see L.W., "Breuer's Beautiful Plan for the Neumanns," *Interiors* (June 1956): 108–11; and "Interiors on the Horizontal in a Breuer House," *Interiors* (January 1957): 118. For the showroom see "The Year's Work," *Interiors* (August 1952): 70; and "How One Space Became Four: Showroom and Offices for Scarves by Vera," *Architectural Record*, 113 (February 1953): 159–64.

91 Cecil Lubell, "Vera: Textile Designer for a Sophisticated Mass Market," *American Fabrics* 63 (Winter/Spring 1964): 87.

92 Cecil Lubell, "Vera," 87. In addition to Vera's own designs and Knoll Textiles, Printex also printed textiles for Schumacher and Herman Miller. See "Breuer's Beautiful Plan for the Neumanns," *Interiors* (June 1956): 111; Isadore Barmash, *The Self-Made Man* (New York: MacMillan, 1969), 301; and Leslie Piña, *Alexander Girard Designs*, 20.

93 Piña, *Alexander Girard Designs*, 20–21. American Art Textile Printing was located at 307 East 22nd Street in New York.

94 Jack Lenor Larsen, interview by the author, February 2, 2010.

95 Eszter Haraszty, interview by Kate Carmel. These photographs show the same loom that appears in Hartmann's photographs of Evelyn Hill.

96 The pattern, renamed *Lazy River Stripe*, was printed on Moygashel linen and pima cotton in different colors (not the Knoll versions) and appeared in B. H. Wragge's summer 1955 collection. It was used for several coat and jacket styles and a sheath dress. For a photograph by Richard Avedon of one of the coats see "The Quilted Linen Coat—Striped in Hot Color," *Harper's Bazaar* (May 1955), offprint, scrapbook in B. H. Wragge Archive, Fashion Institute of Technology Special Collections. The 1955 collection included adaptations of Knoll's *Lazy Lines*, *Chico Stripe*, and *Lima* (renamed *French Quarter*).

97 *Fibra* file, KnollTextiles Archive.

98 Margie Ruddick, email to Paul Makovsky, February 28, 2010; Margie Ruddick, email to author, February 21, 2011.

99 Lesley Jackson, *Twentieth Century Pattern Design* (New York: Princeton Architectural Press, 2002), 100, 126; Bent Salicath and Arne Karlsen, eds., *Modern Danish Textiles* (Copenhagen: Danish Society of Arts and Crafts and Industrial Design, 1959), 50–51. L. F. Foght may have printed *Kon-Tiki* for Knoll; a sample in the collection of the Cooper-Hewitt National Design Museum (fig. 3.44) contains the company's trademark as part of the selvedge marking.

100 NK introduced *Pythagoras* in 1952 and supplied it to Knoll.

101 *Lazy Lines* was printed on linen and later on Fiberglas; the printer is listed as Stonehenge Processing (*Lazy Lines* file, KnollTextiles Archive). *Pythagoras* is still being printed by Ljungbergs in 2011 and requires eighteen screens; see Ljungbergs Textiltryck, www.ljungbergstextil.se/index.php?lang=en&page=sven-markelius.

102 "The Winners: 11th A.I.D. Design Competition," *Interiors* (March 1957): 129.

103 *Prisma* file, KnollTextiles Archive. There are pieces of *Prisma* in the collection of the designer's family marked in the selvedge "NK 'Prisma' Sven Markelius Design Knoll Textiles Inc. Made in Sweden"; Bo Markelius, email to the author, January 31, 2010. In the files at Ljungbergs, there are samples with the same markings, as well as small samples with Knoll cardboard sample tags that could also possibly be the American printing; Bibbi Nilsson, email to the author, January 17, 2008. Two lengths in the collection of the University of Alberta, labeled as having been purchased from Knoll, have no markings at all in the selvedges; see cat. 120.

104 Suzanne Huguenin, interview, ca. 1977, p. 11, Huguenin Designer File, Knoll Archives.

105 Eszter Haraszty, interview, January 25, 1977, pp. 15–16, Haraszty Designer File, Knoll Archives; Suzanne Huguenin, interview, ca. 1977, pp. 3–6, Huguenin Designer File, Knoll Archives; Herbert Matter, interview, ca. 1977, p. 3 ("Graphics"), Matter Designer File, Knoll Archives; Martha Kaihatsu, interview, January 11, 1979, pp. 1–3, Kaihatsu Designer File, Knoll Archives; Richard and Trudy Schultz, interview by the author, April 27, 2010.

106 This fabric was called *Linen Crash Upholstery* in some early Knoll catalogues; see *Knoll Index of Contemporary Design* (New York: Knoll Associates, 1950), 76–77.

107 In the early twentieth century, Arts and Crafts furniture designer Gustav Stickley had been among Donald Brothers' American customers; see Donald Brothers Ltd. Records (GB 582 GB), Heriot-Watt University (Edinburgh), http://archiveshub.ac.uk/ead-html/gb582db-p1.shtml#id448207. See also Lesley Jackson, *Twentieth-Century Pattern Design* (Princeton: Princeton Architectural Press): 78–79, and Helen Douglas, "The Feel for Rugged Texture" in Mary Schoeser and Christine Boydell eds., *Disentangling Textiles* (London: Middlesex University Press, 2002), 177–184.

108 Eszter Haraszty, interview, January 25, 1977, p. 10, Haraszty Designer File, Knoll Archives; Eszter Haraszty, interview by Kate Carmel. Haraszty likely worked with the mill to develop *Kerry Linen* (1953), *Highland Tweed* (1956), and *Highland Stripes* (1956). Numerous trial samples woven for "Miss Haraszty, Knoll New York" survive in Donald Brothers Sample Books 1950-1961, University Archive, Records Management and Museum Service, Heriot-Watt University. For more on Donald Brothers see Peter Simpson, designer biography, in this volume.

109 Little is known about Lorenz or what his connection may have been to Knoll or Donald Brothers. Donald Brothers is known to have invited foreign designers (others included Astrid Sampe) to work in their factory and it is possible he colaborated with them for a short time. See Margaret Duckett, "How Donald Brothers Stay Small and Influence People," *Design* 254 (June 1, 1970): 29.

110 It was described as "a classic in the Knoll collection" in Knoll sales bulletin no. 449, June 29, 1959, *Scotch Linen* file, KnollTextiles Archive. This bulletin also attributed the decline in the popularity of linen upholstery fabrics to their susceptibility to creasing and surface crocking (rubbing off of color).

111 Eszter Haraszty, interview, January 25, 1977, p. 12, Haraszty Designer File, Knoll Archives.

112 For its early history, see Florence Knoll Bassett, "History of Knoll Textiles"; "Transportation Cloth," Suzanne Huguenin, *Knoll Textiles Sales Guide* (1962), KnollTextiles Archive. The *Sales Guide* was prepared by Huguenin for use by Knoll salespeople. For commercial introduction of *Transportation Cloth* see "Merchandise Cues: Stripes and Strength at Knoll," *Interiors* (June 1951): 130. It may have been available before May 1951, as it was selected (from designs "new during the last six months") for *Good Design*, January 1951; see *Good Design* (January 1951), no. 104.

113 Eszter Haraszty, interview, January 25, 1977, p. 12, Haraszty Designer File, Knoll Archives.

114 The name may also have derived from the title of General Motors' first major postwar trade show, "Transportation Unlimited," which was held at New York's Waldorf-Astoria Hotel in January 1949.

115 Knoll sales bulletins, *Transportation Cloth* file, KnollTextiles Archive. According to Jack Lenor Larsen, *Transportation Cloth* was used for some of the original upholstery in Philip Johnson's Glass House, in New Canaan, Conn., but was so weakened by sun exposure that it soon needed to be replaced; Jack Lenor Larsen, interview by the author, Febrary 2, 2010.

116 Strengell received the General Motors Technical Center commission in 1951, and she and her principal weaver, Gerda Nyberg, devoted much of their time to the project over the next several years. See Edwards, "Structure and Surface: Marianne Strengell and Woven Texture," 83.

117 Haraszty later said that she "set up the weaving department just because of this job"; Eszter Haraszty, interview, January 25, 1977, p. 9, Haraszty Designer File, Knoll Archives. She also included an article on this house in a presentation volume about the interiors projects she was responsible for; see The Montreal Museum of Fine Arts, Liliane and David M. Stewart Collection, D88.178.1.29-30.

118 It is not clear how many looms or weavers were involved, or where exactly they worked. Erich Hartmann's photographs of Hill in her studio, taken in 1952, show only Hill's loom, but Hill later described one of her textiles as being "woven by students from Cranbrook" (Hill, handwritten note, Philadelphia Museum of Art, curatorial object file for 69-1983-19), and Haraszty described one of the handwovens as being made "in Long Island [by] a fantastic weaver from Cranbrook" (Eszter Haraszty, interview, January 25, 1977, p. 11, Haraszty Designer File, Knoll Archives). For textiles "hand-woven in Knoll Long Island Factory," see "Drum Beaters for Modern," *Life* (March, 2, 1953): 76.

119 "Special Handwovens," handwritten Knoll price list, KnollTextiles Archive. The list gives prices per yard for orders over 15 yards, but it is not clear where these textiles were woven, or if Knoll received many orders for them.

120 Betty Pepis, "For the Home: Settings in Decorators' Exhibit," *New York Times*, March 29, 1952, 8.

121 "Fabrics to the Fore in Homefurnishings," *Handweaver & Craftsman* 13, no. 3 (Summer 1962): 31; biography of Evelyn Hill Anselevicius (photocopy), n.d., Evelyn Hill designer file, KnollTextiles Archive.

122 Trudy Schultz, who worked in the Planning Unit in the early 1950s, recalls that it was difficult to use small swatches of these fabrics in paste-up plans for this reason, and Richard Schultz remembers similar problems when they were used for upholstery; Richard and Trudy Schultz, interview by the author, April 27, 2010. Some of the handwovens were routinely supplied with a muslin backing for improved stability; Knoll sales bulletin no. 410, February 18, 1959, *Handwoven* file, KnollTextiles Archive.

123 According to Suzanne Huguenin, Hill and Haraszty both favored unusual color combinations, and Hill influenced Haraszty "in her weaves, and in her colorations." Suzanne Huguenin, interview, ca. 1977, p. 26, Huguenin Designer File, Knoll Archives.

124 In 1958, the Planning Unit was "very frequently using the H910 group"; Knoll sales bulletin no. 392, July 31, 1958, *Handwoven* file, KnollTextiles Archive.

125 "Rancocas Fabrics," *Handweaver & Craftsman* 8, no. 2 (Spring 1957): 42. Loring founded Rancocas Fabrics in 1947 as a "handweaving concern on a production basis catering especially to the furniture trade."

126 Jack Lenor Larsen, interview by the author, February 2, 2010.

127 Knoll sales bulletin no. 241, July 30, 1956, *Highland Tweed* file, KnollTextiles Archive.

128 According to handwritten notes accompanying samples of *Rover* (acc. no. 69-1983-16) and *Tara* (acc. no. 69-1983-17) that Evelyn Hill Anselevicius donated to the Philadelphia Museum of Art, these designs were adapted for power-loom production in the early 1960s from samples she had designed in 1953 and 1954. There is no surviving information in the KnollTextiles Archive about their production.

129 *Synthesis* (composed of "Saran, jute and viscose") appeared in a 1953 Knoll price list, and an advertisement described it as a "Remarkable new fabric of warm individuality developed exclusively by Knoll. Spun synthetic vinyl-plastic yarn is designed into a pliable weave of strength and structure . . . in muted tones of . . . Red, yellow, black, tan, green/black, brown/black"; Advertisement for Knoll Textiles, designed by Herbert

Matter, *Interiors* (October 1953): 19; see also "Some Facile Upholstery Plastics for '54," *Interiors* (January 1954): 104 (illus). It was described in the latter as "woven of spun and monofilament Saran."

130 Knoll Textiles price list, June 7, 1954; the finishes may have been available earlier but are not mentioned in earlier price lists. *K-Plus* is later credited to Dow-Corning; see Knoll Textiles wholesale price list, July 15, 1958, p. 19, KnollTextiles Archive.

131 Knoll sales bulletin no. 81, December 27, 1954, KnollTextiles Archive. The Planning Unit worked on Deering Milliken's New York headquarters in 1958 (see chap. 4).

132 *Rugby*, from Huguenin, *Knoll Textiles Sales Guide*.

133 *Lana*, from ibid.

134 Ibid.

135 Knoll sales bulletin no. 327, November 13, 1957, KnollTextiles Archive.

136 Knoll sales bulletins, 1956–60, *Sarano* file, KnollTextiles Archive.

137 Suzanne Huguenin, interview, ca. 1977, p. 8, Huguenin Designer File, Knoll Archives.

138 Naugahyde with plain embossing was offered by Knoll and Herman Miller, each firm having its own exclusive colors; see "Naugahyde," Huguenin, *Knoll Textiles Sales Guide*. According to Knoll textile bulletin no. 6, December 7, 1960, Naugahyde folder, KnollTextiles Archive, the "extra dull" finish was developed at Knoll's request, with Knoll then the only company to offer it.

139 U.S. Rubber introduced *Elastic Naugahyde* in 1950; see "A Flexible Fabric," *Interiors* (November 1950): 166; and *Breathable Naugahyde* in 1955, with versions printed with decorative patterns used in several 1956 Dodge, DeSoto, and Plymouth automobiles; the stripes and colors of *Breathing Naugahyde* were exclusive to Knoll. See "Vinyls Which Breathe," *American Fabrics*, no. 37 (Summer 1956): 110; Knoll press release, ca. 1957, Naugahyde folder, KnollTextiles Archive.

140 "Brigadoon," from Huguenin, *Knoll Textiles Sales Guide*.

141 For "the new low-cost textiles" see Martha Kaihatsu, ed., *Knoll Index of Contemporary Design* (New York: Knoll Associates: 1954), 61.

142 "Merit," from Huguenin, *Knoll Textiles Sales Guide*.

143 Knoll sales bulletin no. 333, December 16, 1957, KnollTextiles Archive.

144 "Domus," from Huguenin, *Knoll Textiles Sales Guide*. *Domus* was woven by Craftex at some point, but this may not have been the original mill; see Knoll questionnaire for *Domus*, n.d. (filled out by Craftex), *Domus* file, KnollTextile Archive.

145 Knoll sales bulletin no. 275, February 21, 1957, *Ombré* file, KnollTextiles Archive.

146 Leslie Piña, *Alexander Girard Designs*, 20. These included *Lattice* (1952) and *Arabesque* and *Gemstones* (both 1954).

147 Martha Kaihatsu, Knoll's publicity director at the time, later recalled, "When Hans died, I thought the best strategy on publicity was to get as much publicity [as possible] on her [Florence Knoll]. . . . We worked very hard to make sure there were important stories"; Martha Kaihatsu, interview, January 11, 1979, p. 6, Knoll Archives.

148 *American Fabrics*, no. 38 (Fall 1956): 36–37. For the Dow Chemical installation see chap. 4 .

149 Suzanne Huguenin, interview, ca. 1977, p. 12, Huguenin Designer File, Knoll Archives.

150 Huguenin's friend Jack Lenor Larsen admired her ability to act as a "one-man department"—he recalls her on her own out on the West Coast selling and training salesmen, while "I had a dozen people doing that"; Jack Lenor Larsen, interview by the author, February 2, 2010. A 1961 newspaper article estimated that she spent half of the year traveling "to Europe and South America, and throughout the United States"; see Charlotte Tapley, "Knoll Color Expert Is a Busy Traveler," *Houston Post*, October 8, 1961, n.p. (clipping), Suzanne Huguenin file, KnollTextiles Archive.

151 Martha Kaihatsu, ed., *Knoll Index of Contemporary Design* (New York: Knoll Associates 1954), 61. This statement appeared in the first Knoll Index in 1950 and was reprinted throughout the 1950s.

152 *Shades* was introduced in July 1956; see Knoll sales bulletin no. 243, July 27, 1956. It was discontinued in June 1958; see Knoll sales bulletin no. 379, June 9, 1958, *Shades* file, KnollTextiles Archive.

153 Knoll sales bulletin no. 294, April 3, 1957, *Wool Casement* file, KnollTextiles Archive.

154 Knoll sales bulletin no. 286, March 25, 1957, *Trellis* file, KnollTextiles Archive.

155 Two agreements between Albers and Knoll, from 1958 and 1964, are in the archives of the Josef and Anni Albers Foundation, Bethany, Conn.: see W. Cornell Dechert to Anni Albers, December 3, 1957 (signed by Albers January 25, 1958); Anni Albers to Robert J. Martin, December 10, 1957; Robert J. Martin to Anni Albers, January 22, 1958; Donald R. Jomo to Anni Albers, January 20, 1964, Albers Foundation. In 1964 Albers agreed to consult on the development of new upholstery fabrics, but none of her designs from that agreement were put into production; it is not clear whether her casement design *Track* (1965) was covered by the first or second agreement. See Anni Albers, interview, [late 1970s], KnollTextiles Archive.

156 "Aerocor: New Potential for Owens Corning's Fiberglas," *Interiors* (February 1958): 126.

157 Anni Albers, interview, [late 1970s], KnollTextiles Archive.

158 Knoll sales bulletin no. 494, January 15, 1960, *Fiberglas Casement* file, KnollTextiles Archive.

159 All three were discontinued from the United States Knoll Textiles collection in 1978. *Rail* was retained in the European Knoll Textiles offerings until at least 1981; see Danielle J. Schroettner (Knoll International) to Anni Albers, May 28, 1982, Josef and Anni Albers Foundation.

160 The Joynel Company, an importer and representative for a number of Belgian mills (Jack Lenor Larsen, interview by the author, February 2, 2010), imported these for Knoll. Joynel also imported the Belgian linen for many Knoll prints, and many other European fabrics carried by Knoll Textiles during the 1950s and 1960s.

161 A sample that appears identical to *Tracey* survives in Donald Brothers' records, marked "sent to Knoll Textiles Inc. NY" and "stocked 13/9/61" (Donald Brothers Sample Books 1950–1961, University Archive, Records Management and Museum Service, Heriot-Watt University); while the mill for *Cirrus* is not known, it was imported from Scotland, and several similar samples were sent to Knoll from Donald Brothers in the late 1950s and early 1960s (ibid.). Donald Brothers was also listed as the supplier of *Tracey* in the early 1970s ("Textile Price List 1972," annotated by Deborah Stoudt of Knoll Textiles, ca. 1972).

162 "'Architectural' window nets" casements from West Germany included *Fence*, *Filigree*, and *Oval*; see "Directions in Fabric and Fashion," *American Fabrics*, no. 63 (Winter–Spring 1964): 11.

163 "The Crème de la Crème: A.I.D.'s Citation of Merit Awards," *Interiors* (May 1959): 12.

164 "New Color Philosophy at Knoll," *Interiors* (May 1959): 144.

165 Suzanne Huguenin, interview, ca. 1977, pp. 14–15, Huguenin Designer File, Knoll Archives.

166 "Nylon Homespun," from Huguenin, *Knoll Textiles Sales Guide*.

167 According to Suzanne Huguenin, the change in yarn occurred after she left Knoll (in 1963), and the later version had "no resemblance to the original"; Suzanne Huguenin, interview by Kate Carmel, October 30, 1987. By the late 1970s, Craftex had replaced Moss Rose as the manufacturer; see Knoll questionnaire for *Knoll Nylon Homespun*, n.d. (filled out by Craftex), *Knoll Nylon Homespun* file, KnollTextiles Archive.

168 For Taslan's introduction see Advertisement for DuPont, *Interior Design* (August 1957): 19. Three new upholstery fabrics by Boris Kroll using Taslan yarns were also announced; see "New Nylons for Boris Kroll," ibid., 116–17.

169 See Advertisement for DuPont, *Interiors* (April 1959): 87.

170 "Sahara," from Huguenin, *Knoll Textiles Sales Guide*.

171 It was sourced through Joynel like several other Knoll imports; see *Furrows* file, KnollTextiles Archive. See also, "Market Spotlight: Ten by Knoll," *Interior Design* (June 1957): 130; and "Fibers and Colors Stripe Fabrics from Two Sources," *Interiors* (July 1957): 114.

172 *Furrows*, from Huguenin, *Knoll Textiles Sales Guide* (1962),. A Saarinen 71 armchair from the General Motors Technical Center, upholstered in orange *Furrows* and Naugahyde, is in the collection of the Cranbrook Academy of Art Museum (acc. no. T 2009.16.1).

173 *Skol* file, KnollTextiles Archive. Little is known about the designer. *Skol*, from Huguenin, *KnollTextiles Sales Guide*.

174 *Skol* and *Furrows*, from Huguenin, *Knoll Textiles Sales Guide*.

175 *Arno*, from ibid.

176 *Cato*, from ibid. Maute's operations were illustrated in a Handwoven Collection brochure, designed by Massimo Vignelli, ca. 1967, Knoll Archives; see chap. 5 and cat. 176.

177 Maute produced *Cato* until 1992.

178 Huguenin, *Knoll Textiles Sales Guide*.

4 The Heart and Soul of the Company: The Knoll Planning Unit, 1944–65

Bobbye Tigerman

The Knoll Planning Unit, design consultants to the architect. A complete planning service that integrates interior and architectural design. Through understanding of specific problems, it coordinates furniture, fabrics, and color to create interiors of utility and beauty.[1]

—Knoll Planning Unit brochure, ca. 1956

In 1958 the magazine *Industrial Design* convened a roundtable of the creative team responsible for the design of the groundbreaking suburban headquarters of Connecticut General Life Insurance Company, to explore how the somewhat unusual design process had played out. The gathering, moderated by editorial director Ralph Caplan, included the client, president of Connecticut General, Frazar B. Wilde; architect Gordon Bunshaft of Skidmore, Owings & Merrill; graphic designer Lester Beall; and interior designer Florence Knoll. To underscore the key contributions of the Knoll Planning Unit led by Florence Knoll, Wilde explained that "most buildings call in an interior decorator *after* all the architectural detail is set. . . . Gordon [Bunshaft] got [Florence Knoll] in early so she could contribute in the execution of architectural details."[2]

The Connecticut General commission was a watershed moment for the Knoll Planning Unit, marking the fulfillment of Florence Knoll's vision of how the Planning Unit would operate, namely as an interior design service working side by side with the architect and client (fig. 4.1). Company brochures emphasized that the purpose of the Planning Unit was "to design and produce furnishings and interiors appropriate to contemporary architecture and suited to the changing needs of modern living," which was reflected in Wilde's comment on the essential role of the Planning Unit and the compatibility of Connecticut General's interior design with its architecture.[3]

Promotional materials for the Knoll Planning Unit stated that it "grew out of a demand by private and architect-clients to provide interiors in which the concept in the Knoll line of furniture and fabrics is carried to its logical conclusion: fusion of architectural space and its contents."[4] Its mission was to create interiors that were sympathetic to modern architecture by using furniture, textiles, and accessories from the Knoll line and often developing new products or customizing existing ones to suit a particular client's needs. Founded in 1944 and headed by Florence Knoll from 1945, it was one of three divisions of Knoll Associates and was the most public branch of the firm, projecting Knoll's image to architects, interior designers, and potential clients.[5] Reflecting later on her tremendous influence on the Knoll firm as a whole, Florence Knoll Bassett affirmed that "the planning unit was the heart and soul of the company because it controlled all the visuals, and it was also its biggest sales tool."[6]

Florence Knoll also oversaw the textile division of Knoll Associates and played a key role in fabric development and specification.[7] As the Planning Unit grew, Knoll Textiles, which had been established as a separate division in 1947, expanded its offerings as well, and the staff of the Planning Unit worked closely with their colleagues in the textile division to develop drapery and upholstery textiles for Knoll interiors and furniture. From her perspective as head of the firm, Florence Knoll ensured that each division worked collaboratively and that product lines were integrated. One example of the way that the textiles and furniture worked together is evident in an advertisement for *Transportation Cloth* (see fig. C.4) in *Architectural Forum*, a magazine

Florence Knoll. Knoll showroom, 575 Madison Avenue, New York, N.Y., 1951.
Photographed by Robert Damora. Courtesy Estate of Robert Damora.

primarily read by architects, proclaiming that the fabric was "designed to correlate with the total architectural scheme."[8] The advertisement showed architects (who, along with interior designers, constituted the bulk of the Planning Unit's client base) how textiles and furniture could work together to create modern interiors. The coordination of the company's divisions was part of Knoll's promotional strategy as well, as seen in a 1954 advertisement that underscored the way that the divisions worked together (fig C.2), asserting that "furniture and fabrics by Knoll are planned for effective integration into the total design."[9]

Olga Gueft, the esteemed editor of Interiors magazine, profiled Florence Knoll in 1957 as she was completing the interiors of the Connecticut General Life Insurance Company. Gueft concluded that Florence Knoll was "the most inspired catalyst of the avant-garde in our field today" because of the widespread influence that she and the Planning Unit exerted on the interiors field.[10] Knoll products and interior design projects were published extensively, displayed at prominent exhibitions, and generally defined the modern office aesthetic. Gueft noted Knoll's domination of the office interior field, writing that "none of Knoll's rivals can claim as many of the great names in the modern design world . . . none can claim as many milestones in modern furniture (esthetic or structural)." Even when the Knoll Planning Unit was not contracted, the selection of Knoll furniture for modern offices led to what Gueft referred to as "a family resemblance," suggesting that Knoll products and Planning Unit idioms defined the visual vocabulary of the high-end office at midcentury.

Knoll's success was substantial despite several obstacles and setbacks, including postwar production challenges, the unexpected death of Hans Knoll in 1955, increasing competition from other companies like the Herman Miller Furniture Company, and the establishment of dedicated interior design teams at large architectural firms like Skidmore, Owings & Merrill. It is difficult to extrapolate statistics for the exact business generated by the Planning Unit, but in 1951, Architectural Forum reported that the Planning Unit's business had increased 87½ times over 1945 levels, and by 1961 Knoll Associates had twenty-nine showrooms in the United States, Europe, and South America, and the firm did $15 million worth of business.[11]

The Knoll Planning Unit fulfilled a demand for innovative office design as the postwar building boom was creating millions of new square feet of office space, particularly in New York City, the site of many Planning Unit projects.[12] The boom in interior design services was also fueled by companies in older buildings that modernized by renovating their interiors.[13] Offices were not just being made over; the nature of the office interior was changing. With space always at a premium, designers had to optimize square footage and worker productivity while maintaining the hierarchies that typified postwar office culture. Planning Unit designs often called for efficient placement of furniture in mid-level executive offices (high-level executives would continue to have roomy suites), and although the grouping of secretaries in work pools was already an established practice, the Planning Unit introduced an extensive line of secretarial desks to meet a variety of office needs.

The Early Planning Unit and Equipment for Living

The earliest documented incarnation of the Planning Unit dates to 1944, when Hans Knoll invited "a group of designers with architectural and engineering backgrounds"—Serge Chermayeff, Charles Eames, Antonin and Noémi Raymond, Joe Johannson, Louis Kahn and Oscar Stonorov, Ralph Rapson, and Eero Saarinen—to submit furniture designs suitable for mass production.[14] Long before the advent of our current celebrity-obsessed culture, Knoll used famous names to develop and market its designs, a practice the company has continued to the present. The project was coordinated by German-born industrial designer Walter Baermann. Hans Knoll may have met Baermann through Florence Schust (later Florence Knoll) and her connections to the Cranbrook Academy of Art, where Baermann was head of the industrial design department from 1941.[15] A 1945 brochure explained that the group's "experience in planning anticipates the 'Equipment for Living' requirements in the home and the community."[16] Such rhetoric reflected the widespread expectation that the conclusion of World War II would usher in an era of mass home building in the United States to satisfy the needs of returning veterans and a growing population.[17] This interest was fueled by exhibitions like Designs for Post-War Living at the Los Angeles County Museum of Art (1943) and Tomorrow's Small House at the Museum of Modern Art (1945), and books like Tomorrow's House by George Nelson and Henry Wright and If You Want to Build a House by Elizabeth B. Kassler.[18] Hans Knoll recognized that there was a lack of furniture and textiles suited for modern homes and, thinking that domestic furnishings would be a large area of postwar growth, sought to develop modern goods for this market.[19] As it turned out, commissions from corporate clients would constitute the bulk of Knoll's postwar business.

An article in the May 1945 issue of Arts and Architecture magazine featured the 1945 Knoll furniture line, marketed under the phrase "Equipment for Living," and outlined the ambitions of the firm. It would be a vertically integrated business with a "new and unified approach in design, production, and merchandising" that would see a design from "the raw product to the consumer's living room."[20] Hans Knoll and Walter Baermann envisioned the Planning Unit would form partnerships with manufacturers who had dramatically increased their productive capacities during World War II and needed to find peacetime conversion uses for their factories.[21] While committed to modern design, the Planning Unit was willing to tackle nearly any problem. An advertisement (fig. 4.2) stated, "Our planning unit with its design associates, is solving our problems and those of our industrial clients. If you have problems susceptible to modern design, modern production, modern materials, we invite your inquiry."[22] The 1945 line consisted of "products which the average American family needs and buys for its home."[23] It was comprised of wood tables and chairs with either webbing or traditional upholstery, including models that furniture designer Jens Risom had developed for Knoll in 1943 (see chapter 2), as well as more recent designs by Ralph Rapson and Abel Sorensen (see figs. 2.17, 2.19).[24]

By October 1945, the Planning Unit as originally conceived was dissolved, and Baermann left to work for designer Norman Bel Geddes. While the "Equipment for Living" initiative was also discontinued, designs by Risom and Sorensen remained in production.[25] Surviving evidence indicates that Florence Schust was involved in this early version of the Planning Unit under Walter Baermann and designed a range of versatile modular storage furniture.[26] It appears that she was assuming a larger role in the company, and the early Planning Unit's focus was incompatible with her vision, which may have contributed to Baermann's departure. In later interviews Florence Knoll Bassett stated that the Scandinavian-influenced wood furniture and Alvin Lustig's advertising campaign did not match her expectations of the direction that the company should take and that she wanted to commission other designers to create new products for the firm.[27]

Organization of the Planning Unit

Florence Knoll Bassett later recalled that she first met Hans Knoll in 1942 through a mutual acquaintance and that she and Hans moved in similar social circles in the relatively small New York design world.[28] As a manufacturer of modern furniture, Hans Knoll was often asked to design spaces for clients, and since his expertise lay in producing and selling furnishings, he hired Florence Schust, who had training in both architecture and design, to handle the interior design work.

Florence Schust and Hans Knoll married August 1, 1946. By this time she had also invested significant capital in the firm, and the name of the company was changed to Knoll Associates. During the war the company's interiors work had consisted primarily of wartime projects for the government, such as designing recreation areas in aircraft plants (see chapter 2 and fig. 2.13). In the postwar period, the client base expanded, with Knoll working on government, corporate, and private commissions (many the result of Florence Knoll's personal connections), and the Planning Unit received growing acclaim for its interior design and space planning projects.

The main Planning Unit offices were located in the company's New York City headquarters, but each Knoll showroom, whether domestic or international, had a Planning Unit branch so that customers around the world could take advantage of space planning services.[29] There were approximately fifteen people on staff at the New York Planning Unit at any given time. Influential figures included designers Lewis Butler, who worked closely with Knoll on design development, and Heino Orro, who focused on showroom design.[30] The process started with client meetings to assess basic needs. The Planning Unit would then prepare a proposal for interior design and furnishings and would develop floor plans, placement drawings, and perspectives to illustrate the proposed interior. With the client's approval, the Planning Unit would select furnishings, color schemes, and accessories and would fabricate custom pieces.[31]

A key tool in the Planning Unit design process was the paste-up, a plan of the interior with fabric swatches and wood chips attached to represent furniture, upholstery, and window treatments, giving the client a sense of how the interior would look and feel. Florence Knoll traced her knowledge of and interest in the technique to a pasted-up model of a dress that Loja Saarinen had given her as a Christmas present in 1935 (fig. 4.3). Knoll recalled that "[Loja] made this enclosed card for Christmas and proceeded to make the actual dress thereafter so she could do the proper fittings."[32] Knoll subsequently used the paste-up technique in a model house that she designed while she was a student at the Kingswood School for Girls at Cranbrook under the tutelage of Rachel DeWolfe Raseman.[33]

Paste-ups were used for nearly every Planning Unit project. Allan Denenberg, a job captain in the Planning Unit from 1956 to 1958, recalled that there was a large worktable in the center of the Planning Unit office on which models and paste-ups were made (fig. 4.4). Underneath the table were boxes of fabrics for paste-up production. For each project, the job captain would make a drawing, and Florence Knoll would select furniture finishes, carpets, upholstery fabrics, and wall colors. Then color and materials specialists Pacita Qua or Rita Litinsky would cut the fabric samples and attach them to the drawing.[34] Describing the paste-up of the executive suite in the Pittsburgh offices of the H. J. Heinz Company (1959), Knoll recalled that the technique was "a typical presentation made for plans or on models. It was extraordinary how small swatches of fabrics and wood could convey a feeling of the space," emphasizing how textiles were integral to the Planning Unit design process (figs. 4.5, 4.6).[35]

Early Projects

After the war, Hans Knoll secured government contracts for the Planning Unit to furnish the interiors of the United

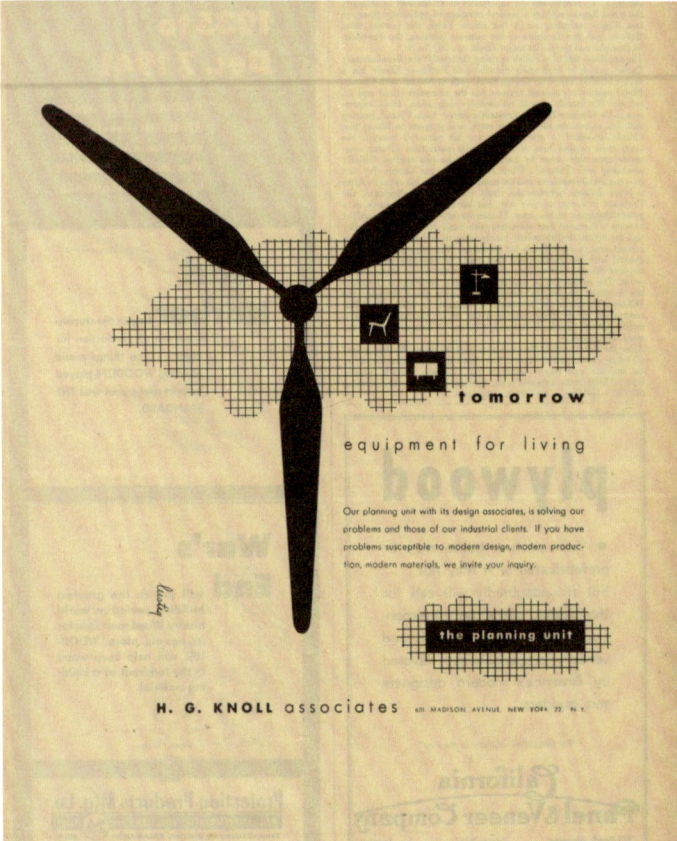

Fig. 4.1 **Top** Florence Knoll (center), Frazar B. Wilde, and others at a conference at Connecticut General Life Insurance Company, ca. 1955. Knoll Archives.
Fig. 4.2 **Bottom left** Advertisement for H. G. Knoll Associates, designed by Alvin Lustig. From *Arts and Architecture*, March 1945.

Fig. 4.3 **Bottom right** Loja Saarinen. Dress paste-up for Florence Schust, 1935. Mixed media on paper. Florence Knoll Bassett Papers, Archives of American Art, Smithsonian Institution.

Fig. 4.4 Knoll Planning Unit textile and work area, Knoll showroom and headquarters, 320 Park Avenue, New York, N.Y., ca. 1961. Knoll Archives.

States Information Services (USIS) offices in Germany, France, and Italy. Taking advantage of incentives to build factories in these countries, Knoll Associates established a woodworking operation in Germany, a metalworking factory in Italy, and both fabric and woodworking plants in France, and the company then used the products to furnish the office interiors. These operations were the genesis of the European Knoll factories and served as the foundation for Knoll International.[36] Hans Knoll also received contracts to design interiors for the United Service Organizations (USO) without knowing their exact locations.[37] Asked later how Hans managed to land such competitive jobs, Florence Knoll recalled that "probably [he] went down to Washington and sniffed it out. I'm not quite sure. He was very good at that. He was an entrepreneur and a great salesman."[38]

Many early postwar projects of the Planning Unit came through the Knolls' friends and connections. The bulk of the orders were from architects specifying Knoll furniture for their new buildings, so Florence Knoll's extensive contacts from her training at the Cranbrook Academy of Art, the Architectural Association in London, and the Illinois Institute of Technology and particularly from her professional experience in the offices of Marcel Breuer in Cambridge, Massachusetts, and Harrison & Abramovitz in New York City, yielded much work. Skidmore, Owings & Merrill partner Gordon Bunshaft, whom the Knolls met in the early 1940s, was a frequent collaborator, working with the Planning Unit on major projects like Connecticut General and Heinz. One of the earliest projects with Skidmore, Owings & Merrill was the 1947 Madison Room, the restaurant at Harry S. Manchester, Inc., a department store in Madison, Wisconsin.[39] Knoll furnished this space with Abel Sorensen chairs with yellow cotton webbing and Isamu Noguchi table lamps (fig. 4.7).[40] The draperies were an Angelo Testa printed fabric with wide yellow stripes and a black linear design.[41] At this early point in the company's life, when the line was limited, Florence Knoll would specify Knoll products as well as designs from other manufacturers. As time passed, though, and the offerings of the Knoll line expanded, Planning Unit projects would increasingly call for Knoll products almost exclusively.

Through Florence Knoll's relationship with architect Wallace K. Harrison, for whom she worked in the early 1940s, the Planning Unit designed the Aluminum Company of America (Alcoa) offices in Pittsburgh (1953) and the Carnegie Endowment for International Peace, International Center, in New York City (1953). For the aluminum-clad Alcoa building, the Planning Unit produced its standard office furniture with custom aluminum frames (even making an aluminum *Barcelona* chair) and covered the furniture with a variety of Knoll upholsteries, including new Evelyn Hill handwoven fabrics.[42] The company celebrated this large and important commission in its first set of advertisements for the Planning Unit (see fig. C.7). At the Carnegie Endowment, where the budget was more limited and the client required a great deal of flexibility, the Planning Unit employed the characteristic features of the "Knoll look"—a primarily neutral palette with accents of bright color in upholsteries and wall treatments and furniture from the Knoll line.[43]

Florence Knoll's friendship with Eero Saarinen (see chapter 2) also resulted in an ongoing business relationship. Knoll Associates not only produced several examples of Saarinen's furniture designs but also largely furnished the massive Saarinen-designed General Motors Technical Center in Warren, Michigan (opened in stages beginning in 1950)—a large commission for the young company. Knoll Textiles developed the durable *Transportation Cloth* for this project, and this fabric became part of the standard line for more than two decades (see chapter 3).[44] The Knoll Planning Unit went on to collaborate with Saarinen on many other projects including Drake University in Des Moines, Iowa (1954), as well as his thirty-five-floor skyscraper for CBS in New York (1965).[45]

The Knoll Planning Unit secured many private and government commissions to design interiors overseas, often through its international branches. Perhaps most significant among these were the interiors of American embassies and consulates in Stockholm, Havana, Copenhagen, Brussels, and other European and Latin American cities.[46] Many of the embassy buildings were designed by architects with whom Knoll had worked previously, including Ralph Rapson, Gordon Bunshaft, and Harrison & Abramovitz.[47] For the United States Embassy in Havana, Cuba (1953), Harrison & Abramovitz designed a monumental seven-story tower of heat-resistant glass and creamy Italian travertine, and the Knoll Planning Unit provided interior planning and furnishings.[48] One of the building's most distinctive spaces was the penthouse conference lounge (fig. 4.8). It featured a predominantly white palette for walls, carpet, and ceiling, with black accents in the furniture frames and some upholsteries, such as black-and-white *Scotch Linen* and *Transportation Cloth*. A few bright color accents were keyed to "the naturally brilliant Cuban spectrum," including the persimmon colorway of Marianne Strengell's *Puli* on one sofa and light blue translucent silk draperies that doubled as a sunscreen. As this space was to be used for both meetings and social functions, Florence Knoll created a retractable room divider using Eszter Haraszty's print *Tracy* in black on white silk gauze. In this way the Planning Unit created dignified yet informal spaces for discussion, negotiation, and socializing.

"A welcoming air of warmth and informality, conducive to the success of agreeable diplomatic relations" characterized the Stockholm embassy designed by the Knoll Planning Unit.[49] The ambassador's office featured neutral tones of off-white, camel, black, and white, with accents of more vibrant colors such as persimmon and blue. While moderately priced textiles such as *Scotch Linen* were employed, this office also exuded a subtle air of luxury through the use of handwoven silk draperies and upholsteries designed by Evelyn Hill. The Swedish embassy project also led to the development of what became a signature Knoll textile. While the Planning Unit had initially specified *Transportation Cloth*, the Avisco rayon fiber required for this fabric was not available to the Swedish manufacturer contracted to weave it. The Planning Unit worked with Astrid Sampe of Nordiska Kompaniet (NK), the Knoll licensee in Sweden and producer of most of the embassy furnishings, to develop a replacement. The result was a durable wool and nylon upholstery fabric that was introduced to the American market in 1954 under the name *Rugby*.[50]

The Rockefeller family was also an important source of early commissions. The first Rockefeller job came through Howard Myers, editor of *Architectural Forum*, and architect Wallace Harrison. In 1946 Nelson Rockefeller invited the Planning Unit to design Room 56, the Rockefeller family offices on the fifty-sixth floor of the RCA Building at Rockefeller Center (see chapter 1).[51] The Planning Unit also designed part of Nelson Rockefeller's own residence, as well as offices and the director's residence in the Rockefeller Institute for Medical Research (1957, now Rockefeller University) in New York City.[52]

Knoll Associates carried out several dormitory furnishing plans in its early years. These projects were an important proving ground for the Planning Unit in fulfilling the complex requirements of such a space: durable furniture for sleeping, studying, and storage, all in a confined space and on a tight budget.[53] The first project was Alice Crocker Lloyd Hall (1948), a women's dormitory at the University of Michigan at Ann Arbor, followed by South Quadrangle Hall (1951), a men's dormitory at the same university, and facilities at the University of Rochester (New York), Trinity University in San Antonio, Texas, and other sites. Solutions included extensive built-ins to deter rearrangement and the resultant damage to furniture and walls; durable materials such as brick walls; washable plastic upholstery on chairs; economically printed cotton textiles for bedcovers, pillows, and draperies; burn-proof desk surfaces; extensive storage in wall-mounted bookshelves; and versatile elements like multidirectional lamps that could shine light on the desk, the bed, or a sitting area (fig. 4.9). All furniture was raised from the floor to allow for easy cleaning. In the dormitory common areas the Planning Unit also employed economical options to create flexible, multifunctional spaces. Furniture in the first University of Michigan installation included lightweight, easily movable chairs and tables designed by Jens Risom and others, with variations of texture and color achieved through webbing and inexpensive printed and textured cotton upholsteries and draperies, including *Chinese Coins*, *Campagna*, and *Prestini* (see chapter 3).

One of the Planning Unit's first comprehensive office installations was for Minneapolis-based North American Life and Casualty Company (1948, architects Lang & Raugland).[54] The importance of this installation to the young firm is evidenced by the fact that it was featured in various Knoll promotional materials of the period.[55] For this project, the Planning Unit furnished the main lobby, reception areas, executive offices, conference room, auditorium, cafeteria, and secretarial areas. For the basement auditorium and cafeteria, a molded plywood stacking chair designed by Ilmari Tapiovaara was specified and upholstered in Knoll Textiles' brown-and-white–striped plastic upholstery (fig. 4.10, see also fig. 3.3).[56] This upholstery was woven from Saran fiber sold under the trade name Lumite and had the benefits of being brightly colored, durable, mildew-proof, and nonflammable.[57] The lobby was furnished with custom-designed desks and tables and pairs of Mies van der Rohe's *Barcelona* chairs, likely the first time they were used in a Knoll installation (fig. 4.11).[58]

Partnerships with Textile Firms

Hans and Florence Knoll's extensive connections in the design community led to several projects for firms that produced or sold textiles, textile fibers, and related products. In a 1948 collaboration with Skidmore, Owings & Merrill, the Knoll Planning Unit and Marianne Strengell furnished the New York City showroom and offices of Owens-Corning Fiberglas, makers of a range of fiberglass products (fig. 4.12).[59] The showroom demonstrated the many uses of fiberglass, then a new material, and the architect and designers employed the company's products throughout, from the vibrant upholstery and curtains designed by Strengell to the acoustic ceiling tile, wall panels, and insulation material. For Dow Chemical's executive offices in Baton Rouge, Louisiana (1956), the new *Sarano* upholstery, woven from Dow's Saran plastic fiber in two-color and striped versions, covered nearly all the upholstered surfaces on the paste-up plan (fig. 4.13).[60]

Another upholstery-related firm that hired the Knoll Planning Unit was Hewitt-Robins, the manufacturer of Restfoam latex foam cushioning. Knoll provided furniture, draperies, and custom wall units for the 1949 renovation of the company's New York City headquarters.[61] The president's office exhibited several aspects that would come to characterize Knoll executive interiors, notably a large table-desk and wall-mounted storage cabinet. In this case the table-desk was custom-designed by Knoll and included a leather top. Textiles were also used prominently to provide texture and subtle decoration as seen in the tweed of the chair upholstery and *Campagna* printed draperies (see fig. 3.14). The Hewitt-Robins project may have come about due to a relationship between Knoll and the company, which provided the cushioning in Eero Saarinen's *Womb* chair (1948), a fact that was proudly advertised by Hewitt-Robins.[62]

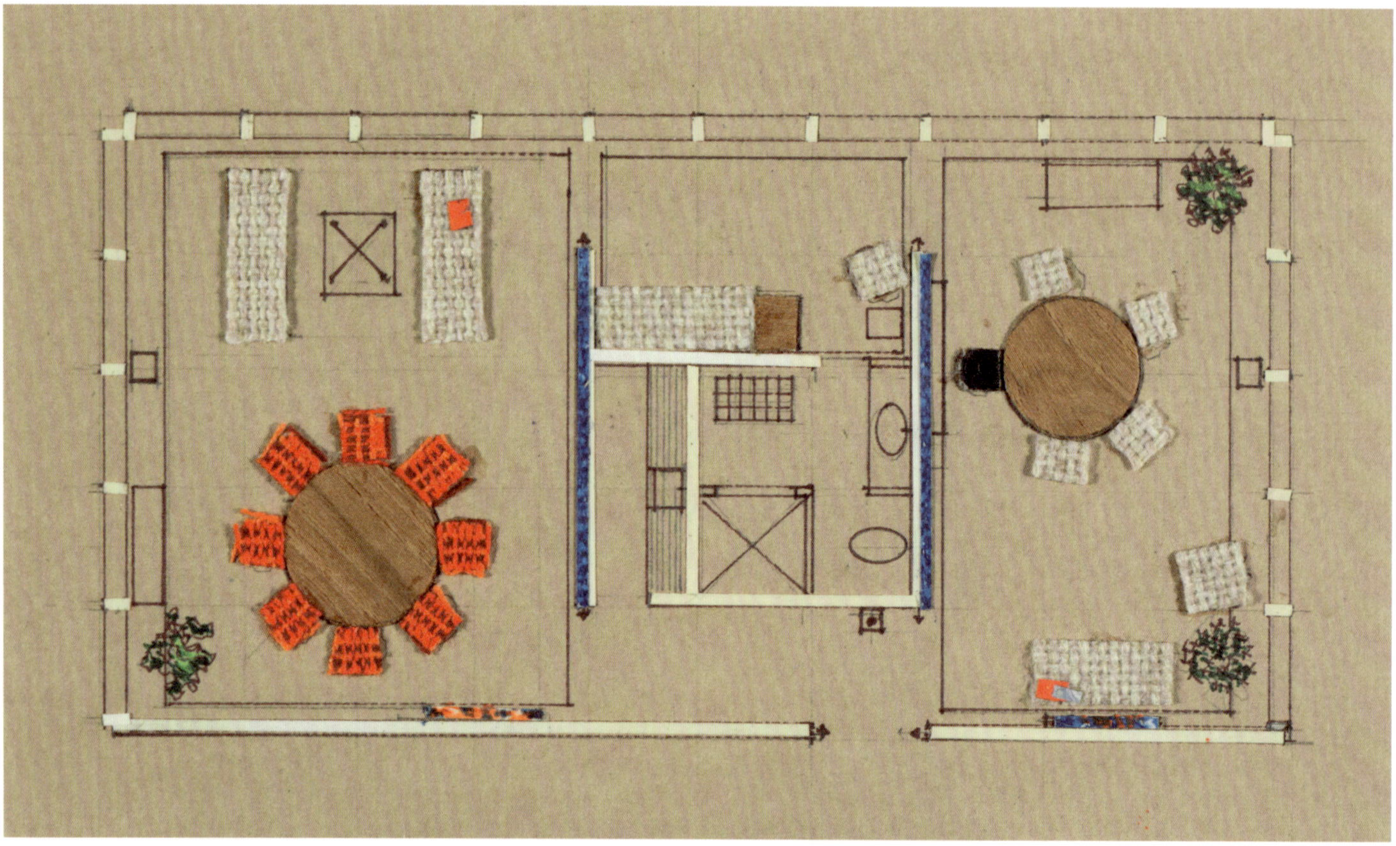

Fig. 4.5 Top Florence Knoll/Knoll Planning Unit. Paste-up plan of the design for Jack Heinz's office at H. J. Heinz Company, Pittsburgh, Penn., ca. 1958. Pen, colored pencil, Knoll *Handwoven* textiles, and wood veneer on paper. Florence Knoll Bassett Papers, Archives of American Art, Smithsonian Institution. Cat. 157.

Fig. 4.6 Bottom Florence Knoll/Knoll Planning Unit. H. J. Heinz Company executive suite, Pittsburgh, Penn., 1959. Photographed by Ezra Stoller. Florence Knoll Bassett Papers, Archives of American Art, Smithsonian Institution.

Fig. 4.7 Florence Knoll/Knoll Planning Unit. The Madison Room, Harry S. Manchester, Inc. department store, Madison, Wis., 1947. Photographed by Smith-Wollin Studio. From "Madison Room," *Architectural Record*, July 1947.

Fig. 4.8 Top Florence Knoll/Knoll Planning Unit. Penthouse conference lounge, United States Embassy, Havana, Cuba, 1953. Photographed by J. Alex Langley. From "U.S. Embassy Office Building, Havana, Cuba," *Progressive Architecture*, February 1955.
Fig. 4.9 Bottom Florence Knoll/Knoll Planning Unit. Dormitory room, South Quadrangle Hall, University of Michigan, Ann Arbor, 1951. Photographed by Arthur Siegel. Knoll Archives.

Fig. 4.10 Top Florence Knoll/Knoll Planning Unit. North American Life and Casualty Company auditorium, Minneapolis, Minn., ca. 1948. From Knoll Associates, "Research Approach to Interior Planning" brochure, designed by Herbert Matter, 1949. The Museum of Modern Art Library, New York.

Fig. 4.11 Bottom Florence Knoll/Knoll Planning Unit. North American Life and Casualty Company lobby, Minneapolis, Minn., ca. 1948. From Knoll Associates, "Research Approach to Interior Planning" brochure, designed by Herbert Matter, 1949. The Museum of Modern Art Library, New York.

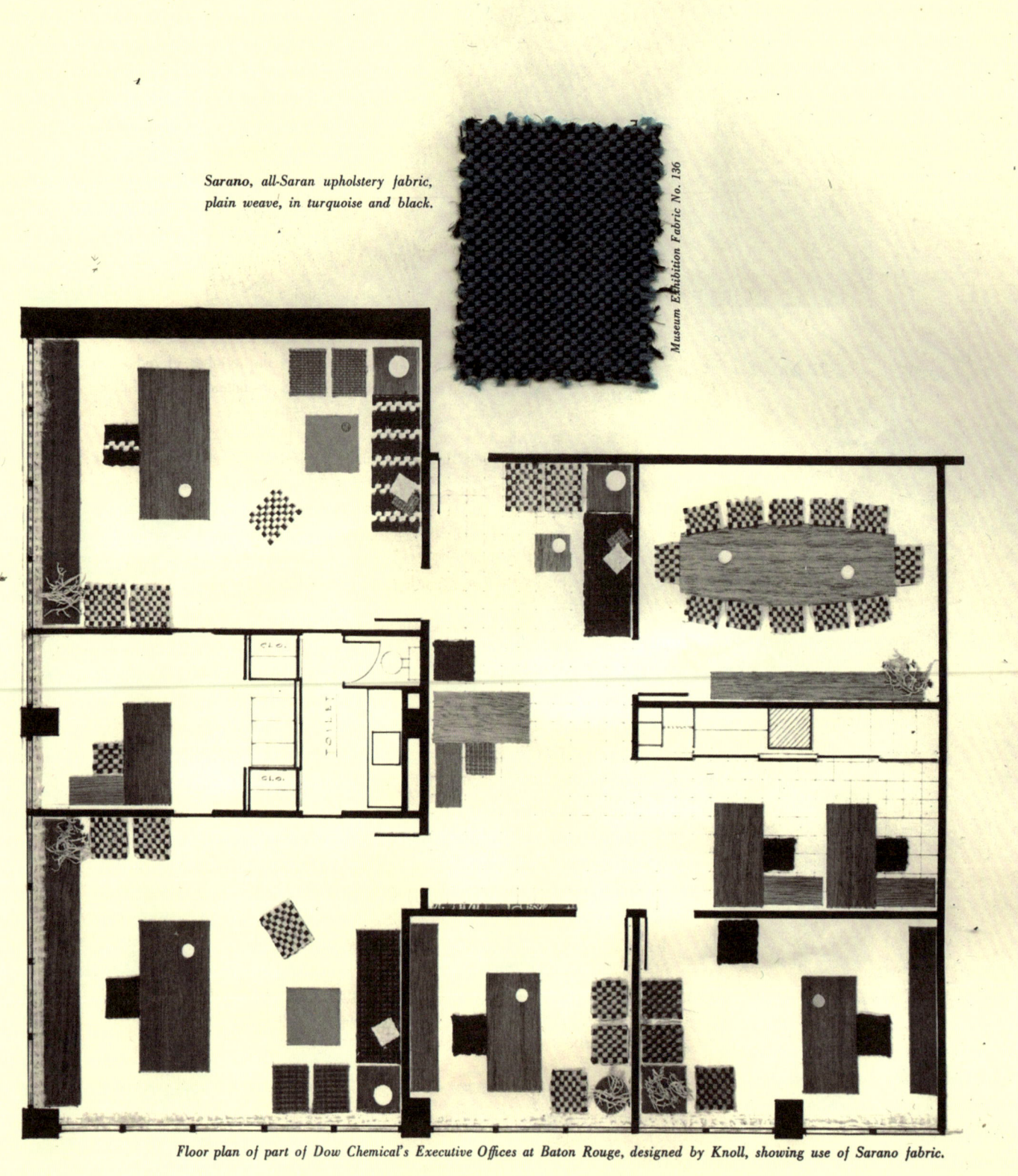

Fig. 4.13 Florence Knoll/Knoll Planning Unit. Paste-up plan of Dow Chemical executive offices, Baton Rouge, La., and swatch of *Sarano*. From *American Fabrics*, Fall 1956.

Fig. 4.12 Top left Florence Knoll/Knoll Planning Unit (designers); Skidmore, Owings & Merrill (architects). Owens-Corning Fiberglas sales office, New York, N.Y., 1948. Photographed by Ezra Stoller. Ezra Stoller © ESTO 8J.006.

Fig. 4.14 Top right Florence Knoll/Knoll Planning Unit. First-floor sales area, Deering Milliken & Company, Avenue of the Americas and 39th Street, New York, N.Y., 1958. Photographed by Herbert Matter. Knoll Archives.

Fig. 4.15 Bottom Evelyn Hill Anselevicious. *Handwoven H950/2* ("Light Grey and White" colorway) on *Model 26* sofa design by Florence Knoll from Deering Milliken & Company installation, ca. 1958. Made for Knoll Associates, Inc. Upholstery: wool; plain weave; sofa: wood frame, metal legs, batting. Courtesy Miliken & Company. Cat. 109.

Deering Milliken & Company, which produced insulated fabrics sold by the textile division, hired the Planning Unit to design the interiors of its New York headquarters, opened in 1958.[63] The photograph for an advertisement widely published by Knoll (fig. 4.14) showed the first-floor sales area, where an array of desks stood before a large wall featuring a Herbert Matter photomural of early spinning machinery. Red wool upholstery provided bright accents of color in this otherwise neutral space. A *Model 26* sofa covered in a Knoll handwoven fabric provided a comfortable and luxurious addition to the executive offices (fig. 4.15).

Frank Stanton and Columbia Broadcasting System

One of the most important Planning Unit projects was the executive floor of the Columbia Broadcasting System's New York headquarters, completed in 1954. It received extensive press coverage and resulted in subsequent commissions from other clients.[64] Like many Planning Unit projects, the impetus came from a singularly charismatic and committed client, company president Frank Stanton, who, together with his wife, Ruth, was interested in design and the arts. Florence Knoll Bassett later recalled, "The most significant planning job Knoll did was the first CBS job. . . . Frank Stanton was unique, he was very contemporary and knew what was going on . . . he found us and gave us a chance. Things like that small job with high visibility led to many other jobs."[65] For this project, the Planning Unit analyzed the needs of the executives and secretaries working on the floor and developed a space plan that accommodated executive offices, reception areas, and secretarial bays.

The Planning Unit lavished much attention on Frank Stanton's own office (fig 4.16). *Architectural Forum* called it "meticulous and exact, without going dead," and reported that it reflected Stanton's particular and refined style.[66] Florence Knoll used sleek yet luxurious furniture and concealed a sophisticated electronic control system and the many devices that a television executive needed close at hand, including a phonograph, telephone, radio, and both color and black-and-white televisions. A marble-topped table desk on steel legs and a wall-mounted control panel and storage unit behind the desk accommodated the built-in technology (fig. 4.17).[67] Custom work such as this exemplified the comprehensive service that the Planning Unit provided—specifying a mix of Knoll furniture and pieces by other firms for general office spaces (fig. 4.18), as well as customized, often more luxurious elements for specialized needs. Stanton's office also included a sitting area with a glass-and-steel Mies van der Rohe coffee table, two *Barcelona* chairs, and a leather ottoman, as well as a Florence Knoll–designed sofa covered in a charcoal Evelyn Hill handwoven upholstery (fig. 4.16).[68] This kind of lounge furniture was similar to that found in high-end modern living rooms, and the creation of such domestic-style spaces within executive offices became a hallmark of a new trend in office design in which Knoll played a major role.[69] The Planning Unit not only specified furniture models and arrangements but also corresponding textiles for upholstery, carpet, window treatments, office accessories, and sometimes even the art for the walls (in the case of CBS, Florence Knoll and Frank Stanton selected the art together). The use of lounge furniture and the rich textures and colors found in Planning Unit offices recalled living rooms more than traditional business offices, and, as a result, the Knoll Planning Unit became well known for designing executive offices that had an air of domesticity.

The CBS executive floor and other prominent projects in this period presented an opportunity for the Planning Unit to publicize its wide range of services to architects and design-minded clients. Projects were extensively advertised in architectural and design periodicals, which raised the profile of the Planning Unit considerably. Shortly after completing the CBS job, Knoll Associates placed an advertisement for the Planning Unit in *Architectural Forum* illustrating Frank Stanton's office and describing how the Planning Unit could remodel a firm's interior to satisfy a company's existing and future needs.[70] In other cases the Planning Unit collaborated with architects on interiors for newly constructed buildings. To appeal to this audience, another advertisement in *Architectural Forum* a few months later featured interiors for the newly built American National Bank in Austin, Texas, and proclaimed, "The Knoll Planning Unit, design consultants to the architect, simplifies his task by co-ordinating interiors with the total plan. Many noted architects have found this Knoll service invaluable in a wide range of major projects."[71] The advertisement, like most Planning Unit promotional materials, acknowledged the architectural firm with which Knoll worked (in this case Kuehne, Brooks & Barr). This business strategy proved particularly effective, as many architecture firms became loyal Planning Unit clients.

Frank Stanton was an important client not only for awarding the Planning Unit a significant and publicity-friendly opportunity, but also for directing other jobs its way. As chairman of the board of the Center for Advanced Study in the Behavioral Sciences at Stanford University in California, Stanton commissioned the Planning Unit to design the interiors of its new building by Wurster, Bernardi & Emmons on the Stanford University campus. Like the CBS project, it was completed in 1954 and widely publicized.[72] The Planning Unit specified many of the same furniture models that it had for the CBS executive floor, but a journalist wrote that "the rooms in California are shaggier, toothier, with a much wider range of finishes—matting on the wood floor, walls of redwood and painted T&G [tongue and groove] ceilings."[73] In contrast to CBS, the budget for the project was relatively

Fig. 4.16 Florence Knoll/Knoll Planning Unit. Office of Frank Stanton, president of CBS, New York, N.Y., 1954. Photographed by Robert Damora. Courtesy Estate of Robert Damora.

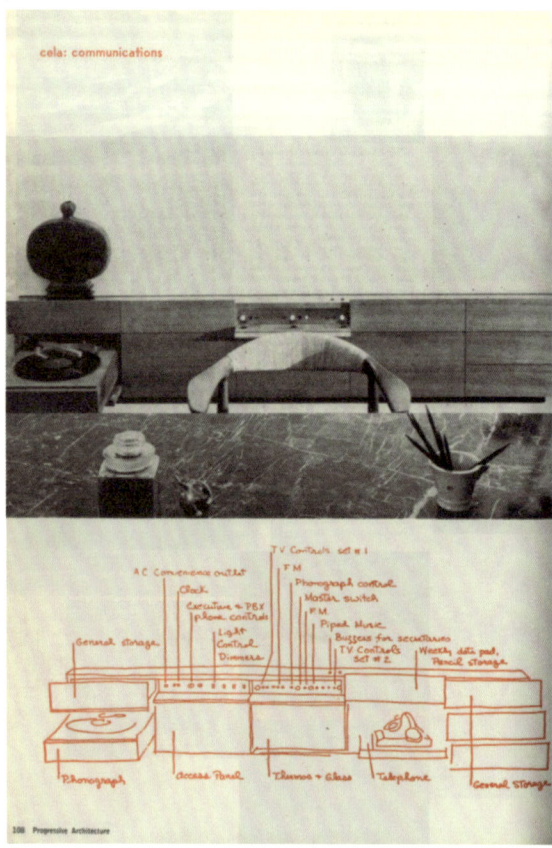

Fig. 4.17 Top left Florence Knoll/Knoll Planning Unit (drawing by Florence Knoll; photograph by Yuichi Idaka). Desk and wall-mounted cabinet, concealing control panel, in the office of Frank Stanton, president of CBS, New York, N.Y., 1954. From "CELA: Communications," *Progressive Architecture*, May 1956.

Fig. 4.18 Top right Florence Knoll/Knoll Planning Unit. Secretarial area, CBS executive floor, New York, N.Y., ca. 1954. Photographed by Robert Damora. Courtesy Estate of Robert Damora.

Fig. 4.19 Bottom Florence Knoll/Knoll Planning Unit (designers); Skidmore, Owings & Merrill (architects). Open office area, Connecticut General Life Insurance Company, Bloomfield, Conn., ca. 1957. Photographed by Ezra Stoller. Ezra Stoller © ESTO 51S.066c.

low, and a Knoll advertisement featuring the center emphasized the Planning Unit's ability to provide more economical design: "The Knoll Planning Unit, design consultants to the architect, collaborates in achieving more efficient use of space, more efficient use of budget."[74] The center's interiors were furnished with standard Knoll furniture and less-expensive Knoll textiles and did not include the customized design found in projects like CBS.

Several years later, Stanton encouraged his friend Gardner Cowles, president of Cowles Magazines and publisher of *Look*, to hire the Planning Unit to design the company's executive offices in New York (1962).[75] The Knoll Planning Unit also designed the interiors of the Eero Saarinen–designed skyscraper for CBS (1965), then under the leadership of Frank Stanton, demonstrating how important loyal and supportive clients were to Knoll's success.

Just when Knoll Associates and the Knoll Planning Unit were gaining widespread recognition for their leadership in the interior design field, the company suffered a significant loss. On October 8, 1955, Hans Knoll was killed in a car accident in Havana, where he had been seeking out Cuban clients.[76] Despite the huge loss of the company's founder, guiding force, and chief salesman, all three divisions of the Knoll firm continued projects that were underway, and the business expanded in subsequent years. Florence Knoll became president and remained director of design, continuing to be the final arbiter on all new textiles, furniture designs, and Planning Unit projects.

Connecticut General Life Insurance Company

Completed in 1957, the Connecticut General Life Insurance Company complex by architects Skidmore, Owings & Merrill, with landscape design by Isamu Noguchi, was the largest project that the Planning Unit had undertaken to date. Located on 260 acres outside Hartford, Connecticut, the 400,000-square-foot office complex was designed for a workforce of 3,000 employees, and, due to its isolated location, the facilities included a cafeteria, auditorium, bowling alley, tennis courts, beauty salon, and other amenities.[77] Company president Frazar B. Wilde had considered building a tower in Hartford, but decided that the rural location would lure employees, and that a horizontal orientation was more conducive to efficient work and would allow for easier expan- sion. As one of the first companies to establish a suburban campus, Connecticut General was the leading precursor to a major trend in office construction in the second half of the twentieth century. In order to maximize space, all offices, secretarial areas, and ceiling and floor panels were based on a six-foot module, as was the custom-designed office furniture. A system of movable walls was installed to allow for flexibility and the reorganization of space when needs changed (fig. 4.19).

The architects and designers built a full-scale mockup of an office interior that allowed executives to experience the space before construction began. Florence Knoll convinced the client that the rather significant $100,000 investment in the mockup would be repaid in more efficient allocation of space. She was proved right in at least one case—the junior executive office. Before the mockup, Wilde had thought that because the building was designed on a six-foot module, the smallest office should measure twelve by eighteen feet. However, the full-size mockup convinced him that a twelve-by-twelve foot office was acceptable if modern furniture were used with the desk placed perpendicular to the window wall (fig. 4.20).[78]

A highlight of the Connecticut General interiors was the penthouse executive suite. The executive lounge and a conference room were designed with neutral-colored carpet, handwoven Indian silk draperies, and a travertine wall and accented with handwoven bright red and blue upholstery on the seating furniture (fig. 4.21). Some rooms in the executive suite also featured brightly colored silk wall panels. While Florence Knoll frequently called for Knoll's power-loomed fabrics, she also specified handwoven textiles because they could be made in small yardages and in highly refined color palettes.[79]

It is very likely that Florence Knoll designed the 1956 *Parallel Bar* system of furniture specifically for the Connecticut General project and its six-foot module (fig. 4.22).[80] After its development and during the multiyear planning process for the huge Connecticut General complex, Knoll made *Parallel Bar* furniture part of the standard line, and it became one of its most frequently specified products. The "parallel bar" consisted of two brushed chrome steel bars riveted to a perpendicular black steel bar which could support seating furniture, desks, or tables (fig. 4.23).[81] The coffee table was introduced to the trade in January 1955, the lounge chair in the fall of that year, and the full line was featured in *Interiors* in January 1956.[82] Acclaim for the design was immediate—Florence Knoll won a 1955 first-place furniture award in the American Institute of Decorators Home Furnishings Competition for the teak coffee table with *Parallel Bar* steel base.[83] For the *Parallel Bar* seating furniture, Knoll developed and patented a unique method of upholstering to create a crisp, tailored look with a clean silhouette, which prevented the fabric from shifting and bunching without traditional buttoning and tufting.[84] The profile of the *Parallel Bar* lounge chair is similar to that of Mies van der Rohe's *Barcelona* chair in its reclining position and the grid of its upholstered cushions. The likeness of form and function, and the similar uses to which both lounge chairs were put in Planning Unit interiors, suggest that Florence Knoll may have designed the *Parallel Bar* lounge chair as a less expensive and less conspicuous version of the *Barcelona* chair.[85] The *Parallel Bar* lounge chair could also be covered in a wide variety of Knoll's upholsteries, offering

Fig. 4.20 Top Florence Knoll/Knoll Planning Unit (designers); Skidmore, Owings & Merrill (architects). Junior executive office, Connecticut General Life Insurance Company, Bloomfield, Conn., ca. 1957. Photographed by Yuichi Idaka. Knoll Archives.

Fig. 4.21 Bottom Florence Knoll/Knoll Planning Unit (designers); Skidmore, Owings & Merrill (architects). Executive lounge, Connecticut General Life Insurance Company, Bloomfield, Conn., ca. 1957. Photographed by Ezra Stoller. Ezra Stoller © ESTO 51S.071c.

Fig. 4.22 Top Florence Knoll/Knoll Planning Unit (designers); Skidmore, Owings & Merrill (architects). Employee lounge with *Parallel Bar* chairs and settees, Connecticut General Life Insurance Company, Bloomfield, Conn., ca. 1957. Photographed by Ezra Stoller. Ezra Stoller © ESTO 51S.060c.

Fig. 4.23 Bottom Florence Knoll. Detail of a *Parallel Bar* settee, 1956. Photographed by George Cserna. Knoll Archives.

Fig. 4.24 Installation featuring models *700* daybed (right) designed by Richard Stein (backrest covered in *Pandanus*), *198* (*Butterfly*) chair (foreground) by Bonet, Hardoy, and Kurchan, *121* cabinets (background) by Florence Knoll, and *654* chair (background) by Jens Risom (covered in *Chinese Coins* by Noémi Raymond) in the Knoll showroom, 601 Madison Avenue, New York, N.Y., ca. 1948. Photographed by Herbert Matter. Knoll Archives.

a greater range of texture and color possibilities than the brown or black leather available for *Barcelona* chairs during this period.

Knoll Furniture

From the outset, Knoll furniture and textiles were the primary revenue stream of the firm. After introducing designs by Jens Risom, Abel Sorenson, and Ralph Rapson in 1945, Hans Knoll encountered manufacturing challenges in the immediate postwar years—"everything seems to take a very long time," he wrote to Ralph Rapson at the end of 1945.[86] In 1946 the company was developing what would become some of its most iconic furniture designs (such as the *Womb* chair) while introducing new designs to the American market, mostly by Jens Risom (see chapter 2). In the same year Hans and Florence Knoll began to seek out additions to the Knoll line from Europe and traveled to Sweden to source furniture and textiles to import to the United States market.[87]

Swedish design had become more widely known in the United States after being exhibited at the 1939–40 World's Fair in New York, and, because of Sweden's neutrality during World War II, Swedish manufacturers of home furnishings had products available to export.[88] Forming a relationship with NK and other Swedish companies, the Knolls selected designs that were modern and could be knocked down and flat-packed to allow for less-expensive shipping. They installed this furniture in an "Authentic Swedish Room" that opened in the Knoll New York showroom in January 1947. The room was then to be exhibited at retail stores across the country.[89]

The collection included furniture designed by Elias Svedberg, Bruno Mathsson, Fritz Hansen, and Erik Wörtz and textiles by Astrid Sampe and Sven Markelius (see fig. 2.23). A living room with a sofa, armchair, and coffee table and a dining area with a table, four chairs, and a storage cabinet were separated by an open shelving unit for the display of objects. Imported Swedish furniture remained available through Knoll Associates for only a few years. Nevertheless, the Swedish interlude was important in establishing Knoll as a leader and tastemaker of modern design. The relationships Knoll formed with NK and Swedish designers would also result in future collaborative work. The relationship cultivated between the Knolls and Astrid Sampe (head of the NK textile division), for example, resulted in the inclusion of many textiles by Swedish designers in the Knoll line through the 1960s.

In late 1947 and 1948, Knoll began to introduce and market a variety of important new furniture designs.[90] Among the most important forms were a cantilevered lounge chair by Eero Saarinen, later dubbed *Grasshopper*; a chair, sofa, and settee by Florence Knoll (*Models 25–27*); a daybed by Richard Stein; and the canvas or leather sling seat on a metal frame, often called the *Butterfly* chair, by Antonio Bonet, Jorge Ferrari Hardoy, and Juan Kurchan (fig. 4.24). In May 1948, Knoll debuted Eero Saarinen's basketlike easy chair (later known as the *Womb* chair), which *Interiors* called "the season's most revolutionary design for sitting."[91] About the *Womb* chair, Florence Knoll Bassett later recalled that she asked Saarinen to create a large metal-frame chair with plastic seat and foam cushions that made it possible to sit in multiple positions.[92] The introduction of this new upholstered furniture also allowed Knoll to promote its new textile collection and generate increased revenue.

By 1950 the line had expanded sufficiently for Knoll to publish the *Knoll Index of Contemporary Design*, a compendium of the firm's furniture and textiles. The publication, notable for its arresting images and primary color accents, was designed and primarily photographed by Herbert Matter, Knoll's graphic designer since 1947 (fig. 4.25). *Interiors* called this substantial wire-bound book "a kind of portable showroom, with its information available in an intelligent, easy to handle layout."[93] The book included sections on chairs, tables, case furniture and beds, office furniture and desks, and textiles. Its introduction announced that "here the architect and the designer of furniture and textiles find common ground," reinforcing the idea that the audience for Knoll products would be composed primarily of architects and designers looking to furnish modern spaces.[94] It also indicated how integrated the furniture and textile businesses had become just three years after the founding of the textile division. Each piece of furniture in the line was represented by a studio photograph or showroom image and also appeared in a line-drawing elevation with dimensions to assist architects and interior designers with space planning (fig. 4.26). In the textile section, some fabrics were artfully arranged on the page; others were photographed in a modernist grid. Prior Knoll brochures, with their loose-leaf sheets, paled in comparison to this lavish publication. With its silver foil cover and abundant images, the *Knoll Index* was not just a reference for the Knoll line but an aspirational guide to modern living.

Architect-designed furniture filled Knoll advertisements and showroom photographs, but the basic office forms of desks and chairs comprised a significant and growing portion of the line and total sales. To fulfill the growing demand for modern office furnishings, in 1952 Florence Knoll and the Planning Unit staff debuted *Office Planned Furniture*, a collection that was developed "through long research and experience in solving the practical needs of hundreds of offices, from those of top executives to the requirements in a secretarial pool" (fig. 4.27).[95] It consisted of a range of designs emphasizing efficiency, including executive and secretarial desks with iron frames and burn- and stain-resistant laminate tops, cabinets, conference tables, the Saarinen–designed *Model 71* armchair, *Model 72* side chair, and *Model 76* secretarial chair, and a suite of desk accessories.[96] The forms were versatile—for example, any desk could be ordered with a pencil tray or multiple-drawer units, and the chairs were available with metal or wood legs or swivel bases on casters, and the cabinet with sliding doors came in lengths of three, four, or six feet. Florence Knoll had also designed a boat-shaped conference table (1946) with curving sides that allowed unobstructed sightlines from each position at the table, and its availability in many sizes and finishes to suit a variety of office needs was heavily promoted (fig. 4.28). For companies that did not have the resources to engage the Planning Unit in a custom job, the *Knoll Office Planned Furniture* was an efficient and less expensive way to furnish an office. That said, these pieces were also used extensively in Planning Unit projects, particularly for secretarial areas and junior executive offices. Furniture catalogues and price lists show that *Knoll Office Planned Furniture* stayed in the product line through the 1960s, testifying to its continued suitability to office needs.

Throughout the 1950s, Knoll continued to commission prominent architects and artists to design furniture for the line on a freelance basis, including Harry Bertoia, Isamu Noguchi, and Eero Saarinen. Knoll also contracted with Mies van der Rohe to put his *Barcelona* chair, ottoman, and coffee table into production.[97] These furniture designs were widely used in both domestic and corporate contexts. While the clientele for the furniture available through Knoll showrooms consisted primarily of architects and interior designers who would specify products for their projects, Hans Knoll was always searching for ways to bring modern furniture to broader audiences. In 1955, just prior to his death, Knoll established Knoll+Drake Furniture with William S. Drake's firm Austin Industries (fig. 4.29).[98] The line of more than thirty pieces was targeted to middle-class consumers and sold through retail stores like Bloomingdale's rather than trade-only showrooms. Ladislav L. Rado designed the first and only group of Knoll+Drake furniture, including metal-framed seating with upholstery by Eszter Haraszty and desks and tables with white plastic laminate tops.[99] While the line was manufactured in 1955 and early 1956, the venture does not appear to have lasted long past Hans's death.

Due to a sophisticated public relations strategy and high design standards, Knoll furniture and textiles were frequently selected for the *Good Design* exhibitions organized by the Museum of Modern Art and shown at the museum in New York and at the Chicago Merchandise Mart between 1950 and 1955. In nearly every showing, the latest Knoll furniture or textiles were displayed, including designs by Florence Knoll, Eero Saarinen, Franco Albini, Harry Bertoia, Marianne Strengell, Ezster Haraszty, and Evelyn Hill. The *Good Design* exhibitions reached Knoll's core audience of architects and designers committed to modern design as well as the broader design-conscious public. In order to build brand recognition, Knoll also placed advertisements in popular, wide-circulation magazines like *The New Yorker* and *Fortune* that reached executives and businesspeople. One of the most striking advertisements was for Saarinen's line of *Pedestal* furniture, which was initially produced with aluminum bases fitted with a fiberglass reinforced plastic chair shell or wood or marble tabletop (fig. 4.30).[100] With its single flaring leg, the design embodied a space-age vision of a technologically sophisticated future. For Saarinen, however, it was about unity of design; he wrote, "the single pedestal seems the answer because it makes the chair *all one thing*."[101] As with many other Knoll products, vivid textiles on the seat, which contrasted with the white chair frame, were key to the furniture's appearance.

The suitability of the *Pedestal* furniture to both home and office use distinguished it from much of the Knoll product line, which was bifurcated between photogenic, vibrantly upholstered, sculptural furniture by prominent designers (often chairs) and the functional office forms of tables, desks, and storage units designed by the Planning Unit staff or Florence Knoll herself. For example, Harry Bertoia's wire furniture (1952), Eero Saarinen's *Grasshopper* and *Womb* chairs, and Pierre Jeanneret's lounge chair (1948) appeared frequently in Knoll showrooms and Knoll advertisements but were rarely found in Planning Unit jobs. It was not an issue of cost, but rather of propriety. The furniture featured in the showrooms was not significantly more expensive than the standard office furniture; in fact sometimes a comparable object was less.[102] The appearance of particular forms in showrooms but not in offices related to modes of acceptance of certain furniture in residential and corporate interiors. Like showrooms, residential interiors offered more latitude in color choice and design whimsy. Offices could not be as playful, demanding more functional-looking furnishings.[103] Standard office furniture, however, was hugely important to the firm—in any Planning Unit job, the relative size of a lobby or reception area, where the more sculptural furniture could be placed, was dwarfed by the extensive secretarial and executive office spaces. For every pair of *Barcelona* chairs specified, many more standard desks and chairs were ordered. The more publicized furniture attracted attention and press, but the core of the business was the sale of modern, functional office furnishings.

Knoll Showrooms

As a key part of the Knoll promotional strategy, Knoll showrooms disseminated the "Knoll look," illustrated how to use the newly available furniture and textiles, and provided decorating ideas to architects and clients. As Florence Knoll Bassett later explained, "[the showrooms] were important because we had to do a lot of convincing. At the time there were very few clients who were interested in these ideas.

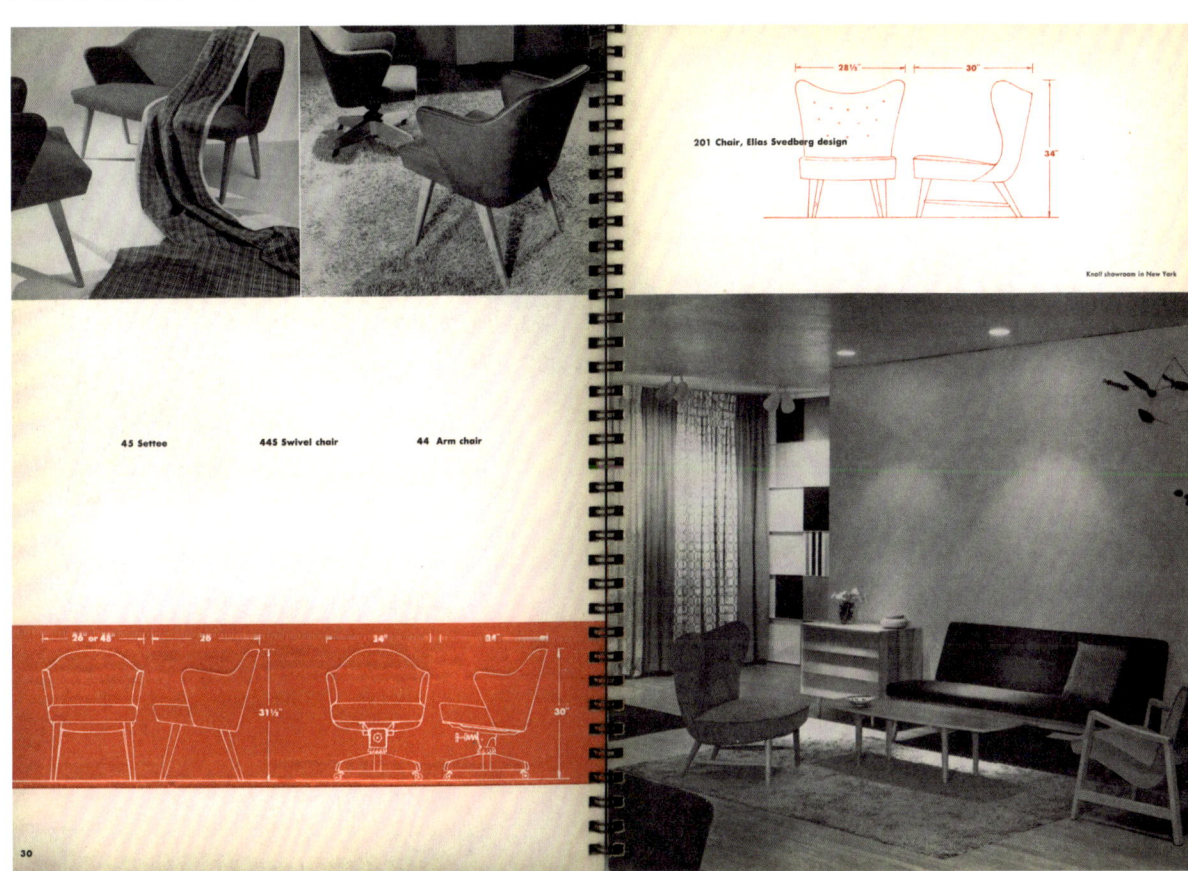

Fig. 4.25 Pages 76–77, featuring textiles, in *Knoll Index of Contemporary Design*, designed by Herbert Matter, 1950. Library, Bard Graduate Center: Decorative Arts, Design History, Material Culture; New York.

Fig. 4.26 Pages 30–31, featuring chair models, *45*, *44S*, *44*, and *201*, in *Knoll Index of Contemporary Design*, designed by Herbert Matter, 1950. Library, Bard Graduate Center: Decorative Arts, Design History, Material Culture; New York.

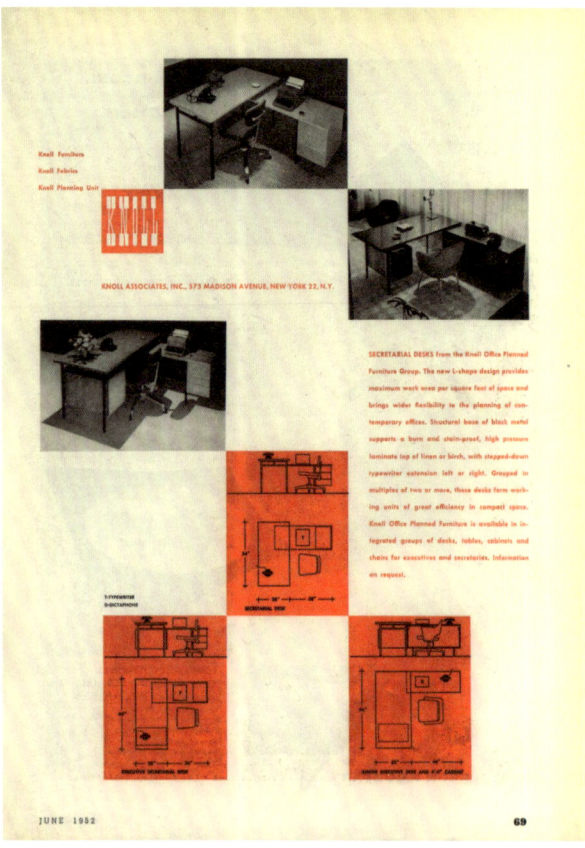
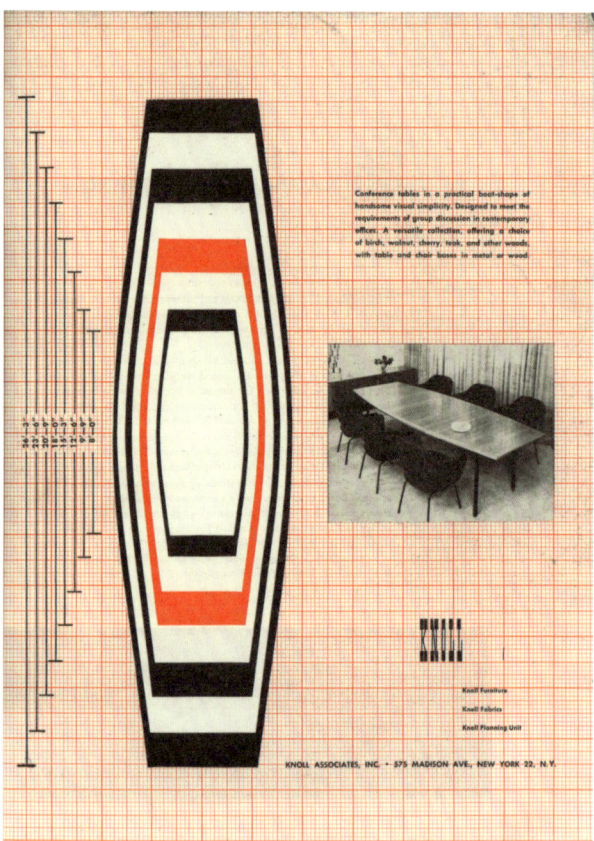

Fig. 4.27 Top left Advertisement for Knoll Office Planned furniture. From *Interiors*, June 1952.

Fig. 4.28 Top right Advertisement for Knoll Associates, designed by Herbert Matter. From *Architectural Forum*, October 1952.

Fig. 4.29 Bottom left Advertisement for Knoll+Drake Furniture, designed by Ladislav Sutnar. From *Interiors*, January 1956.

Fig. 4.30 Bottom right Advertisement for Knoll Associates, designed by Herbert Matter, featuring Eero Saarinen's *Pedestal* chair, ca. 1958. Knoll Archives.

They thought they had to have traditional furniture from Grand Rapids [Michigan]. These showrooms were what really convinced them."[104] The importance of effective showrooms was recognized as early as 1945, when Walter Baermann said that "there is education needed, too, in the merchandising and display of so-called modern furniture" and described how Knoll did not just manufacture furniture but also helped retail outlets display their products.[105] A savvy press strategy capitalized on showroom openings, which were frequently featured in architecture and design trade periodicals like *Interiors*, *Interior Design*, *Arts and Architecture*, *Architectural Forum*, and *Architectural Record*. Mainstream press outlets also covered the showrooms, such as *Life* and *Look* magazines reporting on the advances that Knoll had made in introducing modern furniture to the American public.[106]

Florence Knoll stated that the purpose of the showrooms was "to maintain a Knoll identity with different solutions in interior architecture."[107] The set of aesthetic criteria that governed the showrooms and other Planning Unit projects was known as the "Knoll look." Elements included the characteristic arrangement of furniture from the line and a neutral palette of black, white, gray, and beige with vivid color accents in selected wall treatments, upholstery, accessories, and flowers. These elements became a visual code for Knoll and the modern high-end corporate office. A very important part of the way that Knoll used color was the shadow line between planes to separate and define different elements—a design feature employed in both furniture and architectural details. The shadow line typified Knoll design and reinforced other basic design principles such as geometry and color fields. It was widely used in the 1951 New York showroom, where the metal armature not only defined rooms but also framed furniture vignettes (fig. 4.31). The shadow line indicates how the Knoll Planning Unit understood interior design as space planning, not just furniture arranging. The primary unit of any interior design was space, and the design of the interior required allocating, demarcating, and defining that space. The design of the Knoll showrooms demonstrated that the Planning Unit approached each job without preconception and made each decision according to the demands of the space and the client brief. Used in showrooms and jobs and extensively copied by imitators, the "Knoll look" became a Planning Unit trademark and a symbol of postwar corporate design.

The first showroom that Florence Knoll designed was for the newly founded textile division and opened in February 1947 (fig. 4.32). Located in a single room on East Sixty-fifth Street in New York, the showroom displayed the textile division's new line of drapery and upholstery textiles.[108] Hans and Florence Knoll imported fabrics from Sweden, Switzerland, and the Philippines, and worked with Marianne Strengell, Shirley Fletcher Rapson, and Angelo Testa to produce new designs (see chapter 3). Following the spirit of the products, the showroom was contemporary in style and featured Risom lounge chairs upholstered in the new textiles, tables and stools with webbing designed by Abel Sorensen, and woven rush floor coverings. Florence Knoll also used art as an integral part of her showroom interiors—here an abstract painting was featured prominently on the mantel, and turned-wood bowls by designer-craftsman James Prestini were displayed throughout. The textiles were merchandised in both conventional and more innovative ways. One wall was devoted to printed and plain drapery fabrics displayed as curtains, while, on another wall, upholsteries were wrapped tightly around wood blocks and hung in an abstract geometric pattern. These could be removed to be examined up close, as could larger samples stored in a basket on the floor.[109]

The next year, Florence Knoll incorporated the textile division into her redesign of Knoll's main showroom at 601 Madison Avenue in New York.[110] The space was arranged with the quasi-domestic quality that would soon characterize the company's showrooms; a reporter from *Interiors* wrote that "the patron's first impression is not that furniture is for sale, but how nice it would be to live there."[111] The visitor was greeted by the new Herbert Matter–designed company logo and a screen of interwoven black-and-white string at the entrance (fig. 4.33). A framework of steel partitions divided the space, some of which was hung with string, translucent fabrics, or wood panels, while other parts were left open, allowing the customer to see the expanse of the showroom in a single glance. Brightly colored freestanding walls that defined each furniture group further accented the space. Knoll recalled that "I had become enamored by the T-bar as a structural element and used it to divide the space without visually blocking it. I used wrapped cord and open weave pandanus cloth to further this concept."[112] Furniture was arranged in lounge and office groupings and included extensive textile displays.[113] An L-shaped space just beyond the Matter entrance screen included one long wall devoted to hanging drapery textiles and a shorter wall with a checkerboard display for upholstery fabrics, plant-fiber cloths, and webbings (figs. 4.33, 4.34). In this refinement of the display first used at the Sixty-fifth Street showroom, each square slid horizontally so that samples could easily be added, removed, and compared. Following the reopening of this showroom, plans began in earnest for Knoll outposts in other cities, and, by June 1950 Knoll had established showrooms in Boston (fig. 4.35), Chicago, Atlanta, and Dallas. Each location displayed the complete line of furniture and textiles and also offered Planning Unit services.[114]

On February 9, 1951, Knoll opened a new showroom in New York City that brought renewed attention to Florence Knoll and the Planning Unit and positioned them to take on

Fig. 4.31 Florence Knoll. Knoll showroom, 575 Madison Avenue, New York, N.Y., 1951. View of installation featuring *Barcelona* chairs and ottoman designed by Ludwig Mies van der Rohe. Photographed by Robert Damora. Courtesy Estate of Robert Damora.

Fig. 4.32 Florence Knoll. Knoll textile division showroom, 31½ East 65th Street, New York, N.Y., 1947. Photographed by Phyllis A. Dearborn, Dearborn-Massar. Knoll Archives.

Fig. 4.33 Florence Knoll. Knoll showroom, 601 Madison Avenue, New York, N.Y., 1948. View of installation with string screen by Herbert Matter and textile display. Photographed by Robert Damora. Courtesy Estate of Robert Damora.

Fig. 4.34 Florence Knoll. Knoll showroom, 601 Madison Avenue, New York, N.Y., 1948. View of installation with textile display in the background. Photographed by Ezra Stoller. Ezra Stoller © ESTO, 69J.001c.

Fig. 4.35 Florence Knoll. Knoll showroom, Boston, Mass., 1950. View of furniture and curtain display. Knoll Archives.

larger and more prominent projects (fig. 4.36).[115] The three divisions of the firm—furniture, textiles, and the Planning Unit—came together under one roof, on an upper floor of 575 Madison Avenue. The building was newly constructed, but Florence Knoll had to overcome many design obstacles, including low ceilings and awkwardly located columns and doors. Much like the showroom at 601 Madison Avenue, she painted the walls white and created a grid of black steel tubes from which primary color panels were hung to divide the space into zones. This interior architecture camouflaged the design flaws and provided scale for the furniture, which was arranged in conversation groupings (see fig. 4.31). Due to its sheer improbability and exoticism for the upper floor of a high-rise office building, the most remarked upon element was a shallow reflecting pool with floating tropical plants dividing the furniture area from the textile display (fig. 4.37). Florence Knoll carefully selected the art for this showroom, prominently displaying a sculpture of a horse and rider by Marino Marini as well as several metal abstractions by Harry Bertoia.

In addition to having their own display area, textiles were used throughout. To block an offensive view and create a regular diffusion of light, Knoll hung flexible fiberglass panels layered with *Fishnet* curtains over the window wall and chose upholstery fabrics for furniture and accent cushions. In the office areas, partitions and doors were covered in *Pandanus*, which added an appealing texture and absorbed ambient noise. As in the earlier textiles showroom, fabrics were shown both draped and wrapped on blocks mounted on a wall in the shape of a "fabric tree."[116]

The Planning Unit offices occupied the southwest corner of the space. Designers sat at desks with angled drafting surfaces separated by dividers demarcating individual studios (fig. 4.38). Florence Knoll's own office was adjacent to the Planning Unit. Hans Knoll's office, which was nearby, served both as a place to work and a demonstration of the Planning Unit's efficiency (fig. 4.39). Because space was limited in the new headquarters, Hans's office showed clients how a workspace as small as twelve feet square could be sufficient for an executive. At that time desks in traditional offices were often very bulky and placed cater-cornered, taking up much floor space. Florence Knoll arranged Hans's table-desk square with the walls, placed a cabinet behind him for storage, and selected a black wall and handwoven Indian silk curtains to flatter his ruddy complexion and blond hair (fig. 4.40).[117] In addition to the metal-framed desk with teak top, the office had several Saarinen side chairs and armchairs upholstered in leather and black fabric.

Following the opening of the New York headquarters, a Washington, D.C., branch was inaugurated in 1952 and a new Chicago location in the Merchandise Mart in 1953 (fig. 4.41).[118] By 1955 an advertisement boasted of domestic showrooms in New York, Boston, Chicago, Detroit, Dallas (fig. 4.42), Miami, Washington, D.C., and international ones in Paris (fig. 4.43), Stuttgart, Brussels, Zurich, Stockholm, Copenhagen, Havana, and Caracas. Images and press coverage emphasized that the basic elements of the "Knoll look," particularly the palette of neutral tones with bright color accents in the upholstery, walls, and accessories, characterized every showroom.

Florence Knoll continued to open showrooms in the United States and abroad after the death of Hans Knoll, making a wide variety of building types and styles conform to the "Knoll look." For the San Francisco showroom, opened in 1956 (fig. 4.44), Knoll remodeled a nineteenth-century wood-frame and masonry building; in Milan (1956) it was a renovated palazzo; and in Los Angeles (1960) the Planning Unit installed a white vaulted ceiling in a new building (fig. 4.45).[119] The international expansion continued with new locations in Germany and Rome.[120] In New York, Knoll moved out of its celebrated headquarters at 575 Madison Avenue in 1961 to showrooms and offices in a new building at 320 Park Avenue.[121]

While the primary purpose of the showrooms was to sell furniture and textiles from the Knoll line, they also served another important function. As crucibles of experimentation, showrooms offered the Planning Unit the latitude to work out ideas within real architectural spaces, free from client demands or limitations. They were the place to see and experience the Knoll vision unhampered and served to inspire as well as to sell. Reflecting on the range of her work for Knoll Associates, Florence Knoll Bassett said, "I think the showrooms were more fun than anything else."[122]

Exhibitions

Knoll also publicized its furniture and textiles through domestic and international exhibitions. Following World War II, many American museums organized exhibitions and published books about contemporary design that sought to educate the public about furnishing their homes. Knoll Associates and the Planning Unit were frequent participants in these exhibitions, submitting new designs and, in several cases organizing entire room settings.

One of the first widely publicized exhibitions of this kind was *An Exhibition For Modern Living* at the Detroit Institute of Arts in 1949.[123] Organized by Alexander Girard and containing over 2,000 objects, it was a design show of unprecedented scale. The first section traced a history of modern furniture since the nineteenth century, after which visitors entered the "Hall of Objects," a large display of what the organizers considered "good design." The final section of the exhibition, and the most celebrated, was a series of furnished room settings arranged around an indoor garden. The rooms were designed by the leading figures in American design at the time—

Fig. 4.36 Florence Knoll. Knoll showroom, 575 Madison Avenue, New York, N.Y., 1951. View from entrance. Photographed by Robert Damora. Courtesy Estate of Robert Damora.

Fig. 4.37 Top Florence Knoll. Knoll showroom, 575 Madison Avenue, New York, N.Y., 1951. View of lily pond and textile display. Photographed by Robert Damora. Courtesy Estate of Robert Damora.
Fig. 4.38 Bottom View of Knoll Planning Unit office, 575 Madison Avenue, New York, N.Y., 1951. Photographed by Robert Damora. Courtesy Estate of Robert Damora.

Fig. 4.39 Florence Knoll. Hans Knoll's office, 575 Madison Avenue, New York, N.Y., 1951. Photographed by Robert Damora. Courtesy Estate of Robert Damora.

Fig. 4.40 Florence Knoll. Sketch for Hans Knoll's office, 575 Madison Avenue, New York, N.Y., 1950. Pen, colored pencil, *Pandanus* (cabinet fronts), *Jhuri Silk* (curtains), and leather (chair seats) on paper. Florence Knoll Bassett Papers, Archives of American Art, Smithsonian Institution. Cat. 37.

Fig. 4.41 **Top** Florence Knoll. Knoll showroom, Chicago, 1954. Photographed by Yuichi Idaka. Knoll Archives.

Fig. 4.42 **Bottom** Florence Knoll/Knoll Planning Unit. Knoll showroom, Dallas, 1955. Photographed by Yuichi Idaka. Knoll Archives.

Fig. 4.43 Florence Knoll/Knoll Planning Unit. Knoll showroom, Paris, ca. 1956.
From "Knoll ou Le Triomphe de Modernisme," *Connaissance des Arts*, May 1956.
Photographed by Studio Jean Collas. Library, Bard Graduate Center:
Decorative Arts, Design History, Material Culture; New York.

Fig. 4.44 Florence Knoll/Knoll Planning Unit. Knoll showroom, San Francisco, 1956. Photographed by Morley Baer. Florence Knoll Bassett Papers, Archives of American Art, Smithsonian Institution.

Fig. 4.45 Florence Knoll/Knoll Planning Unit. Knoll showroom, Los Angeles, 1960. Photographed by Yuichi Idaka. Knoll Archives.

George Nelson, Jens Risom, Charles Eames, Alvar Aalto, Bruno Mathsson, and Florence Knoll. Knoll's space was the largest, showing a combination living–dining room and a bedroom and was furnished with designs by Pierre Jeanneret, Eero Saarinen, and others. The display reflected a concern for the rigors of everyday life, as Knoll specified durable materials and washable upholsteries (see fig. 1.32).[124]

The *Good Design* exhibitions (mentioned above) were the most prominent advice exhibitions held in this period, and Knoll furniture and textiles were frequently included (see chapters 1 and 3).[125] Knoll Associates regularly participated in other expositions of museum-approved design as well. The Baltimore Museum of Art presented *Living Up-to-Date* in 1951, spearheaded by trustee Edward M. Benesch, an interior decorator.[126] The exhibition included over 500 examples of modern furnishings and accessories, nearly all of which could be purchased from distributors or retailers who were listed in the catalogue. Like *An Exhibition For Modern Living*, *Living Up-to-Date* featured displays of sanctioned objects, including fourteen Knoll textile designs and room settings furnished by Edward Wormley, Jens Risom, and Florence Knoll. Knoll's room featured a lounge area with Eero Saarinen's *Womb* chair and settee covered in *Scotch Linen*, a slat bench by Harry Bertoia, and a curtain of the Paule Vézelay print *Sequence* (fig. 4.46). A dining area was separated from the lounge area by a screen of *Fishnet* and featured a Saarinen *Model 71* armchair covered in *Transportation Cloth*, a dining table by Hans Bellman surrounded by linen-covered Saarinen *Model 72* chairs, a credenza by Florence Knoll, and a length of Albert Herbert's *Diamonds* pattern hung as drapery.[127]

The Corcoran Gallery of Art in Washington, D.C., followed suit in 1952 with *Hand and Machine Art*, an exhibition organized by Taylor Simmons, an employee of the Washington office of Knoll Associates.[128] The show featured an installation designed by Florence Knoll, with many of the same furnishings displayed in the earlier exhibitions as well as a large group of Evelyn Hill handwoven fabrics in Eszter Haraszty's signature bright palette. Six years later the Corcoran Gallery presented *Living Today*, which included a bedroom designed by Knoll Associates as well as furniture designed by Florence Knoll, Harry Bertoia, and Eero Saarinen, and a selection of Knoll textiles, including *Spectra* in the blue and green colorway, *Nylon Homespun* in orange, and the Sven Markelius print *Pythagoras*.[129]

In 1952 the Dallas Museum of Fine Arts (now the Dallas Museum of Art) held an exhibition devoted exclusively to Knoll that was designed by the Planning Unit and Eszter Haraszty (fig. 4.47). Called *Knoll Furniture and Textiles*, the one-gallery show featured a living room that Florence Knoll described as "a space that is serene and pleasing" and "fosters an atmosphere of relaxation without resorting to cuteness."[130] Although relaxation may have been the goal, the room came alive with vibrant upholstery and textile accents—including Evelyn Hill's handwoven textiles and Haraszty's *Tracy*, a print using an X-ray image of a leaf in its repeat—as well as furniture by Florence Knoll and Eero Saarinen, and an adjustable sofa by the Italian designers Belgiojoso, Peressutti & Rogers.

On some occasions, the Knoll showrooms became venues for exhibitions of the work of designers and artists with connections to the Knoll firm. In 1962, for example, Knoll Planning Unit employee Heino Orro exhibited his paintings, sculptures, and murals made from Knoll textiles.[131] Orro manipulated fabric swatches and yarn to create colorful, abstract compositions. And in 1963, the weavings of Sheila Hicks inspired by ancient Andean textiles were shown at the Knoll Chicago showroom in the Merchandise Mart.[132]

Knoll Associates not only participated in exhibitions to promote its own line of furnishings and textiles but also, in at least one case, contributed to international diplomatic efforts. In a major Cold War–era cultural initiative, the United States government sent exhibitions of American industry and domestic life to Europe. In 1952, the Smithsonian Institution Traveling Exhibition Service (SITES) asked Florence Knoll to curate *Textilien aus USA* (Textiles from the USA), an exhibition of contemporary American fabrics that made several stops in Germany. Knoll selected over 150 printed and woven textiles representing over a dozen American textile manufacturers, including several patterns from the Knoll textile line. Florence Knoll also designed a demountable exhibition structure that was easy to assemble, disassemble, and transport. Textiles were mounted tautly on a cagelike structure of aluminum tubes (similar to the apparatus used to divide areas of the showrooms) to display their pattern and texture (fig. 4.48).[133]

The CBS Building, New York

In 1958, Florence Knoll married Harry Hood Bassett, whom she had met while designing the interiors of the First National Bank of Miami, where he was president. She moved to Miami but remained head of Knoll Associates, commuting frequently to the New York office. The next year, she sold the firm to Art Metal Construction Company, a manufacturer of metal office furniture, continuing as president of Knoll (but delegating some managerial responsibilities) and becoming design and research director of Art Metal.[134]

The Planning Unit continued taking on projects, culminating in its largest and the last under Florence Knoll Bassett's tenure. Eero Saarinen had been commissioned to design a midtown Manhattan skyscraper for CBS at Sixth Avenue and Fifty-second Street, not far from its old Madison Avenue headquarters (fig. 4.49). In the middle of the design process, Saarinen was diagnosed with a brain

Fig. 4.46 Top Florence Knoll. View of installation in the *Living Up-to-Date* exhibition, Baltimore Museum of Art, 1951. The Museum of Modern Art, New York, Architecture and Design Study Center.

Fig. 4.47 Bottom *Knoll Furniture and Textiles* exhibition at the Dallas Museum of Fine Arts. From "Drum Beaters for Modern," *Life*, March 2, 1953. Library, Bard Graduate Center: Decorative Arts, Design History, Material Culture; New York. Cat. 69.

Fig. 4.48 Florence Knoll. View of the *Textilien aus USA* exhibition installation, ca. 1952. Photographed by Alexandre Georges. Knoll Archives.
Fig. 4.49 Eero Saarinen, architect. The CBS Building, 51 West 52nd Street, New York, N.Y., 1965. Photographed in 1967. CBS Photo Archive/Getty Images, #102643369.

Fig. 4.50 Florence Knoll/Knoll Planning Unit. Study for reception lobbies of the CBS Building, New York, N.Y., ca. 1963. Pen and colored pencil on paper. Florence Knoll Bassett Papers, Archives of American Art, Smithsonian Institution.

Fig. 4.51 Florence Knoll/Knoll Planning Unit. Office for John A. Schneider, president of CBS Television, CBS Building, 51 West 52nd Street, New York, N.Y., ca. 1965. Photographed by Robert Damora. Courtesy Estate of Robert Damora.

tumor, and just a few weeks before he died, asked Knoll Bassett and the Knoll Planning Unit to complete the furnishing plan.[135] The opportunity to help out her longtime friend, as well as work with her old patron Frank Stanton, was hard to refuse.

The interior architects Carson, Lundin & Shaw had already developed the interior plan based on a five-foot module.[136] The Planning Unit's task was to select color schemes, furniture, fabrics, and art for the third through thirty-fifth floors.[137] There were several types of spaces to be designed, from secretarial areas to executive suites, and it was important that the design be coherent, but not uniform. Sketches of the elevator lobby reception areas illustrate how color was used to differentiate each floor, while furniture arrangement and forms were the unifying link between them (fig. 4.50). Services consumed the central core of the building, and office space ran along the perimeter, forming what Saarinen called a "square doughnut." Knoll covered the elevator lobby walls with *Oxford*, a durable gray fabric, which created a neutral background and related to the building's granite exterior.[138] In addition to its usual furnishing services, the Planning Unit also specified an annual planting scheme with flowers that were color-coordinated with each floor.[139]

The Planning Unit was less encumbered by the existing architectural plan in their design of the executive suites (fig. 4.51), particularly the office of CBS president Frank Stanton, which was replete with luxurious finishes such as bronze velvet wall coverings, beige linen curtains, and walnut paneling (fig. 4.52).[140] The furniture comprised standard Knoll designs specially made with sumptuous materials such as an oak desk with bronze base, a marble-topped credenza, and a sofa covered in a Knoll handwoven fabric. The office included a lounge area as well as a reception room, pantry, dining room (where antique Tiffany stained-glass windows were installed), dressing room, and bathroom.[141] With these amenities, Stanton's space was as much penthouse apartment as office suite.

Despite an extensive press campaign, the CBS interiors were considered more compromise than success within the Planning Unit and by some critics. Knoll Bassett later remarked, "that job was the culmination of all the refinements that had gone on for many years, but it wasn't the most exciting because . . . we were brought in at the tenth hour when it was really too late. I had no time to develop any furniture or anything, and the planning was all done. . . . The spaces, the ceiling heights, and the lighting were all pretty well set, and we were left with office partitions and office colors that had already been determined."[142] Architecture critic Ada Louise Huxtable went further, commenting that "the inside of C.B.S. is a solid gold corporate cliché; a lavish cocoon, complete to standardized concealed wastebaskets and accredited and almost as equally standardized abstract art."[143] It was clear that the rushed timeframe and predetermined interior architecture had drained much personality from the interiors, and that the pristine design was too sanitized. Planning Unit designer Vincent Cafiero later recalled the ubiquity and uniformity of offices that the Planning Unit and other architecture firms were then producing. He remembered standing in the CBS Building and reflecting that he "was in this white cubicle, looking across the street at other white cubicles and looking in other directions were other white cubicles . . . it was a shattering experience."[144]

Shortly before the opening of the CBS Building, Florence Knoll Bassett submitted her letter of resignation, writing, "I am finding it increasingly difficult to devote the time I would like to give to design supervision. The responsibilities and interests of my private life in Miami and the natural evolution of my professional work lead me to the realistic conclusion that I should step out of my present relationship to Knoll Associates."[145] Her resignation was effective March 1, 1965. Knoll Bassett had been living in Miami for seven years by that point. The CBS Building was undertaken out of loyalty but became a source of frustration and compromise, and Knoll Bassett later reflected that "there are just so many offices one can do in one's life and then it's enough."[146]

After Knoll Bassett resigned in 1965, long-standing Planning Unit designer Lewis Butler was appointed the division's director of design. The Planning Unit continued to work on projects, including interiors for Owens-Corning Fiberglas and Westinghouse, but it never achieved the scale or scope of earlier work.[147] Butler later opined that the Planning Unit should have been phased out at Florence Knoll's departure in 1965 and correctly identified the future of the firm's business as being in sales of contract furnishings and textiles.[148] Planning Unit designer Vincent Cafiero agreed: in hindsight he described the Planning Unit after 1965 as "a boat that had lost its rudder."[149] The Planning Unit ceased operations in 1971.

The "Knoll look" had run its course and become a formulaic cliché even by 1965—even Wallace Harrison said that "when you hire Knoll to do an interior you know what you're going to get."[150] This was a far cry from the late 1940s and early 1950s, when the "Knoll look" epitomized the progressive corporate office and contributed to a wider acceptance of modern design in postwar American life. Under the consummate eye of Florence Knoll, the three branches of the firm—furniture, textiles, and the Planning Unit—became integral players in the creation of innovative and influential corporate interior design.

Fig. 4.52 Florence Knoll/Knoll Planning Unit. Office of Frank Stanton, president of CBS, CBS Building, New York, N.Y., ca. 1965. Photographed by Robert Damora. Florence Knoll Bassett Papers, Archives of American Art, Smithsonian Institution.

1 "Knoll Associates, Inc.: Planning, Chairs, Sofas, Tables, Chests, Textiles," brochure, ca. 1956, Knoll Archives. I have relied on several secondary sources on Florence Knoll, Knoll Associates, and the Knoll Planning Unit in the preparation of this essay, including Eric Larrabee and Massimo Vignelli, *Knoll Design* (New York: Harry N. Abrams, Inc., 1981); Jennifer Komar Olivarez, "Ralph Rapson and Hans Knoll: Missionaries of Modern Design," *Echoes* (Summer 1998): 48–51, 74–75; Bobbye Tigerman, "'I Am Not a Decorator': Florence Knoll, the Knoll Planning Unit and the Making of the Modern Office," *Journal of Design History* 20, no. 1 (Spring 2007): 61–74; Brian Lutz, *Knoll: A Modernist Universe* (New York: Rizzoli, 2010). I also wish to thank Earl Martin and the anonymous reviewer for their very useful comments.

2 Ralph Caplan, "Connecticut General: The Team Approach: A Round-Table Discussion Reveals How Connecticut General Got What It Wanted from Designers," *Industrial Design* (September 1958): 53.

3 "Knoll Associates, Inc. Knoll International, Ltd.," oversize brochure, ca. 1961, p. 3, Knoll Archives.

4 "Text for Planning Unit Brochure," May 11, 1959, Knoll Archives.

5 In many later interviews, Florence Knoll Bassett stated that the Knoll Planning Unit was created when she began working for Hans Knoll in 1943. However, the earliest documented evidence for the Planning Unit relates to a different group by the same name under the direction of Walter Baermann that existed in 1944–45 (discussed in this chapter). The earliest known furnishing projects in which Florence Knoll (then Schust) was involved date to 1942, while the earliest interior design projects by the Planning Unit (as recorded in promotional literature) date to 1945; see Knoll Associates, Inc., "Furniture Price List," November 1, 1948, Brooklyn Museum Libraries and Archives. As there is no written documentation of the transition from Walter Baermann's to Florence Knoll's leadership, I use 1944 as the Planning Unit founding date.

6 Florence Knoll Bassett, interview, ca. 1977, p. 25, Knoll Archives.

7 Knoll received every textile memo, and after the death of Hans Knoll in 1955 and the departure of Eszter Haraszty shortly thereafter, she had final approval for every textile design and colorway. Pattern files, KnollTextiles Archive, New York.

8 Advertisement for Knoll Associates, designed by Herbert Matter, *Architectural Forum* (February 1952): 199. The same advertisement was run the following month; see Advertisement for Knoll Associates, designed by Herbert Matter, *Progressive Architecture* (March 1952): 61.

9 Advertisement for Knoll Associates, designed by Herbert Matter, *Interiors* (February 1954): 21.

10 Olga Gueft, "Florence Knoll and the Avant-Garde," *Interiors* (July 1957): 59.

11 "Furnishing the Dormitory," *Architectural Forum* (December 1951): 176. For the 1961 statistics, which translate to over $100 million in 2011 dollars adjusting for inflation, see Ursula Cliff, "Gallery 4: Florence Knoll," *Industrial Design* (April 1961): 66–71.

12 Between 1945 and 1962, approximately 45 million square feet of office space were developed in Manhattan; see Walter McQuade, "The Booming Office Planners," *Architectural Forum* (January 1962): 83. A 1963 article described the postwar period as an "epochal rush to build in Manhattan's midtown and downtown core"; see "Who Gets What Office?," *Architectural Forum* (February 1957): 118–21.

13 In 1955 Gueft wrote that "the interior has become so important that offices, stores, and banks stuck in twenty-year-old buildings frequently resheathe them in glass downstairs, and do the interior over." Olga Gueft, "The Race to Design," *Interiors* (January 1955): 51.

14 Brochure for H. G. Knoll Associates, design attrib. Alvin Lustig, ca. 1945, Museum of Modern Art, Architecture and Design Study Center. One such invitation still exists—Rapson was asked to become an associate in the newly formed Planning Unit; see Hans Knoll to Ralph Rapson, May 2, 1944, Knoll Archives. This letter names "Joe Johannson," but Knoll could have been referring to the architect John Johansen. See also Bernard Rudofsky, "Modern Doesn't Pay, or Does It?" *Interiors* (March 1946): 66–75.

15 Baermann worked with many industrial designers including Joseph Urban, Norman Bel Geddes, and Henry Dreyfuss, had independent industrial design practices in New York and California, and was the founder and director of the California Graduate School of Design in Pasadena (which merged with the California Institute of Technology in 1941). See "California Schools Merge for Industry," *New York Times*, August 10, 1941, D4; "Forum of Events," *Architectural Forum* (October 1941): 106, 108.

16 Brochure for H. G. Knoll Associates, design attrib. Alvin Lustig, ca. 1945, MoMA, Architecture and Design Study Center.

17 This language, specifically the tagline "Equipment for Living," also recalls the rhetoric of earlier European modernists, perhaps most specifically Le Corbusier, the Swiss architect working in France, who called a house a "machine for living." See Le Corbusier-Saugnier, *Vers une architecture* (Paris: Le Cres, 1923), trans. as *Towards a New Architecture* (New York: Payson and Clarke; London: Rodker, 1927).

18 *Tomorrow's Small House: Models and Plans*, MoMA Exh. 289, May 29–September 30, 1945, curated by Elizabeth Mock; George Nelson and Henry Wright, *Tomorrow's House: How to Plan Your Post-War Home Now* (New York: Simon and Schuster, 1945); Elizabeth B. Kassler [Elizabeth Mock], *If You Want to Build a House* (New York: Museum of Modern Art, 1946). The latter was also a MoMA exhibition curated by Mock (MoMA Exh. 304, January 8–January 30, 1946).

19 Alvin Lustig commented on this lack as well, writing that prior to World War II, "it can be safely said that there were not well designed modern fabrics available in any quantity or at reasonable prices that satisfied the rather demanding needs of the new designers. This could be said of almost everything in the modern furnishing line; there was no modern furniture available at that time either." Alvin Lustig, "Modern Printed Fabrics," *American Fabrics* 20 (Winter 1951–52): 61–62.

20 "Equipment for Living," *Arts and Architecture* (May 1945): 36–38.

21 Hans G. Knoll to Ralph Rapson, May 2, 1944, Knoll Archives. See also Hans Knoll, "Reconversion Responsibility," *Upholstering* (July 1945): 28–30, 57. The first company to which Knoll presented the "Equipment for Living" designs was Kellett Aircraft Corporation in Upper Darby, Penn. Hans G. Knoll to Mr. R. G. Kellett, Kellett Aircraft Corporation, June 25, 1944, Knoll Archives. Kellett did not produce any Knoll designs.

22 Advertisement for H. G. Knoll Associates, designed by Alvin Lustig, *Interiors* (March 1945): 44; and *Arts and Architecture* (March 1945): 26.

23 Program for the H. G. Knoll Associates Planning Unit, May 2, 1944, Knoll Archives.

24 "Forum of Events," *Architectural Forum* (January 1945): 62.

25 Hans Knoll to Ralph Rapson, October 11, 1945, Knoll Archives.

26 A March 1946 article about the Planning Unit highlighted Florence Schust with Ralph Rapson, Eero Saarinen, Abel Sorensen, Jens Risom, and Isamu Noguchi; see Bernard Rudofsky, "Modern Doesn't Pay, or Does It?," *Interiors* (March 1946): 66–75. Although the Planning Unit's focus seems to have shifted by the time this article was published, *Interiors* featured a scale model including Schust's cabinet and storage designs along with designs for metal chairs by Ralph Rapson.

27 Florence Knoll Bassett, interview, ca. 1977, p. 15, Knoll Archives.

28 Ibid., p. 14. The course of events that brought Hans Knoll and Florence Schust together is detailed in chap. 2 of this volume.

29 Ursula Cliff, "Gallery 4: Florence Knoll," *Industrial Design* (April 1961): 66–71.

30 Butler joined the Planning Unit in 1950 as a project manager and retired in December 1970 as the director of design. Lewis J. Butler designer file, Knoll Archives.

31 "Knoll Planning Unit," brochure, ca. 1959, Knoll Archives.

32 Florence Knoll Bassett Papers (cited as FKBP hereafter), series 5, box 3, folder 2.

33 Florence Knoll Bassett, interview ca. 1977, p. 2, Knoll Archives. See also chap. 2 in this volume.

34 Allan Denenberg, interview by author, October 30, 2010.

35 FKBP, series 5, box 3, folder 20. For more on the Heinz project see "An Old Food Company Builds a New Center for Research," *Architectural Record* (February 1959): 173–78.

36 Florence Knoll Bassett, interview, ca. 1977, p. 5–6, Knoll Archives. See also Greg Castillo, *Cold War on the Home Front* (Minneapolis and London: University of Minnesota Press, 2010), 61–64.

37 John D. Morse, "The Story of Knoll Associates," *American Artist* (September 1951): 46–50.

38 Florence Knoll Bassett, interview, ca. 1977, p. 11–12, Knoll Archives.

39 Manchester, Inc. announced plans for a significant expansion to be designed by SOM in 1945; see "Manchester Reveals Plans," *Wisconsin State Journal*, October 7, 1945, 1–2.

40 "Madison Room," *Architectural Record* (July 1947): 112–15. Some of the designs were produced by Knoll; others were specified from other firms.

41 Testa's prints debuted in Knoll Textiles' first collection introduced that spring. It is unclear if this design, which was identified as *Line in Action* when it was published in 1945—see "Textiles," *Arts & Architecture* (October 1945): 42–43—was part of the early Knoll Textiles collection. While Testa's print *Campagna* was kept in the Knoll line for more than a decade, other prints by the designer such as *Indian Heads* and *Filo* only lasted a short time (see chap. 3). The same may have been true for *Line in Action*.

42 "ALCOA Complete," *Architectural Forum* (November 1953): 124–31.

43 "Carnegie Endowment for International Peace International Center, New York, N.Y.," *Architectural Record* (January 1954): 121–31.

44 "Transportation Cloth," from Suzanne Huguenin, "Knoll Textile Sales Guide," 1962, KnollTextiles Archive.

45 For Drake University see "Drake University: Dormitories and Dining Hall," *Progressive Architecture* (April 1955): 96–105. The CBS Building is discussed later in this chapter.

46 William M. Freeman, "She Designs Offices Outside In," *New York Times*, October 15, 1957, 45.

47 "U.S. Architecture Abroad," *Architectural Forum* (March 1953): 101–15.

48 "U.S. Embassy Office Building, Havana, Cuba," *Progressive Architecture* (February 1955): 106–11; "P/A Interior Design Data: Embassy Rooms," *Progressive Architecture* (February 1955): 136–37.

49 "P/A Interior Design Data: Embassy Rooms," *Progressive Architecture* (February 1955): 132–33. Planning Unit member Suzanne Wasson-Tucker managed the design of the Scandinavian embassies; see Olga Gueft, "Swedish Carpentry Supports Swedish Textiles," *Interiors* (June 1958): 110–11.

50 "Rugby," from Suzanne Huguenin, "Knoll Textile Sales Guide," 1962, KnollTextiles Archive.

51 "The Rockefeller Touch in Building," *Architectural Forum* (March 1958): 86–91; Florence Knoll Bassett, interview by Bill Ferehawk (for Eero Saarinen project), March 28–30, 2004, p. 33; Florence Knoll Bassett, interview, ca. 1977, p. 32, Knoll Archives.

52 "The Rockefeller Touch in Building," *Architectural Forum* (March 1958): 86–91; Ursula Cliff, "Gallery 4: Florence Knoll," *Industrial Design* (April 1961): 69.

53 "Furnishing the Dormitory," *Architectural Forum* (December 1951): 176–79; Mary Roche, "Small-Room Décor," *New York Times Magazine* (October 24, 1948): SM44-45; "Alice Crocker Lloyd Residence Hall," *Architectural Record* (April 1951): 112–17.

54 "Office Building—North American Life and Casualty Company Makes a Capital Investment in Minneapolis," *Architectural Forum* (January 1949): 75–81.

55 Knoll distributed a reprint of the *Architectural Forum* article to prospective clients and also featured this project in a 1949 brochure outlining the planning services offered by the firm and its furniture and textiles ("Research Approach to Interior Planning," brochure, designed by Herbert Matter, 1949, MoMA library, http://arcade.nyarc.org/record=b569764~S8).

56 A 1948 textiles price list designates this upholstery as "P1." Knoll Associates, Inc., "Textiles Price List," November 1, 1948, Brooklyn Museum Libraries and Archives; the Tapiovaara chair was a new addition to

Knoll's line; see "A Survey of Furniture from 40-Odd Sources," *Interiors* (March 1948): 104–15.

57 *Upholstering* (September 1949): 98; "Versatile, Long-Wearing and Practical," *Upholstering* (January 1951): 94–95.

58 Knoll planned to put the *Barcelona* chair into production as early as 1947, but it is not clear how successful these early efforts were; see Mary Roche, "Home," *New York Times*, October 12, 1947, SM38. The chair did not appear in the newly redesigned Knoll showroom in New York (opened in May 1948) or in subsequent showrooms in Chicago (1949), Boston (1950), or Dallas (1950). It was only with the publication of the *Knoll Index of Contemporary Design* in late 1950 and the opening of the new 575 Madison Avenue New York showroom in 1951 that the *Barcelona* chair was featured prominently and seems to have been available on an ongoing basis. It is likely that before this the chair was only specified by Knoll for special installations, like the lobby of North American Life.

59 "Deft Remodeling Creates a Compact Sales Machine with a Billboard Front," *Architectural Forum* (June 1948): 88–91; "Fiberglas House: A Depression-Born Industry Demonstrates Its Wares in a Remodeled Brownstone," *Interiors* (October 1948): 112–17.

60 *American Fabrics*, no. 38 (Fall 1956): 36–37. Knoll also later furnished other offices and a showroom for Dow; see "Showroom by Knoll Associates," *Arts and Architecture* (April 1962): 26.

61 "Felt but not Seen," *Interiors* (May 1949): 132–35.

62 Advertisement for Hewitt-Robins Incorporated, *Interiors* (July 1949): 46. It is not clear how long Knoll used Hewitt-Robins Restfoam. By the early 1950s Goodyear was another major supplier of Knoll's foam cushioning: see Advertisement for "Airfoam," Goodyear Tire and Rubber Company, *Interiors* (September 1953): 21.

63 "Design for New Textile Headquarters Deftly Handles Several Problems," *Architectural Record* (December 1958): 119–24; "Company Moves Out And In on Week-End," *New York Times*, June 29, 1958, R1.

64 "Office of Merit: CBS Offices by the Same Designer," *Architectural Forum* (January 1955): 134–39; "Offices on Both Coasts by Knoll," *Interiors* (January 1955): 60–63; "Communication, Electronics, Automation," *Progressive Architecture* (May 1956): 108–9.

65 Florence Knoll Bassett, interview, ca. 1977, Knoll Archives. Version 3, 8–9.

66 "Office of Merit: CBS Offices by the Same Designer," *Architectural Forum* (January 1955): 138.

67 "CELA: Communications," *Progressive Architecture* (May 1956), 108–9.

68 A paste-up of the Stanton office preserved by Florence Knoll records the exact details of leathers and upholsteries used: see Frank Stanton office, CBS, 1952–54, FKBP, Series 5, Box 3, Folder 17.

69 The affinity of executive offices to living rooms has been observed in nineteenth-century offices as well, which resembled middle-class parlors. Angel Kwolek-Folland, "The Gendered Environment of the Corporate Workplace, 1880–1930," in *The Material Culture of Gender, the Gender of Material Culture*, ed. Katharine A. Martinez and Kenneth L. Ames (Winterthur, Del.: Henry Francis du Pont Winterthur Museum, 1997), 157–80.

70 Advertisement for Knoll Planning Unit, *Architectural Forum* (April 1955): 287.

71 Advertisement for Knoll Planning Unit, *Architectural Forum* (June 1955): 265.

72 "A Humane Campus for the Study of Man," *Architectural Forum* (January 1955): 130–34; "Offices on Both Coasts by Knoll," *Interiors* (January 1955): 60–63; "The Center for Advanced Study in the Behavioral Sciences," *Arts and Architecture* (February 1955): 14–16; "Centre d'études et de recherches à Palo Alto," *Architecture d'aujourd'hui* (October 1956): 42–43; "Un 'centro' por la meditazione, in California," *Domus* (April 1957): 3–6.

73 "A Humane Campus for the Study of Man," *Architectural Forum* (January 1955): 134.

74 Advertisement for Knoll Associates, *Architectural Forum* (May 1955): 19.

75 "Model of Office Planning," *Progressive Architecture* (March 1962): 151–57.

76 "Knoll, Textile Man, Dies in Cuban Crash" (obituary), *New York Times*, October 10, 1955, 30; "Havana Crash Kills Modern Furniture Pioneer" (obituary), *Interiors* (November 1955): 134, 136; "Hans G. Knoll" (obituary), *Art News* (November 1955): 68; "Hans G. Knoll" (obituary), *Architectural Forum* (November 1955): 29.

77 "On the Basic Elements of Office Design; And on the Hartford Mock-Ups," *Interiors* (January 1956): 78–79; "Insurance Sets a Pattern," *Architectural Forum* (September 1957): 112–27; L.W., "The Complete Corporation on a 6' Module, Proven by Mockups," *Interiors* (January 1958): 76–85.

78 Caplan, "Connecticut General," 54.

79 "Knoll Textiles: A Flexible Element in Interiors," *Handweaver & Craftsman* (Summer 1958): 12–15.

80 While many Knoll furniture designs were created to fulfill a specific client's need, the fact that a design was developed for a Planning Unit project was never publicized if it entered the general product line. In a profile of Florence Knoll and Knoll Associates, the author asserted that the *Parallel Bar* furniture was developed for Connecticut General. See Ursula Cliff, "Gallery 4: Florence Knoll," *Industrial Design* (April 1961): 66–71. Florence Knoll indicated that new furniture designs often emerged from a specific client need, and the resulting design was then incorporated into the standard line; see Rita Reif, "Pioneer in Modern Furniture is Charting Expansion Course," *New York Times*, June 17, 1959, 29.

81 L.W., "Furniture Flashes," *Interiors* (January 1955): 90–91.

82 L.W., "Furniture Report," *Interiors* (September 1955): 129; L.W., "Knoll's Spare Parallel Bar System," *Interiors* (January 1956): 106–7. In a June 1956 advertisement Knoll indicated that the coffee table was the "First in an important new series of tables, chairs and sofas." See Knoll Associates, Advertisement, *Interiors* (June 1955): 51.

83 "A.I.D. Product Design Awards," *Interiors* (May 1955): 116; Knoll Associates, Advertisement, *Interiors* (June 1955): 51.

84 F. S. Knoll, United States Patent 2,965,160, "Cushion or the Like," December 20, 1960 (originally filed June 29, 1956). Rows of stitching were used to create a grid across the top of the cushion. This grid was tied down where perpendicular rows crossed by threads ran up through the cushion, over the intersections, and then back down through the cushion to anchor the upholstery in place.

85 "Furniture Price List," July 15, 1964, indicates that the *Barcelona* chair sold for $980.00 and the *Parallel Bar* lounge chair in leather sold for $284.00; Knoll Archives.

86 Hans Knoll to Ralph Rapson, December 20, 1945, Knoll Archives.

87 Mary Roche, "New Ideas and Inventions," *New York Times*, February 16, 1947, SM40; "Post-War Trend in Swedish Décor," *Furniture Age* (March 1947): 66, 72; "Swedish Knock-Down Furniture to be Promoted Here," *Upholstering* (February 1947): 64, 66, 76. See also *Interiors* (March 1947): 78; and *Interiors* (August 1947), 87.

88 In addition to the Swedish pavilion, the 1939 World's Fair featured a Finnish pavilion designed by Alvar Aalto. This, combined with an exhibition of Aalto's work at MoMA the previous year, added to American awareness of contemporary Scandinavian design.

89 It is not clear how many retail outlets took part in this promotion. One certain example was Carson Pirie Scott in Chicago, which featured the Swedish room in June 1947; see Advertisement for Carson Pirie Scott, *Chicago Daily Tribune*, June 25, 1947, 20.

90 Knoll's first advertisement designed by newly hired graphic designer Herbert Matter appeared in June 1947 and featured the new *Grasshopper* chair by Eero Saarinen; see Advertisement for Knoll Associates, *Interiors* (June 1947): 9. Many new models were also featured in Mary Roche, "New Chair Offers More Relaxation," *New York Times*, May 19, 1948, 24; "New Furniture," *Arts and Architecture* (July 1948): 38–39; E.B., "Knoll Furniture," *Architectural Forum* (June 1948): 182, 186.

91 "Best of the New Furniture," *Interiors* (October 1948): 92; it was also published in "New Furniture," *Life* (November 15, 1948): 115. The chair had been in development for about two years.

92 Virginia Lee Warren, "Woman Who Led an Office Revolution Rules an Empire of Modern Design," *New York Times*, September 1, 1964, 40; Florence Knoll Bassett, interview, ca. 1977, pp. 3–5, Knoll Archives.

93 "Knoll Associates, Bound and Covered," *Interiors* (December 1950): 126–27.

94 *Knoll Index of Contemporary Design* (New York: Knoll Associates, 1950), 2.

95 *Knoll Office Planned Furniture*, brochure, 1953 or later, Knoll Archives.

96 "Knoll Associates Introduce New Line of Office Planned Furniture," *Upholstering* (August 1952): 112–13; "For Office Flexibility," *Interiors* (June 1952): 140.

97 "Historic Chair Reproduced," *New York Times*, February 9, 1951, 20; see also n. 58.

98 The mayor of Austin, Tex., from 1951 to 1953, William S. Drake was the founder of Austin Industries and president of Calcasieu Lumber Company. See "Furniture Bid," *Business Week* (May 28, 1955), n.p.

99 "Furniture Designs by Rado," *Interiors* (June 1955): 130; "Havana Crash Kills Modern Furniture Pioneer," *Interiors* (November 1955): 134; Betty Pepis, "Communiqué on Fall Furniture," *New York Times*, July 10, 1955, SM38; Betty Pepis, "New Model Rooms Object Lessons in Decorating," *New York Times*, October 5, 1955, 32.

100 L.W., "New Furniture: Part I of our Semi-Annual Survey," *Interiors* (July 1957): 98–99.

101 Eero Saarinen, "If I Could Tell a Woman One Thing About Furnishing a Home," *Family Circle* (March 1958): 33.

102 In a comparative study of lounge chairs, the Florence Knoll designs that appear often in Planning Unit jobs cost more than other lounge chairs from the Knoll line. In the 1958 price list the Florence Knoll lounge chair cost between $275 and $295. In the same year, the Harry Bertoia small diamond chair cost $79 and the large diamond cost $116. The Eero Saarinen *Womb* chair was not included in the 1958 price list, but interpolation between its 1953 and 1961 prices would place it at approximately $280. And by comparison, the Mies van der Rohe *Barcelona* chair, whose price was only available on request in 1958, was $350 in 1951, so presumably had appreciated by 1958.

103 Allan Denenberg, interview by author, January 23, 2005; Vincent Cafiero, interview by author, February 14, 2005.

104 Paul Makovsky, "Florence Knoll Bassett: The Conversation," *Metropolis* (July 2001): 97.

105 Jessie Ash Arndt, "Furniture Is Cued to Living, Not to Period," *Christian Science Monitor*, June 20, 1945, 13.

106 "The Knolls," *Look* (May 22, 1951): 100, 102, 104–6; "Drum Beaters for Modern," *Life* (March 2, 1953): 72–76.

107 FKBP, series 1, p. 25.

108 Mary Roche, "Work of Noted Textile Designers Put on View at New Showroom," *New York Times*, February 27, 1947, 24; "Knoll Associates Introduces Textiles," *Upholstering* (April 1947): 50, 92, 94.

109 "Art Into Living: Integrated Fabrics," *Art News* (May 1947): 36, 60.

110 The separate textile showroom was no longer operated by Knoll after this time.

111 "Eight Solutions to Merchandise Display: Knoll Associates Achieve Intimacy and Openness in Colorful Plan," *Interiors* (October 1948): 108–11.

112 FKBP, series 5, box 3, folder 10. For more about *Pandanus* see chap. 3 in this volume.

113 "Spacious but Intimate; Simple But Subtle: Showroom for Knoll Associates, Inc., New York," *Architectural Record* (November 1948): 92–99.

114 "Furniture Showroom," *Architectural Forum* (July 1949): 79–81; "Richard Revitalizes a Building with Fins, a False Front, and a New Rear End," *Interiors* (September 1949): 96–101; "Outpost in Dallas: Knoll Opens a Lone Star Branch," *Interiors* (June 1950): 90–97; *Interiors* (June 1950): 151.

115 Betty Pepis, "Modern Furniture Put in Room Units," *New York Times*, February 9, 1951, 20; "Walls of Air, Color, Light and Water," *Architectural Forum* (May 1951): 138–43; Olga Gueft, "Knoll Associates Move Into the Big Time," *Interiors* (May 1951): 74–83, 152, 154, 156; "Knoll Associates Inc. Opens New Showroom in New York," *Uphol-*

stering (June 1951): 86–87, 148; "Furniture Showrooms in New York," *Architectural Review* (December 1951): 383–87.

116 "New Knoll Showroom: A Study in Space and Texture," *Interior Design* (April 1951): 30.

117 FKBP, series 1; Virginia Lee Warren, "Woman Who Led an Office Revolution Rules an Empire of Modern Design," *New York Times*, September 1, 1964, 40.

118 *Interiors* (July 1952): 117; "Knoll, Chicago: New Tune in the Same Key," *Interiors* (February 1954): 46–51.

119 "The Knoll Interior," *Architectural Forum* (March 1957): 137–40; "Showroom for Knoll Associates, Inc.," *Arts and Architecture* (May 1957): 22–23; Louise Sloane, "Two Showrooms," *Progressive Architecture* (July 1958): 137–43; "New Showroom for Knoll Associates, Inc.," *Arts and Architecture* (November 1960): 14–15; "Knoll's Newest Showroom," *Interiors* (March 1961): 138–39.

120 Charlotta Heythum, "Ten Years—Knoll International in Germany," *Deutsche Bauzeitung* (October 1961), trans. Else Stone, FKBP series 6, box 4, folder 4; "La nuova sede della Knoll a Roma," *Domus* (November 1960): 51ff.

121 *Interiors* (October 1960), 178; "Executive Offices for Knoll Associates," *Progressive Architecture* (October 1962): 176.

122 Florence Knoll Bassett, interview, ca. 1977, p. 10, Knoll Archives.

123 Mary Roche, "For Modern Living," *New York Times*, September 11, 1949, SM48; Margaret Warren, "Detroit's 'Modern Living' Exhibits, Light in Effect, Heavy in Significance," *Christian Science Monitor*, October 20, 1949, 14.

124 Alexander H. Girard and W. D. Laurie, Jr., with W. A. Bostick, eds., *An Exhibition for Modern Living* (Detroit: Detroit Institute of Arts, 1949).

125 For a general overview of the *Good Design* series see Terence Riley and Edward Eigen, "Between the Museum and the Marketplace: Selling Good Design," in *Studies in Modern Art 4: The Museum of Modern Art at Mid-Century at Home and Abroad* (New York: Museum of Modern Art and Harry N. Abrams, 1994), 150–79.

126 *Living Up-to-Date: An Exhibition of New Designs for the Home from September 25 to October 28, 1951*, exh. cat. (Baltimore: Baltimore Museum of Art, 1951); "Benesch, Drawings He Collected Now Enrich Baltimore Art Museum" (obituary), *Baltimore Sun*, June 24, 1994.

127 "Modern Furniture Exhibition," *Interiors* (October 1951): 12; "Living Up-to-Date," *Arts and Architecture* (December 1951): 20–21; "Furnishings and Rooms in Baltimore Show," *Interiors* (December 1951): 16.

128 Leslie Judd Portner, "Three New Shows at Corcoran," *Washington Post*, October 12, 1952, L4.

129 Leslie Judd Portner, "'Living Today' Outstanding Show," *Washington Post*, April 20, 1958.

130 Knoll Associates, "Dramatic New Design for Leisure at Dallas Museum of Fine Arts," press release, ca. 1952, Jerry Bywaters papers, Southwestern Methodist University.

131 "Art Forms Are Created Out of Fabrics and Yarn," *New York Times*, November 16, 1962, 51.

132 "A Knoll Extra," *Interiors* (June 1963): 14. This was the first of several exhibitions Hicks would have in Knoll showrooms.

133 "Knoll's Kaleidoscopic Knock-Down," *Interiors* (December 1952): 112–15, 175; George Nelson, *Display* (New York: Whitney Publications, Inc., 1953): 39–40.

134 "Art Metal Buys Three Companies," *New York Times*, June 10, 1959, 51; Rita Reif, "Pioneer in Modern Furnishings is Charting Expansion Course," *New York Times*, June 17, 1959, 29.

135 "Interior Design of C.B.S. Building, 51W52, New York," *Architect and Builder* 16 (July 1966): 12.

136 Patricia L. Conway, "Design at CBS," *Industrial Design* (February 1966): 49–51.

137 Mildred F. Schmertz, "Distinguished Interior Architecture for CBS," *Architectural Record* (June 1966): 129–34.

138 "Interior Design of C.B.S. Building, 51W52, New York," *Architect and Builder* 16 (July 1966): 13; and Florence Knoll Bassett, "The Interiors at CBS," reprint from *Office Design* (May 1966): n.p. (courtesy Knoll Archives). *Oxford* was a plain weave introduced in 1959; the colorway used here was called "Banker's Grey."

139 "C.B.S. 'Eye' Zooms In on New Home," *New York Times*, September 12, 1965, R1; "Total Design on a Grand Scale," *Life* (April 29, 1966): 50–58.

140 Florence Knoll, interview, ca. 1977, p. 9, Knoll Archives; "C.B.S. 'Eye' Zooms In on New Home," *New York Times*, September 12, 1965, R1.

141 The Tiffany windows are now in the collection of the Metropolitan Museum of Art, New York, installed in the Charles Engelhard Court of the American Wing.

142 Florence Knoll, interview, ca. 1977, p. 9, Knoll Archives.

143 Ada Louise Huxtable, "Eero Saarinen's Somber Skyscraper," *New York Times*, March 13, 1966, 135.

144 Vincent Cafiero, interview, ca. 1977, p. 5, Knoll Archives.

145 Florence Knoll Bassett to W. Cornell Dechert, January 14, 1965, FKBP, series 6, box 4, folder 4.

146 Florence Knoll Bassett, interview, ca. 1977, p. 15, Knoll Archives.

147 "News: Commissions," *Interiors* (December 1967): 18.

148 Lewis J. Butler designer file, Knoll Archives.

149 Vincent Cafiero, interview by author, June 6, 2004.

150 Ursula Cliff, "Gallery 4: Florence Knoll," *Industrial Design* (April 1961): 71.

5 Knoll without the Knolls: Change and Transformation, 1963–78

Angela Völker

When Florence Knoll Bassett left Knoll Associates in 1965, the firm's future seemed uncertain to many in the industry. According to Olga Gueft, editor of *Interiors* magazine, "The question is whether the pioneering firm will retain its leadership now that its legendary founders have left the scene. . . . Can Knoll remain the symbol of the classic avant-garde without the Knolls?"[1] Under Knoll leadership, the firm had represented an unflinching commitment to design excellence and modernism, a commitment that had continued after Hans Knoll's death in 1955 and even after the company was sold to Art Metal Incorporated in 1959. The next few years, however, proved the solidity of the company and the strength of the Knoll brand. Under new leadership, including several individuals who had shaped their careers at Knoll, the company found expanded markets outside the United States and courted new designers to bring fresh ideas to Knoll Textiles and its other divisions. By examining some of these new textiles and how they came into being, primarily those with designer's names attached to them, changes and developments at Knoll in the late 1960s through the 1970s can be charted.

End of an Era: Knoll Textiles, 1960–65

Although Knoll's reputation for excellence remained intact, the sale of the firm in 1959 had fundamentally changed the culture of the company. After Hans Knoll's death in October 1955, Florence Knoll assumed full leadership and the title of president. She called on Cornell Dechert, who had been with Knoll since 1953, to take over as general manager. In June 1958 Florence Knoll married the Miami-based banker Harry Hood Bassett and began to spend much of her time in Florida. After the sale of Knoll to Art Metal a year later, while she continued to oversee design at Knoll and to head the Knoll Planning Unit, she relinquished the largely administrative role of president to Dechert. The second half of the 1950s and the early 1960s saw the introduction of some of Knoll's most important furniture and textiles and was marked by increasingly large, high-profile interiors projects for the Knoll Planning Unit (see chapter 4). Dominating Knoll's textile collection at this time were durable upholstery fabrics suited to extensive use in office installations—including Astrid Sampe's *Rugby* (1954) and Suzanne Huguenin's *Nylon Homespun* (1958)—as well as sheer and open-weave casements, appropriate for the large window expanses of new office buildings—Reuben Eshkanian's *Trellis* (1957) and Anni Albers's *Rail* (1962), to name just two (see chapter 3). Such fabrics continued to be important parts of Knoll's collection through the 1960s and 1970s.

Suzanne Huguenin, who headed Knoll Textiles from late 1955 through 1963, worked closely with Florence Knoll and the Knoll Planning Unit to shape a collection of textiles suited to the needs of Knoll furniture applications and appropriate for the interiors designed by the company. Huguenin frequently traveled to Knoll's international divisions and licensees in Europe and other parts of the world, and by the early 1960s she was sourcing more and more of Knoll's fabrics from European mills and designers (see chapter 3). One of the most significant of these new European suppliers was Paul Maute, whose mill, located in Heroldstatt near Stuttgart in southwestern Germany, specialized in handwoven fabrics. Maute had been producing Evelyn Hill's *Handwoven* series for Knoll Germany for several years. On a visit to Knoll's Swiss licensee, Huguenin discovered *Arno*, one of Maute's own designs, covering a

Fence, introduced 1964. Made in Germany for Knoll Textiles. Used for drapery; cotton; warp-twining with discontinuous wefts. The Montreal Museum of Fine Arts, Liliane and David M. Stewart Collection, Gift of the American Friends of Canada through the generosity of Ben Short, D87.123.1. Cat. 171.

Fig. 5.1 Left Paul Maute. *Cato* ("Red" colorway) on *72U* side chair designed by Eero Saarinen, ca. 1965. Made by Paul Maute GmbH for Knoll Textiles; chair made by Knoll Associates. Wool, viscose; plain weave with grouped warps and supplemental weft; chair: fiberglas shell, wooden legs, foam rubber. Knoll Museum, East Greenville, Penn. Cat. 164.

Fig. 5.2 Right Paul Maute. Detail of *Cato* ("Red" colorway), introduced 1961. Made by Paul Maute GmbH for Knoll Textiles. Used for upholstery; wool, viscose; plain weave with grouped warps and supplemental weft. Private collection.

Knoll chair, and it was added to the Knoll collection along with *Cato*, another Maute design, in 1961.[2] Throughout the 1960s and 1970s Knoll prominently featured handwoven fabrics produced by the firm, most of which Maute designed himself.[3] Although Maute fabrics took a less prominent role in the 1980s, the firm continued to supply Knoll until 1992.[4]

During the 1960s American textile design for the contract market sector was not particularly original, especially in terms of upholstery fabrics. These tended to be conservative, characterized by formal restraint and simplicity in design and materials. Indeed, Knoll's introduction of the Maute handwoven upholsteries was not groundbreaking. The fabrics were less innovative and experimental than the earlier Knoll handwoven fabrics designed by Marianne Strengell and Evelyn Hill. Those had featured new and unusual fibers and weaving techniques. The Maute handwovens' bold colors and wide range of colorways, however, as well as the superior materials and high-quality weaving, made these luxurious fabrics a mainstay of the Knoll line. Huguenin described their almost immediate success in a company memo in early 1963:

> Of all the new fabrics introduced last fall, none has had a more spectacular success than EBRO, of which we have already sold thousands of yards on furniture and by the yard. CATO's success is also overwhelming. Since it was first introduced in August 1961, we have sold over 10,000 yards. One of CATO's most popular colors is Oyster, and single orders for over 100 yards are frequent, not only of CATO, but also for EBRO and ARNO. . . . I believe that one of the reasons why our Handwovens are so successful is that . . . the quality of the fabrics is outstanding. It is safe to say that nowhere in the US can the wool used for these fabrics be matched. Fabrics very similar to ARNO and EBRO . . . are being produced in other countries . . . notably in South America, Haiti, North Africa . . . [and] are offered by one of our most active competitors at much higher prices, but are much lower quality, because the wool . . . is of a much inferior grade, and in no way compares with the high-grade virgin Merino wool from New Zealand which is used in the Maute collection.[5]

The best-selling design *Cato* is representative of the decades-long popularity of many of Knoll's handwoven textiles in the contract market (fig. 5.1). It is Knoll's oldest fabric in production (as of 2011), although it is no longer handwoven.[6] The hues of *Cato*'s yarns are subtle variations on a basic color, as in one of the earliest colorways, "Red," which was woven with a thin black viscose (a type of rayon) warp and wool weft threads in two tones of red (fig. 5.2). *Cato* eventually was made in more than forty shades of thread-dyed wool.[7]

In addition to introducing the Maute handwoven upholsteries, Huguenin also added a wide range of open-weave casements to the Knoll collection, one of her most important contributions before leaving Knoll in 1963. Significant designs in this category were introduced in the late 1950s and early 1960s (see chapter 3), and additional ones developed by Huguenin were brought out in 1964, just after her departure.[8] These included the first handwoven drapery fabrics designed and manufactured by Paul Maute—*Bourette Silk* and *Horizons*. Both are plain weaves like most Maute fabrics. *Bourette Silk* is a close-woven all-silk fabric, while *Horizons* is composed of linen, wool, and silk. Visual interest was created in *Horizons* by gathering and tying together groups of wefts at regular intervals to create a motif of elongated ovoid shapes (fig. 5.3). In 1964 Knoll also introduced "architectonic net casements" which were intended for use in the large window walls common in modern office buildings.[9] Their wide width (118 inches) would not require seaming together more than one panel for most installations. Machine-woven in West Germany, these included *Filigree* (cat. 172), a polyester weave described by Knoll as "an imaginative counterpoint of major and minor fish nets," as well as *Fence* (see p. 195), a cotton fabric of openwork squares.[10]

When Huguenin left to establish an independent textile consultancy in late 1963, Florence Knoll Bassett became largely responsible for the artistic direction of Knoll Textiles. She is credited with overseeing the development of *York*, an all-wool upholstery woven for Knoll in Denmark by C. Olesen and introduced in 1965.[11] In production until 1978, this houndstooth check pattern was initially available in sixteen colorways (fig. 5.4). It was also featured in a memorable advertisement designed by Herbert Matter (see fig. C.10). By the middle of the 1960s, however, Florence Knoll Bassett, the company's driving force for design innovation, had increasingly withdrawn from day-to-day operations. By the time she formally resigned from Knoll Associates in 1965, there was considerable stagnation in the development of new designs and a more distant relationship between Knoll Associates' leadership and its designers.

New Leadership, New Directions

Knoll without the Knolls was in need of fresh leadership to generate new momentum within the company. While Cornell Dechert would remain president and able administrator of the firm until 1972, an important newcomer, Robert Cadwallader, joined the company's senior leadership in 1965.[12] A native Texan, Cadwallader had worked for Knoll part-time during his college years in Dallas and became a salesman in the Dallas showroom in 1955. In 1960 he founded and headed the new Knoll showroom in Los Angeles and in 1963 was named as the Western sales manager, overseeing sales on

Fig. 5.3 Paul Maute. *Horizons* ("Off-White" colorway), in production 1964–78, this example ca. 1970. Made by Paul Maute GmbH for Knoll Textiles. Used for drapery; wool and linen silk; plain weave with paired wefts and supplemental knots. University of Alberta Clothing and Textiles Collection, 1990.65.22. Cat. 173.

Fig. 5.4 Left *York* sample ("Yellow/Orange" colorway), 1965. Made by C. Olesen for Knoll Textiles. Wool, basket weave. KnollTextiles Archive.

Fig. 5.5 Right Advertisement for DuPont. From *Interiors*, May 1966.

Fig. 5.6 Paul Maute. *Morocco* ("White" colorway) on *Platner* lounge chair designed by Warren Platner, introduced 1966, this example ca. 1971. Made by Paul Maute GmbH for Knoll Textiles; chair made by Knoll International. Wool, plain weave; chair: dark patinated copper oxide on steel rod, foam rubber. Yale University Art Gallery, Gift of Knoll International, Inc., 1971.44.1.

Fig. 5.7 Bottom Sheila Hicks. *Inca* color or weave sample with manufacturer's tag, ca. 1966. Made by Paul Maute GmbH for Knoll Textiles. Used for upholstery; wool; plain weave. KnollTextiles Archive. Cat. 168.

Fig. 5.8 Top Sheila Hicks. *Inca* ("Gold" colorway) on *Stephens* side chair designed by William Stephens, this example ca. 1973. Made by Paul Maute GmbH for Knoll Textiles; chair made by Knoll International. Wool, plain weave; chair: oak frame, plastic shell, foam. Knoll Museum, East Greenville, Penn. Cat. 170.

the West Coast. Cadwallader moved to New York to help Dechert steer Knoll onto a new course. While his title—director of marketing (later vice-president of marketing)—suggests a more limited role, Cadwallader actually assumed many of the duties Florence Knoll had fulfilled before him. He began with speeding up the design development process, focusing first on the furniture division which then had many projects underway but nothing ready for release. Cadwallader set an initial goal of two major furniture introductions each year, to coincide with the important furniture industry markets. In short order, Knoll moved many projects onto the market, including a landmark collection of wire-based furniture designed by Warren Platner and Richard Schultz's *Leisure* collection.[13] Schultz' collection of outdoor furniture was also quite innovative, featuring an early use of a stretch nylon-Dacron mesh to form the seat surfaces of chairs and a chaise lounge (fig. 5.5). Similar mesh fabrics would be widely used decades later in Knoll's and other contract manufacturer's task seating. The cold, bright metal of Platner's seating-furniture frames was often countered with cushions upholstered in chunky textured Maute handwovens, such as *Morocco*, which was also introduced in 1966 (fig. 5.6).

The plain weave of *Morocco* was but one of the upholsteries handwoven by the Maute firm released by Knoll in 1966. In contrast to *Morocco*, the two others, *Inca* and *Harrow*, were not designed by the head of the firm. *Inca* was the first upholstery with a woven pattern not based on stripes or checks that was introduced into the Knoll collection (fig. 5.7). Designed by fiber artist Sheila Hicks, whose weavings had previously been exhibited in Knoll showrooms in Mexico City (1962) and Chicago (1963), *Inca* had been in development since Hicks's initial meetings with Florence Knoll Bassett in 1964. Knoll Textiles contracted Hicks to create fabric designs and act as a color and materials consultant for the firm. While she submitted many designs, only *Inca* was put into production. Its pattern of striped squares that appear to swivel at right angles in opposition to each other was suited to many upholstery applications (fig. 5.8) and had strong appeal—the pattern remained in Knoll Textiles offerings until 1991.

Harrow brought another new designer to the Knoll Textiles roster: Julia Keiner-Forchheimer, a native of Germany, who had spent more than twenty-five years in Israel before coming to the United States in about 1964. A skilled weaver, Keiner-Forchheimer was founder and head of the weaving department at the Bezalel School of Arts and Crafts in Jerusalem. Soon after her arrival in the United States, Keiner-Forchheimer found freelance work with interior fabrics houses such as Knoll and Isabel Scott.[14] *Harrow*, her first design for Knoll, features a fine warp and weft with the addition of a chunky float yarn in the weft, creating a strong contrast to the warp and lending a pronounced dimensional quality to the surface of the fabric (fig. 5.9). Fine blending of the wool yarns used in *Harrow* resulted in a subtle yet elegant textile. It was initially offered in four neutral colorways and with additional colorways in muted earthtones added in 1968.[15] Keiner-Forchheimer also designed two open-weave casement fabrics that were introduced by Knoll in 1967—*Jupiter* and *Stratton*. Both casements were manufactured by Chicopee Mills of seventy percent Verel with smaller amounts of rayon and wool. Verel was the brandname for a type of modacrylic, a fiber that will quickly self-extinguish if it catches fire, making these fabrics "inherently flame retarded," a feature highlighted in Knoll sample tags and literature.[16] *Stratton* (see fig. B.73) has a plain leno-weave structure and *Jupiter* a more intricate one that involved alternately gathering and separating trios of weft yarns (fig. 5.10).

Cadwallader also ushered in a change to the way Knoll products were presented on the market and to Knoll's graphic identity. As the new head of marketing, he focused on refreshing the public image of the company expressed in its graphic identity and advertisements. In developing new press materials, Cadwallader was closely assisted by Christine Rae, who had worked with Florence Knoll and served as director of publications and communications until 1972.[17] Cadwallader had become dissatisfied with the work of Knoll's longtime graphic designer, Herbert Matter, who had significantly shaped Knoll's international image since being hired by Florence Knoll in 1947. In looking for a replacement for Matter, Cadwallader approached Mildred Constantine, a curator at the Museum of Modern Art, for her advice on possible candidates. Among her recommendations was the Italian architect and designer Massimo Vignelli, and Cadwallader hired him in 1966.

Vignelli created an entirely new visual identity and graphic program for the firm—from new fonts and grid formats to the color coding of division materials. Knoll Textiles was designated by "Knoll Red," the orange-red tone heavily used by the company from this point forward.[18] As part of the new graphic program, Vignelli designed a new sample kit and brochure to present the division's handwoven fabrics. The *Handwoven* sample kit and equivalent sample kits for the general upholstery collection, which were developed at the same time, were encased in bright Knoll Red boxes. The *Handwoven* kit contained a series of cards presenting each textile and its various colorways, as well as a larger sample of each handwoven and a booklet on the collection featuring photographs by Cadwallader taken at the Maute mill in Germany (fig. 5.11). The hiring of Vignelli, an innovative Italian graphic designer, reflects the decision to bring an increasingly international orientation and design sense to the company—Knoll would call upon European designers and manufacturers throughout the next decade.

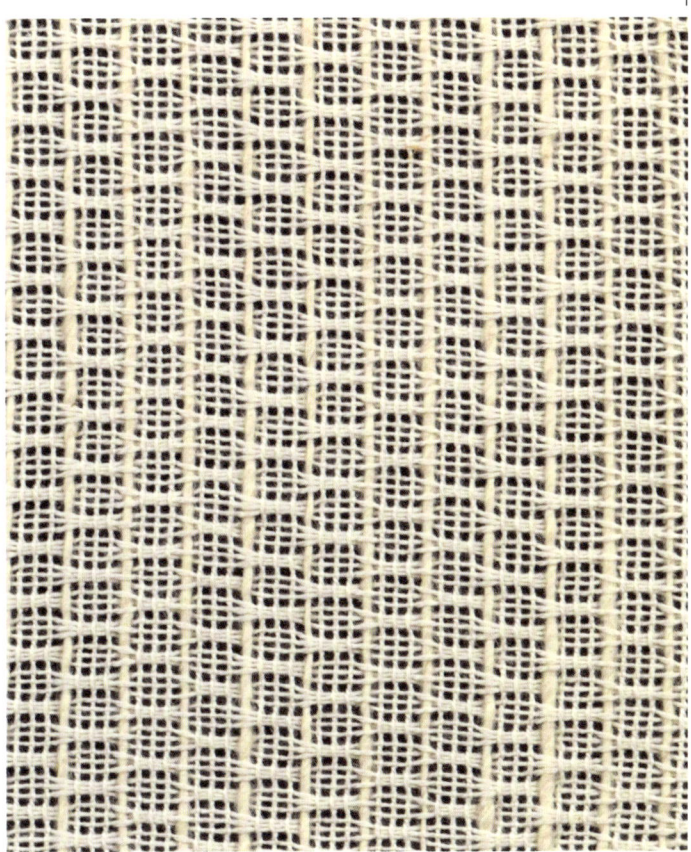

Fig. 5.9 Top left Julia Keiner-Forchheimer. Detail *Harrow* sample ("Oyster" colorway), introduced 1966, this example ca. 1970. Made by Paul Maute GmbH for Knoll Textiles. Used for upholstery; wool, perlon; plain-weave–derived compound weave. Courtesy Paul Makovsky.

Fig. 5.10 Top right Julia Keiner-Forchheimer. Detail *Jupiter* sample ("Off-White" colorway), ca. 1968. Made by Chicopee Mills for Knoll Textiles. Used for drapery, Verel modacrylic, rayon, wool; plain-weave–derived simple weave with alternating warp twining. KnollTextiles Archive. Cat. 174.

Fig. 5.11 Bottom Lella and Massimo Vignelli/Unimark International. Sample kit, "Handwoven Collection," ca. 1967. Made for Knoll Textiles. Cardboard, paper, textile samples. Brooklyn Museum Collection, X1188.3. Cat. 176.

A New Leader for Knoll Textiles

Cadwallader brought in another European to help reinvigorate and expand Knoll's textile offerings—Barbara Rodes (fig. 5.12). Rodes (Rodes-Segerer after 1976), a native of Germany, had been trained in fashion design, textile design, and styling, as well as the more technical aspects of fabric development and manufacturing, before being hired by Knoll at age twenty-one to coordinate the textile operations for Knoll Germany.[19] She brought a focus on textiles, which had not previously existed in the German branch, working with European manufacturers to adapt existing patterns sent from the main office in New York and make them more suitable for the German market.[20] Soon Rodes began originating textiles, rather than just reworking the patterns developed in New York, and quickly came to recognize the advantage of the various European divisions and licensees coming together to share the development of textiles for the European market. In 1962 she began working part of the year from the central Knoll office for Europe in Basel, Switzerland, as a textile development consultant to the various European divisions. Two years later, as her success at textile development grew and textile sales expanded for Knoll in Europe, she was made a member of Knoll's international design and development committee, working with Florence Knoll Bassett and others to develop fabrics for Knoll worldwide. In 1966 Rodes was appointed head of Knoll's International Coordination Office, overseeing textile development for all divisions outside of the United States, although she did work on developing European-made textiles for the United States market.[21] Cadwallader regularly visited the European Knoll divisions and licensees and would often spend time with Barbara Rodes, visiting textile manufacturers, reviewing designs she was considering for inclusion in the Knoll collection, and discussing new designers.[22] In 1971 Rodes was made head of design and development for Knoll Textiles worldwide and began spending about half of the year in New York and half in Stuttgart (where the European central office and warehouse for Knoll Textiles was located from the mid-1970s). In 1973 she was named vice president and director of Knoll Textiles, a position she held until leaving the company in April 1978.

Through her contacts with German and Austrian textile designers, including several professors and former students of the Staatliche Akademie der Bildenden Künste (State Academy of Art and Design) in Stuttgart, Rodes brought new life to Knoll's role as design innovator. During the later 1960s and 1970s, she encouraged Stuttgart-based designer Wolfgang Bauer, a graduate of the Staatliche Akademie and student of designer Leo Wollner (who would soon join the ranks of Knoll designers himself), to see the advantage in designing for a globally networked company such as Knoll. His first collection was likely introduced in late 1967 or early 1968 and consisted solely of printed fabrics. It was released by Knoll's various European divisions, where residential projects and retail customers were more common and such drapery textiles were in high demand.[23] Bauer's first designs for Knoll to be introduced in the United States were upholsteries. Released in 1968, *Mosaic* and *Lumière* were French-made, machine-woven upholstery fabrics, that represented something new for Knoll.[24] They were all-silk and almost twice as expensive as any other upholstery then on offer, but their woven patterning and brilliant colors added to the diversity of Knoll's offerings.[25] *Mosaic* featured a triangular motif arranged in pinwheel fashion (fig. 5.13) while *Lumière* had a linear motif reminiscent of snakeskin (see fig. B.20).

Innovation in printed fabrics was virtually nonexistent at Knoll in the United States during the 1960s; in fact no new printed textiles were introduced there after Huguenin's departure in 1963. This changed in the fall of 1969 when Knoll released a highly publicized collection of Bauer's printed drapery fabrics which had been in development for several years and likely were introduced earlier for Knoll Europe. Cadwallader recalls visiting Rodes in the Stuttgart office in about 1966 and examining a large group of "sensational" designs for print fabrics by Bauer.[26] Together Cadwallader and Rodes chose a few patterns to be put into production. In the fall of 1969 four new patterns by Bauer—*Stones*, *Delta*, *Fragment*, and *Collage*—brought radical change and needed innovations in printed textiles to Knoll.[27] These designs were screen-printed on cotton velvet, a daring and innovative approach. The large-scale patterns of *Fragment* and *Collage* (fig. 5.14) are particularly striking in their sweeping, free composition. The determining form of each pattern resembles a tree trunk, out of which grow various "leaves" reminiscent of colorful, torn pieces of paper. *Stones* (fig. 5.15) has a tight configuration of curvilinear forms resembling two-dimensional stones, whereas *Delta*'s patterning (see page 2) recalls the waterways and tributaries of a river delta. Each print was available in several colorways, many quite vivid, reflective of Bauer's skill as a colorist. Bauer's prints renewed Knoll's claim to the cutting edge of print design after several years of stagnation. Knoll promoted the collection widely in advertisements and through give-away silk scarves printed with the *Collage* motif (cat. 182). *Industrial Design* (*ID*) magazine featured Bauer's prints among the outstanding designs of 1969, and in 1970 they were included in an exhibition of the *ID* selections at the Museum of Science and Industry, Chicago.[28] These Bauer fabrics remained in production for nearly ten years, until 1978 (except for *Stones*, which was discontinued in 1972), representing a resounding success for Knoll.

To manufacture the new Bauer prints, Barbara Rodes turned to the leading textile printing firm Pausa AG in Mössingen, Germany, not far from Knoll's German base in

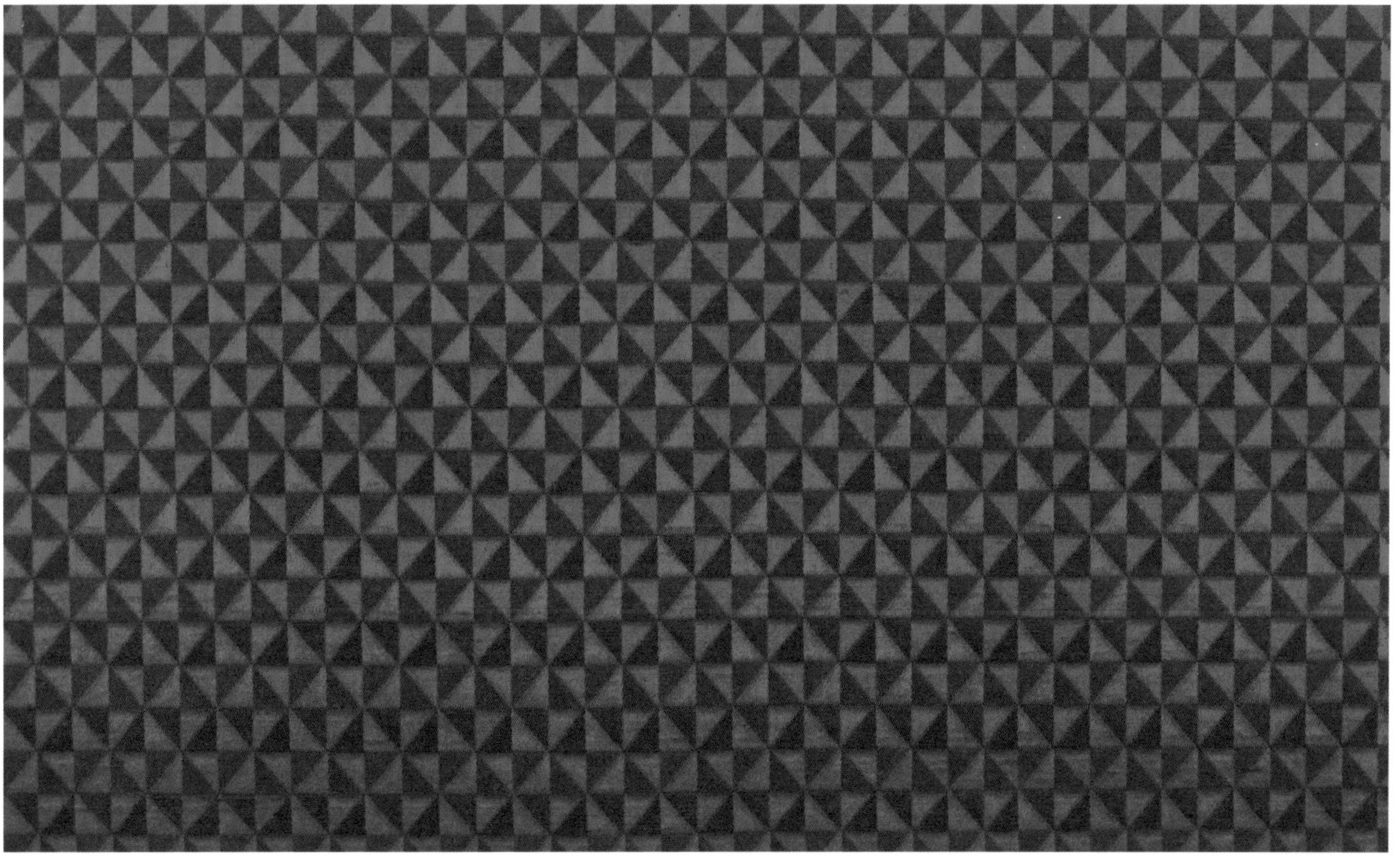

Fig. 5.12 Top Barbara Rodes-Segerer, ca. 1975. KnollTextiles Archive.

Fig. 5.13 Bottom Wolf Bauer. *Mosaic* ("Fuchsia" colorway), in production 1968–74, this example ca. 1970. Made in France for Knoll Textiles. Used for upholstery; silk; plain-weave–derived compound weave. University of Alberta Clothing and Textiles Collection, 1990.65.14b. Cat. 183.

Fig. 5.14 Wolf Bauer. *Collage* ("Yellow" colorway), ca. 1970. Made by Pausa AG for Knoll Textiles. Used for drapery; cotton velveteen; screen-printed. Cooper-Hewitt, National Design Museum, Smithsonian Institution.

 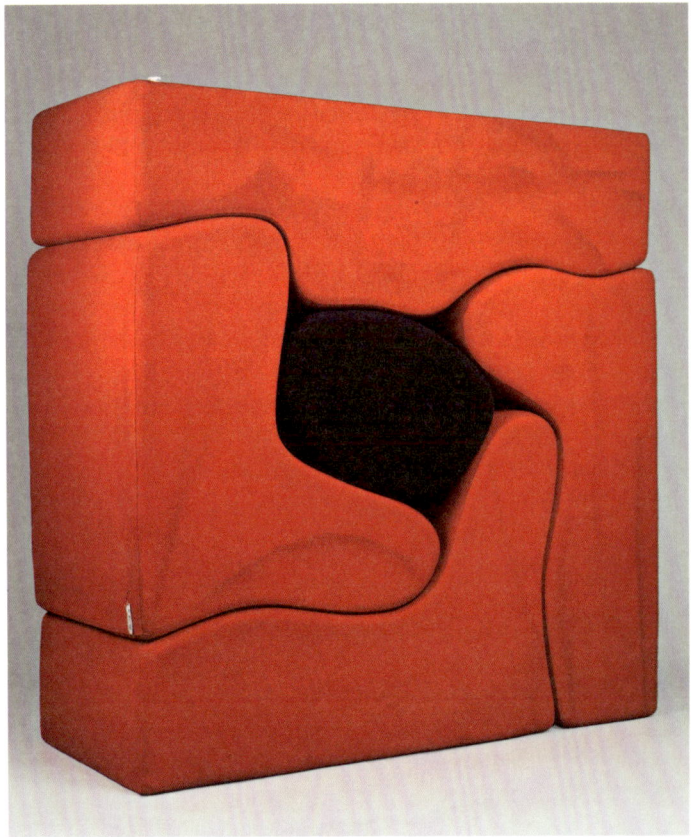

Fig. 5.15 Left Wolf Bauer. *Stones* ("Pink/Red" colorway), ca. 1975. Made by Pausa AG for Knoll Textiles. Used for drapery; cotton velvet; screen-printed. Courtesy Cindia Reyes. Cat. 185.

Fig. 5.16 Roberto Matta. *Malitte* seating system, ca. 1971. Upholstery made by Société Ariégeoise de Bonneterie; seating system made by Gavina division, Knoll International. Nylon and vinyon; seating: polyurethane foam. Brooklyn Museum, Gift of Knoll International, Inc., 78.128.1-5. Cat. 186.

Stuttgart. Pausa had been founded in 1919 and rose to prominence after World War II under the leadership of its director of design Willy Häussler. It had produced fabric designs by such prominent German artists as Willi Baumeister and HAP (Helmut Andreas Paul) Grieshaber, as well as the Danish designer Verner Panton.[29] Bauer's mentor Leo Wollner began working with Pausa in 1952, and after Wollner became head of the textiles department at the Staatliche Akademie in Stuttgart in 1957, a close relationship between Pausa and the school was formed. Bauer worked as Wollner's assistant in the early 1960s and may have helped to foster Knoll's relationship with Pausa. In any event, Pausa remained a leading supplier of printed textiles for Knoll through the 1970s.

In a recent interview Cadwallader suggested that Bauer's and other printed fabrics were not brought into the collection primarily to generate sales, but rather to put Knoll Textiles back in the news and burnish its image as a design innovator.[30] This desire to preserve a progressive and innovative image for the company fueled other major changes at Knoll in 1969 and 1970. During the 1960s, the casual lifestyle adopted by younger consumers with less conventional ideas than their parents presented a challenge for Knoll with its perennial ethos of quality and classics. In 1968 Knoll bought Gavina S.p.A., a furniture company that had been founded by Dino Gavina in Milan in 1960, in part to reflect a new direction for Knoll and in part to have access to Gavina's manufacturing facilities.[31] Knoll's purchase of Gavina included the repro-duction rights to designs by Tobia Scarpa, Achille Castiglioni, Roberto Sebastian Matta, Vico Magistretti, and other innovative designers of their generation, in addition to Marcel Breuer's furniture designs, such as the iconic *Wassily* chair of 1925. In this way, Knoll managed to be associated with the lively Italian design scene which was prominent at the time. In May 1971 the *Interiors* critic Olga Gueft commented: "what Cadwallader wants from Gavina is an opportunity to loosen up the up-tight Knoll perfectionism."[32]

Knoll soon added Gavina's puzzlelike seating system called *Malitte* to its American line, keeping it in production from 1969 to 1976.[33] It had been designed in 1966 by the Chilean sculptor and painter, surrealist Roberto Sebastian Matta, who, like Dino Gavina, had been a follower of Marcel Duchamp. Matta's seating furniture offered the American company an opportunity to participate in the trend toward informality with a true showpiece (fig. 5.16). A monochromatic nylon and vinyon (polyvinyl chloride) stretch fabric was used to cover the rounded, organic furniture forms made of polyurethane foam. This fabric, developed by Gavina, was called simply *Malitte* by Knoll and was among a group of Gavina fabrics that were never officially part of the general Knoll Textiles offerings. They were only available on the Gavina furniture, having been applied to the furniture most likely before it was shipped to United States.[34] With the exception of *Malitte*, the Gavina fabrics were discontinued in the early 1970s. Likely seeing the potential for further sales of a stretch fabric like *Malitte*, in 1971 Knoll contacted the mill that made the fabric for Gavina, Société Ariégeoise de Bonneterie, and eventually procured a similar fabric made by the French mill through its American representative, the Joynel Company, an importer of many other fabrics for Knoll. The new fabric was *Orly*, a nylon and chlorofiber stretch upholstery that remained in the line until 1985.[35]

Knoll International

The transformation of the company founded by Hans and Florence Knoll continued through the late 1960s and early 1970s. In 1968 Walter E. Heller & Company, a Chicago-based "commercial finance company," purchased Knoll's parent company Art Metal.[36] Despite the change in ownership, there were no major leadership changes at Knoll—Cornell Dechert continued as president and Cadwallader as vice president for marketing. In 1971 Cadwallader became president of Knoll when Dechert was made chairman of the board.[37] In the fall of 1969 the company changed its name from Knoll Associates to Knoll International, marking another symbolic move toward making the firm's name synonymous with the best, most innovative designs, sourced from across the world.[38]

The June 1970 opening of a new main showroom at 745 Fifth Avenue in New York City presented a physical manifestation of the reinvented Knoll to match its new name and new graphic program by Vignelli.[39] Olga Gueft noted this change in her review of the space for *Interiors*: "The new showroom is Knoll's formal entry into the seventies, its symbolic casting off of the airy, punchy-hued, puritanically ascetic 'Knoll look' which elicited gasps in the forties, admiring sighs in the fifties, and yawns in the sixties."[40] She praised it as "a barrage of fascinating innovations in interior architecture, space planning, partitioning, detailing."[41] The showroom had been designed by the Italian architect Gae Aulenti who had created Knoll's Boston showroom in 1968 and would renovate the Milan showroom in 1971, later also contributing a number of furniture designs to the company. The 15,000-square-foot space was more than triple the size of the previous New York showroom. Aulenti had turned the interior plan forty-five degrees from the square plan of the building, creating a variety of angular spaces and interesting vistas, which "constantly surprise and delight the visitor."[42] All color came from the furniture, fabrics, and graphics—Aulenti used a silver-white carpet to cover floors, platforms, and partitions, while the walls and ceilings were painted white (fig. 5.17).[43] To the right of the entrance, about 600 square feet of space were devoted to Knoll Textiles. Casements and printed curtain fabrics, including the new

Fig. 5.17 Top Gae Aulenti. Knoll showroom installation, 745 Fifth Avenue, New York, 1970. Knoll Archives.

Fig. 5.18 Bottom Gae Aulenti. Knoll showroom installation, 745 Fifth Avenue, New York, 1970. Knoll Archives.

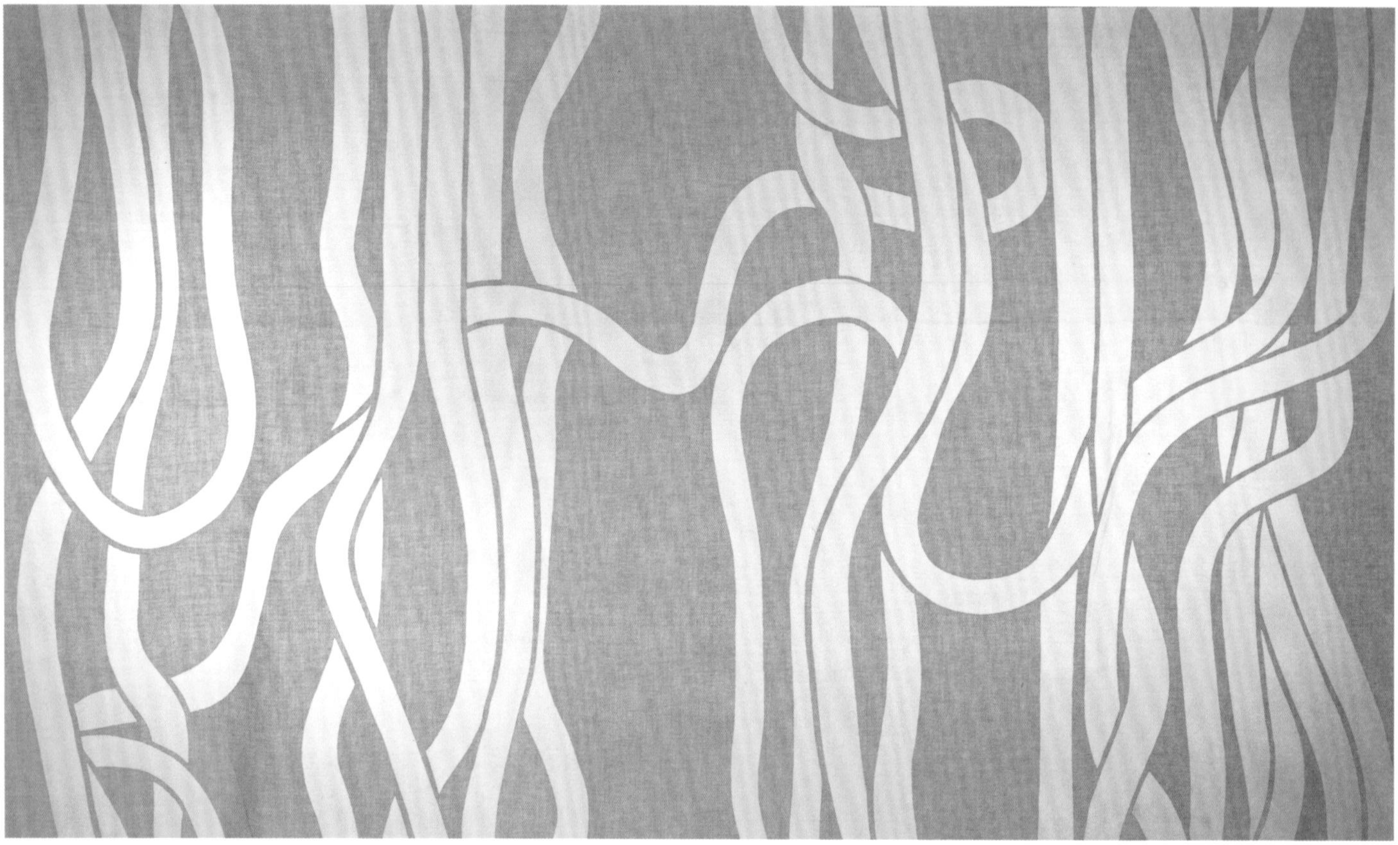

Fig. 5.19 Gretl and Leo Wollner. *Sling* ("White/White" sheer), ca. 1971. Made by Pausa AG for Knoll Textiles. Used for drapery; cotton, polyester; compound plain weave with discontinuous wefts. KnollTextiles Archive. Cat. 192.

Bauer designs, were displayed as panels in front of the windows that ran the perimeter of the showroom (fig. 5.18). The new showroom was a display and marketing success and would remain Knoll's headquarters through the 1970s.

New Prints

New printed fabrics continued to be introduced and heavily promoted by the company in the early 1970s. In the spring of 1971 Knoll Textiles introduced additional prints by Wolf Bauer as well as by four designers new to Knoll. All these designs were developed by Barbara Rodes in collaboration with Pausa in Germany. They included Knoll's first prints using burn-out or etch printing, a technique whereby a cloth with supplementary warps and wefts is "printed" with acid in certain areas so that one set of fibers is burned away leaving the other set, often a sheer, to create a translucent motif. One of the Bauer prints, *Yves*, was printed on a cotton-velvet base cloth, with a large Y-shaped repeat that was more geometric and controlled than previous Bauer velvet prints (see fig. B.21). The other new Bauer design, *Wheels*, featured a delicate, linear motif of circles bisected by radial lines and cross-hatching said to "suggest cobwebs."[44] It was produced in black on polyester and as a burn-out on a white cotton-polyester blend. Also included was *Sling*, the first print for Knoll by Leo Wollner and his wife, Gretl. *Sling* has a meandering linear motif and was made as a white-on-white sheer using the burn-out technique (fig. 5.19) and also printed in several colorways on a cotton ground (see fig. B.147). Another of Wollner's former students from the Staatliche Akademie in Stuttgart, Ulrike Rhomberg, who had begun working at Pausa in 1970, designed *Slant*, a large-scale linear motif printed on cotton velvet (see fig. B.105). Francisca Reichardt Vietsch, a German designer and professor of textile design at Hamburg's Hochschule für bildende Künste (Institute of Fine Arts), contributed *Omahar* to the 1971 collection. This complex pattern required fourteen silkscreens to create its colorful, 30-inch repeat, available in five colorways on a white cotton base cloth (fig. 5.20).[45] François Dallegret, an architect and artist working in Montreal, Canada, designed *Lines*, a print reminiscent of Op Art, which was introduced in two versions, as a polyester sheer with the linear motif silkscreened and a cotton and polyester sheer with the motif created using the burn-out technique. In 1973 a third version printed on a cotton base was introduced (see fig. B.35). With the introduction of this group of new prints from Germany, several older print designs were discontinued. While Suzanne Huguenin's linear prints of the early 1960s (*Quartet*, *Linea*, and *Polystripes*) were kept in the line, formerly successful designs dating to the 1950s by Sven Markelius (*Pythagorus* and *Prisma*), Eszter Haraszty (*Fibra*), and Ross Littell (*Mira*) were dropped.[46]

The new print collection was to be featured the following year at the most prestigious exhibition of Knoll's history: *Knoll au Louvre*, held in the Pavillon de Marsan (part of Palais du Louvre that housed the Musée des arts décoratifs in Paris).[47] On view from January through March 1972, the exhibition had been initiated two years earlier by Gae Aulenti and Yves Vidal, the well-connected director of Knoll France.[48] The installation, designed by Massimo and Lella Vignelli, cunningly exploited the drama of the monumental Napoleon III architecture by opening the exhibition with a twelve-foot high "Knoll" (visitors entered through arch of the "n") and using large cubes of all plastic or plastic and steel as vitrines to display "classic" Knoll furniture by Saarinen, Bertoia, Mies van der Rohe, and others, upholstered in bright Knoll fabrics.[49] An adjacent gallery was divided into seven "trapezoidal shadow boxes" on one side to showcase more recent furniture designs such as those of William Stephens, Matta, and Platner, while on the other side "the wall was covered with Knoll upholstery fabrics, with its casements stretching across the ceiling."[50] With this exhibition, *Interiors* reported that Knoll "was formally accorded official recognition as one of the epoch-making forces in the history of design."[51]

Apparently not shown in Paris was the *Three Meter Print Collection*, which was previewed at the January 1972 interior furnishings market in Chicago before becoming available in the summer of 1972.[52] This group of four prints resulted from a fruitful collaboration between Barbara Rodes, designers Gretl and Leo Wollner, and Pausa. Rodes considered the development of these prints to be one of the most exciting projects of her time at Knoll, both because of the team nature of the process and the "tremendous challenge technically to do it."[53] Knoll decided the 1972 additions to the print offerings should contrast in the size of their motifs with those introduced in 1969 and 1971. Rodes asked the Wollners "to work for two or three months, experimenting with flowing lines of color, on a giant scale."[54] The most interesting pattern the designers developed was "a huge, three meter work of black lines on a white ground," which was to become the print *Rivers*. Rodes and the Wollners were very excited by the prospect of such a large pattern, which had no repeat from floor to ceiling and, although it was then unclear how it was to be printed, Rodes asked the designers to develop their other ideas on this scale. The team took the designs to Pausa, a natural choice both because of the company's willingness to experiment and because of Wollner's long-term relationship with it. The production process involved long printing tables, very large screens that required four workers to maneuver and print and much back and forth to refine the technical process of printing on this scale. Three of the patterns, *Roads*, *Sails*, and *Trails*, were printed on a cotton-viscose sateen base cloth to better retain the brilliance of the colors used.[55] These three had a similar feeling in their use of bands of

Fig. 5.20 Francisca Reichardt Vietsch. *Omahar* ("Brown" colorway), ca. 1971. Made by Pausa AG for Knoll Textiles. Used for drapery; cotton; plain weave, screen-printed. Courtesy Carol Connell. Cat. 188.

Fig. 5.21 Gretl and Leo Wollner. *Trails* ("Brown/Rust" colorway), ca. 1972. Made by Pausa AG for Knoll Textiles. Used for drapery, wall hanging; cotton; 4/1 satin weave, screen-printed. Courtesy Carol Connell.

colors outlined by a related color or black (fig. 5.21, 5.28 and see fig. B.148). *Rivers*, the fourth *Three Meter Print*, was perhaps the most innovative of the group. Its undulating lines were printed on cotton velvet and featured subtle gradations of color that were mixed as the printing was underway, resulting in an effect reminiscent of watercolors (see page 14 and fig. B.149). These extraordinary panels were decorative in design and powerful in scale, appropriate for either office or public interiors, though rather monumental for residential use. Their success was mixed, although they remained in production until 1978.[56] While they recalled certain patterns by the Finnish firm of Marimekko from the 1960s, their free abstraction of forms and color combinations underscored Knoll's leading position in the field of printed textile design in the early seventies.

Casement Innovations

In 1973 Knoll's relationship with Leo Wollner again resulted in the introduction of a series of innovative textiles. A year earlier Knoll had asked Wollner's textile design class at the Staatliche Akademie in Stuttgart to create casement fabric designs—a way of engaging the next generation of designers.[57] Titled "Transparent," the assignment allowed students to create fabrics out of any material, resulting in a diverse range of experimental textiles that incorporated traditional fibers (wool, cotton, linen, silk), synthetic fibers (Lurex, plastic yarns), as well as various other substances including "metal, beads, glass balls, plexiglass, transparent buttons, wire, paper, veneer woods, knitted tubes of silver wire and other fantasy combinations."[58] The results were exhibited in January 1973 at Knoll's Frankfurt office in conjunction with the leading textile trade fair in Germany, Heimtextil.[59] At least three of these textiles were incorporated into the American Knoll Textiles collection (in slightly modified forms), and others were offered by Knoll in Europe.[60] Samples of two of these casements are preserved in the KnollTextiles Archive. *Puzzle* (fig. 5.22), designed by Margarete Warth, features rectangular openings that are made possible through the use of discontinuous wefts (wefts that do not extend across the full width of the fabric). It was manufactured for Knoll by the Swiss mill Linotex. A design by Friedrich Goth, *Comet*, has a similar openwork aspect and was made by the German manufacturer Kreuger using Dralon, a type of acrylic fiber (fig. 5.23).[61] Both of these casements were discontinued in 1977.

The introduction of the open-weave casements by the student designers was part of a significant change in Knoll's casement offerings. Between 1971 and 1974, many older casements, which had been introduced in the 1950s and 1960s, were discontinued, such as *Goatshair Casement* and *Jupiter*, and at the same time more than twenty new open-weave draperies were introduced.[62] Several of these were by the Swiss and German manufacturers who also made *Puzzle* and *Comet* for Knoll, including *Cyclone* made by Linotex (cat. 209), originally introduced in 1972 and then re-released in 2007 as part of Knoll's *Archival Collection*. The leno-weave casements *Durban* (1972) and *Protea* (1973) were the product of a new supplier, Jan-Paul Barnard, a young South African weaver who specialized in mohair textiles, the primary fiber used in these casements. The unevenly spun natural mohair weft yarns give these fabrics a rustic and inviting texture that was unique in the Knoll casement collection (fig. 5.24). Another major contributor was Paul Maute, who designed and manufactured several handwoven casements including *Atoll*, *Almanach*, and *Brabant* (all introduced in 1972) that recalled Maute's previous contribution, *Horizons*, in their use of wool and linen yarns and open-weave structure. *Serenade*, released in 1972, is atypical of the casements then produced by Maute's firm. This plain weave with a supplemental weft that incorporates Hostalen strip, a type of polypropylene, may have been one of the adaptations of the Staatliche Akademie student designs that Knoll had manufactured by Maute (fig. 5.25).[63] Much more in keeping with Maute's own designs is a casement introduced in 1973, *Nebula*, a subtle semi-sheer drapery featuring an irregular, hand-spun wool weft yarn that contrasts with a shiny rayon weft yarn (fig. 5.26). Perhaps the most playful of Maute's contributions to the casement collection in this period was *Loop* (1973), which has regularly spaced intervals without warp yarns between dense sections of warps. In these intervals the large-scale yarns in the weft have been allowed to "loop" out of the surface of the fabric (see fig. B.94).

"The Collection"

From December 11, 1973, to January 4, 1974, Knoll transformed "the New York Showroom into a multi-exhibition of textiles, emphasizing the international character and versatility of Knoll's textile range."[64] Titled "The Collection," this spectacular exhibition ran the gamut of Knoll's print collection, casements, and upholsteries, was well attended by the New York design community, and widely discussed in the press.[65] Perhaps its most controversial aspect was Knoll furniture reinterpreted by well-known New York fashion designers—Stephen Burrows, Calvin Klein, Pinky Wolman and Dianne Beaudry, Betsey Johnson, Ralph Lauren, Clovis Ruffin, Giorgio di Sant'Angelo, Willi Smith, and Willie Woo. Lauren's design was the most conservative, covering Kazuhide Takahama's *Suzanne* lounge chair in leather and belts, while jewelry designer Woo covered Matta's *Malitte* in over 50,000 sequins, and Johnson transformed a drafting stool with a bright yellow ruffled slipcover (fig. 5.27). The inclusion of the fashion designers, Cadwallader's idea, was perhaps the least well-received. The British designer

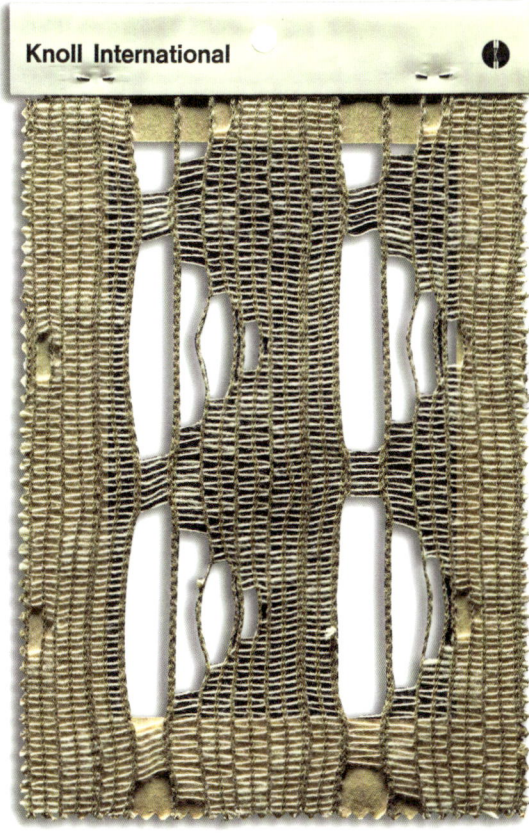

Fig. 5.22 Top left Margarete Warth. *Puzzle* sample ("Natural" colorway), ca. 1973. Made by Linotex for Knoll Textiles. Used for drapery; acrylic, linen; warp twining with discontinuous wefts. KnollTextiles Archive. Cat. 208.

Fig. 5.23 Top right Friedrich Goth. *Comet* sample ("Natural" colorway), ca. 1973. Made by Krueger GmbH for Knoll Textiles. Used for drapery; Dralon acrylic; warp-twining with discontinuous wefts. KnollTextiles Archive. Cat. 210.

Fig. 5.24 Bottom left Jan-Paul Barnard. *Durban* sample ("Beige" colorway), ca. 1973. Made by Barkor for Knoll Textiles. Used for drapery; mohair, cotton; plain gauze (leno) weave. KnollTextiles Archive. Cat. 207.

Fig. 5.25 Bottom right *Serenade* sample ("White" colorway), ca. 1972. Made by Paul Maute GmbH for Knoll Textiles. Used for drapery; wool, Hostalen (polypropylene) strip, spun rayon, perlon; plain weave with supplemental weft pile. KnollTextiles Archive. Cat. 206.

Fig. 5.26 Top Paul Maute. *Nebula* ("White" colorway), ca. 1973. Paul Maute GmbH for Knoll Textiles. Used for drapery; wool, perlon, rayon; plain weave with alternating single and paired wefts. KnollTextiles Archive. Cat. 180.

Fig. 5.27 Bottom Knoll furniture reimagined by Ralph Lauren (foreground), Betsey Johnson (right), and Willie Woo (background, right of center), "The Collection" installation, Knoll New York showroom, 1973. Knoll Archives.

Terance Conran remarked "the whole show seemed based on the questionable premise that modern furniture doesn't have to be dull."[66] Emilio Ambasz, curator of design at the Museum of Modern Art, was even less impressed: "Knoll has a grand tradition and a great responsibility, but I wonder, after seeing all this, what is the cultural role Knoll thinks it intends to play tomorrow."[67]

Knoll's recent innovations in printed fabrics and casement textiles were featured in "The Collection," including the experimental work of Staatliche Akademie student designers. *Interiors* commented in their coverage that "students were allowed to use any materials, disregarding problems of eventual execution. . . . Chicken wire, chicken feathers, wire lace in hot colors, curtains of cotton threads and cigarette papers were some of the exciting inspirations."[68] Floor-to-ceiling lengths of casements, such as Maute's *Loop*, were used throughout the installation. A length of the showroom was devoted to a dramatic display of the Wollners' *Three Meter* prints (fig. 5.28) while Knoll's other print offerings, such as a new group of three designs on Clevyl (a polyvinyl chloride fiber) were also on exhibit, the first to be printed on an "inherently flame retarded fabric."[69] The prints' bold patterns (see fig. B.34) were the creations of British designer Lynne Crosbee.

From Flock to Fabric

Another aspect of "The Collection" exhibition to garner widespread attention was the section titled "From Flock to Fabric," which demonstrated the process of creating textiles (fig. 5.29). At the opening reception, live sheep had been brought in to represent the beginnings of the process. There were also displays of unprocessed wool, yarns, and woven textiles as well as large-scale photographs of the refining and spinning of wool and the weaving of fabrics, largely images taken at the Maute factory and other nearby German mills that were Knoll suppliers. While Knoll's print and casement innovations in the late 1960s through 1970s received much press coverage, upholstery fabrics still formed the core and largest part of Knoll Textiles business. A 1977 issue of the *Knoll Tabloid* (a newspaper-format promotional piece designed by Massimo Vignelli) was devoted to Knoll Textiles and highlighted the diversity of upholsteries available from the company. It noted that the thirty-two machine-woven and sixteen handwoven upholsteries available that year—with all their associated colorways—presented literally hundreds of options, making "Knoll Textiles one of the largest and most complete sources around."[70] The diversity of upholstery color options was highlighted both graphically (fig. 5.30) and in the text: "The color explosion at Knoll has gone on apace. In 1977 you can choose from about 75 reds, 90 blue/purples, 50 greens, 100 yellow/orange/golds . . . and 85 black/browns. We stopped counting the beiges at 75!"[71]

Many of the time-honored machine-woven upholstery fabrics remained in the Knoll collection throughout the 1970s. New products from several of the same manufacturers were also introduced in this period—nearly all without designer credit. *Prestini* marked its thirtieth year in the Knoll collection in 1978. Its manufacturer, Louisville Textiles, contributed new fabrics to the Knoll collection, but in contrast to *Prestini*'s all-cotton composition, the new designs—one upholstery and three casements introduced in 1974 and 1976—were made entirely of artificial fibers, Verel modacrylic and viscose, making them fire-retardant.[72] Another American manufacturer and long-time Knoll supplier, Orinoka Mills, continued to produce *Lana* and *Nylon Transportation Cloth*, Knoll mainstays introduced in the 1950s and in production until 1979. Orinoka also supplied a new wool and nylon upholstery, *Cavalier*, beginning in 1967 which remained in production until 1982.[73] Craftex had purchased Moss Rose (like Orinoka, a Philadelphia-based mill) in the 1960s, inheriting the production of the best-selling *Knoll Nylon Homespun* which continued to be sold in large quantities with new colorways added periodically to keep the pattern fresh. In 1977 Knoll even introduced "Pinstripe" and "Check" versions of this perennial favorite (see fig. C.15).[74] Knoll also added several new upholsteries made by Craftex during the late 1960s and the 1970s. One of the most successful, *Brigadier*, was in production from 1969 to 1984 (fig. 5.31). This ribbed upholstery was warp-faced, meaning that the warp yarns formed the outer surface of the textile. This and the nylon and wool fiber blend made it resistant to abrasion and thus quite durable.[75] Craftex also produced one of the few new upholsteries publicly credited to a designer by Knoll in the 1970s. Barbara Rodes had approached her friend and Knoll designer Anni Albers about creating new designs for Knoll (casement fabrics designed by Albers in the late 1950s and early 1960s were still in the collection). Albers's *Jhet*, introduced in 1975 (see fig. B.8), a slightly patterned weave of nylon and wool, did not sell well, however, and was discontinued in 1978.[76] One of the longest-lasting fabrics from this period was *Cadet*, which was in production from 1973 to 1989. Initially made by Hayward-Schuster Woolen Mills, it was later manufactured by Homestead Fabrics.[77] A small-scale plain weave of wool and nylon, it was marketed as an inexpensive upholstery for contract applications where other more costly Knoll upholsteries were not competitive (fig. 5.32). By 1974 *Cadet* was one of two fabrics offered on chairs in Knoll's "In-Stock Program," for office furniture that could be shipped within three days of receipt of the order.[78] This fabric was also kept up to date by continuous introductions of new colorways.

Fig. 5.28 *Three Meter* prints including *Roads* (foreground) and *Trails* (rear) in "The Collection" installation, Knoll New York showroom, 1973. Knoll Archives.

Fig. 5.29 "From Flock to Fabric" section, "The Collection" installation, Knoll New York showroom, 1973. Knoll Archives.

Fig. 5.30 Top "End of the Rainbow," from the *Knoll Tabloid* for Knoll Textiles, 1977. Promotional piece designed by Massimo Vignelli; photographs by Jim Fesler, Stan Rise. Knoll Archives.

Fig. 5.31 Bottom *Brigadier* (Burgundy colorway), in production 1969–84, this example ca. 1970. Made by Craftex for Knoll Textiles. Used for upholstery; rayon, wool, nylon; plain weave. University of Alberta Clothing and Textiles Collection, 1990.65.12b.

Fig. 5.32 *Cadet* on *Pedestal* armchair designed by Eero Saarinen, this example ca. 1979. Made by Homestead Fabrics for Knoll Textiles; chair made by Knoll International. Wool and nylon; plain weave; chair: plastic, steel, foam rubber. Dallas Museum of Art, Gift of Knoll International, Inc., 1990.133. Cat. 205.

Fig. 5.33 Suzanne Huguenin. *Sequoia* sample ("Cerise" colorway), in production 1974–82, this example ca. 1980. Made by Weberei Eschen AG for Knoll Textiles. Used for upholstery; wool, rayon; twill weave. Courtesy Cindia Reyes. Cat. 203.

New Upholstery Textures and Designers

Textile manufacturers from outside of the United States, mainly based in Europe, increasingly supplied a range of upholstery textiles with both natural and synthetic fibers to Knoll in the second half of the 1960s and through the 1970s. One of the most notable additions to the upholstery collection that was implemented in this period, and distinguished it from the collection as it existed before 1965, was the addition of a number of velvets or other fabrics with a dense pile surface. The first of these was a Belgian-made linen-cotton velvet called *Camelot* that was introduced in 1966 and in production until 1971.[79] In 1972 Knoll introduced *Cuzco*, a stretch velour made in Italy by Lanerie Agnona from Alpaca fiber (likely inspiring the fabric's name), wool, and polyester in four earthtone colorways.[80] The same year, Knoll introduced *Knoll Velvet*, a mohair pile velvet made in the Netherlands, which was initially offered in twenty-eight colorways and is was still in production as of 2011.[81] In 1977 the company introduced another Dutch-made pile fabric, *Knoll Cotton Velvet*, initially offering it in forty-two colorways (see fig. C.14).[82] In 1979 it was renamed *Calais Cotton Velvet*, and by 1980 the colorways on offer had ballooned to a staggering 171.[83] The amazing quantity of color variants for certain plain fabrics, such as velvet, suggests that Knoll was attempting to provide a color option to please a wide range of customers.

The warm relationship that Barbara Rodes had with former head of Knoll Textiles, Suzanne Huguenin, also resulted in new European-made upholstery designs entering into the collection in this period. In 1973 Knoll released *Furrows II*, a revised version of Huguenin's 1957 design in new, brighter colorways, several of which featured strong contrasts between the colors of warp and weft. In 1974 the firm introduced an upholstery designed by Huguenin at the NeoCon trade fair in Chicago that June.[84] *Sequoia* is a large-scale twill weave with a heavyweight wool and rayon weft yarn that dominates the surface, creating a strong textural dimension (fig. 5.33). The yarn was hand-spun and hand-blended before being woven by Weberei Eschen AG in Liechtenstein.[85] After being introduced in the United States, *Sequoia* was also featured by Knoll in the company's display at the leading German textile trade fair, Heimtextil in January 1975.[86] The heavy weight (large amount of wool fiber per square inch) and high-quality materials combined with the handwork made it an expensive fabric. In 1976 it was priced at $52 per yard, making it the most expensive upholstery offered by Knoll that year (the next most expensive was *Mona*, a Maute handwoven of silk and wool at $47.50 per yard).[87] However, the price seems to have been acceptable to many buyers as the fabric stayed in the line until 1982.

Huguenin was also instrumental in bringing another important designer-manufacturer to Knoll Textiles in the 1970s. In the mid-1960s, just after her departure from Knoll, she became the United States representative for rohi, a leading German manufacturer of interior textiles. Founded in 1933 by Marga Hielle-Vatter, the firm specialized in high-quality wool upholstery fabrics, designed by Hielle-Vatter and woven on Jacquard looms at the company's factory in Geretsried just south of Munich. Once the connection was made, Barbara Rodes worked closely with Hielle-Vatter to develop fabrics for Knoll.[88] *Dynamic*, the first Hielle-Vatter design to enter the Knoll collection, was introduced with two other new upholsteries in a special presentation in Knoll's New York showroom in October 1970.[89] The use of a Jacquard loom allowed Hielle-Vatter to produce a fabric that had a rustic, almost handwoven feel with podlike shapes within the weave that seemed irregular but were actually a controlled part of the design (fig. 5.34). This all-wool pattern was offered in a range of vibrant colors, developed in collaboration by Rodes and Hielle-Vatter. By the late 1960s rohi had begun catering to the airline industry upholstery needs, and internal documents indicate that Knoll was attempting to sell *Dynamic* to American Airlines in 1971, although it is not clear whether a deal was brokered.[90] In 1971 Knoll introduced *Tacoma*, the second Hielle-Vatter design for Knoll. It featured an irregular patchwork pattern—a far cry from the geometric lines and checks of patterned upholsteries in the Knoll collections of previous decades.[91] It also represented "the first time Knoll Textiles introduced a fabric in only earthy colors," such as tan/rust, rust/plum, and brown/plum, although a range of brighter colorways was introduced in 1977 (fig. 5.35).[92] In 1974 Hielle-Vatter's only casement fabric for Knoll was introduced—*Align*, a plain-weave sheer fabric that featured "subtle vertical stripes" in gray and brown natural wool.[93] The last Hielle-Vatter fabric introduced by Knoll in the 1970s was *Tournee*, which was released in 1976.[94] This upholstery features a restrained linear pattern and was initially offered in a dozen colorways, each of which relied on two or three different-colored yarns in both the warp and weft (fig. 5.36). These sophisticated weaves were among the costliest of Knoll's offerings, only slightly less than the handwovens, but they seem to have been reasonably successful, remaining in the collection until the early 1980s: *Dynamic* and *Tournee* were discontinued in 1980, *Tacoma* in 1981, and *Align* in 1982.

Paul Maute's relationship with Knoll continued in the 1970s. Maute had worked closely with Barbara Rodes in the 1960s, and Robert Cadwallader was especially enthusiastic over the high-quality textiles the Maute firm produced.[95] The same October 1970 special exhibit in Knoll's New York showroom that included Hielle-Vatter's *Dynamic* also presented the first of Maute's handwovens introduced in the new decade—*Tiber*. The exhibition featured panels of *Tiber* alternating with photographs of the men and women who

Fig. 5.34 Marga Hielle-Vatter. *Dynamic* ("Fuschia" colorway) on *Model 46* chair designed by Max Pearson, this example ca. 1973. Made by rohi for Knoll Textiles; chair made by Knoll International. Wool; plain-weave–derived compound weave; chair: cast aluminum, steel, plywood, plastic shell, latex foam rubber. Private collection. Cat. 197.

Fig. 5.35 Top left Marga Hielle-Vatter. *Tacoma* color sample ("Red" colorway), ca. 1977. Made by rohi for Knoll Textiles. Used for upholstery; wool; plain-weave–derived compound weave. KnollTextiles Archive. Cat. 198.

Fig. 5.36 Top right Marga Hielle-Vatter. *Tournee* ("Brown/Blue" colorway), ca. 1976. Made by rohi for Knoll Textiles. Used for upholstery; wool, cotton; plain-weave–derived simple weave. KnollTextiles Archive. Cat. 199.

Fig. 5.37 Bottom left Paul Maute. *Tiber* sample ("Azure" colorway), ca. 1968. Made by Paul Maute GmbH for Knoll Textiles. Used for upholstery; wool, perlon; plain-weave–derived simple weave. Courtesy Paul Makovsky.

Fig. 5.38 Bottom right *Lasar* sample ("Beige/White" colorway), ca. 1974. Made by McNutt Weaving Company for Knoll Textiles. Used for upholstery; wool; plain weave. KnollTextiles Archive.

wove the fabric for Knoll.[96] Like most Maute fabrics, *Tiber* was a variation on a plain weave with visual interest communicated through the use of varying float yarns as well as yarns in both the warp and weft that varied in thickness, several of them larger in scale. The vibrancy of color was also important, each colorway being composed of three or four different-colored yarns (fig. 5.37). A year later, Knoll released Maute's *Mona*, in which a silk chenille yarn was mixed with wool to create a luxurious, soft surface.[97] *Marabu*, introduced in 1972, featured large-scale yarns similar to those in *Tiber* and *Morocco*, an earlier Maute fabric. *Marabu* was also the second patterned weave manufactured by Maute (after the 1966 introduction of the Sheila Hicks design *Inca*) and featured a large reverse herringbone (a diamond-shaped motif created through a variation on a twill weave). In 1974 Knoll introduced Maute's *Cornaro*, a plain weave of dyed wool blended with white silk creating a subtle random fleck throughout the fabric.[98] Although *Cornaro* was one of Maute's shorter-lived designs (it was discontinued in 1979), the company reintroduced it in 2009, as part of the *Archival Collection*, but had it machine-woven in Scotland.

Lasar, introduced in 1974, was the only handwoven from this period not made by Maute. Extensive correspondence in the KnollTextiles Archive between Gretchen Bellinger, then a manager of textile development for the USA, and Scott McNutt of McNutt Weaving Company records the development of this fabric.[99] McNutt Weaving, a small company in County Donegal, Ireland, specialized in the production of handwoven tweeds. Bellinger apparently met with McNutt during the fall of 1973 and selected two fabrics to develop for Knoll. For what would become *Lasar*, Knoll requested a stronger warp so it would be more useful in contract applications. While development of the second fabric was dropped, Bellinger urged Barbara Rodes not to delay in accepting *Lasar* for the collection before competitors could have a chance to: "I would appreciate your comments on the swatches as quickly as possible as it appears through the fabric grapevine that several other companies are waiting to work with Mr. McNutt should Knoll not follow through on this option rather quickly."[100] *Lasar* was accepted and introduced in June 1974 at NeoCon in Chicago.[101] The upholstery features hand-spun wool in neutral tones. Weft yarns of varied thickness alternated in the weave in a way that appeared to be irregular (fig. 5.38), but there was in fact a repeat approximately every twelve inches initiated by the handweavers from memory.[102] While this was the only fabric made for Knoll by McNutt, it was apparently successful and remained in the line until 1983.

New handwovens by Maute continued to be introduced at an even faster rate as the 1970s wore on. In the fall of 1976 Knoll introduced five new patterns—*Chord*, *Knoll Bouclé*, *Kamee*, *Parsifal*, and *Atlantis*.[103] *Chord* and *Parsifal* featured luxurious, large-scale weft yarns like several earlier Maute upholsteries. *Chord* was a zig-zag twill in both neutral and bright colorways, and *Parsifal* a variation on a plain weave with mottled natural wool weft yarns in neutral colors (see cat. 181). *Knoll Bouclé*, another plain weave, had a loopy surface texture created through the use of a bouclé yarn. *Kamee* was a plain weave on the order of *Parsifal* but in a slightly smaller scale and with less mottled wool yarns in the weft and perlon in the warp. *Atlantis*, an enlarged version of *Inca*, Sheila Hicks's design of 1966, was offered in a variety of neutral colorways. *Cocoon*, added in 1977, differed from Maute's previous mostly wool and wool-and-silk upholsteries by being an all-silk construction.[104] It was the final Maute handwoven to be introduced by Knoll in the 1970s and marked a high point for handwovens in the Knoll Textiles collection. In 1977 sixteen different handwoven upholsteries were offered with a total of 203 varieties when all associated colorways were added together.[105] While Maute fabrics would continue to be sold by Knoll for fifteen more years, they slowly faded from prominence under the new Knoll ownership and management, which began at the end of 1977.

Textiles for Office-Landscape Systems

A new trend in contract furniture gained momentum during the 1960s as the needs of workers began to be taken into account in the design of open-plan offices. The importance of a certain degree of privacy for employees in their workspace was recognized, as well as the need for noise minimization and a cheerful working environment. This meant furniture that was stylish and more ergonomic, and curtains and wall coverings that were attractive, while helping to reduce noise. This trend was incorporated into modular office or office-landscape systems, such as the *USM Haller* system, designed by Swiss architect Fritz Haller in 1963, and the *Action Office System* by Robert Propst for Herman Miller, introduced in 1968.[106] A major component of most of these systems were half-high, movable, textile-covered panels which, with curtains and wall coverings, contributed to the comfortable atmosphere of the office interior and were a significant part of the success of modular office systems.

Textiles thus assumed a more central role in office design, opening new markets for companies such as Knoll, which took up the challenge of absorbing and responding to these new design directions. Knoll began research and development for an office system in 1967 as "part of a continuing search by Knoll designers for better solutions to where and how people work."[107] In 1971 Knoll introduced the short-lived *Christen System*, designed by Andreas Christen, and the much more successful *Stephens Office Landscape System* (also known as the *Stephens System*). Designed by

Fig. 5.39 Top Zapf panel system in use, ca. 1980. Photographed by Dick Frank and Henry Wolf. From Knoll International promotional booklet. Knoll Archives.
Fig. 5.40 Bottom left *Partition Fabric* swatches, ca. 1976. Made by Craftex for Knoll Textiles. Used for panel; modacrylic; plain weave. KnollTextiles Archive.

Fig. 5.41 Bottom right *Zapf Panel Fabric* swatches, ca. 1982. Used for panel; Dacron polyester; plain weave. KnollTextiles Archive.

William Stephens, it had been developed for the Weyerhaeuser corporate headquarters in Washington state, a major installation designed by Skidmore, Owings and Merrill and furnished entirely by Knoll.[108] Knoll's second major office system was the 1975 *Zapf System*, created by the German designer Otto Zapf. This system used fabric-covered panels for the ends of desks and most partition walls (fig. 5.39).[109] From this point forward, office systems constituted one of the most successful sectors in the range of Knoll products.[110] These systems and the millions of yards of textiles that were sold with them became the financial backbone of the company.

Knoll began suggesting multipurpose textiles for office system panels as early as 1973. In that year's price list, a special acrylic backing was offered to make the inexpensive wool and nylon upholstery *Cadet* suitable for use on "sound landscape panels."[111] Textiles developed specifically for use on panel surfaces first entered the Knoll collection a short time later. The 1977 *Knoll Tabloid* devoted to Knoll Textiles outlined the complex set of requirements that must be satisfied in such a fabric: "The specifications require, for instance, that a fabric for Knoll panels be relatively inexpensive, inherently flame retardant, sound absorbing, dimensionally stable, 62 to 63 inches wide, non-directional, and available in small lots for dying to special order."[112] The first panel fabric, called *Partition Fabric*, was produced for use on the *Stephens System*.[113] Its development was overseen by Barbara Rodes's assistant Kristl Reinhardt (later Andrus) and began in the summer of 1974.[114] Knoll approached Craftex, the supplier of *Nylon Homespun* and many other upholsteries, for a suitable fabric. The result was an all-Verel modacrylic plain-weave textile initially offered in fourteen colorways at an inexpensive $7.50 per yard (fig. 5.40). While the first sales of the fabric may have been in 1975, it seems it was officially available beginning in 1976.[115] The following year Knoll introduced a second panel fabric, *Regency*, an all-Dacron polyester textile developed with the *Zapf System* in mind and initially offered in a dozen colorways.[116] *Partition Fabric* was discontinued in 1978, but *Regency* continued to sell well, reaching a high point of forty-seven colorways in 1982 (fig. 5.41). One of Knoll's longest lasting textiles, it sold for more than thirty-three years before being discontinued in 2010.[117]

In 1976 Knoll offered a new group of multipurpose fabrics that could be used for panel application. The first, *Eton*, was introduced in January and could also be used as upholstery.[118] It was a plain weave of Verel modacrylic and viscose produced by long-time Knoll supplier Louisville Textiles. In the fall of 1976 Knoll introduced three more fabrics that could be used for panels, curtains, or wallcovering, all of which were supplied to Knoll by New London Textile Print Works in Newark, Delaware.[119] Named *Galway*, *Glin*, and *Dorset*, these linen-cotton blends were available in natural or white colorways.[120] *Galway*, a twill weave primarily designed for panel, drapery, or wallcovering, could also be used as upholstery. *Dorset* and *Glin* were plain weaves that were stocked in both fire-retardant and non-fire-retardant versions. *Glin*'s small-scale weave was given subtle variation in texture through a slight slub in the yarns used to weave it.

New Directions, 1976–78

In the 1977 *Knoll Tabloid* that featured Knoll Textiles, two pages at the center of the publication discussed Knoll's history of prize-winning printed fabrics (beginning in the 1950s), emphasizing the more recent developments overseen by Barbara Rodes, who was pictured with examples of the *Three Meter Print Collection*. Rodes, who married in 1976, becoming Barbara Rodes-Segerer, had been vice president and director of textiles since 1973 and provided design and development guidance for the company until she resigned in 1978.[121] The *Knoll Tabloid* text hinted that "new directions are emerging."[122] These new directions would be a group of printed fabrics introduced in 1976 and 1977 and the last project Rodes-Segerer would oversee before leaving Knoll.

The first of these prints was a contribution of long-time Knoll designer Anni Albers, who had taken up printmaking in the early 1960s. By the 1970s it had become the primary focus of her artistic practice. In about 1975 Rodes asked Albers to translate her art into a print fabric design for Knoll.[123] Introduced by Knoll in the United States in 1976, this geometric print was offered in two versions—*Eclat* (fig. 5.42), which had a 16-inch repeat and was printed on *Dorset* base fabric, and a smaller-scale version of the same design, *Eclat-S*, with a 3-inch repeat printed on *Glin*. The supplier of the base fabrics, New London Textile Print Works, also printed the *Eclat* designs for Knoll.[124] *Eclat*, intended as both a drapery fabric and for light upholstery applications, was first available in a dozen colorways. In 1978 it was introduced in Europe, where it was printed by Pausa AG on both a linen-cotton base cloth and also as a white-on-white sheer made using the burn-out process. A similar geometric design by Albers, *Epos-T*, was introduced for the European market in 1978. *Eclat*'s initial incarnation in the Knoll collection was short-lived; it was discontinued in 1979 in the United States and in 1981 in Europe. It was, however, re-released twice by the company as part of celebrations marking the fiftieth and sixtieth anniversaries of Knoll Textiles. *Eclat Weave*, an upholstery that re-creates the original printed pattern through power weaving, was the most recent reintroduction, for the inaugural *Archival Collection* of 2007, and is still in production in 2011 (cat. 289).

The final groups of printed fabrics developed by Rodes-Segerer were released in 1977 and 1978. The German designer Christa Häusler had apprenticed with Marga

Hielle-Vatter at rohi from 1962 to 1965 and during this time became friends with rohi's United States representative Suzanne Huguenin. In the mid-1970s Huguenin recommended Häusler to Rodes-Segerer who went on to commission work from the designer.[125] In 1977 Knoll introduced eight Häusler-designed prints, all made for Knoll by Taunus Textildruck. Located in Oberursel, Germany, just outside of Frankfurt, Tanus Textildruck had previously supplied prints to Knoll Europe (as early as the mid-1950s) and would continue to print for Knoll through the 1980s.[126] *Grille*, *Triad*, *Crossroads*, *Ribbon*, and *Interplay* featured large-scale linear motifs and were created as white-on-white sheers through the burn-out process, the first three on Diolen polyester and viscose base cloth, and *Interplay* on polyester and wool base cloth.[127] *Benday*, a large-scale undulating linear motif composed of regular dots in various tones, was the latest in Knoll's prints on a cotton velvet ground. Häusler's *Aquarelle* (see fig. B.51) and *Pyramid* were printed on chintz, a glazed cotton fabric that had not been seen in the Knoll collection since the first half of the 1950s.[128] *Pyramid* features a large-scale diamond pattern (with a 25-inch repeat) composed of bands of color in related tones, resulting in a subdued yet striking drapery fabric (fig. 5.43). In the United States, Häusler's prints were presented along with *Eclat* in 1977 as part of a new initiative at Knoll to cater more to the residential market and provide fabrics that were mostly suited to domestic interiors.[129]

In 1978 Knoll released additional prints by Häusler as well as by another German designer recruited by Rodes-Segerer, Klaus Dombrowski.[130] These were only released in Europe and were likely printed by Taunus Textildruck. Häusler contributed *Don* and *Domino* (see cat. 218 and fig. B.52), small-scale motifs which could be used as upholstery or drapery fabrics, as well as *Giro*, a sheer curtain fabric with a motif of ellipses created through the burn-out process (see fig. B.53). Dombrowski's designs *Flair* and *Flex* were also small-scale geometric motifs, printed on the same fabric as *Don* and *Domino*, and suitable for drapery and upholstery (see cat. 217 and fig. B.36). These two designs were also made as burn-out sheers on a Trevira polyester and cotton base cloth.

A high point in the printed fabrics offered by Knoll in the United States was reached in 1977. With the additions of the Häusler designs, Knoll sold twenty-four print patterns by eight designers that year. However, this was soon to change. By December 1978 all of Knoll's print fabrics had been discontinued in the United States (although they would remain on offer a bit longer in Europe.)[131] This change mirrored a significant shift in the culture of the company that happened in the same period.

In 1973 Walter E. Heller International, the parent company of Knoll, purchased American National Corporation, a holding company for American National Bank of Chicago.[132] Federal Reserve Board regulations required that Heller International divest of all manufacturing arms after it became a bank holding company. This resulted in Knoll International being put up for sale, with a completion deadline set for May 1978. Over several years, many possible buyers were courted by Heller International and Knoll or approached the company (including an unsuccessful bid by Robert Cadwallader and other Knoll executives). In 1975 Marshall Cogan and Stephen Swid, who had made substantial fortunes in the financial industry, became interested in Knoll and ultimately purchased the company. Swid and Cogan also owned General Felt Industries, a large manufacturing firm. Their purchase of Knoll marked a turning point in the culture of the company. When the sale became effective in 1977, Knoll returned overnight to being a privately held company for the first time since 1959, with Swid as chairman of the board and Cogan as president.[133]

The old senior management began to leave Knoll when the new ownership went into effect. Cadwallader left Knoll to work for Hauserman, an office furniture manufacturer. Within a short time, Hauserman purchased Sunar, a Canadian furniture manufacturer, and Cadwallader was asked to head Sunar and transform it into a leader in furniture and fabric for the contract market in the United States. Barbara Rodes-Segerer left Knoll in April 1978 to join Cadwallader in this new venture, running the textile division of Sunar with another former Knoll executive, Duncan South. Sunar soon featured a collection of textiles created by many of the individuals that Rodes-Segerer had worked closely with over the past two decades at Knoll.[134]

The new direction that Cogan and Swid would give Knoll affected Knoll Textiles almost immediately. The print collection was dropped in 1978 and many other fabrics were discontinued. In a single year under the new ownership, the number of patterns offered by Knoll was cut by one-third, from 109 at the end of 1977 to 72 at the end of 1978.[135] Soon a new administrative team would bring new designers and a different focus to Knoll Textiles, leading to a decade of enormous success and expansion in the 1980s.

Fig. 5.42 Anni Albers. *Eclat* ("Orange on Natural" colorway), ca. 1977. Made by New London Textile Print Works for Knoll Textiles. Used for drapery, upholstery; cotton, linen; plain weave, screen-printed. Courtesy Cora Ginsburg LLC.

Fig. 5.43 Christa Häusler-Goltz. *Pyramid* ("Violet/Purple" colorway), ca. 1977. Made by Taunus Textildruck for Knoll Textiles. Used for drapery; cotton; plain weave, screen-printed. Courtesy Cindia Reyes. Cat. 221.

1. Olga Gueft, "Knoll Without the Knolls," *Interiors* (August 1966), 150–151. Although Gueft had always been a staunch supporter of Knoll and never really believed that it would go under, her comments in the influential American design journal must have caused concern for the firm's clients, as well as its employees and designers.
2. "Arno," in Suzanne Huguenin, *Knoll Textiles Sales Guide* (1962), KnollTextiles Archive.
3. Maute is thought to have designed all of the fabrics produced by his firm except for three: *Inca* by Sheila Hicks, *Harrow* by Julia Keiner, and *Serenade*, a 1973 casement. Maute was credited as designer in Knoll press releases and price lists from 1961 through 1964 (see Knoll Textiles, "Wholesale Price List, January 15, 1964," pp. 9–10, KnollTextiles Archive). After 1964 he was not named as designer in Knoll literature for reasons that remain unclear.
4. Paul Maute (grandson of Paul Maute), telephone interview with the author, December 2009. Handwoven upholsteries remained a separate category in Knoll catalogues and price lists until 1988, when they were integrated into the general upholstery lists, having become less important in the Knoll product range.
5. Suzanne Huguenin, "Suzanne Huguenin's Column," ca. 1963, pp. 2–3, Huguenin designer file, KnollTextiles Archive. It is possible that the competitor referenced by Huguenin was Jack Lenor Larsen who was then importing handwoven fabrics from several countries.
6. *Cato* was handwoven until 1993, and since then a Scottish mill has produced it on power looms. The machine-woven version has a more uniform character than the earlier handwoven.
7. The forty shades were not all available at the same time. The earliest colorways (before 1963) had a black warp, but in later colorways warps were coordinated with the weft thread colors.
8. "Merchandise Cues: Knoll's Casement Collection," *Interiors* (February 1964): 120.
9. Ibid.
10. Press release, ca. 1964, *Filigree* file, KnollTextiles Archive.
11. "Bulletin: Upholstery Fabrics Introduction for 1965," ca. January 1965, KnollTextiles Archive. The Bulletin notes that "the exciting range of 16 colors" were "developed under the styling direction of Florence Knoll."
12. Robert Cadwallader recalls that on his first day on the job in the New York offices, he encountered Florence Knoll Bassett leaving the offices and that she told him that she had announced her retirement and unfortunately they would not be working together. Robert Cadwallader, interview with Earl Martin, October 25, 2010.
13. For the Platner collection see Gueft, "Knoll without the Knolls," 152–57; for the Schultz collection see "Knoll's 'Leisure Collection,'" *Interiors* (March 1966): 32.
14. See also Julia Keiner-Forchheimer, in "Knoll Textiles Designer Biographies," in this volume; hereafter cited as "Designer Biographies." For examples of her work for Isabel Scott see "Fall Fabric Report," *Interiors* (August 1966): 165; and "D&D Market Report," *Interiors* (October 1966): 160.
15. "Bulletin: Upholstery Fabrics Introduction for 1966," ca. 1966, p. 3, Knoll Archives. The initial colorways were oyster, beige, brown, and charcoal; in 1968 six additional colorways were added. This group was colorful although still in a muted palette, *Harrow* file, KnollTextiles Archive.
16. *Stratton* and *Jupiter* files, KnollTextiles Archive.
17. Rae had been with Knoll since 1958 as "design liaison to the international companies." She had been Florence Knoll's assistant since 1963 "in furniture and textile design development, graphics and advertising," and until 1972 wrote all copy for the company. Christine Rae file, Knoll Archives.
18. Christine Rae, "Knoll International: Portrait of a Corporation," *Graphis* 26, no. 148 (1970/71): 154–63, 185–94.
19. Nicole Casey (niece of Barbara Rodes), email correspondence with Earl Martin, October 11, 2010; and Toby Rodes (former husband of Barbara Rodes), telephone conversation with Earl Martin, October 21, 2010. Rodes was born Barbara Eckert, September 18, 1938 in Heilbronn, Germany. From 1954 to 1956 she studied fashion and textiles at the Modeschule Szelinsky (Szelinsky Fashion School) in Heilbronn, followed by internships at three textile factories in 1956–57 before completing her studies at the Staatliche Textil-Akademie Hohenstein (State Textile Academy Hohenstein) in Hohenstein, Germany (1957–58), see "Professional Biography of Barbara Rodes-Segerer," Barbara Rodes-Segerer designer file, Knoll Archives. Eckert was hired in 1959 by Toby Rodes, then head of Knoll's international operations. They were married in 1961 and divorced in 1966; in 1976 she married Peter Segerer (Nicole Casey, email correspondence with Earl Martin, October 11, 2010).
20. This section is drawn from Barbara Rodes, interview ca. 1977, pp. 3–6, and "Professional Biography of Barabara Rodes Segerer," ca. 1977, both Barbara Rodes-Segerer designer file, Knoll Archives.
21. Barbara Rodes, interview ca. 1977, p. 5. Correspondence (1964–66) regarding the development of Sheila Hicks's *Inca* and Hicks's other work for Knoll confirm Rodes's involvement in all aspects of Knoll textiles made in Europe (Sheila Hicks designer file, Knoll Archives).
22. Robert Cadwallader, interview with Earl Martin, October 24, 2010.
23. Most of Knoll's European divisions also operated both retail and wholesale; retail customers would often purchase a few yards of fabric, accessories, or other less expensive items (Toby Rodes, interview with Earl Martin, October 21, 2010). Little information about the details of this collection have been discovered, but it was described as "Die neue *Druckstoff Kollektion 1967*" (The new *Print Fabric Collection 1967*) in at least one profile of Bauer and his work; see "Ein Mann will seine Umwelt mit den schönsten Farben schmücken," *Schöner Wohnen* (December 12, 1968): 162–63. It seems likely that some, if not all of the Bauer's print designs released in late 1969 in the United States were part of this initial collection; one of these designs, *Delta*, is illustrated in ibid., 163.
24. One of these designs, *Mosaic*, is illustrated in ibid., 162, with the caption "Knoll 68: Seidenbezug 'Mosaic'" (Knoll '68: silk upholstery "Mosaic"), indicating that these fabrics were available in Europe. The United States fabrics were first recorded in United States price lists in 1968.
25. In 1968 both *Lumière* and *Mosaic* were priced at $47.50 per yard, while the next most expensive fabric, the handwoven *Morocco*, was $27.50 per yard; see Knoll Textiles, "Textile Price List June 15, 1968," pp. 10, 12, KnollTextiles Archive.
26. Cadwallader, interview with Martin, October 24, 2010. One of these 1966 designs is illustrated in "Ein Mann will seine Umwelt mit den schönsten Farben schmücken," *Schöner Wohnen* (December 12, 1968): 162. It bears a strong resemblance to the Knoll pattern *Fragment*.
27. "International Print Collection 1969 Textile Introduction," press release, September 1, 1969, Wolf Bauer designer file, Knoll Archives.
28. "Home/Contract Furnishing," *Industrial Design* (December 1969): 57; "ID's 1969 Design Review," *Interiors* (January 1970): 106–9.
29. Hermann Berner and Werner Fifka, eds., *Pausa, Das Bauhaus kam nach Mössingen: Geschichte, Architektur und Design der einstigen Textilfirma Pausa* (Mössingen, Germany: Talheimer, 2006), 24, 35–42.
30. Cadwallader, interview with Martin, October 25, 2010.
31. Cadwallader has indicated that the Gavina factory with its up-to-date manufacturing capacity was the larger motivating factor in Knoll's decision to acquire the firm (ibid). Dino Gavina began manufacturing in the late 1940s but it was not until the 1950s that he made furniture, and he formed Gavina S.p.A. in 1960; see Martin Eidelberg, ed., *Design 1935–1965: What Modern Was* (Montreal: Musée des arts décoratifs de Montréal; New York: Harry N. Abrams, 1991), 373.
32. Olga Gueft, "Knoll—plus ça change," *Interiors* (May 1971): 122.
33. Eidelberg, *Design 1935–1965*, 334–35, 386. The Gavina collection was introduced in the United States through a special exhibition at the New York Knoll showroom (320 Park Avenue) in February 1969. The installation was designed by Lella and Massimo Vignelli and featured the furniture in combination with the designer's names in "giant letters of neon tubing," see "'Supergraphics' Launch Knoll's Gavina Group Designers," press release, February 19, 1969, *Malitte* object file, acc. no. 473.70.a-e, Architecture and Design Study Center, Museum of Modern Art. See also Rita Reif, "From Italy with Flair, a Furniture Collection in a Neon Setting," *New York Times*, February 19, 1969, 50.
34. Swatches of the various *Gavina* fabrics are preserved in the KnollTextiles Archive (*Gavina Group* file) and are collectively given the title *Gavina Group*, even though these are actually more than five different fabrics. Only *Malitte* is designated as a separate fabric within the *Gavina Group* file.
35. *Gavina Group* file, KnollTextiles Archive.
36. "Walter E. Heller Plans to Acquire Art Metal, Inc.," *New York Times*, September 18, 1967, 96, and "Chrysler Widens Finance Division," *New York Times*, February 10, 1968, 44.
37. Gueft, "Knoll—plus ça change," 122.
38. "Knoll Makes News," *Interiors* (September 1969): 158. In the 1950s and 1960s "Knoll International, Inc.," a division of the firm, encompassed the various Knoll branches outside of the United States.
39. "Knoll Moves to 5th Avenue," press release, June 10, 1970, New York showroom file, Knoll Archives.
40. Olga Gueft, "Stage Setting by Gae Aulenti for the Greatest Modern Furniture Collection of Them All," *Interiors* (August 1970): 96. Ironically this characterization of the "Knoll look" came from one of the greatest champions of Knoll, specifically Florence Knoll, the creator of the "Knoll look," since the early 1950s (see chapter 4 in the volume).
41. Ibid.
42. "Selling Points: Gae Aulenti's Sleight of Hand Transforms a Long Narrow Space for Knoll International," *Industrial Design* (September 1970): 50–53.
43. Aulenti quoted in ibid.
44. "Knoll Expands Imported Print Collection with Bold Designs," press release, May 3, 1971, Wolf Bauer designer file, Knoll Archives.
45. Ibid.
46. A letter and loose-leaf sheet preserved with a 1971 price list in the Brooklyn Museum collection indicates that the patterns on the sheet, including *Prisma*, *Fibra*, *Pythagorus*, and *Mira*, had been discontinued and "will not be available after present stock is exhausted"; see Knoll Textiles, "Textile Price List 1971," May 1, 1971 and J. J. Osborne (marketing, Knoll International), letter, May 15, 1971, Brooklyn Museum Library and Archives.
47. Christine Rae and Massimo Vignelli, *Knoll au Louvre*, exh. cat. (Milan: Amilcare Pizzi S.p.A. for Knoll International, 1971).
48. Cadwallader recalls Aulenti approaching him about the show, and she helped with arrangements in Paris; Cadwallader, interview with Martin, October 24, 2010.
49. See Olga Gueft, "Knoll au Louvre," *Interiors* (April 1972): 136–39, 160–61; "All That Glitters," *Industrial Design* (April 1972): 62–67.
50. "All That Glitters," 63. Research to date has not located photographs of this installation, but Wolf Bauer, Francisca Reichardt, Gretl and Leo Wollner, François Dallegret, and J. P. Garault (designer of the print *Frames*) are mentioned in the exhibition catalogue and their work was apparently shown, see Rae and Vignelli, *Knoll au Louvre*, n.p.
51. Gueft, "Knoll au Louvre," 136. Apart from Knoll, Jack Lenor Larsen was the only American textile producer to whom the Musée des arts décoratifs devoted a solo exhibition in the Louvre (1979–80).
52. Press release, January 9, 1972, KnollTextiles Archive. The prints seem to have been available commercially by the summer of 1972.
53. Barbara Rodes, interview ca. 1977, p. 6.
54. Christine Rae, "Bulletin: Knoll's 'Three Meter' Print Panels and How They Grew," June 1972, Gretl and Leo Wollner file, KnollTextiles Archive. The quotes in this section come from this bulletin unless otherwise indicated.
55. The base cloth would later be changed to an all-cotton one.
56. Jeffrey Osborne, former director of marketing for Knoll, interview with the author, November 2009. Rodes later reflected on these prints for the *Dallas Morning News*, July 12, 1974, p. D1:

"Barbara thinks that 'prints should be used shockingly.' She found people 'thought I was crazy' when she suggested the 10-foot lengths be hung floor to ceiling, with no repeats or 'little' patterns, but they were hits."
57 "Transparente Fantasien," *MD Moebel Interior Design* (December 1972): 45–49.
58 Ibid., 48.
59 Advertisement for Knoll International, *MD Moebel Interior Design* (December 1972): 12. Some of the student designs selected for production were also shown by Knoll at their booth at the Heimtextil fair (Advertisement for Knoll International, *MD Moebel Interior Design* [December 1972]: 12).
60 Six designs were accepted into the Knoll collection; "Transparente Fantasien," 48–49. For illustrations of two textiles that are precursors to *Puzzle* and *Comet*, both released in the United States in 1973, see ibid. An annotated 1973 price list in the KnollTextiles Archive identifies Margarete Warth (*Puzzle*) and Friedrich Goth (*Comet*)—the same designers cited for the prototypes for these fabrics illustrated in the *MD* article—as well as a third student designer also named in the *MD* article, Sybille Dobringer (*Meton*); see Knoll Textiles, "Textile Price List 1973," April 1, 1973, pp. 22, 24–25, KnollTextiles Archive. The 1977 *Knoll Tabloid* devoted to the textile division also highlights the student competition and identifies six designs then in the collection, *Puzzle* and *Tellin* in the United States and *Cross*, *Karo*, *Tree*, and *Circle*; *Knoll Tabloid* for Knoll Textiles, designed by Massimo Vignelli, 1977, p. 10, KnollTextiles Archive. This promotional publication was issued several times between 1976 and 1979, but this 1977 edition was the only one devoted to textiles.
61 Both *Puzzle* and *Comet* were highlighted in "Report of Fabrics," *Interior Design* (November 1973): 89.
62 The manufacturers of the casements in this section are known from three price lists with mill annotations made by Knoll Textiles staff, see Knoll Textiles, "Textile Price List 1972," August 1, 1972; "Textile Price List 1973," April 1, 1973; and "Textile Price List," June 1, 1974; KnollTextiles Archive.
63 "Plastic yarn from Hostalen" is noted as one of the materials that the students used (see "Transparente Fantasien," 48); no student designer for *Serenade* has yet been identified.
64 "Knoll Textiles: The Collection," press release, December 10, 1973, KnollTextiles Archive.
65 See Rita Rief, "More Bewildering Than Bedazzling," *New York Times*, December 13, 1973, 64; "Market: Knoll is a Fabric House," *Interiors* (February 1974): 44; and "Geladene Gäste," *MD Moebel Interior Design* (May 1974): 72–75.
66 Rief, "More Bewildering Than Bedazzling," 64.
67 Ibid.
68 "Market: Knoll is a Fabric House," 44.
69 These were listed as "Flame Retarded Prints" in price lists beginning in 1974, Knoll Textiles, "Textile Price List," June 1, 1974, p. 29, KnollTextiles Archive.
70 Seven hundred options were said to be available; see *Knoll Tabloid* for Knoll Textiles, 1977, p. 5.
71 Ibid., 3.
72 The upholstery, *Eton*, was introduced in January 1976; *Eton* file, KnollTextiles Archive. The three casements, *Terra*, *Aqua*, and *Aire*, first appear in a 1974 price list, Knoll Textiles, "Textile Price List," June 1, 1974, p. 25.
73 *Lana* and *Nylon Transporation Cloth* files, KnollTextiles Archive. *Cavalier* was introduced as a 60-percent wool and 40-percent nylon blend and remained so until 1978. A revised fiber content of 90-percent wool and 10-percent nylon in the same weave, *Cavalier II*, was introduced in 1977 and remained in production until 1982; *Cavalier* and *Cavalier II* files, KnollTextiles Archive.
74 Knoll Textiles, "Textile Price List 1977/78," November 15, 1977, p. 8, KnollTextiles Archive.
75 *Brigadier* file, KnollTextiles Archive.
76 *Jhet* file, KnollTextiles Archive.
77 *Cadet* file, KnollTextiles Archive. *Cadet* last appears in KnollTextiles, "Price Catalogue 1989/90," June 1, 1989, p. 9.
78 Knoll International, "In-Stock Program," brochure, 1974, *Cadet* file, KnollTextiles Archive.
79 *Camelot* file, KnollTextiles Archive.
80 *Cuzco* file, KnollTextiles Archive.
81 *Knoll Velvet* file, KnollTextiles Archive.
82 Knoll Textiles, "Textile Price List 1977/78," November 15, 1977, p. 17, KnollTextiles Archive.
83 Knoll Textiles, "Catalogue 4/80," April 1, 1980, pp. 7–9, KnollTextiles Archive.
84 "Upholstery, casement and leathers mark Knoll Textiles' introductions at NEOCON 6," press release, ca. June 1974, NeoCon 6 file, Knoll Archives.
85 *Sequoia* file, KnollTextiles Archive.
86 Knoll International, press release for Internationale Fachmesse für Heimtextillien, ca. January 1975, Knoll Archives.
87 Knoll Textiles, "Textile Price List," March 1, 1976, KnollTextiles Archive.
88 See Marga Hielle-Vatter, in "Designer Biographies," in this volume.
89 "Knoll Introduces Wool Upholstery Fabrics," press release, October 19, 1970, KnollTextiles Archive.
90 Duncan South to Barbara Rodes (telegram), March 9, 1971, *Dynamic* file, KnollTextiles Archive; M. F. Backus to Barbara Rodes (memorandum), March 10, 1971, *Gavina Group* file, KnollTextiles Archive.
91 Fabric data sheet, *Tacoma* file, KnollTextiles Archive.
92 Knoll Textiles, "Textile Price List 1977/78," November 15, 1977, p. 16, KnollTextiles Archive.
93 "Upholstery, casement and leathers," NeoCon 6 file, Knoll Archives.
94 John J. Flynn, "Knoll Textiles Bulletin" introducing *Tournee*, January 15, 1976, *Tournee* file, KnollTextiles Archive. A "Wear resistance test" dated February 19, 1974 performed by German company Frank Hauser includes *Tournee*, which may indicate that this textile was introduced by Knoll earlier in Europe, *Tournee* file, KnollTextiles Archive.
95 Cadwallader, interview with Martin, October 24, 2010. Rodes began working closely with Maute in the early 1960s when she was coordinating textiles for Knoll Germany.
96 "Knoll Introduces Wool Upholstery Fabrics," press release, October 19, 1970, KnollTextiles Archive.
97 *Mona* file, KnollTextiles Archive.
98 *Cornaro* file, KnollTextiles Archive.
99 *Lasar* file, KnollTextiles Archive. Unless otherwise noted the information in this section comes from this file. Bellinger later left Knoll to found her own textile firm.
100 Gretchen Bellinger to Barbara Rodes (memorandum), January 18, 1974, *Lasar* file, KnollTextiles Archive.
101 "Upholstery, casement and leathers," NeoCon 6 file, Knoll Archives.
102 Gretchen Bellinger, "Knoll Textiles Bulletin" introducing *Lasar*, June 19, 1974. *Lasar* file, KnollTextiles Archive.
103 "New Fabrics + Leather a Feature of Designer's Saturday," press release, October 3, 1976, *Eclat* file, KnollTextiles Archive. See also *Chord*, *Knoll Boucle*, *Kamee*, *Alantis*, *Parsifal* files, KnollTextiles Archive.
104 *Cocoon* file, KnollTextiles Archive.
105 Knoll Textiles, "Textile Price List 1977/78," November 15, 1977, pp. 20–25, KnollTextiles Archive.
106 Stanley Abercrombie, *A Century of Interior Design, 1900–2000* (New York: Rizzoli, 2003), 138, 140, 147.
107 Rae and Vignelli, "1965" in *Knoll au Louvre*, n.p.
108 For the introduction of the *Christen* and *Stephens* systems see "Market Spotlight: For Office Efficiency," *Interior Design* (November 1971): 78; Advertisement for Knoll International featuring the *Stephens System*, designed by Massimo Vignelli, *Interior Design* (September 1971): 84–85; and Advertisement for Knoll International featuring the *Christen System*, designed by Massimo Vignelli, *Interior Design* (November 1971): 24–25. For the Weyerhaeuser project see "Configurations in a Landscape," *Interiors* (March 1972): 76–91; "Wide Open Spaces," *Industrial Design* (March 1972): 38–43.
109 Eric Larabee and Massimo Vignelli, *Knoll Design* (New York: Harry N. Abrams, 1989): 238.
110 Polster and Elsner, *Design Lexikon USA*, 170.
111 Knoll Textiles, "Textile Price List 1973," April 1, 1973, p. 12, KnollTextiles Archive.
112 *Knoll Tabloid* for Knoll Textiles, 1977, p. 11.
113 Ibid.
114 Unless indicated otherwise information in this section is drawn from *Partition Fabric* file, KnollTextiles Archive.
115 Several memos in ibid. indicate that samples were distributed to key Knoll showrooms in late 1974 and one specification sheet indicates "For June '75 Introduction." However, the official announcement of the fabric came in John J. Flynn, "Knoll Textiles Bulletin" January 12, 1976, *Partition Fabric* file, KnollTextiles Archive.
116 *Knoll Tabloid* for Knoll Textiles, 1977, p. 11; Knoll Textiles, "Textiles Price List 1977/78," p. 26, KnollTextiles Archive. Like *Partition Fabric*, *Regency* was also fire-retardant, and both were listed as "Flame Retarded Panel Fabrics" in this price list.
117 Kathryn Gray Gluibizzi, Design Studio Coordinator, KnollTextiles, email to Earl Martin, April 18, 2011. In 1987 Knoll introduced a group of eight panel fabrics based on *Regency* available in custom colorways as *Regency Standard Custom Program*; see Knoll Textiles, "Catalog 1987/1988," June 1, 1987, pp. 59–62.
118 *Eton* file, KnollTextiles Archive.
119 "New Fabrics + Leather a Feature of Designer's Saturday," press release, October 3, 1976, *Eclat* file, KnollTextiles Archive; *Galway*, *Glin*, and *Dorset* files, KnollTextiles Archive. Unless otherwise noted, information in this section is drawn from these files. New London Textile Print Works relocated from New London, Conn., to Delaware sometime in the 1960s.
120 *Glin* could also be ordered in eighteen piece-dyed colorways (dyed after weaving) for an additional cost.
121 Casey, email to Martin, October 10, 2010. Rodes-Segerer's last day with Knoll was April 7, 1978, handwritten notation by Barbara Rodes-Segerer on Jürgen Bargende (Knoll International) to Barbara Segerer (letter), May 19, 1978, Josef and Anni Albers Foundation, Bethany, Conn.
122 *Knoll Tabloid* for Knoll Textiles, 1977, p. 9.
123 Anni Albers, in "Designer Biographies," in this volume.
124 "New Fabrics + Leather a Feature of Designer's Saturday," press release. October 3, 1976, *Eclat* file, KnollTextiles Archive.
125 For more see Christa Häusler, in "Designer Biographies," in this volume.
126 Dieter Gasse, Carl-Wolfgang Schümann, and Manfred Rusche, *"Printed by Taunus Textildruck": 30 Jahre Textildruck in Deutschland am Beispiel einer Firma*, exh. cat. (Krefeld, Germany: Deutsches Textilmuseum Krefeld, 1983), 5, 38–39.
127 Textiles, "Textiles Price List 1977/78," November 15, 1977, p. 38-39. KnollTextile Archive.
128 Paule Vézelay's design *Sequence* (1950–55) was printed on chintz.
129 See "Market: From Knoll Furniture and Fabrics for the Residential Market," *Interior Design* (October 1977): 120.
130 Information in this section is drawn from Knoll France, "Knoll Textiles Tarif 1978/79," October 1978. See also Klaus Dombrowski and Christa Häusler in "Designer Biographies," in this volume.
131 No prints are listed in Knoll Textiles, "Price List 1979," December 1, 1978, KnollTextiles Archive.
132 This section is based on "Corporation Affairs," *New York Times*, August 31, 1977, p. 76; and Cadwallader, interview with Martin, October 24, 2010.
133 "News: Knoll International Bought by General Felt," *Interior Design* (October 1977): 27.
134 These included Albers, Bauer, Häusler, and Hielle-Vatter. Rodes-Segerer would soon return to live and work in Germany and eventually purchased the largely unsuccessful European textile arm of Sunar, which she later renamed S-Collection, operating it first in Schelklingen and then Erbach Germany. She offered a range of upholstery and drapery designs to the European market working closely with designers (including many of those she had worked with at Knoll). Rodes-Segerer devoted the rest of her life to running this business until her death from cancer in 1997. Casey, email to Martin, October 10, 2010. See also Hans Wichmann, *Von Morris bis Memphis: Textilien der Neuen Sammlung Ende 19. bis Ende 20. Jahrhundert* (Basel: Birkhäuser, 1990), 460.
135 Two price lists were used to make this comparison: Knoll Textiles, "Price List 1979," December 1, 1978 and "Textiles Price List 1977/78," November 15, 1977; KnollTextiles Archive.

6 Tradition and Reinvention: Knoll Textiles, 1978–2010

Angela Völker

At the end of 1975, Marshall Cogan and Stephen Swid (fig. 6.1), owners of General Felt Industries, the largest commercial carpet manufacturer in the United States, expressed interest in purchasing Knoll. After the sale became final on August 30, 1977, Cogan and Swid addressed their new employees in a company memo, stating their belief in the company's strong legacy and their hopes for its future growth: "Knoll is a precious institution. The design and quality of its products are unequalled. Its reputation for leadership and innovation in the world of design is towering. The challenge that we accept in purchasing Knoll is to protect the institution, to zealously guard its traditions and to bring about a creative atmosphere which will stimulate both individual growth among Knoll's outstanding employees and corporate growth through increased sales and profits."[1] Within a few months the previous senior leadership of the company had largely resigned, and Swid and Cogan were vetting a new group of men and women to guide the company. Soon, under the new leadership, one of the most successful divisions in the company was Knoll Textiles.

New Directions

The new Knoll owners tapped Arthur Sager to lead Knoll Textiles in new directions, a role he would fulfill for more than a decade (fig. 6.2). After graduating in 1958 with a business degree from the Wharton School at the University of Pennsylvania, Sager was hired by Burlington Industries, one of the largest textile conglomerates in the world.[2] Although he had no background in the industry, Sager became enamored with textiles and the textile business, learning all its aspects from manufacturing to sales. In 1960 he took a leave of absence from Burlington to attend Harvard University, graduating with an MBA in 1962. He returned to Burlington for fifteen years before being asked by his former Harvard classmate, Marshall Cogan, to come to Knoll as a vice president and the general manager of Knoll Textiles. Swid and Cogan had restructured Knoll Textiles into an independently operating division with its own administration and sales force. It marketed its own products as a separate line of business, selling material directly to outside clients as well as producing them for use on Knoll furniture. The division kept up in every way with its national and international rivals, and its products proved to be very successful in their own right, without depending solely on demand from Knoll's furniture and office systems division.

One of Sager's initial tasks was to assess the textile division's existing staff and sales, outlining new goals for Knoll Textiles with Swid and Cogan. After the sale of the company Barbara Rodes-Segerer, who had previously headed design and development for Knoll Textiles, worked for a short time in Knoll's European textile base near Stuttgart before resigning in April 1978. Rodes-Segerer's assistant in New York, Kristl Reinhardt, remained with the company and acted in a stylist role for several more years, but Sager felt that she did not have enough experience to become creative director of Knoll Textiles. For this important position, he hired Richard Wagner in 1978.[3] Wagner, a graduate of Syracuse University's surface pattern design program (1958), had worked for many years at Schumacher & Company, a large residential textile company, and did a brief stint at Cohama Decorative Fabrics. A year later, needing a separate design director for the European Knoll Textiles division, Sager hired Peter Seipelt, a German designer who had previously developed a line of interior fabrics for the leading Swiss textile manufacturer Zumsteg AG.[4] Thus by 1979 the important players in the reconfigured textile division were in place.

Rodarte (Kate and Laura Mulleavy). *Auden* ("Landscape" colorway), introduced 2010. Made in Germany for KnollTextiles. Used for drapery; ramie and polyester; plain gauze with supplemental weft. KnollTextiles. Cat. 297.

Upholsteries and Prints for the Residential Market

Swid and Cogan decided early to place stronger emphasis on creating products for the residential market, certainly a change of focus for the company, and this was reflected in the Knoll Textiles offerings. The 1977 printed drapery textiles by Christa Häusler-Goltz were promoted as part of this new push but were discontinued in 1978 (see chapter 5).[5] By 1979 Wagner had developed a number of new upholsteries that were geared to the residential market, a group dubbed the *Calais Cotton Collection*.[6] In addition to "light upholstery" use (meaning residential), these textiles were considered appropriate for drapery and wallcoverings. The group included a few older patterns, such as *Prestini*, but mostly comprised original designs: *Canton*, *LeMans*, *Lille*, *Marseille*, *Newport*, *Stratford*, and *Toulouse*. Knoll Textiles simultaneously released a highly publicized and innovative collection of drapery fabrics geared to the residential market and created by the Japanese textile designers Nob and Non Utsumi, known professionally as Nob + Non.[7]

In 1978 Jeffrey Osborne, who had been with Knoll since 1969 and was named vice president of design and marketing by Swid and Cogan, had introduced the Utsumis to Knoll executives, and a commission to create a collection for Knoll Textiles soon followed.[8] In June 1979, after a year of development, including close collaboration with the manufacturer New London Textile Print Works to overcome technical challenges in the printing, *Collection 1* was presented to the public to great acclaim from the press and design community. The Utsumis created seven minimalist linear patterns—*Direction*, *In the World*, *Large World*, *Pro*, *Small Space*, *Small World*, and *Vision*—with lines hand-drawn by the designers, "thereby softening all the 'industrial' elements which are synonymous with their designs."[9] These were printed on sheer cotton batiste and a heavier cotton percale in a variety of subtle color variants, such as "Snow/Stripe on White," "Mocha on Natural," and "Rainbow on White" (figs. 6.3 and 6.4). The collection reflected the intense interest in Japanese culture at the time, partially a result of Japanese success in the electronic and automobile industries. The sophisticated, minimalist aesthetic of the Utsumi designs appealed to the taste for simplicity and subtlety, a phenomenon also associated with the economic crisis that had begun earlier in the decade. The Utsumis astutely created a signature look for themselves by dressing solely in white or black outfits, including ensembles made from their Knoll textile designs (fig. 6.5). Their collection was also distributed by Knoll in Europe, where two new patterns were added (*Lights* and *Shades*). Their designs remained in the line with varying success until February 1984.[10]

Knoll Textiles would produce additional collections of printed drapery fabrics for their American collection in the early 1980s. In late 1981 they introduced prints created by Peter Seipelt, the company's European design director.[11] The fabrics—*Zigzag*, *Linea*, and *Basket*—were printed in Germany at Taunus Textildruck, as Häusler-Goltz's designs had been, and were available from Knoll in Europe as well as the United States. Each design was printed on a lightweight solid cotton and also made as a white-on-white sheer on a polyester-cotton base cloth, using the burn-out process (whereby acid is used to burn away part of the fabric and create a translucent pattern). These designs were printed with pastel matte backgrounds overlaid with linear motifs in shiny inks to create a metallic effect (fig. 6.6). Knoll introduced another new group of prints in 1982, a series by the duo Adrian Pulfer and Parry Merkley, working under the name "Adrian Parry." Wagner collaborated closely with the young designers, who had previously focused on graphic design.[12] Like the Nob + Non collection, the Adrian Parry patterns—*Chanel I*, *Chanel II*, *Connection* (fig. 6.7), *Network*, *Shadow*, and *Traffic*—were printed by New London Textile Print Works in Delaware. The series meshed well with the other Knoll print collections, having linear and minimalist motifs and being printed in a range of neutral and pastel colors (fig. 6.8).

While it is not clear from the records whether the *Adrian Parry Collection* was distributed by Knoll in Europe, printed fabrics continued to be an important part of the company's European offerings throughout the 1980s, a fact perhaps attributable to Knoll's more residential client base in Europe. A printed fabric collection by Alexandre Mimoglou, a Greek-born designer living in Paris, was also introduced in 1982. Mimoglou's fabrics—*Sails*, *Festival*, *Crazy Night*, *Morning Sky*, *Uptown*, and *Downtown*—were printed by Taunus Textildruck on solid cotton and as burn-outs on a cotton-polyester blend. Mimoglou's designs included minimalist linear motifs or geometric shapes and were printed in bright colors on the cotton base cloth (fig. 6.9), or as white-on-white motifs on the burn-outs. Unlike Seipelt's prints, this collection was reserved for the European market.[13] Seipelt continued to introduce prints into the European Knoll Textiles collection through the 1980s. Later examples included prints by German designers Jürgen Reichert, Klaus Dombrowski, and Karl Vogelsang (fig. 6.10).[14]

In the United States, when Knoll did not succeed in generating a much larger residential client base, printed draperies were eventually dropped as the company renewed its focus on the contract market. The Non + Non collection was discontinued by 1984, as were prints by Adrian Parry and Peter Seipelt, marking the first time in Knoll Textiles history that printed fabrics were absent from the American collection.[15] They would not return until 2003.

New Spaces, New Looks

In 1980, when Swid and Cogan opened a new Knoll showroom at 655 Madison Avenue in New York, Knoll once again signaled change in the company with a distinctive display space. In true Knoll style, the company under its new owners put the spotlight on architects by engaging Robert Venturi of Venturi and Rauch for the design of the showroom.[16] In selecting Venturi it was clear that Knoll was continuing to align itself with the leading design figures of the day. Knoll remained on this path through the 1980s, opening, for example, a new Houston showroom in 1984 designed by the architectural firm of Stanley Tigerman, Fugman & McCurry.[17]

Venturi also made significant contributions to the Knoll collection when in May 1984 Knoll presented a collection of furniture and two fabrics by Venturi, Denise Scott Brown and Associates. These had been five years in the making.[18] The furniture consisted of chairs and tables fabricated from molded sheets of plywood and were available with a natural finish or with a plastic laminate veneer; there was also an overstuffed couch. The collection's press release stated, "It is a characteristic of Post-Modernism to use familiar and conventional patterns but to use them in an unusual way."[19] The *Venturi Collection* fulfilled this dictum. The outlines of the plywood furniture echoed the historical furniture styles that inspired their names, such as *Chippendale*, as did the patterns in both the plastic laminates and two fabrics used as upholsteries, *Tapestry* and *Grandmother* (fig. 6.11). Both fabrics featured large-scale floral patterns overlaid with small-scale geometric shapes. *Tapestry*, a heavy upholstery fabric, was intended for the couch, while the lighter-weight printed cotton *Grandmother* was used for seat cushions on the *Venturi* chairs and was also translated into a surface pattern for vinyl laminate surfaces on the furniture (see cat. 232). In a press release, Venturi described the origins of *Grandmother*: "We have juxtaposed two conventional patterns—a floral pattern you might find on a faded tablecloth that belonged to your grandmother, and a typical screen pattern used in commercial art but made much bigger."[20] While the Knoll Textiles staff assisted in the development and manufacturing of the *Venturi* fabrics, these two textiles were only offered for sale with the *Venturi* furniture.[21]

The *Venturi Collection*'s introduction was accompanied by brochures and an invitation in a new graphic format, another signature change that communicated the company's new image and kept Knoll's brand fresh. After 1979 Knoll gradually moved away from using an independent graphic design consultant (then Massimo Vignelli) and instead began to rely on an in-house design department. Knoll Graphics, led by Harold Matoussian, was responsible for the new formats and graphic styling that appeared in 1984. One of the key Knoll Graphics designers, Takaaki Matsumoto, created the new Venturi materials as well as a new Knoll Textiles catalogue and logo for the division, introduced in 1985 (see fig. C.15 and cat. 234).[22] More than 350 types of printed promotional and sales material were produced annually, in line with the contemporary trend for ingenious but simple forms. Matsumoto recently commented on the debonair, new-dawn mood at Knoll in the 1980s, as the company renewed its effort to set up a "family" and create design as a synergetic process.[23]

Design Leadership in the Early 1980s

In 1980 Knoll's promotion and education manager, Ursula Dayenian, outlined the place of Knoll Textiles in the contract market, using information compiled from leading Knoll Textiles dealers and specifiers for the department sales staff.[24] "The purpose of this report is so that you will have a better idea as to how we 'stand' regarding the competition," she wrote, presenting a list of Knoll's fifty-seven upholstery patterns and prices along with the comparable fabrics and prices from rival companies. In apprising its sales staff of competitor's products and prices, Knoll set out first to guarantee that they could offer discounts to clients on parallel material and also to inform them about rival products: "Unless we are aware of the competition, we will not be able to present our side of the story."

The report first noted that leading designers and design firms considered Knoll to be in "the top five textile houses" then operating. The detailed list of comparable competitor fabrics identified Knoll's rivals as a veritable "Who's Who" of the interior textile market at the time. The fourteen firms named included companies that had been Knoll's competitors since the 1950s such as Jack Lenor Larsen, Isabelle Scott, and Boris Kroll.[25] Newer additions to the interior textiles field also made the list, such as Gretchen Bellinger, who had previously worked for Knoll and Designtex, a firm that had been founded in the early 1960s.[26] Dayenian noted that Knoll's competitors promoted fabrics that were equivalent in price to many Knoll fabrics, but also products that were both more and less expensive. For example, textile supplier Maharam's equivalent of *Nylon Homespun* was almost half the price of Knoll's. Knoll considered certain of their patterns, however, to have no competition, notably the handwovens made by Paul Maute such as *Atlantis*, *Cato*, *Chord*, *Cocoon*, *Ebro*, *Inca*, *Kamee*, *Parsifal*, and *Tiber*, and the Jacquard-weave designs of Marga Hielle-Vatter produced by rohi, such as *Tacoma* and *Tournee*.

Knoll would soon find a new design leader in Jhane Barnes, who contributed a collection of upholstery textiles in 1983 that were also without competition. Barnes, a young fashion designer, had established her menswear company

Fig. 6.1 Top left Marshall Cogan and Steven Swid, 1983. Photographed by Michele Singer. Knoll Archives.

Fig. 6.2 Top right Textile Management Group: from left, Arthur Sager, Kristl Reinhardt (later Andrus), and Richard Wagner, ca. 1980. Photographed by E. Anthes. Knoll Archives.

Fig. 6.3 Bottom Nob + Non (Nob and Non Utsumi). *Direction* ("Rainbow/Stripe on White" colorway), 1979. Made by New London Textile Print Works for Knoll Textiles. Used for drapery; cotton; plain weave, screen-printed. The Metropolitan Museum of Art, New York, Gift of Knoll Textiles, 1984.547.10. Cat. 225.

Fig. 6.4 Top Nob + Non (Nob and Non Utsumi). *In the World* ("Earthen" and "Rainbow" colorways) promotional photo, 1979. Made by New London Textile Print Works for Knoll Textiles. Used for drapery; cotton; plain weave, screen-printed. KnollTextiles Archive.

Fig. 6.5 Bottom left Nob and Non Utsumi, with their designs for Knoll Textiles, ca. 1979. Knoll Archives.

Fig. 6.6 Bottom right Peter Seipelt. *Basket* and *Zigzag* (various colorways) promotional photo, 1981. Made by Taunus Textildruck for Knoll Textiles. Used for drapery; cotton; plain weave, screen-printed. KnollTextiles Archive.

Fig. 6.7 Top left Adrian Parry (Adrian Pulfer and Parry Merkley). *Connection* sample ("Spruce" colorway), 1982. Made by New London Textile Print Works for Knoll Textiles. Used for drapery; cotton; plain weave, screen-printed, Teflon glaze. KnollTextiles Archive. Cat. 226.

Fig. 6.8 Top right *Adrian Parry Collection* promotional card, 1982. KnollTextiles Archive.

Fig. 6.9 Bottom Alexandre Mimoglou. *Downtown*, 1982. Made by Taunus Textildruck for Knoll Textiles. Used for drapery; cotton; plain weave, screen-printed. Cooper-Hewitt, National Design Museum, Smithsonian Institution, Gift of Taunus Textildruck, 1983-19-5. Cat. 230.

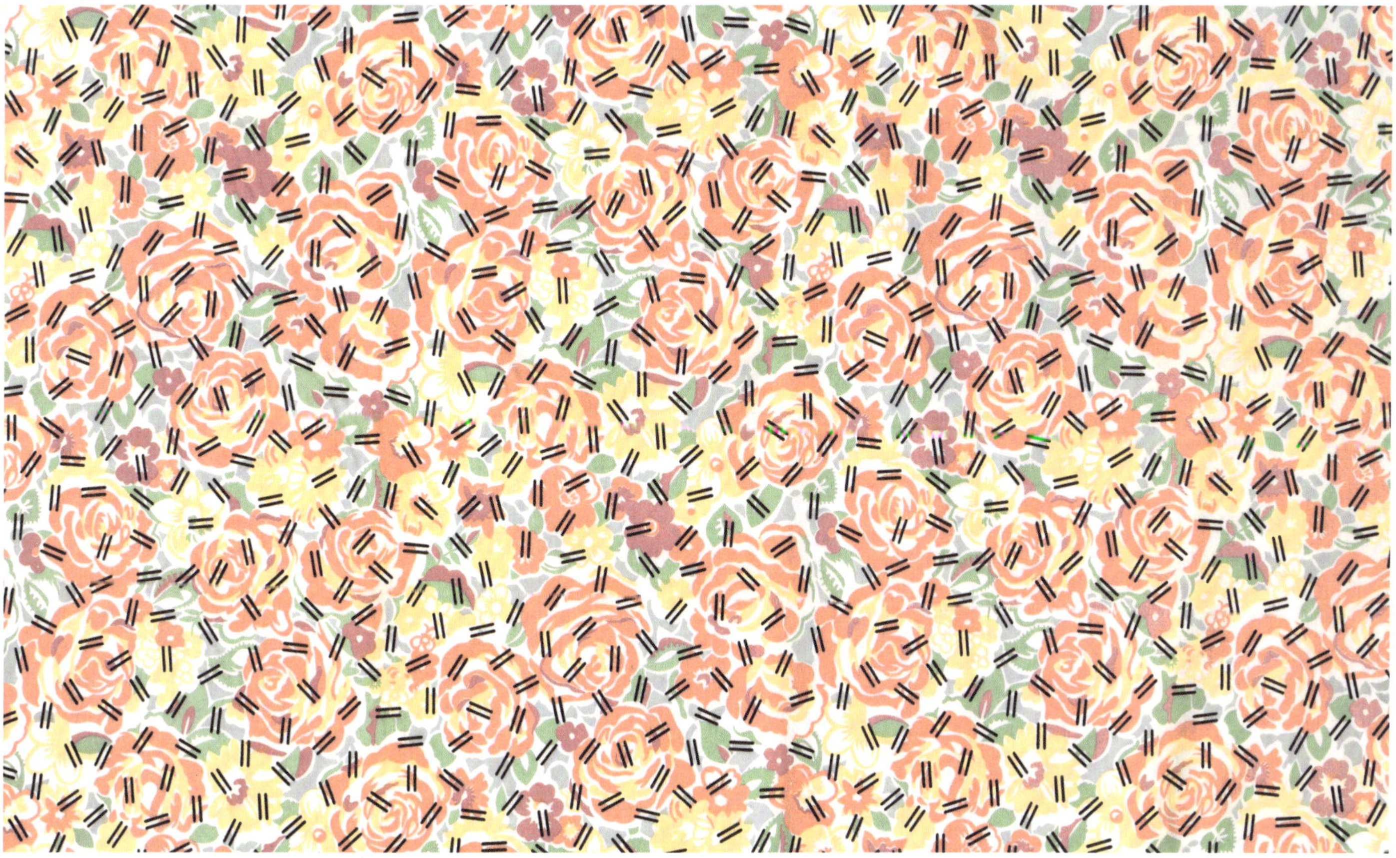

Fig. 6.10 Top Karl Vogelsang. *Fortuna*, 1988. Made by Heberlein Textildruck AG for Knoll Textiles. Used for drapery; cotton; plain weave, screen-printed. Cooper-Hewitt, National Design Museum, Smithsonian Institution, Gift of Heberlein Textildruck AG, Switzerland, 1989-88-1-a. Cat. 231.

Fig. 6.11 Bottom Robert Venturi. *Grandmother*, 1983. Made for Knoll International. Used for upholstery, drapery; cotton; plain weave, screen-printed. Courtesy Joan H. and David E. Bright. Cat. 233.

in 1975 and by the early 1980s was winning prestigious industry awards for her work.[27] She met with Richard Wagner in 1982, who was at first reluctant to engage a designer from the world of fashion until he learned that she was also a handweaver and designed and made her own fabric samples. Barnes presented him with an array of beautiful weaves and textures at their initial meeting.[28] Wagner recalls these samples being very different from anything on the market at that time, with unusual combinations of multiple types of fibers and innovative use of color. Once engaged, Barnes was involved in the entire development of her collection, from design to production. She brought a new supplier to Knoll—Franetta, a small fashion fabrics textile mill with whom she worked. The practice of overseeing the entire development process of her fabrics and bringing in new mills, several from outside the interiors fabric industry, characterized her work with the company over the fifteen years of its duration.

In January 1983, Knoll Textiles presented Barnes's first collection to great acclaim in its new Knoll Design Center showroom which had opened the previous year at 105 Wooster Street in New York's SoHo district (fig. 6.12). Knoll promoted the name of the designer as part of the marketing strategy for the new collection, an approach previously reserved for printed fabric collections and a method that would continue to be exploited by the company in the future. Barnes's collection—*Cobblestone*, *Melange*, *Nuance*, and *Rainbow Twill* (fig. 6.13)—was innovative in both color preferences and weaving techniques. In each fabric Barnes combined three or four individual yarns, primarily of natural fibers, such as the mix of wool, silk, cotton, and rayon in *Cobblestone*. Color was also key in the fabrics—each displayed a subtle range of hues. *Nuance* became the most successful of the collection and remained in production, with later adjustments to its fiber content, for more than fifteen years (fig. 6.14). Barnes recently described the characteristics that made this fabric a success: "*Nuance* had many space-dyed and fancy yarns in it although it was just plain weave. . . . *Nuance* was a 'multi-purpose fabric' to be used on wall, panel, or upholstery, which is probably another reason for [its] long life."[29] The first Barnes collection sold very well and could hardly be kept in stock in its early years.[30] This success led the company to engage Barnes as a contract designer who would regularly contribute both individual designs and collections.

Textiles for the Contract Market, 1979–85

While Knoll attempted to appeal to more residential customers in the late 1970s, its traditional role as a purveyor of high-quality textiles for the contract market continued to be a central focus after the change of ownership in 1977 and throughout the 1980s. One of the first tasks assigned to Sager and Wagner was to find a fabric suitable to upholster a new group of task chairs designed for Knoll by Niels Diffrient.[31] After sourcing possibilities from mills around the globe and an extensive testing process, Sager and Wagner found the best solution in a Dralon acrylic upholstery that had been engineered by the German manufacturer Krall & Roth Weberei GmbH. The fabric, called *Desna* by Knoll, had bi-elastic stretch—the ability to stretch equally in both the warp and weft—which was required of fabrics used to cover the concave seats and rounded edges of the Diffrient seating's cushioning. It also maintained a "lasting tailored appearance" through the ability to return to its original state after being stretched (fig. 6.15).[32] This fabric debuted with the Diffrient chairs in 1979 and remained in the line for more than fifteen years.[33]

Selling fabrics for use on other manufacturer's furniture also became increasingly targeted under Sager and Wagner's leadership. The expansion of Knoll's "cut-yardage" business, as this was known in the trade, would make Knoll Textiles less dependent on orders from the Knoll furniture division. The sale of "cut-yardage" continued to be an important focus for the company as it expanded exponentially in the 1980s.[34] Knoll heralded this new direction in company advertisements such as one that promoted "Knoll Textiles On Steelcase," a major competitor in the office furniture business (fig. 6.16).

Fabrics for vertical applications such as panel-system fabrics and wallcoverings became another major focus of Knoll Textiles after 1980. One of the first new developments in this area was *Furrows Wallcarpeting* which was introduced in the fall of 1981 and signaled Knoll's entry into this part of the market.[35] While its name and ribbed texture recalled the *Furrows* upholstery fabric (1957) designed by Suzanne Huguenin, *Furrows Wallcarpeting* was more akin to carpet, as its name suggests.[36] Wagner worked closely with Troy Mills, a manufacturer in New Hampshire, to develop this nonwoven, needle-punched product made of fire-retardant Trevira polyester. It was also "acoustically absorbent and thermally efficient" and was offered in a wide variety of colors that coordinated with the Knoll upholstery collection.[37] *Furrows Wallcarpeting* linked Knoll to the contemporary trend of interior designers specifying carpeting for wall surfaces, but it offered a better solution because it had been designed specifically for vertical surfaces, an aspect highlighted in the company's advertisements (fig. 6.17). Knoll was the first to bring this type of product to market, and it had huge sales, over three million dollars in the first year.[38]

Wall and panel coverings would become a major sector of growth for Knoll Textiles beginning in the mid-1980s. A new creative director of the textile division, Merle Lindby-Young, brought in by Wagner in 1981, spearheaded Knoll's continued

Fig. 6.12 *Jhane Barnes Collection* promotional card, 1983. KnollTextiles Archive.

Fig. 6.13 Top left Jhane Barnes. *Rainbow Twill* ("Navy" colorway) on *Stephens* armchair designed by William Stephens, ca. 1985. Made by Franetta for Knoll Textiles; chair made by Knoll International. Cotton, wool, rayon, and polyester; twill variation; chair: oak frame, plastic shell, foam. Knoll Museum, East Greenville, Penn. Cat. 239.
Fig. 6.14 Bottom Jhane Barnes. From left: *Nuance* samples ("Rust," "Blue," and "Rainbow" colorways), *Cobblestone* sample ("Multi" colorway), ca. 1983. Made by Franetta for Knoll Textiles. Used for upholstery; *Nuance*: cotton, silk, wool, rayon; plain weave; *Cobblestone*: wool, silk, cotton, polyester; plain-weave–derived simple weave. Courtesy Cindia Reyes. Cats. 235, 237.
Fig. 6.15 Top right "Diffrient Seating Upholstery Fabric" sample folder, featuring *Desna*, ca. 1980. Samples made by Krall & Roth Weberei GmbH for Knoll Textiles. Textile samples (acrylic, doralastan) on paper. Knoll Archives.

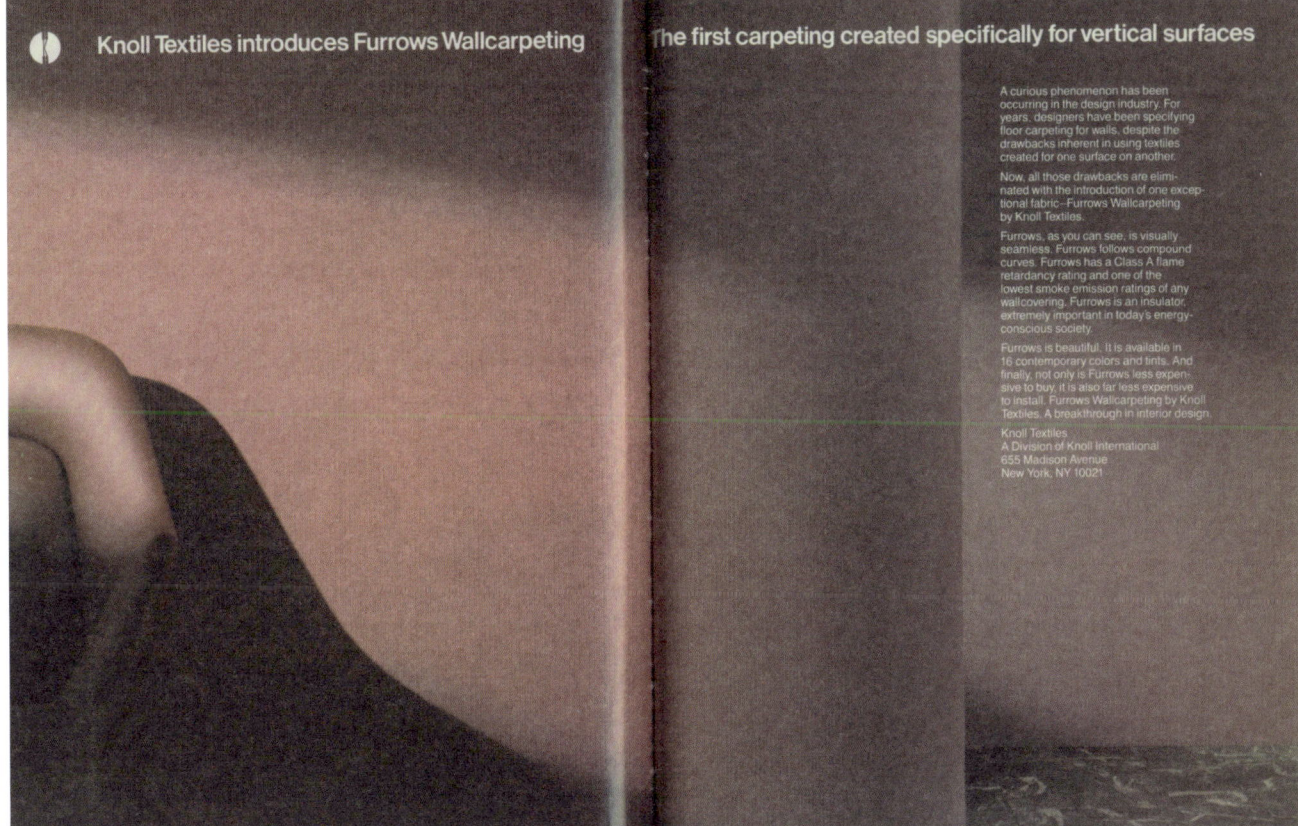

Fig. 6.16 **Top left** Advertisement for Knoll Textiles, ca. 1982. Knoll Archives.
Fig. 6.17 **Bottom** Advertisement for Knoll Textiles, featuring *Furrows Wallcarpeting*. From *Interiors*, January 1981.
Fig. 6.18 **Top right** Merle Lindby-Young, ca. 1983. Knoll Archives.

foray into this part of the market (fig. 6.18).³⁹ Lindby-Young had trained in textile design at the Newark School of Fine and Industrial Art in Newark, New Jersey, graduating in 1964, and had worked at Fieldcrest Mills beginning in 1966, eventually becoming a director of product development and a vice president in the 1970s. At Fieldcrest, she had worked extensively with a variety of designers, including those from the world of fashion such as Geoffrey Beene and Halston, to develop a full range of household textiles from sheets and towels to carpets. When Wagner was named general manager and vice president of Knoll Textiles in 1980, after Arthur Sager left the company, he named Lindby-Young as his successor.⁴⁰ (Sager's departure was brief; he would soon return in a more senior position overseeing Knoll Textiles and other divisions of the company.)

Lindby-Young developed the company's next step into the wallcoverings market in the fall of 1984 with introduction of *Knoll Wall*. This group was described as "a comprehensive fabric collection specifically and exclusively for walls," and included six patterns: *Firenze*, *Panama*, *Mojave*, *Eton*, *Eton Square*, and *Chelsea* (fig. 6.19).⁴¹ The fabrics were designed to address the specific requirements of wallcoverings—a width suited to a single-person installation, backing to ease installation, and "a class 'A' fire rating" that made them appropriate for use in office environments where strict fire codes determined materials. The subtle textures and solids relied on natural fibers like wool, silk, and linen mixed with synthetic yarns like nylon, polyester, and modacrylic, and were offered in color ranges including neutrals and soft pastels.

In the summer of 1986 the company introduced further additions to *Knoll Wall*, the first wallcoverings created by Jhane Barnes, who was becoming increasingly important as a Knoll designer.⁴² These three weaves—*Niji*, *Hashi*, and *Toya*—used the same subtle colorations and distinctive blends of fibers that had been used by Barnes in her upholsteries. The soft-hued wallcovering fabrics were introduced with a companion *Knoll Window Collection*, a new designation for drapery fabrics, including some designed by Barnes: *Fuji*, *Niji Net*, *Nikko*, *Toya*, and *Nuance Leno*. These two groups of fabrics—for walls and windows—were designed to be easily coordinated and could also form an ensemble with such Barnes upholsteries as *Nuance*. The Japanese pattern names for this collection were not coincidental, as Barnes had started to collaborate with Japanese weaving firms that could better interpret her subtle and innovative textile designs. This new relationship was fostered by Barnes's desire for more advanced and reliable millwork for her textiles than could be found in the United States. After 1986 she almost exclusively looked to Japanese mills to execute her textiles for Knoll.

In the summer of 1987 Knoll Textiles introduced the Signature Series, a group of coordinated vertical fabrics.⁴³ Developed under the direction of Lindby-Young, it featured innovative yarns of SRB modacrylic mixed with natural fibers such as linen or wool, creating highly fire-retardant fabrics for corporate interiors. They not only had "the visual and tactile character of the natural fiber with which it's blended," but also met the stringent safety requirements of contract installations.⁴⁴ The Signature Series marked the beginning of a regular feature of the Knoll textile division—customized and coordinated wallcoverings, panel fabrics, and draperies—an effort to appeal to customers wanting more than just the previous small selection of plain-weave panel fabrics and wallcoverings. The Signature Series initially consisted of three panel fabrics, three wallcoverings, and a drapery fabric, all manufactured in the United States in a variety of textures and colorations.⁴⁵

By the fall of 1988 Knoll was offering even more wallcovering, panel fabric, and drapery possibilities under the promotional heading, "Vertical Variations." These drew from the standard products for "woven to order" customization.⁴⁶ They were divided into three groups: Regency, Signature Series, and Jhane Barnes. The Regency group was based on Knoll's *Regency*, the plain-weave solid-color panel fabric that had become Knoll's standard offering for panels after its introduction in 1976. The new Regency group included patterned panel, wall, and window coverings developed from the yarns in *Regency*. The Signature Series used the existing standard line wallcovering fabric yarns to develop coordinated patterned drapery and panel fabrics. The Jhane Barnes Vertical Variations group included eight patterns that could be made as either panel coverings or drapery, featuring an assortment of fibers and colors that would create the intriguing textures and hues characteristic of Barnes. Only one of these fabrics, however, was directly related to a previous Barnes textile—*Nuance*.

Fashioning Fibers: Outside Designers 1985–89

Both Wagner and Lindby-Young courted designers deeply engaged in the art of weaving, pursuing textiles as artistic practice. These included weaver-designer Jhane Barnes, fiber artist Dana Romeis, and production handweaver Robin Whitten. Their creations demonstrated a passion for fibers and unique weave structures, resulting in textiles that propelled the Knoll brand to greater success in the 1980s.

In October 1985 Knoll Textiles presented a striking alternative to the subtle weaves of Barnes, introducing the first collection by Dana Romeis, who had never before designed power-woven fabrics. Lindby-Young had encountered Romeis's work at a craft fair in 1982 and thought she would be an ideal choice for Knoll Textiles: "The contemporary quality made me think instantly of the kinds of fabrics she could create that would be appropriate to the

Knoll collection."⁴⁷ Over the next two years, the two worked closely together to develop a collection of five upholstery fabrics for Knoll: *Tilt*, *Slant*, *Rain*, *Flash*, and *Zag*.⁴⁸ Romeis first created sample patterns on her handloom, then refined those that were chosen by Knoll. The final versions of the fabrics were machine-loomed by a longtime Knoll supplier, Craftex Mills, in a mixture of wool, rayon, and nylon (except for *Slant* which contained no nylon). The collection was notable for its use of intense colors and geometric patterning. In *Tilt*, Romeis used diagonal slashes of bright color on a solid ground (fig. 6.20) while *Slant* had a linear motif, also on the diagonal, with a more subtle blending of colors forming the lines in this twill weave (fig. 6.21). *Zag* had a herringbone motif and was available in a wide range of vibrant tones, while *Rain*, reflective of its name, featured short diagonal lines of color on a solid ground, and *Flash* (cat. 253) had the same motif on a ground bisected by regularly spaced horizontal lines.

In 1986 Lindby-Young contracted another handweaver, Robin Whitten, to create the *American Craftsmen Collection*, a line of five upholstery textiles inspired by Whitten's own handwoven designs. With this collection, introduced in 1987, Lindby-Young was again engaging with a designer outside the traditional contract textiles world. Whitten, whose background in textiles aligned with a craft perspective, had operated a production handweaving studio in Portland, Maine, for more than a decade before being approached by Knoll. Whitten's handwoven samples were translated by Knoll into machine-woven designs in close collaboration with two mills, Franetta, which had previously woven only Jhane Barnes fabrics, and Cascade Woolen Mills of Maine.⁴⁹ Whitten's subtle and engaging weaves included *Watercolor Cord*, a sophisticated neutral fabric, somewhat reminiscent of the work of Marianne Strengell (such as *Puli* for Knoll; see chapter 3) in its use of five different types of fiber: rayon, cotton, linen, wool, and acrylic (fig. B.146). Another striking upholstery was *Cat's Eyes*, a wool and nylon blend, woven with colored and black yarn, that plays with shiny and matte contrasts (fig. 6.22). This collection also marked the final group developed by Merle Lindby-Young before she left the company in 1987.⁵⁰ After her departure, Richard Wagner resumed direct involvement in the design process and hired Candace Key as an assistant to share the responsibilities.

The company's decision to engage Dana Romeis for the 1985 collection was well-taken—her first group of fabrics for Knoll received significant attention in the design press and also sold well. Working with Wagner and Key, she designed a second collection for Knoll using four traditional weaving techniques—tapestry, damask, brocade, and epingle (frieze)—to create six "contemporary, often whimsical" upholstery designs, which were released in 1988.⁵¹ Romeis used a tapestry construction and minute squares of color for *Zana* and *Zana Coordinate* (fig. 6.23), patterned upholsteries based on abstracted floral motifs. *Rampant* and *Tortola*, all-wool frieze weaves or uncut-loop pile fabrics, were "inspired by Carribean topography." *Pandora* and *Cubis* had box motifs constructed with brocade and damask weaves respectively (fig. B.110). After Romeis's second collection, collections of upholsteries with woven decorative patterning became a regular feature of the KnollTextiles line.

In 1989 KnollTextiles introduced additional innovative weaves from Jhane Barnes, as well as those from a newcomer, Anne Beetz. In the spring the company introduced eight new Barnes upholstery fabrics. Four double-knit textiles of wool and polyester—*Waves*, *Pinweels*, *Strata*, and *Luna*—were particularly remarkable. The designer described them as "a personal challenge to do something new and innovative for the furnishing industry."⁵² Developed by Barnes in collaboration with a Japanese mill and available in one or two colors, they seem to have narrow, irregular pleats, giving the ridged knit surface an iridescent character (fig. 6.24). Barnes recently attributed their modest commercial success to their newness. They were just too different for the relatively conservative contract furniture market.⁵³ Despite this, they garnered critical acclaim and received an award from the American Society of Interior Designers. Also part of the 1989 collection were four woven upholsteries including *Romanie* (cat. 244), which was described as a "modern approach to plaid," with contrasts between matte and shiny yarns to create visual interest.⁵⁴

In the fall of 1989 KnollTextiles presented a collection by the innovative Belgian weaver Anne Beetz, one of the few times in the 1980s that Knoll called on a designer from Europe to create textiles for the American collection. The company characterized the collection of eight upholsteries, two wallcoverings, and two textiles that could be used to cover either panels or walls as a "European style collection for the U.S. contract market."⁵⁵ The Beetz textiles had small-scale patterning and a variety of sophisticated weave structures. They were made in a range of muted colors—greens, grays, and off-whites—and were primarily blends of natural fibers, linen, silk, and cotton, with the exception of two panel fabrics that were all-Trevira polyester. One of the upholsteries, *Luberon*, was made in a "plisse-type weave, reminiscent of pleated fabric," creating a subtle, rhythmic design. It was one of the longest-lasting fabrics in the collection, being discontinued only in 2010 (fig. 6.25). The promotional material—a collection sample box and brochure—prominently displayed the designer's name, reflecting the continued importance of designers in the company's marketing strategies (fig. 6.26).

Fig. 6.19 Advertisement for Knoll Textiles, featuring *Knoll Wall*, ca. 1984. Knoll Archives.

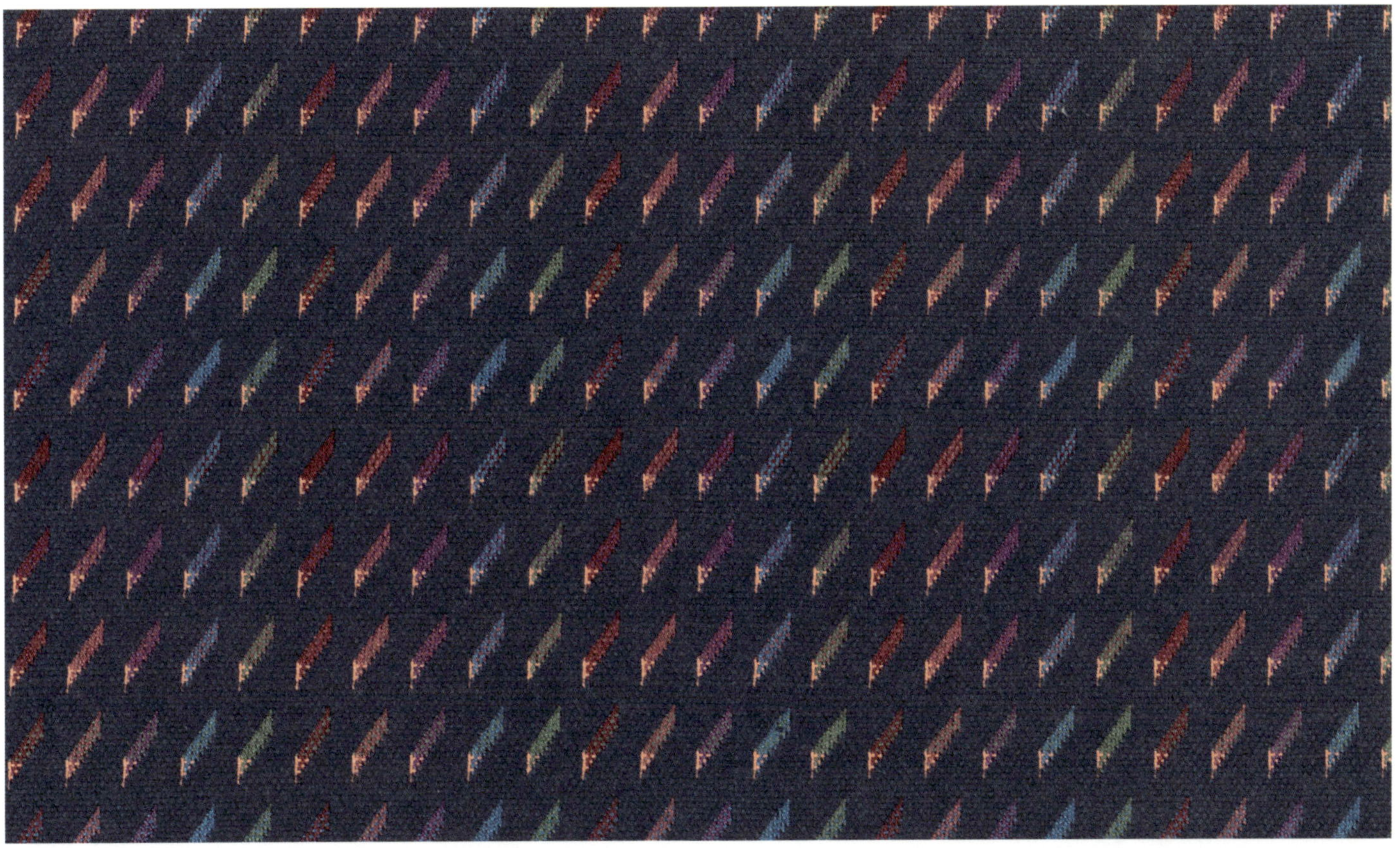

Fig. 6.20 Top Dana Romeis. *Tilt* sample ("Teal" colorway), 1985. Made by Craftex Mills for Knoll Textiles. Used for upholstery; wool, rayon, nylon; plain-weave–derived compound weave. Courtesy Cindia Reyes. Cat. 251.

Fig. 6.21 Bottom Dana Romeis. *Slant* sample ("Charcoal" colorway), 1985. Made by Craftex Mills for Knoll Textiles. Used for upholstery; wool, rayon, nylon; plain-weave–derived compound weave. Courtesy Dana Romeis. Cat. 254.

Fig. 6.22 Bottom left Robin Whitten. *Cat's Eyes* swatch, 1987. Made by Cascade Woolen Mills for Knoll Textiles. Used for upholstery; wool, nylon; plain-weave–derived compound weave. Private collection.

Fig. 6.23 Top left Dana Romeis. *Zana Coordinate* ("Slate" colorway), 1988. Made by Callens Textielfabriek for KnollTextiles. Used for upholstery; cotton; plain-weave–derived compound weave. KnollTextiles Archive. Cat. 256.

Fig. 6.24 Top right Jhane Barnes. Sample package made from *Waves* and containing nine samples, 1989. Made for KnollTextiles. Case: wool, polyester; double-faced knit; samples: wool, cotton, polyester, nylon, rayon, and acrylic; various weaves. Cooper-Hewitt, National Design Museum, Smithsonian Institution, 1990-89-1-a/j. Cat. 242.

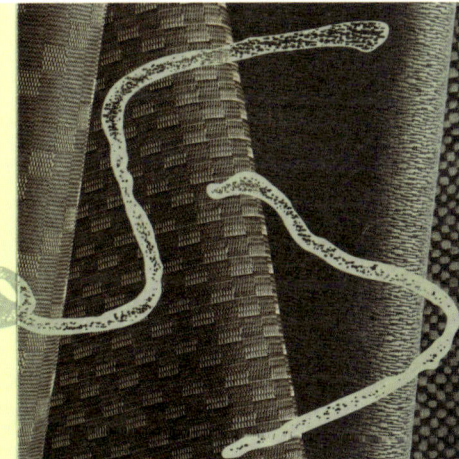

Fig. 6.25 Top Anne Beetz. *Luberon* sample ("Ebony" colorway), introduced 1989. Made in Belgium for KnollTextiles. Used for upholstery; cotton, rayon; plain-weave–derived compound weave with supplemental warp patterning. KnollTextiles Archive.

Fig. 6.26 Bottom *Anne Beetz Collection* brochure, 1989. KnollTextiles Archive.

Fig. 6.27 **Top** Knoll showroom, Los Angeles, with installation of the *Hazel Siegel Collection* for Westweek, 1990. Knoll Archives.

Fig. 6.28 **Bottom** Hazel Siegel. *Blue Night* sample ("Burgundy" colorway), 1990. Made in Germany for KnollTextiles. Used for upholstery; cotton and rayon; compound plain weave with alternating weft and warp floats. KnollTextiles Archive. Cat. 259.

**KnollTextiles
Enters the 1990s**

The late 1980s through the early 1990s was a time of great change throughout Knoll, affecting the textile division along with every other department. In 1986 Steven Swid left the company and Marshall Cogan began to initiate a restructuring. By 1988 a corporate reorganization resulted in new division names—KnollOffice (to sell landscape systems and other office furniture), KnollAccents (office accessories), KnollStudio (to promote and sell "classic" Knoll furniture designs), and KnollTextiles.[56] At the end of the decade Cogan pushed to expand the company and become a major player in the contract office marketplace. In 1990 he commented, "We are competing with the majors, and I have personally invested $50 million in this company to make it an international presence; not only in design in which it will remain a leader, but in terms of volume and affordability."[57] With the corporate focus now trained on volume sales, leadership at various Knoll divisions also changed. After more than a decade, both Arthur Sager and Richard Wagner left in 1989.[58] Cogan named Hazel Siegel as managing director of design for KnollTextiles in the spring of 1989, and she would soon undertake major changes in the division.[59]

Siegel, who had been a consultant to General Felt Industries since 1974, was an experienced designer who specialized in contract textiles. Her career started in 1963 when she was hired by Boris Kroll, considered by many to be the father of contemporary contract fabrics, to work at his eponymous firm. In 1975 Siegel began working for Designtex, another leading contract textile house before leaving in 1989 to join Knoll. Siegel's first decision was to discontinue dozens of existing fabrics, which she considered no longer viable. She then worked "seven days a week" for ten months to develop new fabrics. The *Hazel Siegel Collection* was released in the spring of 1990 (fig. 6.27).[60] According to Knoll it was the "largest single upholstery collection ever introduced in the contract industry," consisting of 38 patterns (with a total of 430 different colorways) divided into twelve "mini-collections."[61] The company promoted it as a "legacy of Knoll and modernism in the 1990s"; however, with the large number of patterns and the stylistic diversity, it represented a clear break from KnollTextiles traditions.[62] This collection related to Knoll's effort to appeal to a much wider segment of the contract market sector. While the majority of the "mini-collections" were oriented to "the high-end market, with pricing above $50" per yard, there were two "mini-collections" oriented to the "medium price points" (under $40 and $30 dollars per yard) and another one targeted to "the low-end high-volume price points" at less than $20 per yard.[63]

While Siegel's approach corresponded to Knoll's market strategies of the early 1990s, it did not exactly match Knoll's historic reputation for elegant luxury and quality, rather than quantity. Nevertheless, some of the new collection's patterns were in production for more than ten years, until at least 2004.[64] One of Siegel's "mini-collections" was based on Paul Klee's paintings which Siegel "translated into textile designs."[65] One of these, the upholstery *Blue Night* (fig. 6.28), based on a painting of the same name, remained in the line until 2004. The four upholsteries in the *Paul Klee Collection* show Siegel working to connect to an historical moment of modernism, while another mini-collection, the *Regal Brocade Collection*, was based on the decorative weaving technique of brocade. Its four patterns retained a high degree of surface decoration (fig. 6.29).

While Siegel's own upholsteries dominated Knoll's offerings in 1990, outside designers were still being engaged by the company. In 1991 KnollTextiles introduced a small collection of upholsteries by architect Peter Eisenman who, at Siegel's suggestion, translated his architectural drawings into designs for upholstery fabrics for Knoll. Siegel had seen his work at the opening of his Wexner Center for the Visual Arts in Columbus, Ohio.[66] The *Snakes and Ladders Collection*, which they developed together, was introduced in the spring of 1991 and included five patterns based on his architectural designs: *Cobra*, *Diamond Back*, *Sidewinder*, *Steppes*, and *Lattice*.[67] *Diamond Back* is characteristic of the group. It derived from Eisenman's design for a hotel in Bayoles, Spain, which would open in 1992 for the Olympic Games. An all-wool upholstery woven on Jacquard looms, it featured an abstracted, geometric motif (fig. 6.30).

Longtime Knoll designer Jhane Barnes regularly contributed large numbers of textiles to the Knoll collection throughout Siegel's tenure, although Barnes worked largely independently on her contributions.[68] In the summer of 1992, Knoll introduced the *Constructions Collection*, an extraordinary group of wallcoverings designed by Barnes. They marked the first foray by Barnes and Knoll into "non-woven, non-textile wallcoverings," a category that continues to be part of Knoll's offerings in 2011.[69] A variety of materials including wood shavings, acrylic resin powder, woven paper, and rayon fiber were bonded onto a paper backing to make delicate relief patterns (fig. 6.31).[70] To create these patterns Barnes again called on a Japanese mill that had the requisite advanced technology to fabricate them and a willingness to work with the designer on experimental materials.[71] In the fall of the same year Knoll introduced another group of Barnes designs, the *Chronology Collection*. This collection included four subtle and richly textured fabrics of wool and wool blends, in line with Knoll's tradition of sophisticated classic upholstery fabrics.[72] Knoll's fact sheet describing the *Chronology Collection* stated that "Jhane Barnes shares Florence Knoll's design aesthetic, and for over nine years has contributed 'timeless' modern-day classics such as Nuance. Today, with 'Chronology,' she continues the

fig. 6.29 Top Hazel Siegel. *Regal Brocade* sample binder, 1990. Samples made in Germany for KnollTextiles. Textile samples (cotton, rayon, polyester), paper, cardboard. KnollTextiles Archive. Cat. 260.

fig. 6.30 Bottom Peter Eisenman. *Diamond Back* on *Model 180* armchair designed by Enrico Franzolini, ca. 1991. Upholstery made in the United Kingdom for KnollTextiles; chair made by Knoll International. Wool; plain-weave–derived compound weave; chair: beech wood, steel, foam. Knoll Museum, East Greenville, Penn. Cat. 262.

Fig. 6.31 Advertisement for KnollTextiles, featuring *Quoinwork* from the *Constructions Collection* by Jhane Barnes, ca. 1992. Knoll Archives.

KnollTextiles tradition . . . coupling new technologies and space dyed yarns with thick and thin wool and wool blend constructions to create a line of new 'handwoven-like' fabrics."[73] Once again Knoll was invoking the reputation of the firm's founder and linking a new collection to its long tradition of handwoven fabrics.

One of the most interesting textiles in this collection was *Transition* (fig. 6.32) which, unlike the other four *Chronology* upholsteries, was of all-polyester construction and could be used in myriad ways—as upholstery, drapery, panel, or wallcovering. It is based on a variation of twill construction with fancy twist and slub yarns that create a monochromatic, textured textile reminiscent of the irregularities of natural woven silk.[74] Barnes also worked with a Japanese mill to weave *Transition*, which has proved its worth as upholstery as well as in vertical applications—it remains in the Knoll collection in 2011, nearly twenty years later. Barnes received a NeoCon Gold Award in 1992 for the *Chronology Collection*.

Corporate Change and KnollTextiles, 1990–97

In the summer of 1990 Westinghouse Electric Corporation purchased Knoll International from Marshall Cogan, ushering in a new era for the company.[75] Before the acquisition, Westinghouse also purchased the office furniture manufacturers Shaw-Walker Company and Reff Inc., merging the three companies into "the Knoll Group," the third largest office furniture manufacturer in the United States after Steelcase and Herman Miller.[76] The new corporate owner soon made a major change in KnollTextiles, closing the European division in 1991 for reasons that remain unclear.[77] While details of all the textiles sold by the European division during the 1980s have yet to be completely discovered, this division remained successful throughout the decade, and its shuttering came as a shock to most European employees and many customers. After this time, textiles were not completely absent from Knoll offerings in Europe, but the focus was on furniture sales, and upholstery was only offered as it related to furniture. One longtime sales manager, J. Christoph Brunzli, purchased the rights to continue manufacturing and selling Knoll's European curtain fabrics through his newly founded company Alato (1991).[78] In the United States curtain fabrics were discontinued in 1991 but returned to Knoll offerings in 1998.[79]

The next several years at KnollTextiles under new ownership were tumultuous ones in terms of leadership. While the company continued to introduce large numbers of upholsteries, panel fabrics, and wallcoverings at regular intervals, the design leadership in the division changed four times in as many years. At the end of 1992, Hazel Siegel left the company because Westinghouse's new emphasis on profits did not match her own goals as design director.[80] In her absence staff designer Suzin Steerman, who Siegel had worked with at Designtex and hired to develop custom textiles, was named "Senior Designer for all product developments" at KnollTextiles, but no new creative director was hired for the division.[81] In February 1995 Deborah Steele was named vice president of marketing and design for KnollTextiles, but she left after little more than a year.[82] By early 1993, Westinghouse had failed to reap the immediate windfall of profits the coporation hoped for from its new Knoll division. Instead it found itself struggling with the many difficulties of managing its large and varied business interests, which included other manufacturing divisions, as well as broadcasting interests. It made the decision to sell the Knoll Group.[83] At the end of 1995 Warburg Pincus Ventures, a leading private equity firm, became the new owner of the Knoll Group.[84] The company, renamed Knoll, Inc., was to be led by a team of managers including Andrew Cogan, son of Marshall Cogan. He had been Knoll's senior vice president of marketing and product development at the time of the sale and was made CEO of the company in 2001.[85] By late 1996 Suzanne Tick, who had been designing textiles for the company since 1995, took a leadership position and was officially named creative director of KnollTextiles in February 1997.[86]

Despite the unsettled design direction and management during this period, the textile division at Knoll established a new area of focus in 1992—textiles for healthcare applications.[87] In that year Siegel and Steerman began to develop custom textiles for a new hospital in Virginia. These textiles, including Siegel's *Sensu*, entered the general line, and in 1993 KnollTextiles initiated a formal collection of healthcare textiles. Knoll called on Jhane Barnes to create a group of eight fabrics dubbed the *Horizon Collection*, to be used for room curtaining in healthcare facilities. Introduced in December 1993, the fabrics were made with Trevira polyester, which is inherently fire-resistant, and featured small- to medium-scale patterning in a range of neutral and pastel colors.[88] Two of these, *Building Blocks* and *Circle Squared*, featured geometric motifs suggested by their names, while other fabrics—*Animal Magnetism*, *Clambake*, *Mum's the Word*, *Room with a View*, *School of Thought*, and *Stripes Forever*—featured animal, shell, and floral decoration that was geared toward a wide range of healthcare applications such as in children's wards at hospitals.[89] Barnes recently recalled that the collection was not very successful initially, but Knoll continued to expand in this new area, and many of the Barnes designs remained in the collection for a decade.[90] In May 1994 KnollTextiles introduced seven new "cubicle" curtains, as these drapery fabrics are informally known, to the *Horizon Collection*, four of which were designed by Steerman.[91] They featured abstract or geometric patterning, except for *Sunrise, Star, Cloud* which had a playful celestial motif related to its name (fig. 6.33).

Healthcare fabrics remained in the line, eventually becoming one of the leading sectors at KnollTextiles.

While several outside designers, such as Tim Van Campen, Brenda Brady, and Claudine Piaget, contributed collections from 1993 through 1996, KnollTextiles relied primarily on contract designer Barnes, to make regular additions to the line, supplementing the designs by Steerman and other staff designers.[92] In these three years alone, Barnes produced more than two dozen new textiles, both upholsteries and panel fabrics, several of which won awards, while her earlier designs such as *Nuance*, a "classic" design, remained strong sellers. In 1994 *Nuance* was produced in yet another iteration—a polyester and silk version dubbed *Spinoff Nuance*—suitable for panel and upholstery applications.[93] It remained in the Knoll collection until 2010. Among her most interesting designs for Knoll in the late 1990s was a group of upholsteries and panel fabrics introduced in the autumn of 1997. The mathematicians Giuseppe Peano (1858–1932) and David Hilbert (1862–1943) inspired two of the fabric's names and motifs (fig. 6.34). Barnes, who had a keen interest in mathematics, had been using a computerized loom in her design practice since the late 1980s and in the early 1990s had collaborated with mathematicians to create special textile design programs.[94] In 1998 Barnes decided to end her fifteen-year relationship with KnollTextiles. She recently cited the company's move away from the natural fibers and high-quality fabrics she favored as a motivating factor in her decision.[95]

In 1996 and 1997 the development of Barnes textiles for Knoll had been facilitated by Nicole Casey, the niece of Barbara Rodes-Segerer (design director of KnollTextiles in the 1970s; see chapter 5). Casey had trained in the United States and Germany and worked with her aunt on her *S-Collection* textile line before becoming a design and development consultant for Knoll.[96] One of her projects at Knoll was the *Decades Collection*, released in 1997 to celebrate the fiftieth anniversary of the founding of Knoll's textile division.[97] The collection comprised five revivals from the company's archive, one from each decade: *Campagna* by Angelo Testa, *Mosaic* by Noémi Raymond, *Stones* by Wolf Bauer, *Eclat* by Anni Albers, and *Arles* by Anne Beetz.[98] In addition, Knoll featured Barnes's *Spinoff Nuance* as part of the *Decades Collection*, introducing eight new colorways. For this collection the earlier printed drapery fabrics (*Campagna*, *Mosaic*, *Stones*, and *Eclat*) were translated into machine-woven upholsteries with their patterns re-created in the weave. As part of the fiftieth-anniversary celebrations the company also released a commemorative brochure titled "Five Decades," which traced the history of KnollTextiles from the 1940s onward.

A New Day: KnollTextiles and Suzanne Tick

By the mid-1990s, after the various corporate upheavals, KnollTextiles was in need of new design direction and leadership. This would come from Suzanne Tick.[99] After studying art and weaving at the University of Iowa, Tick focused on textile design at the Fashion Institute of Technology in New York.[100] In 1982 she began her professional career at Boris Kroll, becoming design director after only a few years. In 1993, after stints at two other leading firms—Brickel Associates and Unika Vaev—Tick founded her own design and consultancy firm, Suzanne Tick Inc. In early 1995 she approached Deborah Steele, then vice president of marketing and design, with a collection of upholstery fabrics she had developed and felt were appropriate for Knoll. The group, named *A New Day Collection*, was released in November 1995.[101] It consisted of six upholstery fabrics woven in cotton-rayon or polyester-viscose blends with subtle patterns, inspired by a "myriad of sources, including traditional Japanese textiles, Buddhist writings and Gregorian chants."[102] The colorways were synchronized so that the fabrics could be used in combination at the designer's discretion, and the entire collection was elegantly presented in a special sample set at its debut (fig. 6.35).

After the release of this collection, Tick continued to bring designs to Knoll. In the spring of 1996, the company introduced two panel fabrics by Tick, representing her first vertical fabrics (panel fabrics, wallcoverings, and draperies) for Knoll, a category that would become the main focus of Tick's design efforts for the company. These fabrics, *Resolution* and *Clarity*, were also Tick's first designs for the company made with innovative new materials that she had sourced—yarn that was colored through minerals dissolved in the molten polyester before it was spun, eliminating the large amount of waste and pollution that can be a byproduct of the dyeing process.[103] The materials were thus environmentally friendly, which became a major focus for Tick and KnollTextiles. The process also resulted in strong colors that were virtually lightfast and could be cleaned with bleach and other products without causing damage, unlike traditionally dyed fabrics. *Resolution* and *Clarity* (fig. 6.36) were extremely successful; profits from *Resolution* soon soared to over $1,000,000 a year.[104] Both textiles remain in the collection in 2011, fifteen years after their introduction.

Steele left Knoll in mid-1996, and in February 1997 the company announced that Suzanne Tick was to be the new design director of KnollTextiles. Tick would soon bring administrative order to the division, assuring it a strong position in the firm's sixth decade. Her first chore was to spend some time "examining the company, taking a look at what the brand stands for, and eventually [she] came

Fig. 6.32 Top left Jhane Barnes. *Transition*, 1992. Made in Japan for KnollTextiles. Used for panels and drapery; polyester; plain-weave–derived simple weave. KnollTextiles Archive. Cat. 245.

Fig. 6.33 Top right Advertisement for KnollTextiles, featuring the *Horizon Collection* by Suzin Steerman, ca. 1994. Knoll Archives.

Fig. 6.34 Bottom Jhane Barnes. *Hilbert* ("Teal" colorway), 1997. Made in the United States for KnollTextiles. Used for upholstery; cotton; plain-weave–derived compound weave. Private Collection. Cat. 247.

Fig. 6.35 Bottom Suzanne Tick. *A New Day Collection* sample kit, 1995. Made for KnollTextiles. Textile swatches, cardboard box, and various media. KnollTextiles Archive. Cat. 263.

Fig. 6.36 Top left and right Details from brochure for *Clarity* (left) and *Resolution* (right), 1996. KnollTextiles Archive.

to the conclusion that the textile collection of this progressive company was no longer up to its own standards."[105] Tick decided to implement a regular program of quarterly introductions each year to include a cohesive group of wallcovering, panel, drapery, and upholstery fabrics that could work together in an interior.[106] In the spring of 1998 Knoll presented the first installment of this program, dubbed the "Integrated Interior," with a collection of three draperies, one wallcovering, and one panel fabric, mostly designed by Tick, as well as four upholsteries, three of them by Claudine Piaget.[107] This marked the first time since 1991 that drapery fabrics had been offered by KnollTextiles. A few months later Knoll debuted another group of fabrics on the Integrated Interior model, this time including three panel fabrics (all woven from recycled polyester), three upholstery fabrics, and one "elegantly sheer drapery."[108] Perhaps the most innovative part of this collection was the drapery, *Silver Screen*, which again demonstrated Tick's innovative, ecologically aware design. It is a gossamer curtain of polyester with an aluminum film adhered to the back in a printing process. This makes the curtain an environmentally friendly solar shield, designed to deflect heat and reduce the need for air conditioning; it also provides a beautiful shimmer (see fig. B.134). Tick recently commented that one goal in bringing draperies back into the Knoll collection was to "soften the corporate interior environment."[109] *Silver Screen* is still part of the KnollTextiles collection today, among the many drapery fabrics the company has since introduced.

Environmental awareness had been growing in the United States since the 1970s, and Knoll was increasingly committed to finding ecologically friendly production methods while meeting the requirements of the contract market. Re-using nonrecyclable or biologically nondegradable materials and minimizing the consumption of raw materials, above all water, in textile manufacture became two important objectives. Fibers and yarns could be made from waste materials, such as plastic bottles, and then dyed in processes that eliminated pollutants as byproducts.[110]

One of the greatest innovations and commercial successes for KnollTextiles was Suzanne Tick's development of *Imago*. It is made through a patented process in which a textile is encased in a high-performance resin, a hard plastic in the polyester family, resulting in a transparent solid panel of "frozen fabric."[111] It was an almost immediate success. Interestingly it had actually originated from a failure.[112] Tick had developed a translucent panel fabric for an office system that was not a success, and she was left with several thousand yards of this fabric and no hopes of selling it. At the same time she was approached by Eastman Chemical Company about the possibility of Knoll using a resin they manufactured. Tick came up with the idea of embedding her fabric in Eastman's resin, and *Imago* was the result. It was released to great acclaim at NeoCon in June 2000, with an installation and promotional literature designed by the New York graphic design firm 2x4, Inc. Tick earned a NeoCon Gold Award and a Chicago Athenaeum Good Design Award for the development and design of this innovative product.[113]

Imago's continued success lies in the fact that it brings a textile dimension to a hard-surface material. It can be easily cut, bent, and drilled for a variety of installations (fig. 6.37). The level of translucency and kind of pattern is determined by the encased fabric as well as the texture that can be applied to the surface of the resin. Knoll regularly introduces new versions of *Imago*, often using drapery textiles from its general line to create these new patterns. *Metallic Mesh*, Tick's drapery released in 2001, for example, was used for an *Imago* version released as *Mirage* later the same year (cat. 270).

Tick continued to develop innovative products over the next few years, including *Foil Rap* and *Heavy Metal* (fig. 6.38), introduced at the end of 2001. These used recycled polyester in a weave with a new tape yarn that Tick developed with the mill. This tape yarn is made from extruded olefin (a type of polypropylene) which is colored with metallic pigments. The fabrics, which could be used for panels, upholstery, and wallcovering, also reflect Tick's interest in merging tradition and innovation—in this case making a traditional "grass cloth" wallcovering with new synthetic materials—to create a fresh and interesting textile.[114] Both textiles are still in the Knoll line in 2011. Tick also used the extruded Olefin tape as the basis for several later designs for Knoll.

During the first few years of Tick's tenure as creative director, KnollTextiles released only a few textiles created by outside designers. In 1998, for example, they introduced three upholsteries by the Belgian weaver Claudine Piaget, who had created a 1996 collection of panel fabrics for Knoll.[115] In 1998 and 2000 Tick revived upholstery designs by Anne Beetz from 1989, reintroducing them with new fiber contents and colorways.[116] Many textiles, however, primarily for upholsteries, were developed in-house, by staff designers who were not credited in company materials but were occasionally acknowledged when fabrics won awards or recognition by trade groups and museums.[117]

In 2002 outside designers began to play a larger role again in KnollTextiles. That year Tick began working closely with Stephen Sprouse on a full collection of fabrics, the first by an outside designer to be introduced during her tenure as design director. Knoll CEO Andrew Cogan had known Sprouse since the 1980s and had invested earlier in his fashion line.[118] He was reponsible for bringing the fashion designer and artist to the attention of Tick and KnollTextiles. The Sprouse collection made its first appearance in June 2003 at NeoCon in Chicago.[119] Four of the five fabrics featured printed decoration, marking the first time in nearly twenty years that printed fabrics were part of a KnollTextiles collection. Two of these—*Camo* and *Graffiti Camo*—could be used as either drapery or upholstery. They were printed on *Extreme Velvet*, a new Trevira polyester velvet designed by Tick and also introduced in 2003. As their names suggest, they consisted of camouflage patterns in Sprouse's signature Day-Glo colors as well as two more subdued combinations. *Camo* featured this motif on its own, while in *Graffiti Camo* it was overlaid with passages from the Declaration of Independence in Sprouse's graffiti-style script (fig. 6.39). Sprouse also reinterpreted *Cato*, the oldest pattern still in production, and called it *Techno Tweed*, using neon and metallic-tape as well as more conventional polyester yarns to create a highly durable upholstery fabric. The draperies *Digital Airwave* and *Static Screen* featured random patterns of television static printed on *Silver Screen*, Tick's sheer curtain fabric. *Techno Tweed*, *Digital Airwave*, and *Static Screen* remained in the line until 2010.

Another 2003 project involved the New York design firm 2x4, Inc., which had designed printed materials, branding, and Knoll's NeoCon installations since 1997. Tick worked with them to develop textile designs.[120] Andrew Cogan had seen a wallpaper designed by 2x4 for the Prada store in New York, and he was certain that they could turn their talents to designs for KnollTextiles.[121] The firm, headed by Michael Rock, Susan Sellers, and Georgianna Stout, contributed two collections of vinyl wallcoverings and upholstery fabrics, which were introduced in 2004: the *Field Theory Collection* and the *Chatter Collection*. The *Field Theory Collection* featured geometric patterns inspired by overhead views of architecture and town planning. *Suburban*, a woven upholstery, had a small-scale motif; *Urban*, another upholstery, a large-scale motif (it was printed on *Una*, a Tick stretch upholstery); while the wallcovering *Exurban* had a mid-sized motif. The *Chatter Collection* was inspired by the stream of online communication that has become part of everyday life. It included one upholstery—*Plus*, a woven featuring a small-scale motif of plus signs—and two wallcoverings: *Command* and *Pause*, both of which were based on punctuation marks. *Pause* consists of large-scale commas and periods, while *Command* was a smaller-scale motif of vertical lines and exclamation points. *Plus* and *Pause* remain part of the KnollTextiles collection in 2011, and *Pause* was used by Knoll in its new showroom and offices in New York City, which opened in the former Port Authority Building at 76 Ninth Avenue in 2004 (fig. 6.40). Both 2x4 collections embraced graphic motifs in bright colors, recalling the bold graphics that Massimo Vignelli had created for Knoll in the 1970s.

At the end of 2004 Suzanne Tick resigned from her position as creative director, citing a need to "design more and manage less."[122] Since that time she has continued to design for KnollTextiles, remaining focused on innovative products and utilizing new materials and processes in order to create both upholsteries and the vertical products (draperies, panel fabrics, and wallcoverings) which have become her specialty at the company. Two of her recent designs, *Air Rights* and *Bandwidth*, demonstrate her ongoing design explorations, particularly her interest in the contemporary trend in architecture to expose the skeletal structure of buildings.[123] *Bandwidth* (fig. 6.41), a panel fabric woven from recycled polyester, was introduced at NeoCon in June 2008 and won a NeoCon Gold Award. Its weave structure inspired the printed and burn-out decoration of *Air Rights*, Tick's sheer drapery fabric (fig. 6.42), released in 2009 and also a NeoCon Gold winner.

Fashion Forward and Reflecting Back: KnollTextiles and Dorothy Cosonas

By the spring of 2005 Dorothy Cosonas had been named successor to Suzanne Tick as creative director of KnollTextiles. Like Tick, she had trained at the Fashion Institute of Technology in New York, focusing on textile design and art. Beginning in 1984 she worked for the leading textile firm Unika Vaev, becoming design director in 1994 and then in 1999 vice president of design, a position she held until moving to KnollTextiles. An experienced designer of upholstery fabrics, Cosonas provided work complementary to the largely vertical fabrics (draperies, panel fabrics, and wallcoverings) by Tick and other outside designers. She often draws inspiration for her work in the contract market from fashion design, where new trends are registered faster than in other design sectors.

One of the first introductions overseen by Cosonas was by an outside designer, Abbott Miller of the design firm Pentagram. David Schutte, then vice president and general manager of KnollTextiles, had contacted Miller about making designs for Knoll, and subsequently Miller created a group of vinyl wallcoverings that debuted in January 2006. The *Grammar Collection* takes its name from *The Grammar of Ornament*, a renowned nineteenth-century pattern sourcebook by Owen Jones.[124] However, instead of drawing on the many ornamental styles contained in Jones's compendium, Miller used typographic compositions as ornament. Both *Merge* and *Filter* employed overlapping type, while *Switch* used repetitions of the letter "I." These bold, graphic patterns are still produced in 2011 and are available in a range of colorways.

Cosonas and Schutte initiated a similar collaboration with the New York architectural firm Lewis.Tsurumaki.Lewis, or LTL, and the resulting *Parallel Lines Collection* was presented in June 2006.[125] It consisted of three vinyl wallcoverings, *Margin*, *Vector*, and *Perimeter*. The printed patterns were based on pencil drawings that were scanned, duplicated digitally, and arranged in linear patterning that has a textural appeal when viewed from a distance (fig. 6.43).

When Cosonas's own first collection for KnollTextiles was released in March 2006, Knoll's promotional materials

Fig. 6.37 *Imago* installed in the Surgical Pavilion, University of Washington Medical Center, designed by Keating Khang Architecture, 2004. Photographed by John Edwards. KnollTextiles.

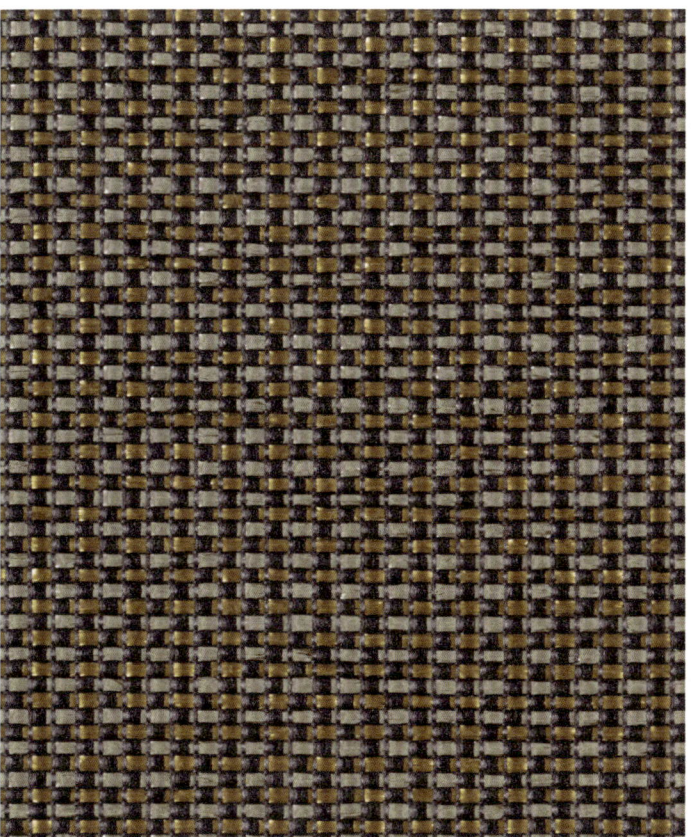

Fig. 6.38 Top left Suzanne Tick. *Heavy Metal* ("Brass Rubbing" colorway), introduced 2001. Made in the United States for KnollTextiles. Used for panel and upholstery; recycled polyester and Olefin; plain-weave–derived compound weave. KnollTextiles. Cat. 266.

Fig. 6.39 Top right Stephen Sprouse. *Graffiti Camo* ("Glo" colorway), ca. 2003. Made in the United States for KnollTextiles. Used for upholstery and drapery; Trevira CS polyester velvet; digitally printed. KnollTextiles Archive. Cat. 274.

Fig. 6.40 Bottom 2×4, Inc. *Pause* ("Orange" colorway) installed in conference room at Knoll Inc., New York City, in 2004. Photographed in 2011.

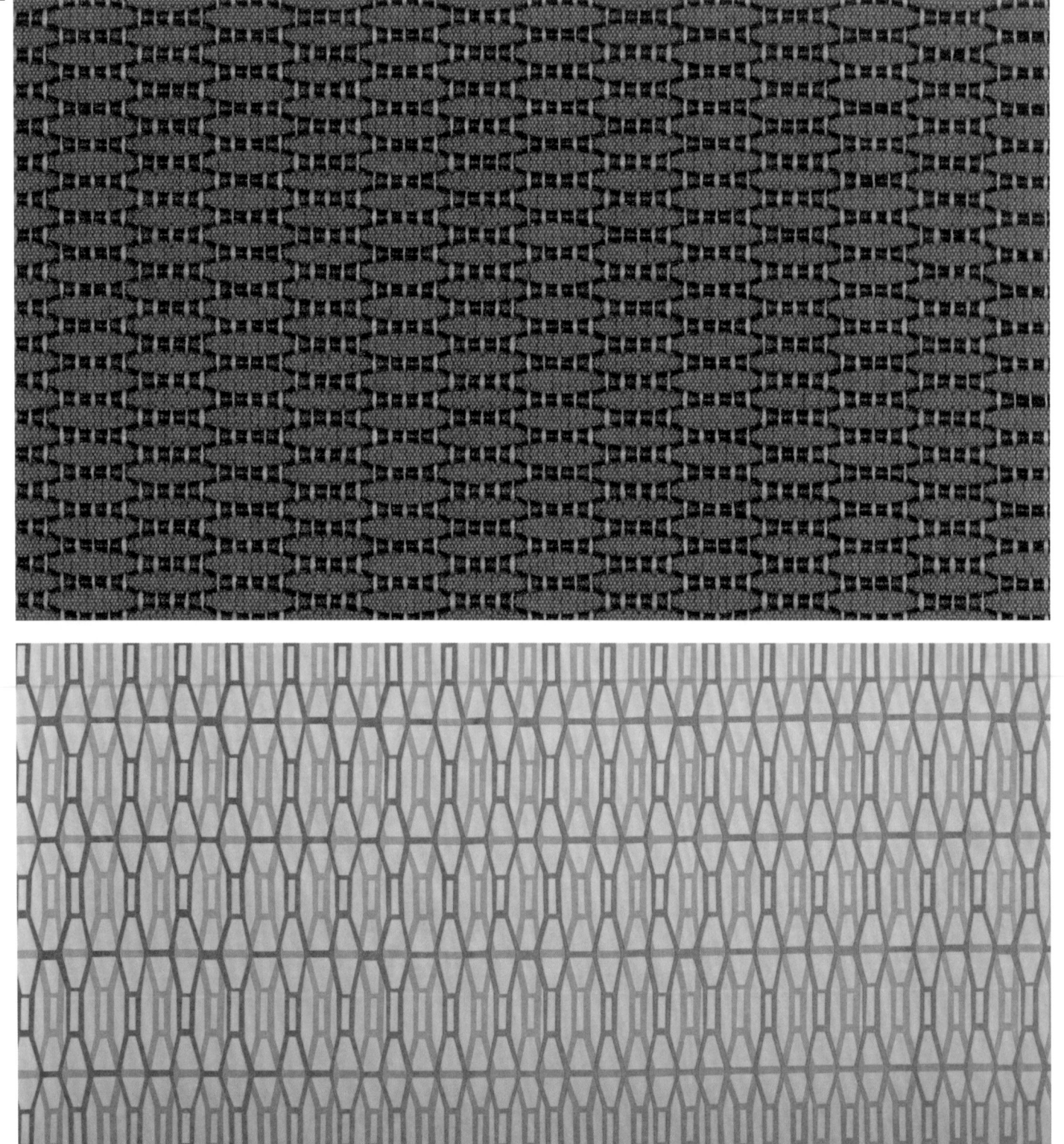

Fig. 6.41 Top Suzanne Tick. *Bandwidth* ("Current" colorway), introduced 2008. Made in the United States for KnollTextiles. Used for panels; post-industrial Terratex recycled polyester; plain-weave–derived compound weave. KnollTextiles. Cat. 272.

Fig. 6.42 Bottom Suzanne Tick. *Air Rights* ("Satellite" colorway), introduced 2009. Made in Japan for KnollTextiles. Used for drapery; polyester; compound plain weave with discontinuous wefts, screen-printed. KnollTextiles. Cat. 273.

Fig. 6.43 Top left LTL. *Vector*, introduced 2006. Made in the United States for KnollTextiles. Used for wallcovering; vinyl. KnollTextiles.

Fig. 6.44 Top right Dorothy Cosonas. Spring 2006 collection, from top: *Icon*, *Coco*, *Cross Stitch*, *Empire Stripe*, and *English Accent*. KnollTextiles.

Fig. 6.45 Bottom left Dorothy Cosonas. *Rivington* samples, introduced 2007. Made in Belgium for KnollTextiles. Used for upholstery; wool, cotton, acrylic, and polyester; plain-weave–derived simple weave. KnollTextiles. Cat. 283.

Fig. 6.46 Bottom right Dorothy Cosonas. *Harrison* samples ("Fulton" colorway), introduced 2007. Made in the United Kingdom for KnollTextiles. Used for upholstery; wool, nylon; plain weave with quadrupled warps and wefts. KnollTextiles. Cat. 282.

Fig. 6.47 Top Dorothy Cosonas. *Courtship* ("Windswept" colorway), introduced 2010. Made in Germany for KnollTextiles. Used for drapery; Trevira polyester; plain weave. KnollTextiles. Cat. 287.

Fig. 6.48 Bottom *Archival Collection* introduction featuring *Mira Sheer*, June 2007. KnollTextiles.

Fig. 6.49 Top Dorothy Cosonas. *Dorothy Cosonas Collection* for Knoll Luxe as installed in the Knoll showroom, New York, including *Galloway* (top row, second from left), *Bavaria* (bottom row, left), and *Jaipur* (second row, left); introduced 2008. KnollTextiles.

Fig. 6.50 Bottom left Proenza Schouler (Jack McCollough and Lazaro Hernandez). *Sandis* ("Caramel" colorway), introduced 2008. Made in the United States for Knoll Luxe. Used for upholstery; linen and cotton; plain-weave–derived compound weave. KnollTextiles. Cat. 295.

fig. 6.51 Bottom right Rodarte (Kate and Laura Mulleavy). *Cummings* ("Shadow" colorway), introduced 2010. Made in the United States for Knoll Luxe. Used for upholstery; cotton and silk; plain-weave–derived compound weave. KnollTextiles. Cat. 298.

outlined her strengths: "The collection showcased her expertise in upholstery—she uses clean, clear color combinations and presents a modern twist on classic motifs and textures. Dorothy uses color to draw the collection together—and to tie in past and future products."[126] Not surprisingly, she aimed for fabrics with classic patterns in the Knoll tradition, and her first collection included examples that lived up to that standard: *Coco*, *Cross Stitch*, *Empire Stripe*, *Icon*, and *English Accent* (fig. 6.44). This group is also exemplary of Cosonas's effort to provide a range of upholstery types in each of her collections—usually a soft textured fabric, a plain fabric, a striped fabric, and a patterned weave—which might be used together in a room. While machine-woven, *Coco* remains well within Knoll's handwoven traditions with the soft texture of its rayon chenille weave, inspired by a classic Chanel suit fabric. *Cross Stitch* and *English Accent* were based on men's suiting or traditional plaids and offered basic motifs. *Empire Stripe*, although reminiscent of a traditional striped fabric, is modern and bold in its color and the various sizing of its stripes. *Icon* was said to be "the signature upholstery pattern in the collection." Its design was inspired by another trend from the world of fashion, namely the use of embroidery and decoration based on "ethnic" motifs.[127] *Icon* was a design departure for Knoll, bringing a new type of motif into the collection that Cosonas would build upon.

Cosonas won the NeoCon Gold Award for 2006 with her first Knoll collection.[128] Since then she has contributed a new collection each year and has overseen the release of new products six times a year. One of her most successful patterns, the upholstery *Rivington*, introduced in 2007, was inspired by the work of textile designer Bernat Klein, who worked primarily in Scotland from the 1940s through 1970s, supplying colorful woven tweeds incorporating many types of fibers to the fashion industry.[129] In *Rivington*, Cosonas translated the various textures and colors found in Klein's work into a wool-cotton-acrylic upholstery that uses space-dyed slubby yarns to create a textural effect (fig. 6.45). *Harrison*, another upholstery that debuted with *Rivington* in the spring of 2007, demonstrates Cosonas's effort to provide basic fabrics to coordinate with other parts of the collection (fig. 6.46). With its regular gridded motif created through a plain weave, *Harrison* is reminiscent of mainstays in the Knoll line from the 1950s through the 1970s such as *Prestini* and *Lana*. While upholsteries formed the main part of Cosonas's work for Knoll, she has contributed several drapery fabrics to the collection as well, including "privacy curtains" intended for healthcare facilities. While most of these have patterned decorations, in her 2010 drapery *Courtship* (fig. 6.47), she used a selection of yarn weights and textures to create visual interest.

In 2007 KnollTextiles celebrated the sixtieth anniversary of its founding. To mark this milestone, the company published *KnollTextiles: Sixty Years of Modern Design*, tracing the history of the textile division. Knoll also introduced the first patterns in their *Archival Collection*, textiles based on the company's extensive archive. Commenting on the introduction of the collection, Cosonas said, "One of my goals is to rediscover the past, what Florence Knoll started, and to expand our language of design but really keep it consistent with the company's heritage."[130] In evaluating archival fabrics for revival, Cosonas often considers how to reinterpret them to meet the requirements of the contract customers who largely comprise KnollTextiles' clientele. For the first *Archival Collection* fabrics, launched at NeoCon in 2007, for example, Cosonas transformed two printed draperies—Anni Albers's *Eclat* (1976) and Eszter Haraszty's *Fibra* (1953)—into woven upholsteries. She has also used the *Archival Collection* as a way to introduce a variety of drapery fabrics into the line. In the first collection, for example, the drapery *Mira Sheer* (fig. 6.48) was a revival of *Mira* (1958) by Ross Littell (see chapter 3). The original had been printed on a heavy slubby linen while *Mira Sheer*, as the name suggests, is printed on diaphanous polyester. Two years later, for Wolf Bauer's *Nova*, a medium-weight cotton of the late 1960s, Cosonas printed a sheer version on fire-retardant polyester.

In 2008 Knoll introduced Knoll Luxe, a separate brand dedicated to fabrics geared to a high-end clientele, using luxurious fibers and pursuing a "fashion-forward modern aesthetic."[131] The first Knoll Luxe collection, presented in March 2008, featured a group of upholstery fabrics by Cosonas (fig. 6.49). *Galloway* (cat. 293), a wool-and-cashmere, striped plain weave, was reminiscent of some of the men's suiting fabrics originally used by Florence Knoll as upholstery in the mid-1940s (see fig. 2.15). *Bavaria*, a weave combining four types of fiber into a colorful textured mix, again underlines Cosonas's fashion-derived inspiration, as does *Jaipur*, a cotton-polyester fabric with embroidery applied in India by artisans using hand-guided machines. In 2008 this collection won her the NeoCon Gold Award for upholstery.[132]

Knoll Luxe, which has its own logo, branding, and link on the Knoll Web site, is promoted separately from the general KnollTextiles line. Since the spring 2008 presentation, Cosonas has engaged outside designers to create collections for the brand, and not surprisingly the first two came from the world of fashion. She characterized her choices as typical of Knoll's long history of commitment "to supporting top American designers."[133] She values the fresh perspective brought by these designers with whom she works closely to meet the challenge of translating fashion textiles into products for use on furniture and windows. In November 2008 Knoll launched a collection of six upholstery fabrics by Proenza Schouler, the youthful design house headed by Jack McCollough and Lazaro Hernandez.[134] The collection was based on details and fabrics from their fashion work, reflecting their signature "nonchalant luxury."[135] Two of these upholsteries featured large-scale patterning in motifs more traditional than those usually seen in the Knoll collection. *Sandis* (fig. 6.50) features a *faux bois*, or woodgrain, pattern in a cotton-linen blend said to be inspired by the animal prints in Proenza Schouler's Spring 2008 fashion collection, while the linen and silk pattern *Mepal* is based, in the broadest sense, on historical pomegranate patterns (see fig. B.98) and was inspired by the fashion house's use of similar patterning on a coat in their Fall 2007 collection.

For the next Knoll Luxe collection, Cosonas engaged Kate and Laura Mulleavy, the sisters behind the fashion label Rodarte. Introduced in the spring of 2010, the *Rodarte Collection* consists of innovative draperies and upholstery fabrics based on the Mulleavys' avant-garde fashion designs, with names derived from the sisters' favorite poets. The five upholstery fabrics include *Cummings* (fig. 6.51), a cotton-and-silk blend that features an abstracted large-scale repeat that plays with the shiny and matte characteristics of the fibers. *Whitman* uses a large-scale twisted yarn in the weft to create a highly textural surface (fig. 6.52). Another upholstery, *Byron*, gets its extraordinary texture from an acrylic yarn that shrinks during the finishing of the fabric to create unique puckering. The line's three casements are also remarkable. The sheer drapery *Emerson* is embroidered with a regular grid of dots created with metallic rayon thread. For *Auden* the designers made sophisticated use of graduated color digitally printed on ramie- and polyester open weave (see page 269). These decidedly new and different designs help to keep Knoll on the cutting edge of the textile industry, but they also present something of a challenge for a contract market unaccustomed to this aesthetic. Cosonas and Rodarte, however, received the NeoCon Gold Award for the collection in June 2010.[136]

Much has changed in the world of textiles and textile design since 1947 when Knoll's textile division came into existence. From the fledgling department born of necessity—to supply appropriate textiles for the modern furniture and interiors Florence and Hans Knoll were producing—KnollTextiles has become one of the leading contract textile suppliers in the world. Growth has been exponential. The first line in 1947 comprised fewer than thirty upholstery and drapery fabrics. By 2011 the KnollTextiles collection had expanded to include about three hundred offerings in six major categories: wallcovering, *Imago*, panel fabrics, healthcare textiles, upholstery, and drapery. The pace of new introductions has also quickened over the years. In the early years the company made introductions of new designs once or twice a year. By the 1990s there were four collection introductions each year, rising in the new millenium, under Dorothy Cosonas, to at least six groups of multiple fabrics being introduced annually.

Despite Knoll's growth and many corporate changes over the decades, KnollTextiles has also maintained a tradition of extraordinary continuity. The company's designers pursue new and innovative materials and methods with the same fervor shown by Florence and Hans Knoll when they introduced Saran plastic upholsteries in 1946 and 1947. The Knoll Luxe line of the twenty-first century can trace its origins to the principles of presenting superior, luxury materials, represented in the early days by Marianne Strengell's exquisite handwovens that were part of the first collection. Market practice has always required the range to be variable, diverse, and comprehensive, and Knoll has made a practice of being in the vanguard of change. In recent years its new luxury collections, created in collaboration with celebrated fashion designers, have won awards and garnered widespread media attention. While this attention is important, Knoll's commercial success actually rests on its fabrics and materials for hospitals, administration buildings, and office furnishings—the miles of curtains, upholsteries, and wall and panel coverings of everyday life. Yet the two directions—commercial and creative—work hand in hand. Part of Knoll's success can be attributed to the stellar reputation earned by the luxury collections but enjoyed by the entire division.

Behind the scenes, close cooperation between executive, marketing, sales, production, and design has been crucial to maintaining the quality of Knoll's products—and thus its reputation. At the end of the day, market success depends on a satisfied clientele, and Knoll has continually demonstrated its ability to meet the demands of innovative design, high quality, and profit. In nurturing this reputation, Knoll remains committed to developing new products—from furnishings to fabric—linked to prominent designers and artists. These artists, past and present, have consistently shown great respect for the company's history and for its determination to uphold the standards set by Florence and Hans Knoll, whose vision of the company remains as KnollTextiles moves forward.

Fig. 6.52 Rodarte (Kate and Laura Mulleavy). *Whitman* ("Teak" colorway) on a *Womb* chair and ottoman designed by Eero Saarinen, introduced 2010. Upholstery: made in the United States for KnollTextiles; chair and ottoman: made by Knoll, Inc. Upholstery: wool, viscose, nylon; plain-weave–derived compound weave; chair and ottoman: fiberglass shell, plywood, urethane foam, polyester fiber, stainless steel. KnollTextiles.

1 Marshall S. Cogan and Stephen C. Swid, "Bulletin to All Knoll Employees," September 1, 1977, Marshall Cogan file, Knoll Archives.
2 Information in this section is taken from Arthur Sager, interview with Earl Martin, October 13, 2010.
3 Kristl Reinhardt Andrus, interview with Earl Martin, September 16, 2010; Richard Wagner, email to Earl Martin, September 9, 2010.
4 See Peter Seipelt in "Designer Biographies," in this volume.
5 "From Knoll: Furniture and Fabrics for the Residential Market," *Interior Design* (October 1977): 120; "Knoll International Makes a Residential Statement," *Residential Interiors* (July/August 1977): 20, 31.
6 Knoll Textiles, "Price List 10/79," October 1979, pp. 24–25, KnollTextiles Archive.
7 "Fact Sheet Casement/Drapery Print Collection," 1979 introductions file, Knoll Archive.
8 Sager, interview with Martin.
9 "Nob + Non Collection 1," press release, ca. June 1979, Knoll Archives.
10 These patterns appear in the 1983 price list but had been dropped by the time the 1984 price list was published, see Knoll Textiles, "Knoll Textiles Catalogue," February 1, 1983, pp. 49–54; Knoll Textiles, "Knoll Textiles Catalogue," February 1, 1984, KnollTextiles Archive.
11 *Basket*, *Linea*, and *Zigzag* files, KnollTextiles Archive.
12 For more on this partnership see Adrian Parry in "Designer Biographies."
13 American price lists do not list Mimoglou's fabrics. They are known through European price lists and from their inclusion in museum collections (primarily European), see Hans Wichmann, *Von Morris bis Memphis: Textilien der Neuen Sammlung Ende 19. bis Ende 20. Jahrhundert* (Basel: Birkhäuser, 1990), 300, 301, 446.
14 For more information on these prints see Jürgen Reichert, Klaus Dombrowski, and Karl Vogelsang in "Designer Biographies."
15 It is not clear how long Nob + Non and Seipelt prints were in production in Europe.
16 "Complexity and Contradiction," *Interior Design* (March 1980): 226–30.
17 "Knoll International Opens New Houston Showroom," press release, January 1984, Knoll Archives.
18 Invitation to the introduction of the *Robert Venturi Collection*, May 1, 1984, Robert Venturi designer file, Knoll Archives. See also Joseph Giovanni, "Venturi, Something Borrowed, Something New," *New York Times*, June 7, 1984, C10.
19 Press release, May 1984, Robert Venturi designer file, Knoll Archives.
20 Ibid.
21 *Venturi Collection* file, KnollTextiles Archive.
22 Mel Silver, Steven Heller, and Eckhard Neumann, "Furniture Design in Congruence with Graphic Design," *Graphis*, no. 237, (May/June 1985): 41–43, 46, 48, 50–51.
23 Takaaki Matsumoto, interview with the author, January 28, 2010.
24 Unless otherwise noted, this section is based on Ursula Dayenian, memo to Knoll Textiles sales staff, ca. 1980, Knoll Archives.
25 The other firms are Arc-Com Fabrics, Inc., Gretchen Bellinger, Inc., Ward Bennett Collection, Clarence House Imports, DesignTex, Inc., Lee / Jofa, Maharam Fabrics, Inc., Herman Miller, Ben Rose, Inc., Scalamandre, Inc., and Sunar, Inc.
26 In 1973 Bellinger was cited as a "recently joined" manager, Textile Development USA; see "Knoll Textiles: The Collection," press release, December 10, 1973, KnollTextiles Archive.
27 For more information see Jhane Barnes in "Designer Biographies."
28 Richard Wagner, phone interview with Earl Martin, September 16, 2010.
29 Barnes quoted in Nurit Einik, *KnollTextiles: 60 Years of Modern Design* (New York: Knoll Inc., 2007), 29, 31.
30 Wagner, phone interview with Martin.
31 This section is based on Sager, interview with Martin; and Wagner, email to Martin, unless otherwise noted.
32 "*Diffrient Seating* Upholstery Fabric, *Desna* sample folder, KnollTextiles Archive.
33 The Diffrient collection was previewed at NeoCon in June 1979 and was available by the fall of 1979; see "Post NEOCON Wrap-Up," *Interior Design* (August 1979): 162. It is not certain when *Desna* was discontinued, but it was still in production in 1994; see Knoll Textiles, "Price List 1994," February 1994, p. 18, KnollTextiles Archive.
34 Sager, interview with Martin; Wagner, email to Martin.
35 *Interiors* magazine characterized it this way: "Knoll International announces its entry into the wallcovering market with Furrows"; see "New Introductions," *Interiors* (October 1981): 58.
36 This section is based on Sager, interview with Martin; Wagner, email to Martin.
37 Knoll Textiles, "Catalogue March 1982," March 1, 1982, p. 55, KnollTextiles Archive.
38 Sager, interview with Martin. *Furrows* was offered by Knoll until the mid-1990s.
39 This section is based on Merle Lindby-Young, phone interview with Ann Marguerite Tartsinis, August 25, 2010; and Merle Lindby-Young, email to Ann Marguerite Tartsinis, September 13, 2010, unless otherwise noted.
40 Wagner, email to Martin.
41 This section is based on Knoll Textiles, "Catalog March 1985," March 1, 1985, pp. 39–42, KnollTextiles Archive.
42 Knoll Textiles "Summer 1986 New Introductions," supplement to price list, KnollTextiles Archive.
43 Advertisement for Knoll Textiles (tearsheet), 1987, Knoll Archives.
44 Ibid. The series was developed in full collaboration with the mill, yarn supplier, and yarn spinning company; Lindby-Young, email to Tartsinis. "SRB" stood for "super retardant bright."
45 Knoll Textiles, "Catalog 1987/1988," June 1, 1987, KnollTextiles Archive.
46 This section is based on "Vertical Variations Wave New Possibilities for Panels, Wallcoverings and Windows," press release, October 6, 1988, Jhane Barnes file, KnollTextiles Archive; and Knoll Textiles, "Price Catalogue 1989/90," June 1, 1989, pp. 59–68, KnollTextiles Archive.
47 "Knoll Textiles Celebrates the Art of Weaving with the Dana Romeis Collection," press release, October 1985, Dana Romeis file, KnollTextiles archives.
48 This section is based on ibid.; and Victoria Geibel, "By Design," *Metropolis* (April 1986): 49–50.
49 These manufacturers are recorded on an annotated price list formerly belonging to Hazel Siegel, see KnollTextiles, "Price List

1988," June 1, 1988, pp. 10, 24–26, 30; KnollTextiles Archive.
50 After leaving Knoll, Lindby-Young founded her own design and development company, Merle Lindby-Young Associates, and provided project management from design to market introduction for a number of high profile clients including Steelcase, Stratford Hall Textiles, Pergo Flooring, and US Gypsom Corporation. She has won several major industry awards for her work. Since 2006 this firm has been known as design[2]. Lindby-Young currently lives and works in Bartonville, Texas.
51 "Dana Romeis Brings Whimsy to Tradition With New Collection for KnollTextiles," press release, May 18, 1988, Dana Romeis file, Knoll Archives.
52 "Jhane Barnes Explores New Dimensions for KnollTextiles," press release, May 23, 1989, Jhane Barnes file, KnollTextiles Archive.
53 Jhane Barnes, interview with the author, February 2, 2010.
54 "Jhane Barnes Explores New Dimensions for KnollTextiles," press release, May 23, 1989, Jhane Barnes file, KnollTextiles Archive.
55 "Neutral Colors, Unusual Weaves Characterize Anne Beetz Collection for KnollTextiles," press release, August 22, 1989, *Anne Beetz Collection* file, KnollTextiles Archive. The upholsteries were *Arles*, *Beaumont*, *Luberon*, *Montserrat*, *Panier*, *Passerelle*, *Raie*, *Tokay*; the wallcoverings, *Chevillon* and *Ghent*; and the textiles that could be used for both wallcovering and panel covering were *Champagne* and *Deauville*.
56 Brian Lutz, *Knoll: A Modernist Universe* (New York: Rizzoli, 2010), 87.
57 Cogan quoted in Michael Wagner, "Getting Out in Front," *Interiors* (August 1990): 74.
58 Sager, interview with Martin.
59 "Hazel Siegel Joins KnollTextiles as Design Director," press release, April 3, 1989, Hazel Siegel file, Knoll Archives.
60 E. D. Smith, "Hazel Siegel's First Collection for Knoll Reveals 33 Inspired Patterns Created in Just 10 Months," *Contract* (March 1990), reprint, Hazel Siegel designer file, Knoll Archives.
61 "Hazel Siegel Textile Collection Perpetuates Knoll Legacy and Modernism in the 1990s," press release, March 21, 1990, *Hazel Siegel Collection* file, KnollTextiles Archive.
62 Ibid.
63 Introduction in "Hazel Siegel Upholstery Collection," March 1990, *Hazel Siegel Collection* file, KnollTextiles Archive.
64 For more details on these patterns and their dates of manufacture see Hazel Siegel in "Designer Biographies."
65 "Hazel Siegel Translates Paul Klee Paintings Into Textile Collection," press release, March 21, 1990, *Hazel Siegel Collection* file, KnollTextiles Archive.
66 Jean Gorman, "Maverick Material," *Interiors* (August 1991): 68.
67 "World Renowned Architect Peter Eisenman Ventures into New Medium for KnollTextiles," press release, May 23, 1991, Peter Eisenman file, Knoll Archives.
68 Barnes, interview with the author. For more on Barnes's textiles from this period see Jhane Barnes in "Designer Biographies."
69 "NeoCon Introductions: Jhane Barnes 'Constructions' Wallcovering Collection,"
June 1992, *Constructions Collection* file, KnollTextiles Archive. In 2011 the nonwoven wallcoverings consist primarily of printed vinyls.
70 The patterns were given names suggestive of their materials or motifs: *Woodwork*, *Paperwork*, *Artwork*, *Marblework*, *Fretwork*, *Quoinwork*, and *Stonework*.
71 Barnes, interview with the author.
72 "Jhane Barnes 'Chronology Collection,'" October 1992, *Chronology Collection* file, KnollTextiles Archive. The four wool and wool-blend upholsteries were *Continuum*, *Era*, *Infinity*, and *Lineage*.
73 Ibid. See also Marilyn Zelinsky, "A Knoll Heritage," *Interiors* (January 1993): 30.
74 Barnes, interview with the author.
75 "Knoll Being Sold to Westinghouse," *New York Times*, July 27, 1990, D3. See also Lutz, *Knoll*, 88.
76 Lutz, *Knoll*, 88.
77 This section is based on Peter Seipelt, interview with Ann Marguerite Tartsinis, October 5, 2010; J. Christoph Brunzli, former sales manager for KnollTextiles in Europe, interview with Ann Marguerite Tartsinis, October 20, 2010; see also Alato Collection Web site, www.alato.ch/Ueber_uns.
78 Ibid.
79 Drapery fabrics were listed in 1990 price list but had disappeared from the list by 1991; see KnollTextiles, "Price Catalogue 1990/91," March 12, 1990, pp. 71–73, KnollTextiles Archive; KnollTextiles, "Price Catalogue 1991/92," February 1991, KnollTextiles Archive. For their reintroduction see "Spring Collection Fabric Introductions," April 1998, KnollTextiles Archive.
80 Hazel Siegel, phone interview with Ann Marguerite Tartsinis, November 15, 2010.
81 Mary Schoeser, ed., *International Textile Design* (New York: John Wiley & Sons, 1995), 185.
82 "KnollTextiles Appoints Deborah Steele," press release, Deborah Steele file, Knoll Archives.
83 Lutz, Knoll, 88; "Westinghouse Rearranges Structure of Its Top Ranks," *New York Times*, February 20, 1993, p. 35.
84 "Westinghouse to Sell Knoll Group to Pare Debt," *New York Times*, December 22, 1995, D3.
85 Lutz, *Knoll*, 88.
86 Suzanne Tick, phone interview with Ann Marguerite Tartsinis, February 7, 2011; "Suzanne Tick Is New Creative Director for KnollTextiles," press release, February 13, 1997, Suzanne Tick file, Knoll Archives.
87 Justin Henderson, "Building Fabric," *Interiors* (August 1992): 54–55.
88 "Jhane Barnes 'Horizon' Collection Healthcare Fabric, December 1993" file, KnollTextiles Archive.
89 Barnes, interview with the author.
90 Ibid.
91 "Cubicles—The Horizon Collection, May 1994" file, KnollTextiles Archive.
92 For more on Steerman, Van Campen, Brady, Piaget, and their designs see "Designer Biographies."
93 "Jhane Barnes 'Mini-Series' Collection Upholstery and Panel Fabric Introductions, April 1994" file, KnollTextiles Archive.
94 For more on her interest in mathematics see Jhane Barnes in "Designer Biographies."
95 Barnes, interview with the author.
96 Nicole Casey, email correspondence with Earl Martin, October 11, 2010.
97 "Decades Collection Upholstery Fabric Introductions, June 1997" file, KnollTextiles Archive.
98 Ironically, the introduction dates of several *Decades Collection* textiles were incorrectly identified by the company.
99 This section is based on Suzanne Tick, interview with the author, February 4, 2010; and Suzanne Tick, phone interview with Ann Marguerite Tartsinis, February 7, 2011.
100 This section is based on "What Makes Suzanne Tick," *Azure* (September/October 1991): 93 and Suzanne Tick, curriculum vitae, mailed to Earl Martin, February 22, 2011.
101 "KnollTextiles Presents a New Day Collection by Suzanne Tick," press release, November 21, 1995, Suzanne Tick file, KnollTextiles Archive.
102 Tick quoted in ibid.
103 This section is based on "Resolution and Clarity by Suzanne Tick, Vertical Fabric Introduction," Spring 1996, KnollTextiles Archive.
104 Tick, interview with the author.
105 "What Makes Suzanne Tick," 94.
106 This section is based on Suzanne Tick, phone interview with Ann Marguerite Tartsinis, February 15, 2011; "Spring Collection Fabric Introductions, April 1988" file, KnollTextiles Archive.
107 Ibid.
108 "NeoCon Collection Fabric Introductions, June 1998" file, KnollTextiles Archive.
109 Tick, interview with the author.
110 In 1976 Knoll appointed an environmental engineer and introduced a recycling agenda into its production, especially in furniture. In 1996 some panel fabrics were made of "100% producer-colored polyester fibers"; in 1997 Terratex materials were made completely of plastic from discarded bottles. It has been Knoll's goal since 2001 to label all products with a GREENGUARD certificate.
111 "Fabrication Techniques KnollTextiles Imago," August 2000, *Imago* file, KnollTextiles Archive.
112 This section is drawn from Tick, interview with the author.
113 *Imago* file, KnollTextiles Archive.
114 Introduction materials for these textiles described them as "technical grass cloths," see "Winter 2001 Fabric Preview: Foil Rap, Heavy Metal" file, KnollTextiles Archive.
115 "Spring Collection Fabric Introductions, April 1988" file, KnollTextiles Archive.
116 The first was *Tokay II*, originally cotton and polyester, revised to be all-polyester ("NeoCon Collection, Fabric Introductions, June 1998" file, KnollTextiles Archive). The second was *Panier II*, originally all linen, revised to all cotton ("January 2000 Fabric Introductions" file, KnollTextiles Archive).
117 Two staff designers, Kathrin Hagge and Sarah Baker, won several awards of recognition; for more on their work see "Designer Biographies."
118 For more on Sprouse see "Designer Biographies."
119 "Stephen Sprouse 2003 Fabric Introductions" file, KnollTextiles Archive.
120 For more on 2x4, Inc. see "Designer Biographies."
121 Tick, phone interview with Tartsinis.
122 Suzanne Tick, "A New New Day," announcement to KnollTextiles staff, December 2004, Suzanne Tick file, KnollTextiles Archive.
123 Tick, interview with the author.
124 "January 2006 Introductions" file, KnollTextiles Archive.
125 "June 2006 Introductions" file, KnollTextiles Archive.
126 "March 2006 Introductions Presentation Strategy" file, March 8, 2006, p. 9, KnollTextiles Archive.
127 "Icon" at KnollTextiles Web site, www.knolltextiles.com.
128 "March 2006 Introductions Presentation Strategy" file, KnollTextiles Archive.
129 Search "Bernat Klein," under "Online Resources," at Scottish Textile Heritage Online, http://scottishtextileheritage.org.uk.
130 Cosonas quoted in Paul Makovsky, "Fresh from the Archives," *Metropolis* (June 2007): 151.
131 "Knoll Inaugurates Knoll Luxe: A New Brand for the Luxury Textile Market," press release, March 26, 2008, online at the Knoll Web site, www.knoll.com/news.
132 Knoll Luxe file, KnollTextiles Archive.
133 "Knoll Luxe Introduces Fall 2008 Proenza Schouler Collection," press release, November 17, 2008, online at the Knoll Web site, www.knoll.com/news.
134 The company name, Proenza Schouler, was coined from the maiden names of the designer's mothers.
135 "Knoll Luxe Introduces Fall 2008 Proenza Schouler Collection," press release, November 17, 2008, online at the Knoll Web site, www.knoll.com/news.
136 "Rodarte for Knoll Luxe Wins Gold and KnollTextiles Wins Silver in the Best of NeoCon 2010 Competition," press release, June 29, 2010, online www.knoll.com/news.

Designer Biographies

This section presents biographies of eighty-four designers known to have created textiles for Knoll since 1942. Their names were found in Knoll Textiles price lists and archival materials as well as through outside sources such as exhibitions checklists, award listings, and personal interviews. While this may be the most comprehensive assembly of Knoll Textile designers to date, it is likely that additional designers remain to be discovered. A chronological list of each designer's textiles has been included along with, where known, the date ranges of its production. Textile designs made for the United States market as well as those produced exclusively for Knoll Europe are addressed. Each biography is also accompanied by a chronological list of relevant awards and exhibitions focused primarily in the period of the designer's work with Knoll. Where identified, the colorways preserve the original wording and style from the Knoll price lists in the KnollTextile Archive. For many European educational institutions mentioned below, we have included the current English translation as identified by the institutions themselves. For further details on style and usage, see the Editor's Note on page 25.

Contributors
CMH	Caroline M. Hannah
HH	Hedvig Hedqvist
CAL	Christian A. Larsen
EM	Earl Martin
AM	Alexis Mucha
CBPP	Catherine Brooke Penaloza-Patzak
ES	Elizabeth St. George
AMT	Ann Marguerite Tartsinis
SAT	Sonya A. Topolnisky
AV	Angela Völker
SW	Susan Ward

Key to Abbreviations
intro.	introduced
disc.	discontinued
AID	American Institute of Decorators
ASID	American Society of Interior Designers
CFDA	Council of Fashion Designers
IBD	Institute of Business Designers
IIDA	International Interior Design Association
Cranbrook	Cranbrook Academy of Art, Bloomfield Hills, Michigan
MoMA	The Museum of Modern Art, New York

Eszter Haraszty. *Fibra* ("Navy, Turquoise, Emerald, and Royal on White" colorway), introduced 1953. Made by Printex for Knoll Textiles. Used for drapery; linen; plain weave; screen-printed. Andy Lin and Larry Weinberg. Cat. 52.

Fig. B.1 Adrian Parry (Adrian Pulfer and Parry Merkley). *Channel II* sample ("Sandbeige" colorway), 1982. Made by New London Textile Print Works for Knoll Textiles. Used for drapery; cotton; plain weave, screen-printed Teflon glaze. KnollTextiles Archive.

Fig. B.2 Adrian Parry (Adrian Pulfer and Parry Merkley). *Network* sample ("Sage" colorway), 1982. Made by New London Textile Print Works for Knoll Textiles. Used for drapery; cotton; plain weave, screen-printed Teflon glaze. KnollTextiles Archive.

Fig. B.3 Anni Albers and Jack Flynn (manager, national textile sales, Knoll Textiles) examining *Eclat*, 1976. Knoll Archives.

Adrian Parry (1978–1983)
Adrian Pulfer (b. 1950)
Parry Merkley (b. 1951)

Graphic designers Adrian Pulfer and Parry Merkley became interested in working for Knoll after reading a magazine article on Nob and Non Utsumi's designs for Knoll Textiles and recognizing a shared aesthetic sensibility.[1] Although neither Pulfer nor Merkley had prior experience designing textiles, they contacted Knoll and in 1982 were awarded a contract to design a collection of printed textiles.

Pulfer and Merkley met in the early 1970s as students at Brigham Young University in Provo, Utah, and began collaborating on architectural signage, advertising, and corporate-identity projects under the name Two's Company, which they changed to Adrian Parry in 1978. Their design strengths were complementary—American-born Merkley had studied illustration and gravitated toward a freer use of line, while Australian-born Pulfer was trained in graphic design and preferred much tighter compositional arrangements.

After contacting Knoll, Pulfer and Merkley were soon working on a design series. Richard Wagner, design director of Knoll Textiles at the time, was searching for innovative new designers to expand Knoll's line of printed textiles for their residential and contract markets and suggested that Pulfer and Merkley submit a design proposal for a print collection. He visited the duo in Salt Lake City and approved several prototypes that had been made by silkscreening. Wagner then commissioned them to expand their proposal with additional colorways and patterns.

Released in October 1982 as the *Adrian Parry* collection (figs. B.1, B.2), it included six patterns (see below). Each one retained the aesthetic appeal of the hand-printed prototypes. Pulfer and Merkley's simple and understated designs consisted of minimal arrangements of loosely defined lines and geometric shapes printed in bright, but soft colorways on a 100-percent cotton fabric. Their goal was to produce neutral, visually flexible patterns that would not dominate a room, but rather would serve as a backdrop for daily life and for other furnishings. Indeed, Knoll Textiles promoted the collection as filling a void for "soft-contemporary" designs that "took the edge off geometrics" and were appropriate for "the residential upholstery market . . . [as well as] hotels, motels, and restaurants."[2]

Although the *Adrian Parry* collection was their only collaboration with Knoll Textiles, Pulfer and Merkley went on to successful design careers, including producing additional lines of printed textiles in the 1980s for Schumacher, Scan Am Imports, and Federated Department Stores.[3] From 1980 to 1985, Pulfer became a design partner at Jonson, Pedersen, Hinrichs & Shakery, Inc. in New York, and in 1985 he moved back to Salt Lake City, where he established the firm Adrian Pulfer Design-A Three (A/3 Corp.) and currently teaches graphic design at Brigham Young University. He has worked on advertising campaigns for American Express, IBM, and Crate and Barrel and designed Salt Lake City's bid book for the 1998 Winter Olympic Games, as well as served as art director and designer for *Graphis* magazine from 1990 to 1992.[4] Merkley has had a successful career in commercial design and advertising in New York, working as design director for Macy's (1981–1983) and Estée Lauder (1983–1985), as well as creative director for the Ogilvy & Mather agency (1985–1991), where he supervised the award-winning 1987 American Express "Portraits" campaign photographed by Annie Leibovitz. In 1993, Merkley co-founded a commercial design firm Merkley, Newman, and Harty (later Merkley and Partners).[5] —ES

Designs for Knoll
Adrian Parry Collection (1982–84): *Shadow, Traffic, Network, Channel I, Channel II, Connection*.

Anni Albers (1889–1994)

Anni Albers's relationship with Knoll Textiles began in 1957 and spanned twenty years, reflecting two artistic periods of her career. In the late 1950s and early 1960s, when her practice reflected the utilitarian principles of the Staatliches Bauhaus, she made open-weave casements for Knoll. Later, in the mid-1970s, when she had shifted her focus from weaving to printmaking and graphic work, she designed printed textiles. Albers was one of several Bauhaus artists hired by Knoll and admired for her sensitivity to the primacy of form, as well as the high standard of design instilled by her Bauhaus training. For the company's textile division, figures such as Albers and Gunta Stölzl represented traditions learned in the Bauhaus weaving workshop.

Albers (née Annelise Else Frieda Fleishman) was born in Berlin, Germany.[1] In 1922 she enrolled at the Weimar Bauhaus where she met Josef Albers; they were married in

1925. Albers studied weaving (the only workshop at the Bauhaus available to women), and she found herself inspired by the structure and possibilities of the medium. The teachings of Bauhaus master Paul Klee, especially his emphasis on Andean textiles, were highly influential and informed her work throughout her career.[2] In the fall semesters of 1929 and 1931 Albers replaced Stölzl as acting director of the Bauhaus weaving department in Dessau.

When the Nazi regime closed the school in 1933—and at the suggestion of architect Philip Johnson—the Alberses immigrated to the United States and taught at Black Mountain College in North Carolina until 1949. After a summer in Mexico City, where Josef had a teaching position at the University of Mexico, they relocated to New York, but a year later, Josef was asked to chair the department of design at Yale University, and the couple moved to Connecticut.

While Albers was at Black Mountain, she also lectured on textile design at MoMA in New York (1944) and the Massachusetts Institute of Technology (1946). During this period she began to collaborate with industrial textile manufacturers such as Patterson Fabrics and Original Textiles (see chapter 1).[3] She was given the first solo exhibition of textiles at MoMA in 1949. The exhibition articulated the evolution of her conceptual underpinnings, highlighting the structural and expository functions of woven threads.[4] It showcased her utilitarian and experimental works from Bauhaus-era drawings to post-Bauhaus samples of commercial textiles and foreshadowed Albers's future constructions by including four of her "pictorial weavings."[5]

Since the 1930s Albers had been a prolific writer, contributing to many contemporary periodicals. She frequently explored the issue of art versus craft, ultimately arguing that woven threads could serve both artistic and commercial endeavors.[6] She also investigated and theorized on the role of textiles in interior architecture, advocating for a more extensive use of textiles in the interior.[7] She anticipated the later trend in partition fabrics (one actively embraced by Knoll) when she called for loose and rigid textile panels to be used in subdividing large spaces for diverse interior needs.

Although perhaps best known for the print *Eclat* (1975/76), Albers also designed commercially successful woven casements for Knoll in the late 1950s and early 1960s (fig. B.3).[8] The first of these, *Fiberglas Casement*, introduced at the end of 1957, was a bit of a false start (see fig. 3.67). The textile was deemed unsuccessful, not because of Albers's plain gauze (leno) weave structure, but because of the coarse nature of the new Aerocor yarn, made of fiberglass and introduced by Owens Corning earlier that year (see chapter 3).[9] Albers had used the gauze weave structure since the 1920s when she developed a modern version of the ancient Peruvian weave by twisting warp threads on the loom to create consistent open areas.[10] Beginning in 1959 Knoll introduced three linen gauze weave casements by Albers: *Lattice* (1959), *Rail* (1962), and *Track* (1965) (figs. B.4, B.5; see also chapter 3).[11] All three casements were imported through Joynel, New York. *Lattice* was produced in Belgium while *Rail* and *Track* were both manufactured by Testori in Italy.[12] They were available in "White," but Knoll also offered *Lattice* in "Oatmeal" and *Rail* in "Natural."[13] *Lattice* and *Rail* were frequently exhibited and remained in production until 1978 in the United States, while *Rail* remained competitive for Knoll in the European market until at least 1981.[14]

At the suggestion of June Wayne from the Tamarind Lithographic Workshop, Albers began to explore printmaking in 1963.[15] With this new graphic language, Albers continued to draw on her abiding interest in Andean textiles and built on the teachings of her mentor Klee, emphasizing positive/negative spatial relationships and a geometric framework. In 1968 Albers featured these motifs

Fig. B.4 Anni Albers. Prototype related to *Rail*, ca. 1959. Plain gauze (leno) weave. The Museum of Modern Art, New York, Gift of Josef Albers, 450.1970.86. Cat. 127.

Fig. B.5 Anni Albers. *Track* ("White" colorway), introduced 1965. Made by Testori for Knoll Textiles. Used for drapery; linen; plain gauze (leno) weave. University of Alberta Clothing and Textiles Collection, 1990.65.11. Cat. 129.

Fig. B.6 Anni Albers (tapestry), Ricardo Legorreta (architect). Lobby bar of the Hotel Camino Real with Albers tapestry, Mexico City, 1968. Photographed by Armando Salas Portugal. The Josef and Anni Albers Foundation, Bethany, Conn.

Fig. B.7 Anni Albers. *Eclat* swatch ("Brown and Beige" colorway), ca. 1975–80. Printed by Pausa AG in Germany for Knoll Europe. Cotton, linen; plain weave. KnollTextiles Archive.

Fig. B.8 Anni Albers. *Jhet* swatches ("Mauve/Copper" and "Red" colorways), 1976. Made by Craftex Mills for Knoll Textiles. Used for upholstery; nylon, wool; twill variation. KnollTextiles Archive.

in a tapestry she created for the lobby bar of the Camino Real Hotel in Mexico City (fig. B.6). The hotel was designed by architect Ricardo Legorreta, with interiors coordinated by Charles Sevigny, Peter Andes, and Barbara Rodes-Segerer of Knoll.[16] The Albers *Camino Real* tapestry was most likely woven by Knoll in Mexico, and Albers saw it as a point of departure for her graphic works, reproducing the design as a print in 1969.[17] Also titled *Camino Real* (1967–69), it was the first of many prints that investigated the rigid patterning of triangular motifs.[18]

By 1970, Albers had abandoned weaving, instead focusing her creative energies toward printmaking. Her graphic language expanded to include intricate patterns of parallelograms and trapezoids as well as triangles. The 1973 screen prints *PO* and *PO II* anticipated her next designs for Knoll Textiles, which included *Eclat*.[19] Both versions of *Eclat*—one with a 16-inch repeat and the other, smaller *Eclat-S* with a 3-inch repeat—were printed at the New London Textile Print Works in Delaware on Knoll's linen-blend multipurpose fabrics *Dorset* (large version) and *Glin* (small version).[20] Although copyrighted in 1975, *Eclat* was not released by Knoll until 1976.[21] In Europe *Eclat* was printed at Pausa AG in Germany and was available on a higher-quality cotton/linen blend that could be used for either upholstery or drapery.[22] Beginning in 1978 *Eclat* was also available in a white-on-white sheer called *Eclat-T* as was *Epos-T*—a related print by Albers—both were produced for the European market as sheer burn-out casements at Pausa (fig. B.7).[23] Though *Eclat* was only in production for two years, it was offered in more than twenty colors on a natural ground. In 1975 Knoll released *Jhet*, a woven upholstery fabric by Albers (fig. B.8), manufactured by Craftex Mills for the American market.[24] Rodes-Segerer had hoped that *Jhet* would be the next *Nylon Homespun*, a classic Knoll textile introduced in 1958 and known for its durability. *Jhet* was much less successful, however, suffering from poor quality and lackluster color palettes and was discontinued by 1978.[25]

A 1977 Knoll brochure welcomed "Anni Albers in her new role of print designer. The association should prove an exciting one."[26] However, the relationship lasted just two years. In 1979 Albers designed *Maze*, a transparent drapery for another firm, the Sunar textile company headed by Rodes-Segerer and Bobby Cadwallader, who had by then left Knoll.[27] *Maze*'s similarity to Knoll's *Epos-T* brought an end to Albers's business relationship with Knoll. She continued to design for Sunar, mostly sheers, including *Monarch* and *Diadem*, which were released in 1989 and lauded as two "most remarkable" machine-embroidered draperies of fine cotton voile.[28]

Josef Albers died in 1976. Despite the emotional setback and immense responsibilities of managing his estate, Anni Albers continued to create new prints with Tyler Graphics, and her graphic work was increasingly admired. Her prints and drawings were exhibited widely over the next nine years, culminating in a 1985 retrospective exhibition, *The Woven and Graphic Arts of Anni Albers* and a 1990 co-exhibition with Gunta Stadler-Stölzl, *Gunta Stölzl and Anni Albers* at MoMA. Albers died four years later in Orange, Connecticut.

Eclat was reinterpreted and reintroduced by Knoll in 1997 in the *Decades Collection*. In making the new version, Nicole Casey, Knoll's interim designer, researched Albers's designs at MoMA and at the Josef and Anni Albers Foundation Archive.[29] The revised textile, a cotton and mohair velvet upholstery fabric, offered a subtle two-tone effect. Manufactured in Holland, it was released in a range of subdued colorways such as "Sandalwood" and "Sage." Dorothy Cosonas, design director of KnollTextiles, selected the design once again when the company introduced its *Archival Collection* in 2007, effectively recognizing it as an iconic Knoll design. It was offered as a woven upholstery fabric in six colorways. As of the spring of 2011 *Eclat Weave* is still in production for KnollTextiles and, with the structural open-weave casements of the late 1950s and 1960s, reflects Albers's formative and lasting contribution to the Knoll Textiles legacy. —AMT

Designs for Knoll
Fiberglass Casement (1957–61); *Lattice* (1959–78); *Rail* (1962–78; disc. in Europe 1982); *Track* (1965–78); *Jhet* (1975–78); *Eclat* (1976–79; disc. in Europe 1981); *Eclat-S* (1976–77); *Eclat-T* (Europe only, 1978–81); *Epos-T* (Europe only, 1978–81); *Eclat* (1997–2006, *Decades Collection*); *Eclat Weave* (intro. 2007, *Archival Collection*).

Selected Awards and Exhibitions
1949 *Anni Albers*, first one-person textile exhibition at MoMA
1950 *Good Design*, MoMA
1956 *Craftsmen in a Changing World*,

Museum of Contemporary Crafts, New York
Textiles USA, MoMA, juror
1961 *Fabrics International*, Museum of Contemporary Crafts and Philadelphia Museum College of Art (*Lattice* shown)
Met Textiel, Stedelijk Museum Amsterdam (*Lattice* shown)
Craftsmanship Medal, American Institute of Architects
1971 *Knoll au Louvre*, Musée des Arts décoratifs, Paris
1975 *Anni Albers*, Kunstmuseum, Dusseldorf, and Bauhaus Archiv Berlin
1978 Award for Knoll International designs, *Eclat* and *Epos*, Design Center Stuttgart
1983 Award for Sunar collection, Design Center Stuttgart
1985 *The Woven and Graphic Art of Anni Albers*, Renwick Gallery, Smithsonian Institution
1990 *Gunta Stölzl and Anni Albers*, MoMA, New York
2006 *Anni and Josef Albers: Latin American Journeys*, Reina Sofía Museum, Madrid (circulating exhibition).

Sarah Baker (b. 1969)

Born in New York City, Sarah Baker first ex-plored weaving in high school. After two years at Hamilton College, she attended the Rhode Island School of Design, graduating in 1992.[1] She then worked at Pallas Textiles under Linda Thompson, a former Knoll and Sunar employee during Robert Cadwallader's tenure at both companies. In 1995 KnollTextiles design director Deborah Steele hired Baker to act as a liaison between Jhane Barnes and Knoll for Barnes's custom fabric production. Steele left the company in 1996, and Baker, with fellow staff designer Kathrin Hagge and interim designer Nicole Casey, managed the design and production of new textiles until Suzanne Tick was hired as creative director in 1997. After Barnes's contract with Knoll ended in 1998, Baker took on additional and varied design work at Knoll, from color coordination to creating textile designs.

While not credited in company materials, as a staff designer, Baker contributed a variety of designs including drapery fabric *Grace Note* (1999), upholstery fabric *Arno* (2000), and patterned woven upholsteries *Stepping Stones* (1999), and *Hula Hoop* (2001), all of which are still in production in 2011.[2] *Arno* is reminiscent of Knoll's classic 1960s and 1970s handwoven textiles by Paul Maute GmbH and even borrows its name from one of Maute's early fabrics for Knoll. It uses specially twisted, thick wool yarns in a simple weave to give the textile a hand-wrought feel.[3] Baker also designed *Field Day*, an upholstery fabric featuring both bouclé and chenille yarns which resulted in a subtle two-tone effect in a grid pattern. The power-loomed fabric was based on a prototype Baker made on her loom at home. Baker's reversible patterned weave *Hula Hoop* features a circular motif in a four-color palette (fig. B.9).

In addition to designing new textile patterns, Baker worked closely with the textile mills, especially the designers and chemists who were responsible for bringing new materials and innovations to Knoll. In 2001 Baker left KnollTextiles for a senior designer position at Maharam, another leading interior textiles company in New York, where she is still employed as of 2011 designing upholstery, panel, and drapery fabrics. —AMT

Designs for Knoll
Foundation (intro. 1998); *Stepping Stones* (intro. 1999); *Arno* (intro. 2000); *Field Day* (intro. 2000); *Hula Hoop* (intro. 2001).

Award
1999 *Good Design* award for *Grace Note*, Chicago Athenaeum

Jan-Paul Barnard (b. 1937)

In 1972 Knoll Textiles introduced *Durban*, an open-weave casement of mohair and cotton (see fig. 5.24). The fabric's name alluded to its country of origin, as it was a product of Barkor, a small handweaving mill in South Africa founded by Jan-Paul Barnard.[1] Born in Morgenzon, Eastern Transvaal (today Mpumalanga), South Africa, Barnard was raised in Uniondale, Western Cape Province. He had initially planned to study law, but after his university studies, he instead applied his natural mechanical abilities and inventiveness to establishing a small facility that manufactured supermarket equipment. After selling this business, Barnard visited a university friend in Alicedale, a village in South Africa's Eastern Cape, where raising Angora goats and the production of mohair was a primary industry. Although he had no experience weaving, he was struck by both the natural beauty of mohair and its production possibilities, as well as the relatively low cost of starting a business in this region. After studies at the Wool and Textile Research

Fig. B.9 Sarah Baker. *Hula Hoop*, reversible, 2001. Made in the United States for KnollTextiles. Used for upholstery; polyester, cotton. KnollTextiles Archive.

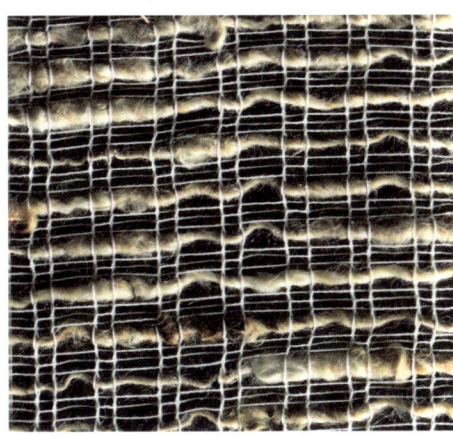

Fig. B.10 Jan-Paul Barnard. *Protea* swatch ("Natural" colorway), ca. 1975. Made by Barkor for Knoll Textiles. Used for drapery; mohair, polyester; plain gauze (leno) weave. KnollTextiles Archive.

Fig. B.11 Jhane Barnes, ca. 1991. Knoll Archives.

Fig. B.12 Jhane Barnes. *Melange* sample ("Sunset" colorway), ca. 1983. Made by Franetta for Knoll Textiles. Used for upholstery; wool, rayon, cotton, silk; plain-weave–derived simple weave. Courtesy Cindia Reyes. Cat. 236.

Fig. B.13 Jhanes Barnes. *Fuji* sample ("Natural" colorway), 1986. Made in Japan for Knoll Textiles. Used for drapery; wool; plain weave with supplemental warp patterning. KnollTextiles Archive. Cat. 241.

Institute branch of South Africa's Council for Scientific and Industrial Research in Port Elizabeth, Barnard developed designs for a more efficient handloom which he began building himself. He also struck on the idea of using the reject mohair that had been stained by the goat's urine for woven products. The urine acted as a natural dyestuff, creating varying ranges of golds, yellows, and bronzes. These luminous natural tones remained after the wool had been cleaned and handspun into yarn. After establishing the Barkor mill, Barnard sold an open-weave casement design to Jack Lenor Larsen, president of the leading American interior fabrics house of the same name, who introduced Barnard's textile as *Colossus* in his 1969 *Reflection Forms and Nature* collection.[2]

Barnard grew dissatisfied with his business relationship with Larsen, and in 1971 he traveled to the United States as part of group sponsored by the South African Department of Trade and Industry. After exhibiting at a trade show in Dallas, Texas, Barnard visited the Knoll showroom there and thought the firm would be a good match for his unconventional fabrics. He met in New York with the president of Knoll, Robert Cadwallader, who selected Barnard's naturally dyed fabric for the Knoll Textile collection, where it was introduced as *Durban* the next year. Barnard would work with Barbara Rodes (later Rodes-Segerer) to develop an open-weave "sunfilter" casement featuring highly irregular hand-spun mohair weft yarns in a leno weave with polyester warps (fig. B.10). Introduced by Knoll in 1973, the casement textile was named *Protea* after the giant or king protea, South Africa's national flower. Both textiles were relatively successful but were dropped from the collection in 1975. By the mid-1970s growing anti-apartheid sentiments and boycotts (later followed by governmental sanctions) had made trade outside of South Africa nearly impossible for Barnard's company, and as a result he was not able to regularly supply Knoll with his fabrics.

Despite a drastic reduction in his overseas sales, Barnard continued to operate his factory and further built up his domestic business, opening a number of showrooms in large South African cities. His company became known for a range of drapery fabrics that take advantage of the natural sheen and durability of mohair. As sanctions on South Africa eased, Barnard again brought his high-quality handwoven fabrics to the international market. Today Barnard's company, now known as Mohair Weavers–Jan-Paul Barnard, sells mohair curtains, throws, and blankets in twenty countries, cultivating its customer base through regular participation in leading European trade fairs such as Heimtextil in Frankfurt and Maison & Objet in Paris. —EM

Designs for Knoll
Durban (1972–75); *Protea* (1973–75).

Jhane Barnes (b. 1954)

In 1983 Jhane Barnes became the first fashion designer to collaborate with Knoll Textiles (fig. B.11). Over the next fifteen years, more than sixteen collections and numerous individual fabrics for upholstery, panel, window-covering, and wallcovering were introduced. Deploying her sartorial expertise, Barnes invigorated the Knoll Textiles collection with a new fashion-forward sensibility. She introduced the company to mills specializing in fashion fabrics, as well as fostered new relationships between Knoll and Japanese mills known for innovative production methods and materials.

Born in Phoenix, Maryland, Barnes designed clothing in high school, including outfits for friends and uniforms for the school band. In 1973 she moved to New York City to attend the Fashion Institute of Technology (FIT). The two-year program focused almost exclusively on fashion design for womenswear, with menswear design covered in the final semester.[1] For Barnes this final semester was the most formative. By the time she graduated in 1975, she had inaugurated a menswear company and received an order for 1,000 trousers from a retail executive.[2] Initially, Barnes experimented with tailoring, offering her customers unusual garments such as lapelless jackets and one-piece sleeves, but she soon decided to experiment with texture and color instead of silhouettes.[3]

As Jhane Barnes, Inc. developed into a multimillion-dollar company, Barnes grew increasingly frustrated with the limited selection of interesting fabrics available for her garments. She learned to weave on a small loom in the back office of one of her textile suppliers, Auburn Mills, in New York. By 1978, with a new cache of technical skills—including yarn spinning—and a newly purchased Macomber loom, she began designing and weaving fabrics for her own use. This helped her assume a role in the vanguard of menswear design, where she became known for distinctive textiles and minimalist silhouettes. In 1980 she became the first woman and youngest designer to receive the prestigious Coty Award, and a year later she was awarded the Council of Fashion Designers of America (CFDA) Outstanding Menswear Designer Award. Her clientele has included celebrities and political figures such as John Lennon, Elton John, Boris Yeltsin, and Rudolph Giuliani.[4]

In 1983 Knoll Textiles sales manager Nelson Spinks approached Barnes about designing a capsule collection. Working with Richard Wagner, general manager of Knoll Textiles, and Merle Lindby-Young, vice president of Knoll Textiles, the *Jhane Barnes Collection* was completed within seven months, a short timeframe for the interior textile industry, but standard for the production of fashion fabrics.[5] Barnes tightened the weave structure of the textiles used in her recent collection of sport coats to make *Nuance*, *Cobblestone*, *Melange*, and *Rainbow Twill* (fig. B.12; see also cats. 235– 238). In addition to space-dying the yarns—whereby sections of the skein are dyed in different colored dye baths for a range of hues and tonal variety—Barnes added luxurious natural fibers such as silk and linen to impart luster and pliability to the upholsteries.[6] The collection was an overwhelming success, and in 1985 Barnes added three textiles to it: *Nomad*, *Rainbow Coordinate*, and *Esplanade*.

Barnes worked with selected textile mills specializing in fashion fabrics. Unlike most freelance designers hired by Knoll, Barnes worked directly with the mills, overseeing and checking samples, textile blankets, and final yardages. Franetta—a small mill in Rhode Island—produced her first collections for Knoll. In 1986 she began to work with Japanese mills, stimulating pioneering approaches to both the design and manufacture of her textiles by bringing in complex weave structures and unique finishing techniques.[7] Overall, Barnes felt that the attitude toward technology in Japan fostered innovative results; in 1990 she stated, "They watch me experimenting with complicated weaves and don't say, 'That's impossible for mass production.' They say, 'If you can do it, we can, too.'"[8]

Barnes's contributions to the summer 1996 windowcoverings released by Knoll— *Fuji*, *Nikko*, *Niji Net*, *Toya*, and *Nuance Leno*—and wallcoverings—*Hashi*, *Niji*, and *Toya*—highlight this new relationship with Japanese mills (fig. B.13, see cat. 240). Only *Niji*, *Niji Net*, and *Nuance Leno* (a drapery version of the wildly popular design from her first collection) were produced in the United States.[10]

In 1987 Knoll added Barnes's woven patterns—*Fenestra*, *Intaglio*, *Maze*, and *Pyramids*—to her eponymous upholstery collection. For these she used an Atari computer to create diverse patterned weaves with geometric decorative motifs, unlike her previously released and highly celebrated woven textiles that offered tonal variety and diverse weave structures. Barnes has been interested in the relationship between mathematics and nature since the early 1980s, and she often based her designs for Knoll on natural and theoretical models of fractals—visually complex, mathematically generated patterns that appear to be similar but are without repeat.[11] To create her designs Barnes often ran fractal patterning sequences on her computer, manipulating a portion of the pattern that would be translated into the textile sample on the loom.

In 1989 KnollTextiles introduced one of Barnes's most innovative collections, a line of patterned knit upholsteries with multi-directional and dimensional surfaces.[12] *Waves*, *Pinwheels*, *Strata*, and *Luna* were manufactured in Japan on specialized knitting equipment that produced durable, tightly woven double-faced "bump-stitch" knits (fig. B.14).[13] The collection's innovative texture and pattern, as well as the elegant binary color relationships of *Waves* and *Pinwheels*, received accolades from ASID and industry press; in commercial sales, however, they were less successful (fig. C.17).[14] Introduced alongside the knit collection was the "modern plaid" *Romanie* (see cat. 244), as well as the woven upholsteries *Fences* and *City Lights*.

A major shift occurred in the corporate structure of KnollTextiles in 1989 when Wagner resigned and Hazel Siegel was hired as the managing director of design of Knoll-Textiles worldwide. Knoll planned to release the largest number of upholstery textiles in the history of the company—all designed by Siegel. With this their overriding concern, Knoll introduced only panel fabrics by Barnes for 1990. However, Barnes resumed her prolific production schedule in 1991 with the *Whimisical Traditions Collection* featuring eleven upholstery patterns. As with many of her previous collections, she relied on computer programs to generate the patterns for *Whimsical Traditions*. Barnes has explained, "I started with various geometric shapes and

Fig. B.14 Jhane Barnes. *Waves* ("Ultramarine" colorway), 1989. Made in Japan for KnollTextiles. Used for upholstery; worsted wool, polyester; double-faced knit, piece-dyed. Cooper-Hewitt, National Design Museum, Smithsonian Institution, Gift of Knoll Textiles, 1990-39-2. Cat. 243.

Fig. B.15 Jhane Barnes. *Paperwork* ("Vellum" colorway), 1992. Made by Aramo for KnollTextiles. Used for wallcovering; woven paper on paper backing; screen-printed.

Fig. B.16 Jhane Barnes. *Rainbow Coordinate* ("Custom Red" colorway), 1985. Made for KnollTextiles. Used for upholstery; wool, polyester, rayon, linen, cotton; basket weave. KnollTextiles Archive.

then used a method of warping . . . them to create a sense of movement. I wanted to achieve a curvaceous, not strict, look."[15]

Knoll launched its first nonwoven wallcovering line with Barnes's *Constructions Collection* in 1992. At the suggestion of her husband, Barnes used the Japanese mill Aramo to create the seven wallcoverings—*Artwork*, *Fretwork*, *Groundwork*, *Marble-work*, *Paperwork*, *Quoinwork*, *Stonework*, and *Wood-work*—all of which featured patterns derived from self-evolving algorithms.[16] While many of the designs were created by applying acrylic resin powder, printed rayon, or wood shavings to the surface, *Paperwork* featured paper in a "basket-like" weave with screen-printed decoration (fig. B.15). *Fretwork*, *Marble-work*, *Quoinwork*, and *Stonework* had a sandpaper-like texture with both marbleized and geometric effects (see cat. 248).

In 1992 Knoll also introduced Barnes's *Chronology Collection*, which returned to both Knoll and Barnes's roots with five upholstery textiles that were reminiscent of men's suiting fabrics.[17] Included in this collection of wool-blend upholstery fabrics was the multipurpose "silk-like" fabric *Transition* with twisted polyester yarns that impart a slightly iridescent sheen and create a subtle vertical pattern (see fig. 6.32).[18] Originally released in fourteen solid colors, it was expanded to six new hues targeted for upholstery use in 1994.[19] *Transition*, along with *Nuance*, is one of Barnes's most successful contributions to the KnollTextiles line, and it remains in the collection in 2011.

Knoll had been producing textiles for the healthcare market since 1991, and in 1993, under senior designer Suzin Steerman, Barnes created a healthcare collection for Knoll, the *Horizons Collection*. The following year Barnes revisited space-dyed yarns for *The Mini-Series Collection*. Both *Spinoff Nuance*—an inexpensive interpretation of the 1983 *Nuance*—and *Wavelength* had space-dyed yarns composed of economical fibers such as polyester and nylon as well as more costly wool and silk.[20] The press release for the collection highlighted the varied nature of the yarns, noting, "This fabric is woven with space-dyed yarns to achieve its distinctive look. Colorations and patterning variations are inherent characteristics of space-dyed yarns; this is most noticeable where colors of greater contrast are used."[21]

The early success of Barnes's textiles for Knoll fostered a demand for custom colorways and encouraged the development of "unique custom-made fabrics for upholstery, walls, panels and floors" for specific projects.[22] Her custom work included special colorways of her best-selling fabrics such as *Rainbow Coordinate* (fig. B.16) and new textile designs for large contract projects. She often worked directly with Alan Olmer, custom development manager at Knoll (and after 1995, with Sarah Baker) to develop colors and designs for such contract interiors clients as IBM, Nestle, Xerox, and Apple Computers.[23] Major projects included the installation of Barnes's *Checkmate* at the Dallas Federal Reserve Bank (ca. 1991) and a custom-colored version of *Starburst* for the Yokohama Convention Center in Japan (1991). Occasionally a custom textile would also be introduced in the Knoll collection. *Morreau*, a polyester tapestry weave originally designed in wool for the Leo Burnett advertising agency in Chicago, was added to the KnollTextiles line in 1989.[24] Partly fueled by Knoll custom orders, Barnes's relationship with the company was highly profitable. By 1996, 15 percent of her 80-million dollar business was with Knoll.[25]

Arguably the most influential event for Barnes occurred at the 1992 Convergence Conference. After speaking on her design process to an audience of over 3,000 people, she met Bill Jones, a mathematics professor from Syracuse University who had created WeaveMaker, a computer-software program designed to create textile patterns. Jones and his colleague Dana Cartwright teamed with Barnes to collaborate on even more sophisticated computer software based on complex algebraic equations and algorithms to generate textile designs. The new program greatly increased Barnes's design output and facilitated the making of panel fabrics that appeared to be without repeat.

In 1996 Barnes invited six mathematicians to a symposium held for the fashion and technology industry press. The event brought Barnes to the attention of *Wired* magazine, which labeled her a "Fashion Nerd."[26] She has also contributed to math textbooks and participated in a video on fractals for a Discovery Channel education series.[27]

Knoll introduced Barnes's *Square Root Collection* in 1996, a group of three upholsteries exploring the concept of a "modernist grid." *Honeycomb* features an architectural motif of small-scale three-dimensional boxes, and *Gordion Knot*, a fine ribbed textile, has a linear network of bouclé lines (fig. B.17). The upholsteries in Barnes's 1997 release—*Hibert*, *Oracle*, and *Pella*—were designed to coordinate with *Gordion Knot* (see fig. 6.34 and fig. C.20). For the 1997 panel fabric introductions, Barnes again drew on her passion for fractals to develop *Criss Cross*, *Labyrinth*, and *Peano*, inspired by nineteenth-century mathematician Giuseppe Peano's theory of two-dimensional space-filling curves.[28] Barnes's final contributions to the KnollTextiles collection were three synthetic-fiber wallcoverings released in 1998: *Foot Prints*, *Flagstone*, and *Walkway*.

Barnes's fifteen-year relationship with KnollTextiles spanned four design directors—Richard Wagner, Merle Lindby-Young, Hazel Siegel, and Deborah Steele. In 1997 Knoll hired Suzanne Tick as design director, heralding a new era for the company. By this time the creative direction had shifted to prioritize technical textiles and synthetic fibers such as polyester and Olefin for its upholstery, panel, and wallcovering fabrics. Barnes, who favored natural fibers, found this focus to be contradictory to her design philosophy and in 1998 dissolved her licensee contract with Knoll. That same year she founded Jhane Barnes Textiles and began to sell her interiors textiles through Bernhardt in North Carolina and since 2010 through Anzea in Texas. Barnes has also explored new arenas for her designs, such as modular carpets for Collins & Aikman, environmentally friendly furniture for Jofco in Indiana, and award-winning carpets for Tandus in Georgia.[29] Her primary focus, however, remains with menswear as it has been since the founding of her first fashion company in 1975, and she continues to distinguish herself as an innovator. —AMT

Designs for Knoll
Jhane Barnes Collection: *Cobblestone* (1983–90), *Melange* (1983–88), *Nuance* (1983–99), *Rainbow Twill* (1983–92); *Nomad* (1985–94), *Rainbow Coordinate* (1985–94), *Esplanade* (1985–92). *Nuance Leno* (1986–88); *Fuji* (1986–90); *Niji Net* (1986–99); *Nikko* (1986–88); *Toya* (1986–92); *Niji* (1986); *Hashi* (1986–88). *Fenestra* (1987–94); *Intaglio* (1987–90); *Maze* (1987–90); *Pyramids* (1987–94). *Vertical Variations Collection*: *Dots* (1988–92), *Diamonds* (1988–92), *Double Dash* (1988–92), *Double Dash Texture* (1988–92), *Nuance* (1988–92), *Shadow Weave* (1989–92), *Silk Texture* (1989–92), *Stacked Boxes* (1989–92). *Chopsticks* (1989–99); *Fences* (1989–92); *Metropolis* (1989–94); *Morreu* (1989–2003); *Romanie* (1989–99); *Gotham* (1989–90); *Gridlock* (1989–90); *Ocillation* (1989–90). *Patterned Knit Collection*: *Luna* (1989–92), *Strata* (1989–92), *Waves* (1989–92), *Pinwheels* (1989–92). *Aerial View* (1990–92); *Coral Reef* (1990–99); *Cosmos* (1990–94); *Cypress* (1990–94); *Jasmine* (1990–94); *Arbor* (1990–93); *Mimosa* (1990–93). *Whimsical Traditions Collection*: *Banners* (1991–94), *CD's* (1991–94), *Checkmate* (1991–2004), *Confetti* (1991–94), *Crosswalk* (1991–99) *Hopscotch* (1991–99), *Starburst* (1991–94), *Confetti Check* (1991–94), *Cord Dot* (1991–94), *Jump Rope* (1991–2003), *Mesh* (1991–94). *Chronology Collection*: *Continuum* (1992–99), *Era* (1992–99), *Infinity* (1992–94), *Lineage* (1992–94), *Transition* (intro. 1992). *Squares* (1992–94), *Swirls* (1992–2004). *Construction Collection* (1992–94): *Artwork*, *Fretwork*, *Groundwork*, *Marblework*, *Paperwork*, *Quoinwork*, *Stonework*, *Woodwork*. *Horizon Collection*: *Animal Magnetism* (1993–94), *Building Blocks* (1993–94), *Circle Squared* (1993–2005), *Clambake* (1993–2004), *Mum's the Word* (1993–2004), *Room with a View* (1993–2004), *School of Thought* (1993–2004), *Stripes Forever* (1993–94). *Formation* (1994–97); *Planet Earth* (1994–99). *Mini-Series Collection*: *Cinema* (1994–97), *Spinoff Nuance* (1994–2010), *Wavelength* (1994–97). *Echo* (1994–97); *Vertex* (1994–97); *Chrysanthemum* (1994–2004); *Odyssey* (1994–2006); *Cubes* (1994–2004). *Academy* (1995–99); *Embassy* (1995–99); *Ivy Field* (1995–2005); *Woven Reeds* (1995–2006); *Flight* (1995–97); *Persia* (1995–97); *Aero* (1996–2007); *Aero Stripe* (1996–2004); *Box Step* (1996–2008); *Eurythmic* (1996–2008). *The Square Root Collection*: *Gordion Knot* (1996–2008), *Honeycomb* (1996–2004), *Sliding Scale* (1996–2003). *Hilbert* (1997–2006); *Oracle* (1997–2002); *Pella* (1997–2007); *Criss Cross* (1997–2008); *Labyrinth* (1997–2011); *Peano* (1997–2004). *Foot Prints* (1998–2006); *Flagstone* (1998–2006), *Walkway* (1998–2004).

Selected Awards and Exhibitions
1980, 1981 Coty American Fashion Critics Award for Menswear
1981, 1982 Outstanding Designer of the Year, Menswear, Cutty Sark
1981 Outstanding Menswear Designer, Council of Fashion Designers of America (CFDA)
1983, 1984, 1986 Gold Award for the *Jhane*

Fig. B.17 Jhane Barnes. *Gordion Knot* sample ("Caladium" colorway), 1996. Made in the United States for KnollTextiles. Used for upholstery; polyester; plain-weave–derived compound weave. Private Collection. Cat. 246.

Fig. B.18 Wolf Bauer, ca. 1970. Knoll Archives.

Fig. B.19 Wolf Bauer. *Nova*, ("Blue" colorway), ca. 1969. Made for Knoll Textiles. Used for drapery; plain weave, screen-printed. KnollTextiles Archive.

Fig. B.20 Wolf Bauer. *Lumière* sample ("Copper" colorway), ca. 1968–69. Used for upholstery; silk; plain-weave–derived compound weave. KnollTextiles Archive.

Barnes Collection for Knoll
1983 International Product Design Award, American Society of Interior Designers, (ASID)
1986 Award for the *Jhane Barnes Collection* for Knoll, ASID
1989 ROSCOE (*Interior Design* Magazine Award for Best Products of the Year) Award for *Vertical Variations Collection* for KnollTextiles
1990 Award for *Patterned Knit Collection* for KnollTextiles, ASID
Color Light Surface: Recent Textiles, Cooper-Hewitt National Design Museum, Smithsonian Institution
1992 Best of NeoCon, Gold Award for *Constructions Collection* for Knoll
Silver Award for *Swirls* for Knoll, IBD
1996 *Good Design* Award for *Honeycomb* for Knoll, Chicago Athenaeum
1998 Best of NeoCon, Gold Award for Jhane Barnes Textiles Collection
2000 *Women Designers in the USA*, Bard Graduate Center, New York (*Spinoff Nuance* shown)
2004 Calibre Awards, Lifetime Achievement Honoree, IIDA
2010 *His and Hers*, Fashion Institute of Technology, New York

Wolf Bauer (1938-1990)

Wolf Bauer (fig. B.18) was born in Neckartenzlingen, Germany, not far from Stuttgart. He studied textile design with Leo Wollner at the Staatliche Akademie der Bildenden Künste (State Academy of Art and Design) in Stuttgart (1959–63) and served as Wollner's assistant from 1963 to 1965.[1] In 1965 Bauer began freelancing, focusing on pattern design for interior and fashion fabrics as well as carpets and wallpapers.[2] Over the course of his career, he worked with many international textile firms including Pausa AG (as did his mentor Wollner), Taunus Textildruck, Fuggerhaus, Heal Fabrics, Weverij de Ploeg, Ascher and Zumsteg, and Sunar/S-Collection.[3] Bauer did not restrict his design practice to textiles but he also developed surface decoration for porcelain manufactured by the German firms Rosenthal, Hutschenreuther, and Arzberg and designed sets and costumes for the theater. As a fine artist he devoted himself to painting and collage throughout his life, exhibiting in galleries as well as in the Knoll France showroom on at least one occasion.

Bauer became involved with Knoll Textiles when Barbara Rodes was directing textile development for the European branches in the 1960s (see chapter 5). His first collection for Knoll was a group of printed drapery designs—including *Nova*, *Collage*, and *Delta*—released in Europe in 1967.[4] *Nova*, a dense pattern of lines that form abstracted floral shapes (fig. B.19), was originally released only in Europe, but in 2009 Knoll introduced it in the United States as part of the *Archival Collection*. *Scope*, a pattern with a similarly dense linear motif forming rectangular quadrants across the surface of the fabric, was available from Knoll's English licensee in early 1968 but may have been part of the 1967 collection.[5] In 1968 Knoll also released woven upholstery designs by Bauer, the first of his Knoll designs to be introduced in the United States. *Lumière* and *Mosaic* (figs. B.20 and see fig. 5.13) are all-silk, small-patterned weaves, manufactured in France in a range of brilliant colors. In 1969 Bauer's printed drapery fabrics—*Delta*, *Stones*, *Fragment*, and *Collage*—were introduced in the United States.[6] These large-scale motifs printed by Pausa AG of Germany in several colorways on cotton velvet marked a significant departure from Knoll's previous printed fabrics for the American market. They were celebrated by the design press, and *Industrial Design* magazine included them in their Best Designs of 1969 issue. As a result they were exhibited in 1970 with the other "Best Designs" at the Museum of Science and Industry in Chicago.[7] In 1971 Knoll introduced two Bauer designs—*Wheels* and *Yves*—among a group of printed drapery fabrics that also included a design by Wollner. *Wheels* featured the familiar dense linear motifs, and *Yves* was a geometric print of large "Y"s on cotton velvet (fig. B.21). Nearly all of Bauer's print designs for Knoll remained in production until 1978.

In 1970 Bauer's work in textile design was featured in a solo exhibition titled *Kunst vom Fließband* (Art from the Assembly Line) at the Design Center in Stuttgart.[8] From the late 1960s through the 1980s, Bauer produced designs for Ewald Kröner, a German manufacturer of carpets, and continued his work with other textile firms. In 1978 he designed a large group of printed fabrics for Fuggerhaus entitled *Articolor*.[9] They reflect the versatility of his design vocabulary, from highly geometric to splintered and chaotic, all in bright colors. In the 1980s Bauer again worked with Barbara Rodes-Segerer, who by this time had left Knoll. He contributed print designs to the collections she developed for Sunar and S-Collection. In 1984 Bauer was appointed professor of design at the Hochschule für Bildende Künste (University of Fine Arts) in Hamburg where he had lived since 1972. In 1989 he participated in the exhibition *Fourteen Designs for Weverij De Ploeg*, celebrating the leading Dutch textile firm's sixty-fifth anniversary.[10] Wolf Bauer died in Hamburg in 1990.[11]

Bauer won a number of design awards, and his work is in several prestigious collections, including the Victoria and Albert Museum, London; the Museum für Kunst und Gewerbe, Hamburg; Neue Sammlung, Munich; and the Cooper-Hewitt, National Design Museum, Smithsonian Institution, New York. He is identified as "one of Germany's most successful freelance designers" in the *Cambridge History of Western Textiles*.[12] —CBPP

Designs for Knoll
Nova (Europe only, intro. 1967, disc. unknown); *Delta* (Europe, intro. 1967, disc. unknown; U.S., 1969–78); *Collage* (Europe, 1967–80; U.S., 1969–78); *Scope* (Europe only, intro. ca. 1968, disc. unknown); *Parallel*, (Europe only, intro. ca. 1968, disc. unknown); *Lumière* (U.S., 1968–71; Europe, disc. unknown); *Mosaic* (U.S., 1968–73; Europe, disc. unknown); *Stones* (U.S., 1969–73; Europe unknown); *Fragment* (U.S., 1969–78; Europe unknown); *Wheels* (U.S., 1969–73; Europe unknown); *Yves* (U.S., 1969–78; Europe unknown); *Stones* (1997- 2003, *Decades Collection*); *Nova* (intro. 2009, *Archival Collection*). This is a partial list (see n. 4).

Selected Awards and Exhibitions
1965 First and Third prizes, Internationalen Gilde-Wettbewerb für Teppichentwürfe (International Guild Competition for Carpet Design)
1969 Award "For Excellence of Design," *Industrial Design* magazine, New York
1970 *Kunst vom Fliessband: Produkte des Textildesigners Wolf Bauer*, Design Center Stuttgart, (several Knoll designs shown)
Best of Year 1969 (*Interior Design* magazine) exhibition, Museum of Science and Industry, Chicago
1972 *Knoll au Louvre*, Musée des Arts décoratifs, Paris
1989 *Fourteen designs for Weverij De Ploeg*, Stedelijk Museum, Amsterdam

Jean Bauret (1907–1990)

Jean Bauret was born into a family of textile manufacturers in Erquinghem-Lys, in northern France. During the 1930s he pursued interests in modern art, literature, and music in Paris and became both a noted collector and friend to numerous artists and gallery owners. Just before the start of World War II, Bauret assumed leadership of his family's textile business, established an office in Paris, and joined with several members of his family to form a new textile company, the Société Industrielle de la Lys. This company quickly earned a reputation for producing high-quality linen and jute fabrics, supplying customers ranging from the French army to couture houses such as Balenciaga.[1]

In 1943 Bauret opened a new design department to focus on decorative and furnishing fabrics, and over the next decade he commissioned decorative textile designs from many of his artist friends including Wassily Kandinsky, Geneviève Asse, Paule Vézelay, and Serge Poliakoff.[2] Bauret also set up a large studio in the rue d'Artois, Paris, where artists could work on their designs. The space was also used for exhibitions of the finished fabrics and became a salon that attracted well-known artists including Jean Dubuffet and Jean Cocteau, along with decorators and architects such as Charlotte Perriand and Le Corbusier.[3] Hans and Florence Knoll likely met Bauret in the late 1940s through colleagues in this artistic circle. Through this connection, the Knolls were also introduced to Bauret's artist-designed fabrics, and Bauret was probably the source for *Sequence*, a pattern by Paule Vézelay, which became part of the Knoll collection in 1950.[4] That same year Knoll imported a series of sturdy cotton twills manufactured by Bauret, with woven stripes in a variety of widths and in a range of unusual colors, and released under the name *Bauret Stripes* (fig. B.22). Knoll credited the design of these textiles to Jean Bauret. In the late 1950s, Bauret retired from the Société Industrielle de la Lys, and although he continued as a collector and patron of the arts, no further artist-designed textiles were produced by the company after that time.[5] —SW

Design for Knoll
Bauret Stripes (1950–51).

Fig. B.21 Wolf Bauer. *Yves* ("Ochre and Navy on Beige" colorway), ca. 1969–78. Used for drapery; cotton velvet; screen-printed. KnollTextiles Archive.

Fig. B.22 Jean Bauret. *Bauret Stripes* archive page with 4 colorways attached, ca. 1950. Made for Knoll Textiles. Used for drapery; cotton; one-third twill. KnollTextiles Archive.

Fig. B.23 Anne Beetz. *Beaumont* ("Ivory" colorway), 1989. Made for KnollTextiles in the United States. Used for upholstery; cotton, rayon; plain-weave–derived simple weave. KnollTextiles Archive. Cat. 257.

Fig. B.24 Anne Beetz. *Passerelle* ("Lichen" colorway), 1989. Made in Belgium for KnollTextiles. Used for upholstery; cotton, linen; plain-weave–derived simple weave. KnollTextiles Archive. Cat. 258.

Anne Beetz (b. 1939)

Anne Beetz's career as a weaver and textile designer bridges craft and industry as she explores new boundaries and experimental materials for the commercial textile market.[1] She initially sold her woven textiles for the residential market through her own atelier, Tissus Anne Beetz.[2] She expanded into contract textiles through KnollTextiles, with a collection released in 1989.

Beetz was born in Brussels, where she continues to live and work. She studied weaving and textile design at the École Superiure d'Art et d'Architecture de la Cambre, while also working at the Brussels Design Center.[3] She was hired by the progressive manufacturer De Gryse et Façon to work with designer Jeanine Coppens in 1962 and left the company to open her own studio in 1968.[4] By 1980 Beetz had received a Signe d'Or award from the Brussels Design Center, and five years later she received a commission to design textiles for the Magritte Room at the Museum voor Moderne Kunst (Museum of Modern Art) Brussels.[5]

Beetz earned a reputation as a superior handweaver, producing handwoven textile designs that appealed to fashion and interior designers alike.[6] Jack Lenor Larsen noted that "her complete understanding of the loom gives her total command."[7] In the 1980s industrial designer and writer Kenji Ekuan aligned her work with the thriving craft-weaving being produced in Japan and Italy, particularly in her restrained use of color and emphasis on intricate weave structures.[8]

In the mid-1980s Beetz presented samples of her work to Maurice Meunier, president of Knoll France, at the Knoll International Paris showroom.[9] A few years later, the company contracted Beetz to design a collection. Richard Wagner, vice president of Knoll Textiles, had apparently been interested in Beetz's work for some time.[10] After his visit to her display at the Heimtex trade fair in January 1987, Knoll purchased her entire collection.[11] Wagner and Peter Seipelt (Knoll Textiles European director) then worked with Beetz to tailor the line for the American contract market.[12] While Seipelt and Candace Key (assistant to the vice president of Knoll Textiles) sourced the mills, Beetz selected the colorways for the line. The collaboration included making a few adjustments to the designs, such as changing the linen and silk content of *Champagne* and *Deauville* to Trevira Polyester FR, while preserving the original weave structure for each textile. The color range of the collection reflected Beetz's preference for a muted color palette, with offerings in black, gray, olive green, and cream (figs. B.23., B.24, see figs. 6.25, 6.26). After almost two years of development, in 1989 the *Anne Beetz* collection was released as part of Designers Saturday in New York.[13] It comprised eight earth-toned fabrics for upholstery and four suitable for use as wallcoverings, which were produced in eight mills in Belgium, France, Ireland, Switzerland, and the United States.

In 1992 Beetz and Hazel Siegel (managing director of design) discussed the possibility of another collection for KnollTextiles, but the project was never realized. Knoll continued to produce many of the textiles from her collection and later reissued *Arles* (1997) in a version restyled by Nicole Casey for the *Decades Collection*.[14] Creative director Suzanne Tick also reinterpreted two Beetz designs and released them as *Tokay II* (1998) and *Panier II* (2000).[15] Adjustments included changes in fiber content and more diverse color palettes. A few of Beetz's designs—*Luberon* and *Beaumont* as well as *Tokay II*—remained in the line until 2010.[16]

Beetz's initial break into the American market led to work beyond Knoll. In 1993 she produced a series of five panel fabrics, the *Brussels Collection*, for Stratford Hall.[17] She has also designed for Millikin & Company, KI Textiles, Carnegie Fabrics, and Rogers & Goffigon, Ltd.[18] —AMT

Designs for Knoll
Anne Beetz Collection: *Arles* (1989), *Beaumont* (1989–2010), *Luberon* (1989–2010), *Monserrat* (1989), *Panier* (1989–94), *Passerelle* (1989–2003), *Raie* (1989–92), *Tokay* (1989–99), *Chevillion* (1989–92), *Champagne* (1989–99), *Deauville* (1989–99), *Ghent* (1989–92). *Arles* (1997–2005, *Decades Collection*); *Tokay II* (1998–2010, reinterpreted by Suzanne Tick); *Panier II* (2000–2002, reinterpreted by Suzanne Tick).

Selected Awards and Exhibitions
1980 Signe d'Or award, Brussels Design Center
1984 *Anne Beetz*, exhibition in conjunction with the opening of the Brussels Museum of Modern Art

Emily Belding (1903–1999)

Emily Belding began weaving professionally in 1945, after spending twenty years as a physical education and modern dance teacher. Although she had little formal training in weaving, within five years she was selling designs to prominent New York mills and converters, and her textiles were regularly selected for MoMA's *Good Design* exhibitions. After 1956, when she went to work for the Philadelphia mill William Whitaker & Sons, her name faded from public view, but her designs remained well-known within the trade, and her fabrics were featured in the collections of leading interior designers and fabric houses.

Born in Troy, New York, Belding studied at the New York State College for Teachers in Albany (now the University at Albany–SUNY), the Cortland Normal School (now SUNY–Cortland), and the Chalif Russian Normal School of Dancing in New York City. While teaching in the Albany public schools, she began to weave as a hobby in the mid-1930s, and later studied briefly at the Universal School of Handicrafts in New York City.[1] In 1945, after being told she would have to wait two years to study at Cranbrook Academy of Art, she decided to start weaving professionally on her own. Working from her Selkirk, New York, studio, she assembled a portfolio of samples, and began showing her work to textile mill offices in New York City. By September 1948 several of her handwoven designs, made with "a pot pourri of old and new yarns—silk, wool, cotton, nylon and plastic coated Fiberglas" (Tensolite)—were featured in the showroom of Arundell Clarke.[2] In 1950, one of her designs for Clarke, a linen and Tensolite casement cloth called *Linten Lace*, was selected by MoMA for a *Good Design* exhibition (the first of several to include her work—see list below), and also received an Honorable Mention in the annual design competition sponsored by AID.[3] Clarke continued to purchase designs from Belding over the next several years.

In about 1952 Belding began to work directly with mills to put her designs into power production, rather than selling designs to converters such as Clarke.[4] That same year a line of her designs, including casement fabrics of jute, ramie, and linen mixed with synthetic fibers, was available (in minimum orders of 50 yards) through the New York showroom of agent John C. Milne, but this arrangement was short-lived.[5] Belding's work, including a critically acclaimed series of ramie casement fabrics, was next prominently featured by Habitat Associates, a New York showroom founded by designers Warren Nardin, Albert Radoczy, and Paul Mayen in 1953. One of the Habitat fabrics, *Belding Blocks*, was a casement cloth made up of three horizontally striped 18-inch-wide strips staggered and sewn together. This system of construction allowed for a variety of pattern configurations, while also preventing the fabric from sagging when used across large window areas.[7] *Belding Blocks* and another casement fabric for Habitat were chosen for *Good Design* in January 1954 and included in the *100 Museum Selections* that marked the series' fifth anniversary.

Shades and Tints, originally for Habitat, was shown in the final edition of *Good Design* in January 1955 and became part of the Knoll Textiles collection in 1956, renamed *Shades* (see fig. 3.65). It was exhibited in *Textiles USA* at MoMA in the same year. In January 1956 Belding moved to Philadelphia to design casement and upholstery fabrics for William Whitaker & Sons.[8] This collaboration was so successful that the mill sometimes found it difficult to keep up with the demand for her fabrics.[9] Knoll especially appreciated her signature "tailored, almost plain" style of weaving and asked her to develop an upholstery fabric for them, but it was never produced (see chapter 3).[10] Other customers for her Whitaker fabrics included Dan Cooper, Jack Valentine, Kravet, Dunbar, Jofa, and Jens Risom.[11] Belding remained with Whitaker until she retired, probably in about 1970, when the mill closed down.[12] In about 1989 she moved to Holland, Pennsylvania, where she spent her last decade. —SW

Design for Knoll
Shades (1956–58).

Selected Awards and Exhibitions
1950–55 *Good Design* exhibitions: Merchandise Mart (June 1950, January 1951, January 1952, January 1954) and MoMA (1950, 1951, 1952)
1950 Design Award, Honorable Mention, AID
1951 *Living Up-to-Date*, Baltimore Museum of Art
1954 *Good Design, 100 Museum Selections*, Merchandise Mart (June) and MoMA
1956 *Textiles USA*, MoMA (*Shades* shown)

Fig. B.25 Michela Bronzini. *Italian* silk, or *Handwoven Silk from Italy*, 1950. Photographed by Herbert Matter. Knoll Archives.

Fig. B.26 Vibeke Bruun de Neergaard. *Skol* swatches ("Persimmon" and "Azure" colorways), ca. 1965. Made by C. Olesen for Knoll Textiles. Used for upholstery; wool, cotton; twill weave. Private collection.

Brenda Brady (active 1990s)

Brenda Brady's relationship with KnollTextiles began in 1993 when her firm B. Brady Designs created three custom woven fabrics for Lomas Financial, in Dallas, Texas.[1] They were presented by Andrea Almond at the KnollTextiles national sales meeting in 1994. *Linkage*, one of the original designs for Lomas, as well as the three new designs *New Leaf*, *Intertwine*, and *Pendulum*, were released as a "transitional" collection for both residential and contract markets in 1995. Brady's *Traditions Collection* was aimed at the broader contract market and featured neutral and mid-tone colorways coordinated for furniture finishes from Knoll, Steelcase, and Herman Miller. *Linkage* featured an architectural design of horizontal stripes and an "X" motif, while *New Leaf* and *Pendulum* were striped and geometric patterns, respectively. *Intertwine* departed from the other patterns in the collection by including an organic "freeform leaf motif." The woven textiles were made of cotton and rayon blends, except *Linkage*, which had a more durable blend of cotton and polyester. Brady also designed the color rotation for the collection.[2] —AMT

Designs for Knoll
Traditions Collection: Linkage (1995–2004), *Intertwine* (1995–99), *New Leaf* (1995–99), *Pendulum* (1995–99).

Michela Bronzini (active 1940s–1980s)

In 1950 Knoll imported a group of luxurious silks handwoven in Italy. Designed by Michela Bronzini, these were available in a small range of coordinated solids and horizontal stripes in brilliant colors (fig B.25). According to contemporary photographs, they appear to have been plain weaves or twills.[1] They were favorably received in the press (see chapter 3), and one was selected for the June 1950 *Good Design* exhibition at the Merchandise Mart in Chicago. Intended for both upholstery and drapery, the Bronzini group was described as "select, small, inspirational," recalling "the great Renaissance tradition of luxury fabrics with glints of gold and bronze in the silken threads."[2]

Little is known of Michela Bronzini's life.[3] Both her mother, Gegia Bronzini (1894–1976), and sister Marisa Bronzini (1920–2007) are better known than Michela for their work in silk and other handwoven textiles.[4] In the early 1930s Gegia taught weaving and set up a small workshop near Venice, Italy. Marisa learned to weave from her mother and in 1946 founded a handweaving workshop in Cantù, near Como, Italy. She named the workshop Gegia Bronzini after her mother who joined her in this enterprise. Michela Bronzini is known to have created designs for handwoven silks and woolens, along with silk scarves, men's ties and accessories, and women's skirts, beginning in the 1940s. They were largely made by the family workshop, and Michela sold her work through a shop in the Piazza San Marco in Venice which was still in operation as late as 1985.[5] It is not clear how Hans and Florence Knoll became aware of Michela Bronzini's designs, but it seems likely that these silk textiles were woven at the Gegia Bronzini workshop. Textiles by the workshop had been included in *Decorative Arts Today* exhibition at the Newark Museum in New Jersey in 1949 and were being imported for sale in the United States in the same year.[6] The Gegia Bronzini workshop is still in operation in 2011, creating handwoven silk textiles.[7] —SW

Design for Knoll
Italian silk, or *Handwoven Silk from Italy (K605)* (1950–51).

Exhibition
1950 *Good Design*, Merchandise Mart (June)

Vibeke Bruun de Neergaard (active 1950s)

In the 1962 "Textiles Sales Guide," Suzanne Huguenin identified Vibeke Bruun de Neergaard as the designer of *Skol* (fig. B.26).[1] This was the only time any designer was identified for *Skol* in Knoll materials and research thus far has uncovered little about Bruun de Neergaard. It is likely that she was employed as a staff designer at the textile manufacturer C. Olesen in Copenhagen, Denmark, the makers of *Skol*. Founded in 1892, Olesen Domestic Textiles—eventually renamed C. Olesen Boligtextiler (furnishing fabrics)—grew to be one of Denmark's largest textile firms.[2] By the 1950s C. Olesen had taken a leading role in design as well, and beginning in 1956, the firm engaged several Scandinavian architects and designers such as Arne Jacobsen, Liz Ahlmann, and Vibeke Klint to create both printed and woven textiles for its new *Cotil Collection*.[3]

C. Olesen supplied Knoll with two suc-cessful upholstery fabrics, *Skol* (1959) and *York* (1965). They were enduring contribu-tions to the Knoll Textiles collection, each remaining in the collection more than a decade—*York* (fig. 5.4) was discontinued in 1978 and *Skol* in 1985. Knoll introduced *Skol* as a replacement for the more expensive *H930* and *H980* series of handwoven fabrics in April 1959.[4] *Skol* featured a cotton warp and wool weft and was marketed as a sturdy fabric, suitable for both contract and res-idential use.[5] Before 1962 *Skol* was awarded the Cotil Prize, a Danish award for fabric design.[6] Initially released in eleven colors ranging from "Beige" to "Water Blue," by 1985 (the year it was discontinued) *Skol*'s color offerings had been increased to twenty-eight colorways including more contemporary hues such as "Henna" and "Copper."[7] —AMT

Design for Knoll
Skol (1959–85).

Award
ca. 1960 Cotil Prisen (Cotil Prize)

Lois Bryant (b. 1955)

Best-known as a fiber artist, Lois Bryant designed a single pattern for Knoll Textiles in 1982—*Somerset*—which represents a rare example of her early commercial work. Bryant was born in New Jersey but grew up in southeastern Michigan and attended the Cranbrook Kingswood School until grad-uating in 1974.[1] She studied design at the Rhode Island School of Design (1979), after which she moved to New York, dividing her time between art weaving and commercial projects.[2] Before Knoll, she designed a line of interior fabrics for P. Kaufmann and apparel textiles for Hatema, both located in New York.

In the early 1980s Kristl Reinhardt Andrus, stylist for Knoll Textiles, encouraged Bryant to submit fabric samples to the com-pany. Using her computerized loom and wor-sted wool yarns, Bryant sought to create a "Knoll Textiles's look" in her prototypes. Of the twelve designs she presented to Knoll, four were selected for consideration, and ult-imately *Somerset* was chosen for production (fig. B.27). The design featured a simple motif of regular dots on a solid ground and was available in twelve colorways (selected by Reinhardt) that coordinated with the broader Knoll Textiles collection. This under-stated upholstery fabric proved successful and remained in the line until 1989.

Bryant slowly turned away from commer-cial textiles to focus on fiber art commis-sions. A year after *Somerset* was released, she designed large tapestries, including *Rising Bubbles Falling Squares* (Art Institute of Chicago) and completed major commis-sions for corporations such as Liz Claiborne and IBM.[3] In 1986 she started to investigate lampas-style weaving—a double weave composed of ground weave and pattern weave—at the suggestion of Milton Sonday, then curator of textiles at the Cooper-Hewitt National Design Museum.[4] She transformed her computerized loom to work in this com-plex and demanding technique as well as to create weft-backed weaves and warp brocades. Bryant has since created tap-estries with expressive geometric designs as well as playful and evocative weavings with spiritual underpinnings.[5] In addition to her studio work, she has taught weaving and surface design at Parsons The New School for Design (1983–95) and the Uni-versity of Michigan, School of Art and Design (2003–5). She currently lives in Ann Arbor, Michigan, and will be completing her MFA degree at Eastern Michigan University in 2011. —AMT

Design for Knoll
Somerset (1982–89).

Selected Awards and Exhibitions
1983 *Contemporary Continuous Pattern*, Cooper-Hewitt National Design Museum, Smithsonian Institution
1984 *Damask*, Cooper-Hewitt National Design Museum, Smithsonian Institution
Textiles for the Eighties, Museum of Art, Rhode Island School of Design
1987 *Interlacing: The Elemental Fabric*, American Craft Museum
1990 *Color, Light, Surface: Recent Textiles*, Cooper-Hewitt National Design Museum, Smithsonian Institution
1991 Artist's fellowship, New York State Foundation for the Arts
1992 *Unanswered Questions*, one-person show, Center for Tapestry Arts
1994 *Contemporary Textiles from the Collection*, Art Institute of Chicago
1998 *20 Years of Collecting*, Art Institute of Chicago
2010 *Fiber Art: Selections from the Perm-anent Collection*, Art Institute of Chicago

Fig. B.27 Lois Bryant. *Somerset* swatch ("Gray" colorway), 1982. Made in the United States for Knoll Textiles. Used for upholstery; worsted wool, nylon; plain-weave–derived compound weave. KnollTextiles Archive.

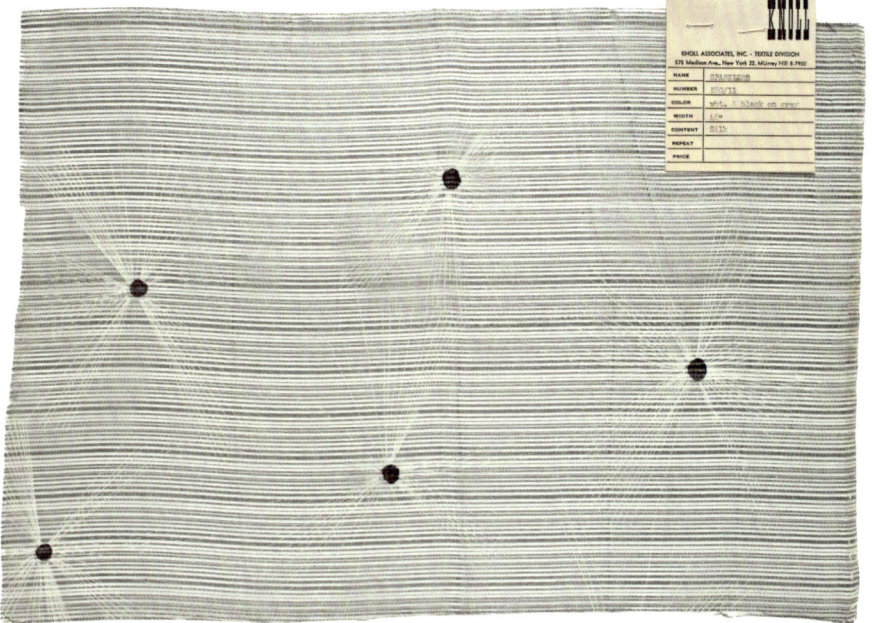

Fig. B.28 Colcombet Fois or Buchet-Colcombet (Bucol). *Sparklers* sample ("Black and White on Grey" colorway), ca. 1953. Made for Knoll Textiles. Used for drapery; silk gauze; plain weave, screen-printed. Cranbrook Art Museum, Bloomfield Hills, Mich. T 2010.13.2. Cat. 59.

Fig. B.29 Dorothy Cole Ruddick. Dress in *Filigree* ("Black and White" colorway), ca. 1950. Made for Knoll Textiles. Used for drapery; rayon; plain-weave, screen-printed. Estate of Dorothy Cole Ruddick. Cat. 54.

Colcombet

François Colcombet founded the Societé Colcombet Fois et Cie., a ribbon-weaving company in the city of Saint-Étienne, France, in 1804.[1] Under the direction of Alexandre Colcombet (1852–1928), the company became world-famous for its ribbons and silk fabrics, exhibiting at international expositions including the World's Columbian Exposition in Chicago (1893) and the Exposition internationale des arts décoratifs et industriels modernes in Paris (1925).[2] Alexandre's son, Johan Colcombet (1877–1949), succeeded him as president in 1928. In 1933 Johan opened a new showroom on the Place Vendôme in Paris.[3] Like his father, Johan experimented with new synthetic fibers as they became available. He also created fabrics in collaboration with leading couturiers such as Elsa Schiaparelli.[4] After Johan's death in 1949, Colcombet Fois continued under the direction of two of his sons, Alexandre and Yves.[5]

In 1924 Johan's brother Carlo (1890–1962) joined with a silk manufacturer in Lyon to form a new company—the Societé Buchet Fils et Charles Colcombet, later shortened to Buchet-Colcombet, or Bucol. They too established a reputation for the innovative use of new fibers, such as nylon, and for producing high-quality textiles for the couture and decorative fabric markets. In 1962 Carlo was succeeded as president by his son Hilaire Colcombet. As of 2011 Bucol remains in operation, and has been owned by the Hermès Group since 2003.[6]

It is not clear which of the two companies should be credited with *Sparklers*, a printed design released by Knoll in 1953. Both were manufacturing luxury textiles under the direction of members of the Colcombet family, and both had promoted their fabrics in the United States. Colcombet Fois exhibited at the Golden Gate Exposition in San Francisco (1939), and Buchet-Colcombet opened a showroom in New York's Rockefeller Center in 1937.[7] In addition, both companies appear to have been printing designs quite similar in feeling to *Sparklers* during the 1950s (fig. B.28).[8] Because the two companies have frequently been confused with each other, and because Knoll simply credited *Sparklers* to "Colcombet, France," the exact source of the design remains unknown. *Sparklers*, a design of spidery lines reminiscent of contemporary dress fabrics, was printed by Knoll in two colors on "antique satin" (a satin weave with slub yarns in the weft) and on three colors of silk gauze, but the pattern did not sell well and was discontinued in March 1954.[9] —SW

Design for Knoll
Sparklers (1953–55).

Dorothy Cole Ruddick (1925–2010)

Dorothy Cole Ruddick worked in a variety of media. Although her only foray into the field of textile design was a pattern for Knoll, she often explored textile imagery and materials in her other art, producing works that blurred the lines between drawing, fiber art, and sculpture.

Dorothy Cole was born and raised in Winnetka, Illinois. While in high school, she spent a summer in San Miguel de Allende, Mexico, studying with painter Rufino Tamayo, probably at the Escuela Universitaria de Bellas Artes (University School of Fine Arts).[1] From 1943 to 1945 she majored in art history at Radcliffe College in Cambridge, Massachusetts, and in 1945 she transferred to Black Mountain College in North Carolina, where she studied painting with Josef Albers and Ilya Bolotowsky. In 1947, the year she graduated, she won a contest to become the "guest editor" for the annual college issue of *Mademoiselle* magazine, moved to New York City, and began working as a freelance illustrator.[2] She quickly found assignments, and over the next several years contributed illustrations not only to Mademoiselle, but also to *Look*, *Flair*, and *Interiors*, for which she designed a cover (August 1948). She also created illustrations for books, including *How to Meet a Millionaire* by Doris Lilly (1951). In December 1950 Cole married Dr. Bruce Ruddick, a Canadian psychiatrist and poet, and shortly thereafter the couple moved to Ruddick's native Montreal, at which time Dorothy Ruddick gave up illustration assignments to focus on her studio work.

Earlier in 1950, Hans Knoll had hired Dorothy Cole to develop a design for Knoll's print collection. Knoll, like other manufacturers of printed textiles at the time, was looking to designers from other fields to expand the range of the firm's textile offerings. Cole produced a group of delicate, tracery-like patterns, and from these Knoll selected a single design that was then reworked in collaboration with the designer.[3] The finished pattern, *Filigree*, reflects the draftsmanship for which Cole was known and also the contemporary interest in lightness and transparency—as seen in the wire sculptures of Ruth Asawa (Cole's fellow student at Black Mountain College) and the wire chairs by Harry Bertoia, which Knoll introduced in 1952. *Filigree* was selected for the January 1951 *Good Design* exhibition, and Cole Ruddick was among a group of Knoll designers featured in *Look* magazine in May of that year.[4] The scale of the pattern, composed of web-like interconnected forms, made it equally effective when used as a dress fabric, as can be seen in a *Filigree* dress that the designer made (or had made) in the early 1950s (fig. B.29).

The Ruddicks returned to New York in 1957 and thereafter divided their time between the city and their summer home in Amagansett, New York. Beginning in the mid-1950s, Dorothy Cole Ruddick displayed her artwork regularly in group and one-person gallery exhibitions. Major museums, including the Metropolitan Museum of Art, the Art Institute of Chicago, and MoMA, showed and acquired examples of her work. In the 1970s and 1980s Ruddick continued to draw and paint and also used embroidery on linen to create abstract fiber art pieces. In the 1990s, she further expanded into sculpture, and much of her later work reflected her "long fascination with cloth and clothing," using classically draped female figures as subject matter.[5] Her final project, made with her daughter Margie Ruddick (a landscape designer), was a group of four landscape sculptures in the Bank of America tower at One Bryant Park in New York City, completed shortly before her death in 2010. —SW

Design for Knoll
Filigree (1950–54).

Selected Exhibitions
1951 *Good Design*, Merchandise Mart (January) and MoMA (*Filigree* shown)
Living Up-to-Date, Baltimore Museum of Art (*Filigree* shown)
1952 *Textilien aus USA*, Smithsonian circulating exhibition (*Filigree* shown)
1955 Galerie Agnes Lefort, Montreal
1963, 1965 Weyhe Gallery, New York
1970 Graham Gallery, New York (first of several)
1981 Allentown Art Museum, Pennsylvania
1989 *Gift, Bequest and Purchase: A Selection of Textile Acquisitions from 1982–1987*, Art Institute of Chicago
1993 Cleveland Museum of Art
2003 *Dorothy Ruddick: Recent Work*, Richard York Gallery, New York

Dorothy Cosonas (b. 1961)

Dorothy Cosonas became KnollTextiles's creative director in 2005 (fig. B.30). Since then she has infused a fashion-forward flair into the collection, most notably with the introduction of a new brand, Knoll Luxe, in 2008. She has sought to capitalize on the growing international interest in fashion trends and the cult celebrity of fashion designers with collaborations with Proenza Schouler and Rodarte. Cosonas has also instituted a new focus on the production of upholstery fabrics. She has expressed her deep respect for the company's history, apparent in the *Archival Collection*, which was introduced in 2007 to celebrate the company's sixtieth anniversary.

Born in New York, Cosonas pursued an education in fine arts and textile design at the Fashion Institute of Technology (FIT), receiving a dual degree in 1984.[1] During her final semester, she was recommended to the American textile firm Unika Vaev in New York and, upon graduation, she commenced a twenty-one year relationship with the company.[2] While she held positions ranging from sales representative to manager of Unika Vaev's custom fabric division, she perceives her role as the assistant to Sina Pearson—then design director—as the most formative. Working directly with Pearson for five years, Cosonas gleaned much from the senior designer, including a particular appreciation for meticulous design processes that favored color over texture or pattern. She recently

Fig. B.30 Dorothy Cosonas, ca. 2005. KnollTextiles Archive.

Fig. B.31 Dorothy Cosonas. *Topography* sample ("Lake" colorway), 2006. Made in Germany for KnollTextiles. Used for upholstery; polyester, cotton, acrylic, rayon; plain-weave–derived compound weave. KnollTextiles. Cat. 281.

Fig. B.32 Dorothy Cosonas. Detail of *Gibson* ("Grenadine" colorway) upholstery on *Armless Tulip Chair* designed by Eero Saarinen, this example ca. 2007. Upholstery made in Germany for KnollTextiles; chair manufactured by Knoll, Inc. Upholstery: cotton, polyester; plain-weave–derived compound weave with supplemental warp pile; chair: cast aluminum and molded fiberglass shell, foam rubber cushion. KnollTextiles. Cat. 285.

Fig. B.33 Dorothy Cosonas. *Bavaria* ("Holly" colorway), 2008. Made in Austria for Knoll Luxe. Used for upholstery; acrylic, wool, cotton, cotton chenille, polyester; plain-weave–derived simple weave. KnollTextiles. Cat. 292.

recalled, "a great pattern or texture badly colored will never sell. Color trumps all."[3]

In 1994 Cosonas became the design director at Unika Vaev and five years later was named vice president of design for the entire collection, which featured many that received awards.[4]

After the departure of Suzanne Tick in late 2004, KnollTextiles hired Cosonas as her successor, looking to impart a fresh aesthetic while honoring the company's iconic history and dedication to good design.[5] Cosonas was charged not only with pre-serving Knoll's modernist aesthetic, but also with charting new ventures that would fuel growth for the company. To this end she has endeavored to create textiles that reflect a popular fashion sensibility, yet designed to coordinate with the broader KnollTextiles line.

Since joining the company, Cosonas has been a prolific contributor to the Knoll brand, largely focusing on upholsteries. Her first collection was introduced in 2006 and featured five upholstery fabrics of various textures and patterns, but coordinated in color, offering both diversity and the possibility of integrating the interior. Cosonas drew upon the legendary couture brand Chanel for *Coco* and *Icon*. *Coco*, a bouclé and chenille upholstery fabric, was based on a classic Chanel jacket, while *Icon* was inspired by the lace trim of a 2005 dress Karl Lagerfeld designed for Chanel.[6] Harkening back to Florence Knoll's early use of men's suiting fabrics for upholstery, *Cross Stitch*, *English Accent*, and the warp stripe fabric *Empire Stripe* looked to classic menswear for inspiration.[7] In fall 2006, Knoll introduced another coordinated collection by Cosonas featuring the designs *Topography*, *Century*, and *Decade*. *Topography* easily betrays its sartorial inspiration, employing a multicolor scheme woven with thick weft yarns of various fibers and thin warps in a manner similar to the renowned Italian fashion house Missoni (fig. B.31). For her spring 2007 upholstery collection, Cosonas designed *Gibson*, *Harrison*, *Madison*, and *Rivington* (fig. B.32). The design source for the latter was *Copper Beach* (1964), a multicolored weaving by the well-known fashion textile designer Bernat Klein.[8] Her 2010 upholstery introductions, such as *Spectator* and *Spot On*, employ circular motifs in both regular and irregular patterns. *Round Trip* was inspired by African beadwork, and the coordinating fabric, *Pony Up*, featured an array of undulating lines.

While focusing primarily on upholstery designs, Cosonas has also contributed to Knoll's healthcare collection of privacy curtains with, for example, *Enchantment* (2007), featuring a cloverlike motif, and *Sundial* (2011), with "drawn" motifs of circles, boxes, and starbursts. Coordinating with outside designers, including the architecture firm LTL and the graphic designer Abbott Miller, Cosonas oversaw the creation of two collections of vinyl wallcoverings.[9] She also works with her predecessor Suzanne Tick, who has continued to create vertical fabrics for KnollTextiles as a freelance designer since her departure in 2005.

To commemorate the sixtieth anniversary of Knoll Textiles, Cosonas culled five classic Knoll designs by celebrated designers from the extensive archive, restyling them for the *Archival Collection* in 2007. The printed textiles *Eclat* (1976) by Anni Albers and *Fibra* (1953) by Eszter Haraszty were reinterpreted as woven designs, while Ross Littell's *Mira* (1958) was released as a sheer casement (see cats. 289, 290). The *Archival Collection* also featured the reintroduction of the open-weave casement *Cyclone* (1972), and five colors were added to the offerings of Paul Maute's *Cato* (1961), Knoll's longest-produced fabric.[10] In 2009 Cosonas added the upholstery fabrics *Plain Linen* (1953) and *Cornaro* (1972), as well as the draperies *Quartet* (1963) by Suzanne Huguenin and *Nova* by Wolf Bauer (1969) to the *Archival Collection*.

The *Archival Collection* has been particularly well-received, but Cosonas's most significant contribution to Knoll may prove to be the creation of Knoll Luxe. The new brand, aimed at the high-end contract and residential luxury markets, offers fashion-forward textiles with a "far more bespoke feel" than the regular collection.[12] The inaugural Knoll Luxe introduction in the spring of 2008 was created by Cosonas and featured ten upholstery textiles in luxurious blends of mohair, silk, wool, and cashmere.[13] The collection pays homage to Knoll handwovens of previous decades with the tactile weaves *North Island* and *Bavaria* (fig. B.33). Cosonas's interest in fashion was not absent from this collection; the circular motif of *Garden City* was inspired by the decorative patterning of an Oscar de la Renta gown, and the embroidered decoration of *Jaipur* refers to the ornament found on traditional Indian tunics.[14] Cosonas released two additions to her Knoll Luxe collection in 2010: *Ravello*, a cashmere upholstery, and *Double Vision*, her first drapery for Luxe, featuring a motif of horizontal stripes in a cotton, lambswool, and polyester blend.

Seeking to further the connection between fashion and interior textiles and feeling that fashion designers bring fresh perspectives and sensitivity to luxury materials, Cosonas selected the up-and-coming design duo Proenza Schouler to collaborate on the next Knoll Luxe collection.[15] Proenza Schouler was a natural fit. The two partners, Jack McCollough and Lazaro Hernandez, had already demonstrated their understanding of color and structure and had used textiles of high character and quality in their fashion collections.[16] McCollough and Hernandez worked closely with Cosonas to create upholstery textiles based on highlights from their previous fashion collections, and the result was the *Proenza Schouler Collection* (2008).[17]

For the next collaborators for Knoll Luxe, Cosonas was drawn to Rodarte for their experimental use of textiles. She engaged this celebrated avant-garde American fashion house to design the third Knoll Luxe collection.[18] The Mulleavy sisters—the creative duo behind Rodarte—pulled designs from their former fashion collections for their Knoll Luxe collection.[19] The resulting *Rodarte Collection* was a success for both Cosonas and Knoll, winning the Best of NeoCon Gold Award, while receiving wide exposure in both interiors and fashion industry press.[20] —AMT

Designs for Knoll
Coco (intro. 2006); *Cross Stitch* (intro. 2006); *Empire Stripe* (intro. 2006); *English Accent* (intro. 2006); *Icon* (intro. 2006); *Century* (intro. 2006); *Decade* (intro. 2006); *Topography* (intro. 2006); *Divine* (intro. 2007); *Enchantment* (intro. 2007); *Fable CR* (intro. 2007); *Gibson* (intro. 2007); *Harrison* (intro. 2007); *Legend CR* (intro. 2007); *Madison* (2007-2011); *Rivington* (intro. 2007); *Whimsy* (intro. 2007). *Kalidescope CR* (intro. 2008); *Compass CR* (intro. 2008); *Garland* (intro. 2008); *Lanterns* (intro. 2008). *Passages* (intro. 2009); *Roundtrip* (intro. 2010); *Spectator* (intro. 2010); *Entourage* (intro. 2010); *Courtship* (intro. 2010); *Pony Up* (intro. 2010); *Spot On* (intro. 2010). *Bloom* (intro. 2011); *Sundial* (intro. 2011); *Jubilee* (intro. 2011).
Knoll Luxe, *Dorothy Cosonas Collection*: *Bavaria* (intro. 2008), *Brugge* (intro. 2008), *Galloway* (intro. 2008), *Garden City* (intro. 2008), *Hampshire* (intro. 2008), *Jaipur* (intro. 2008), *Lyon* (intro. 2008), *Mohair Prima* (intro. 2008), *North Island* (intro. 2008), *Stirling* (intro. 2008). *Ravello* (intro. 2010); *Double Vision* (intro. 2010).

Selected Awards and Exhibitions
2000 *Women Designers in the USA*, Bard Graduate Center, New York
2006 Best of NeoCon Gold Award (Knoll upholstery)
2008 Best of NeoCon Gold Award (Knoll Luxe, *Dorothy Cosonas Collection*)
Interior Design Magazine Award (Knoll Luxe, *Dorothy Cosonas Collection*)

Lynne Crosbee (active 1970s)

In late 1974 Knoll International released three flame-retardant printed draperies by the British artist Lynne Crosbee, who was credited with their design in Knoll price lists and press materials.[1] The rigid geometry of the patterns is anchored in the Art Deco revival of the 1970s.[2] They were produced in contrasting, vibrant and muted color combinations such as gold, orange, and sand.[3] *Casino*, *Caravel*, and *Catena* all have a 24-inch repeat on 48-inch wide fabric (fig. B.34). Knoll promoted Crosbee's textiles as a new direction for the print collection, and the bold rectangles, squares, and triangles made them a departure from the more organic patterns then in production by the company.[4] In an article about the Knoll International headquarters in Stuttgart, lise Gray noted that the textiles are "scaled for perfect alignment when used as pleated constructions, flat panels, or laminated to wide, vertical Venetian Blinds."[5]

Crosbee's patterns are printed on *Cara*, a fabric composed of Clevyl, a flame-retardant fiber.[6] Both Crosbee's textiles and *Cara* were produced by the well-known French textile manufacturer Bianchini-Férier.[7] The collection was launched as part of the firm's new relationship with the British distributor Form International as the licensee for Knoll International in the United Kingdom.[8] —AMT

Designs for Knoll
Caravel (1974–78); *Casino* (1974–78); *Catena* (1974–78).

François Dallegret (b. 1937)

François Dallegret was born in Morocco, where his father was an engineer on the

Fig. B.34 Lynne Crosbee. *Caravel* page from "Print Collection" binder ("Copper/Mauve/Mocha" colorway) ca. 1977. Textile sample made by Bianchini-Férier for Knoll Textiles. Used for drapery; Clevyl; screen-printed. KnollTextiles Archive. Cat. 195.

Fig. B.35 François Dallegret. *Lines* sample ("Brass" colorway), ca. 1970. Made by Pausa AG for Knoll Textiles. Used for drapery; cotton; plain weave, screen-printed. KnollTextiles Archive.

Trans-Saharan Railroad and his mother worked as a journalist.[1] In 1945 the family moved to Paris, where Dallegret earned his bachelor's degree in mathematics and studied architecture at the École Nationale Supérieure des Beaux-Arts (1958–63).[2] He then spent a year in New York before settling in Montreal in 1964.[3] Despite his architectural background, Dallegret and his work resist easy categorization. Instead the boundaries between architecture, product and graphic design, drawing, sculpture, and multimedia installation are blurred. Dallegret's cultivation of various sobriquets only heightens the ambiguity of his creative pursuits. He has labelled himself an "aestheticien acid" ("aesthetician" a quasi-official designation from the Canadian Ministry of Industry, and "acid" an acronym for Association of Canadian Industrial Designers), and trademarked the identity GO Dallegret, often shortened to GOD & CO.

In 1962 Dallegret had his first gallery exhibition at the Galerie Iris Clert, featuring mechanical drawings for "astrological automobiles"—vehicles based on astrological signs.[4] His work combined the techniques of architectural drafting with a critical eye toward contemporary materialism and a fascination for technology, a direction he has continued to pursue.[5] He was a frequent contributor of drawings, montages, and texts to such magazines as *Art in America* and *Industrial Design* through the mid- to late 1960s. *Architectural Forum* editor Peter Blake introduced Dallegret to architectural critic and theorist Reyner Banham, and the two collaborated on several projects including the article "A Home Is Not a House" (1965) that observed the liberation of architecture through mechanical technologies.[6] Banham proclaimed that Dallegret's drawings "demonstrate the hollowness of the fear of many architects that acceptance of the dominance of environmental machinery will be 'the end of creativity.'"[7] Since the 1960s, Dallegret has worked on numerous urban structures and architectural interventions.[8]

Dallegret's textile design *Lines* for Knoll was one of the few mass-produced objects he created. His furniture designs, for example, such as *Chaise Ressort* (1967) and *Table Électrique* (1980) remained prototypes, while others, such as the decorative object *Atomix* (1966), were produced in limited series.[9] The invitation to design for Knoll came from his acquaintance with Barbara Rodes-Segerer, a Knoll Textiles executive. Knoll publicized Dallegret's "seemingly ephemeral printed cloth" as an addition to their international print collection in 1971 (fig. B.35).[10] *Lines* was initially released as a black-printed cotton casement and a cotton and polyester white sheer burn-out, but by 1972 the colorways included "Brass," "Grey," "Stone," "Camel," "Charcoal," and "Copper."[11] Printed at Pausa AG in West Germany, the European versions offered more colorways such as vibrant greens and blues.[12]

The pattern for *Lines* developed from Dallegret's earlier projects such as his *Wave* graphic (1966) which was reproduced as a reversed negative montage on the cover of *Art in America* (March–April 1966). Another source was his prototype for *Kiik*, which he described as a "hand-pill"—a barbell-shaped object that would "help cure body discomforts and mind obsessions" when handled.[13] *Kiik* inspired several subsequent designs, from the textile *Lines* to a series of lamps. —CAL

Design for Knoll
Lines (1971–78).

Selected Exhibitions
1962 Solo exhibition, Galerie Iris Clert, Paris
1963 Solo exhibition, PVI Gallery, New York
1965 Solo exhibition, Museum of Contemporary Art, Montreal
1966 *La Machine*, Waddell Gallery, New York
1967 Expo '67, Montreal
2001 *Les années Pop*, Centre Georges Pompidou, Paris
2007 *Tomorrow Now*, MUDAM, Luxembourg
2009 *Environnement Total*, Canadian Center for Architecture, Montreal

Sybille Dobringer (active ca. 1970)

Sybille Dobringer studied textile design under Leo Wollner at the Staatliche Akademie der Bildenden Künste (State Academy of Art and Design) in Stuttgart during the early 1970s. She was one of his students to submit proposals for "Transparent," a 1972 project to create woven textile designs for Knoll International.[1] The juried selections were exhibited in January 1973 at Knoll's Frankfurt office (see chapter 5). Wollner, perhaps in concert with Barbara Rodes, then head of Knoll Textiles, selected three designs to be produced for Knoll's casement collection. Dobringer's submission for the competition was released as *Meton* in 1973.[2] Made of Leavil, a fire-retardant fiber, it was manufactured in West Germany and remained in production for only a year. —CBPP

Design for Knoll
Meton (1973).

Klaus Dombrowski (b. 1938)

Klaus Dombrowski was born in Labiau, Germany, which became part of Russia in 1945 and today is known as Polessk. In 1962, after studying exhibition and window design and spending a year in that field, he enrolled in the Folkwangschule für Gestaltung (Folkwang School of Design) in Essen to study textile design, graduating in 1966.[1] He then worked for a design company before becoming an independent designer in 1967.[2] His earliest freelance work was with Rasch, a leading German wallpaper and textile manufacturer. The firm's roster of designers included Maria and Ernst May, Josef Hoffmann, and Salvador Dali.[3] These early projects helped establish Dombrowski's reputation within the textile industry and brought him in contact with other artists and diverse companies, such as the porcelain manufacturers Hutschenreuther and Arzberg, for whom he created designs in the 1980s.[4]

Dombrowski was particularly influenced by the minimalist forms of Mies van der Rohe and the rationalist architecture of Richard Meier, which were based on a visually concise vocabulary in keeping with Dombrowski's own design aesthetic.[5] By the early 1970s he gained a reputation as a versatile designer, as comfortable working in glass and ceramics as in textile design.[6] In 1972 he was appointed professor in the art and design department at the Universität Essen (University of Essen), and he currently works and lives in Essen, Germany.

In 1978 Dombrowski created his first designs for Knoll. These two printed upholsteries—*Flair* and *Flex*—are repetitive patterns enhanced by binary color contrast. *Flair* is composed of a series of geometric nesting S-forms. *Flex* has short, curving lines on a solid background that create an impression of row after row of deconstructed zig-zags (fig. B.36 and see cat. 217). Both patterns were also introduced as cotton draperies and burnout sheer casements (*Flair-T* and *Flex-T*). In 1987 Dombrowski designed two additional casement patterns—*Square* and *Screen*—which were printed with lacquer on white fabric at Heberlein & Co. AG, a Swiss textile manufacturer, and offered a more traditional "seersucker look."[7] Dombrowski's reduced palette and dexterous manipulation of line in these Knoll designs reflect a Bauhaus sensibility. In addition to Knoll, he has worked with a number of international textile firms including Taunus Textildruck, Jab Anstoetz, Fuggerhaus, Pausa, and Vereinigte Werkstätten.[8] —CBPI

Designs for Knoll
Introduced in Europe only; it is uncertain when these designs were discontinued: *Flair* (1978); *Flair-T* (1978); *Flex* (1978); *Flex-T* (1978), *Square* (1987); *Screen* (1987)

Selected Awards and Exhibitions
1977–78, 1981–82, 1984, 1986, 1987, 1991
Award for textiles, Design Center Stuttgart
1978–79, 1980, 1982, 1984–85, 1988, 1989
Design Center Nordrhein Westphalia Award
1983 German Textile Museum, Krenfeld
1985/86 Bundespreis Guteform, German Federal Good Design Award
Museum of Decorative Arts, Zurich
Kunstgewerbemuseum, Zurich
1989 Stedelijk Museum, Amsterdam; German Textile Museum, Krenfeld
Museum of Decorative Arts, Belgium
1990 German Textile Museum, Krenfeld
Museum voor Sierskunst, Ghent

Peter Eisenman (b. 1932)

Born in Newark, New Jersey, Peter Eisenman has had a distinguished career as architect and academic. He earned his bachelor of architecture at Cornell University (1955), master of science in architecture at Columbia University (1960), and an MA at Cambridge University (1962), as well as a doctor of philosophy a year later. From 1982 to 1985, he was the Arthur Rotch Professor of Architecture at Harvard University. He was the first Irwin S. Chanin Distinguished Professor of Architecture at the Cooper Union School for Advancement of Science and Art and has taught at Cambridge, Princeton, Ohio State University, and Yale, where he currently holds the Louis I. Kahn Professor of Architecture Chair.

From the beginning of his career, Eisenman has been a prolific contributor to theoretical and historical architectural thought.[1] In 1967 he founded the Institute for Architecture and Urban Studies (IAUS), an international think-tank for architecture and architectural criticism, and served as director until 1982. He also edited IAUS publications,

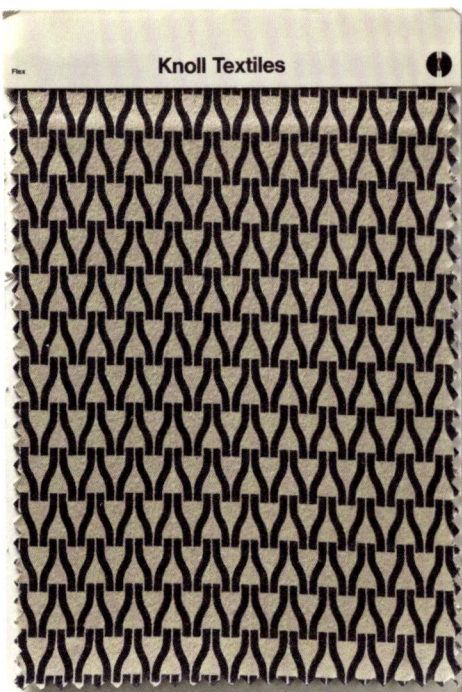

Fig. B.36 Klaus Dombrowski. *Flex* swatch, ("Blue and Beige" colorway) ca. 1978. Made in Europe for Knoll Textiles. Used for upholstery; polyester, cotton; warp-faced compound weave (5/1 satin weave and 1/2 twill weave). KnollTextile Archives. Cat. 216.

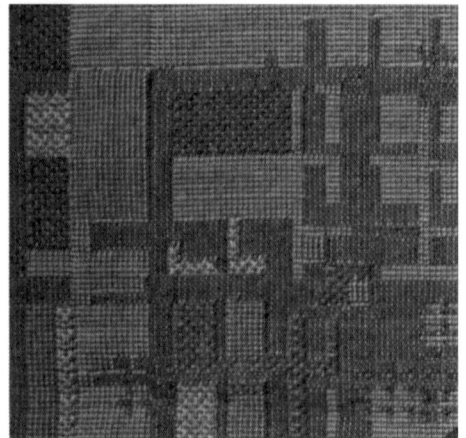

Fig. B.37 Peter Eisenman. *Lattice* ("Nickle" colorway), 1991. Made in the United Kingdom for Knoll Textiles. Used for upholstery; wool. KnollTextiles Archive.

notably the influential journal *Oppositions*. During this period he became associated with architects Charles Gwathmey, Richard Meier, Michael Graves, and John Hejduk, known as the "New York Five." Their work, while unique to each architect, came to represent an interest in pure architectural form elevated through intellectual discourse and theoretical underpinnings.[2]

In 1980 Eisenman established his full-time architectural practice—Eisenman Architects—and soon won many design competitions and awards, most notably for the Wexner Center for the Visual Arts (1983–89) and more recently for the Memorial to the Murdered Jews of Europe (1998–2005). The firm's projects include large-scale housing, urban design schemes, facilities for educational institutions, and private residences.[3] While attending the opening of Eisenman's Wexner Center in 1989, Hazel Siegel (KnollTextile's managing director of design worldwide) was struck by the affinities between his architecture and textile design.[4] She approached the architect about translating his architectural drawings into fabric patterns. The result was *Snakes and Ladders*, a collection of five textiles released by Knoll in 1991. The Jacquard weaves *Cobra*, *Diamond Back*, *Steppes*, and *Lattice* are wool, while *Sidewinder* represents a cotton alternative.

The Wexner Center's L-shaped window grid served as the basis for the interlocking L-pattern in *Steppes*, and the site plan informed the linear interplay of *Lattice* (fig. B.37).[5] *Cobra* and *Diamond Back* derive their designs from the site plan of the unbuilt Banyoles Olympic Hotel in Spain.[6] The Boolean cube geometries of the Carnegie Mellon Institute in Pittsburgh inspired the intricate pattern of *Sidewinder*.[7] Taking a cue from the philosopher Jean Baudrillard, Eisenman explained his concept behind the fabrics as a corrective to "a generation of instant-replay junkies who have lost their capacity to experience the subtleties and complexities of reality."[8] He envisioned the Knoll collection as having a sensorial grounding: "By re-emphasizing the tactility, the sensuality of experience, we are subtly trying to arouse those stimulants that bring a person back in touch with the material world."[9]
—CAL

Designs for Knoll
Snakes and Ladders collection: *Cobra* (1991–99), *Diamond Back* (1991–99), *Lattice* (1991–94), *Sidewinder* (1991–99), *Steppes* (1991–93).

Selected Awards and Exhibitions
1967 *The New City: Architecture and Urban Renewal*, MoMA
1985 *Stone Lion*, Third International Architecture Biennale, Venice, Italy
1988 National Honor Award, American Institute of Architects
Deconstructivist Architecture, MoMA
1994 *Cities of Artificial Excavation: The Work of Peter Eisenman, 1978–1988*, Canadian Center for Architecture, Montreal
2001 National Design Award, Cooper-Hewitt National Design Museum, Smithsonian Institution
2004 Jencks Award for Architectural Theory, Royal Institute of British Architects
Golden Lion for Lifetime Achievement in Architecture, Ninth International Architecture Biennale, Venice, Italy
2010 Wolf Foundation Prize

Ruben Eshkanian (b. 1929)

Ruben Eshkanian designed a single casement fabric for Knoll, *Trellis*, introduced in 1957. Sold by the company for more than twenty years, this lasting contribution to the Knoll Textiles collection was a highpoint of Eshkanian's early career.[1] Eshkanian was born and spent his childhood in Highland Park, Michigan, attending Highland Park Junior College and receiving a B.A. from Wayne State University. His career in textiles began in the late 1940s when he worked for the celebrated textile designer Ruth Adler Schnee in her Michigan retail store and textile printing studio, assisting with window displays and screen-printing fabrics. Eshkanian then attended Cranbrook Academy of Art (1950–52), with a letter of reference from Schnee (an alumna), who noted that he was talented and hard-working and would "be an asset to the Academy's high standards."[2] At Cranbrook, he studied weaving with Marianne Strengell. His enthusiasm for the discipline was sparked by the rigor and variety it afforded. He recalled being "spoiled" by a luxurious display of colored yarns shown to him by fellow student Jack Lenor Larsen.

In 1952 Eshkanian left Cranbrook (without completing his thesis) and relocated to New York City where he opened a weaving studio and textile shop with Cranbrook alumna Jeanne McIntyre in Greenwich

Village. They were soon recognized in the media for their tweedlike handwovens and jewel-toned prints.[3] They designed textiles for Thaibok, Inc. and the Troy Yarn and Textile Co.[4] In 1953 Eshkanian worked as an assistant to the chief designer at Cohn-Hall-Marx Fabrics (Cohama), which also employed Knoll designer Evelyn Hill for a short time during this period. In 1954 Eshkanian left Cohama to freelance for New York textile and rug companies such as Spectrum Fabrics and Rugcrafters, Inc.[5]

As part of his freelance work Eshkanian designed an open-weave linen casement for Joynel Co. (see chapter 3). Joynel showed it to Knoll, and it was included in the Knoll Textiles collection in 1957. Aptly named *Trellis* for its gridlike construction, it stayed in production until 1978 (fig. B.38).[6] Woven on a box loom, *Trellis* offered a more sophisticated alternative to Knoll's *Fishnet* and was appropriate drapery for the large window walls of modern buildings with new window air conditioners.[7] In 1959, with the approval of Eshkanian and Florence Knoll, the weave structure of the design was adjusted—a special knot was introduced to prevent slippage of the weave's fibers over time. The adjustment allowed for more structural stability, and resulted in a more standardized and gridlike aesthetic (see fig. 3.66).[8]

In 1961 *Trellis* was included alongside some of Knoll's most celebrated textiles, such as designs by Anni Albers, Sven Markelius, Suzanne Huguenin, and Ross Littell, in the exhibition *Met Textiel* at the Stedelijk Museum in Amsterdam.[9] The exhibition aimed to demonstrate the integration of modern textiles and architecture, one of Knoll's primary commercial aims.

In early 1957, just prior to *Trellis* being picked up by Knoll, Jack Lenor Larsen hired Eshkanian as an executive assistant who soon took on more design-related responsibilities at the company. Within a year Larsen selected Eshkanian—whom he would later call his "protégé"—to assist in a special project administered by the International Cooperation Administration (ICA), an organization that aimed to stimulate cottage industries in developing countries.[10] The American design firm Russel Wright Associates was assigned to Southeast Asia and after surveying the native craft products in the region and assessing their marketability in the United States, Wright gave Larsen a three-year contract to develop grass-weaving projects in Taiwan and South Vietnam.[11] Larsen appointed Eshkanian to be junior designer on the project, and the young designer moved to Southeast Asia, settling in Saigon and Taiwan, where he established deep and lasting connections with indigenous weavers. He remained in the region after Larsen returned to the United States.[12]

After completion of the ICA project Eshkanian worked with the Peace Corps design initiative in Puerto Rico and participated in the International Development Alliance for Progress program in Peru in 1961.[13] These experiences influenced his practice, leading him to experiment with exotic materials including cypress shavings, coconut wood fibers, and sisal.

After returning to the United States in the early 1960s, Eshkanian established himself as a designer-craftsman and educator. In 1962, on Larsen's recommendation, he joined the faculty of the Fibers Art Department at the Philadelphia Museum School of Art (renamed the Philadelphia College of Art in 1964).[14] He was appointed chair of the department in 1977 and retired in 1979.[15]

Despite his move to academia, he continued to exhibit extensively and to work with commercial clients. By 1964, however, he had sold designs to Galey and Lord, Inc. and also was a frequent color consultant to the industry throughout 1960s and 1970s.[16] After his retirement from teaching, he worked as a weaver and designer from his Connecticut studio through the 1980s; he now lives in Muncie, Indiana. —AMT

Design for Knoll
Trellis (1957–78).

Selected Awards and Exhibitions
1952 *Exhibition for Michigan Artist-Craftsman*, Detroit Institute of Arts
1953 *Designer-Craftsmen U.S.A.*, Brooklyn Museum
1956 *Craftsmen in a Changing World*, Museum of Contemporary Crafts, New York
1957 *Object Art '57*, Zabriskie Gallery, New York
1961 *Fabrics International*, Museum of Contemporary Crafts and Philadelphia Museum College of Art
Met Textiel, Stedelijk Museum, Amsterdam (*Trellis* shown)
1964 *Designed for Production: The Craftsman's Approach*, Museum of Contemporary Crafts, New York
1967 *Craftsman '67*, Museum of the Philadelphia Civic Center

Fig. B.38 Ruben Eshkanian. *Trellis* swatch from archive memo, original weave version, 1957. Made in Belgium for Knoll Textiles. Used for drapery; linen; plain-weave–derived simple weave. KnollTextiles Archive.

Fig. B.39 Shirley Fletcher Rapson (later Nickerson). *Isles* (two colorways), 1947. Photographed by Phyllis A. Dearborn, Dearborn-Massar. Knoll Archives.

1970 *Objects: USA*, Johnson Collection of Contemporary American Crafts, Smithsonian Institution, Washington D.C.
1977 *American Craft '77*, Philadelphia Museum of Art
1979 *Selected Works*, Helen Drutt Gallery, Philadelphia

Shirley Fletcher Nickerson (born 1923)

Shirley Fletcher was born in Santa Monica, California, and raised in Marblehead, Massachusetts, and Wilmington, Delaware.[1] Daughter of Theodore Fletcher, a prominent architect in Wilmington, Fletcher took courses in art at the Wilmington Academy of Art before enrolling in the fall of 1941 at the Cranbrook Academy of Art in Bloomfield Hills, Michigan.[2] She studied weaving and developed a series of block-printed textile designs under the guidance of Marianne Strengell, head of the weaving department. Fletcher also met Ralph Rapson, a graduate of the University of Michigan's architecture program, who had studied architecture and design at Cranbrook and was working in the architectural office of Eliel Saarinen (head of Cranbrook), and his son Eero.[3] Fletcher and Rapson were soon married.

In 1942 Shirley Fletcher Rapson moved to Chicago to join her husband, who had been appointed head of the architecture program at the Institute of Design. Florence Schust (later Knoll), who attended Cranbrook at the same time as Ralph Rapson, introduced him to Hans Knoll, and Knoll asked Rapson to submit furniture designs to the company in 1944. In their correspondence, Knoll shared with Rapson his interest in starting a textile division after the war. Rapson brought some of his wife's designs to Hans Knoll's attention and one of these, *Isles* (fig. B.39), was among the earliest print fabrics developed by the company. It was used by Florence Knoll in 1946 in the offices of the Rockefeller family at Rockefeller Center and was featured in Knoll's first textile collection in 1947 (see chapters 2 and 3). *Isles* was printed on a textured rayon-cotton blend in at least four colorways and its designer was credited as "Shirle Rapson" by Knoll.[4]

In 1946 the Rapsons moved to Marblehead, Massachusetts, so that Ralph could take a professorship at Massachusetts Institute of Technology and Shirley could be closer to her family. However, the couple soon divorced, and she later remarried, becoming Shirley Nickerson. Although she continued to experiment with weaving and block-printing as a hobby, she devoted much of her time to raising her children and maintaining her home in Marblehead, where she resides in 2011. —EM

Design for Knoll
Isles (1946–ca. 1950).

Josef Frank (1885–1967)

Josef Frank was born in Baden and raised in Vienna, Austria. He studied architecture at the Technische Hochschule (Institute of Technology, today University of Technology) in Vienna, receiving his undergraduate degree in 1908, and his doctoral degree in 1910. While still a student, Frank began working on architectural and interior projects on his own and in collaboration with architects Oskar Strnad and Oskar Wlach, who belonged to a circle of like-minded architects seeking new directions in the design of modern interiors. Before World War I they participated in several important Viennese design exhibitions.[1] After serving as an officer in the Austro-Hungarian army during the war, Frank resumed his architectural practice and was appointed professor at the Vienna Kunstgewerbeschule (School of Arts and Crafts). In 1925 he started a home furnishings business, Haus & Garten, together with Wlach and Walter Sobotka.[2] The business was a commercial and critical success, but by the early 1930s Frank, who was Jewish, found his position in Vienna endangered by the rise of the German Nazi party and anti-Semitism in Austria. Frank and his Swedish wife, Anna, moved to Stockholm in 1933.

Frank had first designed textiles around 1910 and after the war worked on patterns for the textile workshop of the Wiener Werkstätte. During the 1920s he turned more of his attention to textile design and designed many successful patterns for Haus & Garten.[3] In 1932, while Frank was still in Vienna, Estrid Ericson, the founder of the Swedish interior design shop Svensk Tenn, asked him to create some furniture. Shortly thereafter she offered him a permanent position, and they began a fruitful collaboration that would last through the 1960s. Frank is today best remembered for the exuberant textile patterns he designed for Svensk Tenn. These drew on a variety of historical styles, as well as influences such as the work of William Morris, but were given a distinctive character by Frank's stylized yet naturalistic treatment of botanical motifs and masterful handling of scale and pattern repeats.

After the German invasion of Denmark and Norway in 1940, the Franks no longer felt safe in Sweden, and late in 1941 they moved to New York City, where they remained for the duration of World War II. Frank taught at the New School for Social Research (now the New School University) and created many new textile designs, including a group of fifty patterns that he sent to Estrid Ericson in 1944. These designs formed the core of Svensk Tenn's postwar textile collections, and many remain in production in 2011.[4] Several of Frank's New York patterns, including US Tree, based on the field guide Trees of North America, and Manhattan, featuring cartouchelike details of the Manhattan street map connected by winding ribbons of text, took their inspiration from American themes.[5] Manhattan was put into production by Svensk Tenn after the Franks returned to Sweden in 1946. It was also part of the first textile collection offered by Knoll in 1947, the only Svensk Tenn design known to have been retailed by Knoll.[6] Frank's connection to Knoll remains unclear, but it is possible that the design was in a packaged group of home furnishings from Sweden that Knoll also introduced in early 1947 (see chapter 2).

After the war Frank's work for Svensk Tenn largely concentrated on the design of furniture and interiors. Although Frank designed few new textile patterns, Ericson released his wartime patterns a few at a time, thereby providing "new" Frank designs at regular intervals, while keeping the more successful patterns in continuous production. Frank continued to design for Svensk Tenn through the early 1960s. He died in Stockholm in 1967. —SW

Design for Knoll
Manhattan (1947; designed 1943–44).

Selected Awards and Exhibitions
1927 Weissenhofsiedlung, Stuttgart
1939 Swedish Pavilion, New York World's Fair
Swedish Pavilion, Golden Gate Exposition, San Francisco
1952 *Josef Frank: Twenty Years at Svensk Tenn*, Nationalmuseum, Stockholm
1958 *Josef Frank: 25 Years in Sweden*, Svensk Tenn, Stockholm
1965 Austrian State Prize for Architecture
1968 *Josef Frank, 1885–1967*, Nationalmuseum, Stockholm
1998 *Josef Frank, Architect and Designer*, Bard Graduate Center, New York

Jean Pierre Garrault (b. 1942)

Born in Paris, Jean Pierre Garrault was largely self-taught as an artist, learning basic drawing and painting skills under the guidance of his father, an amateur painter.[1] He attended secondary school and spent a year at the Prépa IDHEC film school. At age seventeen he was given a travel grant from the Zellidja (Bourses de Voyages) Scholarship Foundation to pursue photography and painting. Throughout his career he has been prolific in a wide range of fields, from the design of interiors, textiles, and ceramics, to installation art, video, computer art, and painting.

In 1964 Garrault began his professional career in the research office of the furniture company Roche & Bobois in Paris working in interior design. There he met Maryvonne Jeanne, another artist, and the two were married in 1966. A year later, he left his job and began to work as a freelance designer. Under the label JMP Garrault, he and his wife designed upholstery fabrics for Roche & Bobois, as well as carpets, wallpaper, furniture, and interiors for various clients, including the fashion designer Pierre Cardin for whom they designed the interior of a Simca automobile in 1969. In 1968 Garrault designed modular seating, armchairs, and lighting for the department store chain Prisunic, and these were featured in their first mail-order furniture catalogue and years later included in a Prisunic exhibition.[2] In 1968 he also created several ceramics for the Milan firm Cedit Ceramiche, winning a Compasso d'Oro for *Garrault 34* and *Garrault 35*.

In 1969 he began producing textiles, carpets, and wallpapers for several design companies, including Conran's, Heal's, Urgé, Tapisift, and Kröner. Most of his patterns were bold, colorful geometric designs. By 1970 he had established the design studio Garrault-Delord-Design with Henri Delord. The studio produced textiles, wallpaper, carpets, furniture, and interiors until the partnership dissolved in 1977. Many Garrault-Delord designs were exhibited at the Musée d'art moderne de la Ville de Paris (1971), Eurodomus Milan (1970), Eurodomus Turin (1972), and the Salon des Artistes Decorateurs in Paris (1972). In 1971 Knoll Textiles introduced *Frames*, a printed polyester

Fig. B.40 J. P. Garrault. *Frames* sample ("Brown" colorway), 1971. Made in Europe for Knoll Textiles. Used for drapery; polyester; screen-printed. KnollTextiles Archive.

Fig. B.41 Alexander Girard. *Links* ("Gray on White" colorway), late 1940s. Made for Alexander Girard. Used for drapery; cotton; plain weave, screen-printed. Cooper-Hewitt, National Design Museum, Smithsonian Institution, Gift of Alexander H. Girard, 1969-165-16.

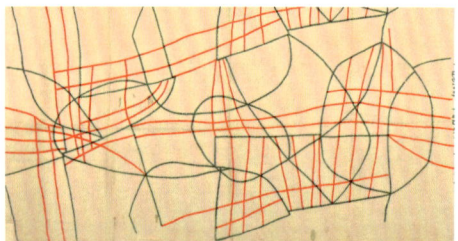

Fig. B.42 Alexander Girard. *Wires*, late 1940s. Made for Alexander Girard. Used for drapery; linen; plain weave, screen-printed. Cooper-Hewitt, National Design Museum, Smithsonian Institution, 1969-165-18.

casement based on a design by Garrault, for the European Market (fig. B.40). In 1978 *Frames* was shown at the Third Triennial Tkaniny in Lodz, Poland, and the same year, Garrault was contacted by Arthur Sager, vice president of Knoll's Textile Division, about the possibility of managing the company's design and development in Europe.[3] Garrault declined, preferring to remain an independent designer.

From 1982 until 1996, Garrault was a freelance design consultant and the artistic director for Formica International, and then at Buflon-Solvay from 1996 until 2003. He became interested in computer art and graphics in 1978, leading to the formation of the artist collective Art Virtuel in 1987. Since 2003, he has focused his artistic production on pain-ting, video making, and installations based in his atelier in Massoult, Burgundy.
—CAL

Design for Knoll
Frames (Europe only, 1971–81).

Selected Exhibitions
1970 Salon des Artistes Decorateurs (SAD), Grand Palais, Paris
1971 *Espaces Urbains*, Musée d'art moderne de la Ville de Paris
1972 *Knoll au Louvre*, Musée des Arts décoratifs, Paris
1978 Third Triennial Tkaniny, Lodz, Poland
1980 *Création Graphique et Ordinateur*, Centre George Pompidou, Paris (circulating exhibition)
1998 *Prisunic*, Le Musée d'art moderne de Saint-Etienne
2008 "Prisunic & Design, A Unique Adventure," VIA (Valorisation de l'Innovation dans l'Ameublement), Paris

Alexander Girard (1907–1993)

Alexander Girard was a prolific designer, whose influence was felt in many areas of twentieth-century design. He is today best remembered for the textile collections he designed for Herman Miller between 1952 and 1973, and as the creator of such iconic projects as the New York restaurant La Fonda del Sol (1960) and the redesign of Braniff International Airlines (1965). Before joining Herman Miller, however, Girard played an important role in the postwar development of modern textile design. He also worked on several important midcentury exhibitions and participated (if indirectly) in the formation of Knoll Textiles.

Girard was born in New York City and grew up in Florence, Italy, the son of an American mother and a French-Italian father. He studied at the Architectural Association in London beginning in 1925. After graduating in 1929 he returned to Florence on a traveling scholarship and won a Gold Medal for his work on the Italian Pavilion at the 1929 International Exposition in Barcelona. He continued his studies at the Royal School of Architecture in Rome (1930–31) and at New York University (1932–35). In 1937 he opened an office in Detroit and over the next decade practiced architecture and interior design, including work for Ford Motor Company and the Detrola Corporation. In 1949 Girard organized and designed the landmark *Exhibition For Modern Living* at the Detroit Institute of Arts. He went on to design several important exhibitions for MoMA, including the 1953 (and January 1954) editions of *Good Design*. During his tenure at Herman Miller he would continue to work on a variety of architectural, exhibition, and interior projects.

Girard's textiles first came to public attention through the two Honorable Mentions he received in MoMA's *Competition for Printed Fabrics* (1946)—one for his own entry, the other for a pattern he designed with Eero Saarinen ("coordinated" by Charles Eames).[1] Girard's textiles were again exhibited in January 1947 at the annual AID meeting.[2] That same year he established a new office and retail shop in Grosse Pointe, Michigan, and expanded his textile production. Later in 1947 his prints *Spines* and *Links*, although probably printed by Girard or for his own distribution, were promoted as available through Knoll Textiles (figs. B.41, B.42; see chapter 3).[3] Girard also sold them through his own shop, along with a comprehensive collection of fabrics by Angelo Testa, June Groff, Goodall (Dorothy Liebes), Harry Schulke, Antoinette Lackner Webster, and Knoll.[4] His patterns from this period were looser in feeling than his later designs for Herman Miller, but by 1949 he was already taking a more systematic approach to his print collection than many of his contemporaries, offering his designs printed on a choice of two base fabrics and in twelve standard colors.[5]

When Herman Miller established its Textile Division in 1952, the company hired Girard as the new division's director and sole designer, a position he would hold until he retired in the mid-1970s. His textile collections for Herman Miller reflected his love of folk art and traditional textiles from Mexico and India and were distinctive for their clear, bright colors and playful sensibility. They also demonstrated his practical experience with how fabrics are used; in designing drapery fabrics, for example, he consciously chose simple patterns that would not be distorted by drapery folds.[6] His first collection—a carefully coordinated range of woven and printed fabrics with over thirty small-scale geometric patterns and 120 colorways in a palette of related "spectrum" and neutral colors—was an immediate success.[7] Girard would build upon this basic vocabulary over the next two decades. In 1971 Herman Miller released Girard's final major project—the *Environmental Enrichment Panels*—a series of forty decorative screen-printed panels that allowed customers to personalize the standardized elements of the company's *Action Office 2* cubicle system.

For much of his time with Herman Miller, Girard worked from his home in Santa Fe, New Mexico, where he had moved in 1953. There, he and his wife, Susan, assembled a collection of over 100,000 folk art objects from around the world, which became the basis for the Girard Foundation. In 1978 the Girards donated the collection to the Museum of International Folk Art in Santa Fe. Alexander Girard designed the installation in the museum's now Girard Wing which opened in 1982. —SW

Designs for Knoll
Links (1947); *Spines* (1947); *Wires* (1947–49).

Selected Awards and Exhibitions
1929 Gold Medal, International Exposition, Barcelona
1947 *Printed Textiles for the Home*, MoMA; awarded two Honorable Mentions (one shared with Eero Saarinen and Charles Eames)
AID exhibition, Art Institute of Chicago
1949 *Modern Textiles*, Everyday Art Gallery, Walker Art Center, Minneapolis, Minnesota (*Links* shown)
Second National Biennial of Contemporary Textiles and Ceramics, Cranbrook (*Spines* shown)
An Exhibition for Modern Living, Detroit Institute of Arts (*Wires* shown)
Modern Art in Your Life, MoMA (*Wires* shown)
1952–55 *Good Design*, Merchandise Mart (January and June 1952, January and June 1953, January 1955), MoMA (1952, 1953)
1952 *Textilien aus USA*, Smithsonian circulating exhibition
1954 *Good Design, 100 Museum Selections*, Merchandise Mart (June) and MoMA
1956 *Textiles USA*, MoMA
1975 *Nelson, Eames, Girard, Probst: The Design Process at Herman Miller*, Walker Art Center, Minneapolis
1983 *Design Since 1945*, Philadelphia Museum of Art
1995 *Design 1935–1965: What Modern Was*, Musée des Arts décoratifs de Montréal
2001 *The Opulent Eye of Alexander Girard*, Cooper-Hewitt, National Design Museum, Smithsonian Institution

Friedrich Goth (active 1970s)

Friedrich Goth studied under Leo Wollner at the Staatliche Akademie der Bildenden Künste (State Academy of Art and Design) in Stuttgart in the early 1970s. He was one of the textile design students who in 1972 participated in "Transparent," whereby students submitted woven casement designs to Knoll. Goth's design for the competition was later selected for mass production and called *Comet* by Knoll. It was one of three student designs known to have been introduced commercially by the company.[1] Knoll produced it as a wide-width casement made from Dralon acrylic fiber; it was manufactured by Krueger GmbH in Germany (see fig. 5.23). Another design by Goth appeared in *Zwischen Industrie und Kunst* (Between Industry and Art), a 1976 exhibition held at the Design Center Stuttgart.[2] —CBPP

Design for Knoll
Comet (1973–77).

Fig. B.43 Kathrin Hagge. *Crystal Pleat,* 2001. Made for KnollTextiles in the United States. Used for upholstery; polyester, rayon, acrylic. KnollTextiles Archive.

Fig. B.44 Eszter Haraszty wearing a dress made from her design *Fata Morgana,* ca. 1949. Photographed by Erich Hartmann. Magnum Photos.

Fig. B.45 Eszter Haraszty. *Triad* ("Black, Navy, Royal, White, on Blue" colorway), introduced ca. 1954, this example 1955. Used for drapery; cotton; plain weave, screen-printed. The Museum of Modern Art, New York, Gift of Knoll Associates, SC25.1975.2.

Exhibition
1976 *Zwischen Industrie und Kunst* (Between Industry and Art), Design Center Stuttgart

Kathrin Hagge (b. 1963)

Born in Bonn, Germany, Kathrin Hagge studied textile design at the Fachhochschule Reutlingen (University for Economics, Technology, Computer Science, and Design)in Reutlingen, Germany, receiving a Diplom Ingenieur (FH) in 1984.[1] She relocated to Italy in 1987 to work as an assistant textile stylist and then textile researcher at Setterie Riccardo Mantero S.p.A. in Como.[2] Two years later she moved to New York City to study at the Fashion Institute of Technology.[3] After receiving her bachelor's degree in 1990, Jhane Barnes hired Hagge to assist in the development of woven fabrics for Barnes's collections of men's apparel, as well as upholstery and wallcoverings for KnollTextiles.[4] Hagge returned to Germany in 1993 and worked freelance for European textile companies such as Christian Fischbacher in Switzerland and former Knoll supplier Taunus Textildruck in Germany.[5]

In 1996 Deborah Steele, director of design at KnollTextiles, hired Hagge for a designer position. She worked with sales representatives to develop custom textiles for specific projects, and as a staff designer, she often collaborated with fellow staff designer Sarah Baker on textiles for the general line. She remained in this dual role until 1998 when the new director of design, Suzanne Tick, shifted her responsibilities to designing textiles solely for the main collection. While Hagge was not credited with many of the textiles she helped to create during her tenure at Knoll, she has received accolades for three upholstery fabrics: *Arras* (1999), *3-D* (2000), and *Crystal Pleat* (2001) (fig. B.43).

Arras, a tapestry weave in a cotton, rayon, and polyester blend, featured both organic and geometric abstract motifs with subtle three-color palettes and was targeted for both modern and transitional interiors.[6] *3-D* and *Crystal Pleat* employed an innovative finishing technique that resulted in a three-dimensional surface pattern. Both the accordion texture of *3-D* and the rectangular pattern of *Crystal Pleat* were created by weaving acrylic yarn into the back of the fabric, which shrinks during the finishing process resulting in the puckered relief effect of the textiles.[7] Both were woven in the United States and composed of polyester, rayon, and acrylic fibers.[8] Each textile featured subtle two-tone effects and was offered in both subdued and vibrant colorways.[9] When *Crystal Pleat* was included in Knoll's 2001 NeoCon installation, it garnered attention in the trade press, including such publications as *Interiors* and *Contract*.[10]

After leaving Knoll in 2002, Hagge worked at Jack Lenor Larsen as the senior textile designer until 2008. During this time she focused on designs for the hospitality and residential markets and until 2004 worked directly with Larsen on design and development projects.[11] Beginning in 2009 she was the design director for woven textiles at Stroheim & Romann. When the company was sold a year later, Hagge relocated to India for a one-year contract position with Eastern Silk Industries in Bangalore. —AMT

Designs for Knoll
Arras (1999–2004); *3-D* (2000–08); *Crystal Pleat* (2001–08).

Selected Exhibitions and Awards
1999 *Good Design* Award for *Arras*, Chicago Athenaeum
2000 *Good Design* Award for *3-D*, Chicago Athenaeum
2001 *US Design 1975–2000*, Denver Art Museum (circulating exhibition, *Crystal Pleat* shown)

Eszter Haraszty (1920–1994)

Eszter Haraszty was the leading force within Knoll's textile division in the first half of the 1950s. In addition to creating iconic textile designs, she was adept at promotion and became Knoll's color authority—using her distinctive palette and keen color sense to create some of Knoll's most memorable installations and color combinations.

Born to a well-to-do Jewish family in Budapest, Hungary, Haraszty studied painting and art history at the Magyar Képzómúvészeti Egyetem (Royal Academy of Fine Arts) and also undertook "a thorough study of color theory and the I. G. Farben dyes."[1] She began designing and making clothing while in school and then branched out into making sets and costumes for the stage. World War II made living in Hungary difficult, and as a young Jewish woman, Haraszty was lucky to escape with her life under the German occupation that began in

1944. The "liberation" of Hungary by Russian forces made life only slightly better. In 1947 Haraszty visited her sister, the wife of a Hungarian diplomat in Washington D.C., and during her visit a Soviet-controlled election turned Hungary into a satellite state of the Communist regime.[2] Facing an uncertain future in her homeland, Haraszty decided to remain in the United States.

She settled in New York City, staying with her compatriots Marcel and Constance Breuer, whom she would later describe as "my godparents in this country."[3] Haraszty found work at Drago Studio, a small fabric decorating and screen-printing firm about which little is known, and by 1949 she was designing textile patterns hand-screened on "silk shantungs, organdy, Egyptian cotton or linen" under the name "Eszter."[4] One of these was *Fata Morgana* (ca. 1949), a densely concentrated linear pattern that recalled medieval stained glass (fig. B.44).[5] Arundell Clarke, former showroom manager for Knoll's textile division (1947), included some of Haraszty's fabrics in his own textile line and supplied one of her designs, a fabric printed with broad horizontal stripes, for use as drapery in Marcel Breuer's landmark "House in the Museum Garden," at MoMA in 1949.[6] That same year, at Breuer's suggestion, Haraszty contacted Hans Knoll about design work, and she was offered a "Good job at Knoll, part time, consultant, $75 a week."[7]

Over the next six years, Haraszty contributed several of the most notable Knoll textiles and regularly brought acclaim to the company through the many awards given to her fabrics. *Cinders*, her first design for Knoll, introduced in November 1950, was a drapery print reminiscent of her previous work in its composition of black solid lines and organic shapes on a white or colored base cloth (see fig. 3.29).[8] Haraszty later recalled the print's origin: "I sat in [the] Breuer house, watched rain on glass, painted it, [and] somehow it was [a] perfect repeat."[9] Haraszty reworked the horizontal stripe design she had created for Breuer's "House in the Museum Garden," and named it *Knoll Stripes*. Suitable for both drapery and small-scale upholstery applications, this print fabric debuted in early 1951 and was recognized for its unique color combinations—"all very vivid."[10] In late 1949 and 1950 Haraszty developed *Transportation Cloth*, an upholstery initially created for use in the General Motors Technical Center, an important Knoll Planning Unit project at the time, and it became part of the Knoll Textiles collection by 1951. Haraszty later noted that this hard-wearing, all-rayon upholstery "was the first industrial fabric, the first one that stood all the tests."[11] It remained in the Knoll line through the late 1970s, becoming one of Knoll's standard fabrics.[12] Both *Transportation Cloth* and *Knoll Stripes* were included in the 1951 *Good Design* exhibitions jointly sponsored by MoMA and Merchandise Mart, Chicago.[13]

In 1952 and 1953 Haraszty created several innovative print fabrics for the Knoll collection. For *Tracy* (1952) she used the ribs and veining of a leaf, a literal "tracing" of a natural form, as the pattern's abstracted linear repeat. Printed on a variety of sheer and heavier-weight fabrics suited for drapery use, it was one of her most important designs for Knoll (see chapter 3). Haraszty again used a motif from nature in her 1953 pattern *Spruce*, which had a repeat of pine needles in two closely related colors printed across a base cloth of linen or silk gauze (fig. B.46). *Fibra*, Haraszty's other 1953 print introduction, became one of her most successful designs for Knoll and is among the best-known print fabrics of the 1950s. *Fibra*'s motif, derived from an enlarged photo of the heddles of a loom, was initially printed on linen in a variety of striking colorways (fig. B.47). Both *Tracy* and *Fibra* won great acclaim for Haraszty and Knoll: they were honored by AID, and *Fibra* was also selected for MoMA's *Good Design* exhibition in 1953.[14] It remained in production until 1971.

Haraszty's later designs for Knoll included several fabrics that would long outlast her time with the company. In 1955 her print *Triad*—a vertical linear motif in three colors and black on a white or colored base fabric—was introduced to immediate accolades (fig. B.45).[15] Knoll debuted three other Haraszty designs the same year.[16] The upholstery fabric *Spectra* and a related drapery *Spectra Magna* feature a woven pattern repeat of small squares in a range of related tones of the same color (fig B.49). *Spectra Magna* became one of Haraszty's longest-lasting designs for Knoll; although it was discontinued in the United States in 1961, it was offered by the firm's international divisions into the 1980s.[17] *Ombre*, which was designed for both upholstery and drapery, combined the textures and natural colors of wool, cotton, jute, and viscose.

Knoll introduced Haraszty's designs *Façade* and *Sarano* in early 1956, just after her departure from the company at the end

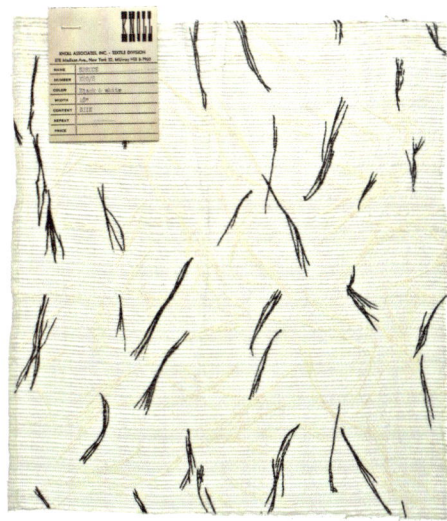

Fig. B.46 Eszter Haraszty. *Spruce* sample ("Black and White on White" colorway), ca. 1953. Made for Knoll Textiles. Used for drapery; silk gauze; plain weave, screen-printed. Cranbrook Art Museum, Bloomfield Hills, Mich., T 2010.13.3. Cat. 61.

Fig. B.47 Eszter Haraszty. *Fibra* sample ("Pink, Red, Cream, on Orange" colorway), introduced 1953. Made by Printex for Knoll Textiles. Used for drapery; linen; plain weave, screen-printed. Cooper-Hewitt, National Design Museum, Smithsonian Institution, Gift of Mae Festa, 1991-157-6-b. Cat. 51.

Fig. B.48 Eszter Haraszty. *Lana* sample ("Persimmon" colorway), ca. 1960. Made by Orinoka Mills for Knoll Textiles. Used for upholstery; wool, nylon; basket weave. KnollTextiles Archive, donated by Doreen Rose Stempien. Cat. 117.

Fig. B.49 Eszter Haraszty. *Spectra Magna* ("Blue and Green" colorway), introduced 1955. Made by Orinoka Mills for Knoll Textiles. Used for upholstery; linen, cotton; twill variation. Courtesy Richard and Trudy Schultz. Cat. 115.

of 1955. *Façade*, a linear print design reminiscent of the geometric glass and steel exteriors of modern office buildings, was described by *Interiors* magazine as "black lines with brilliantly colored blocks on a white ground."[18] *Sarano* was another in Knoll's efforts to provide the market with a hard-wearing synthetic upholstery, this time composed of Saran fiber. *Sarano* was available in a tweedlike weave with a black warp and strong color in the weft, as well as a version with a narrow stripe. *Sarano* seems to have sold well, but after the introduction in 1958 of the popular and very durable *Knoll Nylon Homespun*, it was discontinued, not being able to match the sales of this competitive textile.[19] While not publicly attributed to Haraszty, *Lana*, her final design for Knoll, is credited to her in internal company memos.[20] The upholstery textile features a gridded pattern resulting from a basket weave of yarns in close tonal variations (fig. B.48). *Lana*'s initial all-wool fiber content was adjusted to wool and nylon in the late 1950s, and it remained in the line until 1978.[21]

Less tangible today are the other skills that Haraszty brought to Knoll—her keen color sense, interior design abilities, and talent for promotion. Haraszty's use of color often drew comment in the period press, likely contributing to Knoll's reputation as a style leader during the first half of the 1950s. Her rethinking of Knoll Textiles' promotion during this period led to several key innovations. One of her first undertakings after joining Knoll was to recolor some of the firm's successful prints. Haraszty developed new colorways for Stig Lindberg's *Apples*, Noémi Raymond's *Chinese Coins*, and Marianne Strengell's *Shooting Stars*. *Interior Design* magazine noted the "sharp, clear, paint-box colors," referring to the brighter primary tones Haraszty developed to replace the original muted ones.[22] The *Chicago Tribune* described the "wintry tones" of Haraszty's new colorings of *Apples*, such as black on blue and black on brown, as well as the "deep colors" of Haraszty's new combinations for *Chinese Coins*—black on red, blue on red, and brown on gray (see chapter 3).[23] The *Tribune*'s review of these fabrics was within an article on Knoll's "Roving Fabric Show," a new promotional tour that was circulating to Knoll showrooms and retailers of Knoll fabrics across the country.[24] Developed by Haraszty, this tour highlighted the versatility of the Knoll textile collection and presented drapery prints with coordinating upholstery fabrics. A similar effort was carried out by Haraszty in the Knoll "Fabric Color Guides," which were announced at the end of 1950.[25] These handy references, available to architects and interior designers, promoted the collection for the next several years (see chapter 3).

By the end of 1950 Haraszty's skills at design and color had been noticed by Hans Knoll, and she was named the coordinator for Knoll Textiles as well as Knoll's chief colorist.[26] One of her initial color design projects was her work on the new flagship showroom in New York that opened in February 1951 (see chapter 4).[27] Olga Gueft of *Interiors* magazines remarked on the transformation in Knoll's color range, noting pillows covered in "fuschia, pink, flame, citron and violet blue" textiles, "not in Mrs. Knoll's usual Mondrian colors."[28] Haraszty continued to provide color schemes for Knoll showrooms, including those in Miami, Detroit, Paris, Brussels, and Havana.[29]

While Hans Knoll asked Haraszty to work on color schemes for Planning Unit projects, these were often radically changed or dismissed entirely, and she instead specialized in the design and colors for special exhibitions and displays presented by Knoll. As she later recalled, "I always did exhibitions, showy things where you could play around."[30] In 1952 Haraszty worked with Evelyn Hill to develop a collection of handwoven textiles that featured striking color combinations. *Interiors* magazine characterized them as "dramatic and vivid—not primary colors, but exotic, striking hues, hot and vibrant . . . wonderful, eye stopping pinks, often combined unexpectedly with brilliant orange, or come up against jewel-bright sapphire, and lucid emerald."[31] These fabrics debuted in March 1952 at AID's national convention (fig. B.50). For Knoll's display, Haraszty and Herbert Matter (the firm's graphic designer) designed what the *New York Times* described as a "modern maze of handwoven textiles creating a fabric composition" that was "brilliantly exciting in color and depth, with orange, purple, chartreuse and deep-blue greens clashing in heady fashion" (see fig. 3.53).[32] In December 1952 Haraszty created the display for Knoll's introduction of Harry Bertoia's wire shell chairs. She set them in the New York showroom in dark backgrounds dramatically lit to highlight the metallic gleam of the chair frames and the brilliant colors of the seat cushions.[33] In the fall of 1952 she helped to create the installation for *Knoll Furniture and Textiles*, an exhibition at the Dallas Museum of Art (see fig. 4.47 and cat. 72).[34] Her characteristic concentrated splashes of rich colors against a dark or neutral background were used throughout and highlighted in the Knoll brochure for the exhibition: "an all-over effect of black and white is a perfect foil for concentration of brilliant color provided by the pinks and oranges of the upholstered pieces."[35]

While at the textile division, Haraszty oversaw the introduction of many different patterns by other designers and mills—shepherding them from initial designs to final products. Period press accounts credited her with color decisions for many Knoll textiles, including *Diamonds* by Albert Herbert, *Ringles* by Carol Summer, *Citronnade* by Jacqueline Iribe, and *Shogi* by Dennis Lennon (see chapter 3). Haraszty, who enjoyed a close relationship with Herbert Matter, also collaborated on graphics and advertisements for Knoll Textiles, such as the 1952 advertisement for the new Hill *Handwoven* collection, (see fig. B.50).[36] Toward the end of her time at Knoll, Haraszty developed a new promotional device for the division. As she later remembered, "we always had this terrible problem of how to present the textiles," and in 1954 she, with graphic designer Ladislav Sutnar, devised the Knoll Textile Kit.[37] It consisted of two small booklets, one devoted to the upholstery fabrics, the other to multipurpose fabrics (drapery, casements, sheers), and a third, larger booklet on Knoll's print collection, all packaged together in a fitted box (cat. 38). This innovative kit featured swatches of each fabric mounted in paper cards and provided designer names and textile data such as fiber content and, in the case of prints, photo cards showing how the textile would appear in multiple repeats.[38] *Industrial Design* magazine featured the kit in its annual design review for 1954 and fifteen years later included it in a retrospective of design highlights.[39] Haraszty would later recall that it "went over very big."[40]

In 1954 personal tensions within the company resulted in a difficult atmosphere for Haraszty, and she became a part-time consultant for Knoll.[41] She began to work with other clients, including Fuller Fabrics and the fashion house B. H. Wragge, for whom she developed a line of women's sportswear that featured modified forms of Knoll prints such as *Fibra*. This line became quite successful and was even featured in *Harper's Bazaar*.[42] With Hans Knoll's death on October 8, 1955, Haraszty lost her chief champion in the firm. Her relationship with Florence Knoll became increasingly difficult, and at the end of 1955, Knoll Associates terminated her consultant contract.

Haraszty spent only a few more years in New York. In 1956–57 she was director of interior design for Michael Saphier Associates, a leading design firm.[43] After this, she again served as a consultant to a variety of architects and companies, taking on such noteworthy projects as the interiors of the American restaurant annex in the United States pavilion (designed by Edward Durell Stone) at the 1958 Brussels World's Fair (Expo '58).[44]

In 1960 Haraszty moved from New York to Los Angeles and indulged in her passion for gardening. Inspirations from her flower gardens were incorporated into her design work from the 1960s through the 1980s. She created extravagantly colorful interiors for herself as well as private clients, often featuring oversized floral motifs in bright, clear tones. In the early 1960s she took up embroidery, often translating floral inspirations into embroidered cushions and upholstery for her interiors. In 1974 she published *Needlepainting: A Garden of Stitches*, co-authored with her husband Bruce David Colen, and in the late 1960s she again entered the realm of fashion, creating a group of critically acclaimed but financially unsuccessful designs under her own short-lived line. Haraszty's passion for flowers and needlework led to two other books—*Living with Flowers* (1980) and *The Embroiderer's Portfolio of Flower Designs* (1981). She spent the last decade of her life in relative obscurity in her Malibu, California, home and died of non-Hodgkin's lymphoma on November 24, 1994. —EM

Designs for Knoll
Cinders (1950–52); *Transportation Cloth* (1950–78); *Knoll Stripes* (1951–61, disc. in Europe after 1963); *Tracy* (1952–58, disc. in Europe after 1963); *Spruce* (1953–55); *Fibra* (1953–71); *Triad* (1954–64, disc. in Europe after 1963); *Ombre* (1955–58); *Spectra* (1955–59); *Spectra Magna* (1955–61, disc. in Europe after 1980); *Merit* (1955–71); *Façade* (1956–61, disc. in Europe after 1963); *Sarano* (1956–60); *Lana* (1956–78); *Fibra Weave* (intro. 2007, Archival Collection).

Fig. B.50 Eszter Haraszty. Presentation volume page with "The Knoll Handwovens" advertisement and AID invitation, ca. 1955. Samples of *Handwovens H900* and *H930*, paper, printed paper, graphite, mounted on paper. The Montreal Museum of Fine Arts, Liliane and David M. Stewart Collection, Gift of the American Friends of Canada through the generosity of Eszter Haraszty, D88.178.2.7. Cat. 70.

Fig. B.51 Christa Häusler-Goltz. *Aquarelle* ("Grey / Gold" colorway), 1977–78. Made by Taunus Textildruck for Knoll Textiles. Used for drapery; cotton; plain weave, screen-printed. KnollTextiles Archive. Cat. 220.

Fig. B.52 Christa Häusler-Goltz. *Domino* swatch ("Blue-Brown" colorway), 1979. Made in Europe possibly by Taunus Textildruck for Knoll Textiles. Used for drapery and upholstery; cotton; warp-faced compound weave. KnollTextiles Archive. Cat. 219.

Selected Awards and Exhibitions
1949 "House in the Museum Garden," MoMA
1951 *Living Up-to-Date*, Baltimore Museum of Art
Good Design, MoMA (*Transportation Cloth*, *Knoll Stripes* shown)
1952 *Textilien aus USA*, Smithsonian circulating exhibition (*Tracy*, *Knoll Stripes* shown)
1953 *Good Design*, MoMA (*Fibra* shown)
Fourth Biennial Exhibition of Textiles and Ceramics, Cranbrook (*Tracy* shown)
AID Honorable Mention, Printed Fabrics (for *Tracy*)
1954 AID First Award, Printed Fabrics (for *Fibra*)
1955 *Good Design*, MoMA (*Triad* shown)
AID First Award, Printed Fabrics (for *Triad*)
1956 *Textiles USA*, MoMA (*Transportation Cloth*, *Ombre*, *Sarano* shown)
Design by the Yard, Cooper Union Museum (*Triad*, *Fibra* shown)
1983 *Design Since 1945*, Philadelphia Museum of Art (*Tracy* shown)
2000 *Women Designers in the USA*, Bard Graduate Center (*Fibra* shown)

Christa Häusler-Goltz (b. 1943)

Born in Nuremberg, Germany, Christa Häusler (later Christa Häusler-Goltz) pursued a career in textiles from a young age.[1] From 1962 to 1965, she worked as an apprentice for Marga Hielle-Vatter at rohi, a textile manufacturer in Geretsried near Munich.[2] There she learned the textile trade, while developing her own design aesthetic. She also met Suzanne Huguenin, representative for rohi in the United States and former Knoll Textiles design director (1955–63). In 1965 Häusler left rohi and enrolled in the Hochschule für Bildende Künste (University of Fine Arts) in Hamburg, studying with well-known print designer Margaret Hildebrand and earning a master of design degree. Häusler worked as a freelance designer for major European companies and also began a ten-year association with Taunus Textildruck, a textile manufacturer near Frankfurt.

Häusler frequently visited Huguenin in New York, and in the mid-1970s Huguenin suggested that she show her designs for printed casements to Barbara Rodes-Segerer, then vice president of design for Knoll Textiles who commissioned Häusler to create a collection of prints to be produced by Taunus Textildruck.[3] The collection featured five burn-outs, two chintz casements, and a velvet drapery fabric. They were introduced to great acclaim at the Heimtextil contract and residential textiles trade fair in Frankfurt in 1977, by which time she had married.[4]

Häusler-Goltz described her practice: "when I design drapery fabrics (patterns) . . . I put special value on the harmony of form, color, and material."[5] She credits the static geometric forms juxtaposed with a dynamic use of color with creating a vitality in the final design.[6] Two chintz casements in the collection—*Aquarelle* and *Pyramid*—as well as the printed cotton velvet drapery *Benday*, demonstrate this quality. *Aquarelle*'s large swaths of color reflect brush strokes and overlap with a translucency and sheen suggestive of the watercolor technique (fig. B.51). *Pyramid* alternatively employs a subtle geometric pattern with bold steps of color in horizontal stripes (see fig. 5.43). *Benday*, its name a reference to the graphic process of using pointillist techniques to create tints and shadows, features undulating tonal areas created by large repeats of regular dots.[7]

Knoll released the remaining designs—*Triad*, *Grille*, *Ribbon*, and *Crossroads*—as all-white sheer burn-out prints on a synthetic fabric of Diolen (polyester) and viscose blend. *Interplay* was manufactured as a wool and polyester burn-out. *Interplay* and *Crossroads* feature geometric spirals, while *Ribbon*'s pattern was suggestive of basketweave. *Triad* and *Grille* were more straightforward—one, a series of V-shapes, and the other, irregular vertical stripes.

In 1978 Knoll released three more textiles—*Don*, *Domino*, and *Giro*—designed by Häusler-Goltz for European distribution. *Don* was a lattice design and *Domino* a polka-dot and square in muted colors. Both were produced as upholstery and casement fabrics (fig. B.52, see cat. 218). *Giro*, another burn-out print, featured a repeat of bold ellipses (fig. B.53). It was available in "White on White" as well as earth tones such as "Sand" and "Brown" on the sheer fabric.[8]

Rodes-Segerer left Knoll in 1978 and became head of the textiles division at Sunar, for whom Häusler-Goltz designed a number of textiles. She has also created prints for other textile companies such as Alato and Weverij de Ploeg, made woven prototypes for rugs and tapestries with Kinnasand, and automobile upholstery for De Witte Lieter in Belgium.[9] In addition she designed a successful porcelain collection for Rosenthal as well as wallpaper for Fuggerhaus and Marburger Tapeten.[10] In 1988 she started teaching design courses at the Hochschule Angewandte Wissenschaften Hamburg (Hamburg University of Applied Sciences). In 2010 she began to divide her time between Berlin and the Isle of Sylt, Germany, and in the spring of 2011 she and her family were renovating a medieval vineyard in the Sonnhof district of Austria. —AMT

Designs for Knoll
Aquarelle (1977–78, disc. Europe 1981); *Benday* (1977–78, disc. Europe 1981); *Crossroads* (1977–78); *Grille* (1977–78, disc. Europe 1982); *Interplay* (1977–78, disc. Europe 1981); *Pyramid* (1977–78, disc. Europe 1981); *Ribbon* (1977–78, disc. Europe 1982); *Triad* (1977–78, disc. Europe 1982). Introduced in Europe only; it is uncertain when these designs were discontinued: *Domino* (1978), *Don* (1978), *Giro* (1978).

Selected Awards and Exhibitions
1980 Awards for *Aquarelle*, *Grille*, *Pryamid*, and *Triad*, Design Center Stuttgart
1981 Awards for textiles, Design Center Stuttgart
1983 Awards for textiles, Design Center Stuttgart
Printed by Taunus Textildruck: 30 Jahre Textildruck in Deutchland am Beispiel einer Firma, Krefeld Textile Museum (*Pyramid* and *Giro* shown)
1984 Awards for textiles, Design Center Stuttgart
1985 Bundespreis Gute Form, German Federal Good Design Award
1986 Awards for textiles, Design Center Stuttgart

Albert E. Herbert Jr. (1928–2008)

Albert Herbert was born in Detroit, Michigan, and later moved to New York City to study industrial and interior design at Pratt Institute, graduating in 1950.[1] His first design job in New York was with the Knoll Planning Unit where he worked from 1950 to 1952. He left to serve in the U.S. Air Force during the Korean War.[2]

In 1951 Knoll introduced Herbert's printed drapery design *Diamonds* (see fig. 3.42).[3] It features alternating positive and negative diamond-shaped voids outlined in an uneven white line, creating contrast and moving the viewer's eye along the zig-zagged edges of the motifs. Hand-printed on linen, *Diamonds* was originally produced in six colorways including "Humus" and "Parma Violet," but in 1954 Eszter Haraszty, then fabric coordinator and color stylist of Knoll Textiles, revised the fabric in seven new colorways including "Tan and Hazel Brown" (fig. B.54).[4] She also introduced a slightly less graphic interpretation of the original design, maintaining the white outline, but reducing the contrast between paired tones.

Although Herbert was employed at the Knoll Planning Unit only for a brief period, he maintained professional and personal connections throughout his career with designers and staff, especially his friend Haraszty.[5] The two of them collaborated on the interior design of the American restaurant in Edward Durell Stone's U.S. Pavilion at Expo '58 in Brussels. In the late 1950s, Haraszty, who was then a design consultant for V'Soske, a maker of luxury handmade carpets, commissioned Herbert to design for the company, which he continued to do throughout the 1960s. He created several series of brightly colored, geometrically patterned rugs, including the *Palace* collection (1960–61), with patterns such as *Turkish Delight*, *Sahara Sun*, *Peking*, *Baroda*, *Alhambra*, and *Mecca*, inspired by "famous palaces around the world" and incorporating Herbert's romantic notions of the Near and Far East.[6]

Although most of Herbert's later work was for residential and commercial interiors, he continued to design printed textiles as well as furniture and jewelry. He was also a graphic artist, whose practice included the cover of *Interiors* magazine (May 1954).[7] In 1956–57, he worked alongside Haraszty for the architecture and interior design firm Saphier, Lerner, Schindler, Inc. (now SLS Environetics). In 1956 two leading textile companies (L. Anton Maix and Arundell Clark) released Herbert's geometric linen casement fabrics: *Variations* for Maix and *Miss Prism* for Clark.[8] A year later Herbert established his own design firm, Albert Herbert Designs, which remained open until 1970, when he relocated to East Hampton, New York. Herbert designed three lines of casement fabrics for Rowen, including the patterns *Alhambra*, *Trestles*, and *Palette* for the 1959 collection; *Reflections*, *Fantasia*, *Galaxies*, and *Meadowlands* in 1960; and *Flower Stripe*, *Anemones*, and *Jardin* in 1963.[9] Through his own design office, he worked for V'Soske and produced interior designs for private residences, showrooms

Fig. B.53 Christa Häusler-Goltz. *Giro* swatch ("White on White" sheer), ca. 1977. Made by Taunus Textildruck for Knoll Textiles. Used for drapery; polyester, cotton; burn-out. KnollTextiles Archive. Cat. 212.

Fig. B.54 Albert Herbert. *Diamonds* ("Tan and Hazel Brown" colorway), design introduced 1951. Made for Knoll Associates. Used for drapery; linen; plain weave, screen-printed. Courtesy Richard and Trudy Schultz.

Fig. B.55 Sheila Hicks. *Inca*, color or weave sample, ca. 1965. Made by Paul Maute GmbH for Knoll Textiles. Used for upholstery; wool; plain weave. KnollTextiles Archive. Cat. 166.

Fig. B.56 Sheila Hicks. *Inca* sample ("Red" colorway), ca. 1965. Made by Paul Maute GmbH for Knoll Textiles. Used for upholstery; wool; plain weave. Private collection. Cat. 169.

(such as one for the Danish textile firm Unika-Vaev) exhibition spaces, and offices.[10] In 1963 he earned an Honorable Mention for his design of the interior of his own home in Manhattan in the "Outstanding Interior of the Year" competition sponsored by the S. M. Hexter Company.[11] His furniture included glass tables for Cumberland (1960) and "executive" office furniture for Jim Eppinger (1968).[12]

After moving to East Hampton, Herbert designed a prefabricated house which was published in *Interiors* (November 1965), wrote cookbooks, and collaborated on several novels and short stories with his long-time partner Roger Myers. He also supervised the merger of AID with the National Society of Interior Designers (NSID) to form the American Society of Interior Designers (ASID) in 1975, serving as president of the New York Metro Chapter (1974–75).[13] —ES

Design for Knoll
Diamonds (1951–59).

Selected Awards
1956, 1959, 1960 Honorable Mention, textile design, AID
1963 Honorable Mention, Outstanding Interior of the Year Award,
S. M. Hexter Company
1965 Honorable Mention, Interior Design of the Year Award, S. M. Hexter Company

Sheila Hicks (b. 1934)

Sheila Hicks has traveled the world—visiting Central and South America, Morocco, India, and Israel—in pursuit of handweaving techniques and traditions. She frequently lived with the community from which she received instruction, gaining appreciation for their craftsmanship.[1] Her first opportunity to adapt ethnological textiles to the commercial market came when she collaborated with Knoll Textiles in the mid-1960s.

Born in Hastings, Nebraska, Hicks has spent most of her working career in Europe, largely in Paris where she has maintained a studio since 1964. She attended Syracuse University (1952–54), followed by Yale University (1954–58), where she studied painting with Josef Albers and Rico Lebrun.[2] Hicks also met Anni Albers, who shared a love of South American textiles and helped to refine Hicks's understanding of linear structures. While at Yale, she took classes with designer and photographer Herbert Matter, Knoll's long time graphic designer, and the architect Louis I. Kahn.

Encouraged by Josef Albers, Hicks explored the textiles of Central and South America through coursework on the art of Andean cultures and developed an appreciation for challenging color combinations. She traveled to Central and South America on a Fulbright Scholarship and from 1957 to 1958 visited pre-Columbian archeological sites, making detailed photographic studies of architecture, which further fostered her ideas on integrating architectural ornament into weaving compositions and structuring designs with complex combinations of yarns.[3] After graduating from Yale with an MFA, she relocated to Taxco, Mexico, where she established an experimental weaving studio and began producing woven miniatures that incor-porated traditional Zapotec techniques of "twining, knotting, netting, and wrapping."[4]

In 1962 some of these wall hangings and miniatures were shown in Knoll's Mexico City showroom, and the following year she was invited to display her work in their showroom at the Chicago Merchandise Mart during Market Week.[5] Florence Knoll Bassett then met with Hicks in New York and subsequently contracted her to produce fabric designs for Knoll Textiles and to act as a color and materials consultant.[6] Between April 1964 and early 1965, Hicks sent several proposals to Christine Rae, a design and marketing consultant to Florence Knoll Bassett, and of these designs, *Inca* (1966) was selected for the line (fig. B.55).[7]

Inca was adapted from Hicks's 1957 master's thesis, "Pre-Incaic Textiles," which was inspired by illustrations in *Les textiles anciens du Pérou et leur techniques* (1934), by Raoul d'Harcourt.[8] In designing *Inca*,

Hicks reinterpreted an Andean pattern from the book that consisted of a block sequence formed through a basket weave, alternately emphasizing the design's vertical and horizontal axis and reflecting Hicks's sensitivity to playful structures (fig. B.56). Hicks had made an earlier version of *Inca*, using the fabric for a skirt and jacket that she wore to her initial meeting with Knoll Bassett.[9] The final version of *Inca* maintained the block sequence and created visual dynamism and tension through the isolation of the warp and the weft threads. It was made with handspun wool in the weaving workshop of Paul Maute—supplier of handwoven upholstery and drapery textiles to Knoll since the early 1960s—and dyed in a variety of colors and neutral tones. *Inca* was an upholstery fabric used, for example, on a William Stephens side chair (see fig. 5.8.).[10]

Hicks also designed hand-embroidered cushions for Saarinen pedestal chairs for Knoll France's clientele in 1964–65.[11] As a consultant for the company, she proposed programs to research and develop new designs and production methods. Her collaboration with Knoll Textiles, however, was short lived. Changes in the corporate structure at Knoll's New York office in the mid-1960s relegated her to a freelance-designer role.[12] Although Hicks's ambitions for a fruitful and lucrative collaboration were cut short, the Knoll Textiles commission was an early outlet for her work, in a career that has now spanned over five decades. —ES

Design for Knoll
Inca (1966–90).

Selected Awards and Exhibitions
1963 *Woven Forms*, Museum of Contemporary Crafts, New York (ongoing 1963, 1967, 1969, 1971, 1973, 1975, 1977)
1969 *Wall Hangings*, MoMA
Perspectief in Textiel, Stedelijk Museum, Amsterdam
1971 solo exhibition, Bab Rouah, Rabat, Morocco
1974 Stedelijk Museum, Amsterdam
Musée des Arts décoratifs, Nantes
Modern Masters Tapestry, New York
1975 solo exhibition, Galerie Alice Paul, Lausanne Art and Architecture Medal, American Institute of Architects
1979 Fil, Montreuil
Musée des tapisseris, Aix-en-Provence
1985 Medal, Académie d'Architecture, Paris
1986 *High Styles: American Design Since 1900*, Whitney Museum of American Art, New York
Man Ray and Sheila Hicks, Lunds Konstall, Lund, Sweden
1993 Officier, l'Ordre des Arts et des Lettres, National Ministry of Education and Culture, Paris
2006 *Sheila Hicks: Weaving as Metaphor*, Bard Graduate Center, New York
2010–11 *Sheila Hicks: 50 Years*, Addison Gallery of American Art, Andover
Institute of Contemporary Art, University of Pennsylvania

Marga Hielle-Vatter (1913–1997)

Marga Vatter was born in the Schönlinde region, in Bohemia, then part of the Austrian Empire (today Krasná Lípá, Czech Republic). This region has been an important center for the textile industry, primarily linen weaving, since the mid-seventeenth century. By the late nineteenth century Schönlinde was a manufacturing center, and in 1882 Vatter's family founded I. H. Vatter, a hosiery manufacturing firm.[1]

Vatter studied arts and crafts at the Hochschule für Bildende Künste (Academy of Fine Arts) in Dresden beginning in 1927 and completed her studies in Vienna in 1932. She returned to Krasná Lípá, and in 1933 she and partner Rolf Hielle, another Krasná Lípá native, whom she married a year later, established rohi, a textile manufacturing business, its name derived from four letters of *Rolf Hielle*'s name.[2] Hielle's family was also involved in the textile industry. Hielle & Dittrich, a linen-spinning and weaving company, had been founded in 1849, and Hielle & Wünche, a manufacturer of wool and cotton textiles, in 1856. The rohi firm took over part of a Hielle & Wünsche mill, where they both spun the yarn and handwove the fabrics. As demand for their textiles grew, however, much of the fabric production was done off-site by local weavers who were supplied with yarn and production instructions.

By World War II, a large portion of Krasná Lípá's population had become decidedly anti-German, and when the war ended the city expelled its German citizens.[3] Marga Hielle-Vatter moved to Ammerland in Lower Saxony, Germany, in 1946 and resumed production on a single handloom. Rolf Hielle did not accompany the family, and the couple soon divorced.[4] In 1951 Hielle-Vatter relocated again, this time to Geretsried, Germany, just south of Munich and north of the German-Austrian

Fig. B.57 Marga Hielle-Vatter. *Dynamic* swatch ("Fuchsia" colorway), ca. 1975. Made by rohi for Knoll Textiles. Used for upholstery; wool; plain-weave–derived compound weave. KnollTextiles Archive. Cat. 196.

Fig. B.58 Marga Hielle-Vatter. *Tacoma* swatch ("Gray" colorway), ca. 1975. Made by rohi for Knoll Textiles. Used for upholstery; wool; plain-weave–derived compound weave. KnollTextiles Archive.

Fig. B.59 Marga Hielle-Vatter. *Tournee* sample ("Orange/Cinnamon" colorway), 1976–81. Made by rohi for Knoll Textiles. Used for upholstery; wool, cotton; plain-weave–derived simple weave. KnollTextiles Archive. Cat. 200.

Fig. B.60 Marga Hielle-Vatter. *Severin* ("Lilac" colorway), ca. 1982. Made by rohi for Knoll Textiles. Used for upholstery; wool, rayon; plain-weave–derived simple weave. KnollTextiles Archive.

border, where the company remains today. Beginning in the early 1950s Hielle-Vatter headed rohi's design and development department. It was a period of rapid progress and innovation within the company, and Hielle-Vatter was soon recognized as a leader in the textile industry, winning several prestigious awards.[5] Throughout rohi's history Hielle-Vatter maintained the firm's reputation by focusing on creating distinctive woolen textiles woven from high-quality raw materials processed on the premises. In the late 1950s the company began production with power looms.

During her tenure, Hielle-Vatter had the firm concentrate on Jacquard weaving and in the 1970s began courting business from airlines and designer furniture companies.[6] The decision to incorporate Jacquard weaving was especially important. The Jacquard mechanism facilitates the weaving of complex patterns by providing a high degree of control over individual warp yarns. Unlike the constraints of most other modern weaving machines, contemporary Jacquard weaving has made it possible to create nonrepeating, asymmetrical designs with a discernibly more sophisticated textile structure and without sacrificing durability.[7]

The relationship between rohi and Knoll Textiles came about through Suzanne Huguenin and Barbara Rodes-Segerer. Although Huguenin left Knoll in 1963, she remained in contact with the company and its designers.[8] By the early 1970s she represented rohi in the United States and brought the company's textiles to the attention of Rodes-Segerer, who was then responsible for textile development at Knoll.[9] Dividing her time between New York and Germany, Rodes-Segerer worked alongside Hielle-Vatter at rohi to develop the color palette for the fabrics Hielle-Vatter designed and produced for Knoll. The relationship that developed between Knoll and rohi is unusual in that Hielle-Vatter was both owner and artistic director of the firm, which gave her complete creative control over the design of the textiles and their manufacture. The collaboration with Knoll resulted in several Jacquard-woven upholsteries and one drapery that married utility with design. They were introduced over the span of a decade, from 1971 to 1982.[10]

Dynamic, the first rohi textile for Knoll, was introduced at Knoll's new Fifth Avenue showroom in October 1970.[11] Hielle-Vatter's textiles of this era often featured vibrant colors such as oranges and purples, and *Dynamic*, a wool upholstery fabric, was no exception (fig. B.57, see fig. 5.34). The fifteen colorways included a range of multihued yarns; the "Blue" colorway, for example, had solid warps and colored wefts of bright blue, navy, kelly green, and gold.[12] In 1972 Knoll introduced *Tacoma*, another all-wool Jacquard-woven upholstery, featuring a patchwork-like pattern in neutral tones such as "Gray" and "Tan" as well as more vibrant colors such as "Blue and Plum" (fig. B.58, see fig. 5.34).[13] *Align*, introduced in 1974, was a plain weave with white, beige, and gray stripes created through the use of different natural wool yarns.[14] *Tournee* (1976), an upholstery of 94 percent wool and 6 percent cotton, was offered in at least twelve colorways (fig. B.59, fig. 5.36).[15] Like *Dynamic*, *Tournee* used a sophisticated range of colored yarns in creating the overall design, but it featured contrasting tones in both the warps and wefts to create a vertical ladder-like pattern.

Although Rodes-Segerer left Knoll in 1978, Hielle-Vatter continued to work with Knoll Textiles. The final rohi textile for the line was *Severin*, a wool-and-rayon blend upholstery offered in muted colorways such as "Mist" and "Oyster" (fig. B.60).[16] *Severin* was woven with thin, tightly twisted yarns, like the weave of *Dynamic*, and the design was created by the layering of different colored wefts in an organic linear fashion.

Hielle-Vatter worked with Rodes-Segerer again in 1979, when she (along with Knoll designers Huguenin, Anni Albers, Wolf Bauer, and Christa Häusler-Goltz) contributed to Sunar's first textile collection.[17] Hielle-Vatter worked as an advisor for design and development at rohi until just before her death in Kempfenhausen on Starnberger See, Germany. The success of her designs—and of rohi in general—is reflected in the numerous honors her work has earned during the course of her career, including seven awards from the Design Center Stuttgart between 1981 and 1989. Today rohi uses computer-controlled looms to create their Jacquard weaves and prides itself on the sturdy and timeless textile designs that it supplies to the airline, furniture, and entertainment industries. Rohi manufactures textiles for Lufthansa, Singapore Airlines, and Aeromexico, and its fabrics have been used in a number of public institutions across Europe. The company is now under the ownership of the third generation of the Hielle family.

Hielle-Vatter's son Bernd Hielle is president of the board of directors and her granddaughter Katrin Hielle-Dahm is artistic director. —CBPP

Designs for Knoll
Dynamic (1970–80); *Tacoma* (1972–82); *Align* (1974–82); *Tournee* (1976–81); *Severin* (1982–88).

Selected Awards and Exhibitions
1943 Exhibition, Städtisches Kunstgewerbemuseum, Leipzig
1952 Gold medal, the Bavarian State Government
1957 Silver medal, Milan Triennale
1958 Certificate of distinction, Brussels World's Fair
1981–86, **1989** Awards, Design Center Stuttgart
1983 *Design Since 1945*, Philadelphia Museum of Art

Evelyn Hill Anselevicius (1923–2003)

Evelyn Hill Anselevicius succeeded in two distinct areas of the textile arts. In the early 1950s, she developed a series of award-winning handwoven fabrics for Knoll Textiles. A decade later she gained renown as a master tapestry weaver, exhibiting her work internationally during the formative years of the fiber art movement, and receiving numerous commissions for her monumental architectural hangings. Although she only concentrated on designing furnishing fabrics for a brief period, her distinctive and imaginative designs for Knoll heightened Knoll's reputation as a textile innovator and had a lasting influence on the textile collections that followed.

Evelyn Jane Hill was born in Hobart, Oklahoma, and grew up in Texas (see fig. 3.51). In 1946 she received a BA in design from the Texas State College for Women (now Texas Women's University) in Denton. She worked as an art instructor in the public schools of Fort Sumner, New Mexico (1946–48), and Spokane, Washington (1948–49), and pursued a variety of advanced studies in art and design, while her interests "fluctuated from painting to sculpture to furniture to fashion."[1] In 1946 she also studied for a time with Josef and Anni Albers at Black Mountain College in North Carolina and later cited Josef Albers's teaching as a major influence on her work.[2] She attended summer sessions at Highlands University in Las Vegas, New Mexico, beginning in 1947, earning an MA in arts and crafts in 1950. Moving to Chicago in 1949, she took classes at the Institute of Design, pursuing a new interest in architecture and its relationship to woven fabrics. She also worked as a weaver for Cranbrook-trained Majel Chance, who specialized in custom drapery and upholstery fabrics.[3] Inspired by Chance's enthusiasm for weaving, she began to concentrate on textiles and to work on her own designs.[4]

In the summer of 1951, Hill moved to New York City where she was hired by Knoll to develop a new line of handwoven fabrics (fig. B.61), the first of which were introduced with great fanfare at the AID national conference in March 1952 (see chapter 3). They were prominently featured in press accounts of the event, including full-page illustrated articles in *Interiors* and *Handweaver & Craftsman*.[5] Eszter Haraszty, then head of Knoll Textiles, also included Hill's vibrant handwoven textiles in her design for the *Knoll Furniture and Textiles* exhibition held at the Dallas Museum of Art in the fall of 1952 (figs. B.62, B.63).

In describing her design approach, Hill wrote that she used architecture as a frame of reference when designing textiles: "Visualizing space in this way, there are no inhibiting factors regarding the use of pure color in fabric design. Color is used relatively, as it is in painting. Even radiant pinks and orange may be used if used in proportion to the surrounding space—and in relation to the surrounding colors."[6] The same principle applied to the relationships between different textures and between texture and color—as, for example, when she used close color combinations to emphasize contrasts in texture. Hill's two *Handwoven* series, woven for Knoll by Rancocas Fabrics, and *Kerry Linen* (figs. B.64, B.65), introduced in 1953, helped to establish Knoll's reputation for rich colors and strong tactile and visual texture, setting the stage for classic Knoll fabrics of the 1960s such as *Cato* and *Morocco*.

Hill also worked as a designer and color consultant for textile manufacturer Cohn-Hall-Marx (Cohama) and made custom fashion fabrics for clients such as the well-known milliner Mr. John. After three years in New York, a time she later described as both exciting and exhausting, Hill moved to St. Louis, Missouri, and married architect George Anselevicius.[7] At Knoll she felt limited by the need to fit her ideas into a process governed by function and cost. Hill continued

Fig. B.61 Evelyn Hill Anselevicius. *Handwoven* Panel, 1951. Made for Knoll Textiles. Used for upholstery; wool, viscose, rayon, synthetic raffia. Philadelphia Museum of Art, Gift of Mr. and Mrs. George Anselevicius, 1983, 1983-42-2. Cat. 74.

Fig. B.62 Evelyn Hill Anselevicius. *Handwoven* textile, 1952. Used for edging on pillows, displayed at *Knoll Furniture and Textiles*, Dallas Museum of Art, 1952. Used for upholstery; wool filament, nylon. Philadelphia Museum of Art, CTK1. Cat. 73.

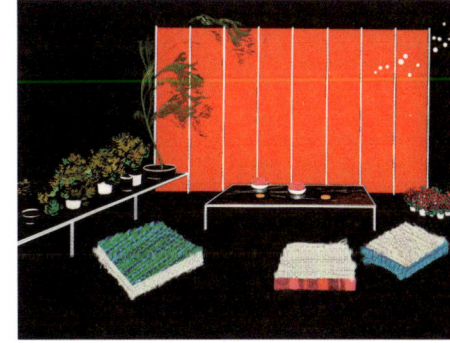

Fig. B.63 Eszter Haraszty. Presentation volume page "Perspective of Dallas exhibition" (view 1), ca. 1953–55. Paper, handwovens, paint, fabric, cardboard, adhesive tape on paper. The Montreal Museum of Fine Arts, Liliane and David M. Stewart Collection, Gift of the American Friends of Canada through the generosity of Eszter Haraszty, D88.178.1.10. Cat. 71.

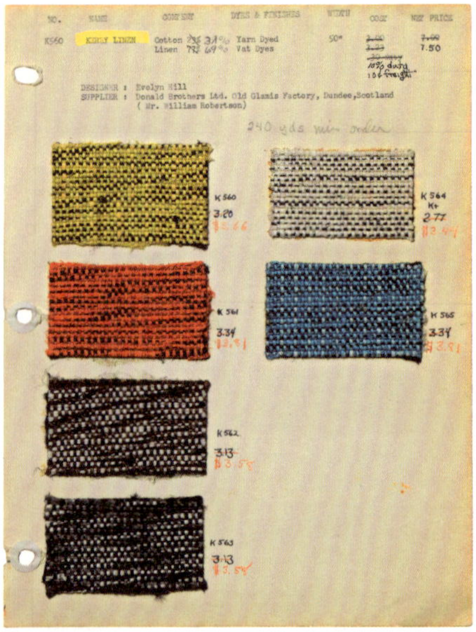

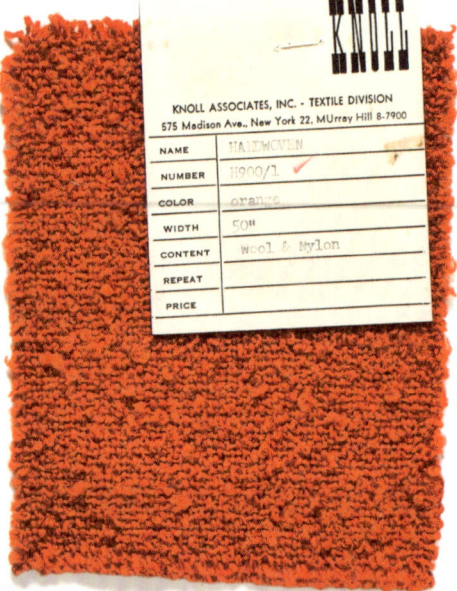

Fig. B.64 Evelyn Hill Anselevicius. *Kerry Linen* data page with samples, ca. 1953. Made by Donald Brothers for Knoll Textiles. Textile samples, linen, cotton; plain weave; mounted on paper. KnollTextiles Archive. Cat. 103.

Fig. B.65 Evelyn Hill Anselevicius. *Handwoven H900* swatch ("Burnt Orange" colorway), ca. 1953. Made by Rancocas Fabrics for Knoll Textiles. Used for upholstery; wool, nylon; plain weave. Cranbrook Art Museum, Bloomfield Hills, Mich., T 2010.13.7. Cat. 97.

to design furnishing textiles for Knoll and other clients but began to focus on weaving as art, and on teaching, which she did for many years at the People's Art Center in St. Louis.[8] Around 1960 she started weaving tapestries to be used as wall hangings, and this became her primary medium. Hill established a studio in San Miguel de Allende in Guanajuato, Mexico, in the 1960s and over the next twenty years spent much of her time living and working there. She worked with local hand-spinners and weavers to produce her large rugs and tapestries, and established a dyeing workshop, using the knowledge of modern dye chemistry she had acquired in New York.[9]

Hill's celebrated "linear faces"—large-scale images resembling printed black-and-white photographs, made with varying heights of black knotted pile against a white ground—were woven in the 1960s and early 1970s. They were included in *Wall Hangings* at MoMA (1969), one of the first major museum exhibitions devoted to textiles, and a year later were featured in a solo exhibition at Jack Lenor Larsen's New York showroom. They became widely known through *Beyond Craft: The Art Fabric* (1972), a seminal book by Larsen and MoMA curator Mildred Constantine. Hill created monumental tapestries for Harris Bank in Chicago (1974) and the Colorado School of Mines (1975), among other architectural commissions.[10] In 1981 the Anseleviciuses moved to Albuquerque when George Anselevicius was named dean of architecture at the University of New Mexico. Two years later Evelyn Anselevicius moved her studio from Mexico to Albuquerque as well, continuing to weave and to exhibit until her death in 2003.[11] —SW

Designs for Knoll
Handwoven series (1952–62); *Synthesis* (1953); *Kerry Linen* (1953–66); *Wool Casement* (1957–62); *Rover* (1963–64); *Tara* (1963–71).

Selected Awards and Exhibitions
1952 Knoll *Handwoven* installation, AID national conference, Waldorf Astoria, New York
Good Design, Merchandise Mart (June) and MoMA (*Handwoven* blanket and samples shown)
Knoll Furniture and Textiles, Dallas Museum of Art (*Handwovens* shown)
Textilien aus USA, Smithsonian circulating exhibition (*Handwovens* shown)
1953 *Good Design*, Merchandise Mart (June) and MoMA (*Kerry Linen* shown)
Honorable Mention, woven fabrics (*Kerry Linen*), AID
Fourth Biennial Exhibition of Textiles and Ceramics, Cranbrook (*Handwovens H900* and *H930* shown)
1954 Second Award, woven fabrics (*Handwoven* series, *H960–H978*), AID
1955 *Good Design*, Merchandise Mart (January) (*Handwoven* samples shown)
1969 *Wall Hangings*, Museum of Modern Art, New York
1970 *Woven Wall Hangings* (solo exhibition), Jack Lenor Larsen showroom, New York
1971 Fifth International Biennial of Tapestry, Lausanne, Switzerland
1972 *Fibre Art by American Artists*, Ball State University Art Gallery, Muncie, Indiana
1983 *Design Since 1945*, Philadelphia Museum of Art (Handwoven prototypes shown)
1992 15th International Biennial of Tapestry, Lausanne, Switzerland

Suzanne Huguenin (1916–2008)

Suzanne Huguenin (fig. B.66) was born in Lucerne, Switzerland, where her family owned a successful restaurant and patisserie.[1] Huguenin had intended to study art in Geneva, but her father's death while she was a teenager put a strain on the family's finances, and instead she enrolled in a trade school to learn secretarial skills. One of her early secretarial jobs was in the planning offices of Landi '39, the landmark 1939 Swiss national exhibition in Zurich. There she met architects and designers such as Armin Meili and Hans Fischli and as a result became determined to work in the design world.[2] In 1947 Huguenin came to the United States, where her brother and other relatives were already living, and found work as a trilingual secretary for a variety of companies.[3] In 1949 she became an assistant to Charles Maurice Gourdon, a designer and owner of C. M. Gourdon, Inc., an importer of fashion fabrics, primarily French silks, and here Huguenin received her first exposure to "fabric styling, printing, [and] dyeing."[4]

In June 1952 Hans Knoll hired Huguenin as an assistant to Eszter Haraszty.[5] Huguenin's minimal amount of experience in textile design and development was at first a challenge, but her organizational skills were immediately put to good use as she later recalled: "[Hans Knoll] knew I had no qualifications as far as textiles were concerned, I didn't bluff... I started totally from scratch. The only thing I knew how to do was to run this department, purchase orders, quality control, etc., when I came to Knoll there was not even a file about textiles."[6] Huguenin learned much on the job, working closely with Haraszty over the next three years and also taking classes in night school to gain technical knowledge. After Haraszty's departure from Knoll in late 1955, Huguenin was tapped to take her place and remained head of the department until the summer of 1963.

Huguenin would usher in significant additions to the Knoll Textiles line, working closely with Florence Knoll and the Knoll Planning Unit to develop textiles suited to large office installations (see chapter 3). Among the new drapery fabrics, for example, were open-weave casements that worked well in the large windows of modern office buildings. One of these fabrics was Huguenin's own *Tracey* (1962), made of wool and cotton for Knoll by the Scottish mill Donald Brothers. Huguenin developed a number of highly durable upholsteries in the second half of the 1950s that used artificial fibers such as Saran, nylon, and viscose. The most significant of these, and one of the best-selling fabrics in Knoll's history, was *Nylon Homespun* (later renamed *Knoll Nylon Homespun*), introduced in 1957. Huguenin considered it "the most important contribution I made to Knoll."[7] She discovered this fabric, made from a nylon fiber developed for use in carpets, at the Philadelphia mill Moss Rose. Its tactile appeal, resembling hand-spun, handwoven wool, combined with its resistance to wear, resulted in millions of yards sold over its thirty years in the line.

During her tenure, Huguenin also increasingly sourced textiles from European manufacturers, in part reflecting a decline in the American textile industry. The first among the several high-quality upholsteries Knoll imported from Europe was Huguenin's *Furrows*, a wool, viscose, and cotton upholstery made for Knoll in Belgium and introduced in 1957 (fig. B.67). *Furrows* would remain in the Knoll line until 1973, when Barbara Rodes (later Rodes-Segerer) reworked the ribbed fabric in brighter colors, naming it *Furrows II*. With both *Furrows* and *Nylon Homespun*, Huguenin introduced a wider range of hues into the Knoll collection including more muted tones and darker colors, diverging somewhat from Knoll's earlier reputation for bright primary hues. Huguenin considered the addition to the Knoll collection of high-quality German handwoven fabrics by Paul Maute among her major achievements. This contribution echoes even in 2011 as *Cato*, first introduced by Huguenin in 1961, marks its fiftieth year in the collection.

Occasionally, Huguenin would be asked to originate textiles for specific furniture lines being developed at Knoll. When the Richard Schultz *Leisure Collection* furniture (1966) was still in the early design stages, Schultz called upon Huguenin to help him develop a stretch fabric that could withstand regular exposure to sunlight, a requirement for this line of outdoor furniture. Huguenin assisted in the design and sourcing of a Dacron polyester and nylon stretch fabric, which was then realized by a small manufacturer in East Hampton, New York, with whom she had previously worked.[8]

Huguenin would later say "I feel always uneasy if I am labeled 'designer'," preferring to define her contribution as having "conceived" designs such as those for a number of printed draperies released at the end of the 1950s and the early 1960s.[9] Huguenin created three striped patterns, *Polystripes* (1959), *Linea*, and *Quartet* (both 1963), which are fairly straightforward in their linear motifs but show her skill as a colorist in their subtle blending of tones. *Linea* was unique in that it used a "printing technique without repeat" to create varied combinations of trios of colored bands across the width of the fabric (fig. B.68).[10] For the motif of her 1959 drapery *Peru*, she drew upon "a handwoven rug which I discovered around 1954 at the famous local Indian Sunday market in Pisac in the Andes." *Peru* was printed on a highly textural linen base fabric that was known in the trade as "Peruvian," even though Knoll's version was actually made in Belgium (see fig. 3.73). Huguenin's affinity for South American textiles is evident in a photo taken around 1960 of the studio (fig. B.69) in her Greenwich Village apartment, where she would often work when not at Knoll. Huguenin, however, spent much of her time traveling to Knoll showrooms and manufacturers across the United States, Europe, Central and South America—as much as six months out of each year.[11] In the late 1950s she became the public face of Knoll Textiles, presenting new collections at Knoll locations around the world and often being featured in press accounts.

Although she considered Florence Knoll "the best critic I could have," Huguenin

Fig. B.66 Suzanne Huguenin, ca. 1963. Photographed by Steven Trefonides. Knoll Archives.

Fig. B.67 Suzanne Huguenin. *Furrows* swatches, introduced 1957, these examples ca. 1965. Made in Bolgium for Knoll Textiles. Used for upholstery; wool, cotton, rayon; plain weave. Private collection. Cat. 155.

Fig. B.68 Suzanne Huguenin. *Linea* sample ("Aqua/Turquoise/Reseda" colorway), in production 1963–77, this example ca. 1965. Made by Winston Prints for Knoll Textiles. Used for drapery; linen; plain weave, screen-printed. KnollTextiles Archive, donated by Doreen Rose Stempien. Cat. 139.

Fig. B.69 Suzanne Huguenin's home studio, ca. 1960. Courtesy Christina Laubi.

felt restricted at times by the company head's opinions and strict artistic vision, which made the Knoll collection more tailored and less diverse than Huguenin would have preferred.[12] By 1963 Huguenin found these limitations too much and left Knoll to start her own independent textile consulting business.[13] Her early clients included La France Industries, a large textile mill located in South Carolina, and long-time Knoll sup-plier, Donald Brothers.[14] In 1966 Huguenin also became a "special design consultant," who would act "in a promotional, advisory capacity" to Jack Lenor Larsen, a leading Knoll competitor in the interior fabrics business. Huguenin represented the firm in a variety of capacities both in the United States and Europe, including sourcing and designing fabrics for the company.[15] She and Larsen became lifelong friends. Huguenin also represented the German manufacturer rohi and its designer-owner Marga Hielle-Vatter in the United States, and most likely introduced the firm to Larsen.[16] Huguenin would later identify Hielle-Vatter as "without any doubt the most gifted production fabric designer that I know of."[17] Huguenin helped to foster Knoll's strong relationship with rohi in the 1970s by bringing the prototype for Hielle-Vatter's *Dynamic* (1970) to the company, where it would go on to become a best seller.

Huguenin enjoyed a warm relationship with later executives in Knoll's textile division, including Barbara Rodes (later Rodes-Segerer) in the 1970s and Merle Lindby-Young in the 1980s. In her capacity as United States representative for several small European mills, Huguenin supplied a variety of fabrics to Knoll, her last design for the company being the 1974 heavy twill fabric, *Sequoia* (fig. B.70). This textural weave was produced for Knoll by Weberei Eschen AG in Liechtenstein and earned Huguenin a jury award for contemporary fabrics from the Resources Council Product Design Award Program in 1974.[18]

Huguenin continued to be active in the interior textiles community in the 1980s, supplying fabrics to Larsen, Gretchen Bellinger and Carnegie Fabrics.[19] She divided her time between New York and Menzingen, Switzerland, where she had also had a residence. One of her final, most lasting contributions to Knoll Textiles was assisting creative director Merle Lindby-Young in organizing the company's textile archive in the mid-1980s, preserving many of the earliest records that she herself had created beginning in 1952.[20] In her later years she collected modern art and spent time with her family in Switzerland, where she died in September 2008. In 2009 KnollTextiles re-introduced Huguenin's 1963 drapery *Quartet* as a part of the *Archival Collection*, a marker of the timelessness of her artistic vision in textiles. —EM

Designs for Knoll
Furrows (1957–73); *Ghent* (1958–62); *Maja Stripes* (1958–60); *Knoll Nylon Homespun* (1958–88); *Domus* (1959–71); *Polo* (1959–64); *Breeze* (1959–71); *Wisp* (1959–60); *Peru* (1959–64); *Polystripes* (1959–76); *Brigadoon* (1960–67); *Tracey* (1961–73); *Kinna* (1961–73); *Quartet* (1963–78; intro. 2009 *Archival Collection*); *Linea* (1963–76); *Furrows II* (1974–76); *Sequoia* (1974–81); *Quartet II* (1979–81).

Awards
1973 Outstanding Design for Fabrics, National Contract Interior Design Competition, Institute of Business Designers
1974 Product Design Award for Contemporary Fabrics (*Sequoia*), Resources Council, New York

Jacqueline Iribe (b. 1925)

Knoll Associates opened its first Paris show-room in the early 1950s and during this time, Eszter Haraszty—then head of Knoll Textiles—asked Jacqueline Iribe to create a fabric design for the company.[1] Iribe, "a specialist in tapestry and printed textile design," was also known as a talented color-ist.[2] She and her husband—lighting and furniture designer Alain Richard—may have come to Knoll's attention as part of a circle of designers and architects Knoll contacted in France or Haraszty may have learned of her through Yves Vidal, who joined the firm in 1952 to head Knoll's French division.[3] Though the nature of the contract remains unclear, Haraszty and Vidal may have commissioned Iribe to make a printed textile for the residential market, a commercial aim of Knoll France during this period.[4] In any event, Knoll introduced Iribe's *Citronnade* in 1953.

The print is somewhat of an anomaly in Iribe's work in general as well as within the Knoll line, which had been dominated by an austere modernist aesthetic. *Citronnade*'s motif of lemon slices and bright colors is more akin to the organic aesthetic of Iribe's father, painter Paul Iribe, than of the geometric patterns typical to her other known textile designs (fig. B.71).[5] The design's 9-inch repeat was hand-printed on heavy cotton and produced in vibrant colorings typical of Eszter Haraszty.[6] *Citronnade* was featured in Knoll advertisements, displayed in the New York showroom in 1954, and included in a Knoll + Drake catalogue maquette (designed by Ladislav Sutnar) as well as in advertisements for the same branch of Knoll Associates in 1955.[7] Knoll Associates discontinued the print in 1955, but it made an appearance in a French interior by Gustave Gautier in 1958, suggesting that it had a longer release in Europe as was typical of Knoll's drapery prints.[8]

In the late 1950s Iribe's textile designs were sold by the leading Dutch department store Metz & Co.[9] She was one of many French designers hired by Metz—they carried designs by Sonia Delaunay and fellow Knoll designer Paule Vézeley.[10] Iribe's work was widely available in France, appearing in popular French magazines such as *La Maison Française* and *L'Officiel de la mode*.[11]

When Alain Richard opened a research and consulting firm in 1952, Iribe often collaborated on his commissions and frequently was credited as a color consultant.[12] Beginning in 1964, both Iribe and Richard began teaching at the École Nationale Supérieure des Arts Décoratifs.[13] The couple also went on to teach at the Ecole supérieure de Design, d'art Graphique et d'Architecture Intérieure (ESAG), Penninghen, where Iribe served as a board member in 1974, 1984, and 1986. —AMT

Design for Knoll
Citronnade (1953–55 in U.S., later in Europe).

Arne Jacobsen (1902–1971)

Arne Emil Jacobsen was born in Copenhagen and as a young student exhibited a talent for the arts and an interest in the natural world. With his parents' encouragement, he studied architecture at Teknisk Skole I Kobenhavn (Copenhagen's Technical College), graduating in 1924, and the Kunstakademiets Arkitektskole (Royal Danish Academy of Fine Arts) from 1924 to 1927. Jacobsen, one of Denmark's most important architects in the post–World War II period, completed many significant commissions.[1] Careful attention to form and space, combined with the ability to shape design details into a harmonious whole, can be observed throughout his oeuvre, including his textile designs. Jacobsen always identified himself as an architect whose other design work was part of an inclusive architectural project. Many of his most important designs—lamps, furniture, textiles, and tableware—originated within specific architectural projects.

Jacobsen began a long and fruitful collaboration with the prestigious Danish furniture manufacturer Fritz Hansen in 1934, producing some of the twentieth century's most recognizable modern furnishings. He continued designing furnishings, single-family homes, and larger municipal projects in Denmark until 1943 when the German occupation of Denmark forced him to flee to Sweden with his wife Jonna.

Jonna Jacobsen, who was a textile designer and printer, encouraged Arne to pursue textile and wallpaper design in Sweden, architectural assignments being scarce. Some of his original designs were acquired by the Nationalmuseum in Stockholm, as well as commercial textile firms.[2] Inspired by his love of botany, Jacobsen created several patterns for printed textiles featuring stylized flowers, leaves, and grasses, including *Foxtail* (1943) and *Hyacinth* (1945) later manufactured by Grantex, as well as others for Nordiska Kompaniet. *Waves*, produced for Knoll, was possibly designed during Jacobsen's time in Sweden (fig B.72). It is likely that Knoll acquired it through Nordiska Kompaniet, a regular supplier at this time. *Waves* was also produced by Grantex in 1948.[3] The fabric, with its simple, undulating lines and pleasing visual rhythm, was suitable for a variety of treatments. The continuous organic curves seen in *Waves* were a recurring motif in Jacobsen's work; the seating at the Bellevue Theater in Klampenborg (1937) represents a three-dimensional version.

Jacobsen returned to Denmark in 1945 and began to rebuild his architectural prac-

Fig. B.70 Suzanne Huguenin. *Sequoia* ("Copper" colorway), 1974–82. Made by Weberei Eschen AG for Knoll Textiles. Used for upholstery; wool, rayon; twill weave. KnollTextiles Archive. Cat. 202.

Fig. B.71 Jacqueline Iribe. *Citronnade*, 1954. Used for drapery; cotton; plain weave, screen-printed. Photographed by Herbert Matter. KnollTextiles Archive.

Fig. B.72 Arne Jacobsen. *Waves*, ca. 1950. Used for drapery; linen; plain weave, screen-printed. Photographed by Herbert Matter. KnollTextiles Archive.

Fig. B.73 Julia Keiner. *Stratton* swatch ("Off-White" colorway), ca. 1975. Made by Chicopee Mills for Knoll Textiles. Used for drapery; Verel Modacrylic, rayon, wool; plain gauze weave with supplemental warp. KnollTextiles Archive. Cat. 211.

tice. He did not abandon textile design, however, recognizing this to be critical to creating balanced and cohesive interiors. In 1948 Lord and Taylor carried a collection of Jacobsen's textiles, an international collaboration intended to appeal to a range of consumers. Some designs were printed in the United States on cotton by Cyrus Clark and available at lower prices than those printed on linen in Denmark by Graucob Textiles. This was the first large-scale group of textiles to be sent directly from Denmark.[4] Described as having a "fresh-from-the-fields look," the floral and foliate designs show that Jacobsen continued to use vital natural forms in contemporary novel ways.[5]

Jacobsen's printed textiles were featured in numerous small exhibitions around New York City in the late 1940s. His textiles were exhibited at *Decorative Arts Today* at the Newark Museum in New Jersey in 1948. Moreley-Fletcher, an importer of European fabrics, featured Jacobsen's printed textiles in the AID exhibition at the Pierre Hotel in New York in 1949 and included Jacobsen's "amusing series of toadstools" in their New York showroom the same year.[6] Also in 1949 *Hyacinth* was included in an Architectural League installation, and the Jacobsen prints *Crow's Nest* and *Water Level* were presented at the Hambro House of Design in 1950.[7]

During the postwar period, Jacobsen's work gained international acclaim as a leading exemplar of "Scandinavian Modern," a modernist sensibility characterized by softer, organic forms and natural materials.[8] Every design detail was given careful consideration; function, texture, and color were equally important. Commissions for private housing, furniture, and industrial design—including the SAS Royal Hotel in Copenhagen (1950) and St. Catherine's College at Oxford (1963)—helped popularize this modern aesthetic. The *Ant* chair (1952) and *Swan* chair (1958), both produced by Fritz Hansen, have become iconic examples of simple modern furnishing and are still available today. Jacobsen never stopped working. He died suddenly in March of 1971, leaving several projects to be completed by others. —SAT

Design for Knoll
Waves (1948–50).

Selected Awards and Exhibitions
1925 Silver medal for a chair at the Exposition Internationale des Arts décoratifs et Industriels, Paris
1929 "The House of the Future" winning design (with Flemming Lassen), Denmark
1937 Competition winner, Arhus Town Hall (with Erik Moller)
1945 Prize for design of YMCA athletic center, Borough of Copenhagen
1948 *Decorative Arts Today*, Newark Museum
1953 Grand Prix for Massey-Harris Project, International Architect Exhibition
1957 Silver medal for chair *3140*, Grand Prix, Eleventh Triennale, Milan
1966 Competition, first prize for design of Christianeum Grammar School, Hamburg Denmark (with Otto Weitling)
1970 Träpriset–The Wood Prize, an architectural prize instituted by the Swedish Forest Industries Federation (Skogsindustrierna)
1971 Gold Medal, Académie d'Architecture de France

Julia Keiner Forchheimer (1900–1992)

Born in Wilhermsdorf, Germany, Julia Keiner (later Forchheimer) started weaving at a young age on her uncle's hand loom. After finishing college, Keiner studied at local art schools in Munich and Nuremburg before opening a studio for textile design and embroidery in Wilhermsdorf.[1] Keiner commenced formal weaving studies in 1927 at Frankfurt's Kunst und Kunstgewerbeschule (School of Arts and Crafts, part of the State Academy of Fine Arts) and, two years later, she joined the institution's faculty, conducting a workshop on experimental and commercial weaving.[2] Keiner traveled throughout Europe and pursued advanced weaving studies in Sweden. In 1932 she settled in Frankfurt, opening a private weaving studio which remained in operation until 1936 when, fleeing the increasingly difficult political climate in Germany, she immigrated to Palestine.[3]

In 1941 Keiner founded a weaving workshop at the Bezalel School of Arts and Crafts in Jerusalem, serving as the workshop's director from its inception until the early 1960s.[4] The school, which had closed in the late 1920s due to financial difficulties, reopened in 1935 as the "New Bezalel," emulating the principles and workshop platform of the Bauhaus and enjoying a period of resurgence.[5] Keiner, an influential teacher, had a lasting impact on her students at Bezalel and in the broader weaving community of Jerusalem.[6]

Her work received widespread recognition when, in 1952, she was commissioned to weave curtains for the new General Assembly Building at the United Nations in New York.

During the late 1950s, Keiner continued to travel and expand her craft, spending a short period in the latter part of the decade in the United States and Canada, while still maintaining a presence in Jerusalem. Israeli architect and designer Nathan Shapira selected Keiner's weavings for the 1958 traveling exhibition, *Forms from Israel*, sponsored by the Israeli Government, the America-Israel Cultural Foundation, and Crafts from Israel, Inc.[7]

Keiner remained at Bezalel until about 1964 when she relocated to New York and married the philanthropist Leo Forchheimer. Resuming her weaving practice, she supplied woven textile designs to notable textile firms such as Isabel Scott Fabrics Corporation and Knoll Textiles. Both companies were producing Keiner Forchheimer's fabrics by 1966. That same year Isabel Scott introduced Keiner's reversible all-wool casement *Janus* and her sheer casement *Vermeil* of metallic and linen threads. Isabel Scott followed these releases with the introduction of wool and mohair blend upholsteries designed by Keiner in 1968 and 1969.[8]

Knoll unveiled *Harrow*, the first of three designs by Keiner, in 1966 (see fig. 5.11).[9] Handwoven in West Germany, the refined yet textural upholstery was initially offered in "Oyster," "Beige," "Brown," and "Charcoal"; six additional colorways such as "Saffron" and "Olive" were added in 1968.[10] The fire-retardant textiles *Jupiter* and *Stratton*, both woven with Verel modacrylic, were added to the Knoll casement collection in 1967.[11] *Stratton* featured a plain gauze (leno) weave with an alternating chunky warp, while *Jupiter* had twisted weft yarns, creating a more dimensional feel (fig. B.73, see fig. 5.10).

As she settled in the United States, Keiner joined her husband as an active philanthropist, forming the Leo and Julia Forchheimer Foundation which has funded major institutions such as Yeshiva University Museum and the Museum of Jewish Heritage, both in New York.[12] Keiner survived her husband (who died in 1981) by eleven years.
—AMT

Designs for Knoll
Harrow (1966–78); *Jupiter* (1967–71); *Stratton* (1967–78).

Selected Awards and Exhibitions
1958 Milan Triennale
1958–60 *Forms from Israel*, Hartford Art Museum, Connecticut, and Museum of Contemporary Crafts, New York
1961 Gold Medal, International Handworkers, Munich

Steffi Kiessling-Plewa (b. 1953)

Steffi Kiessling-Plewa designed seven delicately wrought woven casements for Knoll International beginning with *Lucena* in 1979. Knoll was the first company to purchase a design from Kiessling-Plewa after she finished her studies in Hamburg.[1] Born in Heilbronn in southern Germany, Kiessling-Plewa studied industrial design and art history at the Hochschule für Bildende Künst (University of Fine Arts) in Hamburg in 1972; two years later, however, she shifted her focus to textile design and studied with printed-textile designer Margaret Hildebrand and her assistant Gerda Kock.

Upon graduation in 1978 Kiessling-Plewa showed her designs to major textile companies throughout Germany. The European division of Knoll, located in Mürr, made the first purchase in July 1978 when Kiessling-Plewa brought her samples to Arthur Sager (vice president of Knoll Textiles) who happened to be visiting. He immediately selected one of the designs to be included in the *Wool Casement Collection* of Knoll Textiles.[2] The textile, *Lucena*, was woven in Switzerland with five different wool yarns of varying thicknesses (fig. B.74).

After this initial contribution to the Knoll Textiles line, Peter Seipelt, director of design for Knoll Textiles Europe, asked Kiessling-Plewa to create a collection of woven casements for European release in 1982. The result included six different patterns of white-on-white vertical stripes, whose names—*Adagio*, *Allegro*, *Glissando*, *Largo*, *Pizzicato*, *Staccato*—derive from classical music. Seipelt named the collection and sourced the mills. Both *Glissando* and *Pizzicato* were still in production when Knoll Textiles stopped offering casements for the European market in 1991.[3]

After her work with Knoll, Kiessling-Plewa designed textiles for a variety of important textile companies including Heal Fabrics Ltd., Stuttgarter Fabric, Taunus Textildruck, and Nordiska Kompaniet. In 1987 she developed a patented woven leather textile used by BMW for its M-3

Fig. B.74 *Wool Casement Collection* promotional material featuring *Lucena* by Steffi Kiessling-Plewa, 1979. Knoll Archives.

Fig. B.75 Susan Kimber. *Knoll Irish Tweed* and *Knoll Irish Tweed Grid*, (both "Orange and Natural" colorway), ca. 1978. Made in Ireland for Knoll Textiles. Used for upholstery; wool; plain weave. KnollTextiles Archive.

Fig. B.76 Antoinette Lackner Webster (Toni Prestini), ca. 1948. Courtesy of Margaret Webster.

series. The leather textile was subsequently sold under various names—*Technikleder*, *Nappa-Textil-Webstruktur*, and *Log-100*, among others.[4] In 1986 Kiessling-Plewa and her husband, industrial designer Jan Plewa, established Designkontor in Hamburg, and the leather textile earned the fledgling company third prize in the Baden-Württemberg International Design Competition the following year. Kiessling-Plewa no longer designs textiles but now focuses on collaborative industrial design projects with her husband, under a new company name, Plewaworks, since 2010.[5] —AMT

Designs for Knoll
Lucena (1979–82, *Wool Casement Collection* in the U.S.); designs introduced in Europe only: *Glissando* (1982–91); *Pizzicato* (1982–91); designs introduced in 1982 in Europe only with unknown discontinued dates: *Adagio*; *Allegro*; *Largo*; *Staccato*.

Selected Awards
1985 Bundespreis Guteform, German Federal Good Design Award
1988 Third Prize, Baden-Württemberg International Design Competition

Susan Kimber (active ca. 1978)

In 1978 Knoll Textiles introduced *Knoll Irish Tweed*, designed by Susan Kimber (Susan Kimber Kiviat), and its variant *Knoll Irish Tweed Grid*. Kimber had worked as an interior designer at Skidmore, Owings, & Merrill, concentrating on the application of textiles to the built environment. This work later inspired her to study "how textiles are put together."[1] Exploring different combinations of materials, colors, and textures, she enrolled in a weaving class and purchased a handloom, working in different combinations of materials, colors, and textures.[2]

Throughout the 1970s and 1980s, Kimber's wall hangings and tapestries were featured in exhibitions and design showcases, such as the Robert Tait and Steelcase showrooms in Manhattan and the Silo Gallery in New Milford, Connecticut.[3] In Kimber's noncommercial fiber art, she incorporated strips of color photographs into linen and sisal weavings, as in *Portrait of an Irish Cow*.[4]

For *Knoll Irish Tweed* and *Knoll Irish Tweed Grid*, Kimber drew from her handweaving experience and knowledge of the way finished textiles are used in the design of commercial interiors (fig. B.75). The fabrics were manufactured in wool and issued in several different colorways, including a range of neutral tones and two-color offerings such as "Persimmon" and "Natural." In *Knoll Irish Tweed* the design was composed of similarly colored warp and weft yarns or was slightly altered by introducing a more richly colored yarn for the warp and a neutral tone for the weft. Kimber designed additional variants with *Knoll Irish Tweed Grid*, which used black warp and weft yarns to superimpose a grid over a neutral ground color. —ES

Designs for Knoll
Irish Tweed (1978–84); *Irish Tweed Grid* (1978–84).

Antoinette Lackner Webster (1909–1998)

Antoinette Lackner Webster (fig. B.76) was an award-winning designer and teacher, who during her brief career as a professional weaver created an iconic Knoll fabric—*Prestini*. It was released in 1948 just as she dropped "Prestini," her first husband's surname, from her name, having remarried. The identity of "Toni Prestini" (as she was credited in Knoll press materials and price lists) thus became obscured over the decades, while the fabric she designed remained a key component of Knoll's textile collections for over thirty years (fig. B.77).[1]

Antoinette Lackner was born in Winnetka, Illinois. At the age of sixteen, she entered Vassar College, graduating with a bachelor's degree in art in 1930. After graduation, she apprenticed briefly with a Chicago fashion house, then opened her own custom dressmaking business which operated successfully until 1936, when she became interested in teaching.[2] Between 1936 and 1942, she taught at the Lake Forest Day School and Lake Forest Academy in Lake Forest, Illinois. In 1941 she married designer-craftsman James Prestini, who at the time was teaching mathematics and woodworking at Lake Forest Academy and was also an instructor at the School of Design in Chicago. While continuing to teach, Antoinette Prestini attended summer and night classes at the School of Design.[3]

The couple moved to Denton, Texas, in 1942, when James Prestini was hired to teach at North Texas State Teachers College (now the University of North Texas).[4] There Antoinette Prestini studied art with an emphasis on weaving. When her husband returned to Chicago in 1943, she stayed on in Denton to finish her degree, earning a master's degree in 1944, and she taught at the college during the 1943–44 school year.[5] She continued teaching after returning to Lake Forest, and enrolled as a weaving student at Cranbrook Academy of Art in the summer of 1945. She may have separated from James Prestini around this time.[6] At Cranbrook (1945–47), her work was highly regarded, and in 1947 she won the academy's first prize for weaving.[7] She was hired by department head Marianne Strengell to teach the weaving course in Cranbrook's summer session that year.[8] In the fall of 1947 she organized and became design director for a new weaving program at Plymouth Colony Farms, an experimental agricultural and craft industry venture in Plymouth, Michigan.[9] During the late 1940s Antoinette Prestini was awarded prizes in several national design competitions and exhibited throughout the United States (see chapter 1 and list below).

In January 1948 Antoinette Prestini married Frank J. Webster and later that year moved back to Lake Forest, Illinois, where she set up her own weaving studio. One of her designs for Plymouth Colony Farms was exhibited in *For Modern Living* (1949) at the Detroit Institute of Arts. It was praised in the new journal *Handweaver & Craftsman* as "an unusually beautiful upholstery fabric" of wool, cotton ratiné, flax and rayon yarns in plain weave, "proving that imagination in the use of yarns can produce unusual textures in the simplest technique."[10] These qualities are also present in Prestini (fig. B.78, see chapter 3). She continued to weave and exhibit (as Antoinette Lackner Webster) but not professionally after the early 1950s. In 1953 the Websters moved to Bedford Hills, New York, and again in 1960 to Mount Kisco, New York, where she worked as a teacher and school librarian at the Cisqua School.[11] She retired with her husband to East Poultney, Vermont, in 1972, living there until her death in 1998.
—SW

Design for Knoll
Prestini (1948–82).

Selected Awards and Exhibitions
1946 *International Textile Exhibition*, Greensboro, North Carolina
1947 Honorable Mention (for woven textile design), Moss Rose competition
Fifth amateur prize, La France textile design competition
First prize for weaving, Cranbrook
First award, Woven Clothing Fabrics, and second award, Woven Synthetics, *International Textile Exhibition*, Greensboro, North Carolina
1949 Second National Biennial Exhibition of Contemporary Textiles and Ceramics, Cranbrook
An Exhibition for Modern Living, Detroit Institute of Arts
1951 *Alumni Exhibition*, Cranbrook
1952 *Textilien aus USA*, Smithsonian circulating exhibition (*Prestini* shown)
1959 *20th Century Design, U.S.A.*, Albright Art Gallery, Buffalo, and Cleveland Museum of Art (*Prestini* shown)

Dennis Lennon (1918–1991)

John Dennis Lennon was born in London, and between 1936 and 1939 he studied architecture at the University College of London. Like many young men of his generation, Lennon served in the British military during World War II. By 1946 he had resumed his career in architecture, working as an assistant designer in the offices of Maxwell Fry and Jane Drew, British architects devoted to the modern movement, where his talents were recognized. Architect Theo Crosby recalled that "Lennon always had style—I remember him in the office of Maxwell Fry and Jane Drew in 1948.... We could all see that he would go far."[1]

While in Fry and Drew's office, Lennon assisted in the construction of the new Rayon Design Centre, an industrial campus that housed a design studio and exhibition space, and he became acquainted with participants in Britain's growing rayon industry. His designs for a modern interior in a Georgian building impressed the clients, especially the sensitivity he displayed in balancing two seemingly contradictory styles. Lennon was offered the role of director of the Design Centre where he devoted himself to designing textiles as well as interior spaces, exhibition stands, and *Rayon and Design*, the industry's publication. He hired a young design student, Terence Conran, to work for him. Conran, now a renowned designer, restaurateur, and retailer, credits Lennon with allowing him to experiment and expand his boundaries, and he adopted Lennon's view that a good designer should be able to turn his hand to anything.[2] Conran later recalled their shared enthusiasm for contemporary modern designers, identifying

Fig. B.77 Antoinette Lackner Webster (Toni Prestini). *Prestini* ("Orange-Yellow" colorway), introduced 1948, this example 1958. Made by Louisville Textiles for Knoll Textiles. Used for upholstery; cotton; plain weave. KnollTextiles Archive. Cat. 23.

Fig. B.78 Antoinette Lackner Webster (Toni Prestini). Detail of *Prestini* upholstery on *Small Diamond* chair designed by Harry Bertoia, this example ca. 1952–61. Upholstery made by Louisville Textiles for Knoll Textiles; chair made by Knoll Associates, Inc. Upholstery: cotton; plain weave; chair: plastic-coated wire frame, foam rubber. Private collection. Cat. 110.

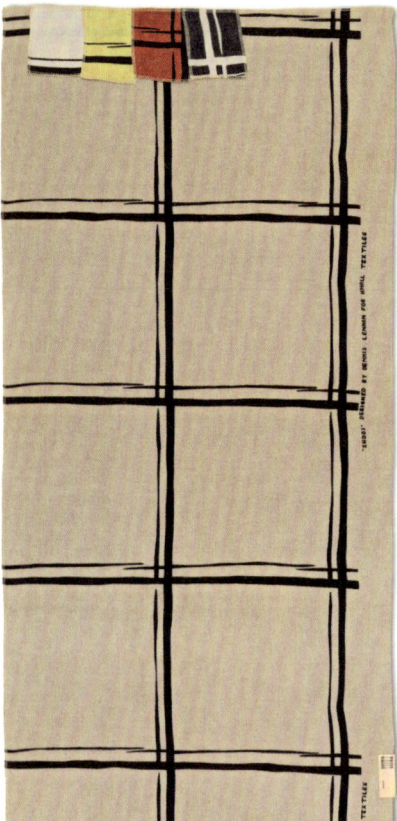

Fig. B.79 Dennis Lennon. *Shogi* sample ("Black on Natural" colorway), ca. 1954. Made by American Art for Knoll Textiles. Used for drapery; linen; plain weave, screen-printed. Private collection. Cat. 65.

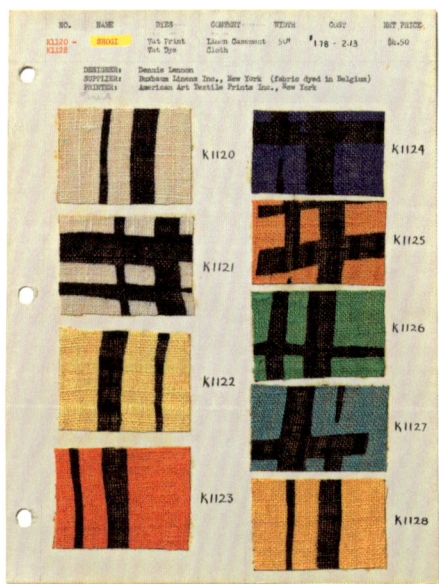

Fig. B.80 Dennis Lennon. *Shogi* data page with 9 colorways attached, 1954. Used for drapery; linen; plain weave, block- or screen-printed; mounted on paper. KnollTextiles Archive. Cat. 42.

Scandinavian modern furniture, the Eameses' designs, and Knoll as key sources of inspiration at this time.[3]

Lennon also created printed textiles for the English firm Haworths, and while retaining a position at the Rayon Design Centre, he also established his own firm, Dennis Lennon & Partners in 1950.[4] As an architect Lennon worked on large-scale projects such as the Royal Opera House in Covent Garden (1960). The interiors he designed included retail spaces for the Jaeger stores in London, Glasgow, and Oxford (1954–59), showrooms for Sekers, a London textile design firm (1964), and opulent reception areas on the RMS *Queen Elizabeth II*, which were highly publicized when the ocean liner was launched in 1968.[5] He also turned his hand to modern furnishings for Scottish Furniture Manufacturer's Ltd. and Dunn's of Bromley (1950), and to set design in the theater, particularly for the Glyndebourne Opera House in East Sussex.[6] The range of these projects reflects his conviction that designers should be able to work with different materials. The dual nature of textiles, at once flat surfaces but also with the potential to hold volume in space, allowed Lennon to enrich his holistic interior designs.

Shogi (1953–59), produced by Knoll Textiles, was named after a Japanese architectural element—the screens that serve as sliding doors or room dividers and are constructed of rice paper stretched over a bamboo grid.[7] In *Shogi*, a printed textile, horizontal and vertical lines in a large-scale repeat suggest the regularity and simplicity of a grid, but the lines have a loose hand-drawn quality, contributing to an organic feel (fig. B.79). *Shogi* was printed on two weights of Belgian linen that were standard plain drapery cloths in the Knoll line: a heavier weight version simply called *Linen* and a sheer called *Linen Casement Cloth*.[8] The heavier weight cloth was available in white, natural, yellow or "Paprika Red" with the design printed in black, as well as in charcoal with the design printed in white. The sheer cloth had vibrant colored grounds such as paprika or turquoise with the design also printed in black (fig. B.80). Bernard Wiehan, an architect working with Lennon, noted that he "always liked to have the best of any particular material or product, and he had an affinity with strong primary colors—reds, yellows, strong blues."[9] These qualities made his designs a good fit for Knoll. Although it is unclear how Knoll and Lennon were connected, Knoll was producing many one-off prints around the time they included Lennon in their textile line. Dennis Lennon died in the United Kingdom in 1991.
—SAT

Design for Knoll
Shogi (1953–58).

Selected Awards and Exhibitions
1951 Festival of Britain Exposition, London
Fellow of the Royal Institute of British Architects

Elizabeth Levin Ossip (b. 1955)

Elizabeth Levin (later Ossip) was born in Johnstown, Pennsylvania. She first became interested in textile design at High Mowing School in Wilton, New Hampshire, where she took classes in handweaving and ordered her first handloom from Sweden. She studied textile design and production at several venues: the Sharon Arts Center in Peterborough, New Hampshire (1973); Penland School of Crafts in Penland, North Carolina (1974); and Keene State College in Keene, New Hampshire (1974–76).[1] From 1977 to 1981, Levin was enrolled in the textile program at the Rhode Island School of Design (RISD) where she developed technical skills in Jacquard and multiharness weave construction and studied color application and surface-print design.[2] After graduating with a BFA from RISD, Levin relocated to New York City and from 1981 to 1985 ran her own freelance design and consulting business— Elizabeth Levin Woven Textile Design—for the contract and residential markets.

Through her firm, Levin actively pursued commissions from commercial textile firms, in addition to her custom work, circulating her portfolio of handwoven samples throughout the textile industry. In 1981 Kristl Reinhardt (later Andrus), design stylist, and Richard Wagner, design director at Knoll Textiles, hired her to produce two designs based on prototypes in her portfolio— *Accord* (1984) and *Façade* (1984).[3]

Both textiles displayed Levin's affinity for designs with complex weave structures. The prototypes had been woven on an *haute-lisse* loom—a traditional tapestry loom. Although adapted to meet Knoll Textile's abrasion standards for contract market upholsteries, Levin's work remained textural.[4] The Jacquard-woven pattern for *Façade* consists of small cells of concentric squares and creates a sense of depth through the juxtaposition and layering of dark and neutral colors, while *Accord* features a gridlike pattern in four contrasting colors (fig. B.81). Like the textiles of her Knoll contemporaries Dana Romeis and Robin Whitten, Levin's designs also emphasized some aspects of the aesthetic and technical traditions of American craft culture such as an interest in natural fibers and handwoven prototypes. *Accord* and *Façade* were composed of a blend of wool and synthetic fibers in several different colorways.[5]

In addition to her work for Knoll, from 1981 to 1983 Levin served as manager and co-owner of Green Mountain Spinnery in Putney, Vermont, supervising the development and quality control of custom yarns for handknitting and handweaving. From 1983 to 1985 she worked as director of specifier sales at Guilford Industries in New York, where she marketed Guilford's services and products, including their many lines of upholstery fabrics, to the architecture and design community and was also the firm's color and design director, managing product development and coordinating Guilford's New York showroom designs.[6] Levin stopped working as a textile designer in 1985 and now resides in Boca Raton, Florida, where she is a social worker. —ES

Designs for Knoll
Accord (1984–87); *Façade* (1984–87).

Stig Lindberg (1916–1982)

"Exuberant," "whimsical," "playful" are words that characterize the remarkable textile patterns and ceramic designs of Stig Lindberg. Although he was recognized as one of the most imaginative Swedish designers of the twentieth century, Lindberg is not well known in the English-speaking world.

Born in Umeå, Sweden, Lindberg studied ceramics at the Konstfackskolan (School of Arts, Crafts, and Design) in Stockholm in 1935. Two years later, Hjalmar Olson, director of the Gustavsberg porcelain works outside Stockholm, arranged for Lindberg to meet Wilhelm Kåge, the artistic director, who hired the young student as a designer.[1] After World War II, Lindberg's designs for painted faience at Gustavsberg attracted the attention of Astrid Sampe, director of the textile department of Nordiska Kompaniet (NK), Stockholm's premier department store. Ten textiles with Lindberg designs were printed by Erik Ljungberg for NK by May 1947, when they were displayed with work by NK's other contemporary designers. In the imaginative installation, the colorfully patterned textiles were draped on 10-foot-high mannequins, made by Lindberg himself, and were also hung on clotheslines.

How Hans Knoll first learned of Lindberg's textiles remains unknown. Sampe may have introduced Lindberg's work to him, or Knoll may have seen the installation at NK in 1947, during a period when he was making regular trips to Europe to find items for Knoll and to meet with potential contacts. In any case, in 1948 Knoll began selling Lindberg's *Fruktlada* design, changing the name to *Apples*, in both upholstery and drapery fabric. The inspiration for the rhythmically stylized motifs derived from the neatly arranged fruit counter at the local Konsum, a cooperative grocery store chain in Stockholm; as described in the *New York Times*, the "one-color print on a white ground by Stig Lindberg depicts cross-sections of apples packed cheek to cheek in a shipping crate."[2] The playfully graphic pattern was printed on a linen, jute, and cotton blend in two colors, red and graphite gray, which was typical of Knoll's colorways in the late 1940s. When Eszter Haraszty became head of the textile division in 1950, one of her first decisions was to recolor *Apples*, producing it in darker grounds, such as "Black and Blue" (fig. B.82).

By the 1950s, Bonniers in New York was also importing Lindberg's textile and furniture designs for its fashionable Madison Avenue store while his ceramics designs were included in *Design in Scandinavia*, an exhibition which opened at the Virginia Museum of Fine Arts, Richmond, in 1954, and traveled to twenty museums.[3] Lindberg also created textiles for AB Heyman & Olesen, a leading Swedish manufacturer. He served as artistic director at Gustavsberg (1948–57), continuing to work there until 1980, and was principal teacher at Konstfack in Stockholm (1957–72). He died in Italy in 1982. —HH

Design for Knoll
Apples (1948–54).

Selected Awards and Exhibitions
1939 New York World's Fair
1947 Lindberg Exhibition, Nordiska Kompaniet
1948, 1957 Gold Medal, Milan Triennale
1951, 1954 Grand Prix, Milan Triennale
1954 *Design in Scandinavia: An Exhibition*

Fig. B.81 Elizabeth Levin. *Accord* sample ("Aztec" colorway), 1984. Made in the United States for Knoll Textiles. Used for upholstery; cotton, nylon; plain weave with alternating single and paired warps and wefts. KnollTextiles Archive.

Fig. B.82 Stig Lindberg. *Apples* (*Fruktlada*), ("Black on Blue" colorway), designed ca. 1947, manufactured ca. 1952. Made for Knoll Textiles. Used for drapery and upholstery; cotton; plain weave, screen- or block-printed. The Cleveland Museum of Art, The Harold T. Clark Educational Extension Fund 1952.402.

Fig. B.83 Ross Littell. *Mira* ("Red, Orange and Persimmon" colorway), introduced 1958. Made by Winston Prints for Knoll Textiles. Used for drapery; linen; plain weave, block- or screen-printed. Private collection. Cat. 131.

Fig. B.84 Ross Littell. *Discs* sample ("White on White" colorway), introduced 1959. Made by Winston Prints for Knoll Textiles. Used for drapery; linen, cotton; plain weave, block- or screen-printed. Courtesy the family and friends of Ross Littell. Cat. 138.

Fig. B.85 Ross Littell. *Chess* ("Tan on White" colorway), introduced 1959. Made for Knoll Textiles. Used for drapery; linen; plain weave, block- or screen-printed. Courtesy the family and friends of Ross Littell. Cat. 137.

of Objects for the Home—From Denmark, Finland, Norway, and Sweden, Virginia Museum of Fine Arts (circulating exhibition)
1957 Gregor Paulsson Trophy, Swedish Society of Industrial Design
1968 Prince Eugen Medal
1982 *Scandinavian Modern: 1880–1980*, Cooper-Hewitt Museum
2007 *©Stig Lindberg*, Nationalmuseum, Stockholm

Ross Littell (1924–2000)

Ross Franklin Littell was born in Los Angeles. He studied there at the Art Center School (now the Art Center College of Design) in Pasadena on a scholarship in 1942. During World War II he served in the U.S. Coast Guard (1943–46), and when he returned to his studies, it was at Pratt Institute in Brooklyn, New York, where he graduated with an industrial design major in 1949.[1]

Littell formed a partnership that year with two other Pratt graduates—William Katavolos and Douglas Kelley. They soon began working with Laverne, Inc., an interior design firm with showrooms on Fifty-seventh Street in New York. Laverne sought the best examples of new design, and Littell made creative contributions to textile, wallpaper, and furniture designs. Littell's textile designs for Laverne, such as *Day Star* and *Holiday*, exhibit a sophisticated graphic sensibility and a skill for combining simple lines, dots, and circles in innovative ways.[2] One of Littell, Katavolos and Kelley's most celebrated and novel designs for Laverne was the *T-Chair* (1952), a lightweight three-legged armchair with a seat and back composed of a piece of leather suspended across a three-point bent-steel structure. The *T-Chair*, and the pieces that accompanied it, were dubbed "The New Furniture" in re-cognition of their forward-thinking design and minimalist simplicity.[3]

By 1956 the partnership had ended, and Littell was working freelance. The following year he was awarded a Fulbright scholarship to study in Italy where he focused his attention on patterns and textures found in nature—from the visible to the microscopic.[4] This close inspection of the intricacies of geometric shapes—especially the fractal patterns of crystalline forms and the precision of cellular structure—would inform the repeat patterns of his textile designs and other work. Three designs, *Fugue*, *Eclipse* and *Daystar* for Laverne, were included in the *Textiles USA* exhibition at MoMA in 1956.[5] In 1957, while still in Italy, Littell participated in the Milan Triennale where he became acquainted with several influential Danish furniture designers—Finn Juhl, Hans Wegner, Borge Mogensen, and Ole Wanscher. He also met the Danish architect Inger Klingenberg whom he would later marry.[6] Littell forged strong symbiotic connections to the art and design community in Denmark, but he worked in Italy and the United States throughout the rest of his life, contributing designs to various companies including furnishings for Herman Miller in the United States and De Padova in Italy. His textile designs were produced by such notable Danish companies as Unika Vaev and Kvadrat, as well as by Knoll Textiles.

Littell's print designs for Knoll such as *Mira* (1958) and *Spheres*, *Chess*, *Discs*, and *Criss Cross* (all introduced in 1959) are excellent examples of his virtuosity with form and line. Geometric shapes combine in unexpectedly sophisticated ways. *Mira*, for instance, uses three colors such as "Red/Orange/Persimmon" on a white linen ground (fig. B.83). The subtly pointed half-circle forms suggest the regularity of a honeycomb but without its rigidity. *Discs* is simply circles arranged in rows, but the subtle shading gradient provides a textured appearance (fig. B.84). It was printed in five colors ranging from "Turquoise" to "Beige" on a linen and cotton sheer fabric.[7] *Spheres* also plays upon the optical effects of permeable grids and interlocking circles and was available in one or two colors such as "Black on Natural" and "Lemon and Gold on White," both on linen and cotton.[8] *Chess* playfully expands on the simple grid of a chessboard, but by recombining and adjusting the scale in novel ways, Littell creates a new dynamism (fig. B.85). *Chess* was released in "Tan," "Yellow," "Aqua," or "White," on a white ground, on a Dacron and linen sheer.[9] Littell described *Criss Cross* as part of "a series of visual adven-tures, an exploration of texture pattern and form based on vissualogies or systems incorporating arithmetic or geometric fundamentals or progressions."[10] It is a design that exemplifies the striking visual impact of straight lines combined with mathematical precision. *Criss Cross* was printed on Belgian linen, in colorways such as "Charcoal on White," or "Olive on Oatmeal," and was awarded a citation of merit from AID.[11]

Littell's designs for Kvadrat exhibit the same passion for the optical interplay as those for Knoll. Many were the result of a successful collaboration with the Danish artist Finn Skodt, who worked closely with Kvadrat for years.[12] His textiles, including many collaborative projects with Skodt, continued to be featured in publications such as *Interiors* and *Living Architecture* through the 1990s, and many remain in production, including *Tomoko 2*, which is offered in a wide range of colorways by Kvadrat.[13] KnollTextiles reinterpreted *Mira* as a sheer drapery fabric for the *Archival Collection* in 2007. Littell returned to California in 1995, settling in Santa Barbara where he died in 2000. —SAT

Designs for Knoll
Mira (1958–72); *Chess* (1959–64); *Criss Cross* (1959–64); *Discs* (1959–64); *Spheres* (1959–64).

Selected Awards and Exhibitions
1949 Citation of Merit, American Institute of Decorators
1953 *Good Design* exhibition, MoMA
1955 *Good Design* exhibition, MoMA
1956 *Textiles USA*, MoMA
1957 Milan Triennale
1958 American Pavilion, Brussels World's Fair
1957–58 *Fulbright Designer's Show*, Museum of Contemporary Crafts (now Museum of Arts and Design, New York)
1959 Citation of Merit Award for *Criss Cross*, AID
1983 *Design Since 1945*, Philadelphia Museum of Art

Franz Lorenz (active ca. 1950)

Franz Lorenz has been credited with the design of the early Knoll upholstery fabric *Scotch Linen* (fig. B.86, see fig. 3.48). While little is known about him, he is thought to have been the founder or director of an eponymous handweaving workshop in Düdingen, Switzerland, and a member of the Swiss Werkbund.[1] His connection to Knoll or to Donald Brothers, the mill that wove *Scotch Linen*, has not yet been clearly established. Lorenz may have collaborated with the mill, which had many international connections and clients throughout its history, or the design may have been licensed from Lorenz for production in Scotland.[2] It is also possible that Knoll learned of Lorenz's textiles through the Swiss modernist retailer Wohnbedarf. Knoll imported a tripod table (*Model 103*) designed for Wohnbedarf by Hans Bellman beginning in 1948 and about the same time Wohnbedarf became the Swiss licensee for Knoll furniture.[3] Original samples of *Scotch Linen* from 1950 (along with later trial samples for proposed additional colorways) survive in Donald Brothers' sample books (listed as "No. 2529, Plain Linen Crash"), but designer credits are not included nor is there any reference to the Franz Lorenz company.[4]

Scotch Linen was a heavyweight linen upholstery fabric of a type known as "crash" meaning a fabric with a rough irregular surface, woven of thick, uneven yarns. It was initially named simply *Linen Crash* in known Knoll publications.[5] A plain weave available in one-, two- and three-color versions, and in coordinated plaids, *Scotch Linen* was a perennial favorite in the Knoll collection—along with the visually related designs *Prestini* (1948–82, cotton) and *Lana* (1956–78, wool)—until it was superseded in contract installations by more durable fabrics in the 1960s. —SW

Designs for Knoll
Scotch Linen (1950–66).

Selected Awards and Exhibitions
1951 *Good Design*, Merchandise Mart (January) and MoMA (*Scotch Linen* shown)
Living Up-to-Date, Baltimore Museum of Art (*Scotch Linen* shown)
1952 *Textilien aus USA*, Smithsonian circulating exhibition (*Scotch Linen* shown)

LTL Architects (established 1997)
Paul Lewis (b. 1966)
Marc Tsurumaki (b. 1965)
David J. Lewis (b. 1966)

Lewis.Tsurumaki.Lewis (LTL) Architects, a relatively young firm based in New York, was founded by three graduates of Princeton University's master of architecture program. A "design intensive firm" by their own estimation, LTL's varied work ranges from large-scale public commissions and speculative projects to interiors and product design, including lighting for Ivalo Lighting, Inc. and wallcoverings for KnollTextiles.

The firm's notable architectural projects include a residence hall for the College of Wooster in Ohio (2004), an updated interior for New York University's department of social and cultural analysis (2009), and a contemporary art space in downtown Austin,

Fig. B.86 Franz Lorenz. *Scotch Linen* ("Black/White Check" colorway), 1951–66. Made by Donald Brothers for Knoll Textiles. Used for upholstery; linen; plain weave. KnollTextiles Archive. Cat. 35.

Fig. B.87 LTL. *Margin* ("Copper" colorway), 2006. Made in the United States for KnollTextiles. Used for wallcovering; vinyl. KnollTextiles Archive.

Fig. B.88 Sven Markelius. *Markelius* sample ("Blue" colorway), designed ca. 1943, manufactured 1948–50. Used for drapery; linen, jute, cotton; plain weave, screen-printed. The Museum of Modern Art, New York, P382. Cat. 18.

Texas (2010). LTL also realized several award-winning restaurant interiors, created an art installation for Memorial Sloan-Kettering Cancer Center, New York (2009), and participated in notable exhibitions, from the Cooper-Hewitt, National Design Museum's first National Design Triennial (2000) to MoMA's *Rising Currents* (2010).[1]

LTL's approach is to embrace the "constraints of each project into the design trajectory."[2] This working philosophy "recast[s] architectural practice as a form of restricted play" and seeks to negotiate demands of "overlapping agendas of program, spatial form, and inhabitation while generating sensory environments that engage the user"—ideas more fully explored in their monograph, *Opportunistic Architecture* (2008).[3] This experimental method encourages exploration of different surfaces and materials, an element of LTL's practice that attracted consultant Marybeth Shaw. After hearing Marc Tsurumaki speak in Baltimore, Shaw brought LTL to the attention of Dorothy Cosonas and David Schutte of Knoll.[4]

LTL's 2006 *Parallel Lines* wallcovering collection for KnollTextiles, "explore[s] the boundaries between the hand-crafted and the digital" by scanning hand-drawn pencil lines and digitally duplicating them.[5] Viewing the patterns up-close reveals the detailed logic of the pencil markings, while from afar their physicality fades into a textural rhythm, what LTL calls "field condition[s]."[6] The three patterns of *Parallel Lines* offer variations of this effect. The shifting gradients of *Vector*'s vertical lines suggest motion while horizontal lines make up *Margin*'s columns (fig. B.87). *Perimeter*, the most complex of the three, uses nine different overlapping rectangles, outlined in broken lines to give depth to an otherwise flat pattern and create a sense of vertical movement.[7] The wallcoverings are printed on vinyl in a mostly neutral palette, accented with bronze, copper, and bright green.[8] —CMH

Designs for Knoll
Parallel Lines Collection (intro. 2006): *Vector*, *Perimeter*, *Margin*.

Selected Awards and Exhibitions
1998 The Mercedes T. Bass Rome Prize in Architecture, American Academy in Rome (Paul Lewis)
2001–2 *Architecture + Water*, Van Alen Institute, UCLA Department of Architecture, San Francisco Museum of Modern Art, The Heinz Architectural Center of the Carnegie Museum of Art
2004 Selected Architects, Venice Biennale—U.S. Pavilion
2007 National Design Award, Interior Design, Cooper-Hewitt National Design Museum, Smithsonian Institution
2010 *Rising Currents*, MoMA
Lawrence Israel Prize, Fashion Institute of Technology, New York
Design USA, Cooper-Hewitt National Design Museum, Smithsonian Institution

Sven Markelius (1889–1972)

Sven Markelius emerged as one of the leading modern architects in Sweden at the 1930 Stockholm Exhibition, where he designed various buildings and pavilions. His ideas about standardization in architecture had gained him recognition as a proponent of modern architecture in the 1920s, and by invitation, he had attended the 1929 CIAM (Congrès internationaux d'architecture moderne) meeting in Frankfurt. Markelius and his colleagues promoted a distinguished social agenda for modern architecture and design in Sweden. He co-authored *Acceptera* (1931), a landmark manifesto for Swedish Functionalism, the Funkis movement that defined progressive architecture in Scandinavia in the 1930s.[1] He became widely known in the United States as the architect of the highly acclaimed Swedish Pavilion at the New York World's Fair in 1939, and in 1947 he was part of the design team that planned the United Nations Headquarters in New York.[2]

Markelius (born Sven Jonsson) graduated from the Royal Institute of Technology in Stockholm in 1913. His architectural career during the interwar years corresponds to the shift from the Swedish classicism of the 1920s, practiced by Gunnar Asplund, for example, to a modern idiom that was already evident in Markelius's work—especially in the Student Union building at the Royale Institute of Technology, which he designed with Uno Åhren (1930), and the Helsingborg concert hall of 1932, perhaps his greatest project. Markelius is also well known for housing projects initated before World War II, such as the Kollektivhus (Collective Housing, 1935) and the Folkets Hus (People's House) community centers. In the 1940s he became an active city planner and in 1944 was appointed director of city planning and head of the Stockholm City Planning Office. He was thus positioned at the center of polemical and ongoing debates about urbanism—from concerns over extensive traffic congestion to decisions about heritage and preservation of the historic city center. Markelius also main-tained his own architectural office (1910s–72), completing more than fifty buildings in Sweden.

Markelius's first textiles were for Nordiska Kompaniet (NK), Sweden's largest department store in the late 1930s. While Astrid Sampe, the dynamic visionary head of the store's textile department, had encouraged him to create a few designs, his real impetus in designing textiles was the dearth of existing fabrics that he considered appropriate for the interiors of the buildings he created. Commissioned to design the main office for the company AB Turitz in Gothenburg in 1940, he worked with Sampe to develop textiles and furniture for the office interiors. NK produced the furniture, and the textiles were woven by Konstfliten–Bohusslöjd Konstfliten in Gothenburg.[3]

NK and Knoll Textiles became acquainted when Florence and Hans Knoll visited Sweden as newlyweds in 1946. Through this connection, Knoll introduced a sampling of textiles by Swedish designers. The first of these designs—*Markelius* (originally *Markeliusruta* or *Markelius Square*) and a selection of textile designs by Astrid Sampe—was featured in "The Authentic Swedish Room," an installation at the Knoll Textiles New York showroom in 1947.[4] *Markelius* was another design prom-pted by the designer's need for appropriate materials and furnishings for his projects, in this case, the headquarters of the Stockholm Building Society which he designed in 1937.[5] Knoll included the print in its first textile collection, and it remained in the line until about 1950 (fig. B.88).

Necessity also inspired the creation of two of his most famous patterns, *Pythagoras* and *Prisma*, each of which was based on an abstract geometric form. Initialy designed in the 1950s for Folkets Hus in Linköping, Sweden, *Pythagoras* was a collaboration between Markelius and his wife, Ka Markelius. Approaching textile design through the creative lens of the architect, Markelius often made elaborate prototypes that would enable him to work out complex geometric patterns. The Markeliuses laboriously created paper models of *Pythagoras* to help them properly position the complex geometric pattern which would require eighteen screens to print. Markelius was proprietary about *Pythagoras*, using it almost exclusively for his own buildings. He installed it in 1952 as a cotton and linen blend stage curtain at the Royal Institute of Technology and on velvet for a similar installation at the Linköping Trade Union Hall (fig. B.89).[6] *Pythagoras* was also chosen for installation in the ECOSOC Council room at the United Nations headquarters, where it continues to be used as of 2011.[7]

Knoll Textiles added *Pythagoras* to the line in 1953. Printed in three colorways—"Spectrum Red," "Spectrum Blue," and "Spectrum Yellow"—the print was manufactured solely by Erik Ljungbergs in Sweden for Knoll until being discontinued in 1971 (fig. B.90).[8] *Prisma* was introduced by Knoll in 1956 to almost instant acclaim (see cats. 120, 121).[9] It was initially imported from Sweden, but in late 1957 Knoll began to print the design on fiberglass in the United States. This second iteration of *Prisma* was discontinued in 1959, while the linen version remained in the collection until 1971.

In 1954 Markelius retired as Stockholm's director of city planning. His late architectural projects included the Skogsindustrihuset, Stockholm (1958), and the Arts and Congress Centre, "Bürgerhaus" in Giessen, West Germany (1962–66), both of which featured curtains in Markelius's print *Timber*. He died at age eighty-two, while designing plans for the City Theatre in Överkikaren; this final project was never constructed.[10] —HH

Fig. B.89 Curtain of *Pythagoras* textile by Sven Markelius in the cinema of the Linköping Trade Union Center, ca. 1952. Building designed by Markelius. Photographed by Egerborn ca. 1952. Knoll Archives.

Fig. B.90 Sven Markelius. *Pythagoras* color sample ("Spectrum Red," "Spectrum Yellow," "Spectrum Blue" colorways), 1954–72. Made by Ljungbergs for Knoll Textiles. Used for drapery; linen, cotton; plain weave, screen-printed. KnollTextiles Archive, donated by Doreen Rose Stempien.

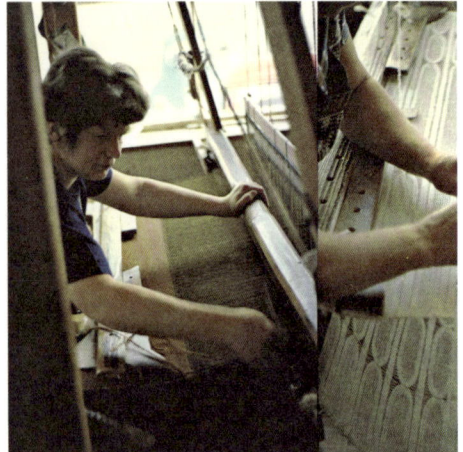

Fig. B.91 Weaving of *Horizons* at Paul Maute GmbH factory. From *Handwoven Collection* brochure designed by Massimo Vignelli/Unimark International. Photographed by Robert Cadwallader. Printed in Switzerland by Conzeti and Huber through Chanticleer Press for Knoll Textiles, ca. 1967. Knoll Archives.

Fig. B.92 Paul Maute. *Cato*, color or weave sample with manufacturer's tag, ca. 1965. Made by Paul Maute GmbH for Knoll Textiles. Used for upholstery; wool, viscose; plain weave with grouped warps and supplemental weft. KnollTextiles Archive. Cat. 163

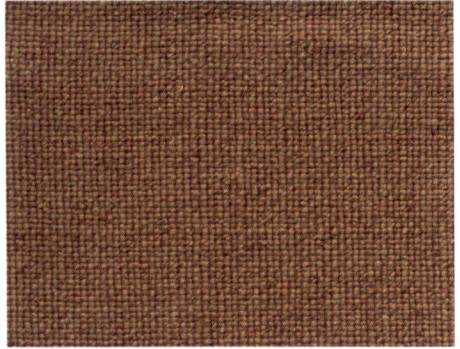

Fig. B.93 Paul Maute. *Morocco* ("Copper" colorway), introduced 1966. Made by Paul Maute GmbH for Knoll Textiles. Used for upholstery; wool; plain weave. Private collection.

Designs for Knoll
Markelius (designed ca. 1943; 1947–50);
Pythagoras (designed 1952; 1953–71);
Prisma (designed 1952; 1956–71).

Selected Awards and Exhibitions
1939 Swedish Pavilion, New York World's Fair
1944 *VÄNDERKORSET* (The Turnstile) film, (*Markelius* shown on set)
1953 *Good Design*, Chicago Merchandise Mart and MoMA (*Pythagoras* shown)
1956 AID Award for Printed Design for *Prisma*
1957 *Interbau* exhibition, Berlin (*Prisma* shown)
Award for Best Decorative Textile for *Prisma*, AID
1958 *Möbler, Mattor Och Tygtryck*, Nationalmuseum, Stockholm
1961 *Met Textiel*, Stedelijk Museum Amsterdam (*Prisma* and *Pythagoras* shown)
1967 AID Award
2000–02 *Utopia and Reality—Modernity in Sweden, 1900–1960*, Moderna Museet, Stockholm and the Bard Graduate Center, New York (*Markelius* shown)
2006–07 *Bruno Mathsson: Architect and Designer*, Swedish Museum of Architecture (*Prisma* shown)

Paul Maute (1897–1982)

Paul Maute contributed designs of lasting influence to Knoll Textiles. Handwoven at his factory beginning in the 1950s, his finely wrought drapery and strongly textural upholstery designs such as *Cato* and *Arno* had remarkable longevity in the Knoll collection.

Maute was born in Heroldstatt, a town southeast of Stuttgart which had been traditionally associated with linen weaving.[1] After serving in World War I, he studied weaving with a neighbor and set up a workshop for making rag rugs in the basement of his parents' home. In 1927 he founded his own firm in one of the town's old weaving schools. The workshop did all its own spin-ning and dying, as well as handweaving, a practice that was still common in the years between the wars and one that Maute con-tinued through his time supplying Knoll. This inclusive all-in-one production process allowed manufacturers to be far more responsive to their client's requests for specific fibers, textures, and colors. At first, Maute mainly produced simple woven car-pets, but as his design and manufacturing skills improved and the size of his operation increased, he began to specialize in high-quality handwoven upholstery and casement fabrics.

Maute's relationship with Knoll began in the 1950s when his company made Evelyn Hill–designed *Handwovens* for Knoll Germany.[2] The first textile Maute both designed and made for Knoll was *Arno*, an upholstery in production from 1961 to 1977. During a visit to Wohnbedarf, Knoll's licensee in Zurich, Suzanne Huguenin saw *Arno*, on a *Womb* chair and a *Model 96* sofa, and this led her to its creator.[3] From this time until 1993, Maute's company, Paul Maute GmbH, supplied handwovens of his own design to Knoll. From the early 1960s to 1978, when his fabrics enjoyed great prominence in the Knoll collection, Maute worked closely with Barbara Rodes on new designs and colorways. Maute was identified as a designer in Knoll press releases and price lists only in the early years of their collaboration; after 1964, while his fabrics continued to be featured in the Knoll offerings, they were listed without a designer name. Internal company records, however, document the many fabrics he designed and wove for Knoll.

The same year that Knoll introduced *Arno*, they also released *Cato*, one of the most successful fabrics ever produced for Knoll—it is still in production in 2011 (fig. B.92).[4] Two weaves related to *Arno*—*Ebro* and *Heather*—were introduced in 1962 and 1964 respectively (see chapter 3). *Morocco*, a plain weave introduced in 1966, featured a large-scale yarn (fig. B.93). Maute continued to contribute handwoven upholsteries to the Knoll collection throughout the 1970s (see chapter 5), several of which nearly matched the popularity of his earlier designs: *Tiber* (in production for eighteen years), *Parsifal* (sixteen years), *Cocoon* (seventeen years), *Mona* and *Atlantis* (both twelve years), and *Kamee* (nine years). Some of Maute's 1970s upholsteries did not survive the change of Knoll ownership in 1977: *Marabu* (in production until 1978), *Cornaro* (until 1979) and *Chord* (until 1979). Maute also wove two upholstery fabrics not of his own design for Knoll: *Inca* designed by Sheila Hicks and *Harrow* by Julia Keiner Forchheimer, both introduced in 1966.

In addition to the upholsteries, Maute produced handwoven drapery fabrics for Knoll. The first two of these—*Bourette Silk* and *Horizons*—were released in 1964. Between then and 1976 Knoll introduced a number of open-weave casements by Maute, of which *Horizons* and *Nebula* were particularly successful (see figs. 5.3 and 5.26). Maute's 1973 casement, *Loop* is outstandingly original with its three-dimensional loose looped pile (fig. B.94).

Maute lost his close connection with Knoll executives after the 1977 purchase of the company by Marshall Cogan and Stephen Swid and the departure of his close friend Barbara Rodes-Segerer in 1978.[5] There followed a gradual erosion in relations with Knoll, and Paul Maute delivered his last new design to the company in 1977, *Cocoon*, an all-silk upholstery. However, his firm continued to manufacture existing designs for Knoll through the 1980s. Maute would still go into the mill every day until about two weeks before his death at the age of eighty-five in 1982. His son, Oskar Maute, took over the helm and was followed in 1992 by Paul Maute, grandson of the founder (his namesake).[6] Maute designs that remained in the Knoll collection after 1992 and 1993 began to be produced by other manu-facturers. *Cato*, which was made by Maute GmbH as a hand-woven until 1993, has been woven since then in a Scottish mill on power looms.[7] Still in operation in 2011 Paul Maute GmbH con-tinues to specialize in handwoven tufted carpets and upholstery fabrics and promotes its ability to customize its products to suit the individual client. —AV

Designs for Knoll
Arno (1961–77); *Cato* (intro. 1961); *Ebro* (1962–94); *Heather* (1964–77); *Bourette Silk* (1964–66, 1973–75); *Horizons* (1964–78); *Morocco* (1966–88); *Tiber* (1970–87); *Mona* (1971–82); *Almanach* (1972–73); *Atoll* (1972–73); *Brabant* (1972–76); *Marabu* 1972–78); *Serenade* (1972–76); *Nebula* (1973–82); *Loop* (1973–78); *Cornaro* (1974–79); *Carré* (1976–82); *Atlantis* (1976–87); *Chord* (1976–79); *Knoll Bouclé* (1976–79); *Kamee* (1976–84); *Parsifal* (1976–91); *Cocoon* (1977–93). Manufactured by Paul Maute GmbH for Knoll, designed by others: *Inca* (1966–92), design Sheila Hicks; *Harrow* (1966–78), design Julia Keiner Forchheimer.

Exhibition
1972 *Knoll au Louvre*, Musee des Arts décoratifs, Paris

Abbott Miller (b. 1963)

In 1981 Abbott Miller left his home state of Indiana to study design—as both practice and intellectual discourse—at the Cooper Union School for the Advancement of Science and Art in New York City. Miller met fellow classmate Ellen Lupton and thus began their ongoing professional collaborations; they were married in 1991.[1] After earning BFA degrees in 1985, Miller and Lupton started Design/Writing/Research, a multi-disciplinary studio that allowed them to pursue freelance work while holding day jobs elsewhere.[2] Miller began his career working with Richard Saul Wurman, while also designing identity graphics and adver-tising for New York art galleries.[3] A year-long retainer paid by the New Museum of Con-temporary Art freed him to pursue more sustained projects, and he began designing for the visual and performing arts magazines, *Dance Ink* and *2wice*.[4]

By 1989 Design/Writing/Research had become a full-time endeavor. Miller and Lupton co-authored T*he Bathroom, The Kitchen, and the Aesthetics of Waste* (1992) and *Design/Writing/Research: Writing on Graphic Design* (1996). Miller has taught graphic design since 1997 at the Maryland Institute College of Art in Baltimore, Maryland, where Lupton serves as director of the Graphic Design MFA Program. They often collaborate on exhibitions, another important venue for communicating and applying their design ideas, most recently *Design for a Living World* (2009) at the Cooper-Hewitt National Design Museum, New York, where Lupton is curator of contemporary design. On his own, Miller has curated and designed a number of exhibitions, including *Printed Letters: The Natural History of Typography* (1992) at the Jersey City Museum, and the Harley-Davidson 100th Anniversary Open Road Tour (2002–3). He is also creative director at Steuben Glass.

In 1999 Miller joined the design consultancy firm Pentagram as a partner in their New York office, where he leads the design of books, magazines, catalogues, identity graphics, exhibitions, and various editorial projects.[5] Miller takes a fluid design approach between media in two and three dimensions, about which he quotes the artist Lawrence Wiener: "words, images, and artifacts arranged on a wall, in a space, or in a book."[6] His clients have included the Whitney Museum of American Art, the Guggenheim Museum, Vitra, and Knoll.[7]

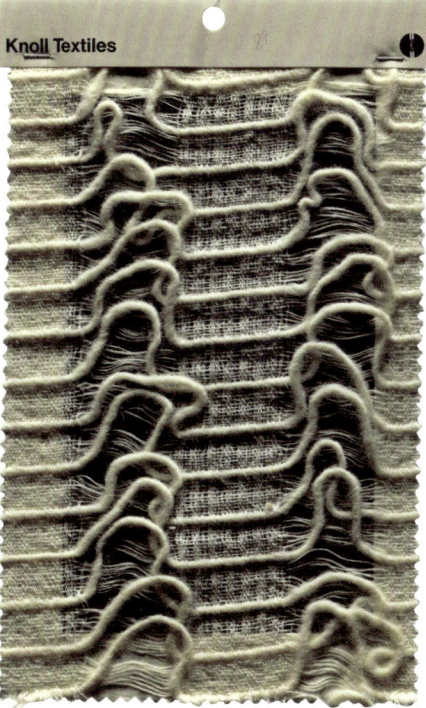

Fig. B.94 Paul Maute. *Loop* large swatch ("Natural" colorway), ca. 1973. Made by Paul Maute GmbH for Knoll Textiles. Used for drapery; wool, nylon; plain-weave–derived simple weave. KnollTextiles Archive. Cat. 213.

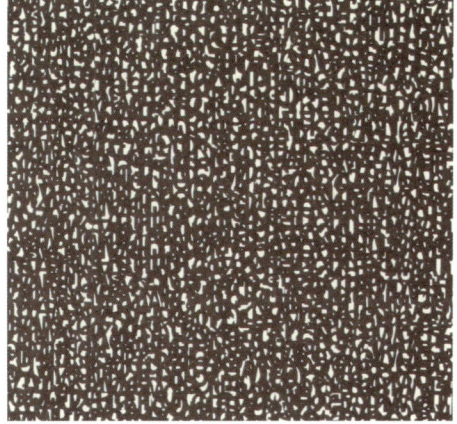

Fig. B.95 Abbott Miller. *Merge* wallcovering ("Mars Black" colorway), introduced 2006. Made in the United States for Knoll Textiles. Used for wallcovering; vinyl, cotton. KnollTextiles Archive.

In 2006 Knoll released the *Grammar Collection* of vinyl and cotton wall coverings designed by Miller for KnollTextiles. They were developed from the idea of swarming as a social effect, a theme which he investigated in *Swarm* (2005) an exhibition he curated shown at the Fabric Museum and Workshop in Philadelphia. *Grammar* consists of three patterns, *Filter*, *Merge*, and *Switch*, each of which densely overlaps typographic letterforms to generate variations on abstracted and textural decorative fields (fig. B.95). Miller explains that "this is an appropriate theme for any room where there is conversation."[8] For his second collection of vinyl wallcoverings for KnollTextiles, Miller explored the movement of ink in three patterns—*Run*, *Drip*, and *Drop*.[9] The new collection was released by KnollTextiles in 2011. —CAL

Designs for Knoll
Grammar Collection (intro. 2006): *Filter*, *Merge*, and *Switch*. *Ink Collection* (intro. 2011): *Run*, *Drip*, and *Drop*.

Selected Awards and Exhibitions
1992 *Printed Letters: The Natural History of Typography*, Jersey City Museum, New Jersey
1994 Chrysler Award for Innovation in Design
2003 *National Design Triennial*, Cooper-Hewitt National Design Museum, Smithsonian Institution
2005 *Swarm*, Fabric Museum and Workshop, Philadelphia
2009 Saint-Gaudens Award for Professional Achievement, Cooper Union School of Art
Design for a Living World, Cooper-Hewitt National Design Museum, Smithsonian Institution

Frances Breese Miller (1893–1985)

Frances Miller enjoyed the distinction of being Knoll's first textile designer. Her printed sheers on synthetic fibers appeared in the first Hans Knoll Furniture catalogue in 1942 (see fig. 2.6). Their inclusion marks an important turning point for the fledgling firm. Identified therein as a "well-known textile designer," Miller came to the profession relatively late, with little in her background suggesting such a career path.

Born to a wealthy New York family, Frances Breese had a privileged upbringing and education—by a French governess, at day schools, and a Paris boarding school for American girls. Her father, James L. Breese, was a photographer and close friend of architect Stanford White. Conforming to the conventions of her class, she spent summers at the family's Stanford White–designed house in Southampton, Long Island, made her debut in society in 1912, and married stockbroker Lawrence Miller three years later, followed by the birth and rearing of three children. Her social circle included well-known society decorator Dorothy Draper; philanthropist Aileen Osborne Webb, who founded the American Craft Council (and in whose wedding Miller was a bridesmaid); Gertrude Whitney, sculptor and founder of the Whitney Museum of American Art; among others. Miller began painting in the 1920s, taking a two-week class at the Hawthorne School in Ogunquit, Maine. This, and a 1939 summer course in dynamic symmetry at the Taos School of Art, seems to have been her only formal artistic training.[1]

In the fall of 1928, Miller opened Books and Things at 333 East 57th Street with her partner Ian McEwen. In addition to publications, the shop sold craft, Native American and Mexican objects, and contemporary American design—notably Russel Wright's ceramics, Gilbert Rohde's furniture, and Walter Van Nessen's lamps and other accessories.[2] Sourcing American-designed rugs proved challenging, and Miller turned to Ralph Pearson and George Biddle, a painter designing hand-hooked rugs.[3] Uncomfortable with "putting a painting on the floor," she began experimenting on her own.[4] "What did appeal to me," she admits in her autobiography, "was to use an old American technique in a totally new way. . . . [She] visualized unobtrusive patterns, relying largely on texture, to complement, simple contemporary furniture."[5] She soon developed a line of sheared, tooled, and bas-relief rugs. This aspect of her business—renamed Frances T. Miller, Inc. to accommodate interior design work—became her focus after the 1929 stock market crash, at which time her marriage also dissolved.[6]

During the 1930s Miller's specially designed handmade rugs, made-to-order stenciled fabrics, innovative printed and woven curtains, and occasional machine-made textiles gained increasing recognition.[7] She also promoted work of other designer-craftsmen, such as San Francisco–based handweaver Dorothy Liebes, who was not yet widely known—a favor that was returned when Liebes included Miller's textiles in the exhibition she organized for the Golden Gate International Exposition in 1939. Miller exhibited in several other world's fairs as well as museum-sponsored industrial arts exhibitions.[8] Her work could also be seen in her showroom, which she closed during World War II. By this time, Miller had established business relationships with other distributors (before Knoll), such as the Persian Rug Manufactory.[9] *Interiors* and its predecessor, *Interior Decorator*, regularly featured Miller's rugs and draperies. She was also an early member of the Design Group, which evolved into the *American Way* line, spearheaded by Russel Wright and other designers to promote American design.[10]

Despite steady industry exposure, Miller's entry in MoMA's home furnishings competition in 1940–41 was probably what brought her to Knoll's attention. This landmark competition and exhibition included established designers, such as Charles Eames and Eero Saarinen, alongside newcomers. Many, like Saarinen, would later work with Knoll's textile and furniture division.[11] With the war on and her shop closed, Miller had a short-lived arrangement with Knoll. Yet her textile designs appear in the first photographs of Knoll's furniture collection, ensuring her place in its history.[12] —CMH

Design for Knoll
Printed Sheers (1942).

Selected Awards and Exhibitions
1933 Century of Progress International Exposition, Chicago
1937 Gold Medal for Decorative Textiles, Exposition Internationale des Arts et Techniques, Paris
Fourteenth Annual Exhibition of American Industrial Arts, The Metropolitan Museum of Art
1938 Fifty-second Exhibition of the Architectural League of New York
1939 American Decorative Arts, Museum of Modern Art Gallery, Washington, D.C.
Decorative Arts Exhibition, Golden Gate International Exposition
New York World's Fair
1941 Honorable Mention for Printed Fabric, *Organic Design in Home Furnishings*, MoMA

Alexandre Mimoglou (b. 1954)

In 1982, Knoll International released a collection of drapery fabrics by Alexandre Mimoglou. The designs, including *Sails*, *Uptown*, *Downtown*, *Crazy Night*, *Festival*, and *Morning Sky*, were exclusively distributed in Europe and produced as burn-outs and screen-prints on cotton plain-weave fabric by the German textile manufacturer Taunus Textildruck.[1]

Born in Greece and educated in France, Mimoglou was trained as an architect and urban planner. He studied aesthetics and art at the Sorbonne and has exhibited his paintings at museums, galleries, and other cultural institutions throughout Europe.[2] During the 1980s, he was deeply interested in systematic studies of real and imagined environments. He employs a visual vocabulary of brightly colored lines, circles, crescents, and dots against a bare, white background to create graphic assemblages of abstracted and intuitive space.[3] In his Knoll designs *Festival* and *Downtown* (fig. B.96, see fig. 6.9), Mimoglou explored his theoretical concepts of spatiality, linking straight and curved lines in shades of blue, yellow, pink, and red to replicate the sense of movement and dynamism flowing through urban spaces. Mimoglou's print collection for Knoll was featured in 1983 at Knoll International's showrooms in Frankfurt and Paris.[4]

In addition to his textile designs for Knoll International, Mimoglou has also adapted his ideas to a range of industrially manufactured products, including home-furnishing textiles for the French manufacturers Bucol and Pierre Frey in 1982 and porcelain prototypes for Rosenthal in 1984. His work has been recognized by the Association of Friends of the City of Paris' Modern Art Museum in 1985 and was exhibited at the *Salon des Artistes Décorateurs* 1985, held at the Grand Palais Museum in Paris.[5] In 1994, he founded European Art Networks (EURAN), an initiative to create electronic information and sales systems using communications technologies.[6] —ES

Designs for Knoll
Introduced in Europe only; it is uncertain when these designs were discontinued, (1982): *Uptown*; *Downtown*; *Crazy Night*; *Morning Sky*; *Festival*; *Sails*.

Selected Exhibitions
1982 Institut Français, Copenhagen
Institut Français, Thessaloniki, Greece
Greek Embassy, Oslo
Cassina showroom, Paris
École Spéciale d´Architecture, Paris
1983 Knoll International showroom, Frankfurt

Fig. B.96 Alexandre Mimoglou. *Festival*, 1982. Made by Taunus Textildruck for Knoll Textiles. Used for drapery; cotton; plain weave, screen-printed. KnollTextiles Archive.

Fig. B.97 Claudine Piaget. *Screenplay Collection*, 1996. Made in the United States for KnollTextiles. Used for wallcovering and panel; vinyl, polyester. KnollTextiles Archive.

Knoll International showroom, Paris
Metz & Co., Amsterdam
Printed by Taunus Textildruck: *30 Jahr Textildruck in Deutschland am Beispiel eirner Firma*, Krefeld Textile Museum (*Morning Sky* shown)
1985 Salon des Artistes Décorateurs, Grand Palais Museum, Paris
1988 Charlottenborg Museum, Copenhagen Design Center, Stockholm
2000 Voksenåsen, Oslo

Claudine Piaget (b. 1957)

Born in Brussels, Belgium, Claudine Piaget has focused her career on the design and weaving of furnishing and installation fabrics using new technology. Her work is often stimulated by innovations in materials, as well as an ongoing interest in the restructuring of traditional fabric weaves by mixing typical yarn fibers with unconventional manufacturing methods and materials, creating dynamic and vibrant plays of texture and light.[1]

From 1976 to 1980, Piaget studied woven textile design and fine arts at La Cambre, École nationale supérieure des arts visuels (ESAV) in Brussels. She began her professional career at the Création Baumann studio in Langenthal, Switzerland, where she worked as a colorist (1980–83).[2] Piaget also collaborated with O.J. Van Maele on a line of linen wallcoverings and tablecloths (1984–88), and she served as a consultant for Steelcase Strafor in France, directing textile research for seating and paneling and coordinating the surface coloring and finishing of office furniture designs (1987–93).[3]

Piaget produced two collections of fabrics for KnollTextiles. Deborah Steele, then design director for KnollTextiles, saw Piaget's work at Surtex (1995), the annual "Surface and Texture" art and design market fair held in New York City, and recruited her to design textiles for Knoll that would incorporate her knowledge of technical weaving and new materials.[4] For the 1996 *Screenplay Collection*, Piaget designed vertical fabrics—*Animation*, *Mezzanine*, *Digital Tape*, and *Fast Forward*—to "be used for wrapped acoustical panels, as well as stretched wall applications" (fig. B.97).[5] By using high temperatures to fuse vinyl-coated, polyester warp and weft threads at their crossing points, Piaget created textiles with great "dimensional stability" and "acoustic properties," while also reducing the potential for the fabric to fray.[6] In April 1998 Knoll introduced upholstery textiles by Piaget: *Rain Check*, *Watermark*, and *Windfall*. *Rain Check* and *Watermark* offered diminutive ribbed and diamond-patterned weaves respectively. In *Windfall*, Piaget blended rayon bouclé with wool and cotton yarns to create a texturally rich surface with a pattern "rhythmically balanced on its diagonal."[7]

Beginning in 1993 Piaget also conceived textile designs for a variety of companies around the globe: B&T Textilia in Belgium; Camborne Fabrics Ltd., and Hield Brothers Ltd. in Great Britain; Kawashima in Japan; Himatsingka in India; and Guilford of Maine and Glen Raven Inc. in the United States.[8] Piaget completed technical research for Delcar Industries France, experimenting with the specialized knitting and general production of textiles manufactured for automobiles, while for the Belgian company Helioscreen, she designed a collection of fiberglass sunscreens.[9] In 2001, she designed a collection of four wallcoverings for Composites, a line of affordable, durable, and technically advanced fabrics made of vividly colored plastic fibers. Distributed by the American firm Maharam, Piaget's collection for Composites was for application to public seating, especially in sports facilities which have a high volume of use.[10] In 2008 Piaget suspended her activities as a textile designer.[11] —ES

Designs for Knoll
Screenplay Collection: Animation (1996–2006), *Mezzanine* (1996–2005), *Digital Tape* (1996–2010), *Fast Forward* (intro. 1996). *Rain Check* (1998–2004); *Watermark* (1998–2004); *Windfall* (1998–2005).

Proenza Schouler (established 2002)
Jack McCollough (b. 1978)
Lazaro Hernandez (b. 1978)

Proenza Schouler began as the senior thesis collection that Jack McCollough and Lazaro Hernandez presented at Parsons The New School for Design in 2002, winning Parsons' Designer of the Year award. Barneys department store purchased the entire collection, and *Women's Wear Daily* featured it on their cover, a rare coup for new designers who had not yet formally launched their line.

Before enrolling in Parsons in 1999, Jack McCollough, who grew up in New Jersey, studied glassblowing at the San Francisco Art Institute.[1] Lazaro Hernandez was raised in Miami and began as a pre-med student at the University of Miami, but changed direction and transferred to Parsons in 1999.[2] While in school, they interned with prestigious fashion houses (Marc Jacobs, Michael Kors, United Bamboo) before teaming up for their thesis.[3] After selling their collection, McCollough and Hernandez founded their company, Proenza Schouler, in New York, combining their mothers' maiden names to do so—Proenza (Hernandez), Schouler (McCollough).[4]

After its initial success, Proenza Schouler continued to receive critical recognition, representing the "Future of Fashion" at the fortieth-anniversary celebration of the Council of Fashion Designers of America (CFDA) in 2002. In 2004 the designers won the first CFDA / Vogue Fashion Fund prize of $200,000 and a mentorship with Burberry CEO Rosemarie Bravo.[5] After their Fall 2005 collection, Target approached Proenza Schouler to design a capsule collection based on reinterpretations of the best pieces of their previous collections as part of Target's Go International Series for 2007. The reception of their 2005 collections generated other collaborations as well, such as with Movado and Hewlett-Packard.[6] In 2007, with outside financing from the Valentino Fashion Group SpA, Proenza Schouler expanded, opening a Paris showroom and developing accessory and footwear collections.[7] The strength of their designs won them the CFDA Accessory Designer of the Year Award in 2009.

In 2007 Dorothy Cosonas of KnollTextiles approached McCullough and Hernandez about creating interior textiles for Knoll Luxe—a new high-end brand for Knoll featuring luxury fabrics by Cosonas and collaborations with cutting-edge fashion designers (Proenza Schouler would be the first). The designers worked with Knoll for over a year to develop a collection of six upholstery fabrics, introducing them in the fall of 2008. The color palette of these fabrics reflected Proenza Schouler's use of neutrals, with rich purples and deep berry colors added for drama, as well as their characteristic mixing of pattern scales and textures.

The signature pattern of the collection, *Mepal*, is inspired by the Poiret-esque coat—black-and-white Jacquard-woven wool, fur-trimmed—that closed the Fall 2007 collection. *Mepal*, a silk and linen damask, had a large-scale repeat and was produced in eight colorways (fig. B.98). The historic foliate pomegranate pattern on which *Mepal* is loosely based was first popular in Renaissance Italy and spread throughout Europe. This historicizing source represented a departure for Knoll which favors more modern textile patterns. *Mepal* was the inspiration for the Bard Graduate Center's installation on KnollTextiles at the International Art and Design Fair in New York in 2008 (fig. B.99).

The other five upholstery fabrics in the collaboration are also based on existing fabrics in Proenza Schouler's 2007 and 2008 runway collections. *Sandis* (fig. 6.50, see cat. 295) is a faux bois pattern that is inspired by an animal print from the Spring 2008 collection, while *Gates*, a solid high-sheen fabric made with cotton, linen, silk, and Lurex, derives from a sequined fabric used in an evening ensemble in the Fall 2008 collection. *Worth*, the most substantial texture in the line, combines thick yarns to emulate the brocade that was used in their 2007 Resort Collection suit neckline and pockets. *Walker* is an opposing twill motif in a rectangular grid formation that is Jacquard woven to create a structured geometric aesthetic.[8] *Canaan* displays a linear based motif and is based on a vest from the Spring 2007 collection.

The collaboration with Knoll was appropriate for Hernandez and McCollough in light of their on-going interest in developing pattern and texture rather than new silhouettes for their fashion collections. Reflecting on their more recent fashion collections, Hernandez stated, "We are really interested in the surface more than anything. That's what feels relevant to us . . . developing textiles, the two dimensional aspect of things."[9] McCollough added, "That's our biggest thing right now. We develop all of our fabrics from scratch."[10] Hernandez and McCollough, used to the rapid production schedules for fashion, were surprised by the unexpectedly lengthy process of realizing the upholstery designs from concept to product for Knoll Luxe. Hernandez summed this up by saying, "In the year and a half it took to create this . . . line, we did nine fashion collections!"[11]

Since their Knoll collection, Proenza Schouler has remained committed to showcasing skilled craftsmanship and textiles that play with scale, color, and materials in their designs. Their fabric choices have ranged from soft and delicate to forceful and thick. Their pronounced aesthetic and high standards have garnered widespread industry recognition, and they continue to receive accolades and awards for their work. —AM

Fig. B.98 Proenza Schouler (Lazaro Hernandez and Jack McCollough). *Mepal* ("Willow" colorway), introduced 2008. Made for Knoll Luxe. Used for drapery; linen, silk; plain-weave–derived compound weave. KnollTextiles Archive. Cat. 294.

Fig. B.99 Alejandro Cardenas. Installation featuring textiles by Proenza Schouler for Knoll Luxe and the coat that inspired *Mepal*, Art and Design Fair at the Park Avenue Armory, New York, 2008. Courtesy Bard Graduate Center: Decorative Arts, Design History, Material Culture, New York.

Designs for Knoll
Proenza Schouler Collection for Knoll Luxe (intro. 2008): *Mepal, Sandis, Gates, Worth, Walker, Canaan.*

Selected Awards and Exhibitions
2002 Designer of the Year, Parsons The New School for Design
CFDA, "Future of Fashion"
2004 CFDA/Vogue Fashion Fund winner
2007 CFDA, Womenswear Designer of the Year
2008 International Art and Design Fair, Knoll Luxe exhibition
2009 CFDA, Accessory Designer of the Year

Elisha Prouty (b. 1927)

Elisha Prouty was born in Brattleboro, Vermont. He served in the United States Army's 252nd Corps of Engineers in Berlin from 1945 to 1947. When he was discharged, he enrolled in the Ray-Vogue School of Design in Chicago.[1] He also studied space planning at the New Bauhaus Institute of Design (started by László Moholy-Nagy in 1937, now the Illinois Institute of Design), under the designer Marianne Willisch, and he worked for S. M. Hexter, a leading interior textile company, at its showroom in the Chicago Merchandise Mart. In addition he took weaving classes and began creating luxurious handwoven fabrics, many of which were manufactured and sold by the Clara Castle Studio in Guilford, Vermont.

After spending two years in Chicago, Prouty moved to New York where he held a variety of jobs, beginning in the local S.M. Hexter office. He also worked outside the textile industry at, for example, Idlewild Airport (now John F. Kennedy International Airport). He eventually secured a staff designer position at the Isabel Scott Fabrics Corporation in the mid-1950s.[2] The firm was well-known for producing handwoven textiles expressly for architects and interior designers, and Prouty, an adept weaver and designer, soon became head of their design department. Prouty's *Vermont Collection* (1958), composed of wool and rayon blend fabrics in vibrant colors, was favorably reviewed in industry periodicals such as *Progressive Architecture* and *Interiors*, as well as in the *New York Times*.[3] By late 1965, Prouty had left Isabel Scott to start Tweedsmuir, Inc.. The company primarily focused on the design of upholstery fabrics but also produced some casement and drapery fabric designs, which were purchased by large converters, including Knoll. In 1967 Knoll Texiles introduced a Prouty-designed casement, *Belaire*, a translucent, plain-weave alternative to open-weave draperies, such as the leno-weave designs by Anni Albers, which typified the Knoll line until the late-1970s.[4] *Belaire* was woven in a North Philadelphia mill on a "pick and pick" loom and featured a sheer cotton warp with all-wool wefts.[5] A multiple-language description of the textile in the KnollTextiles's archive suggests a European distribution after 1969.[6] Prouty rarely communicated with Knoll representatives, but recalls seeing the textile displayed in a ceiling-to-floor panel in a Knoll showroom at the Chicago Merchandise Mart in 1971. *Belaire* was discontinued in 1974.

In 1971 Prouty returned to Chicago and formed Prouty Design, Inc. In addition to designing textiles, he consulted on commercial and residential interior design work. He collaborated with the renowned architectural firms Skidmore, Owings, & Merrill and Keck + Keck (celebrated for their work at the 1933–34 Century of Progress World's Fair in Chicago). Prouty mostly consulted for William Keck on residential interiors. By 1976 Prouty Designs became known for "architectural" casements and fire-retardant fabrics.[7]

In the late 1970s the Saudi Arabian government awarded Prouty Design a major commission to design casement and upholstery fabrics for the new palace buildings in Riyadh.[8] Soon after completing this profitable commission, Prouty sold his company to the drapery manufacturer Duchess and Co. and returned to Vermont in about 1985. He has since owned a small weaving studio and run a bed and breakfast, as well as led National Trust tours of local historic sites. In the early 1990s Prouty became a curator at the Grafton Vermont Historical Society and remains in this position in 2011. —AMT

Design for Knoll
Belaire (1967–74).

Noémi Raymond (1889–1980)

The careers of Noémi Raymond (fig. 1.10) and her husband, Antonin (1888–1976), with whom she collaborated from the 1910s to the 1970s, were closely intertwined with the development of modern architecture, interiors, and textile design in the United States, Europe, and Japan. Their contributions, while significant, have only recently received scholarly attention in part because the international, collaborative, and multidisciplinary nature of their careers has made it difficult to locate their work within a particular national or stylistic context.[1] Noémi Raymond's printed textile designs of the 1940s and early 1950s were highly influential and were featured in many key American design exhibitions and publications of the period, but they too defy easy categorization. In terms of chronology, character, and inspiration, they stand apart from the work of younger and arguably better-known American print designers such as Angelo Testa and Ben Rose. While Noémi Raymond's designs for Knoll can perhaps best be understood in the context of the Raymond's long, multinational career, they also came to epitomize the kind of modern textiles that Knoll's textile division was commited to providing, and they played a key role in defining the character of Knoll's early print collections.

Noémi Pernessin (later Raymond) was born in Cannes, France, and spent her early years in France and Switzerland with her mother (her father died in 1892). In 1899 her mother married an American language teacher on sabbatical in Geneva, and the following year the family moved to New York City where Noémi attended the Horace Mann School. From 1907 to 1909 she studied art at Columbia Teacher's College, where her instructors included Arthur Wesley Dow, whom she later credited with inspiring her with "his enthusiasm for the Japanese concept of nature and design."[2] Dow's compositional principles, largely derived from his study of Japanese art, played an important role in forming Raymond's artistic sensibility and the approach that she would later bring to the design of textile patterns.[3] In 1909, Raymond went to Paris to study for a year at the École de la Grande Chaumière and on her return to New York in 1910 she opened a graphic design studio. Over the next few years, she worked as a commercial artist, producing cartoons, posters and advertising art for clients including the *New York Sun*, one of the city's premiere news-papers, and the Lily Cup Company. In 1914 she met and married Antonin Raymond, a Czech-born architect who had been working in New York since 1910. From 1914 until 1973, when both Raymonds retired, the couple collaborated closely on architectural projects in both the United States and Japan. As Antonin Raymond later put it, "Noémi had her finger in every single job since [1914].... she became a source of inspiration for me, a teacher and a most faithful companion in our combined search for eternal values."[4]

In 1916 the Raymonds spent eight months living and working with Frank Lloyd Wright at Taliesin, Wright's home and studio in Spring Green, Wisconsin, and in 1919 they accompanied Wright to Japan to supervise the final design work and construction of the Imperial Hotel in Tokyo. Noémi Raymond's contributions included designs for a series of decorative peacock murals.[5] In early 1921 Antonin founded an independent architectural firm in Tokyo, and the couple remained in Japan for much of the next two decades while maintaining international connections through regular travels to Europe and the United States.[6] From the beginning, Noémi Raymond pursued an interest in Japanese art, culture, and philosophy, studying traditional techniques of woodblock printing, calligraphy, and brush painting. In the mid-1920s she became interested in textile and furniture design, and her contribution to the Raymond firm's interiors soon became considerable. Her highly individual rug and textile designs from the early 1930s, like the interiors for which they were created, combined references to Japanese culture with quiet abstract textural effects prefiguring the designs she submitted in 1941 to *Organic Design in Home Furnishings*, the groundbreaking MoMA exhibition and related competition (see chapter 1).[7] Raymond took inspiration partly from stencil-printed text-iles with traditional small-motif patterns (komon), transforming them into modern abstractions by reinterpreting the scale and composition. Antonin Raymond later described these as "the first successful textiles that could be called modern."[8]

The Raymonds left Japan in 1938 to work on a project in India and from there traveled through Europe to New York City. In 1939 they opened an office in the city and purchased a farm in New Hope, Pennsylvania, where they lived during World War II. Antonin Raymond worked on architectural projects throughout the war, and in 1946 he joined with Ladislav Rado to form the New York–based firm of Raymond & Rado. During these years, Noémi Raymond largely concentrated on textile design and for the first time sought to market her designs independently of specific projects. Beginning with *Organic Design*, she entered and won prizes in most of the major textile design competitions and exhibitions of the 1940s. By 1948 she had sold designs to both Knoll and Schumacher.

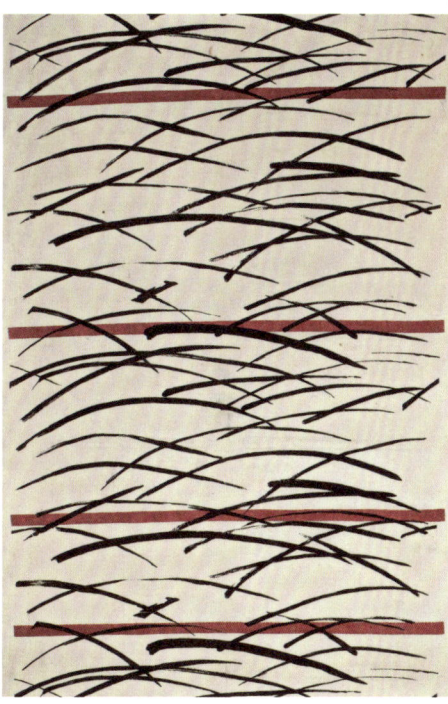

Fig. B.100 Noémi Raymond. Printed textile length, combination of "Reeds and Horizontal Lines," ca. 1941. Probably made by Cold Spring Bleachery for Noémi Raymond. Used for drapery; cotton; plain weave, screen-printed. Raymond Collection, The Architectural Archives, University of Pennsylvania. Cat. 2.

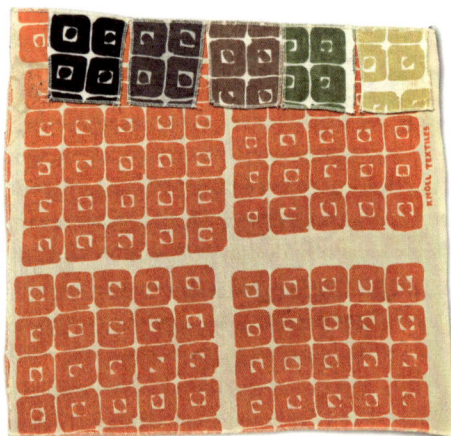

Fig. B.101 Noémi Raymond. *Mosaic* sample ("Persimmon on Sand" colorway), ca. 1950. Made for Knoll Textiles. Used for drapery; rayon; plain weave, screen-printed. KnollTextiles Archive. Cat. 12.

It is unclear how the early sales to Knoll came about, but the Knolls and the Raymonds knew each other socially.[9] Noémi Raymond's prints may also have been recommended to the Knolls by Marianne Strengell, who had invited Raymond to participate in the *First Biennial Exhibition of Contemporary Textiles and Ceramics* at Cranbrook in 1946. Knoll initially produced two of her larger-scale designs, *Reeds and Bars* and *Reeds*, but had more success with *Chinese Coins* and *Mosaic*, two simple patterns with smaller repeating motifs and an unobtrusive, textured appearance (figs. B.100, B.101; see figs. 3.15, 3.16). *Chinese Coins*, which was used extensively by architects in the late 1940s and early 1950s, fell out of favor and was discontinued by Knoll in 1955. Perhaps its informal, freehand quality, so suited to residential interiors and wooden furniture, made it less appropriate for use in the corporate interiors that made up the majority of Knoll's business during this period.

Raymond also created pictorial, naturalistic designs for other companies during the postwar period. Two of these, *Strip Fields* and *Mesh and Starfish*, were released by Schumacher in 1948. In 1950 she began to experiment with screen-printing in her New Hope studio with the idea of finding other buyers for her designs. In 1951 she sold at least seven designs to Arthur Brill, of Golding Decorative Fabrics, including a leaf design and one of pear trees in blossom.[10] The Brill's purchases brought in extra income, and Raymond found her work for him to be "a relief from the pedantic sophisticated Knoll's type of thing, where either nothing is supposed to look like anything or on the contrary must be a naïve-like reproduction of nature."[11] She also sold at least one design to Arundell Clarke, who released her *10,000 B.C.* as a Jacquard-woven fabric in 1952.[12]

The Raymonds reopened their Tokyo office in 1949, and from 1952 to 1973 they lived and worked primarily in Japan. Noémi Raymond again focused on designing textiles, furniture, and interiors for the firm's architectural projects, with her role as designer and collaborator receiving more recognition than it had before the war.[13] She continued to play a central role in the firm until 1973 when both Raymonds retired from practice to their New Hope farm, where she died in 1980 at the age of ninety-one. —SW

Designs for Knoll
Chinese Coins (1948–55, possibly disc. later in Europe); *Reeds* (1948–ca.1950); *Reeds and Bars* (1948–ca. 1950); *Mosaic* (1950–59, reinterpreted as woven upholstery, 1997 Decades Collection).

Selected Awards and Exhibitions
1936 Exhibition, Kanebo Service Company, Tokyo (furniture and textiles shown)
1941 First Place for Printed Textiles, MoMA "Organic Design Competition" (designs mistakenly credited to Antonin Raymond) *Organic Design in Home Furnishings*, MoMA (precursors of Knoll's *Chinese Coins*, *Mosaic*, and *Reeds and Bars* shown)
1944 Second Place for Printed Textiles, *International Textile Exhibition*, Woman's College of the University of North Carolina
1945 *Modern Textile Design*, MoMA, circulated 1947–48 (precursor of *Chinese Coins* shown)
1946 First Biennial Exhibition of Contemporary Textiles and Ceramics, Cranbrook (included precursors of *Chinese Coins*, *Mosaic*, and *Reeds and Bars*)
1947 Award, Philadelphia Print Club printed fabric design competition
1948 *American Textiles '48*, The Metropolitan Museum of Art
1949 Second Biennial Exhibition, Cranbrook (*Chinese Coins*, *Reeds and Bars* shown) *Exhibition For Modern Living*, Detroit Institute of Arts
1951 *Good Design*, Merchandise Mart, of Chicago (January) and MoMA (*Mosaic* shown)
Living Up-to-Date, Baltimore Art Museum (*Chinese Coins*, *Mosaic* shown)
1956 *Textiles USA*, MoMA
2006 *Crafting a Modern World: The Architecture and Design of Antonin and Noémi Raymond*, University Art Museum, University of Pennsylvania (circulating exhibition *Chinese Coins*, *Mosaic* shown)

Francisca Reichardt Vietsch (b. 1936)

Francisca Reichardt (later Vietsch) was born in 1936 in Eisenbach, Germany, and in 1954 began taking art courses at the Werkkunstschule (School of Applied Arts) in Wiesbaden. In 1956 she transferred to the Staatliche Hochschule für Bildende Künste (University of Fine Arts) in Hamburg, studying textile design under the renowned German print designer Margaret Hildebrand, and received her diploma in 1959. Reichardt recalls Hildebrand emphasizing the importance of creating designs for mass production, which greatly influenced Reichardt's later design practice.[1] After receiving her degree in 1959, Reichardt worked as a freelance textile designer and taught a course on fabric printing at the Staatliche Hochschule (1964–69), as well as substituting for Hildebrand as a lecturer (1969–70).

After 1970 Reichardt concentrated on her design work and became acquainted with Barbara Rodes (later Segerer). In 1971 Knoll introduced Reichardt's design, *Omahar*, in the United States (fig. B.102).[2] It had been manufactured by Pausa AG in Mössingen, Germany, which had printed Wolf Bauer's designs for Knoll beginning in 1967. *Omahar*, a large-scale design on cotton, required fourteen screens to print. Its bold, almost psychedelic print is composed of a series of arcs and lines arranged along a central axis in a 30½ inch repeat and was produced in five color combinations.[3] The chromatic intensity within each combination varies, drawing the eye along the pattern through the use of stacked clusters of color connected at regular intervals by less dense, neutral arcs. In 1971 Reichardt was included in *Knoll au Louvre*, an exhibition of Knoll designs at the Musée des Arts décoratifs in Paris, *Omahar* won a certificate of recognition. It was discontinued in 1978.

In 1977 Reichardt co-founded der Bettwäscheladen, a shop located in Hamburg, which, as she later recalled, served as a "trendsetter for the ever-neglected [industry of] home textiles." By 1984 Reichardt returned to the studio but, having grown "weary of [designing] patterns," she began "free painting" or "design painting," exploring still-life motifs featuring decorative and culinary objects. As a textile designer, Reichardt has worked with several well-respected German textile and design firms including Stuttgarter Gardinenfabrik, Grimes International, Taunus Textildruck, Marburger Tapetenfabrik, Rasch, Resopal, and Anker Teppichfabrik. Between 1991 and 2000 she published five instructional craft books through Englisch Verlag GmbH, and until 2008 she also designed two collections a year for Graser, German manufacturer of exclusive bed linens company located in Merklingen. Reichardt currently resides in Hamburg. —CBPP

Design for Knoll
Omahar (1971–78).

Awards and Exhibitions
1971 *Knoll au Louvre*, Musée des Arts décoratifs, Paris (*Omahar* shown, certificate of recognition)
Texhibition, V-Studio, Hamburg
1984 *Textildesign 1934–1984 am Beispiel Stuttgarter Gardinen*, Design Center Stuttgart

Jürgen Reichert (b. 1953)

Jürgen Reichert was born in Mannheim, Germany. He attended the Freie Universität (Free University) in Berlin and studied painting at the Universität der Künste (University of the Arts) in Berlin from 1975 to 1980. In the early 1980s Reichert became interested in textile design.[1] He attended the Royal College of Art in London (1982–83) and in 1984 began working with KARO, a branding and communication design firm.[2] The visual structure of Reichert's vibrant paintings, often based on indefinite grid patterns, translates well to the context of textile design as evidenced by his five printed casements for Knoll. *Pergola*, *Vulcano*, and *Pittura* (ca. 1987) reflect his interest in the interplay of color and shape. In *Vulcano* energetic daubs overlap on a darkly contrasting background, while *Pittura*, a discharge print on cotton velour, though similar, reveals Reichert's ability to render subtlety through the use of muted colors and reduced contrast between fore- and background (fig. B.103). Introduced in 1988, *Metro* and *Polis* (fig. B.104), along with their sheer counterparts *Metro-T* and *Polis-T*, feature linear motifs and monochromatic coloring but continue Reichert's exploration of line and overlapping forms.

In 1990 Reichert lectured at the Hochschule für Bildende Künste (University of Fine Arts) in Berlin and was awarded a work stipend from the Senats für Kulturelle Angelegenheiten (Senate for Cultural Affairs). Reichert has also designed printed textiles for Taunus Textildruck, Karonis, and other European firms.[3] In 1994 he collaborated with the textile designers Andrej Kupetz and Heike Huster to produce *Extra Virgine* for Karonis, a cotton-linen blend textile printed with black "artistically drawn stick-figures" on a white ground.[4] Reichert served as a visiting professor at the Hochschule für Bildende Künste (University of Fine Arts) in Hamburg (2002–3) and was awarded an

Fig. B.102 Francisca Reichardt Vietsch. *Omahar* page from "Print Collection" binder, ca. 1977. KnollTextiles Archive. Cat. 190.

Fig. B.103 Jurgen Reichert. *Vulcano*, 1987. From "Knoll's Curtain Call," *Designers' Journal*, (1987), 6.

Fig. B.104 Jurgen Reichert. *Polis*, 1988. Made for Knoll International. Used for drapery. KnollTextiles Archive.

Fig. B.105 Ulrike Rhomberg-Greiner. *Slant* ("Brown" colorway), ca. 1970. Made by Pausa AG for Knoll Textiles. Used for drapery; cotton velvet; screen-printed. Private collection. Cat. 187.

artist-in-residence position at Utsira Fyr in Norway in 2009. He has participated in solo and group exhibitions in Germany and internationally, and his work has been published in numerous exhibition catalogues. He currently lives and works in Berlin. —CBPP

Designs for Knoll
Introduced in Europe only (1987); it is uncertain when these designs were discontinued: *Pergola*, *Pittura*, and *Vulcano*; (1988): *Metro*, *Polis*, *Metro-T*, and *Polis-T*.

Selected Awards and Exhibitions
1981 Gallery Linneborn, Bonn
1982 Kunstverein Hamburg
1983 Royal College of Art, London
1982/83 DAAD stipend for study at the Royal College of Art, London
1986 Karo Gallery, Berlin
Gallery Walzinger, Saarlouis
1987 Award for *Vulcano*, Design Center Stuttgart
1988 Galerie Scheffel, Bad Homburg
Galeria d'arte contemporanea, Suzzara, Italy
Award for *Pittura*, Design Center Stuttgart
1989 Awards for *Metro*, *Polis*, *Metro-T*, *Polis-T*, Design Center Stuttgart
1990 Work stipend from the Berlin Senate for Cultural Affairs
1991, 1993, 1995, 1997, 1999, 2001, 2003, 2010 Gallery Walzinger, Saarlouis
2000, 2002, 2004, 2008 Linneborn Gallery, Berlin
2004 Orangerie Blieskastel
2006 Kunsthaus Fischer, Stuttgart
2009 "Meer oder weniger" Kunstverein Rotenburg

Ulrike Rhomberg-Greiner (b. 1941)

Ulrike Rhomberg was born on July 26, 1941, in Dornbirn, Austria. In the early 1960s she studied textile design at the Staatliche Akademie der Bildenden Künste (Academy of Art and Design) in Stuttgart, Germany, under Leo Wollner and briefly attended the École des Beaux Arts (School of Fine Arts) in Paris. From 1965 to 1969 she lived in New York City, where she designed textiles and wallpaper in the studio of Berlin-born textile designer and agent Lily Furst.[1]

In 1969 Rhomberg returned to Germany and worked as a freelance designer for various textile companies, including Pausa AG, a connection made through the firm's affiliation with the Staatliche Akademie der Bildenden Künste. Later that year she married Werner Greiner Jr., who was the stepson of Pausa's creative director Willy Häussler, and soon to become chief executive of the firm.[2]

In 1970 Rhomberg-Greiner began designing and coordinating collections of interior and fashion fabrics exclusively for Pausa.[3] In 1971 Knoll International released *Slant*, her first design for the company. This boldly elegant print on velvet features thick groupings of diagonal color stripes on a light background (fig. B.105). By 1978 Knoll introduced *Graffiti* by Rhomberg-Greiner, specifically for the European market. It was printed in both gold and silver luster inks on sheer fabric, and in a white-on-white burn-out sheer. In 1983 Pausa began to expand its product range by venturing into textile production for the high end of the garment industry. *Filathron* by Pausa, one of the earliest textiles printed using technology that produced a metallic effect, was created in 1986, becoming one of Pausa's most successful ventures into the fashion fabric industry.

During the 1980s Rhomberg-Greiner created a subsidiary of Pausa called Panorama which specialized in table linens, and soon became an integral part of the firm.[4] Rhomberg-Greiner continued to work with Pausa until it ceased production in 2001. She currently lives in Reutlingen, Germany. —CBPP

Designs for Knoll
Slant (1970–76); *Graffiti* (intro. ca. 1978, disc. date unknown).

Rodarte (established 2005)
Kate Mulleavy (b. 1979)
Laura Mulleavy (b. 1980)

Since the Rodarte label was introduced in 2005, its founders Kate and Laura Mulleavy have been the subjects of two museum exhibitions, the first fashion designers honored with a National Art Award by Americans for the Arts, and the first Americans and first women designers of any nationality to win the Swiss Textiles Award.

Kate and Laura Mulleavy graduated from the University of California, Berkeley, in 2002, where Kate studied art history and Laura literature. After graduation they moved back in with their parents in Pasadena and for over a year undertook a self-styled course of study with the goal of becoming fashion designers despite having no formal training. They culled reading lists from design school Web sites for books on couture design construction, while learning basic sewing skills from their mother, an artist, whose maiden name Rodarte became their fashion moniker.[1]

By mid-2004, the sisters started their business with $16,500 dollars, and within six months, with the help of two seamstresses and a patternmaker, they had created seven dresses and three coats.[2] Through the assistance of Cameron Silver, owner of the vintage store Decades in Los Angeles, the Mulleavys made their first trip to New York City at the end of January 2005 to show their collection to members of the fashion industry and press. The trip proved to be extraordinarily fruitful—three days after meeting with editors at *Women's Wear Daily*, their designs were featured on the cover (February 3, 2005), and three stores soon placed orders for the ten-piece debut collection.[3] A few weeks later Anna Wintour, the editor of *Vogue*, came to see their collection in Los Angeles, becoming one of their most influential champions. Rodarte presented their first complete collection (Spring 2006) at New York fashion week in September 2005.

Rodarte is a family business, and until mid-2006, when they rented a loft in Los Angeles, the Mulleavys designed and produced the collection at their parent's home. Their mother, Victoria, designs jewelry and their father, Perry, a botanist, acts as CFO and business advisor. The company has no outside funding and has supported itself through fashion industry prizes awarded since 2006. Sponsors, such as Lexus, MAC Cosmetics, and Aveda, are often used to underwrite their fashion shows.[4]

Rodarte produces about one thousand pieces a year, each retailing for upwards of hundreds of dollars.[5] A single garment often features multiple materials, techniques, and adornments that take many hours to complete. The Mulleavys frequently spend months altering their fabric through their own self-developed methods or working with artisans to dye, pleat, and bead it to their exacting specifications. The company now includes three seamstresses, a patternmaker, dyer, leather-worker, and three knitters, and a handful of interns. For their Spring 2010 collection, the Mulleavys worked with a costume "ager" from the film industry to stain, burn, shred, sandpaper, and distress each custom fabric. A single custom fabric might be further sandpapered, stained, burned, and have its edges treated by razor blade upon delivery. Each of the garments in the Spring 2010 collection was composed of at least nine fabrics, including silk, linen, leather, velvet, cheesecloth, crystal-encrusted cotton, sequined lace, and some, such as "wool cobweb" and a corrugated fake leather "bird skin" of their own making.[6]

Rodarte was the only design house Knoll-Textiles creative director, Dorothy Cosonas considered approaching for the second Knoll Luxe designer collaboration: "They are more artists than fashion designers. Laura and Kate have a true understanding of materials, color combinations, craft and technique."[7] Their collection for Knoll which debuted in the spring of 2011 recalls their signature looks from 2008 and 2009 and is named after poets. The Mulleavys were excited to have an opportunity to focus intently on the design of textiles, and the collection reflects their sense of texture and structure. As they explain, "Fabrics always take on a life of their own for us. We're constantly reworking our fabrics and are very open to how things are created."[8]

The Rodarte Collection for Knoll Luxe consists of five upholstery and, a first for Knoll Luxe, three drapery patterns, produced by mills in Italy, Switzerland, Germany, the United Kingdom, and the United States.[9] *Parker*, a drapery fabric composed of fine viscose, linen, cotton, and lurex threads encapsulated between two layers of polyester gauze, references the "spider web" knits from their Fall 2008 collection (figs. B.106, B.107). According to Laura Mulleavy, "instead of looking like a perfect weave, it looks broken and tattered and makes a connection to our spider-weave dresses."[10] The suspended strands and threads of *Parker* also reflect the way the Mulleavys "play with wool in its raw form, pulling it to make it stringy."[11] The hand-dyed ombré fabric used for gowns in their Spring/Summer 2009 collection inspire the drapery fabric *Auden*. Digital printing creates the large vertical bands of nonrepeating color which blend subtly on the semi-sheer polyester and ramie base cloth (see page 269). Inspiration for the collection's third drapery, *Emerson*, is the studded surfaces in the Fall/Winter 2009 collection, such as the sequined and beaded armorlike sleeves. The studs were translated into raised metallic embroidered dots on a sheer ground. *Keats*, an upholstery fabric with embroidered tone on tone viscose nailheads on cotton ground is based on the same inspirational vein of embroidered and studded bodices from the 2009 Fall/Winter collection as

Fig. B.106 Rodarte (Kate and Laura Mulleavy). *Parker* ("Tint" colorway), introduced 2010. Knoll Luxe, *Rodarte Collection*. Made in Switzerland for Knoll Luxe. Used for drapery; polyester, viscose, linen, Lurex, cotton; plain weave face and back encapsulating laid vertical and horizontal elements. KnollTextiles. Cat. 296.

Fig. B.107 Rodarte (Kate and Laure Mulleavy). Fall 2008 and Spring 2009 ready-to-wear. From *Quicktake: Rodarte* at Cooper-Hewitt, National Design Museum, February 11–March 14, 2010. Cooper-Hewitt, National Design Museum, Smithsonian Institution.

Fig. B.108 Dana Romeis, ca. 1985. Photographed by Ben Rosenthal. KnollTextiles Archive.

Fig. B.109 Dana Romeis. *Tilt* ("Navy" colorway), introduced 1985. Made by Craftex Mills for Knoll Textiles. Used for upholstery; wool, rayon, nylon; plain-weave–derived compound weave. Courtesy Dana Romeis. Cat. 252.

Emerson. The texture of *Byron*, inspired by sequined strands and the textured knits in the Fall/Winter 2008 collection, is created through a shrink-yarn technique of weaving acrylic yarn into the back of the fabric. The tonal dyeing used in the Fall/Winter 2008 collection is the inspiration for *Cummings*. The interplay of matte and shiny yarns in this silk and cotton upholstery is reminiscent of frost on window glass or the mottled surface of cowhide (see fig. 6.51). *Whitman*, a wool-viscose blend upholstery fabric, is based on the knit collars from the 2009 Fall/Winter collection and has a strikingly chunky texture resulting from the nubby, large-scale yarns. The mohair upholstery *Lowell* has a lengthy, loopy pile that was based on a fabric the Mulleavy sisters custom-designed for a private client. Much as Rodarte combines many differently textured and treated fabrics in a single garment, the collection they designed for Knoll Luxe can be combined for use within a single interior. The "Copper," "Violet," "Beige," "Steel Blue," "Smoke," and "Silver Gray" colorways were chosen for cohesion within the overall collection. Immediately after the collection's debut, seven of the textiles were acquired for the collection of the Cooper-Hewitt National Design Museum. —AM

Designs for Knoll
Rodarte Collection for Knoll Luxe (intro. 2010): *Auden, Parker, Emerson, Byron, Keats, Whitman, Cummings, Lowell.*

Selected Awards and Exhibitions
2005 Award, EccoDomani Fashion Foundation
2007 Gap and CFDA/Vogue Fashion Fund collaboration
2008 Swarovski Emerging Womenswear Designer award, CFDA
Swiss Textile Award, Swiss Textile Foundation
2009 Womenswear Designer of the Year, CFDA
Go International collection, Target
2010 Award Fashion Design Winner, Cooper-Hewitt, National Design Museum
Quicktake: Rodarte, Cooper-Hewitt, National Design Museum, Smithsonian Institution
National Art Award, Americans for the Arts
NeoCon Gold Award for Knoll Luxe line, Best of NeoCon 2010
2011 *Rodarte: States of Matter*, Museum of Contemporary Art, Pacific Design Center, Los Angeles

Dana Romeis (b. 1948)

Dana Romeis designed two collections for Knoll Textiles, one in 1985 and another in 1988 (fig. B.108). Born Dana Horner in Oklahoma, Romeis first experienced the craft of weaving while in college at the Oklahoma State University, when her husband gave her a two-harness rug loom. After graduating in 1970, she taught art and art education in the Syracuse Public School system, while honing her weaving practice.[1] She was soon creating one-of-a-kind fiber art pieces that explored the relationship between textiles and architecture.[2] In 1977 Romeis briefly attended the fiber arts program at Northern Illinois University, before taking a position as the program director at the Arts & Crafts Association in Winston Salem, North Carolina, which she held until 1980. By 1985 Romeis had received corporate commissions for her wall hangings from clients such as R. J. Reynolds Industries and Barclay American.[3] In addition to corporate commissions, Romeis sold her work through artists' representatives and a variety of art and craft fairs.

In 1983 at a craft fair in Rhinebeck, New York, Merle Lindby-Young, head of Knoll Textiles, discovered Romeis's weavings which she viewed as "wonderfully crafted woven paintings."[4] Lindby-Young recently recalled Romeis's textiles as "modern and unique" and appropriate for translation into the Knoll Textiles collection.[5] Romeis often used spatial limitations to dictate a framework for her designs, a methodology well-suited to the Knoll aesthetic. While Romeis was initially skeptical of a Knoll collaboration, Lindby-Young was persistent and ultimately convinced her to submit designs to the company. Working on her home loom, Romeis wove samples and presented them to Lindby-Young and Richard Wagner, general manager of Knoll Textiles, in early 1984.

Exploring color, texture, and surface tension, Romeis designed five upholstery fabrics: *Flash, Rain, Slant, Tilt*, and *Zag*. The graphic designs featured linear motifs exploring variations on the diagonal line and dash, ranging from *Zag*, a herringbone pattern, to *Tilt*, a repeat of slant marks in a range of colors with pink highlights (fig. B.109). To create the clean, simple, graphic language of *Tilt* and *Slant*, she used the color and design flexibility afforded by the Mexican double-weave technique later translated for industrial Jacquard looms.[6] The textiles were made in a blend of wool, rayon, and nylon, with the exception of *Zag* which was comprised of rayon and wool. Romeis selected yarns with both matte and glossy finishes to play up the jewellike colorways of the collection such as "Teal" and "Crimson."⁷ At the large party Knoll hosted to launch Romeis's collection in October 1985, they installed her unique wallhangings and panels to further attract orders. The *Dana Romeis Collection* was a critical and commercial success and led to a second collaboration between the firm and designer.

Romeis's next set of textiles debuted in 1998, featuring six paired designs that drew more overtly on postmodernist aesthetics, especially the patterning and names of each design. For example, the damask fabric *Cubis* and the brocade *Pandora* employed pattern repeats of dimensional boxes (fig. B.110), while *Zana Tapestry*, an abstract, pixilated floral pattern, played on the vernacular design of a cabbage rose with its checkered motif. *Zana Coordinate* has the same checkered design as an allover pattern (see fig. 6.23). The last offerings of the collection, *Rampant* and *Tortola*, were uncut looped pile fabrics in an irregular stripe and interlocking grid pattern respectively, with colorways evoking natural landscapes such as "Big Sur" and "Bryce Canyon."⁸ Unlike the first Romeis collection, these fabrics were woven at mills in the United States, Belgium, and West Germany.⁹ Again, Romeis's designs received accolades from the design community. Jack Lenor Larsen included *Pandora* and *Cubis* in his 1989 text *Material Wealth*.¹⁰

Knoll was the only commercial company that contracted Romeis to supply textile designs. During and after this collaboration, she continued to exhibit her fiber art and remained active in the design community, serving on the board of the American Craft Council in the late 1980s. Around this time Romeis began to take on color consulting contracts and slowly transitioned to work as an interior designer. This became her full-time occupation by the mid-1990s, and she remains a principal in her interior design company Fibercations, in St. Louis, in 2011. —AMT

Designs for Knoll
Dana Romeis Collection: Flash (1985–90), *Rain* (1985–90), *Slant* (1985–90), *Tilt* (1985–92), *Zag* (1985–90). Second collection: *Cubis* (1988–92), *Pandora* (1988–91), *Tortola* (1988–91), *Rampant* (1988–91), *Zana Coordinate* (1988–99), *Zana Tapestry* (1988–92).

Selected Awards and Exhibitions
1970 Contemporary Arts Foundation, Oklahoma City
1976 The Syracuse Show, Everson Museum, N.Y.
1977 Craftsman, Inc. Winston-Salem, N.C.
1982, 1983 The Fair at Rhinebeck, Rhinebeck, N.Y.
1982 Fiber Sculpture National, Rochester, N.Y.
1984 American Craft Council Craft fair, West Springfield, Mass.

Astrid Sampe (1909–2002)

Astrid Sampe, one of the most prominent Swedish textile designers in the twentieth century, was a technical innovator and "linking force" in international design, two qualities that benefited Knoll in the early postwar period.¹ Born in Stockholm to a family of industrialists and brought up in Borås, Sweden's textile center, Sampe studied textile design between 1928 and 1932 at the Konstfackskolan, Sweden's leading design school, and the Royal College of Art in London. She was hired as a textile designer in 1936 at Nordiska Kompaniet, or NK, Stockholm, Sweden's largest department store. A year later she helped to establish its textile department (Textilkammare).²

Under Sampe's direction NK's Textilkammare became a leading producer and retailer of innovative modern textiles. Sampe experimented with unusual materials during the war when there were supply shortages of natural fibers; she introduced the first fiberglass fabrics at NK in the 1940s.³ Other innovations included the "Signerad Textile" (signed textile) collection (1954), for which she commissioned designs from leading artists and architects, such as Alvar Aalto, Sven Markelius, Karl Axel Pehrson, and Viola Gråsten.⁴ This initiative was part of Sampe's efforts to bring greater recognition to textiles as objects of art. NK sold many of Sampe's upholstery and drapery fabrics as well as those by other leading Scandinavian designers she recruited, such as Markelius, Arne Jacobsen, and Stig Lindberg. Sampe remained head of the Textilkammare until it closed in 1971.

Sampe's textile designs were shown at the Exposition Internationale des Arts et Techniques dans la Vie Moderne, held in Paris in 1937. Two years later, her printed fabrics were used in the celebrated Swedish Pavilion designed by Sven Markelius for the New York World's Fair, bringing Sampe to

Fig. B.110 Dana Romeis. *Pandora* ("Blue" colorway), introduced 1988. Made by Craftex for KnollTextiles. Used for upholstery; spun rayon; plain-weave–derived simple weave. Courtesy Dana Romeis.

Fig. B.111 Detail of various fabrics designed by Sampe displayed in the Nordiska Kompaniet/Astrid Sampe installation in the Knoll showroom, 1948. Nationalmuseums Stockholm, Konstnärsarkivet, Astrid Sampes arkiv, pärm 418/2002.

Fig. B.112 Nordiska Kompaniet/Astrid Sampe installation in the Knoll showroom, 1948, including a *Model 652U* chair (right) in striped fabric, possibly *Sampe Stripe*. Nationalmuseums Stockholm, Konstnärsarkivet, Astrid Sampes arkiv, pärm 418/2002.

the attention of the American design community. Following World War II, Hans and Florence Knoll visited Sweden, seeking new designers and business contacts. At NK they met Sampe, initiating a long and productive relationship.[5] Starting in 1947, Swedish textiles were displayed at the Knoll showrooms in New York City. Sampe created eight patterns for Knoll, both printed drapery and upholstery fabrics. Florence Knoll included a selection of them—*Raindrops*, *Honeycomb*, and *Ciphers*—in the February 1947 launch of the textile product line at the new Knoll textile showroom on East Sixty-fifth Street in New York. Press coverage of the first collection suggests that Knoll scourced other Swedish textiles through Sampe.[6] Sampe's upholstery textiles and rugs were exhibited in "The Authentic Swedish Room" installation at Knoll, which represented the first collaboration between NK and Knoll. It also included furniture from the NK Trivia Series and designs by Bruno Mathsson (see chapter 2).[7] The installation traveled to several department stores across the United States.

In 1948 Florence Knoll devoted an entire exhibition to NK textiles in the Knoll showroom in which Sampe's work featured prominently and received much acclaim (figs. B.111 and B.112).[8] Sampe traveled to New York for the opening (fig. B.113). According to the *New York Times*, the exhibition included fifty designs, many of which revealed Sampe's innovative use of materials, including Tensolite, a fiberglass-coated yarn, and a cotton fabric that was made from the remnants of cotton and linen found in textile mills. One of the fiberglass textiles, *American Rand* (American Stripe), prefigures Knoll's *Sampe Stripe*, designed by Sampe and also introduced in 1948.[9]

Sampe brought extensive knowledge of textile structure to her work for Knoll. She experimented with weaves to create new textural and color effects. She collaborated closely with Knoll, holding regular meetings in Stockholm and New York. In the early 1950s NK became the licensee for Knoll products in Sweden, and as a result NK manufactured the Knoll furniture designs that were used in the United States embassies in Stockholm, Copenhagen, and Oslo, and also retailed these through the NK store.[10] *Rugby* (fig. B.114), a woven wool and nylon upholstery fabric that Knoll introduced in the United States in 1954, was originally made for the American embassy in Stockholm. It had been developed by Sampe when it was determined that Knoll's *Transportation Cloth* could not be made in Europe. Of her designs for Knoll, her print *Lazy Lines* and *Rugby* were particularly successful and remained in production for many years: *Lazy Lines* (1953–63) and *Rugby* (1954–71).

In addition to the Scandinavian embassy projects for Knoll, Sampe received prestigious commissions in the United States in the 1950s and 1960s. In 1954 she designed the printed drapery *Modular* for Eero Saarinen's Kresge Auditorium at M.I.T., and almost a decade later designed a group of five large area rugs based on flora from around the world for the Dag Hammarskjöld Library at the United Nations. Sampe also worked for major American industries, such as IBM, who commissioned her in 1970 to create a computer-generated textile that was printed on fiberglass, a project reflecting her lifelong commitment to innovation.[11] —HH

Designs for Knoll
Honeycomb (1947); *Raindrops* (1947); *Ciphers* (1947); *Rings* (1947); *Sampe Stripe* (1948–ca. 1951); *Crossbars* (ca. 1948); *Lazy Lines* (1953–63); *Rugby* (1954–71).

Selected Awards and Exhibitions
1937 Textiles for the Swedish Pavilion, Exposition Internationale des Arts et Techniques, Paris
1939 Printed fabrics for the Swedish Pavilion, New York World's Fair
1946 "Modern Swedish Home" installation, Building Centre, London
1947 Grand Prix, Milan Triennale
Elected Royal Designer for Industry, London
1955 "Linenline" at the H55 exhibition in Helsingborg, Sweden
1956 Gregor Paulsson Trophy, from the Swedish Society of Industrial Design
1967 Retrospective exhibition at the Borås Museum, Borås, Sweden
1980 His Majesty The King's Medal, Sweden
1984 *Astrid Sampe—Svensk Industritextil* (Swedish Industrial Textiles), Nationalmuseum, Stockholm

Peter Seipelt (b. 1937)

Peter Seipelt was born in Königsberg (Germany, today Kaliningrad, Russia). He studied architecture at the Technische Hochschule (Technical University) in Munich (1957–59) and industrial design at the Werkkunstschule (School of Arts and Crafts) in Krefeld (1960), under the aegis of former Bauhausler Gerhard

Kadow.¹ He attended a master class in textile design with Elisabeth Kadow at the textile engineering school in Krefeld (1961–63) and augmented his studies with a four-month practicum at a local weaving mill. From 1963 to 1975 he was chief designer at Storck, a textile manufacturer in Krefeld, creating designs for major projects such as the Olympic Games in Munich (1972) and collaborating with such well-known designers as Tobia Scarpa and Mario Bellini.²

In 1975 Seipelt was hired by Zumsteg AG in Zurich—a renowned converter for luxury fashion fabrics—to create a decorative textile collection for interiors. Seipelt selected the designers, printers, and weavers for the new line. After this was completed, Arthur Sager (general manager and vice president of Knoll Textiles) and Maurice Meunier (Knoll France executive) recommended Seipelt to Knoll executives Marshall Cogan and Steven Swid, to discuss opportunities with Knoll. In 1979 Seipelt was hired as director of design for the European textile collection of Knoll International.

Seipelt was responsible for the creative direction and product development of Knoll Textiles in Europe, which meant anticipating needs for residential and contract textiles, procuring designers, and facilitating production. He worked closely with Knoll's furniture designers to determine their product needs; he also sourced new mills and textile printers and tested prototypes in Knoll facilities in Pontoise, France, and Foligno, Italy.

Seipelt re-colored some of Knoll Europe's "classic" textiles such as selections of handwoven fabrics by Paul Maute. He also updated the colors of *Quartet* by Suzanne Huguenin for the European market with the designer's permission in 1980.³ He sourced new leathers, resulting in the introduction of *Vitello* and *Toscana* in 1988, and contributed to the European development of textiles for the Zapf panel system. Under Seipelt's direction, Knoll International released printed casements by Alexandre Mimoglou (1982), Klaus Dombrowski (1987), and Jürgen Reichert (1987).

In addition to finding new designers, Siepelt also produced his own textile designs. Knoll released his first series of printed textiles in 1981. The prints *Basket* (fig. B.115), *Linea*, and *Zigzag* (see cat. 228), as well as their burn-out sheer counterparts *Basket-T*, *Linea-T*, and *Zigzag-T*, in polyester and cotton, comprised the collection. The textiles were screen-printed at the Taunus Textildruck in Germany. *Basket*, *Linea*, and *Zigzag* featured a network of linear designs printed in reflective ink on a pearlescent marbled ground in a variety of pastel colorways— evoking basket weaves or zig-zag line motifs. The sheers were made through the burn-out process to play with translucent and opaque qualities. Knoll design stylist, Kristl Reinhardt (Andrus), recently recalled Seipelt's prints as having "elegant colors with wonderful sheen and vibrancy" and being ostensibly "very European and residential."⁴

Although Seipelt's designs were also released in the United States, as with most of the print collections since the 1970s, the line was more successful in Europe, where there was a strong residential client base as well as more extensive European promotion. The collection was discontinued in the United States in 1985. Seipelt also designed casement fabrics introduced in 1987 and 1988 for the European market. The 1987 prints offered two opposing aesthetics: *Cirrus* was a light and airy print while *Vetro* offered dark and luminous effects.⁵ A year later, Knoll Europe released *Duo* and *Trio*, both of which were austere pigment prints on polyester voile.⁶

In 1987 Knoll executives asked Seipelt to relocate to New York to succeed Merle Lindby-Young as the vice president of Knoll Textiles, but he declined, preferring to stay in Europe. He remained at Knoll Europe until the corporate structure was modified in the early 1990s and much of the European textiles division was reduced.⁷

Shortly after Knoll recalibrated its European priorities, the rights for many of Seipelt's prints—namely, the 1982 collection and *Duo* and *Trio*—along with a selection of drapery and decorative fabrics from the European collection were purchased by Alato AG of Switzerland.⁸ Simultaneously, Seipelt relocated to Italy, where he still resides, and was hired to consult for Bute Fabrics in Scotland until 2005. In concert with Catherine Murray, design director at Bute, he contributed designs to large commissions, including durable textiles for Hong Kong's Chek Lap Kok Airport, as well as colored textile lines such as *Elgin*, *Pentland*, and *Clyde*.⁹ Over the years, Seipelt has also consulted and designed for Kinnasand in Sweden and Ruckstuhl in Switzerland. —AMT

Designs for Knoll
Print Collection (1981–85): *Basket*, *Basket-T*, *Linea*, *Linea-T*, *Zigzag*, *Zigzag-T*.

Fig. B.113 Astrid Sampe, wearing a dress made from her print design *Rings*, in the Nordiska Kompaniet/Astrid Sampe installation in the Knoll showroom, 1948. Nationalmuseums Stockholm, Konstnärsarkivet, Astrid Sampes arkiv, pärm 418/2002.

Fig. B.114 Astrid Sampe. *Rugby* ("Two-Tone Orange" colorway) on *Model 71* armchair designed by Eero Saarinen, ca. 1955. Chair introduced 1948; upholstery introduced 1954. Upholstery made by Orinoka Mills for Knoll Textiles; chair made by Knoll Associates, Inc. Upholstery: cotton, wool, nylon; basket weave; chair: wood legs, plastic shell, latex foam. Private collection. Cat. 108.

Fig. B.115 Peter Seipelt. *Basket* sample ("Lilac" colorway), 1982–85. Made by Taunus Textildruck for Knoll Textiles. Used for drapery; cotton; plain weave, screen-printed. KnollTextiles Archive. Cat. 229.

Fig. B.116 Hazel Siegel, 1990. Knoll Archives.

Introduced Europe only; it is uncertain when these designs were discontinued: *Scala* (1982); *Setalana* (1982); *Cirrus* (1987); *Vetro* (1987); *Duo* (1988); *Trio* (1988).

Selected Awards
1962 Rome Scholarship through Meisterklasse Textilkunst, Krefeld
1969 Art Prize, City of Krefeld
1982 Award for *Basket-T*, Design Center Stuttgart
1988 Award for *Duo* and *Trio*, Design Center Stuttgart

Hazel Siegel (b. 1942)

Hazel Siegel became the managing director of design of KnollTextiles worldwide in 1989. She introduced the largest single release of textiles in both Knoll's and contract market history, adding over 900 new skus (stock keeping units) to the company's inventory. She has held key posts not just at Knoll but at some of the most notable textile companies in the United States.

Born Hazel Kaplan in New York City in 1942, she married architect Robert Siegel in 1962 (fig. B.116). After graduating from Skidmore College in 1963, she began working at Boris Kroll—one of Knoll Textiles's early competitors—where she "cut her teeth" and eventually became the design director. In 1975 she accepted a similar position at another prominent textile company, Designtex Fabrics.[1] A year prior to working at Designtex, Siegel began consulting for General Felt Industries, which became Knoll's parent company in 1977, bringing Siegel in contact with Knoll for the first time. She also had a stint as product manager for General Felt carpets in 1982.[2] Her relationship with General Felt most likely stemmed from her friendship with the company's owner Marshall Cogan who, along with Stephen Swid, purchased Knoll in August 1977. In 1989, when Cogan sought to refocus the textile division, he looked to Siegel, hiring her to manage KnollTextiles and precipitating the resignation of Richard Wagner (general manager, Knoll Textiles).

Siegel's first decision was to discontinue many of the existing patterns and invest the division's resources in producing new collections.[3] She hired Suzin Steerman (also hailing from Designtex) to assist with custom product development. Foremost, Siegel focused on wallcovering fabrics and task-seating upholstery, with innovative weave structures and a contemporary feel.[4]

Throughout her career Siegel has aimed to design textiles that promote a modern ethos while also articulating the architectural foundation of interior environments. A dialogue with architects has been particularly influential to her design aesthetic. At the center of her relationship with architects is her husband, Robert Siegel, who, along with his partner, Charles Gwathmey, designed the Knoll Boston showroom at 37 Newbury Street (1980) and the *Derby Desk* for KnollOffice (1990).[5] In April 1990 the Siegels traveled to Tokyo for Knoll Japan's introduction of Gwathmey Siegel–designed furniture and Hazel Siegel textiles.[6]

The introduction of the *Hazel Siegel Collection* was a seminal moment for KnollTextiles (fig. B.117, see fig. 6.27). E. D. Smith of *Contract* magazine called this unprecedented, large release of contract upholstery collections "an unequivocal paean to modernism in the 1990s."[7] The collection included twelve "mini" collections and thirty-three individual patterns. Based on distinct themes that drew from a variety of points of inspiration, they shared a coordinated color system.

The *Hazel Siegel Collection* targeted the products of Knoll's competitors as well as offering textiles that filled product gaps in the contract market. In Knoll internal sales materials, key competitors were mentioned in the description for each "mini" collection. For example, *Spirited Classics Collection*—said to be inspired by silk designs from the Art Nouveau and Art Deco periods—cited competing fabrics from Unika Vaev and Deepa Textiles.[8] Other collections, such as the *Paramount Collection*, were new developments in the textile industry. Knoll had exclusive rights to the Olefin yarn system they used in the collection, creating a new market and releasing innovative textiles without parallel.[9] In addition to bringing in new materials, Siegel also updated the Knoll color palette to include more timely and "relevant" hues. She colored the *Cross Cultures Collection* with subtle hues such as "Pewter" or "Celadon." One example from this mini-collection, the large-scale repeat *Bauhaus Geometric*, was released with subtle color variations, resulting in a "balance of pattern and texture" (fig. B.118).[10]

In the late 1980s and early 1990s, the company frequently aligned itself with a Bauhaus heritage.[10] To this aim and seeking to reinterpret early twentieth-century modernism through a contemporary lens, Siegel designed the *Paul Klee Collection*.

She selected four paintings by Bauhaus master Paul Klee—*Polyphony*, *Colorful Life Outside*, *Monument in a Fertile Country*, and *Blue Night*—to interpret as upholstery textiles (see fig. 6.28). In keeping with her preference for architectural frameworks, Siegel emphasized Klee's grid system in the designs' repeats.

Siegel sourced mills in the United States and Europe to produce her collection. For the *Regal Brocade Collection* she contracted Rohleder in Germany to weave four patterns on their Jacquard looms. Fascinated by the intricate weave structure of brocade construction (fig. B.119, see fig. 6.29), she considered the relationship between the dense construction and the thick "almost embroidered" design as "modernist in theory."[12] The four *Brocade Collection* textiles had diverse and anachronistic historical references suggested by their names, such as *Etruscan Brocade* and *Byzantium*.[13]

In 1990 Siegel drew on her strong connections to the architectural community and commissioned Peter Eisenman to create a collection for KnollTextiles. That year at the opening of Eisenman's Wexner Center for Visual Arts in Columbus, Ohio, she had been struck by the graphic potential of the imbedded grids formed by the building's dimensional steel scaffoldings.[14] Together, Eisenman and Siegel created the *Snakes and Ladders Collection* with designs based on his architectural models and drawings. In the following year Siegel, created the *Sensu Collection*, a group of three upholstery textiles—initially designed for the Augusta Medical Center.[15]

Siegel left Knoll in late 1992, and in 1994 she formed Textus, a textile firm focused on the architectural and interiors contract market. To build the company, Siegel purchased the seminal textile company Ben Rose Ltd.—both the company name and the rights to market its woven fabrics—from G. & T. Industries.[16] Major textile clients included USB Swiss Bank and Merrill Lynch.[17] In 1998 the Momentum Group acquired Textus, and since then Siegel has taught at Pratt Institute of Art in New York. She has also served on numerous boards of interior design associations including the Association of Contract Textiles and International Interior Design Association. —AMT

Designs for Knoll
Paul Klee Collection: *Blue Night* (1990–2004), *Polyphony* (1990–94), *Colorful Life Outside* (1990–94), *Monument in Fertile Country* (1990). Regal Brocade Collection: *Anatolia* (1990–91), *Byzantium* (1990–93), *Etruscan Brocade* (1990–93), *Nouveau Foliage* (1990–93). English Propriety Collection: *Berkshire* (1990–2003), *Bristol* (1990–2003), *Westminster* (1990–99). Cross Cultures Collection: *Bauhaus Geometric* (1990–2005), *Dardinelles* (1990–99), *Marmara* (1990–94), *Quadrate* (1990–2004), *Tesserae* (1990). Classic Worsteds: *Bandeau* (1990–93), *Maelstrom* (1990–94). Spirited Classics: *Meteor* (1990–94), *Orion* (1990–94), *Pavo* (1990–94), *Quasar* (1990–94), *Umbrage* (1990–99). Luxe Wools: *Cavalier* (1990), *Meridian* (1990–92), *Syncopation* (1990–92). Anthology Collection: *Penumbra* (1990–94), *Pointillage* (1990), *Tempest* (1990–94), *Pastiche* (1990–94). Paramount Collection: *Genesis* (1990–99), *Poseiden* (1990–99), *Mariner* (1990–2007). Overture Collection: *Vanguard* (1990–94), *Prism* (1990–94). New World Wools: *Parquet* (1990–99), *Pluma* (1990–99), *Aerial* (1990–99). Wallcoverings: *Charmont* (1990–94), *Collage* (1990–99), *Corniche* (1990–99), *Flambeau* (1990–92), *Hokkaido* (1990–2004), *Kyoto* (1990–2004), *Motion* (1990–99), *Nara* (1990–2004), *Oblique* (1990–92), *Paradigm* (1990–92), *Paradox* (1990–99), *Primo* (1990–94), *Proscenium* (1990–99), *Sorrento* (1990–94). Sensu Collection: *Sensu* (1992–94), *Suna* (1992–2003), *Feathers* (1992). Circuits (1992–94), *Express* (1992–94), *Goliath* (1992–2005).

Fig. B.117 Knoll NeoCon Showroom featuring the *Hazel Siegel Collection*, Chicago, 1990. Knoll Archives.

Fig. B.118 Hazel Siegel. *Bauhaus Geometric* sample ("Buff" colorway), introduced 1990. Made in West Germany for KnollTextiles. Used for upholstery; cotton, rayon, polyester; plain-weave–derived compound weave. KnollTextiles Archive. Cat. 261.

Fig. B.119 Hazel Siegel. *Etruscan Brocade* advertisement, 1989. KnollTextiles Archive.

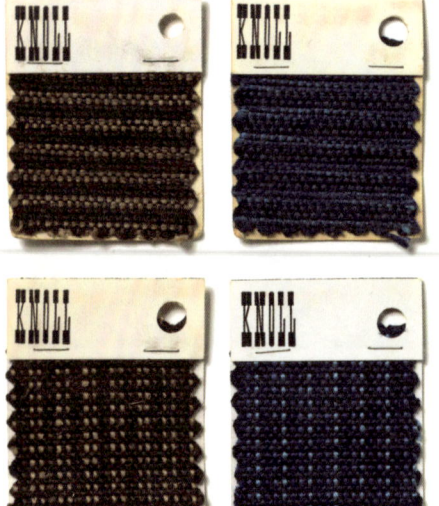

Fig. B.120 Evelyn Hill Anselevicius. *Highland Tweed* and *Highland Stripes* swatches ("Blue" and "Brown" colorways), ca. 1952. Made by Donald Brothers for Knoll Textiles. Used for upholstery; linen, cotton; plain weave. Private collection.

Selected Awards and Exhibitions
1980, 1981, 1987, 1988 ASID International Products Design Award
1987 IBD Judges Citation for 25 Years of Design Excellence
1990 Exhibition of Gwathmey Siegel furniture with Hazel Siegel textiles, Knoll Japan
2004 Leadership excellence in Contract Design Industry from the International Interior Design Association

Peter M. Simpson (1921–1988)

Over the course of his career, Peter Simpson helped shape the histories of two leading Scottish textile manufacturers—Donald Brothers Ltd. and Bute Fabrics. Serving as the creative director at both companies, first at Donald Brothers in the 1950s and 1960s and then at Bute Fabrics in the 1970s and 1980s, Simpson has been credited with individual designs as well as major shifts in textile production. His designs for both companies received professional recognition time and again, earning many awards from the British Council of Industrial Design (CoID). Significantly, both companies have longstanding relationships with Knoll Textiles, ties undoubtedly nurtured by Simpson during his tenures.

Simpson's design career began after he served in the Royal Air Force in World War II. After the war, he enrolled at the Duncan of Jordanstone College of Art in Dundee, Scotland.[1] He then traveled abroad and worked for JOFA, a leading textile firm in New York, from 1950 to 1953.[2] Returning to Scotland he spent the next twenty years at Donald Brothers. The company had a long history of catering to the modern interior with its use of "rugged . . . and . . . constructed texture," offering a rich visual and tactile quality.[3] Building upon this legacy, Simpson (as the chief designer and later the design director) shifted the focus of the small firm away from exclusive limited-production weaves in an effort to court the larger contract textile market. As part of this new direction, Donald Brothers expanded the range of weaves it produced and ultimately cornered the market for both tightly woven weaves offering a modern "Scandinavian" aesthetic as well more "chunky, natural weaves."[4] These changes suited an illustrious list architects, designers, and textile and furniture companies including Jack Lenor Larsen, Arne Jacobsen, Jens Risom, Nordiska Kompaniet, and Knoll.[5]

Knoll Textiles' relationship with Donald Brothers began with the production of *Scotch Linen* designed by Franz Lorenz in 1950. Company records at the Heriot-Watt University, Edinburgh, however, suggest that Knoll's relationship with the Scottish mill entered a more profitable phase in 1953, the year Simpson joined the firm. Their sample books contain an extensive list of designs presented to Knoll—often identified as trials for "Knoll Associates, New York" and in some cases for "Miss Haraszty, Long Island"—and confirm the production of a selection of these textiles.[6] Textiles manufactured for Knoll after Simpson joined the firm included Evelyn Hill's *Kerry Linen* (1953–66); Suzanne Huguenin's *Tracey* (1962–74); *Highland Tweed* and *Highland Stripes* (1957–62) (fig. B.120); *Major and Minor* (1956–60) (see fig. 1.39); as well as Simpson's own design *Scotch Mist* (1962–75).[7] The trials for *Scotch Mist*—a plain-weave wool-and-linen blend fabric—were produced in late 1961, and the textile was released by Knoll in January 1962 (fig. B.121).[8] Though the initial sampling of colors included a natural gray, Knoll sold the textile only in "Off-white" until its discontinuation in 1975.

In addition to the woven textiles, Simpson designed several printed textiles for Donald Brothers, including *Woodlands* (1955) and *Kenya* (1958).[9] Thanks in part to Simpson's connections in New York, Donald Brothers also sold extensively to JOFA and Dan Cooper.[10] Beginning in 1960 Simpson was frequently honored by CoID for individual textiles, as well as for full collections for Donald Brothers: first for *Ely* (1960)—a textile sold by Terrence Conran as *Orlando*—and continuing with *Cawdor* (1962) and *Glendale* (1964). He was celebrated for the *Hebridean Collection* in 1970.[11] The universal acclaim for his designs resulted in his appointment as a Royal Designer for Industry in 1975.

Simpson's numerous successes and extensive experience led to his consulting for a new venture of the Fifth Marquess of Bute.[12] Drawing on his experience at Donald Brothers, where he remained design director, Simpson advised the marquess on transforming Bute Looms Ltd.—a boutique handwoven textile company with a focus on making handwoven fashion fabrics—into a profitable manufacturer for the contract industry. When he joined Bute in 1974 he brought another Donald Brothers designer, Ian Ross, with him and perhaps more importantly, he brought key contacts at major furniture companies.¹³ There were instant contracts with both Scandinavian and American companies such as Steelcase, Herman Miller, and Knoll International.¹⁴ In 1977 the company renamed itself Bute Fabrics and made Simpson the design director, a position he retained until his retirement in 1986.¹⁵ Under Simpson's direction, the company produced *Scotchwool* (1977–85) as well as *Fife* and *Berwick* (1985–91) and other upholsteries for Knoll.¹⁶

In addition to his positions at Donald Brothers and Bute, Simpson traveled to Thailand and India to work with native weavers in 1967, and three years later as a member of the Scottish Committee of Design Council, he visited Swaziland weavers in South Africa.¹⁷ While advancing professionally within private industry, Simpson managed to serve as a governor of Duncan of Jordanstone College of Art from 1972 until 1982. In 1984 he was hired as the director of the Edinburgh Tapestry Company.¹⁸ In 1986, after Simpson retired, the Scottish Development Agency invited him to be a design counselor for the group, and he was also appointed a governor of the Glasgow School of Art.¹⁹ A year before his death, he was awarded an Honorary Doctorate of Literature by the Scottish College of Textiles, Galashiels. He died at his home in Perthshire, Scotland in 1988. —AMT

Design for Knoll
Scotch Mist (1962–75).

Selected Awards and Exhibitions
1956 Elected Member of Society of Industrial Artists and Designers (S.I.A.D.)
1960 CoID award
1961 Designed collection for Hilton Hotels
1962–64, 1968, 1970, 1972 CoID Awards
1966 CoID Award for Best Fabric Collection Membership in Scottish Committee of the Council of Industrial Design
1975 Royal Designer for Industry, Woven Textile Design
Elected Fellow of S.I.A.D.
1976 Exhibition of work for Bute Fabrics, I.D.I. Olympia
1987 Awarded an Honorary Doctorate of Literature by Scottish College of Textiles, Galashiels

Stephen Sprouse (1953–2004)

Fashion designer Stephen Sprouse's five-textile collection for Knoll in 2003 served as a reflection of his career, revisiting motifs that comprised his signature style: Day-Glo colors, graffiti, camouflage, photo transfer, TV static, and the use of unconventional materials. Growing up in Indiana, Sprouse went to New York City at age twelve to meet the fashion designers Norman Norell and Bill Blass. Two years later, Blass hired him as a summer apprentice.¹ Sprouse attended the Rhode Island School of Design (RISD) briefly before moving to New York City in 1971, landing a job as the main assistant to Halston. He transcribed the architecture of Halston's draped forms to paper, in the process learning about the construction of the designer's minimalist silhouettes and developing a penchant for luxury materials.²

After two and a half years with Halston, Sprouse left to pursue his own design career. He moved into a loft on the Bowery where his neighbors included Debbie Harry and Chris Stein of Blondie. Sprouse, who made one-of-a-kind clothes for friends and art-world acquaintances, helped Harry create and polish her look, designing the dress she wore in the 1978 *Heart of Glass* video, for example (fig. B.122). To make this dress, Sprouse photographed static lines off his television screen and then photo-printed the image onto a layer of fabric that was placed between cotton and a layer of chiffon. Around this time Sprouse was developing his signature style while focusing on his artwork. The static-line motif was revisited years later in his designs for KnollTextiles.

In the 1970s he befriended Steven Meisel, then a fashion illustrator, and the two formed a symbiotic identity, creatively inspiring and influencing each other. With the tall blonde transsexual Teri Toye, they formed an influential downtown New York trinity of cool. Sprouse showed Meisel sketches of what would become his first collection in 1982.³ Meisel suggested Sprouse to publicist Kezia Keeble for *Image by Design* (April 1983), a show of emerging designers that included Anna Sui and Vivienne Tam.⁴ Fifteen Sprouse designs were included, introducing his Day-Glo palette, 1960s-inspired silhouettes, and graffiti prints on luxurious fabrics. The positive response to the small collection led Sprouse to start his business with $1.4 million from his parents.⁵

Sprouse showed his first full collection for Spring 1984 in his new West Fifty-seventh Street studio to critical acclaim, and his clothing began appearing in major fashion magazines and retailers. For the highly theatrical

Fig. B.121 Peter Simpson. *Scotch Mist* sample card, ca. 1970–75. Made by Donald Brothers for Knoll Textiles. Used for drapery; wool, linen; plain weave; on paper card. KnollTextiles Archive.

Fig. B.122 Debbie Harry of Blondie, wearing a "scan line" dress designed by Stephen Sprouse, filming the video for *Heart of Glass* at Studio 54, 1979. Photographed by Roberta Bailey.

launch of his Fall 1984 collection, fifteen hundred people packed the Ritz nightclub on East Eleventh Street. Andy Warhol was in attendance that night and traded two portraits for the whole collection; afterward Sprouse became part of Warhol's circle.[6] Before Warhol's death in 1987, the two collaborated on a camouflage print for fabrics to be used in Sprouse's designs.[7]

Despite critical recognition, Sprouse's collection was not a commercial success due to the contradictory nature of his designs. His approach appealed to a youthful downtown crowd, but his use of luxury materials, custom techniques, and his uncompromising attitude toward production—such as personally hand-painting the graffiti on the garments—resulted in fashion that was priced for a wealthier demographic.[8] By the summer of 1985, he was forced to close his company, burdened by escalating debt and merchandise delivery problems.[9]

In February 1987, Sprouse announced a partnership with Andrew Cogan, the twenty-four-year-old son of Marshall S. Cogan, chairman of GFI/Knoll International Holdings Inc. That fall, Sprouse and Cogan opened a tri-level store at 99 Wooster Street a few doors away from the Knoll Design Center at 105 Wooster. Three differently priced lines were sold in the store: S, Sprouse, and Steven Sprouse. In October 1988, however, Sprouse was again forced to close. Not only was there the same disconnect between pricing and potential buyers, but he was also plagued by the same merchandise delivery problems.[10]

Sprouse reverted to freelance designing and spent more time on his pop-influenced paintings. He also designed costumes, album covers, and set backdrops for rock bands. In 1992 his critically successful Cyber-Punk collection of thirty looks for men and women was marketed exclusively by Bergdorf Goodman. The influence of computers and technology on Sprouse was reflected in the use of large Velcro closures, lightweight metals, and reflective fabrics.

To relaunch his label in 1998, Sprouse entered into an agreement with the Italian manufacturing and distribution company Staff International. His first runway show (Spring 1998) again featured Warhol artworks printed on chiffon and plastic. He followed with two more collections incorporating prints based on Warhol's *Oxidation* paintings as well as a print of satellite photographs taken by NASA's Mars Pathfinder mission.

Marc Jacobs, the creative director of Louis Vuitton, approached Sprouse in 2000 to collaborate on handbags, accessories, and textiles for the Spring 2001 collection, resulting in Sprouse's iconic trademark graffiti scrawl of "louis vuitton paris," over the Vuitton monogram on handbags. The collaboration sold out before it even reached stores.[11] The success of this collaboration led to commercial offers from high-profile companies such as Target and KnollTextiles.

Andrew Cogan, Sprouse's former partner and now the CEO of Knoll, Inc., approached Sprouse in 2002 about designing for Knoll. Cogan wanted a second chance to work with Sprouse and looked to him to create progressive fabrics for Knoll, which would "attract a younger generation that appreciates edgy design."[12] The results, introduced in 2003, were a departure from Knoll's more subdued modernism, resulting in some of the first new prints launched by Knoll since the 1980s.

To begin his design work, Sprouse studied all of the textiles in the line. He was particularly drawn to *Cato* and *Silver Screen*. Reinterpreting *Cato*, he used his signature Day-Glo colors as well as new materials that would appeal to the eclectic environment of the new millennium.[13] Suzanne Tick, creative director, KnollTextiles, suggested using tape yarn made by the same extrusion method developed for *Foil Rap* and *Heavy Metal*. The resulting upholstery fabric, *Techno Tweed*, was also produced in neutral colorways (see cat. 275).

Silver Screen inspired Sprouse to revisit his TV scan-line prints. Though initially hesitant to spend a day looking at a static TV screen, Tick described the process of working with Sprouse on *Digital Airwave* and *Static Screen* as an "alternative way of getting design imagery—and it's beautiful."[14] To capture the pattern, Tick focused a digital camera on a TV screen tuned to static while Sprouse jostled and twisted the cable to create different patterns. A series of 10-by-12-inch photographs was created. The patterns were then printed onto heat-transfer paper and applied to *Silver Screen* (fig. B.123).

For his trademark graffiti style, Sprouse chose *Extreme Velvet*, which was then under development. To create the pattern, archival camouflage patterns were researched as a starting point, and the proper repeat required to work with the rotary screen printer was designed. Sprouse then wrote—and re-wrote—with thick markers, the passages from the Declaration of Independence that he found to be most poignant (see fig. 6.39). When asked in an interview with the *New York Sun* if scrawling the Declaration of Independence on *Graffiti Camo* was a political statement, Sprouse explained, "It seemed pretty timely when I started doing it last fall," after the start of the post-9/11 Iraq War. But beyond the political implications, he continued, "I like the "inalienable rights" thing—it's just a great word, inalienable— pretty sci-fi for the Declaration of Independence."[15] He also added, "America's been an interesting place for the last couple of years, so I'm looking back in time for an extraction of goodness, of optimism."[16]

The collaboration with Knoll was well received in the press but commercially less successful, and Sprouse's patterns were all discontinued by 2010. The draperies sold better than the upholstery fabrics, of which *Techno Tweed* was found to be "too plastic" for Knoll's market.[17] In addition to the five textile patterns, Sprouse applied his signature graffiti, this time featuring words about art and culture such as Mies van der Rohe's "less is more," to two Saarinen pedestal tables and two Mies *Barcelona* chairs and ottomans, and two *Barcelona* sofas. These were auctioned online in 2003 to benefit Design Industries Foundation Fighting AIDS (DIFFA), garnering press attention to the Knoll/Sprouse collaboration in general.

While working on the Knoll designs, Sprouse was diagnosed with lung cancer, a condition he kept private. At the time of his death in 2004, he was collaborating with NASA on, for example, paintings of the International Space Station. Before his cremation, friends covered his coffin in graffiti, inside and out, and left the marker in his hand so he could have the last word.[18] —AM

Designs for Knoll
Camo and *Graffiti Camo* (2003–8); *Techno Tweed* (2003–10); *Digital Airwave* (2003–9); *Static Screen* (2003–10).

Selected Awards and Exhibitions
1984 Award for Fashion Design, CFDA Coty Award nomination
1987 Costumes for New York City Ballet "Ecstatic Orange"
1995 Exhibition of silkscreen paintings, Cleveland Center for Contemporary Art
2002 "Americaland" for Target
2004 Hospitality Design Award Honorable Mention for *Digital Airwave* and *Static Screen*, International Interior Design Association
2006 *Anarchy to Affluence: Design in New York, 1974–1984*, Parsons The New School for Design
2009 *Rock on Mars*, Deitch Projects, New York
2011 *Jet Boy*, Dorian Grey Gallery, New York

Gunta Stadler-Stölzl (1897–1983)

Gunta Stölzl was born Adelgunde Stölzl in Munich, Germany. She studied at the Königliche Kunstgewerbeschule (Royal School of Arts and Crafts) in Munich from 1913 to 1917, then volunteered as a nurse for the Red Cross until the end of the First World War. In 1919 she enrolled at the Staatliches Bauhaus in Weimar, where she was strongly influenced by the teaching of Paul Klee and Johannes Itten, who encouraged students to explore the tactile as well as the visual aspects of materials. In 1920 Stölzl was asked to supervise the new Women's Department and thereafter played a central role in the organization of the Weaving Workshop. As craft master in 1925, and *Jungmeister* (Young Master) at the Dessau Bauhaus in 1927, she developed a systematic method of professional training and built the Weaving Workshop into the school's most financially successful division.[1] Through her pioneering tapestries, wall hangings, and designs for industry, as well as her teaching, she had a profound influence on the development of modern textile design.

In 1931 internal politics at the Bauhaus forced Stölzl to resign her position, and she moved to Switzerland.[2] With two other Bauhaus weavers, Gertrud Preiswerk and Heinrich Otto Hürliman, she founded a handweaving studio in Zurich, S-P-H Stoffe, which became S-H Stoffe in 1933.[3] The studio designed and produced textiles and fabrics for the home for a variety of Swiss companies. They exhibited at the 1937 *Exposition Internationale des Arts et Techniques* in Paris. From 1938 until 1967, Stölzl continued to run the workshop independently, under the name Handweberei Flora. In 1942 she married Willy Stadler, and became a Swiss citizen. Commissions continued to be plentiful during and after World War II, although materials were difficult to come by. Stadler-Stölzl often used local hand-spun wool, either leaving it natural (undyed), dyeing it herself, or having it custom-dyed.[4] In her upholstery fabrics, she used natural

Fig. B.123 Stephen Sprouse. *Static Screen* ("Plasma" colorway), 2003. Used for drapery; polyester. KnollTextiles Archive.

Fig. B.124 Suzin Steerman. *Shibai* sample ("Autumn" colorway), ca. 1994. Made in the United States for Knoll Textiles. Used for upholstery; plain-weave–derived compound weave. KnollTextiles Archive.

wool in all-wool fabrics with small woven patterns, and also in combination with fibers such as jute and cellophane.[5]

Stadler-Stölzl was listed among the designers of the first Knoll Textiles collection in 1947 advertisements and probably designed the upholstery fabric *Vallis* (see fig. 3.25), which was described as being made of handspun wool from a "special breed of Swiss mountain sheep."[6] The fabric's name probably refers either to Valais (Wallis in German), a mountainous canton in southwest Switzerland, or to one of its namesake breeds of sheep, the Wallis blacknosed or Wallis country sheep (*roux du Valais*). Stadler-Stölzl's connection with Knoll is unknown, but Florence Schust (Knoll) may have become aware of Stadler-Stölzl's work while interning and studying with her former Bauhaus colleagues Walter Gropius, Marcel Breuer, and Mies van der Rohe (1939–41, see chapter 2).[7] It is also possible that the Knolls encountered her work when they set up their business relationship with Wohnbedorf, Knoll's Swiss licensee, just after World War II.

Through the 1950s and 1960s, Stadler-Stölzl made a good living designing furnishing and upholstery fabrics through the Handweberei Flora and also returned to making handwoven tapestries and wall hangings. In 1967 she closed her weaving workshop and thereafter concentrated on her own work.[8] She participated in numerous solo and group exhibitions through the 1970s, when her work from the Bauhaus period began to be rediscovered. She died in Zurich in 1983. —SW

Design for Knoll
Vallis (attributed; 1947–ca. 1948).

Selected Awards and Exhibitions
1937 *Exposition Internationale des Arts et Techniques*, Paris
1976–77 *Gunta Stadler-Stölzl*, Bauhaus-Archiv, Berlin
1987 *Gunta Stölzl: Weberei am Bauhaus und aus eigener Werkstatt*, Bauhaus-Archiv
1990 *Gunta Stölzl and Anni Albers*, MoMA
1997 *Gunta Stölzl: Meisterin am Bauhaus Dessau*, Bauhaus Foundation, Dessau
1999 *Das Bauhaus Webt*, Bauhaus-Archiv
2009 *Bauhaus 1919–1933: Workshops for Modernity*, MoMA

Suzin Steerman (Levy) (active 1990s)

Although Suzin Steerman worked at Knoll for just five years, she created and guided the production of award-winning designs for both the general collection and custom projects. In 1993 she was named senior designer for KnollTextiles.

Steerman initially taught herself basic weaving methods and structures, but recognizing her need for a more supervised and specific course of study and training, she enrolled in Philadelphia University's textile design program (formerly the Philadelphia College of Textiles) in 1979. It was at this time that Steerman first crossed paths with Knoll Textiles, working as a sales assistant for a Knoll representative. In 1984, after completing her undergraduate degree, Steerman relocated to New York City, where she was employed in the sales and textile design departments of Designtex, a division of Steelcase.[1]

At Designtex, Steerman worked with Hazel Siegel, who would later become manager of KnollTextiles, worldwide (1989–92), and then recruited Steerman to work for Knoll.[2] Beginning at Knoll in 1990, Steerman primarily worked on specific projects as director of custom development. When Siegel departed in late 1992, Steerman was named senior designer and supervised all fabric design and production for KnollTextiles.[3]

During her tenure with KnollTextiles, Steerman created three wallcoverings for the *Hemisphere Collection* (1993), as well as the upholstery textiles *Curves* (for the *Urban Geometry Collection*, 1994) and *Pavilion* (for the *Bauhaus Collection*, 1994), among others. Her textile designs featured playful geometric and abstract figural forms, using different yarn weights and complex weave structures for texture and dynamic visual interest. In *Isho* (from her 1994 *Kabuki Collection*), for example, Steerman used chenille yarns in a plain weave of subtle, contrasting colors to form a small-scale circle pattern with a slightly raised and "light-reflective" surface, while *Shibai*, a coordinating fabric to *Isho*, offered a slightly iridescent quality created by the blend of rayon and cotton (fig. B.124).[4] Steerman also contributed the cubicle fabrics *Harlequin*, *Picketfence*, *Portico*, and *Sunrise*, *Star*, *Cloud* to the *Horizon Collection* a line targeted at the healthcare industry.

Steerman left Knoll in 1995. The American Society of Interior Designers and the International Interior Design Association awarded her special recognition, and her Knoll wallcoverings and upholstery fabric designs won NeoCon Gold Awards in 1993 and 1994.[5] —ES

Designs for Knoll
Orbit (1990–99), *Freefall* (1992–2007), *Casual Elegance* (1992–2008). *Hemisphere Collection*, (1993–2000): *Constellation, Galactic, Orbit. Horizon Collection: Harlequin* (1994), *Picketfence*, (1994–2005), *Portico* (1994), *Sunrise, Star, Cloud* (1994). *Urban Geometry Collection: Curves* (1994–2000). *Bauhaus Collection: Pavilion* (1994–2004). *Kabuki Collection* (1994): *Butai* (1994–2006), *Isho* (1994–2000), *Shibai* (1994–2008).

Awards
ca. 1993 AID Awards for KnollTextiles
IIDA Awards for KnollTextiles
1993, 1994 NeoCon Gold Awards for KnollTextiles

Marianne Strengell Hammarström (1909–1998)

Introduced for a short time, beginning with the first collection in 1947 and terminating in about 1951, Marianne Strengell's woven and printed fabric designs made a critical contribution to the early offerings at Knoll. Her focus on the utility and aesthetic qualities of handwoven textiles, particularly as they were translated for machine production, and her embrace of a "Scandinavian Functionalism" were major themes throughout her career.[1] They also aligned well with Florence Knoll's approach to textile design. Strengell's commitment to experimentation and to working with commercial clients and architects dominated her practice.

Strengell was born in Helsinki, Finland, in 1909. Her father—architect, writer, and theorist Gustaf Strengell—had a formative impact on her aesthetic principles and her approach to design.[2] Her mother, Anna Strengell (née Wegelius), was a successful interior designer in Finland, who imparted a strong sense of color and design to her daughter, and was also the local agent for the leading British firm Liberty and Company.[3] Her parents' influence would prove a strong foundation for Strengell, who built on it at the Taideteollinen Korkeakoulu (Central School of Industrial Design) in Helsinki, where her progressive upbringing was challenged by the vernacular ideals of her professor Arttu Brummer. He urged the budding designer to embrace self-expression and fantasy.[4] After her graduation in 1929, she was hired by the Svenska Slöjdföreningen (Swedish Society of Arts and Crafts) as an assistant to Swedish textile artist Elsa Gullberg in the preparation of the seminal 1930 Stockholm Exhibition of Industrial Art. Gullberg introduced Strengell to experimental weaving techniques with new artificial yarns.[5]

From 1930 to 1936 Strengell designed and handwove textiles for a number of companies throughout Scandinavia. During this formative period, she not only garnered critical acclaim for her textiles, but also gained an acute understanding of the complex relationships between textiles, architecture, and industry. Early on, her mother hired her as the chief designer at Ab Hemflit Kotlahkerruus OY.[6] Strengell's Functionalist aesthetic was also popular in commercial markets outside of Finland. In 1934 Kaj Dessau made her the artistic director of the weaving workshop at BO Aktieselskab, the interior design house in Copenhagen, Denmark.[7] From 1934 to 1936, she was also the head designer for the interior design studio of Koti Hemmet in Helsinki, a retail store she co-owned with the architect Elna Kiljander.[8]

In late 1936, during a vacation in the United States, Strengell received an invitation from fellow Finn and close family friend, Eliel Saarinen, to teach weaving at the Cranbrook Academy of Art (founded in 1932). She accepted, joining the largely Scandinavian faculty and forging close ties with many innovative designers and students (fig. B.125). Strengell gradually departed from the established curriculum set by Loja Saarinen (Eliel's wife and head of the weaving department), which emphasized figural imagery and Nordic or Islamic motifs. Instead, Strengell began to emphasize patterns created by the weave structure and to encourage experimentation within the predetermined limitations set by material constraints or environmental conditions such as "available labor . . . raw materials, . . . climate and end use."[9] This methodological template developed further through Strengell's own experiences during World War II when there were many material shortages, as well as in her diverse architectural and industrial commissions.

In 1942 Strengell succeeded Loja Saarinen as the head of the weaving department, the appointment coinciding with Cranbrook being granted graduate level accreditation by the state of Michigan. Strengell formulated a new advanced curriculum, which not only focused on hand- and power-loom weaving but also added printing on textiles. She placed new emphasis on producing

Fig. B.125 Marianne Strengell in the Cranbrook Studio, 1952. From the *Detroit News*, n.d. Private collection.

Fig. B.126 Marianne Strengell's *Propellers* in the conference room of the Glass Container Manufacturers' Institute, 1949. Photographed by Lionel Freedman. From *Interiors* (August 1949).

Fig. B.127 Marianne Strengell. *Cartree* swatches, introduced 1947. Made by Louisville Textiles for Knoll Associates, Inc. Used for upholstery; cotton, plain weave with alternating single and paired wefts. KnollTextiles Archive. Cat. 26.

Fig. B.128 Marianne Strengell. *Buster* swatches, introduced 1947. Made by Louisville Textiles for Knoll Associates, Inc. Used for upholstery; cotton; plain weave. KnollTextiles Archive. Cat. 25.

designs for industrial production, a major motive in her own work, including hand-weaving samples of "utilitarian goods—upholstery, drapery, clothing—which were neatly mounted to show clients."[10] This training greatly benefited many of her students, who would become successful textile designers, including Jack Lenor Larson, Ed Rossbach, and Robert Sailors.

In keeping with her educational platform, throughout her tenure at Cranbrook, Strengell nurtured important relationships with industrial designers, manufacturers, and architects alike. In the 1940s her projects included woven fabrics for Russel Wright's *American Way* line and upholstery for United Airlines, a Raymond Loewy project.[11] Additionally, in 1949 textile firm Judd Williams, Inc. sought to capitalize on the trend for the nubbly "hand-loomed" look and translated three of Strengell's woven samples for machine production.[12] She worked with the company again in 1950, designing a series of "tweed" upholstery fabricated entirely out of the synthetic fiber Saran.[13]

The architectural firm Skidmore, Owings & Merrill commissioned Strengell to create interior textiles for the Terrace Plaza Hotel in Cincinnati in 1945 and Manhattan House in New York City in 1948.[14] Their most ambitious project together, however, was the new interior of the Owens-Corning Fiberglas building in New York, for which Strengell designed innovative wall fabrics as well as handwoven curtains and upholstery. Evincing the playful aesthetic of Brummer and adhering to her "framework of limitations," Strengell experimented with various combinations of Fiberglas, asbestos, cotton, mohair, and wool for the suite of Owens-Corning textiles.[15] The interiors of the building were coordinated and installed with a variety of Knoll furniture by the Knoll Planning Unit (see chapter 3).[16]

In the late 1940s Strengell became a key contributor and advisor to the nascent Knoll textiles division. When she was traveling with the Saarinens, Florence Knoll had met Strengell many years earlier in Finland, and later at Cranbrook the two shared a dorm room.[17] It is no surprise, therefore, that Florence Knoll asked Strengell to contribute to Knoll's inaugural textile collection along with other notable American and Scandinavian textile designers.

Strengell's first design for Knoll, *Shooting Stars*, was also her first printed textile design.[18] It featured a repeat of multidirectional dark brown lines, suggestive of the tails of shooting stars, on a solid natural cotton or gray linen ground. Over the next four years, new color choices were added, including "Dark Gray on Light Gray," "Black on White," and "White on Persimmon." The print was also produced on rayon shantung fabric.[19] The option to purchase this print in cotton, shantung, or linen was typical of Knoll's practice of aiming for both high-end clients and the mid-market.

Knoll included *Shooting Stars* along with *Propellers*, Strengell's second screen-print for the firm, in their first collection in 1947.[20] *Propellers* was less successful and was discontinued before 1950. The print, comprised of crescent-moon and propeller shapes on a solid ground, was produced in three colorways: "White and Green on Yellow," "White and Brown on Gray," and "White and Red on Beige."[21] Despite its limited years in production, the print was featured in Knoll promotional material from 1949 and was used in office installations (fig. B.126).[22]

In addition to her printed textiles, Strengell designed three power-loomed upholstery fabrics for Knoll: *Devil*, *Cartree*, and *Buster*. *Devil* and *Cartree* highlighted Strengell's sophisticated use of differing combinations of mohair, cotton, and wool while adhering to simple weave structures (figs. B.127, B.128, see figs. 3.17, 3.18). With an eye to the luxury market, Florence Knoll also commissioned Strengell to create a line of handwoven upholstery and curtain fabrics beginning with the initial 1947 textile collection, and these remained in the Knoll line until about 1952.

Strengell's handwovens for Knoll were used in the "House in the Museum Garden" installation designed by Marcel Breuer at MoMA in 1949. The exhibition house featured a bed and several pieces of furniture upholstered in *Devil* and another unidentified brown hand-loomed fabric.[23] Just a few years later Strengell created *Puli*, her last textile for Knoll and perhaps the one most closely related to Strengell's handweavings, with the varied use of fibers to create visual interest and texture (see chapter 3).[24] In 1950 Strengell also designed the short-lived *Pebble Weave* webbing for Knoll.[25]

Building upon the success of her Knoll designs, Strengell embarked on a monumental project, one that demonstrated her belief in the aesthetic unity between woven textiles and modern architecture. Beginning in 1951 she designed rugs, curtains, and vast yardages of upholstery for Eero Saarinen's General Motors Technical Center complex in Warren, Michigan (fig. B.129). As with other Saarinen projects, the many interiors were furnished by Knoll. From the outset and possibly in concert with Knoll, Strengell aimed to soften the complex's austere architecture and to "humanize the great expanses of glass, the pre-fabricated units of the walls, the use of stainless steel and aluminum."[26] By offsetting the hard surfaces of these interiors with dark striped rugs or brilliantly colored upholstery she adroitly created unique individual spaces sensitive to their respective needs.

In contrast to this massive corporate commission, Strengell's relationship with industry and handcraft was reshaped in the early 1950s. Along with her second husband, Finnish-American architect Olav Hammarström, Strengell participated in the United States Economic Cooperation Administration's joint project with the United Nations to sponsor cottage industries in Japan and the Philippines.[27] The opportunity to work with new materials, such as abaca and pineapple fibers, intrigued Strengell, and while in the Philippines, she also introduced block-printing as an alternative to the embroidery of indigenous motifs.[28] Her largest contribution to the Philippine project, however, was the creation of a small loom that she and her husband designed, which would allow the width of textiles to be increased from 18 to 42 inches, a width more in keeping with commercial textile dimensions.[29]

Always a promoter of industrial relationships, Strengell designed a cotton and abaca upholstery, woven at the Chrysler automobile plant in Manila for their Southeast Asian models.[30] According to a U.N. report, Strengell designed another upholstery fabric that was produced in the Philippines expressly for a furniture series developed for the international division of Knoll.[31] Her commitment to stimulating cottage industries continued throughout the 1960s, when the government of Jamaica invited her to help resuscitate their local weaving production. In the United States, she also worked with weavers in Appalachia with similar aims.

The automobile fabric produced in the Philippines prefigured one of Strengell's most celebrated textiles, *Taj Mahal*, a black and gold-flecked lurex and cotton upholstery fabric made in close consultation with the in-house design team at Chatham Manufacturing for the 1959 Lincoln Continental.[32] Strengell continued to work with many companies and manufacturers over the next two decades. She created an all-aluminum rug for Alcoa Industries' "Home of Tomorrow" project in 1956.[33] She also consulted on projects for Forster Textile Mills, Fieldcrest, Darnsworth Yarns, and Karastan Rug Mills in New York, as well as international clients such as Artek and Pori Cotton Mills in Finland and the Chinese textile firm Tai Ping, based in New York.[34] Strengell left her position at Cranbrook in 1961 and relocated with her husband to Hamden, Connecticut, where she continued to design for industrial clients.[35] At the end of the decade, she retired to the modernist enclave of Wellfleet, Massachusetts, on Cape Cod and continued to research and experiment with indigenous fibers, as well as explore personal weaving projects and photography until her death in 1998.[36]
—AMT

Fig. B.129 Eero Saarinen, architect. Executive Office Lobby at the General Motors Technical Center, Warren, Mich., featuring Marianne Strengell's *Rug within a Rug*, 1956. Photographed by Ezra Stoller. © Esto 99Q.050C.

Designs for Knoll
Devil (1947–55); *Cartree* (1947–59); *Buster* (1947–59); *Propellers* (1947–ca. 1950); *Shooting Stars* (1947–52); *Pebble Weave Webbing* (1950); *Puli* (1951–57); *Handwovens*, including *Silvertone* (1947–51).

Selected Awards and Exhibitions
1929 Bronze Medal, Barcelona International Exposition
1932 Silver Medal, Antwerp International Exhibition
1934 *Rags to Riches*, Swedish Nationalmuseum

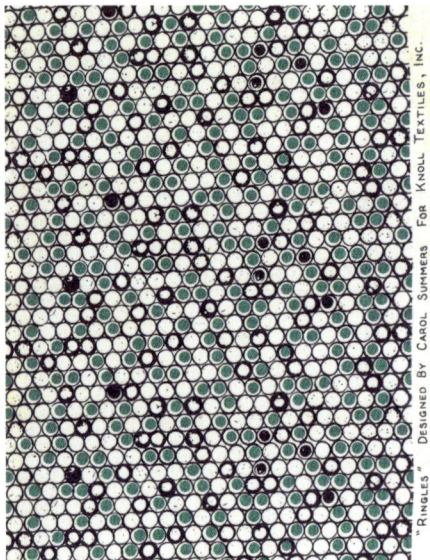

Fig. B.130 Carol Summers. *Ringles* prototype, ca. 1954. Made for Knoll Textiles. Used for drapery; cotton; plain weave, screen-printed. Courtesy Richard and Trudy Schultz. Cat. 64.

1939 New York World's Fair
Golden Gate International Exposition, San Francisco
Contemporary American Industrial Art, The Metropolitan Museum of Art
George Walter Smith Art Gallery, Springfield, Mass.
1941 *Organic Design in Home Furnishings*, MoMA
1945 *Modern Textile Design*, MoMA (circulating exhibition)
International Textile Exhibition, The Women's College, Greensboro N.C.
1946, 1949, 1951 Biennial Exhibition of Contemporary Textiles and Ceramics, Cranbrook (*Shooting Stars* shown, 1951)
1948 *American Textiles '48*, Metropolitan Museum of Art
1949 "House in the Museum Garden," MoMA (*Devil* and other Knoll fabrics shown)
For Modern Living, Detroit Institute of the Arts
1950 Solo exhibition, Cranbrook (*Shooting Stars*, *Propellers*, *Devil*, *Silvertone*, and *Strengell Handwoven* shown)
1951 *Living Up-to-Date*, Baltimore Art Museum (*Devil* and *Buster* shown)
Good Design, MoMA (*Puli* shown)
1961 *Masters of Contemporary Crafts*, Brooklyn Museum
Fabrics International, Museum of Contemporary Crafts and Philadelphia Museum College of Art
1965 AID scholarship and award for "An Exploration of Textile Fibers for Use of as Architectural Components"
1982–83 *Design in America: The Cranbrook Vision*, Detroit Institute of Art (circulating exhibition)
1983 *Design Since 1945*, Philadelphia Museum of Art
1991 *Design 1935–1965: What Modern Was*, Musée des Arts décoratifs de Montréal, Canada
1993 Gold Medal for Distinguished Achievement, American Craft Council

Carol Summers (b. 1925)

Carol Summers was born in Woodstock, New York.[1] He recalls childhood experiments with woodcuts and painting, and these techniques have informed his lifetime of creative output. Summers's father, an artist who worked in painting and etching, supported the family during the lean years of the Depression by making illustrations for medical publications. The family moved frequently throughout the United States during this period.

Summers served in the United States Marine Corps during World War II, and once discharged, he returned to New York to attend Bard College in Annandale-on-Hudson in 1948, where he studied painting with Stefan Hirsh and woodcutting with Louis Schanker.[2] He also took classes in Woodstock offered by the Art Student's League of New York as well as the New York School of Ceramics at Alfred University. In 1951, after attaining a degree in painting and printmaking from Bard, he moved to New York City, where he lived and worked for twenty years.

Summers became acquainted with artists who occasionally designed textile patterns for commercial production, and he decided to try his hand at this to supplement his income. Working through an agent who paid him when a design was purchased, Summers did not know which companies produced his textiles. Asserting that "artists will do anything to feed themselves," Summers recently stated that he considered his textile designs from this period as merely a way of getting by, like the freelance carpentry he also did during this period. His textile designs paid for what he considers his more significant artistic practice.

In 1954 Knoll produced one of his designs, *Ringles*, a name attributed to it either by his agent or by Knoll. *Ringles*, a rhythmic composition in bold colors, exhibits Summers's distinctive style of execution and construction of image.[3] Introduced in 1954, the pattern features small rings and circles of color on a background of a similar tone or on white (fig. B.130, see fig. 3.30). Eszter Haraszty at Knoll selected the colorways—"Daffodil Yellow," "Cornflower Blue," "Geranium Red," and "Aquamarine"—which were hand-printed on cotton.[4]

Summers favors vivid blocks of color and dynamic effects. He employs texture to create painterly abstract compositions. His work has been widely collected and is in many important collections including the Art Institute of Chicago; Bibliothèque National, Paris; Metropolitan Museum of Art; and MoMA, to name just a few.[5] Summers also taught printmaking at Pratt Institute, Hunter College, the School of Visual Arts, and Columbia University, all in New York City as well as Pennsylvania State University and the Art Institute of San Francisco.[6]

Since 1973, Summers has made his home in Santa Cruz, California, but has traveled extensively since that time. He taught art classes and gave instructional tours for artists in India between 1974 and 1979, familiarizing himself with local dyes and printmaking techniques. He is also an avid collector of Indian folk textiles and Mexican folk art. In 1999 his diverse woodcuts were displayed in a fifty-year retrospective exhibition titled *Carol Summers Woodcuts: 50 Year Retrospective* in Woodstock, New York and Santa Cruz. —SAT

Design for Knoll
Ringles (1954).

Selected Awards and Exhibitions
1955 Grant from Italian Government to work in Sienna, Italy
1956 *Textiles USA*, MoMA, (*Ringles* shown)
1959 John Simon Guggenheim Foundation Fellowship
1993–94 Awarded grant for research in India, Council for the International Exchange of Scholars
1999 *Carol Summers Woodcuts: 50 Year Retrospective*, Woodstock Artists' Association, and Museum of Art and History, Santa Cruz

Angelo Testa (1921–1984)

Throughout his career, Angelo Testa helped popularize and commercialize modernist aesthetics in the United States. His mass-produced printed textiles widely influenced textile and interior design, where he made his greatest contribution, although he was also a lifelong painter and sculptor. Testa designed his textiles with sensitivity to the integration of arts and architecture, later writing: "To be fully realized, it must be the synthesis of the combined efforts of architects, engineers, artisans, sculptors, artists, and craftsmen. Only through this collaborative effort can the total integration of all parts result in a Whole Statement."[1]

Testa, whose parents were Italian immigrants, was born in Springfield, Massachusetts. In 1939 he enrolled in a summer course at the New York School of Fine and Applied Arts (now Parsons The New School for Design).[2] The following year, he moved to the University of Chicago to study archaeology but soon transferred again, this time to László Moholy-Nagy's School of Design.[3] By the time Testa graduated in 1945, the school had undergone a name change to the Institute of Design and eventually became part of the Illinois Institute of Technology. These formative years under the guidance of former Bauhaus master and artist Moholy-Nagy, as well as Bauhaus-trained weaver Marli Ehrman and architect Ralph Rapson, established the direction of Testa's career. In Rapson's screen-printing class, Testa produced the pattern *Little Man* (1942), which would become one of his first commercial textile patterns.[4] He continued to produce freelance designs while still a student and even after he established Angelo Testa & Company in 1947.[5] Among these early patterns was *Campagna* (1943), which Testa sold to Knoll Associates for their first textile collection in 1947 (fig. B.131). *Campagna* became one of Knoll's longest-running printed drapery fabrics and remained part of the collection until 1964. Knoll also produced three earlier designs by Testa dating to about 1942, *Filo*, *Animal Forms*, and *Indian Heads* (fig. B.132), but these were in the collection only briefly, around 1947 and 1948. Both *Filo* and *Indian Heads* were later manufactured by other companies.[7]

In about 1943 Testa and others affiliated with the Institute of Design rented a building close to the school as a living and working space. At some later time, Testa invited Hans Knoll to use his office in the complex as a base while in Chicago since Knoll did not yet have a showroom in the city. It was likely during this time that Knoll decided to carry Testa's fabric designs.[8] In filling his early commissions, Testa would perform "all the necessary functions of a small company: he would create a design, sell it to an architect or interior designer, run home to cut the stencil himself, screen-print the fabric, steam it, and then deliver it as well."[9] As his orders increased, Testa hired Ruben Aguilar as his printer. In keeping with his training in Marli Ehrman's weaving workshop, Testa produced handwoven samples for upholstery on his own loom and contracted the production of commercial quantities to Theodore Lowitz. Testa's screen-printed fabrics on cotton or linen were by far more numerous than his handwovens.[10] While he always intended to make his products available to the mass market, Testa mostly designed for contract clients, producing upholstery, sheers, wall hangings and coverings, draperies, and carpets for large institutional facilities such as hotels, schools, and dormitories. He also made clothing fabrics and patterns for paper and plastic manufacturers.[11] In addition to Knoll Associates, Testa's client list included furniture firms such as Herman Miller Furniture Company and Jens Risom; textile

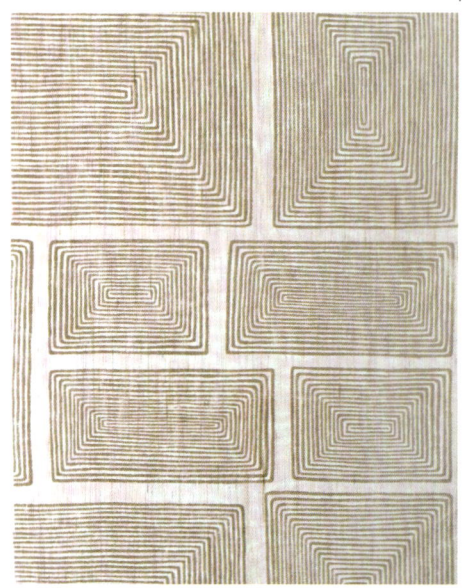

Fig. B.131 Angelo Testa. *Campagna* ("White on White sheer" colorway), this example ca. 1958. Made for Knoll Textiles. Used for drapery; Dacron polyester, linen; plain weave, screen-printed. Richard and Trudy Schultz. Cat. 122.

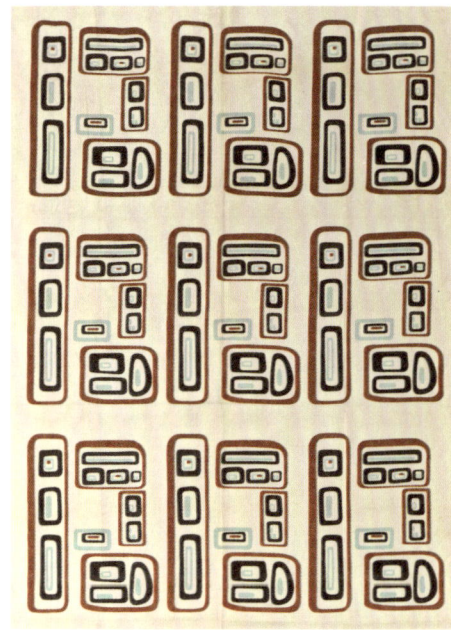

Fig. B.132 Angelo Testa. *Indian Heads* ("Rust, Black, Turquoise on White" colorway), ca. 1948. Made for Knoll Textiles. Used for drapery; cotton; plain weave, screen-printed. Cora Ginsburg LLC.

Fig. B.133 Suzanne Tick, ca. 2009. Photographed by Jeff Barnett-Winsby. Courtesy Suzanne Tick.

Fig. B.134 Suzanne Tick. *Silver Screen* ("Gold" colorway), introduced 1998. Made in Switzerland for KnollTextiles. Used for drapery; polyester, metallic backing; plain gauze (leno) weave. KnollTextiles.

companies Cohn-Hall-Marx, F. Schumacher and Co., and Greeff; and custom work notably for IBM, TWA, Container Corporation of America, Playboy International, and Sunbeam Corporation.[12] Testa designed new textile patterns until 1960, after which he turned his attention increasingly to painting, printmaking, and large-scale sculpture, as well as weaving.[13] Production of his existing designs continued.

Testa received professional accolades from the start. *Little Man* brought him to the attention of Fernand Léger and Sigfried Gideon.[14] MoMA regularly featured his textiles in their *Good Design* exhibitions, and by 1982 Testa's work was in the permanent collections of numerous museums and had been exhibited extensively at museums and colleges.[15] In 1982 the Art Institute of Chicago named him one of eight of "America's Living Treasures." He remained a staunch defender of modernist principles, believing that the "universal truths" revealed in the "catholic relationships to man and to his visual world have even a greater importance today than perhaps any other period in the history of man."[16] He died at his mother's home in Springfield, Massachusetts, in 1984.
—CAL

Designs for Knoll
Campagna (1947–64); *Filo*, *Indian Heads*, and *Animal Forms* (ca. 1947–48).

Selected Awards and Exhibitions
1946 Everyday Art Gallery, Walker Art Center, Minneapolis
First Biennial Exhibition of Contemporary American Fabrics and Ceramics, Cranbrook
Award, Philadelphia Print Club (again in 1947)
1947 Award, AID
1948 *Decorative Arts Today*, Newark Museum, New Jersey
1949 *Contemporary Textiles and Ceramics*, Cranbrook
Angelo Testa, George Walter Vincent Smith Art Museum, Springfield, Massachusetts
1952 *Textilien aus USA*, Smithsonian circulating exhibition
1953–55 *Good Design* Awards for textiles, MoMA
1982 *Selected Textiles Acquisitions since 1978*, Art Institute of Chicago
1983 *Angelo Testa*, College of Architecture, Art and Urban Planning Gallery, University of Illinois, Chicago
Angelo Testa: Forty Years in Art, Temple Buell Architecture Gallery, University of Illinois, Urbana-Champaign
1990 *Designed by the Yard: Twentieth-Century Pattern Repeats*, Art Institute of Chicago
1997 *Rooted in Chicago*, Art Institute of Chicago

Suzanne Tick (b. 1959)

As the creative director at KnollTextiles from 1997 to 2005, Suzanne Tick transformed the division's design and development processes, created an extensive array of textile designs, instituted the "Integrated Interior" program, and shepherded the innovative *Imago* line to success. At a time when KnollTextiles was lacking leadership, Tick reinvigorated the company with a unique combination of business savvy and commitment to quality and innovation.

Born in Bloomington, Illinois, Tick enrolled at the University of Iowa to study printmaking, but after taking a weaving class, she switched disciplines (fig. B.133).[1] She graduated in 1981 with a BFA and relocated to New York to attend the Fashion Institute of Technology (FIT) where she received an associates degree in textiles in 1982. Tick was hired as a staff designer at Boris Kroll and was soon promoted to design director, a position she retained until her departure in 1986. Over the next six years, she served as design director at Brickel Associates (1986–89) and Unika Vaev (1989–93). In 1993 Tick founded her own consultancy and design firm, Suzanne Tick, Inc., and in 1996 she opened the carpet design firm Tuva Looms with her partner Terry Mowers.[2]

Tick built upon her connections with textile mills and jobbers to fuel her start-up consultancy company. In 1995, during this transitional period, she designed a small collection, aptly named *A New Day*, that embodied her aspirations for the future. The collection was purchased by Knoll, initiating a ten-year relationship with the firm (see fig. 6.35).[3] Released during the tenure of design director Deborah Steele, the collection initially comprised six upholstery fabrics suited to the KnollTextiles collection. Designs for panel fabrics followed. In 1996 Tick created the vertical fabric *Resolution* for Knoll, a benchmark design using a groundbreaking manufacturing process that eliminated waste and resulted in 100-percent solution-dyed polyester in myriad colors (see cat. 264).[4] Tick developed these innovative yarns with the spinning mill.

She also sourced the manufacturers and oversaw the production of *Resolution* and its coordinated panel fabric *Clarity*.[5] *Resolution* was an overwhelming success, selling over a million yards in its first year.

Although her appointment as KnollTextiles's creative director was not formally announced until February 1997, Tick started to assume directorial responsibilities in 1996.[6] Unlike her predecessors (and her successor), she took the position as a consultant, continuing to run her own company and to manage other clients, such as the residential textile firm Groundworks, a division of Lee Jofa. As creative director, Tick instituted a new design management platform that helped streamline the KnollTextiles production processes. In the spring of 1998 she introduced the "Integrated Interior," a quarterly release of related panel fabrics, wallcoverings, draperies, and upholsteries. This was not only the first time that Knoll coordinated the entire range of textile products into an integrated scheme, but it also represented the return of drapery fabrics to the collection for the first time since 1991.

Tick contributed numerous designs to the KnollTextiles collection, as well as such innovations as the four-way stretch fabric, *Una*, the drapery *Silver Screen*, and the *Imago* line of resin-encapsulated textiles. She viewed *Una* as a "change agent," replacing a stagnant product in the collection.[7] Tick sourced the knitted material from an Italian fashion mill, adjusted the fabric content to a blend of elastin, polyurethane, polymid, and polyester for more durability and less luster, and introduced it in 1999.[8] She demonstrated her innovative and functional approach with the polyester and aluminum, printed *Silver Screen* drapery, which deflects heat and sunlight from the interior (fig. B.134). The resin panel *Imago* (see chapter 6) was initially offered in seven designs, including three textiles created expressly for the product: *View*, a fishnet grid; *Chimera*, an open gauze weave; and *Progeny*, a grass cloth.[9] The *Imago* design titled *Lucere* was made with *Silver Screen* embedded in the resin base with embossing of the fabric pattern on the surface of the resin panel, creating a moiré effect. The new *Imago* line immediately garnered accolades and sold well when it was introduced in 2000; it remains in the collection with regular additions.

Tick's textiles designs have often been informed by her studio work. In 1998 her handwoven fiber piece, made of spun stainless-steel yarns was included in *Surface and Structure: Contemporary Japanese Textiles* at MoMA. The stainless-steel fiber—a Japanese material used to line tires—was made by Bridgestone Metalpha and fueled the development of a new technical tape for KnollTextiles.[10] Tick sought to replicate the look of the steel fibers for a more interesting and beautiful panel fabric but was unable to use the stainless-steel yarns for production textiles. The concept, however, was readily translated into Olefin (polypropylene) extrusion tape that was pliable enough for weaving but retaining the look of metal. Tick employed this tape in multiuse textiles—*Heavy Metal* (2001), *Foil Rap* (2001), and *Hard Rock* (2006)—which were colored with metallic flakes resulting in a glimmering surface (fig. B.136, see fig. 6.38).

As creative director, Tick worked with outside designers Stephen Sprouse (2003) and 2x4, Inc. (2004), and staff designers such as Kathrin Hagge and Sarah Baker.[11] Though Tick resigned as KnollTextile's creative director in late 2004, she continues to work for the company as a freelance designer and consultant. Coordinating with Dorothy Cosonas, her successor as creative director, today Tick mostly designs vertical fabrics for the collection, such as *Macro*, *Mezzo*, and *Micro*—coordinated, recycled polyester panel fabrics featuring the same weave in three different scales (fig. B.135). Recent introductions have included the recycled polyester vertical fabric *Bandwidth* (2008) and the drapery it inspired, *Air Rights* (2009), among others (see figs. 6.41, 6.42). The 2009 upholstery introduction *Earthwork* exemplifies the interplay between Tick's art practice and her commercial designs. To create *Earthwork*, Tick scanned a piece of her fiber art, *Refuse DC*—a weaving created out of the packaging materials used by drycleaners—to generate an organically gridded pattern.[12] In addition to this recent project, Tick, working with industrial designer Harry Allan, experimented in 2007 with weaving monofilament and fiber optics to create delicate, ethereal lamps.[13]

Since 2005, Suzanne Tick, Inc. has remained active, taking on other corporate clients. In addition, Tick serves as the design director, alongside her partner Mowers, creative director of Tandus, a carpet company based in Georgia. She has also contributed award-winning designs to the architectural glass manufacturer, Skyline Design since 2008. —AMT

Fig. B.135 Suzanne Tick. *Macro* ("Sheet Metal" colorway), *Mezzo* ("Oxide" colorway), *Micro* ("Silver" colorway), introduced 2005. Made in the United States for KnollTextiles. Used for panels; recycled polyester; plain-weave–derived simple weave. KnollTextiles Archive. Cat. 267–69.

Fig. B.136 Suzanne Tick. *Hard Rock* ("Patina," "Ochre," and "Tiger Eye" colorways), introduced 2006. Made in the United States for KnollTextiles. Used for panel; recycled polyester, Olefin; plain weave with paired wefts. KnollTextiles Archive. Cat. 271.

Designs for Knoll

A New Day Collection: Flower Toss (1995–2004), *Insight* (1995–2003), *Jitters* (1996–2006), *Square One* (1995–2003), *Starryeyed* (1995–2003), *The Light Dawns* (1995–2004). *Bardo* (1996–2008); *Chain Reaction* (1996–2004); *Heatwave* (1996–2006); *Satin Sketch* (1996–1999); *Resolution* (intro. 1996); *Clarity* (intro. 1996). *Utopia Collection* (with Louise Russell): *Shangri-La* (1996–2007), *Atlantis* (1996–2007), *Avalon* (1996–2007), *Narnia* (1996–2010), *Chiron* (1997–2005), *Delphi* (1997–2006). *Parallax* (1997–2004); *Sabian* (1997–2006). *Horizontal* (1997–2008); *Spin* (1997–2006); *Weave Three* (intro. 1997). *Breeze* (1998–2005); *Chimes* (1998–2004); *Domino* (1998–2005); *Gaze* (1998–2007); *Harmony* (intro. 1998); *Palmetto* (1998–2002); *Sennit* (1998–2009); *Silver Screen* (intro. 1998); *Striae Epinglé* (1998–2009); *Synthesis* (1998–2005); *Veil* (intro. 1998). *Balance* (1999–2005); *Bamboo* (1999–2004); *Brava* (1999–2006); *Charade* (1999–2010); *En Route* (1999–2006); *Fishnet* (1999–2008); *Forum* (1999–2006); *Method* (1999–2006); *Progression* (1999–2003); *Streetwalk* (1999–2005); *Technical Stripe* (1999–2004); *Transport* (1999–2010); *Una* (intro. 1999); *Versatility* (intro. 1999). *Allegory* (intro. 2000); *Dialogue* (2000–2005); *Equinox* (2000–2004); *Kybos* (2000–2008); *Odeon* (2000–2009); *Progression Striae* (2000–11); *Rattan* (intro. 2000); *Sequel* (intro. 2000); *Transit* (2000–2009); *Transparency* (2000–2005); *Tsunami* (2000–2009). *Basket Draft* (intro. 2001); *Elan* (2000–2008); *Foil Rap* (intro. 2001); *Gem* (2001–10); *Giza* (2001–10); *Heavy Metal* (intro. 2001); *Luxe* (2001–8) *Lyonese Velvet* (intro. 2001); *Metallic Mesh* (intro. 2001); *Pindot Zap* (2001–3); *Zap* (2001–6); *Slicker Zap* (2001–8); *Tweed Frieze* (intro. 2001); *Zap* (2001–10). *Analogy* (2002–8); *Box Garden* (intro. 2002); *Dristi* (intro. 2002); *Forza* (intro. 2002); *Horizon Line* (2002–9); *Metaphor* (2002–8); *Waters Edge* (intro. 2002). *Altered Lines* (2003–10); *Ikat Blocks* (2003–10). *Andante* (2003–9); *Autobahn* (2003–10); *Beveled Square* (2003–5); *Diamond Plate* (2003–8); *Extreme Velvet* (2003–9); *Groove Line* (intro. 2003); *Growth Spurt* (intro. 2003); *In the Loop* (intro. 2003); *Orchestra* (2003–06); *Roots and Rhythms* (2003–9); *Satin Chisel* (intro. 2003); *Symbolic Details* (intro. 2003). *Pixelated* (2004–10); *Bifold CR* (intro. 2004); *Broadcloth* (intro. 2004); *Cadena* (2004–7); *Close Knit* (intro. 2004); *Fine Print* (2004–5); *Flanders* (2004–8); *Wide Angle* (intro. 2004). *Adaption* (2005–6); *Alexandria* (2005–10); *Aperture* (2005–7); *Argos* (2005–10); *Astria* (intro. 2005); *Bollywood* (intro. 2005); *Double Feature* (2005–11); *Ithaca* (2005–10); *Macro* (intro. 2005); *Mezzo* (intro. 2005); *Micro* (intro. 2005); *Second Shift* (intro. 2005); *Troy* (2005–08). *Echo* (intro. 2006); *Hard Rock* (intro. 2006); *Leda* (intro. 2006); *Notion* (intro. 2006); *Palladium* (intro. 2006); *Scene Change* (2006–09); *Skye* (2006–09); *Soundtrack* (intro. 2006); *Subtitle* (intro. 2006). *Aperture Emboss* (intro. 2007); *Divided Light* (intro. 2007); *Enmesh* (intro. 2007); *Glam* (intro. 2007); *Glaze* (intro. 2007); *Glisten* (intro. 2007); *Interknit* (intro. 2007); *Modular* (intro. 2007); *Perception* (intro. 2007); *Periphery* (intro. 2007); *Triple Lace* (2007–10); *Wiretap* (intro. 2007). *Amplify* (intro. 2008); *Bandwidth* (intro. 2008); *Domus* (intro. 2008); *Escala* (intro. 2008); *Etching* (intro. 2008); *Illume* (intro. 2008); *Lintel* (intro. 2008); *Mantilla* (intro. 2008); *Louver 2007* (intro. 2008); *Air Rights* (intro. 2009); *Biota* (intro. 2009); *Candela* (intro. 2009); *Cosma* (intro. 2009); *Earthwork* (intro. 2009); *Gem II* (intro. 2009); *Gravity* (intro. 2009); *Nematic* (intro. 2009); *Photon* (intro. 2009); *Transport II* (intro. 2009); *Triose* (intro. 2009). *Prague* (intro. 2010); *Petra* (intro. 2010); *Logic* (intro. 2010); *Guild* (intro. 2010).

Selected Awards and Exhibitions
1998 *Structure and Surface*, MoMA
1998, 1999, 2000, 2001, 2003 *Good Design* Award, Chicago Athenaeum

1999, 2000 *Interior Design Magazine*, Design Distinction Award
1999, 2000, 2002, 2004, 2005, 2006 Best of NeoCon Gold Award
2001 *US Design 1975–2000*, Denver Art Museum (circulating exhibition, *Imago* shown)
2003 Cooper Hewitt National Design Awards, Finalist, Product Design
2006 ASID Design Distinction Award
Women in Design Award, VNU Business Media
Design Life Now National Design Triennial, Cooper-Hewitt, National Design Museum Smithsonian Institution (*Adaptation* and *Aperture* wallcovering shown)

Inge Toft (1929–1996)

In 1954 Knoll introduced *Kon-Tiki*, a printed drapery fabric by the Danish designer Inge Toft. Born in Copenhagen, Toft first encountered textiles as a discipline in Helga Foght's eponymous screen-printing workshop in Copenhagen. Toft also took window decoration classes at the cooperative workshop *Den Permenente* (1948–50) and oversaw the print studio at *Havemanns Magasin*, a department store in Copenhagen (1952–52). Beginning in 1954 she served as manager of the Foght print workshop.[1]

Along with other small-scale workshops, Foght's studio helped shape the Danish textile industry during the 1940s and 1950s.[2] Foght had been a pupil of the influential designer and teacher Marie Gudme Leth (1895–1997) who, alongside architect Arne Jacobsen (1902–1971) and designer Ruth Hull (1912–1996), transformed the aesthetics of printed textiles in Denmark after World War II.[3] These designers often produced hand-printed textiles in small print workshops and acted as consultants to industry. By 1950 the new bridge between industry and individual workshops had effectively shifted the aesthetic idiom of Danish textiles from naturalistic and dense floral patterns to linear abstraction and rhythmic repeats.[4] Exemplary of this relationship and dominant in this new idiom were Toft's printed designs.

Throughout her design career, Toft produced textiles under the commercial name Ingetoft. Her designs were often extremely restrained and employed subtle color schemes.[5] Despite her austere use of linear pattern and ornament, she frequently gave her textiles exotic names such as *Congo* or *Lahos*.[6] Many were commercially produced by the progressive textile printer firm L. F. Foght (possibly owned by Helga's uncle). The firm had been producing and exporting the designs of Jacobsen, Helga Foght, and Axel Salto (1889–1961), among others since the late 1940s.[7] One such design was *Kon-Tiki* by Toft (fig. B.137, see fig. 3.44).

First sold in 1953, *Kon-Tiki* was available in green, gray, and black on a white ground.[8] Possibly at the suggestion of Astrid Sampe, the head of Nordiska Kompaniet Textilkammare NK, who had a close relationship with Knoll as both a supplier and designer, Knoll acquired and introduced *Kon-Tiki* in 1954. Sampe had included a selection of Helga Foght's textiles in NK's textile offerings since the mid-1940s.[9] Eszter Haraszty, head of Knoll Textiles and the firm's chief color stylist, restyled the print in colors more typical of the Knoll collection at the time such as "Turquoise" and "Tomato."[10] Although it is unclear what manufacturer produced the print for Knoll in the United States, Knoll enlisted the German company Taunus Textildruck to print *Kon-Tiki* for local distribution in Germany and possibly for other Knoll European divisions and licensees.[11] *Kon-Tiki* remained a part of the Knoll collection until 1957.

Toft soon broadened her practice. She is credited with designing furniture for L. F. Foght in 1957, and she contributed wallpaper designs to the Dahls Kunstner Tapet collection alongside noted designers such as Hull and Rolf Middleboe (1917–1995).[12] As Toft expanded her oeuvre and became well known, she increasingly exhibited through the Landsforeningen Dansk Kunsthaandværk (Danish Society of Applied Arts) in Denmark and abroad.

Toft and Helga Foght became business partners in 1967, and Toft assumed ownership of the workshop after Foght's death in 1974. In addition to textile design, Toft accepted graphic design commissions. Clients included the National Institute for Life, Elizabeth Arden, and the L. F. Foght Memorial Fund.[13] Beginning in the 1970s, she shifted her creative energies to the production of liturgical textiles, designing church vestments and altar hangings for an extensive list of churches throughout Denmark until her death in 1996.[14]
—AMT

Design for Knoll
Kon-Tiki (1954–57).

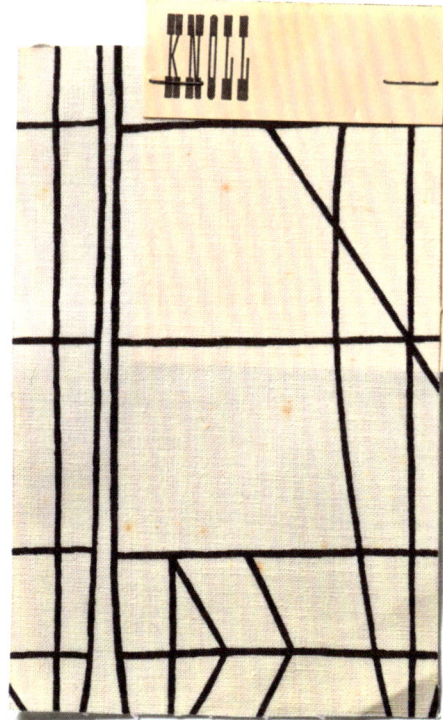

Fig. B.137 Inge Toft. *Kon-Tiki* swatch ("Black on White" colorway), ca. 1954. Made for Knoll Textiles. Used for drapery; cotton; plain weave, screen-printed. Private collection.

Fig. B.138 2x4, Inc. *Plus* ("Red" colorway), and *Pause* ("Orange" colorway), both 2004. Made in the United States for KnollTextiles. *Plus*: used for upholstery; cotton, polyester. *Pause*: used for wallcovering; vinyl. KnollTextiles Archive.

Selected Awards and Exhibitions
1957 Gold Medal, Milan Triennale
1957, 1977 Solo exhibition, *Den Permanente*, Copenhagen
1960 *The Arts of Denmark*, Metropolitan Museum of Art
1970 Solo exhibition, Helligåndshuset, Copenhagen
1974–81 Appointed member of the board of executives, *Den Permanente*, Copenhagen
1976 Solo exhibition, Olivia Holm Møller-museet, Holstebro

2x4, Inc. (established 1994)
Michael Rock (b. 1959)
Susan Sellers (b. 1967)
Georgianna Stout (b. 1967)

The design studio 2x4, Inc., a collaborative team of art directors, writers, graphic designers, architects, and programmers, produces a broad range of work—from print, web, and video graphics to signage and environmental design. Their clients are drawn primarily from the art, design, architecture, and cultural sectors.[1] The studio's creative process typically begins with a research phase marked by prolific production of design solutions, followed by an intensive period of editing and refining the design.

Michael Rock received a BA in humanities from Union College in New Jersey and an MFA from the Rhode Island School of Design.[2] He leads the studio's projects for such clients as Prada and Condé Nast in association with AMO/Rem Koolhaas and served as principal-in-charge of the Illinois Institute of Technology McCormick Tribune Campus Center and Vitra Branding/New York Headquarters. He writes for several design magazines, including *I.D.*, *Print*, *AIGA Journal*, and *Eye*, and was named professor of design at Yale University School of Art in 1991 and visiting artist at the Jan Van Eyck Akademie in Maastricht from 1993 to 2001. He currently heads the Graphic Architecture Project at Columbia University Graduate School of Architecture, Planning, and Preservation. Awards include the Rome Prize in Design (1999/2000) from the American Academy in Rome.

Susan Sellers holds a BA from the Rhode Island School of Design and an MA in American studies from Yale University. Her work at 2x4 includes graphic identities for the Isabella Stewart Gardner Museum and the Museo Picasso Málaga, as well as brand strategy and packaging for Kiddo, a toymaker, and environmental and Web site design for the Guggenheim Museum in collaboration with YouTube. She has worked in several design studios, including Total Design and UNA in Amsterdam, and was appointed senior critic at Yale University School of Art in 1998. She is also a contributor to *Eye*, *Design Issues*, and *Visible Language*.

Georgianna Stout received a BA from the Rhode Island School of Design, where she has also served as a visiting design critic. Her work at 2x4 varies from large-scale identity and environmental graphics (Nasher Sculpture Center, Dia:Beacon, and Brooklyn Museum), to retail interiors, graphics and packaging (Vitra New York, Malin+Goetz), as well as textiles and wallcoverings for KnollTextiles. In addition she collaborates with her husband, David Weeks, in his lighting, furniture, and product design studio.

Beginning in 1997 2x4 contributed branding and printwork for Knoll furniture product catalogues as well as print and multimedia installations for Knoll's NeoCon installations. Inspired by 2x4's wallcoverings for the New York Prada Store, Knoll asked the firm to design a collection for KnollTextiles in 2003.[3] Initially 2x4 culled inspiration from such diverse sources such as the ASCII code—a character encoding scheme for computers—resulting in the prototype *ASCII Love* featuring a motif of "cabbage roses" and tangles of electronic wires for *Snarl*.[4] Working closely with KnollTextiles's creative director Suzanne Tick, 2x4 further developed a vocabulary of simple graphic elements that investigate physical space in the *Field Theory Collection* and virtual space in the *Chatter Collection*.[5] *Field Theory* comprises two upholstery patterns, *Urban* and *Suburban*, as well as the vinyl wallcovering *Exurban*, which each reproduce at varying scales a repeated motif that resembles a building abstracted axonometrically.[6] *Chatter* explores the idea of linguistic and virtual space in three patterns. The upholstery pattern *Plus* extends an infinite field of "+" signs in alternating colors (fig. B.138). The collection includes two cotton and vinyl wallcoverings. *Command* is an imagined conversation in which vertical bars and exclamation points replace words. *Pause* is a play on supersized punctuation marks, the period and the comma (fig. 6.40).
—CAL

Designs for Knoll
Field Theory Collection: Urban (2004–7), *Suburban* (2004–10), *Exurban* (2004–9). *Chatter Collection: Command* (2004–9), *Pause* (intro. 2004), *Plus* (intro. 2004).

Selected Awards and Exhibitions
2005 *Design Series 3: 2x4*, San Francisco Museum of Modern Art
2006 National Design Award for Communication Design, Cooper-Hewitt National Design Museum
2008 *Just In: Recent Acquisitions from the Collection*, Museum of Modern Art, New York
2009 *It is What It Is* Eye of Gyre Gallery, Tokyo, Japan

Nob + Non
Nob Utsumi (b. 1945)
Non Utsumi (b. 1944)

Although Knoll's reputation for producing well-crafted woven upholstery fabrics for the contract market had been long established, in the late 1970s the company hoped to expand its selection of products for residential interiors. Many market competitors had issued lines of printed textiles for this sector, and Knoll Textiles sought a greater share of the market.[1] The introduction of *Collection 1* by Nob and Non Utsumi would signal this new focus on the residential market for Knoll Textiles in the United States.

Prior to working for Knoll, Nob and Non Utsumi, a married design duo, were independent fashion textile designers in Japan. While living in Kyoto, Nob worked for Ukon Textile Studio, where he created the Hanae Mori butterfly print that was introduced in the United States in 1967. Shortly after, he moved to New York City to work for Leslie Tillett but returned to Japan after only a year to open his own textile design studio. In 1969, he met Non, who was hand-dying couture-quality silks for Sakon Giken K.K. in Kyoto, and they began their design partnership. From 1970 to 1975 they worked in New York for Belle Fabrics and Leslie Tillett, after which they began to design independently under the "Nob + Non" moniker.[2] Their shift to freelance work coincided with a new focus on textile designs for home furnishings, and interior design in general.[3] Jeffrey Osborne, vice president of design and marketing of Knoll Textiles, coordinated the initial development of Nob + Non's screen-printed patterns for Knoll production.[4] It is difficult to isolate the work and creative input each designer contributed to the project, as they were deliberately vague about their design process in interviews. Kristl Reinhardt (Andrus), design assistant and stylist at Knoll Textiles during the 1970s and 1980s, has remarked that "Non was the business side of the couple.... she was extremely pointed, knew what she wanted to do, and also had a head for numbers and money."[5]

In 1979 *Collection 1* was released and exhibited at the NeoCon trade fair in Chicago.[6] The seven designs in the collection—*Direction*, *Small Space*, *Small World*, *Large World*, *In the World*, *Vision*, and *Pro*—were rotary printed on two different fabric weights, a sheer cotton batiste and a heavier cotton percale, and were issued in multiple colorways plus "White on White" and "White on Natural" (figs. B.139, B.140, and see figs. 6.3, 6.4).[7] In Europe, the collection included two additional drapery designs, *Lights* and *Shades*.[8]

Nob + Non's minimal, softly colored designs for *Collection 1* consisted of lines arranged into various grid and diagonal patterns and emphasized a dynamic, ascending movement of motifs to express "the upward direction of an advanced contemporary lifestyle . . . an explosion of geometric design ever growing, ever expanding and looking ahead."[9] To humanize and soften the industrially printed designs, the designers hand-drew the motifs, assuring variation in the linework throughout the range of patterns.[10] While the bright primary hues of *Direction*'s slash motifs created an air of light-heartedness, the coloring of other patterns, such as *Vision* and *Pro*, was much more subtle, using a single tone and exploring texture and light through contrasts created between the matte surface of the ground fabric and the shiny dye of the print. Nob + Non planned for consumers to embrace the versatility of the designs and to layer different patterns and fabric weights building texture.[11]

Designing *Collection 1* "with the Total in mind," Nob + Non's overall design philosophy conceived "life as a total concept [wherein] the things you live with, the things you eat, and the things you wear, all show your concept of life."[12] While it is easy to assess Nob + Non's aesthetic as stereotypically "Japanese minimalist" or "modern," their view was much more jovial and open to the element of discovery. As evident in the patterns for *Collection 1*, especially *Direction*, they have used clean, bare backgrounds to provide the framework for spontaneity and

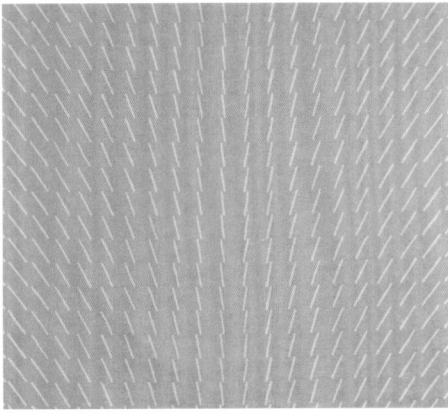

Fig. B.139 Nob + Non (Nob and Non Utsumi). *Vision* ("White on White" colorway), 1979. Made by New London Print Works for Knoll Textiles. Used for drapery; cotton; plain weave, screen-printed. The Metropolitan Museum of Art, New York, Gift of Knoll Textiles, 1986, 1986.41.1. Cat. 224.

Fig. B.140 Nob + Non (Nob and Non Utsumi). *Pro* ("White on Natural" colorway), 1979. Made by New London Print Works for Knoll Textiles. Used for drapery; cotton; plain weave, screen-printed. The Metropolitan Museum of Art, New York, Gift of Knoll Textiles, 1984, 1984.547.7. Cat. 223.

Fig. B.141 Tim Van Campen. *American Mosaic Collection*, 1993. Made in the United States for KnollTextiles. Used for upholstery. KnollTextile Archives.

play. Their lifestyle also reflected this "concept of life": they dressed in matching white clothes punctuated with bursts of neon color, and their minimalist apartment in New York had a neutral palette, but a collection of found objects and household items provided accents of bright colors.[13] Sarah Booth Conroy, who interviewed the couple in their apartment in 1980 for an article in the *Washington Post*, described Non performing behind panels of their Knoll textiles, creating movement of light and shadow across the fabric in a celebration of their work, of performance, and of play.[14]

Although a creative success, *Collection 1* was Nob + Non's only line for Knoll Textiles, as the collection did not sell well in the American market despite its commercial success in Europe.[15] In 1979 Nob + Non were engaged in developing a residential furniture system for Knoll, but plans did not progress past a preliminary stage.[16] After their work with Knoll Textiles, Nob + Non continued to experiment with texture, light, and harmony in shaping interior spaces. In 1983 V'Soske produced a collection of their minimal and sculptural rugs, and in 1988 Nob + Non designed white ceramic wall tiles, for the Japanese company Toto, hand-painted with a light brushstroke of color, strongly referencing their design for *Direction*.[17] They have also been contracted to design furniture and domestic, commercial, and airline interiors, and have served as color consultants.[18] —ES

Designs for Knoll
Collection 1, (1979–84): *Direction, Small Space, Small World, Large World, Vision, In the World, Pro*; Europe only (1979–after 1984): *Lights, Shades*.

Award
1980 Award for *Collection 1*, Design Center Stuttgart

Tim Van Campen (b. 1947)

Although the *American Mosaic Collection* (1993) displays visual continuity with traditional American craft and textile production, its creator, Tim Van Campen, designed the patterns via technology that was anything but conventional at the time. Using Adobe Photoshop and Pixel Paint Professional on his Macintosh II computer, Van Campen enlarged color images to the point of pixilation. He then adjusted the images' color, scale, and arrangement of forms, resulting in abstracted, geometric designs for application to textiles.[1]

Van Campen trained as a painter and printmaker, studying at the Pennsylvania Academy of Fine Arts in Philadelphia, the Skowhegan School of Painting and Sculpture in Maine, and the Provincetown Workshop in Massachusetts. He largely abandoned painting for textile design, however, when Michaelin & Kohlberg Inc. began producing hand-stitched wool needlepoint carpets using his computer-generated patterns in 1992.[2] Although Van Campen's design methods are decidedly technocratic, the coloring, themes, and textures in his work were inspired by "nature, the beauty and ever-changing weather of Maine," as well as the diversity of America's cultural heritage.[3]

Van Campen approached KnollTextiles about collaborating on a line of textiles and subsequently developed the *American Mosaic Collection* with the assistance of Suzin Steerman, then senior designer at KnollTextiles, and Michael Laessle, director of marketing (fig. B.141).[4] After viewing preliminary computer drawings at Knoll's New York office, Steerman visited Van Campen in Maine and selected a set of patterns, fine-tuning and rescaling some of the repeats. The patterns were then colored in a scheme based on the rich, nature-inspired tones typical of Van Campen's designs.[5]

The *American Mosaic Collection* debuted at NeoCon '93 in Chicago and was awarded a NeoCon Gold Award.[6] Van Campen's designs, which juxtaposed abstracted figural forms and geometric shapes to create a "mosaic" of highly symmetrical, but visually complex patterns, were manufactured on Jacquard looms in Guilford, Maine. While primarily intended for the contract market, the collection's upholstery designs were also used in home interiors.[7]

This was Van Campen's only collaboration with KnollTextiles. However, Van Campen continues to produce designs based on computer imaging in a diverse array of materials and techniques, including textiles, rugs, decorative paintings and prints, and ceramics. His work has been produced by Michealin & Kohlberg, and he has received contracts for textile and rug design work with HBF, Revman, West-Point, Collins & Aikman, and Durkan.[8] —ES

Designs for Knoll
American Mosaic Collection (1993–99): *Cascade, Iroquois, Susquehanna, Olympic, Mystic, Acadia*.

Selected Awards and Exhibitions
1991 Interior Design Roscoe Award for "Best Contemporary Rug"
Milliken Design Award, Chicago
1993 Best of NeoCon Gold Award for the *American Mosaic Collection*
1994 First Place, ASID Interior Design Product Award
2009 Icon Gallery, Brunswick, Me.
2010 Cadbeck Gallery, Rockland, Md.

Robert Venturi (b. 1925)
Denise Scott Brown (b. 1931)

After their purchase of Knoll in 1977, Stephen Swid and Marshall Cogan aimed to reposition the company on the cutting edge of design. They hired leading architects and designers to create furniture designs for Knoll, among them Robert Venturi and Denise Scott Brown, who contributed a collection in 1983.[1] Venturi had studied architecture at Princeton University and worked in the offices of Eero Saarinen (1951–53) and Louis Kahn (1954, 1956–57) before forming his own architectural firm, Venturi and Rauch, with John Rauch in 1964. As winner of the Rome Prize, he spent two years at the American Academy in Rome (1954–56). Scott Brown was a student at the Architectural Association in London (1952–55) and earned a master's degree in city planning and architecture from the University of Pennsylvania (1960). She worked in the London firms of Ernö Goldfinger and Dennis Clarke-Hall and in Rome with Giuseppe Vaccaro. In 1969 she became a partner at Venturi and Rauch. Venturi and Scott Brown met in 1960 while both were faculty members at the University of Pennsylvania.[2]

In 1980 the firm Venturi and Rauch was officially changed to Venturi, Rauch, and Scott Brown, and the office remained based out of Philadelphia. Through their projects and writings on architecture and urban design, Venturi and Scott Brown profoundly influenced American architecture and urbanism at the end of the twentieth century.[3] Employing aesthetic qualities and theoretical models that have become synonymous with the postmodernist idiom, the architects inject a sense of historicism, pluralism, humor, and the vernacular into their architecture and industrial design projects.

In 1978 Venturi approached Knoll about creating a line of furniture that adapted "a series of historical styles involving wit, variety, and industrial process" to spur "an evolutionary change in [the design of] Modern furniture."[4] The resulting *Venturi Collection* (1984) consisted of two designs for textile patterns (*Grandmother* and *Tapestry*), nine molded-plywood-and-plastic-laminate chairs named after historical styles (*Queen Anne*, *Chippendale*, *Sheraton*, *Hepplewhite*, *Empire*, *Biedermeier*, *Gothic Revival*, *Art Nouveau*, and *Art Deco*), a sofa, coffee table, and two high tables, one with cabriole legs, the other with urn-shaped supports.[5] While the collection bears Venturi's name—and in the past has been attributed solely to him—Scott Brown and several other members of their firm made important contributions to the development of the Knoll line.[6]

The pattern for *Grandmother* was derived from a tablecloth that had once belonged to the grandmother of Frederic Swartz, an associate in the firm. Both this pattern and *Tapestry*, however, have conceptual ties to Venturi, Rauch, and Scott Brown's 1977 façade for the Best Products Showroom in Langhorne, Pennsylvania, which was covered in a floral pattern derived from a commercial wallpaper design, enlarged to a massive scale.[7] *Grandmother* combines two patterns: a figural, pastel floral ground based on the grandmother's tablecloth and a scheme of black dashes adapted from the inside of a business envelope (see fig. 6.11). *Grandmother* was intended to be a design "that was explicitly pretty in its soft, curvy configurations and sweet combinations of colors, and represented . . . something with nice associations, those of flowers," as well as having a dynamic sense of contrast, scale, and rhythm.[8] For *Tapestry*, they again superimposed geometric forms on a floral ground, but using squares instead of dashes and a darker, much more saturated color scheme (fig. B.142). When used on the round contours of the *Venturi Collection*'s sofa and viewed from a distance, the upholstery creates the illusion of being a tufted sofa.

The patterns were completed in 1983, and Venturi copyrighted the designs and licensed them to Knoll that same year.[9] The *Grandmother* pattern was transferred onto plastic-laminate for the Knoll *Queen Anne* chair (see cat. 232), and Knoll Textiles restricted distribution of both *Grandmother* and *Tapestry* to the Venturi furniture.[10] *Grandmother* was printed onto plain-weave cotton, and *Tapestry* was produced on a Jacquard loom at Textielfabriek in Belgium.[11]

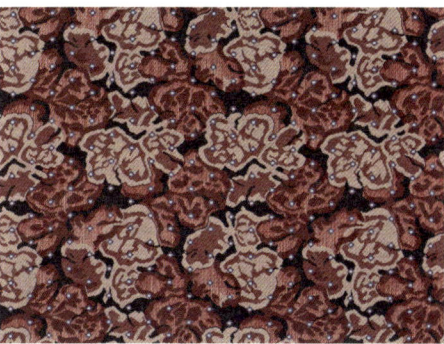

Fig. B.142 Robert Venturi. *Tapestry*, 1983. Made for Knoll Textiles. Used for upholstery; cotton, synthetic fibers. The Metropolitan Museum of Art, New York, Gift of Knoll International, Inc., 1987, 1987.383.

Venturi later licensed the *Grandmother* surface design to Swid Powell and Fieldcrest Cannon, both subsidiaries of General Felt Industries, for application to tableware and bedding.[12]

Although the *Venturi Collection* received acclaim, it was never a financial success and was discontinued in 1990.[13] In addition to the design collection for Knoll, Venturi also supervised the creation of Knoll's new showroom at 655 Madison Avenue in 1980. Venturi and Scott Brown later collaborated on the interior design of the Hotel Mielmonte Nikko Kirifuri in Nikko, Japan (1992–97), a project in which Knoll International Japan manufactured custom furnishings and modified standard products, and DesignTex printed Venturi and Scott Brown's made-to-order fabric designs.[14] —ES

Designs for Knoll
Venturi Collection (1984–1990): *Grandmother*, *Tapestry*.

Selected Awards and Exhibitions
1980 Award, Best in Retail/Showroom Design, *Interiors Magazine* Annual Awards Program, for Knoll Showroom
2001 *US Design, 1975–2000*, Denver Art Museum (circulating exhibition, *Tapestry* shown)
2002 *Out of the Ordinary: Robert Venturi, Denise Scott Brown and Associates: Architecture, Urbanism, Design*, Carnegie Museum of Art, Pittsburgh, Penn. (circulating exhibition)
2008 *The Architect's Table: Swid Powell and Postmodern Design*, Yale University Art Gallery

Paule Vézelay (1892–1984)

Born Marjorie Watson-Williams, Paule Vézelay made her mark as one of the first British artists to fully embrace abstraction and also as a progressive textile designer in the postwar period. Her pioneering geometric compositions slowly developed in the 1920s and 1930s, and by the end of World War II, both her personal artwork and her commercial designs evinced a mature abstract visual language. In 1912 she moved from Bristol to London where she briefly attended the Slade School and then the London School of Art, which closed at the outbreak of World War I.[1]

Vézelay abandoned painting and sculpture in favor of the graphic arts and received professional acclaim as a printmaker and illustrator. She returned to painting in the early 1920s after a visit to Paris. This decade was a period of rapid artistic growth for the budding British artist. In 1926 she immigrated to Paris to join the progressive art circles of France, abandoning what she regarded as the stodgy artistic community in England.[2] Upon her arrival, she officially changed her name to Paule Vézelay to assert her connection to French culture and to embrace a certain gender ambiguity pervasive in French avant-garde circles at this time.[3] Over the next eight years, Vézelay continued to paint and exhibit as she experimented with abstract art movements then prevalent in Paris—slowly discarding the visual tropes of realist painting.[4] Making a fundamental shift from surrealism to a more geometric style, she aligned herself with the international art group Abstraction-Création, which had been founded to unite the diverse groups of artists who favored abstraction.[5] The outbreak of World War II forced Vézelay to return to England in 1939, but the connections she made in Paris would benefit her career after the war.

Back in London, Vézelay made her first foray into textile design in 1944 when she created patterns for the French firm Études Représentation de la Société Industrielle de la Lys, established by textile manufacturer Jean Bauret in 1943.[6] A year later in 1945 and 1946, alongside prominent artists such as Henry Moore, Henri Matisse, and Felix Atlan, Vézelay produced patterns for dress fabrics for Ascher, Ltd.[7] In 1950 Knoll added *Sequence* by Vézelay to its growing collection of printed textiles by a range of international designers (see figs. 3.43, 4.46). The exact details of Vézelay's connection to Knoll are not clear. It is possible, however, that *Sequence* was sold to Knoll by Bauret through the Société Industrielle de la Lys.[8]

The initial production of the textile featured "muted colors typical of the line." In 1954, presumably at the direction of Eszter Harastzy, the head of Knoll, the company added richer tones to the line including "Pimento Red" and "Deep Turquiose."[9] The linear design of *Sequence* played with changes of scale; the vertical motif was alternately printed in miniature and magnified form across the textile. In early 1953 the Knoll Planning Unit installed the fabric as drapery in the reception room of the CBS Radio executive offices.[10]

Vézelay created a similar textile design

for the leading Dutch department store Metz & Co. around 1952. Both designs reflected the restrained linearity of Vézelay's mixed media work of the decade, such as *Lines in Space*—a series created with wire, thread, glass, and cutout wooden shapes. Both textile designs also drew from the increasingly abstract visual language in her paintings.[12] Like the wire constructions, the textiles created spatial tension by articulating repeated motifs on a solid ground.

Metz & Co. was the first to market Knoll International furniture in the Netherlands.[13] In 1954 the company presented a new collection of furniture that included designs by Florence Knoll, Alvar Aalto, and Gio Ponti, along with fabrics by newly inducted Groupe Espace members, such as Silvano Bozzolini and Edgard Pillet.[14] The Groupe Espace was inspired by De Stijl as well as the Bauhaus and pursued a constructivist agenda. When Vézelay became a member in 1953, she was appointed the "London *délégué*."[15] The growing trend in the postwar period for prominent abstract artists to create textile designs articulated the Groupe's aim for nonfigurative art to "serve the conditions of private and public life and engages in direct interaction with the human community" and, most importantly, mark an "essential presence of the plastic arts."[16] Most notably, in 1953, the relationship between abstraction and commercial production was evident at *Painting into Textiles*, an exhibition at the Institute of Contemporary Art in London. Shortly afterward, Vézelay sold a design to the leading British interiors company Heal Fabrics, beginning a fruitful yet tumultuous relationship with the popular firm.[17]

Vézelay's textile designs, which were included in international exhibitions throughout her career, resulted in her participation in the British Society of Industrial Artists beginning in 1949.[18] Vézelay continued to produce a variety of commercial work and experiment in mixed media in the following decades, yet her career went largely unnoticed. It was not until shortly before her death that she received the attention and acclaim afforded to her contemporaries. The belated professional recognition culminated in a retrospective exhibition held at the Tate Gallery in 1983. Vézelay died a year later in Britian.
—AMT

Design for Knoll
Sequence (1950–55).

Selected Awards and Exhibitions
1930 *The Independents: Invitational with French and Belgian Surrealists*, Stedelijk Museum, Amsterdam
1938 *Abstract Art*, Stedelijk Museum, Amsterdam
1951 *Living Up-to-Date*, Baltimore Museum of Art (*Sequence* Shown)
1953 *Paintings into Textiles*, ICA in London
1956 *Textile as Art*, Stedelijk Museum, Amsterdam
1968 Retrospective, Grosvenor Gallery, London
1983 Retrospective, Tate Gallery, London
2008 *Post-war to Pop, Modern British Art: Abstraction, Pop and Op Art*, Whitford Fine Art, London

Karl Vogelsang (1932–2006)

Born in Essen, Germany, Karl Vogelsang studied painting from 1952 to 1954 at Universität Bonn, and in 1955 began studying textile design under Maria May at the Hochschule für bildende Künste (University of Fine Art) in Hamburg. May was a textile designer who had become well known for her name-branded textiles and wallpaper, "May-Stoff" and "May-Tappeten," produced for the Munich-based Vereinigte Werkstätten in the mid-1920s. She encouraged Vogelsang's freelance work and continued to mentor him after he left the academy.[1] She also introduced Vogelsang to Vereinigte Werkstätten, and this leading design firm became one of his earliest clients.[2] In 1955, after completing his studies with May, Vogelsang spent a year in Paris as a textile design intern at Atelier Thominet.[3] In 1961 he completed his textile training at the Akademie der Künste (Academy of the Arts) in Berlin, and spent the next two years designing for Christoph Andreae, a textile firm in Viersen, Germany.

In 1963 Vogelsang began working exclusively as a freelance designer and painter, and in 1969 was awarded a stipend from the Kulturkreis im Bundesverband der deutschen Industrie (Federal Association of German Industry). In addition to his work with Vereinigte Werkstätten, he established strong working relationships with other leading European textile firms, including Heberlein & Co. AG, Taunus Textildruck, Rothrist, and JAB Anstoetz.[4] In 1983 six of Vogelsang's designs were displayed at the Deutsches Textilmuseum in Krefeld, Germany, alongside those of Raoul Dufy, Verner Panton, and

Fig. B.143 Karl Vogelsang. *Atrium*, 1988. Made by Heberlein Textildruck AG for Knoll Textiles. Used for drapery; cotton; plain weave, screen-printed. KnollTextiles Archive.

other European artists and designers.[5] By the mid-1980s Vogelsang had earned a reputation for his innovative textile designs, and in 1985 he was awarded a prize for his textiles by the Salon International d´Editeur in Paris.

In 1988 Knoll International introduced two of Vogelsang's designs, *Fortuna* and *Atrium*, in Europe (fig. B.143, see fig 6.10). They were produced by the Swiss textile manufacturer Heberlein, which had been established in 1836 and, in its prime, was the largest textile printing firm in Switzerland (it closed in 2001).[6] Both of Vogelsang's prints use small-scale areas of color that are organized to create an overarching rhythmic quality. Compared to Vogelsang's paintings from this period, the textiles have a vibrant palette and display more marked interest in the use of dark tones to demarcate color sequences and create the illusion of shallow pictorial space.

In 1990 *Fortuna* was exhibited in *Color, Light, Surface: Contemporary Fabrics*, an international retrospective of avant-garde fabric designs created in the 1980s, held at the Cooper-Hewitt National Design Museum in New York. Vogelsang's designs have also been exhibited internationally, and his work has received awards from a number of institutions including the Haus der Industrieform, Essen, and the Design Center Stuttgart (1986, 1987, and 1989).[7] Late in life, Vogelsang returned to working solely as a painter; he died in Kronberg im Taunus, Germany, in 2006. —CBPP

Designs for Knoll
Introduced in Europe only (1988); it is uncertain when these designs were discontinued: *Fortuna*, *Atrium*.

Selected Awards and Exhibitions
1966, 1970 Galerie Baukunst, Cologne
1969 Textile Design Award, Federal Association of German Industry (Kulturkreis im Bundesverband der deutschen Industrie)
1983 Beletage Gallery, Dusseldorf
Boisseree Gallery, Cologne
1985 Decorative Print Design Award, Grand Palais, Salon International d'Editeur, Paris
First Prize, International du Tissu d'Ameublement, Paris
1986, 1987 Awards for textiles, Design Center Stuttgart
1989 Award for *Fortuna* and *Atrium*, Design Center Stuttgart
1990 *Color, Light, Surface: Contemporary Fabrics*, Cooper Hewitt National Design Museum, Smithsonian Institution

Margarete Warth (b. 1951)

Margarete Warth was born in Nagold, Germany. She studied textile design at the Staatliche Akademie der Bildenden Künste (State Academy of Art and Design) in Stuttgart (1970–75) under Leo Wollner who had a profound impact on her artistic practice, particularly his persistent refrain in the studio—"less is more."[1] In 1972 Warth was among a group of Wollner's students to create design proposals for "Transparent," a call for casement textiles commissioned by Knoll. The company provided the students with a wide variety of materials and challenged them to create a design that expressed the theme of transparency. The results were later exhibited at the Design Center Stuttgart, the Knoll Frankfurt Showroom, and in the "Collection" and exhibition of Knoll designs in 1973.[2]

Warth's prototype for the competition was a machine-knit pattern of off-set checks in linen. Knoll selected it for commercial manufacture by Linatex of Switzerland, naming it *Puzzle*, and in 1973 began selling it in a polyester and linen blend.[3] After graduating from the Staatliche Akademie, Warth and former classmate Liisa Moser collaborated on freelance design projects. In 1981 Warth received a scholarship to study textile design at the École nationale d'Art Décoratif in Aubusson, France. Warth spent the following year as an Aubusson tapestry weaver in the Robert Four studio, and in 1983 she was honored by the French Ministry of Culture for her weavings.

From 1984 to 1999 Warth was a lecturer in the textile department at the Freie Kunstakademie (Free Academy of Arts) in Nürtingen, Germany, and since 1988 she has been lecturing at the Fachhochschule für Kunsttherapie (University of Applied Sciences for Art Therapy) in Nürtingen. In 1999 she co-founded Werkraum Textil, an arts organization located in Nürtingen, offering textile workshops that focus on technical and methodological exchanges between participants. Warth currently lives in Tübingen, Germany. —CBPP

Design for Knoll
Puzzle (1973–77; disc. in Europe after 1981).

Selected Awards and Exhibitions
1981 Scholarship, École nationale d'Art Décoratif, Aubusson, France
1983 Decorative arts award, Ministère de la

Culture, France
2000 *European Felt Art*, Baden State Museum, Karlsruhe, Germany
2007, 2009 Baden–Würtenberg artists exhibition, Stuttgart

Henning Watterston (1916–2009)

Henning Watterston was one of the most sucessful weaver/designers active during the postwar period, participating in many landmark competitions and exhibitions. He was also one of the first contemporary handweavers to build a career and reputation as a freelance designer for industry, and he sustained that career longer than many of his contemporaries. Although few records and even fewer examples of his work remain, the surviving evidence reveals he was a remarkably versatile designer, whose importance has been largely overlooked.

Henning Watterston was born in Appleton, Minnesota, and as a child moved with his family to Los Angeles, California.[1] He studied painting and textile design in San Francisco at the Rudolph Schaeffer School of Design, an innovative academy best known for its courses in color and interior design. In the late 1930s, he married and formed a partnership with Carolyn Rees, designing and exhibiting handwoven fabrics under the name of Henning-Rees. In 1941 they received an Honorable Mention in MoMA's *Organic Design* competition.[2] The January 1941 issue of *The Weaver* included two articles—"Texture Identity in Weaving" by Henning-Rees and "Handweaving Today: Textile Work at Black Mountain College" by Anni Albers—which prompted a lively debate between traditional and "contemporary" handweavers.[3] By 1941 Watterston and Rees had joined Frank Lloyd Wright's Taliesin Fellowship, in Spring Green, Wisconsin. There, they designed and wove curtains for projects such as Wright's Rose Pauson house in Phoenix, Arizona (1940), and also may have taught weaving and textile design.[4]

By 1945 Rees and Watterston had separated, and having returned to San Francisco, Watterston began weaving under his own name.[5] Over the next several years, he produced custom handwoven textiles and designed for power-loom production.[6] Among his first clients was Menlo Textiles, a small manufacturer in Menlo Park, California, for whom he created handwoven collections in 1947 and 1948. Another early client, Cohn-Hall-Marx, Inc., was a large converter in New York City.[7] In 1949 he moved his studio to New York and designed hand- and power-woven fabrics for Henod Textiles.[8] Through the 1950s, Watterston sold designs and handwoven textiles from his New York studio and created custom fabrics for decorators and a diverse group of clients, including La Salle Silk Mills; Rodoma; Jack Valentine, Inc.; F. Schumacher & Co.; and the Dunbar Furniture Corporation.[9] In 1952 he was hired by Craftex Mills in Philadelphia to design "a new group of high-style fabrics for the decorator trade," and he was still working for Craftex when the mill developed *Bangkok* for Knoll in 1961 (fig. B.144).[10]

Early in his career, Watterston was known for his inventive transparent casements, such as the "strange and richly textured gauzes" he designed for Menlo Textiles in 1948, and a dramatic 1946 openwork textile woven of looping plastic Koroseal filaments.[11] Such work reflected Watterston's central concerns in textile design: understanding the qualities of the threads used to construct the fabric—or as he called it, "the texture identity of the thread"—and organizing the fabric's construction to clearly express those qualities, rather than "swallowing them up" in a complex structure.[12] As he later branched out into designing a wider range of fabrics, he continued to be guided by these principles. *Bangkok*, for example, was simply a plain weave, but one carefully designed to showcase the distinctive qualities of the nylon yarns from which it was made (see chapter 3).

In 1960 Watterston joined with Peter Leavitt, a longtime purchasing and sales representative for F. Schumacher & Co., to found the Leavitt, Watterston Corporation based in Woodstock Valley, Connecticut.[13] Leavitt, Watterston continued to work with Schumacher and some of Watterston's previous clients and also acted as both design consultants and sales representatives for several large mills. In the 1960s and 1970s, three of their major clients were Virginia Mills, Novelty Textile Mills, and the Stevens Linen Company.[14] In both modern and stylized traditional designs, Watterston and the firm established a reputation for creating varied and unusual color and texture effects.[15] In 1977 Watterston retired to concentrate on oil painting. With his second wife, Kathleen, he moved to Seillons, France, and after her death in 1984, he returned first to Connecticut, moving again in 2000 to Cloverdale, California, where he died in 2009.[16] —SW

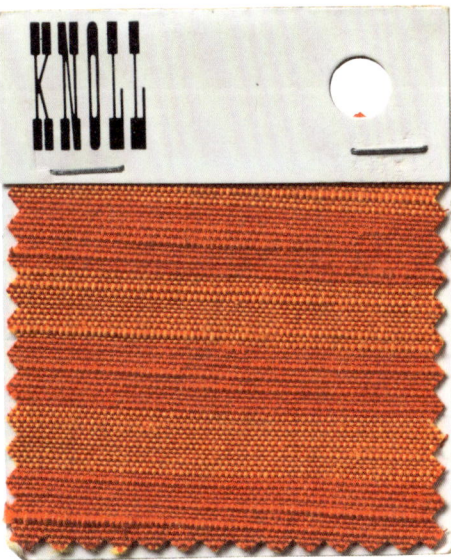

Fig. B.144 Henning Watterston. *Bangkok* and *Bangkok Stripe* swatches, ca. 1965. Made by Craftex for Knoll Textiles. Used for upholstery; nylon; plain weave with doubled warps. Private collection.

Fig. B.145 Elizabeth Whalen. *Paper Shift* ("Mahogany" colorway) and *Shuffle* ("Silver Pine" colorway), 2004. Made in Mexico for KnollTextiles. Used for wallcoverings; paper, polypropylene backing; plain weave. Courtesy Elizabeth Whalen. Cats. 276, 277.

Designs for Knoll
Bangkok (1962–71); and *Bangkok Stripe* (1963–71).

Selected Awards and Exhibitions
1941 *Organic Design in Home Furnishings*, Honorable Mention for Woven Fabrics (with Carolyn Rees), MoMA
1945 *Exhibition of Modern Textiles*, MoMA (circulating exhibition)
1949 *An Exhibition For Modern Living*, Detroit Institute of Arts
Modern Textiles, Everyday Art Gallery, Walker Art Center, Minneapolis
1950 *Good Design*, Merchandise Mart, Chicago (January)
1951 *Third Biennial Exhibition of Textiles and Ceramics*, Cranbrook
1952 *Textilien aus USA*, Smithsonian circulating exhibition
1953 *Fourth Biennial Exhibition of Textiles and Ceramics*, Cranbrook

Elizabeth Whelan (b. 1961)

Born in Boston, Elizabeth Whelan earned a BA at Trinity College in Connecticut and an MFA at the Rhode Island School of Design (RISD) in 1991.[1] She then worked for textile firms such as Designtex and Raxon Mill. By 1997 she had established a design studio in New York City and since 1999 has created Olefin wallcoverings for Wolf Gordon and award-winning mesh textiles for Humanscale's Niels Diffrient chair line.[2]

In the early 2000s Whelan discovered a unique mill in Mexico that specialized in weaving paper yarns on dobby looms from the 1930s and 1940s. The mill had used this process to make hats for U.S. postal workers as well as clothing hampers but had not yet attempted wallcoverings or other applications.[3] Whelan, intrigued by the paper yarns, requested samples from the mill to experiment with woven structure. Overcoming material constraints, she tailored her designs to maximize the yarns' potential.

Whelan came to KnollTextiles at the suggestion of Roger Wall, president of Spinneybeck Leathers (a Knoll, Inc. division, that had hired Whelan to recolor the *Prima* line of high-end leathers). Wall saw Whelan's early woven-paper prototypes and encouraged her to present them to KnollTextiles. After submitting handwoven samples to Suzanne Tick (creative director) and Miles Glidden (vice president and general manager) at KnollTextiles, Whelan and Tick worked together closely to produce the two woven-paper wallcoverings in the *Woodlands Collection*.

To create the designs, Whelan engaged in a dialogue of "low tech/high tech interplay" aimed at "processing utilitarian materials through the latest in manufacturing technologies to create intriguing modern textures."[4] The two resulting wallcoverings, *Shuffle* and *Paper Shift*, featured patterns that were tweedlike and linear, respectively (fig. B.145).[5] Offered in eleven colors, the collection signaled its origin with colorway names such as "White Pine," "Cypress," and "Cedar."[6] For all its ingenuity and effort, however, the *Woodlands Collection* was not a success. The designs suffered from poor backing material and, since the wallcoverings were made of a natural fiber, they were susceptible to fading with exposure to light.

While this was Whelan's only contribution to KnollTextiles, she continues to work with Spinneybeck. Most recently, the company introduced a line of woven leathers for upholstery and panels that combine strips of differing leather textures and finishes in a basketlike weave to highlight the diversity of the material. Since 2001 Whelan has taught at Parsons The New School for Design, Pratt Institute, and RISD. —AMT

Designs for Knoll
Woodlands Collection (2004–5): *Paper Shift*, *Shuffle*.

Award
2005 Design Distinction Award, *I.D. Magazine*

Robin Whitten (b. 1949)

In the 1980s, in a move reminiscent of the Knoll collections of the 1940s and 1950s, the company began commissioning designers trained in traditional handweaving to generate machine-woven fabrics that would infuse "craft [into] contract."[1] Under this initiative, Robin Whitten designed the *American Craftsman Collection* (1987) for Knoll, a group of five textiles that were structurally simple but articulated Whitten's signature blend of proportion, color, and texture into a balanced design.

After graduating from Vassar College in 1970 with a degree in art history, Whitten worked as an apprentice in a small fabric store and studio in Sandwich, New Hampshire, owned and operated by Roberta Ayotte.[2] While there Whitten trained in textile production and developed an appreciation for the handweaving process. Wanting to further explore ideas about natural fibers and yarns that would create unique surface variations and aesthetic sensations, Whitten enrolled at the Philadelphia College of Textiles (now Philadelphia University) in 1973. Although the formal coursework strengthened her technical knowledge of production methods, two design workshops with Jack Lenor Larsen in 1976 and 1984 at the Haystack Mountain School of Crafts on Deer Isle, Maine, helped Whitten cultivate a more sophisticated design sensibility, allowing her to bring color and texture into textiles using basic weave structures.[3] In 1973 she opened a seasonal shop and studio in Damariscotta, Maine, and in 1976 founded Linekin Bay Fabrics in Portland, Maine, employing five weavers working on hand-operated looms. Spurred by freelance design commissions from companies such as Ralph Lauren, L. L. Bean, J. P. Stevens, and Lily Pulitzer, Whitten began to consider commercial fabric design for apparel and domestic furnishings.[4]

In 1986, Merle Lindby-Young, design director of Knoll Textiles, approached Whitten about working for the company, likely after seeing Whitten's work at a San Francisco trade show that year. Whitten's emphasis on handweaving and natural fibers paralleled the company's plans to revisit "Knoll's tradition of hand-woven textiles and the [American] craft culture."[5] The result was Whitten's *American Craftsman Collection*, which debuted in January 1987 during CONDES '87, a design showcase at the Dallas Market Center in Texas.[6]

Whitten's independent work was influenced by the colors and textures of Maine, and the *American Craftsman Collection* also employed combinations of bright and muted natural and synthetic fibers to create contrasting and rich surface effects (fig. B.146).[7] The designs also drew on the heritage of the American weaving traditions and were similarly aligned with the historical craft and design traditions of Scandinavia, especially the vibrant colors used in textiles.[8] Although the *American Craftsman Collection* was industrially produced, Whitten collaborated with Lindby-Young to preserve the qualities of the original handwoven samples in the final designs.[9]

The *American Craftsman Collection* was Whitten's only project for Knoll Textiles and her fabrics were discontinued after a change in the division's leadership. Shortly after its debut, she closed down Linekin Bay Fabrics and left the textile industry altogether. In the early 1990s, Whitten started Audiofile, an online magazine dedicated to audiobooks, where she is currently chief editor and publisher. —ES

Designs for Knoll
American Craftsman Collection: Rapture (1987–89), *Cat's Eyes* (1987–89), *Rollover* (1987–90), *Silk Twill* (1987–90), *Watercolor Cord* (1987–92).

Gretl Wollner (1920–2006)
Leo Wollner (1925–1995)

Gretl and Leo Wollner were both born in Vienna, Austria, five years apart.[1] There are few published sources that document Gretl's life or career, but she is mentioned as a collaborator on most of her husband's projects, and through these some sense of her biography can be ascertained. In 1939 Leo Wollner began studying at the Höhere Bundeslehr- und Versuchsanstalt für Textilindustrie (Federal Training and Research Institute of the Textile Industry) in Vienna, but he took a mandatory two-year leave of absence to serve in the Wermacht.[2] After this, he enrolled at the Hochschule für angewandte Kunst (University of the Applied Arts) in Vienna. The Wollners met (and married) in the late 1940s while studying textile design and technology under Eduard Josef Wimmer-Wisgrill, founder of the fashion division of the Wiener Werkstätte in the early twentieth century.[3] In 1947 Leo Wollner began working for Austrian architect and designer Josef Hoffman.

At the close of his studies in the spring of 1949, Leo Wollner was awarded the state prize for his work at the university.[4] The same year, the Wollners began collaborating on freelance textile design projects for companies such as Taunus Textildruck, Sanderson, and Fuggerhaus.[5] Although primarily concentrating on pattern design, the Wollners also made woven textiles. During the 1950s they became well known for their work with Pausa AG, the innovative textile design company based in Mössingen, Germany.

They began working with Pausa in 1952. Willy Häussler (previously of the design firm Vereinigte Werkstätten) was Pausa's art director, and he teamed with Leo Wollner and Walter Mathaysiak as the company's artistic

Fig. B.146 Robin Whitten. *Watercolor Cord* ("Natural" colorway), 1987. Made by Franetta for Knoll Textiles. Used for upholstery; rayon, cotton, linen, wool, acrylic; plain weave. Private collection.

Fig. B.147 Gretl and Leo Wollner. *Sling* sample ("Orange" colorway), 1971. Made by Pausa AG for Knoll Textiles. Used for drapery; cotton; plain weave, screen-printed. KnollTextiles Archive. Cat. 193.

Fig. B.148 Gretl and Leo Wollner. *Trails* ("Flame/Orange" colorway), 1972. Made by Pausa AG for Knoll Textiles. Used for drapery, wall hanging; cotton; 4/1 satin weave, screen-printed. KnollTextiles Archive. Cat. 191.

team.[6] Together they helped usher in what would become Pausa's most fiscally successful era, developing the legendary Pausastil, which was advertised under the slogan "interior decoration designed by artists."[7] The Wollners soon established a strong connection with Häussler through their creative approach to textile design and were encouraged to experiment with new techniques and formats.[8] In 1953 the Wollners were awarded both first and second prizes as well as an honorable mention at the Fleischman International Carpet Design Competition.[9] In 1957 Leo Wollner was appointed head of the textiles department at the Staatliche Akademie der Bildenden Künste (Academy of Art and Design) in Stuttgart, Germany, and began dividing his time between Stuttgart and Vienna.[10] Häussler, who became involved with the academy through Wollner, partly funded the designer's theoretical teaching program and helped to develop design competitions.[11] Over his long career, Wollner trained many important textile designers whose work would benefit both Pausa and Knoll; these included Wolf Bauer and Ulrike Rhomberg-Greiner, to name just two.[12]

In 1958 Leo Wollner was commissioned to redesign the interior of the Festspielhaus (Festival Theatre) in Salzburg, including new wallcoverings, carpets, and stage curtains. This commission helped earn Wollner the Vienna prize for visual arts in 1959.[13] In 1958 Wollner had a solo exhibition, *Leo Wollner Textiliontwerper*, at the Stedelijk Museum in Amsterdam. The catalogue describes his approach to his work: "Wollner is not a drawing designer, he lives between loom, fabric bags and paint pots, and in terms of weaving he is quite at home."[14] Wollner used varied materials—pencil, pen, crayon and even photography—according to his vision for a specific design. He worked with experimental color palettes and enjoyed testing color combinations. In the late fall of 1959, the Wollners' work was exhibited jointly at the Österreichisches Museum für Angewandte Kunst (MAK) in Vienna. The exhibition catalogue includes a portrait of the couple on the first page, followed by a series of actual textile samples cut from their latest prints.[15]

In 1959 German interior design magazine *Die Kunst und das schöne Heim* cited the influence of the Bauhaus on the Wollners' designs and characterized their work as a "naturalized" realization of the Bauhaus legacy.[16] The Wollners' designs from the 1950s generally used between twelve and twenty colors, allowing for patterns that could perform in various interior contexts. Throughout their careers, the Wollners explored functionality, creating, for example, large-scale designs that could be sewn without causing pattern inconsistencies, thus minimizing fabric waste. The Wollners won awards for their textile designs during this period, both for those made in collaboration with textile firms and for those created independently. In 1966 Gretl Wollner won first place in the International Competition for Carpet Designs, Class 2, for her design *Mikado*.[17] In the early 1970s the Wollners designed *Sling* (1971) for Knoll (fig. B.147).[18] This innovative design received numerous awards and accolades, including a feature in *Industrial Design*.[19]

In 1972 the Wollners were involved with two important projects for Knoll. The first of these was a collaboration with Pausa. The couple's strong working relationship with Häussler had afforded them many opportunities to break from traditional manufacturing mandates to realize their designs. With Pausa they developed new printing technologies that allowed them to produce large-scale prints that ran from floor to ceiling with no repeat of the pattern.[20] Working with this technology and with Barbara Rodes of Knoll International, they created the impressive *Three Meter Prints Collection*, comprising *Rivers*, *Roads*, *Sails*, and *Trails* (figs. B.148, B.149, see fig. 5.28).[21] The collection remained in production until 1978. A second project for Knoll was the "Transparent" challenge, an open call for designs from Wollner's students at the Staatliche Akademie der Bildenden Künste. The single parameter stipulated by the company was that students develop their own concepts for how transparency might be realized materially. Although some designs were not usable in the mass-production context, at least three of them were manufactured as casement fabrics for the Knoll Collection.[22]

In 1991 Leo Wollner retired as professor and head of the department of textiles at the German Academy of Art and Design in Stuttgart. He died in 1995; Gretl Wollner died eleven years later in Vienna.[23] —CBPP

Designs for Knoll
Sling (1971–78; disc. in Europe 1981). *Three Meter Prints Collection* (1972–78): *Rivers*, *Roads*, *Sails*, *Trails*.

Selected Awards and Exhibitions
1949 State prize for work at the University for Applied Arts (Leo Wollner)
1951 Silver medal, Milan Triennale
1953, 1955 AID Awards
1954 Gold medal, Milan Triennale
1958 *Leo Wollner Textiliontwerper*, Stedelijk Museum, Amsterdam
1959 Prize of the City of Vienna for Visual Arts, contributions to the applied arts (Leo Wollner)
Textilausstellung Grete und Leo Wollner im Österreichischen Museum für angewandte Kunst MAK, Vienna
1961 Silver medal, Milan Triennale (Gretl Wollner)
1966 First place, International Competition for Carpet Designs (Gretl Wollner)
1972 *Knoll au Louvre*, Museé des Arts décoratifs, Paris
1988, 1999 Awards, Design Center Stuttgart (Gretl Wollner)

Fig. B.149 Gretl and Leo Wollner. *Rivers* page from Print Collection binder, ca. 1977. KnollTextiles Archive.

Adrian Parry

1   Adrian Pulfer, interview by Elizabeth St. George, January 24, 2011; Parry Merkley, interview by Elizabeth St. George, January 27, 2011. This entry is based on the interviews unless otherwise noted. I am grateful to both designers for their kind assistance.—ES
2   "Knoll Textiles Moves in NEW Directions with Designer's Saturday Introduction," press release, October 1982, Adrian Parry designer file, Knoll Archives.
3   "Adrian Pulfer: Clearness, Delicateness, and Simplicity," *Idea* [Japan] 36 (September 1988): 78, 80–81.
4   "Adrian Pulfer," 78; Kevin Ryan, "Going for Gold," *Graphis* 48 (January–February 1992): 78–83.
5   Lynn Snowden, "American Express: Do You Know Me? Becomes 'You Should Know Me'," *Graphis* 44 (March–April 1988): 32–49.

Anni Albers

1   Albers's life and the history of her years at the Bauhaus and subsequent artistic successes have been well chronicled. See, e.g., Virginia Gardner Troy, *Anni Albers and Ancient American Textiles* (Aldershot, England, and Burlington,Vt.: Ashgate Press, 2002); Nicolas Fox Weber and Pandora Tabatabai Asbaghi, eds., *Anni Albers* (New York: Guggenheim Foundation, 1999); and Brenda Danilowitz and Heinz Liesbrock, eds., *Anni and Josef Albers: Latin American Journeys* (Ostifildern: Hatje Cantz Verlag; New York: D.A.P., 2007). Biographical details in this entry are drawn from these, especially Pandora Tabatabai Asbaghi, "Anni Albers 1899–1994" in Weber and Tabatabai Asbaghi, *Anni Albers*, 152–79; and Anni Albers, curriculum vitae, February 1949, artists' scrapbooks, MoMA Library, New York.
2   Jenny Anger, "Anni Albers's Thank You to Paul Klee," in Danilowitz and Liesbrock, eds., *Latin American Journeys*, 159–74. I would like to thank Brenda Danilowitz for her assistance with this research.—AMT
3   *Interiors* (February 1950): 142.
4   Troy, *Anni Albers*, 128.
5   Ibid.
6   Ibid., 129. For compilations of Albers's essays see Anni Albers, *On Designing* (New Haven,: Pellango Press, 1959); Albers, *On Weaving* (Middletown, Conn.: Wesleyan University Press, 1965).
7   Anni Albers, "The Pliable Plane in Architecture" *Perspecta* 4 (1957): 40.
8   Eric Larrabee and Massimo Vignelli, *Knoll Design* (New York: Harry N. Abrams, 1990), 96; Brian Lutz, *Knoll: A Modernist Universe* (New York: Rizzoli, 2010), 191. Larrabee also neglects to mention any involvement Albers may have had with Knoll before *Eclat*; Lutz notes her creation of samples but not the production of *Track* and *Rail*; fig. 5.42, selvege marked 1975, *Eclat* first appears in the March 1, 1976 price list.
9   Anni Albers, interview, n.d., Knoll Archives.
10 Mary Jane Jacob, "Anni Albers: A Modern Weaver as Artist" in *The Woven and Graphic Art of Anni Albers* (Washington, D.C.: Smithsonian Institution Press, 1985), 72.
11 See Knoll price lists, Knoll Archives.

A new contract for *Track* was drawn up in March 1976.
12 *Lattice*, *Rail*, and *Track* folders, KnollTextiles Archive.
13 Knoll Textiles, "Textile Price List," February 15, 1967, pp. 13–15, Knoll Achives.
14 See Danielle J. Schroettner (Knoll International) to Anni Albers, May 28, 1982, Josef and Anni Albers Foundation.
15 Tabatabai Asbaghi, "Anni Albers," 176.
16 Victor R. Zevallos, "Camino Real," *Architectural Forum* (November 1968): 90. Rodes-Segerer was head of textiles for Knoll's international licensees, as well as head of the International Coordination Office; in 1971 she was appointed director of the Knoll International textile design.
17 Brenda Danilowitz, "Towards an Ending: Anni and Josef Albers's Final Journey to Mexico," in Danilowitz and Liesbrock, *Latin American Journeys*, 202. She was given permission by the architect to print her design; see Anni Albers to Ricardo Legorreta, July 21, 1969, Josef and Anni Albers Foundation Archive.
18 Prints *A*, *B*, *C*, *D*, and *F* (1968–69) and *TR I*, *TR II*, and *TR III* (1970) follow the graphic language of *Camino Real*; see Brenda Danilowitz, "Catalogue of Prints, 1963–1984" in *The Prints of Anni Albers: A Catalogue Raisonné, 1963–1984* (Bethany, Conn.: Josef and Anni Albers Foundation; Mexico City: Editorial RM, 2009), 46–59, 73–77.
19 For her contract with Knoll, see Duncan South to Anni Albers, May 9, 1975, Josef and Anni Albers Foundation Archive.
20 Knoll International, "Textile Price List" March 1, 1976," p. 41, KnollTextiles Archives.
21 *Eclat* was released in the United States with the ground fabrics *Dorset* and *Glin*, Knoll Textiles, press release, October 3, 1976, KnollTextiles Archive.
22 Barbara Rodes-Segerer to Jürgen Bargende (manager of Knoll International, Germany), May 5, 1978; Rodes-Segerer to Bargende, May 23, 1978, Josef and Anni Albers Foundation Archive; a woven sample of *Eclat*, though never put into production, also survives in the Josef and Anni Albers Foundation Archive, see Kelly Feeney to Nicolas Weber, August 27, 1996, Josef and Anni Albers Foundation Archive.
23 Knoll International, "Textile Collection January 11, 1978," Knoll International file, KnollTextiles Archive; see also Knoll International European price lists, 1978, 1980, KnollTextiles Archive.
24 Knoll International purchase order, ca. 1974, KnollTextiles Archive.
25 Gin Richter to Barbara Rodes-Segerer, August 12, 1974, Josef and Anni Albers Foundation Archive.
26 Knoll Textiles brochure, designed by Massimo Vignelli, 1977, p. 12, Josef and Anni Albers Foundation Archive.
27 Sunar "News," supplement, April 1979, Josef and Anni Albers Foundation Archive.
28 Jack Lenor Larsen, *Material Wealth* (New York: Abbeville Press, 1989), 56.
29 Kelly Feeney (Josef and Anni Albers Foundation Archive) assisted Casey with this research; see Kelly Feeney to Nicolas Weber, August 27, 1996, Josef and Anni Albers Foundation Archive.

Sarah Baker

1   Sarah Baker, telephone conversation with the author, April 11, 2011. Unless otherwise noted the information in this biography was drawn from this interview. Many thanks to Sarah Baker for her assistance on this project. —AMT
2   Baker was publicly credited for *Grace Note* when it won the Chicago Athenaeum's Good Design Award; see "Good Things," *Interior Design* (December 1999): 74.
3   KnollTextiles, "September 2000 Fabric Introductions," KnollTextiles Archive.

Jan Paul Barnard

1   Unless otherwise noted this biography is drawn from Jan Paul Barnard, emails to the author, April 13, 2011, and April 21, 2011. Many thanks to Mr. Barnard for his kind assistance on this project. —EM
2   Larsen also exhibited this fabric in a 1969 retrospective of his work in textiles, see *Retrospective: Jack Lenor Larsen, An Exhibition* (Fort Wayne, Ind.: Fort Wayne Museum of Art, 1969), cat. 101.

Jhane Barnes

1   Jhane Barnes, interview with the author, February 18, 2011. Unless otherwise noted the information in this biography comes from this interview. Many thanks to Jhane Barnes for her kind assistance with this project. —AMT
2   Diane Wintroub Calmenson, "2+2 = Design," *IS, the magazine for Interiors and Sources* 7 (May 1997): 46.
3   Michael Sand, "Fashion Nerd," *Wired* (June 1996): 135. Jhane Barnes designer file, KnollTextiles Archive.
4   Sand, "Fashion Nerd," 135. Christine Valhouli, "Fiber Fusion" *I.D.* (May 2001): 60. For more on Barnes's career as a fashion designer see Sandra Schroeder, "Jhane Barnes" in *Contemporary Fashion*, ed. Taryn Benbow-Pfalzgraf (Farmington Hills, Michigan: St. James Press, 2002), 49–50.
5   Barnes first encountered Knoll Textiles in 1981 when she created a men's jacket with Knoll Textiles's *Marseille* for *Collaboration '81*, a benefit fashion show that paired interior textile firms with fashion designers to create one-of-a-kind garments, see "Resources Council Presents Collaboration '81' *Interior Design* (November 1981): 136.
6   "Jhane Barnes designs for Knoll Textiles," press release, January 1983, KnollTextiles Archive.
7   Barnes began using Japanese mills in 1979 for specialty fashion fabrics. See the March (2011) Newletter, under "News" on her Web site, www.jhanebarnes.com. Barnes's husband Katsuhiko Kawasaki is a textiles manufacturing agent whose family owns a mill that has produced many of Barnes's textiles.
8   Julie V. Iovine, "Dream Weaver," *Metropolitan Home* (March 1990): 92.
9   Knoll Textiles, "New Introductions," Summer 1986, Knoll Archives.
10 Ibid.
11 Catherine Amidon, "Materializing the Invisible," *Surface Design Journal* 26 (Summer 2002): 29.
12 "Jhane Barnes Takes on New Dimensions for KnollTextiles," press release, February 28, 1989, KnollTextiles Archive.
13 Ibid.
14 Perhaps due to criticism by competitors, consumers perceived the double cloth upholstery to be structurally weak; Barnes recalls representatives literally pulling apart the two cloths at a trade show.
15 "Jhane Barnes Designs New Collection for KnollTextiles," press release, 1991, Knoll Archives.
16 Phil Patton, "Jhane Barnes," *I.D.* (January/February 1996): 49; "NeoCon Introductions, Jhane Barnes "Constructions" Wallcovering Collection," KnollTextiles press release, June 1992, KnollTextiles Archive.
17 Marilyn Zelinsky, "A Knoll Heritage," *Interiors* (January 1993): 30. See also chap. 2 in this volume.
18 "Chronology Collection," press release, October 1992, KnollTextiles Archive.
19 KnollTextiles, "NeoCon Introductions Echo, Transition, and Vertex," June 1994, KnollTextiles Archive.
20 "Jhane Barnes Mini-Series Collection," KnollTextiles press release, April 1994, KnollTextiles Archive.
21 Ibid., 6.
22 As early as 1982, Knoll advertised the availability of custom colors in their price lists, and by 1985 the custom program had expanded to include the development of "unique custom-made fabrics for upholstery, walls, panels and floors" for specific projects. Knoll Textiles, "Catalogue March 1982," March 1, 1982, p. 56, KnollTextiles Archive; Knoll Textiles, "Catalog March 1985," March 1, 1985, p. 55, KnollTextiles Archive.
23 Clients also included Nestle, Kellogg, Quaker Oats, and Olivetti. See "Jhane Barnes," Knoll International press release, ca. 1989, Jhane Barnes deisgner file, Knoll Archives.
24 KnollTextiles, "Price Catalogue 1989/90," March 1989, p. 23. KnollTextiles Archive.
25 Sand, "Fashion Nerd," 135.
26 Ibid.
27 She contributed a lesson titled "Sequences and Series: Fractals for Fashion" in *Algebra II: Explorations and Applications* (New York: Houghton Mifflin / McDougal Littell, 1997); and she was featured in "Playing by the Rules…of Fractal Design," *Discovering Math (9–12)*, segment 70, Discovery Education (Discovery Channel, 2007); see Sandra Schroeder, "Jhane Barnes," in *Contemporary Fashion*, ed.Taryn Benbow-Pfalzgraf (Farmington Hills, Michigan: St. James Press, 2002), 50.
28 KnollTextiles, "*Criss Cross, Labyrinth, Peano*" Panel Fabric Introductions, p. 1, October 1997, KnollTextiles Archive.
29 Calmenson, "2+2," 43.

Wolf Bauer

1   Wolf Bauer designer file, Knoll Archives. See also Lesley Jackson, *Twentieth-Century Pattern Design: Textile and Wallpaper Pioneers* (New York: Princeton Architectural Press, 2002): 176; Charlotte Fiell and Peter Fiell, eds., *Seventies Decorative Art* (Cologne: Taschen, 2000), 449.
2   Hans Wichmann, ed., *Von Morris bis Memphis: Textilien der Neuen Sammlung Ende 19. bis Ende 20. Jahrhundert*, exh. cat, Die Neue Sammlung, Munich, Germany (Basel: Birkhauser, 1990), 438.

3   For Taunus see Dieter Gasse, Carl-Wolfgang Schümann, and Manfred Rusche, *Printed by Taunus Textildruck: 30 Jahre Textildruck in Deutchland am Beispiel einer Firma*, exh. cat. (Krefeld, Germany: Deutsches Textilmuseum Krefeld, 1983).
4   This collection was cited as "Die neue Druckstoff Kollektion 1967" (The new Print Fabric Collection 1967) in "Ein Mann will seine Umwelt mit den schönsten Farben schmücken," *Schöner Wohnen* (December 12, 1968): 163. Research to date has not uncovered all the Bauer prints that were part of this collection. *Nova* and *Delta* are illustrated in ibid. Examples of *Collage* in the KnollTextiles Archive and Cooper-Hewitt Museum are marked in the selvedge with a 1967 copyright date indicating this pattern was also part of the initial Bauer collection.
5   Elizabeth Williamson, "Fabric Survey" *Design* 230 (February 1968): 29. It is likely *Scope* was part of the 1967 Bauer collection.
6   "International Print Collection 1969 Textile Introduction," press release, September 1, 1969, Wolf Bauer designer file, Knoll Archives. It is likely that these designs had been introduced in Europe two years earlier.
7   "Home/Contract Furnishing," *Industrial Design* (December 1969): 57; "ID's 1969 Design Review," *Interiors* (January 1970): 106–9.
8   Amelie Duras, *Kunst vom Fliessband: Produkte des Textildesigners Wolf Bauer* (Stuttgart: Design Center, 1970).
9   Wichmann, *Von Morris bis Memphis*, 278–79.
10 Helen Boterenbrood, Patricia Wardle, and Wolf Bauer, *Fourteen Designs for Weverij De Ploeg / Veertien ontwerpen voor Weverij De Ploeg* (Amsterdam: Stedelijk Museum, 1989).
11 "Textildesigner Wolf Bauer gestorben" (obituary), *Hamburger Abendblatt*, August 14, 1990, 12.
12 David Jenkins, ed., *The Cambridge History of Western Textiles* (New York: Cambridge University Press, 2003), 1098.

Jean Bauret

1   Gaël Bonzon, "À la découverte de Jean Bauret, éditeur de tissus d'artistes, de Kandinsky à Geneviève Asse," *Histoire de l'Art* 44 (June 1999): 65–66.
2   Ibid.
3   Ibid., 66–67.
4   Vézelay began to design for Bauret in 1944 (ibid.); an image of *Sequence* was captioned "K375 'Bauret' chintz" in *Knoll Index of Contemporary Design* (1950), 78.
5   Bonzon, "À la découverte de Jean Bauret," 67, 76.

Anne Beetz

1   Many thanks to Anne Beetz for her kind assistance with this project. —AMT
2   Marilyn Zelinsky "Neutral Powers," *Interiors* 152 (March 1993): 46.
3   "Anne Beetz Collection," press release, October 1989, KnollTextiles Archive.
4   Lise Coirier, *Label-Design.BE* (Legeweg, the Netherlands: Stichting Kunstboek, 2005), 70; Anne Beetz, email correspondence with the author, November 16, 2010.
5   Anne Beetz, email correspondence with the author, October 17, 2010.
6   "Neutral Colors, Unusual Weaves Characterize Anne Beetz Collection for KnollTextiles," press release, 1989, Anne Beetz designer file, Knoll Archives.
7   Jack Lenor Larsen, *Material Wealth* (New York: Abberville Press, 1989), 152.
8   Kenji Ekuan, "Anne Beetz Biography," n.d., Anne Beetz designer file, KnollTextiles Archive.
9   Anne Beetz, telephone conversation with the author, October 14, 2010. Meunier seems to have replaced Yves Vidal as president of Knoll France in the late 1970s and remained until the early 1990s. The exact dates of his employment are unknown.
10 Candace Key, telephone conversation with the author, November 4, 2010. Key worked for the company from 1987 to 1989, and has provided further details into this collaboration with Beetz.
11 Anne Beetz, email conversation with the author, October 18, 2010.
12 Beetz continued to sell the original collection in Europe through her atelier.
13 The collection was introduced under Hazel Siegel, managing director of design of KnollTextiles worldwide, who started at Knoll that same year. She was not, however, involved in the production of the collection.
14 Press release, 1996, *Decades Collection* file, KnollTextiles Archive. Casey was an interim designer at the time; she changed the silk content to cotton and recolored the textile to coordinate with other designs in the *Decades Collection*.
15 KnollTextiles, fabric introduction price lists, 1998 and 2000, KnollTextiles Archive. *Tokay II* is polyester; Tick kept three best-selling original colors and added seven new ones. *Panier II* is cotton in three of the original colors. Knoll Archives.
16 KnollTextiles price list, 2010, at www.knolltextiles.com/textiles/index.
17 Zelinsky, "Neutral Powers," 46.
18 Coirier, *Label-Design*, 70.

Emily Belding

1   Biographical facts are from "Emily Belding: Textile Designer," *Handweaver & Craftsman* 7, no. 1 (Winter 1955–56): 26; and Herb Drill, "Emily Belding, Teacher Turned Fabric Designer," obituary, *Philadelphia Inquirer*, January 28, 1999.
2   Mary Roche, "Decorators' Work is Displayed Here," *New York Times*, September 2, 1948, 26.
3   For *Linten Lace* see "Textile Awards: Fourth A.I.D. Design Competition," *Handweaver & Craftsman* 1 (April 1950): 31 (illus.).
4   "New Weaves Available," *New York Times*, September 23, 1952, 22.
5   Emily Belding to Eva Ingersoll Gatling, December 31, 1952 and January 26, 1953, curatorial exhibition files, Cranbrook Academy of Art Museum. Belding enclosed a note with the December letter indicating that John C. Milne was no longer the agent for her fabrics.
6   "New Home for Habitat," *Interior Design* (April 1954): 36; Habitat advertisement, *Interiors* (January 1954): 123.
7   Whitaker had probably been weaving her designs for Habitat Associates; a 1956 letter from a mill representative to Belding reported that Knoll had placed an order for *Shades and Tints*, implying that Whitaker had already been weaving it. Evelyn B. Donaldson to Emily Belding, May 18, 1956, Emily Belding Collection, Thousand Islands Arts Center, Home of the Handweaving Museum, Clayton, N.Y.
8   Belding's nephew later recalled that the mill had a four-year backlog of orders at one point (David B. Grinell, quoted in Drill, "Emily Belding").
9   Donaldson to Belding, May 18, 1956.
10 See correspondence between Evelyn B. Donaldson and Emily Belding, May 18, 1956 to June 26, 1957, Emily Belding Collection, Thousand Islands Arts Center, Home of the Handweaving Museum, Clayton, NY.
11 William Whitaker & Sons Records 1809–1970, Hagley Museum and Library, online catalogue record.

Brenda Brady

1   Unless otherwise noted, the information in this biography is from "Traditions Collection," press release, March 1995, KnollTextiles Archive. Research thus far has yielded little information about the designer.
2   Linda Castiglione, "Color Rotation for the Traditions Collection," memorandum, April 6, 1995, KnollTextiles Archive.

Michela Bronzini

1   For black-and-white photographs of two of these silks, see *Knoll Index of Contemporary Design* (New York: Knoll Associates, 1950), 79; and "In the Showrooms: New Cuttings," *Interiors* (September 1950): 110. A photo caption identifies K605/5 as Italian silk in *Knoll Index of Contemporary Design* (1950), 79; a partial "Textile Price List," ca. 1950–51, KnollTextiles Archive, lists *Handwoven Silk from Italy* in six colorways (K605/1-6). No examples of them are known to survive.
2   "Rare Italian Silks Add Home Luxury," *Dallas Morning News*, July 10, 1950, 1.
3   Information in this section, unless otherwise noted, is based on Lalla Colombo Borzatta, Gegia Bronzini division of Punto Como, email to Earl Martin, September 1, 2010.
4   For Gegia and Marisa Bronzini, see Doretta Davanzo Poli, *Twentieth-century Fabrics: European and American Designers and Manufacturers* (Milan: Skira, 2007), 289.
5   Colombo Borzatta, email to Martin. Michela Bronzini does not seem to have had any connection to the American company Bronzini, a manufacturer of men's ties, scarves, and silk robes, which was founded in 1947 by designer Brooke Cadwallader; see Caroline Rennolds Milbank, *New York Fashion: The Evolution of American Style* (New York: Harry N. Abrams, 1989), 149.
6   "For Your Information: Newark Museum Displays," *Interiors* (January 1949): 14; "Retail Story: Italian Modern in Chicago," *Interiors* (March 1949): 125.
7   The workshop was purchased in about 2002 by the Punto Como company and is its handwoven textile division; see www.gegiabronzini.com.

Vibeke Bruun de Neergaard

1   Suzanne Huguenin, "Textile Sales Guide: Part I, Upholstery Fabrics," August 15, 1962, Dan Kroger Collection.
2   For a brief company history, see the Olesen Web site, www.c-olesen.dk/en_profil.html. C. Olesen is now under the guidance of Gro and Bjarne Sachse.
3   Arne Karlesen and Anker Tiedmann, *Made in Denmark* (Copenhagen: Jul. Gjellerup, 1960), 73. Bodil Bødtker-Næss, "Textiles, Weaving and Printing," in *Danish Design*, ed. Svend Erik Møller (Copenhagen: De Danske Selskab, 1974), 121–22; Lesley Jackson, *Twentieth-century Pattern Design: Textile and Wallpaper Pioneers* (New York: Princeton Architectural Press, 2002), 93; Thomas Dickson, *Dansk Design* (Copenhagen: Gyldendal, 2006), 168.
4   Huguenin, "Textile Sales Guide."
5   "Wide New Collection of Designs and Colors Introduced in Knoll Textiles," press release, April 26, 1959, Knoll File, MoMA Archives.
6   Huguenin, "Textile Sales Guide."
7   Knoll Textiles, "Wholesale Price List," November 15, 1959, KnollTextiles Archives; Knoll Textiles, "Catalogue March 1984," March 1, 1984, KnollTextiles Archives. The 28 colorways were not all in production at the same time.

Lois Bryant

1   Lois Bryant, email interview with the author, August 16, 2010. Unless otherwise noted the information in this biography is from this interview. I would like to thank Lois Bryant for her kind assistance with this project. —AMT
2   Marie A. Giles and Marion Marzolf, *Fascination with Fiber* (Ann Arbor: University of Michigan Press, 2006), 32.
3   Art Institute of Chicago, www.artic.edu/aic/collections/artwork/artist/3774; and "Informed Sources" *Surface Design Journal* (Fall 1994): 22.
4   Mary McCoy, "Exhibition Review: Lois Bryant," *American Craft* 52, no. 5 (October/November 1992): 64.
5   Betty Freudenheim, "Tapestries Warm Up Modern Buildings" *New York Times* (March 3, 1988); and the artist's Web site, http://loisbryantstudio.com/node/4.

Colcombet

1   "Paris se souvient–Johan Colcombet," *l'Officiel de la Couture*, no. 333–34 (1949): 154, online at Jalou Gallery, http://patrimoine.jalougallery.com/lofficiel-de-la-mode-numero_333-334-detail-13-287.html.
2   Alexandre Colcombet, "Proposition pour la Grade d'Officier, Legion d'Honneur," 1926, Archives nationales, Fontainebleau, (Fonds de la Légion d'Honneur) online: www.culture.gouv.fr/leonore/leonore.htm.
3   *L'Officiel de la Couture de la Mode de Paris*, no. 148 (1933): 98, online at Jalou Gallery, http://patrimoine.jalougallery.com.
4   Dilys E. Blum, *Shocking! The Art and Fashion of Elsa Schiaparelli* (Philadelphia: Philadelphia Museum of Art, 2003), 71–72.
5   "Paris se souvient," 154.
6   Daniela Gilbert, "Old School," *Women's Wear Daily*, October 21, 2003, 13.
7   "Textile Firm Enters Rockefeller Center," *New York Times*, December 30, 1937, 36.
8   See, e.g., Marguerite Duguet de

Laprade, *French Textiles* (Leigh-on-Sea, Eng.: F. Lewis, 1955), figs. 1, 2, 60.
9   Knoll Sales bulletin no. 25, March 8, 1954, *Sparklers* file, KnollTextiles Archive.

Dorothy Cole Ruddick

1   *Interiors* (August 1948): 208; Margie Ruddick, personal communication, February 19, 2011.
2   See also Dorothy Cole, "She's the Type," *Mademoiselle* (August 1947): 239–40.
3   Dorothy Cole Ruddick and Margie Ruddick, pers. comm., February 28, 2010. A group of drawings related to the Knoll *Filigree* design survives in the collection of the artist's family. *Filigree* was released in the fall of 1950; see "Fall Fabrics 1950," *Interior Design and Decoration* (October 1950): 62.
4   See "The Knolls," *Look* (May 22, 1951), 100-105.
5   Kevin Scott, "Dorothy Ruddick," in *Dorothy Ruddick: Recent Work*, exh. brochure, Richard York Gallery, New York, January 31–March 1, 2003.

Dorothy Cosonas

1   Dorothy Cosonas, email to Earl Martin, January 11, 2011. Many thanks to Dorothy Cosonas for her assistance with this project. —AMT
2   Though now an American company, Unika Vaev originated in Denmark in the 1950s.
3   Cosonas, email to Martin.
4   Ibid.
5   Tick would remain a freelance designer for Knoll, primarily focusing on vertical textiles.
6   Jean Lin "Dorothy Cosonas & Knoll Textiles Introduce . . . ," *officeinsight* (May 8, 2006), 11.
7   Ibid.
8   *Rivington* File, KnollTextiles Archive.
9   See Suzanne Tick, LTL, and Abbott Miller biographies herein.
10 Paul Makovsky, "Fresh from the Archives" *Metropolis* (June 2007), 150-53; *Archival Collection* folder, KnollTextiles Archive.
11 KnollTextiles "June 2009 Introductions" presentation strategy, KnollTextiles Archive.
12 David Kaufman, "Material Girl" *Hospitality Design* 30 (October 2008): 143.
13 "Market Talent," *Interior Design* (May 2008): 177.
14 Ibid.
15 Cosonas, interview with Martin.
16 Dorothy Cosonas, email to Earl Martin, January 11, 2011.
17 See the Proenza Schouler biography herein.
18 Dorothy Cosonas, interview with Earl Martin and the author, January 21, 2011.
19 Ibid.
20 See Rodarte biography herein.

Lynne Crosbee

1   Research has thus far uncovered little information about the designer. She seems to have been one of a number of designers whose work was intended to appeal to an international audience; see Lesley Jackson, *Twentieth-Century Pattern Design: Textile and Wallpaper Pioneers* (New York: Princeton Architectural Press, 2002), 189; a review of her work for Knoll identifies her as British, *Interior Design* 43 (November 1973): 89.
2   The revival may have been spurred by *Les Années "25,"* an exhibition at the Musée des arts décoratifs in Paris, held in 1966 to commemorate the Exposition internationale des arts décoratifs et industriels modernes, Paris, 1925.
3   Knoll International, "Textile Price List June 1, 1974," Knoll Archives.
4   Knoll International, press release, ca. 1974, Knoll Archives.
5   Ilse Gray, "Message to Stuttgart," *Design* 319 (July 1975), 35.
6   Knoll released *Cara* in 1977 as a plain fabric; see Knoll International, "Textile Price List 1977/78," November 15, 1977, p. 37, KnollTextiles Archives.
7   Knoll International, "Textile Price List," June 1, 1974, Knoll Archives.
8   Gray, "Message," 35.

François Dallegret

1   François Dallegret, telephone interview by the author, March 30, 2011; artist's Web site, www.arteria.ca. Biographical details in this entry are based primarily on these two sources. I thank the artist for his assistance.—CAL
2   Press release, Waddell Gallery, September 1966; Grace Glueck, "Little Shows, Big Themes," *New York Times*, November 20, 1966, D26.
3   "François Dallegret in Conversation with Alessandra Ponte," *AA Files*, no. 58 (2009).
4   "Astrological Automobiles of François Dallegret," *Automobile Quarterly* 3, no. 1 (1964); see also Sarah K. Rich, "François Dallegret's Astrological Automobiles: Occult Commodities for France in the 1960s," *Oxford Art Journal* 31, no. 1 (2008): 27-49.
5   Projects have included the *L'iNtro coNvers oMAtic* (1963), Space City "Astronef 732" (1963), and the sculpture-sound machine *La Machine* (1966), see "Gallery: The Visions of Mr. Dallegret," *Architectural Forum* (May 1964): 109–114.
6   Reyner Banham and François Dallegret, "A Home Is Not a House," *Art in America* (April 1965): 70–79.
7   Ibid.
8   "Le Drug," *Architectural Forum* (April 1965); see also artist's Web site, www.arteria.ca.
9   *Atomix* has recently been re-released, see William Bostwick, "The New Executive Toys," *I.D.* (January/February 2009): 22.
10 Knoll International press release, May 3, 1971, Knoll Archives.
11 Knoll Textiles, "Textile Price List," May 1, 1971, p. 25, KnollTextiles Archive.
12 Knoll Textiles, "Textile Price List," June 1, 1974, Knoll Archives; Knoll International, "Printed Casements" sample binder, ca. 1974, KnollTextiles Archive.
13 *Kiik* 69 document, www.arteria.ca.

Sybille Dobringer

1   "Transparente Fantasien," *MD Moebel Interior Design*, (December 1972): 45–49.
2   Student names— Friedrich Goth, Margarete Warth, and Sybille Dobringer— were handwritten below three separate textile entries; see Knoll Textiles, "Textile Price List," April 1, 1973, pp. 22, 24–25, KnollTextiles Archive.

Klaus Dombrowski

1   Schwarz, Erne. " 'Galaxis 94' — harmonische Kombination von Tapeten, Borten und Dekostoffen," *Objekt*, no. 11 (November 1992): 126.
2   Klaus Dombrowski email to the author, March 9, 2011. Many thanks to Klaus Dombrowski for his kind assistance with this text.
3   *Bauhaus-Rasch bringt aus deutschen Ateliers 1939*, brochure designed by Jupp Ernst and featuring the Bauhaus line as well as *Weimartapeten* designed by Paul Schultze-Naumburg and Wiener Künstlertapeten, Klaus Dombrowski archive (private) Essen, Germany.
4   " 'Galaxis 94'."
5   "I was impressed by the Bauhaus because of the reduced forms of its architects led by Mies van der Rohe or for example, Bauhaus disciple Richard Meyer who built the new Frankfurt Museum of Decorative Arts. Here I see a strong connection with my intentions [to create] a clear language of form." " 'Galaxis 94,' " 128.
6   Ibid., 127.
7   "Knoll's Curtain Call," *Designer's Journal* (April 1987): 6.
8   Klaus Dombrowski, email to the author, March 9, 2011.

Peter Eisenman

1   For an Eisenman bibliography, see "Architect Bibliographies: Writings by and about Peter D. Eisenman," Canadian Center for Architecture Web site, search "Peter Eisenman Archive," at www.cca.qc.ca/en.
2   Paul Goldberger, "Architecture View: A Little Book that Led Five Men to Fame," *New York Times*, February 11, 1996, book review.
3   For a list of all projects and awards, see Eisenman Architects Web site, www.eisenmanarchitects.com.
4   Jean Gorman, "Maverick Material," *Interiors* 150 (August 1991): 60.
5   Ibid.
6   "Peter Eisenman Ventures into New Medium for Knoll Textiles," press release, ca. 1991, KnollTextiles Archive.
7   Ibid.
8   Gorman, "Maverick Material," 60.
9   Ibid.

Ruben Eshkanian

1   Unless otherwise noted the information in this biography is from Ruben Eshkanian, telephone conversation with the author, August 27, 2010. I would like to thank the artist for his kind assistance with this project. —AMT
2   Ruben Eshkanian, Cranbrook Academy application for enrollment, ca. 1949, Cranbrook Archives.
3   "Gay Fabric Items Shown in 2 Shops," *New York Times*, December 11, 1953, 39; "Primary Accents," *New York Times Magazine* (February 14, 1954): 46.
4   Eshkanian exhibition announcement, Helen Drutt Gallery, 1983, Ruben Eshkanian folder, MoMA Library Archive.
5   Ibid.

6   *Trellis* last appears in Knoll Textiles, "Textiles Price List," November 15, 1977, KnollTextiles Archive.
7   Sales Bulletin, March 25, 1959, Knoll Archives.
8   Knoll Associates, "Trellis" sample sheet, January 9, 1959, KnollTextiles Archive.
9   *Met Textiel* (Amsterdam: Stedelijk Museum and Kunstwerkstede, 1961), Brooklyn Museum Library and Archives.
10 Jack Lenor Larsen, Oral history interview by Arline M. Fisch, February 6–8, 2004, Archives of American Art, Smithsonian Institution.
11 Arthur J. Pulos, *The American Design Adventure: 1940–1975* (Cambridge, Mass.: MIT Press, 1988), 236–37; Larsen, *Weaver's Memoir*, 61. ICA selected five design organizations for each set of developing countries. Russel Wright Associates went to Hong Kong, Taiwan, Thailand, Cambodia, and Vietnam.
12 Larsen, *Weaver's Memoir*, 61; and Larsen, Oral history interview. Larsen visited during the winters of 1959 and 1960.
13 His brother, Dickran Eshkanian, was head designer for the Peace Corps project in Lima.
14 He replaced Larsen in this teaching position. In 1987 the school changed its name to the University of the Arts.
15 Eshkanian exhibition announcement.
16 "Fabrics International: Catalogue of the Exhibition," *Craft Horizons* 21 (September/October, 1961): 46; and *Craft Horizons* 24 (March/April 1964): 18, 38, 64.

Shirley Fletcher Nickerson

1   Unless otherwise noted this biography is based on Shirley Fletcher Nickerson, phone interview with the author, August 30, 2010, and Shirley Fletcher, student file, Office of the Registrar (1990-19), Cranbrook Academy of Art, Cranbrook Archives. I wish to thank Shirley Nickerson and her daughter Terry Larson for their kind assistance with this project—EM
2   "Class Scene at Art Academy," *Sunday Morning Star*, June 16, 1940, 16.
3   This section is based on Jane King Hession, Rip Rapson, and Bruce N. Wright, *Ralph Rapson: Sixty Years of Modern Design* (Afton, Minn.: Afton Historical Society Press, 1999), 47–48, 59–64.
4   Knoll Associates, Textiles price list, November 1, 1948, Brooklyn Museum Library and Archives. The colorways listed are "Green and Brown," "Grey and Brown," "Yellow," and "Red."

Josef Frank

1   For more on Frank's architecture and interior design before and after World War I, see Christopher Long, "The Wayward Heir: Josef Frank's Vienna Years, 1885–1933," in *Josef Frank, Architect and Designer*, ed. Nina Stritzler-Levine (New York: Bard Graduate Center for Studies in the Decorative Arts, 1998), 44-61; and Christopher Long, *Josef Frank: Life and Work* (Chicago: University Of Chicago Press, 2001).
2   Kristina Wängberg-Eriksson, *Josef Frank: Textile Designs*, trans. Christopher Long, Jan Christer Eriksson, and Kristina Wängberg-Eriksson (Stockholm: Bokförlaget Signum I Lund, 1999), 12.

3 Frank's patterns were primarily block-printed (some by the London firm G. P. & J. Baker) until screen-printing began to be adopted in Sweden in the mid-1930s; see ibid., 47–84.
4 Ibid., 24–28. While in New York Frank evidently also had several designs printed by F. Schumacher & Co. but the arrangement was not successful. For the current offerings of Frank's textile designs see the Svensk Tenn Web site, www.svenskttenn.se.
5 In the late 1940s Frank was commissioned by the Stockholms Enskilda Bank to create a similar design featuring the map of Stockholm; see Stritzler-Levine, *Josef Frank, Architect*, 258, and Wängberg-Eriksson, *Josef Frank*, 31.
6 The inclusion of *Manhattan* in the Knoll collection is known from Mary Roche, "Work of Noted Textile Designers Put on View at New Showroom," *New York Times*, February 27, 1947, 24; it was no longer offered by Knoll in 1948.

Jean P. Garrault

1 Jean Pierre Garrault, email correspondence with the author, February 25, 28 and March 10, 2011. Unless otherwise noted, the details in the text are based on this correspondence. I am grateful to the artist for his kind assistance. —CAL
2 For Garrault and the *Prisunic & Design* exhibition, see VIA Web site, www.via.fr/gb/evenements_prisunic.asp.
3 Arthur Sager to Jean Pierre Garrault, June 21, 1978, J. P. Garrault personal papers.

Alexander Girard

1 Registrar Exhibition Files, Exh. 98, MoMA. Both designs were shown in *Printed Textiles for the Home* (1947; see "Textures," *Interiors* (April 1947): 23 (illus. Girard/Saarinen design).
2 "3 Receive Awards for New Design," *New York Times*, January 4, 1947, 12.
3 "The Good Word on Fabrics," *Interiors* (November 1947): 106, 108.
4 "Where to buy Well Designed Objects," *Everyday Art Quarterly* 7 (Spring 1948): 3. There may have been some kind of cooperative arrangement between Knoll and Girard.
5 *Furniture Forum* (Winter 1949): Section 4, 2 (illus. *Links* and *Wires*).
6 See Alexander Girard, quoted in Terence Conran, *Printed Textile Design* (London: Studio Limited, 1957), 40.
7 "Merchandise Cues: Girard Collection at Herman Miller," *Interiors* (July 1952): 100; "The Market: Fabrics Too At Herman Miller," *Interior Design* (July 1952): 17.

Friedrich Goth

1 Six designs were reportedly accepted into the Knoll collection; see "Transparente Fantasien," *MD Moebel Interior Design* (December 1972): 48–49 (includes an illustration of the *Comet* prototype). An annotated 1973 price list in the KnollTextiles Archive identifies Margarete Warth (*Puzzle*) and Friedrich Goth (*Comet*)—the same designers cited for the prototypes for these fabrics illustrated in the *MD* article—as well as a third student designer also named in the *MD* article, Sybille Dobringer (*Meton*); see Knoll Textiles, "Textile Price List 1973," April 1, 1973, pp. 22, 24–25, KnollTextiles Archive.
2 Leo Wollner, ed., *Zwischen Industrie und Kunst*, exh. cat. (Stuttgart: Design Center Stuttgart and Staatliche Akademie der Bildenden Künste, 1976).

Kathrin Hagge

1 The Diplom Ingenieur (FH) is the equivalent of a BA degree in the United States. Kathrin Hagge, telephone conversation with the author, April 7, 2011. Unless otherwise noted the information in this entry is primarily from this interview. Many thanks to Kathrin Hagge for her assistance with this project. —AMT
2 Kathrin Hagge, curriculum vitae, 2010, (Hagge, email to the author, April 7, 2011).
3 Melissa Martin Marsh, "Kathrin Hagge," *US Design 1975–2000*, exh. cat. (New York: Prestel Verlag in association with the Denver Art Museum, 2001), 242.
4 Hagge, curriculum vitae.
5 Ibid.
6 KnollTextiles, "NeoCon 1999 Introductions," 1999, p. 3, KnollTextiles Archive.
7 KnollTextiles, "January 2001 Fabric Introductions," 2001, KnollTextiles Archive.
8 Ibid.; Knoll Textiles "Spring 2000 Introductions," 2000, KnollTextiles Archive.
9 Ibid.
10 Neither journal credits Hagge with the design; see Melissa Feldman, "The Inn Crowd," *Interiors* (May 2001), 46; "NeoCon" *Contract* (May 2001), 72.
11 Hagge, curriculum vitae.

Eszter Haraszty

1 Quote from Olga Gueft, "The Exhilarated World of Eszter Haraszty," *Interiors* (June 1956): 94. Other information from Eszter Haraszty, conversation with David Hanks, handwritten notes, August or September 1989, Stewart Collection Archives, Montreal Museum of Fine Arts, courtesy David A. Hanks & Associates. Unless otherwise noted, the biographical data in this text derives from Eszter Haraszty, interview, January 25, 1977, Eszter Haraszty Designer file, Knoll Archives; and Eszter Haraszty, interview with Kate Carmel, May 1989 (notes by Christine Laidlaw), Stewart Collection Archives, Montreal Museum of Fine Arts, courtesy David A. Hanks & Associates. Haraszty's date of birth is somewhat uncertain, being given as 1922, 1923, or 1925; it is entered on her United States Certificate of Naturalization as September 28, 1920; see Bruce David Colen, with Kristine B. Pietersma, *A Colorful Woman, Eszter Haraszty: A Life of Design* (n.p.: Lost Art Productions, 2006), 9.
2 The end of the war brought a brief period of freedom in Hungary and in 1946 Stephen Borsody, Haraszty's brother-in-law, became a press attaché to the Hungarian delegation to the United States; see "Stephen Borsody, 89, Scholar of Hungary," *New York Times*, November 18, 2000, A17.
3 Quoted in Colen, *Colorful Woman*, 4. The Breuers were family friends.
4 "Hand-Screened Fabrics," *Interior Design and Decoration* (July 1949): 8. Haraszty later recalled "doing hand painting [on] plastic aprons for Christmas" during her time at Drago Studio; see Haraszty, interview with Carmel. In 1957 Haraszty said she began work in New York as "a $25-a-week helper in a dress manufacturing firm"; see Edith Evans Asbury, "Brussels Fair Restaurant Next Project for Designer, *New York Times*, October 7, 1957, 24. It is unclear if this comment refers to Drago Studio or another job.
5 "The New Fabrics," *Interiors* (March 1950): 106. This design was also identified as *Stained Glass*; see "Hand-Screened Fabrics," *Interior Design and Decoration* (July 1949): 8.
6 "The House in the Museum Garden," *Bulletin of the Museum of Modern Art* 16, no. 1 (1949): 5. Arundell Clarke is credited with providing "Fabrics for draperies & floor cushions; striped material designed by Eszter; bamboo shades" for the house installation. As Haraszty later recalled "Marcel asked me to design [a] textile for his MoMA house, Knoll Stripe" (Haraszty, interview with Carmel). For Haraszty's fabrics displayed Clarke's showroom; see "Hand-Screened Fabrics," 8.
7 From "Eszter's Diary, 1950–1955," in Colen, *Colorful Woman*, 170.
8 "Chicago First Stop on This Fabric Tour," *Chicago Daily Tribune*, November 5, 1950, SW-AA.
9 Haraszty, interview with Carmel.
10 "Merchandise Cues-Stripes and Strength at Knoll," *Interiors* (June 1951): 130.
11 Haraszty, interview, January 25, 1977, Knoll Archives.
12 The rayon fiber of *Transportation Cloth* was adjusted in the mid-1950s to improve wear, and in 1959 the fiber content was changed to a rayon and nylon blend, making it more durable. This new version was called *Nylon Transportation Cloth*.
13 For *Transportation Cloth* see *Good Design January '51*, exh. cat. (New York: Museum of Modern Art, 1951), 11. For "Knoll Stripes" see *Good Design June '51*, exh. cat. (New York: Museum of Modern Art, 1951), 7. See also chap. 3 in this volume.
14 For awards see also "For Your Information: A.I.D. Conference," *Interiors* (May 1953): 16; "Results of the A.I.D.'s Annual Homefurnishings Competition," *Interiors* (May 1954): 94.
15 For *Good Design* inclusion see Betty Pepis, "Good Design Exhibit Opens in Chicago," *New York Times*, January 5, 1955, 20. See also Pepis, "Textile Designs Dominate Home Furnishing Contest," *New York Times*, April 14, 1955, 35.
16 Information in this section comes from Knoll Associates, "Knoll Textiles Introduces Three New Fabrics Designed by Eszter Haraszty," press release, June 20, 1955, Haraszty designer file, Knoll Archives.
17 Knoll Textiles, "Preisliste Textilien 80/81," January 1, 1980, pp. 12, 25, KnollTextiles Archive.
18 "Precise Prints and Neat Weaves," *Interiors* (February 1956): 132.
19 *Sarano* file, KnollTextiles Archive.
20 *Lana* file, KnollTextiles archive.
21 Ibid.
22 "Fall Fabrics 1950," *Interior Design and Decoration* (October 1950): 60.
23 "Chicago First Stop on This Fabric Tour."
24 Ibid. While it is unclear how many stops were made after Chicago, one of them was at the Knoll retailer Contemporary House in Dallas; see "For Your Information: Contemporary Fair in Dallas," *Interiors* (November 1951): 16.
25 Advertisement for Knoll Associates, *Interiors* (December 1950): 161. *Interior Design* noted the introduction of the guides in their review of the new New York showroom; see "New Knoll Showroom: A Study in Space and Texture," *Interior Design and Decoration* (April 1951): 30.
26 It is not clear when Haraszty went from being a consultant to head of textiles and chief colorist for Knoll. For the first published identification of Haraszty as "colorist" see "The Knolls: Furniture-Designing Team," *Look* (May 1951): 104.
27 Haraszty later remembered her "first big" color project was the 575 Madison Avenue showroom, see Haraszty, interview, January 25, 1977, Knoll Archives.
28 Olga Gueft, "Knoll Associates Move Into the Big Time," *Interiors* (May 1951): 79.
29 Haraszty, interview, January 25, 1977, Knoll Archives.
30 Haraszty, interview with Carmel. Haraszty remembered that after she put in the colors, the plans "went back to [the] Planning Unit, by the time they got back to Hans, my colors had been removed." It is likely Haraszty's colors were rejected because they were thought too dramatic and daring for the largely conservative business customers of the Planning Unit.
31 "Merchandise Cues: Fantasies of the Loom," *Interiors* (May 1952): 126.
32 Betty Pepis, "For the Home: Settings in Decorators' Exhibit," *New York Times*, March 29, 1952, 8.
33 This dramatic atmosphere was noted in Betty Pepis, "Sculptor Designs Wire-Shell Chairs," *New York Times*, December 10, 1952, 46.
34 "Drum Beaters for Modern," *Life* (March 2, 1953): 72–73.
35 Knoll Associates, "Dramatic New Design for Leisure at the Dallas Museum of Art," brochure, 1952, courtesy Jerry Bywaters Research Collection on American Art, Southern Methodist University.
36 Knoll Associates, Advertisement, *Interior Design* (October 1952): 33. This advertisement also appeared in *Interiors* (December 1952).
37 Haraszty, interview, January 25, 1977, Knoll Archives.
38 Haraszty later recalled that Herbert Matter assisted her on the Textile Kit by designing the photograph cards for the print booklet; see ibid. Ladislav Sutnar was identified as Haraszty's co-designer in *Industrial Design*, "Selling" (December 1954), 92.
39 Ibid.; and "Fifteen Years in Retrospect," *Industrial Design* (April 1969): 42, 92.
40 Haraszty, interview, January 25, 1977, Knoll Archives.
41 From "Eszter's Diary," 177–78; see also *Interiors* (March 1954): 140.
42 From "Eszter's Diary," 179–80.
43 See "Trade Notes," *Interior Design* (May 1956): 147, 149.
44 See "Bold Colors and Aboveboard Cuisine for the American Restaurant at Brussels," *Interiors* (May 1958), 128–29. Interestingly, former Knoll alum Albert Herbert provided a mural design for the space.

Christa Häusler-Goltz

1 Christa Häusler-Goltz, email to the author, February 2, 2011. Unless otherwise noted the information in this biography is from this email correspondence. I would like to thank Christa Häusler-Goltz and her daughter Anne Garber for their assistance with this project. —AMT
2 Christa Häusler-Goltz, email to the author, February 24, 2011. For more on rohi see the Marga Hielle-Vatter biography herein.
3 Designs by Häusler may have been included in the Knoll International textile offerings before 1977. A catalogue for an exhibition of textiles by Taunus identifies *Anda* (1975) and *Kobe* (1976) as designs by Häusler made for Knoll, however, research thus far has not been able to confirm that these textiles were included in the Knoll line. See Dieter Gasse, Carl-Wolfgang Schümann, and Manfred Rusche, *Printed by Taunus Textildruck: 30 Jahre Textildruck in Deutchland am Beispiel einer Firma*, exh. cat. (Krefeld, Germany: Deutsches Textilmuseum Krefeld, 1983), 38–39.
4 "Knoll International macht das Wohnen wohnlicher," Knoll International press release, January 13, 1977, Knoll Archives.
5 Quoted and translated in Barbara Segerer to Christine Rae, December 31, 1976, Knoll International interoffice memo, Knoll Archives.
6 Ibid.
7 "Weltpremiere der Knoll International Textilcollection 1977 in Frankfurt," Knoll International press release, ca. January 1977, Knoll Archives.
8 Knoll International, "Preisliste Textilien 80/81," Textiles Price List, January 1980, KnollTextiles Archive.
9 Design Christa Häusler-Goltz, artist Web site, haeusler-goltz.com/.
10 Ibid.

Albert Herbert

1 Unless otherwise noted the information in this biography comes from Roger Myers, interview by Elizabeth St. George, March 26, 2011. I am very grateful to him for his assistance with this project. —ES
2 He served as staff artist for *Air Training* magazine and took classes at the USAF Drafting School. See "Interiors' Cover Artists," *Interiors* (May 1954): 10.
3 *Diamonds* press release, n.d., *Diamonds* textile file, Knoll Archives.
4 Photographs and textile sample cards, 1951–59, *Diamonds* textile file, Knoll Archives.
5 Others included Yves Vidal (president of Knoll France) and furniture designer Harry Bertoia, whose chairs Herbert had in his own apartment. For photographs of Herbert's residence, see "Albert Herbert," *Interiors* (August 1956): 82–83; "For Your Information," *Interiors* (March 1963): 12; "The Year's Work; Residence 2. Albert Herbert's all-in-1 Headquarters," *Interiors* (August 1963): 50; "Six Stories in Four," *Interiors* (August 1965): 52–57.
6 "Merchandise Cues," *Interiors* (February 1961): 138, 172; For V'Soske, see "Merchandise Cues," *Interiors* (March 1960): 136, 152; "Merchandise Cues," *Interiors* (August 1965): 174, 199; "Market," *Interiors* (January 1968): 58. Also advertisements for V'Soske, *Interiors* (August 1960): 46; (September 1960): 47; (January 1961), 59.
7 Although Herbert was prolific, his work is underresearched, and it is uncertain which of his designs from this period were actually produced.
8 For Arundell Clark, see "Arundell Clarke's 'Miss Prism,'" *Interiors* (May 1956), 130; "The Winners," *Interiors* (April 1956): 107; For L. Anton Maix, see "Precisely Delineated Patterns for Small Scale Prints," *Interiors* (June 1956): 118. For Saphier, Lerner, Schindler, Inc., see "The Year's Work," *Interiors* (August 1956): 64.
9 "Merchandise Cues," *Interiors* (April 1959): 150, 153; advertisement for Rowen, *Interiors* (October 1959): 211; "Merchandise Cues," *Interiors* (December 1960): 118, 133; "Merchandise Cues," *Interiors* (February 1963): 114.
10 "For Your Information [A.I.D. National Decoration and Design Show, 1963]" *Interiors* (November 1963): 8; "For Your Information [A.I.D. apartment at the National Decoration and Design Show, 1966]" *Interiors* (November 1965): 8; "Two-Danes at D & D: Unika-Vaev," *Interiors* (November 1967): 31; "Designers Without Clients—an Open-plan Office by Albert Herbert," *Interiors* (November 1967): 89–91.
11 "For Your Information, Awards and Competitions," *Interiors* (March 1963): 12.
12 Advertisement for Cumberland, *Interiors* (March 1960): 176; "Albert Herbert Designs for Jim Eppinger," *Interiors* (April 1968): 154-55.
13 He was long active in the society both before and after the merger and was made a life member in 1991. Herbert died in Williamsburg, Va. Obituaries, *East Hampton Star*, March 2008; John Elmo, "Remembering Albert E. Herbert, Jr.," *New York Metro*, March 2008, online at ASID Web site, www.asidnymetro.org/files/summer_2008.pdf.

Sheila Hicks

1 Joan Simon and Susan C. Faxon, eds., *Sheila Hicks: 50 Years* (New Haven: Yale University Press, 2010); Nina Stritzler-Levine, ed., *Sheila Hicks: Weaving as Metaphor* (London: Yale University Press; New York: Bard Graduate Center, 2006). See also Betty Werther, "Sheila Hicks at Rabat," *Craft Horizons* 31 (June 1971); "The Weaving of Sheila Hicks," *American Fabrics*, no. 53 (1961): 30–33.
2 "1997 American Craft Council Awards," *American Craft* 57, no. 5 (October/November 1997): 85; Joan Simon, "Frames of Reference," in Stritzler-Levine, *Sheila Hicks*, 59–64; Nina Stritzler-Levine, "A Design Identity," in Stritzler-Levine, *Sheila Hicks*, 351.
3 Ibid.
4 "Knoll Previews Art Institute Exhibit of Woven Forms," press release, ca. 1963, Sheila Hicks designer file, KnollTextiles Archive. Edith Weight, "Art Form," *Chicago Tribune*, November 10, 1963; "For your Information," *Interiors* (June 1963): 14.
5 Stritzler-Levine, "Design Identity," 354.
6 Ibid., 359.
7 Christine Rae and Sheila Hicks, Knoll internal memos, April 1964–January 1965 (esp. April 1964), Sheila Hicks designer file, Knoll Archives. This correspondence suggests that Hicks was unsure of her role in the company, but consistently performed as "consultant," identifying worthy new designers or interesting exhibitions.
8 Joan Simon, "Unbiased Weaves," in Simon and Faxon, *Shelia Hicks*, 100, illus. 101. Anni Albers shared her interest in this source.
9 The prototype for *Inca* was dyed using the exact color scheme of the skirt: rust threads combined with brown and white natural wools; Sheila Hicks to Christine Rae, April 1, 1964, and April 7, 1964, Sheila Hicks designer file, Knoll Archives.
10 "Upholstery Fabrics, Introduction for 1966," press release, n.d., Sheila Hicks designer file, Knoll Archives.
11 The Saarinen chair cushions were hand-embroidered in France. Because they were deemed too expensive to be exported to the U.S., they were produced solely by Knoll France; Rae and Hicks, Knoll internal memos, April 1964–January 1965, Sheila Hicks designer file, Knoll Archives.
12 Duncan H. South, internal memo, January 15, 1965 (in reference to Sheila Hicks's letter, January 11, 1965), Sheila Hicks designer file, Knoll Archives.

Marga Hielle-Vatter

1 Unless otherwise noted the information in this biography comes from Bernd Hielle, emails to the author, March 7, 2011, and March 12, 2011. Many thanks to Bernd Hielle, son of Marga Hielle-Vatter for his kind assistance with this project. —CBPP
2 "Aus einer Passion wurde eine erfolgreiche Firma," *Merkur*, Region Wolfratshausen, June 17, 2003.
3 Gordon Huelin, ed., *Old Catholics and Anglicans, 1931–1981* (London: Oxford University Press, 1983), 116.
4 During this time Hielle was imprisoned in the former Czechoslovakia for more than a year and a half, and the couple divorced shortly after his release.
5 Jutta Beder, *Zwischen Blümchen und Picasso: Textildesign der fünfziger Jahre in Westdeutschland* (Muenster: Lit Verlag, 2002), 292.
6 In 1971 Knoll was seeking to sell *Dynamic* to American Airlines; Duncan South telefax to Barbara Rodes, March 9, 1971, *Dynamic* textile file, KnollTextiles Archive.
7 For an example of a long-repeat Jacquard weave by Hielle-Vatter see *Parquet*, illustrated in Jack Lenor Larsen and Jeanne Weeks, *Fabrics for Interiors* (New York: Litton Educational Publishing, 1975), 72; see also "Hielle-Vatter, Marga" in Mel Byers, *The Design Encyclopedia* (London and New York: Laurence King Publishing and MoMA, 2004), 324.
8 Cherie Fehrman and Kenneth R. Fehrman, *Interior Design Innovators, 1910-1960* (San Fransisco: Fehrman Books, 2009), 68; Lesley Jackson, *Twentieth-Century Pattern Design: Textile and Wallpaper Pioneers* (London: Mitchell Beazley, 2002), 114.
9 Huguenin may also have introduced rohi to Jack Lenor Larsen who presented rohi's textiles beginning in 1965; see Advertisement for Jack Lenor Larsen Inc., *Interiors* (September 1965): 47.
10 The Hielle-Vatter textiles discussed in this biography are those known to be designed by her as identified in the records for Knoll Textiles in the United States. However, it is likely that Knoll introduced other textiles manufactured by rohi for distribution in Europe.
11 "Knoll Introduces Wool Upholstery Fabrics," Knoll International press release, p. 2, October 19, 1970, KnollTextiles Archive.
12 Ibid.
13 Knoll Textiles, "Textiles Price List August 1, 1972," p. 10, KnollTextiles Archive.
14 Five years after its introduction, Knoll included *Align* in the *Wool Casement Collection* in the United States; Knoll Textiles, "Price List October 1979," p. 29, KnollTextiles Archive.
15 Knoll Textiles, "Bulletin," January 15, 1976, *Tournee* design file, KnollTextiles Archive.
16 *Severin* design file, KnollTextiles Archive.
17 Hielle-Vatter designed *Jamaica* and *Norwalk* for the collection. See Sunar "News," April 1979, supplement, Josef and Anni Albers Foundation Archive; and "Materials, Components, Processes" *Industrial Design* 26 (July/August 1979): 64.

Evelyn Hill Anselevicius

1 Evelyn Hill, "Autobiography," ca. 1952, Evelyn Hill designer file, KnollTextiles Archive. The dates given by Hill for her activities during the late 1940s vary slightly on this and several other biographies that she provided to Knoll between the 1950s and early 1970s (see Hill designer file, KnollTextiles Archive).
2 Hill does not appear to have been formally enrolled at the college; see "Faculty and Student Roster," in Mary Emma Harris, *The Arts at Black Mountain College* (Cambridge, Mass.: MIT Press, 1987), 263–76.
3 In 1950 Chance had four weavers (including Hill) working for her; Majel Chance Obata, telephone interview by Susan Ward, February 10, 2011.
4 Evelyn Anselevicius, quoted in Patricia Degener, "Modern Tapestries and Ancient Ways," *Saint Louis Post-Dispatch*, August 3, 1972: 4; Chance Obata, telephone interview.
5 "Merchandise Cues: Fantasies of the Loom," *Interiors* (May 1952): 126; "Fabrics to the Fore in Homefurnishings," *Handweaver & Craftsman* 3 (Summer 1952): 30-31.
6 Hill, "Autobiography."
7 He had a distinguished career in teaching; see "Obituary: George Anselevicius, Former Dean of Architecture School," Washington University Web site, http://news.wustl.edu/news/Pages/12856.aspx.
8 Degener, "Modern Tapestries and Ancient Ways," 4.
9 Ibid.
10 The 1974 tapestry is now in the collection of Koehnline Museum of Art, Oakton Community College, Chicago; see www.oakton.edu/museum/anselevicius.html.
11 Evelyn Anselevicius to Kathryn Hiesinger, February 17, 1983, *Design Since 1945* curatorial exhibition files, Philadelphia Museum of Art; Paul Logan, "Weaver Evelyn Anselevicius Left Powerful Tapestries Worldwide" (obituary), *Albuquerque Journal*, July 12, 2003, Albuquerque Journal Web site, www.abqjournal.com.

Suzanne Huguenin

1   Information in this section is taken from Christina Laubi (niece of Suzanne Huguenin), email to the author, December 9, 2010, and Christina Laubi, phone interview with the author, December 10, 2010. I extend my warmest thanks to Ms. Laubi for sharing memories of her aunt and for providing archival documents and photographs that form the basis of this biography. —EM
2   Ursina Jakob, "Suzanne Huguenin: ein Auge – und Glück," *ProLitteris Gazeta*, no. 23 (June 1998): 58–59.
3   Ibid.; and Suzanne Huguenin to Christine Rae, October 23, 1979, Suzanne Huguenin designer file, Knoll Archives.
4   Huguenin to Rae. For Gourdon see "Charles Maurice Gourdon, Silk Manufacturer, 88," *New York Times*, May 11, 1991, 10.
5   Huguenin to Rae. Unless otherwise noted this section is drawn from this letter and from Suzanne Huguenin, interview, ca. 1977, pp. 1–25, Huguenin designer file, Knoll Archives. Huguenin's aunt Berta (Huguenin) Sekula was a friend of Hans Knoll's uncle and they knew each other socially. Huguenin's cousin, the noted painter Sonia Sekula, acted as Haraszty's assistant for a short time, but Sekula suffered from schizophrenia and had to leave the company (Laubi, phone interview; Huguenin, interview, ca. 1977, p. 1).
6   Huguenin, interview, ca. 1977, 3.
7   Suzanne Huguenin, interview by Kate Carmel, October 30, 1987, Stewart Collection Archives, Montreal Museum of Fine Arts, courtesy David A. Hanks & Associates.
8   Huguenin, interview, ca. 1977, p. 16. This textile was not part of the Knoll Textiles collection but was used exclusively on the Schultz furniture.
9   Suzanne Huguenin to Jennifer Toher, David A. Hanks & Associates, Inc., May 12, 1987, Stewart Collection Archives, Montreal Museum of Fine Arts, courtesy David A. Hanks & Associates.
10 Ibid.
11 Ruth Wagner, "Transcripts to Textiles," *Washington Post/Times Herald*, December 9, 1962, F25.
12 Huguenin, interview, ca. 1977, pp. 6–7, 16–17.
13 "Textile Consulting Service," *Interiors* (October 1963): 172.
14 "People in the Showroom," *Interiors* (July 1964): 123; "Market Report: Small Scaled Weaves," *Interiors* (January 1965): 130; Nancy Lane Kerr, "Suzanne Can Do Anything—But Vote," *Greensboro Record*, November 2, 1964; Annie Lee Singletary, "She Takes Color to Market," *Winston Salem Journal*, October 31, 1964.
15 "People in the Trade," *Interiors* (April 1966): 180.
16 Larsen first featured rohi fabrics in 1965. see Advertisement for Jack Lenor Larsen, Inc., *Interiors* (September 1965): 47.
17 Huguenin, interview, ca. 1977, pp. 22–23, Huguenin Designer File, Knoll Archives.
18 Knoll International, Press release for Internationale Fachmesse für Heimtextilien, ca. January 1975, Knoll Archives.
19 Huguenin, interview by Carmel.
20 Merle Lindby-Young, phone interview with Ann Marguerite Tartsinis, August 25, 2010.

Jacqueline Iribe

1   Laurence Bartoletti, "La Scène Internationale," in *Mobi Boom*, exh. cat. (Paris: Musée des arts décoratifs, 2010), 191. Research thus far has uncovered little about Jacqueline Iribe.
2   Anne Bony, *Furniture and Interiors of the 1960's* (New York: Flammarion, 2004), 101.
3   Brian Lutz, *Knoll: A Modernist Universe* (New York: Rizzoli, 2010), 62.
4   Ibid.
5   D'Arlette Barré-Despond, "Alain Richard," *Dictionnaire International Des Arts Appliqués et du Design* (Paris: Editions du Regard, 1996), 507.
6   Advertisement for Knoll featuring *Citronnade*, *Lazy Lines*, *Diamonds*, and *Shogi*, *Interior Design* (November 1953): 21. The text of the ad claims all of the colors were coordinated by Haraszty; also ran in "Merchandise Cues," *Interiors* (February 1954): 100.
7   Lutz, *Knoll*, 58–59; Knoll + Drake advertisement, *Interiors* (September 1955): 25.
8   George Eudes, *Modern French Interiors*, transl. M. I. Martin (New York: Cromwell, 1958), 1.
9   Petra Timmer, *Metz & Co: de Creatieve Jaren* (Rotterdam: Uitgeverij 010, 1995), 157, 164. Under the guidance of owner Henk de Leeuw, Metz & Co. was the sole Dutch representative of Knoll International in the Netherlands.
10 Ibid., 157.
11 A drapery fabric by Iribe was featured on the 1954 cover of *La Maison Française*, see *Mobi Boom*, 264; Another design by Iribe was included in a fashion photograph in the article "Les Collections et l'évolution de la mode," in *L'Officiel de la mode*, no. 449 (1959): 297.
12 Barré-Despond, "Alain Richard," 507.
13 "Alain Richard," in *Mobi Boom*, 287.

Arne Jacobsen

1   Christopher Mount, *Arne Jacobsen* (San Francisco: Chronicle Books, 2004), 8.
2   Tobias Faber, *Arne Jacobsen* (New York: Praeger, 1964), xv.
3   "Chronology," in Poul Erik Tojer, *Arne Jacobsen: Architect and Designer* (Copengagen: Dask Design Center, 1995).
4   "Fabrics Designed in Denmark Here," *New York Times*, November 20, 1948, p. 8.
5   Ibid.
6   Mary Roche, "Decorators Hold Luncheon, Exhibit" *New York Times*, March 23, 1949, p. 33; and "Belgian Linen, Printed in Sprightly Colors," *New York Times*, October 10, 1949, p. 26.
7   Walter Rendell Storey, "Exhibit Presents Home Furnishings," *New York Times*, November 5, 1948, p. 28; "Modern Furniture From 8 Lands in Show at Architectural League," *New York Times*, May 26, 1949, p. 36; and "New Fabrics From Europe are Presented at the Remodeled Hambro House of Design," *New York Times*, April 26, 1950, p. 45.
8   For Scandinavian Modernism see Mount, *Arne Jacobsen*, 11; Faber, *Arne Jacobsen*, xix.

Julia Keiner-Forchheimer

1   "Fabrics from Israel by Julia Keiner," *Handweaver & Craftsman* 5 (Fall 1954): 30.
2   Ibid.
3   Sarah L. Schmerler, "Julia Keiner Forchheimer" in *Aishet Hayil*, exh. cat. (New York: Yeshiva University Museum, 1993), n.p.
4   "Fabrics from Israel by Julia Keiner," 30.
5   Dr. Ran Sapoznik and Curt Arnson, "Design of Jewish Ritual Objects and the Bezalel Academy of Arts and Design" in *Continuity and Change: 92 Years of Judaica at Bezalel* (Jerusalem: Department of Culture, Jerusalem Fairs and Conventions Bureau, Bezalel Academy, Ministry of Education, 1998), n.p.
6   Schmerler, "Julia Keiner Forchheimer," n.p.
7   Ralph Saul Caplan, "Forms from Israel," *Industrial Design* 6 (February 1959): 67.
8   "Isabel Scott: The Many Faces of Janus," *Interiors* (August 1966): 165; "D&D Market Report," *Interiors* (October 1966): 160. In 1968 and 1969 she also contributed wool and mohair upholsteries to the Isabel Scott collection; see "The Resources Council Preview '69," *Interiors* (November 1968): 146; and Advertisement for "Yampa Valley Collection" by Isabel Scott Fabrics, *Interiors* (May 1969): 68.
9   "Bulletin: Upholstery Fabrics Introduction for 1966," ca. 1966, p. 3, Knoll Archives.
10 Knoll Textiles, "Textile Price List," June 15, 1968, KnollTextiles Archive.
11 Knoll Textiles, "Textile Price List," February 15, 1967, KnollTextiles Archive.
12 Sylvia Axelrod Herskowitz, "Aishet Hayil Revisited," in *Aishet Hayil*, n.p.; and see list of founders, the Museum of Jewish Heritage Web site, mjhnyc.org.

Steffi Kiessling-Plewa

1   Steffi Kiessling-Plewa, phone conversation with the author, February 2, 2011. Unless otherwise noted this biography is based on this interview. Many thanks to Steffi Kiessling-Plewa for her assistance on this project. —AMT
2   Knoll International, "Textile Price List," 1979, and Knoll Textiles (U.S.), "Textile Price List," 1979, KnollTextiles Archive. In Europe Lucena was marketed as a single design.
3   J. Christophe Brünzli, telephone conversation with the author, October 20, 2010.
4   Steffi Kiessling-Plewa, email correspondence with the author, March 9, 2011.
5   Plewaworks Web site at www.plewaworks.de.

Susan Kimber

1   "Partners in Residence: Stephen Kiviat and Wife Susan Kimber Co-Design Their City Apartment," *Interior Design* 44 (December 1973), 85.
2   Ibid.
3   Vivien Raynor, "Tapestries, Inge Morath Photo Exhibited," *New York Times*, April 12, 1981; Patricia Leigh Brown, "Currents; So What Came First, the Art or the Furniture?," *New York Times*, July 20, 1989. Kimber's affiliation with Steelcase was likely through their subsidiary Atelier International which was headed by Kimber's husband, Steve Kiviat.

4   "Tapestry," *Interior Design* 55 (November 1984): 242.

Antoinette Lackner Webster

1   The designer spelled her nickname, by which she was known for much of her life, "Tony" (Margaret Webster, email to Susan Ward, February 18, 2011); Knoll, for reasons unknown, spelled it "Toni." Many thanks to Margaret Webster and Hollis Webster for their assistance on this project.—SW
2   Antoinette Lackner Prestini, application for admission, Cranbrook Academy of Art, May 23, 1945, Cranbrook Academy of Art Office of the Registrar (1990–19), Cranbrook Archives.
3   Ibid. The School of Design was renamed the Institute of Design in 1944.
4   For Denton as a center for progressive art education, see Kendall Curlee, "Corpron, Carlotta," in The Handbook of Texas Online, Texas Historical Association, www.tshaonline.org.
5   Among other subjects, she taught mechanical drawing, which her husband had been hired to teach; see Antoinette Lackner Prestini, application for admission; and Margaret Webster and Hollis Webster, conversations with Susan Ward, May 8 and 11, 2010.
6   Margaret Webster and Hollis Webster, conversations with Susan Ward, May 8 and 11, 2010.
7   Majel Chance Obata recalled that both students and faculty admired Prestini's work; Chance Obata, telephone interview by Susan Ward, February 10, 2011.
8   Prestini was replacing Robert Sailors, who left Cranbrook at the end of the 1947 school year; see Christa C. Mayer Thurman, "Textiles," in *Design in America: The Cranbrook Vision 1925–1950* (New York: Harry N. Abrams, 1983), 201–5.
9   Cranbrook Academy of Art Student News Letter, 1947, Cranbrook Archives (1998-05c), 2:4. She apparently continued to design for the Farms after returning to Lake Forest in 1948; see "Handweavers Design for the Power Loom," *Home Furnishings Merchandising* (June 1948); 49, and "Plymouth Colony Farms," *Handweaver & Craftsman* 1 (April 1950): 38–39.
10 "Plymouth Colony Farms," 38.
11 Margaret Webster, email to Susan Ward, February 18, 2011.

Dennis Lennon

1   Theo Crosby, Obituary: Dennis Lennon, *The Independent*, May 1, 1991, p. 27; see also Colin Naylor, ed., *Contemporary Designers* (Chicago: St. James Press, 1990). Lennon was born on June 23, 1918.
2   Nicholas Ind, *Terence Conran: The Authorized Biography* (London: Sidgwick and Jackson, 1995), 47.
3   Ibid., 49, 51.
4   *Decorative Art* 45 (1955–56): 75.
5   Michael DeCourcy Hinds, "High Living on The QE2," *New York Times*, June 29, 1978, p. C1; Paul Sargent Clark, "Vestments of a Queen," *Industrial Design* 15 (September 1968): 28–31.
6   Project dates recorded online at DesignInform, www.designinform.co.uk/dp.htm.
7   "Hand Printed Fabrics are Bold in

Colors," *New York Times*, November 17, 1953, p. 34.
8   Knoll Textiles, "Price List," June 7, 1954, pp. 3, 5, KnollTextiles Archive.
9   Ind, *Terence Conran*, 49.

Elizabeth Levin Ossip

1   Elizabeth Levin Ossip, interview with the author, April 13, 2011. Unless otherwise noted the information in this biography is derived from this interview. Many thanks to Elizabeth Levin Ossip for her assistance with this project.—ES
2   Elizabeth Levin curriculum vitae, Elizabeth Levin designer file, KnollTextiles Archive.
3   Levin Ossip designed a third textile for Knoll, but it was never put into production; Ibid.
4   Ibid.
5   Ibid.; Sample card, Elizabeth Levin designer file, KnollTextiles Archive.
6   Levin, curriculum vitae.

Stig Lindberg

1   See also Martin Eidelberg, ed., *Design 1935–1965: What Modern Was* (Montreal: Musée de L'Arts décoratifs de Montréal; New York: Harry N. Abrams, 1991): 259; Kathryn B. Hiesinger, ed., *Design Since 1945* (Philadelphia: Museum of Art, 1983): 220; and Karin Linder et al., *©Stig Lindberg* (Stockholm: Nationalmuseum, 2006). Lindberg also gained recognition as an illustrator of children's books.
2   Mary Roche, "New Chair Offers More Relaxation," *New York Times*, May 19, 1948, 26.
3   "Textile Imports Offered: Bonniers Shows Lines Designed by Scandinavian Artists," *New York Times*, November 24, 1949, 53; "European Fabrics in Bright Designs: Danish and Swedish Cloth Shown Here—Dreams and Fairy Tales are Themes," *New York Times*, October 13, 1950, 28; Betty Pepis, "The Fabric Picture," *New York Times Magazine*, April 29, 1951, 27; and "Scandinavia Gets Museum Display: Stores Duplicate Some of the 700 Items in Show of Design in Brooklyn," *New York Times*, April 21, 1954, 32.

Ross Littell

1   Ross Littell, curriculum vitae, Ross Littell file, KnollTextiles Archive.
2   Alvin Lustig, "Modern Printed Fabrics," *American Fabrics*, no. 20 (Winter 1951–52): 70.
3   *Interiors* (June 1956): 108–11. The name "New Furniture" was given by Laverne; see Kathryn B. Hiesinger, ed., *Design Since 1945* (Philadelphia: Museum of Art, 1983): 217; Aase Holm, "Ross Littell: Portrait of an International Designer," *Living Architecture*, no. 8 (1989): 99.
4   Obituary: Ross Littell, *Los Angeles Times*, May 17, 2000.
5   *Textiles USA: A Selection of Contemporary American Textiles*, exh. cat. (New York: MoMA, 1956).
6   "Designers: Ross Littell," at the Kvadrat Web site, www.kvadrat.dk.
7   Knoll Textiles, "Wholesale Price List" November 15, 1959, p. 19, KnollTextiles Archive.
8   Ibid., 18–19.
9   Ibid., 18.
10 Ross Littell file, Knoll Textile Archive.
11 "The Crème de la Crème: A.I.D.'s Citation of Merit Awards," *Interiors* (May 1959): 12.
12 Holm, "Ross Littell," 104.
13 "Designers: Ross Littell."

Franz Lorenz

1   The trademark design for "F. Lorenz, Handweberei und Textilien [Handweaving and Textiles], Düdingen" appears in *Schweizer Signete/Trademarks and Symbols* (Zurich: Amstutz & Gerdeg, Graphis Press, 1948). Textiles credited to "Franz Lorenz SWB, Düdingen" were apparently published and mentioned in several contemporary Swiss journals such as *Bauen und Wohnen*.
2   Margaret Duckett, "How Donald Brothers Stay Small and Influence People," *Design* 254 (June 1, 1970): 29. See also chap. 3 in this volume, and "Peter Simpson" biography herein.
3   See Brian Lutz, *Knoll: A Modernist Universe* (New York: Rizzoli, 2010), 119; Alfred Roth, "Neue Möbel von Wohnbedarf AG und Heimatwerk," *Werk* (August 1948): 248–52. Bellman and Gunta Stölzl (see "Gunta Stadler-Stölzl" biography herein) were also members of the Swiss Werkbund (SWB).
4   Donald Brothers Sample Books 1950–1961, University Archive, Records Management and Museum Service, Heriot-Watt University.
5   It is listed under this title in the *Knoll Color Guide* (1950), KnollTextiles Archive, and *Knoll Index of Contemporary Design* (New York: Knoll Associates, 1950), 76–77.

LTL

1   For a list of all projects and awards, see LTL's Web site, www.ltlwork.net.
2   LTL Architects, firm profile, April 25, 2011, ibid. Paul and David Lewis are twin brothers.
3   Ibid. Paul Lewis, Marc Tsurumaki, David J. Lewis, *Lewis.Tsurumaki.Lewis: Opportunistic Architecture* (Princeton: Princeton Architectural Press, 2008), 11.
4   Paul Lewis, telephone interview with Ann Marguerite Tartsinis, January 11, 2011.
5   Paul Lewis, quoted in Aric Chen, "Currents: Wallcoverings, Experimental Architects Draft New Looks for the Wall," *New York Times*, June 26, 2006, F3.
6   Knoll Wallcoverings, LTL Web site, www.ltlwork.net.
7   Ibid.
8   "Product Briefs: NeoCon Review, The Writing's on the Wallpaper," *Architectural Record* (August 2006): 191.

Sven Markelius

1   The manifesto was written with Bruno Paulsson, Uno Åhrén, Gunnar Asplund, Wolter Gahn, and Eskil Sundahl; see Lucy Creagh, Helena Kåberg, and Barbara Miller Land, *Modern Swedish Design: Three Founding Texts* (New York: MoMA, 2008).
2   For Markelius's career see Eva Rudberg, *Sven Markelius, Architect* (Stockholm: Arkitektur Förlag, 1989).
3   According to the protocol in Sven Markelius's file, Architect Museum archives, Stockholm.
4   See chaps. 2 and 3 in this volume.
5   Rudberg, *Sven Markelius*, 123.
6   Ibid., 126.
7   ECO-SOC Council room at the U.N. headquarters in New York was designed with architects Hans Borgström and Bengt Lindroos, 1951–52.
8   A letter and loose-leaf sheet in a 1971 price list in the Brooklyn Museum collection indicates that *Prisma* and *Pythagoras* had been discontinued; see Knoll Textiles, "Textile Price List 1971," May 1, 1971; and J. J. Osborne (marketing, Knoll International), letter, May 15, 1971, Brooklyn Museum Library and Archives; see also chap. 5 in this volume.
9   Marilyn Hoffman, "Decorators Bestow Awards" *Christian Science Monitor*, April 3, 1957, 14.
10 Rudberg, *Sven Markelius*, 180.

Paul Maute

1   Unless otherwise noted details of Paul Maute's biography and the history of the company derives from Oskar Maute (b. 1924), telephone interview with the author, September 1, 2010. For more on Maute see also chap. 5 in this volume.
2   "Arno," from Suzanne Huguenin, *Knoll Textiles Sales Guide* (1962), courtesy Daniel Kroger. In describing *Arno* Huguenin wrote about Maute's history with the company: "Actually, he had been weaving some of our early H900-H930 handwoven series for Knoll Germany for several years." These are likely the fabrics mentioned by Toby Rodes, Barbara Rodes-Segerer's first husband and head of Knoll Europe 1955-1966, in a telephone conversation with Earl Martin, October 21, 2010. Rodes remembered Maute was weaving for Knoll in the 1950s, making Evelyn Hill *Handwovens* for Knoll Germany.
3   "Arno," from Huguenin, *Knoll Textiles Sales Guide*.
4   *Cato* file, KnollTextiles Archive. See also chap. 5 in this volume.
5   O. Maute, telephone interview.
6   Paul Maute (grandson), telephone conversation with the author, May 4, 2011.
7   *Cato* file, KnollTextiles Archive.

Abbott Miller

1   Caitlin Dover, "Design Couples: Ellen Lupton and Abbott Miller," *Print* 64 (June 2010), online at magazine Web site, www.printmag.com.
2   John L. Walters, "Interview with Pentagram's J. Abbott Miller," *Eye* 45 (Autumn 2002), online at magazine Web site, www.eyemagazine.com.
3   Ibid.
4   Ibid.
5   Miller profile, under "Partners," at Pentagram Web site, www.pentagram.com.
6   Walters, "Interview with Pentagram's J. Abbott Miller."
7   Debbie Millman, "Design Matters Today with Abbott Miller," transcript of radio broadcast, March 28, 2008, online under "Archives, March 2008" at www.debbiemillman.blogspot.com. See also "Abbott Miller," under "Designer Bios," Knoll Web site, www.knoll.com.
8   Quoted in "The Grammar Collection for KnollTextiles," under "All Work / Products," Pentagram Web site, www.pentagram.com.
9   For more about Miller's 2011 collection see John Pavlus, "The Legendary Abbott Miller Unveils Wallpaper Drawn with Dripping Ink," *Fast Company's Co. Design* (March 24, 2011), online journal, Web site, at www.fastcodesign.com.

Frances Breese Miller

1   All biographical details, unless otherwise noted, are drawn from three autobiographies: Frances Miller, *"Tanty": Encounters with the Past* (Sag Harbor, N.Y.: Sandbox Press, 1979); *More About "Tanty": A Second Growing Up* (Sag Harbor, N.Y.: Sandbox Press, 1980); *"Tanty": The Daring Decades, Completing the Tanty Trilogy with a Haitian Interlude* (Sag Harbor, N.Y.: Sandbox Press, 1981).
2   Miller, *More About "Tanty,"* 36.
3   Other American artists designing hooked rugs include Thomas Hart Benton, Hugo Gellert, Ilonka Karasz, Yasuo Kuniyoshi, Henry Varnum Poor, Ruth Reeves, Henriette and Winold Reiss, and Marguerite Zorach. See Cynthia Fowler, *Hooked Rugs and American Modernism* (Surrey, Eng,. and Burlington, Vt.: Ashgate, forthcoming).
4   Miller, *More About "Tanty,"* 36.
5   Ibid.
6   The "T" in Frances T. Miller stands for either for her nickname, Tanty, or for Tileston, her middle name prior to marriage.
7   See chap. 2, in this volume.
8   She also exhibited at Guild Hall in East Hampton, N.Y., in the early 1930s and at Gump's in San Francisco in the late 1930s.
9   Advertisement, *Interior Decorator* (June 1939): 2; Advertisement, *Interior Decorator* (September 1939): 6.
10 "Activities in Brief," *Interior Decorator* (February 1940): 30; "American-Way," *Interior Decorator* (May 1940): 28.
11 Such as Noémi Raymond, Marianne Strengell, Oscar Stronorov, and Henning Watterston. Eliot F. Noyes, *Organic Design in Home Furnishings* (New York: MoMA, 1941).
12 See, e.g., "Interiors Selection of 1942 Furniture," *Interiors* (February 1942): 38; and "Today's Modern Furniture," *Interiors* (May 1942): 37.

Alexandre Mimoglou

1   Dieter Gasse, Carl-Wolfgang Schümann, and Manfred Rusche, *Printed by Taunus Textildruck: 30 Jahr Textildruck in Deutschland am Beispiel eirner Firma*, exh. cat. (Krefeld, Germany: Deutsches Textilmuseum Krefeld, 1983), 61.
2   Hans Wichmann, ed., *Von Morris bis Memphis: Textilien der Neuen Sammlung, Ende 19. bis Ende 20. Jahrhundert* (Basel: Birkhäuser, 1990), 446.
3   "Alexandre Mimoglou," *Architecture Intérieure-Créé*, no. 203 (Winter 1984/85): 18-19.
4   Alexandre Mimoglou biography and career synopsis, EURAN (European Art Networks) Global Cultural Networks Web site, www.euran.com.
5   "Alexandre Mimoglou," 19–20; Wichmann, *Von Morris bis Memphis*, 446.
6   Alexandre Mimoglou biography and career synopsis, EURAN Web site, www.euran.com.

Claudine Piaget

1   Claudine Piaget, email correspondence with Elizabeth St. George, April 11, 2011; Claudine Piaget curriculum vitae and Piaget fax to Nicole Casey, July 25, 1996, Claudine Piaget designer file, KnollTextiles Archive.
2   Ibid.; Lise Coirier, ed., *Label-Design.Be: Design in Belgium after 2000* (Oostkamp: Stichting Kunstboek, 2005), 218.
3   Ibid.
4   Piaget correspondence with St. George.
5   "The Screenplay Collection," press release, November 1996, textile folder (1996), KnollTextiles Archive.
6   Ibid.
7   "Spring Collection, Fabric Introductions," Knoll press release, April 1998, textile folder (1998), KnollTextiles Archive.
8   Piaget curriculum vitae and fax; Coirier, *Label-Design.Be*, 218.
9   Piaget curriculum vitae and fax.
10 Diana Mosher, "Fantastic Plastics," *Contract* 43 (November 2001): 34.
11 Piaget correspondence with St. George.

Proenza Schouler

1   Phoebe Eaton, "Proenza Schouler grows up: Jack and Lazaro, Fashion's 29-year-old Wunderkinder, take it to the next level with new backing from the Valentino Group," *Harper's Bazaar* (September 2007): 551+, consulted online via General OneFile database, New York Public Library (NYPL).
2   Meenal Mistry, "Fashion Flash: Boy Wonders: Fashion's Newest Duo, Lazaro Hernandez and Jack McCollough, Are Wowing the Critics," *W* (September 2002): 366+, consulted online via General OneFile database, NYPL.
3   Their internships proved beneficial when putting together the collection as Michael Kors donated all of the fabric for their thesis show.
4   Hernandez explained that they did not want to put their own names on the company in case it failed, Eaton, "Proenza Schouler Grows Up."
5   The award process was documented in *Seamless*, a 2005 film that followed three of the ten finalists as they competed. In addition to Proenza Schouler, Doo.Ri and Alexandre Plokhov of Cloak were profiled.
6   Eric Wilson, "At Fashion Week, The Sponsors are Stealing the Spotlight," *New York Times*, February 4, 2005.
7   Marc Karimzadeh, "Jack McCollough and Lazaro Hernandez for Proenza Schouler," *Womens Wear Daily* 195, no. 112, 2008, 22. consulted online via General OneFile database, NYPL.
8   "United States of America: Proenza Schouler Creates the First Interior Textile Collection for Knoll Luxe," January 5, 2009, online at www.Fibre2fashion.com/news/printstory.asp?news_id=67855.
9   Chloë Sevigny, "Lazaro Hernandez & Jack McCollough," *Interview*, March 2011, 207. online at www.interviewmagazine.com.
10 Ibid.
11 Rima Suqi, "Dress Code," *Elle Décor* (November 2008): 70.

Elisha Prouty

1   Elisha Prouty, telephone conversation with the author, January 10, 2011. Unless otherwise noted the information in this biography comes from this interview. Many thanks to Elisha Prouty for his kind assistance on this project. —AMT
2   For more on Isabel Scott see chap. 1 in this volume.
3   "New Upholstery Fabrics Introduced," *Progressive Architecture* (January 1959): 8, 87; "Three Fabric Houses Show Variations on Stripes and Textures," *Interiors* (February 1959): 114; "Bright Hues Mark Upholstery Fabrics," *New York Times*, November 13, 1958.
4   "Description of Knoll Fabrics," January 28, 1969, KnollTextile Archive.
5   Ibid.
6   *Belaire* was described in English, French, and German, see ibid.
7   "Prouty Designs, Inc.," *Interiors* (October 1976): 131.
8   Riyadh witnessed a construction boom during the 1970s and 1980s as a result of rising oil prices. Prouty's contract came through the United States government.

Noémi Raymond

1   See Kenneth Frampton, Foreword: Belated Recognition," in Kurt G. F. Helfrich and William Whitaker, eds., *Crafting A Modern World: The Architecture and Design of Antonin and Noémi Raymond* (New York: Princeton Architectural Press, 2006), 10–11; Kurt G. F. Helfrich and Mari Sakamoto Nakahara, introduction to ibid., 14–15.
2   Noémi P. Raymond, "Draft Autobiography," n.d., Raymond Collection, Architectural Archives, University of Pennsylvania.
3   For Dow's approach to creating harmonies of line, "notan" (light and shade), and color, see *Composition: A Series of Exercises in Art Structure for the Use of Students and Teachers*, 9th rev. ed. (Garden City, NY: Doubleday, Page & Co., 1913).
4   Antonin Raymond, *An Autobiography* (Rutland, Vt., and Tokyo: Charles E. Tuttle Co., 1973), 318.
5   Helfrich and Nakahara, introduction, 23.
6   See William Whitaker, "Chronology of the Raymonds' Lives and Careers," in Helfrich and Whitaker, *Crafting a Modern World*, 263–76.
7   A photograph of Raymond's textile designs from 1935 shows small-motif patterns similar to the design later issued by Knoll as "Chinese Coins," see A. Raymond, *Autobiography*, 319.
8   Ibid., 320.
9   See Brian Lutz, *Knoll: A Modernist Universe* (New York: Rizzoli: 2010), 52.
10 The New Hope silkscreening project and designs sold to Brill are known only from Antonin Raymond/Noémi Pernessin Raymond correspondence (specifically, NPR to AR, November 7/8, 1949; October 16, October 20, November 7, November 12, November 18, and December 12, 1950; February 9, February 15, February 19, March 1, March 5, April 7, and April 10, 1951), Architectural Archives, University of Pennsylvania.
11 Noémi Raymond to Antonin Raymond, March 5, 1951, ibid.
12 This design was included in *Textiles USA* (MoMA, 1956) and published in *American Fabrics* 38 (Fall 1956), 40–41. A related pencil drawing survives in the Architectural Archives, University of Pennsylvania.
13 Helfrich and Nakahara, introduction, 19–20.

Francisca Reichardt Vietsch

1   Francisca Vietsch, email to the author, April 14, 2011. Unless otherwise noted the information in this biography is derived from this email. The designer's name has been spelled incorrectly as Franziska Reichardt in Jutta Beder, *Lexikon der Textildesigner 1950–2000* (www.bkm.uni-paderborn.de/php/textildesigner.php); and as Francisco Reichardt in Lesley Jackson, *Twentieth-Century Pattern Design: Textile and Wallpaper Pioneers* (London: Princeton Architectural Press, 2002), 189. Many thanks to Francisca Vietsch for her kind assistance with this text. —CBPP
2   Knoll International, "Knoll Expands Imported Print Collection with Bold Designs," press release, May 3, 1971, KnollTextiles Archive.
3   The colorways were identified as: "Blue/Turquoise," "Brown," "Red/Gray," "Purple/Ochre," "Gold/Ochre" in "Francisca Reichardt," *Industrial Design* 18 (1971): 52.

Jürgen Reichert

1   *Design Report*, no. 10 (1994): 22.
2   Reichert curriculum vitae, artist's Web site, http://juergenreichert.com/about.
3   *Design Report*.
4   Quote translated from German in ibid.

Ulrike Rhomberg-Greiner

1   Ulrike Rhomberg-Greiner, telephone interview with the author, March 13, 2011. Many thanks to Ulrike Greiner-Rhomberg for her kind assistance with this project. — CBPP
2   In 1936 Pausa ownership transferred from the Löwenstien brothers to Richard Burkhardt and Werner Greiner Sr. as part of the government's "Aryanization" program. Werner Greiner Sr. was married to Richard Burkhardt's daughter Gerda, and the two had a son also named Werner. After the death of Werner Sr., Gerda Greiner married Willy Häussler, creative director of Pausa. Rhomberg-Greiner, telephone interview; and Hermann Berner and Werner Fifka, eds., *Das Bauhaus kam nach Mössingen: Geschichte, Architektur und Design der einstigen Textilfirma Pausa* (Mossingen: Talheimer, 2006), 34, 41, 46, 161, 166, 167.
3   Rhomberg-Greiner, telephone interview.
4   Berner and Fifka, *Bauhaus*, 47.

Rodarte

1   Kavita Daswani, "Two of a Kind; Kate and Laura Mulleavy Launched Label Rodarte with No Formal Training, Just a Love of Workmanship and a Gut Feeling," *South China Morning Post* [Hong Kong], March 17, 2010, 6.
2   Amanda Fortini, "Twisted Sisters: The Designers Behind Rodarte," *The New Yorker* 85 (January 18, 2010): 32ff; Nandini D'Souza, "Sister Act," *WWD*, February 3, 2005, 14.
3   Susan in San Francisco, Kirna Zabete in New York, and Satine in Los Angeles placed the first orders; six more stores placed orders following the Spring 2006 collection.
4   Fortini, "Twisted Sisters."
5   Ibid.
6   Ibid.
7   Leila Brillson, "Material Girls: Rodarte," *Interview*, June 2, 2010, search "Material Girls," at www.interviewmagazine.com.
8   Kate Mulleavy quoted in Brooke Hodge, "Seeing Things: Rodarte for Knoll Luxe" *T: New York Times Style Magazine*, April 30, 2010.
9   Edie Cohen, "A Family Outing," *Interior Design* 81 (April 2010): 156.
10 According to Laura Mulleavy, "the way that instead of looking like a perfect weave, it looks broken and tattered and makes a connection to our spider-weave dresses," quoted in Hodge, "Seeing Things."
11 Cohen, "Family Outing."

Dana Romeis

1   Dana Romeis, telephone conversation with the author, October 21, 2010. Unless otherwise noted the information in this biography is derived from this interview. Many thanks to Dana Romeis for her assistance with this project. —AMT
2   Jan Detter, "Dana Romeis: Spatial Problem-Solving," *Fiberarts* (January/February 1987), 18.
3   "During October 1985 Knoll Introduces the Dana Romeis Contract Upholstery Collection," press release, October 1985, KnollTextiles Archive.
4   Ibid.
5   Merle Lindby-Young, telephone conversation with the author, August 25, 2010.
6   Quote in Suzanne Slesin, "Home Beat," *New York Times*, October 17, 1985, C3; Victoria Geibel, "By Design," *Metropolis* (April 1986): 51.
7   Geibel, "By Design," 49.
8   Knoll Textiles, "Price List" June 1, 1988, KnollTextiles Archive.
9   Ibid.
10 Jack Lenor Larsen, *Material Wealth* (New York: Abbeville Press, 1989), 138.

Astrid Sampe

1   David Revere McFadden, "An American Perspective," in Helena Dahlbäck Lutteman, ed., *Astrid Sampe-Svensk industritextile/ Swedish Industrial Textiles*, exh. cat. (Stockholm: Nationalmuseum, 1984): 16.
2   Details of Sampe's life and career are drawn from Lesley Jackson, *Twentieth-Century Pattern Design: Textile and Wallpaper Pioneers* (New York: Princeton Architectural Press, 2002), 121–22; Alan Powers, *Modern Block Printed Textiles* (London: Walker Books, 1992), 64-65; Inez Svensson, *Tryckta Tyger från 30-tal tll 80-tal Liber* (Stockholm: LiberFörlag, 1972). Gisela Eronn, *Tidlösa Mönster: Textilekonst frå 1950-talet* (Stockholm: Norstedts, 2009), 16–31; Dahlbäck Lutteman, *Astrid Sampe*; Carsten Thau and Kjeld Vindum, *Arne Jacobsen* (Copenhagen: Danish Architectural Press, 2001).
3   Examples of these are in binder 50 (Glassfibertyger 1945–1956), Astrid Sampe Archive, Nationalmuseum Library, Stockholm; for discussion see Marianne Erikson, "Glass and Milk: New Materials in Astrid Sampe's

Textiles," *Scandinavian Journal of Design History* 6 (1996): 103–9.
4   See Gisela Eronn, *Tidlösa Mönster*, 38–43.
5   See chap. 2 in this volume.
6   Mary Roche, "Work of Noted Textile Designers Put on View at New Showroom," *New York Times*, February 27, 1947, 24.
7   See "H. G. Knoll Associates, New York City," *Interiors* (August 1947): 87.
8   "Swedish Fabrics Go on Exhibition," *New York Times*, July 9, 1948, 12; "Textiles by Astrid Sampe-Hultberg," *Arts & Architecture* (August 1948): 36.
9   *American Rand* may be the 1948 striped textile designed by Sampe in MoMA collection; see cat. 19 in this volume. This pattern is included in Nils G. Wollin, *Swedish Textiles, 1943–1950* (Leigh-on-Sea, Eng.: F. Lewis, 1952), 20 and fig. 62.
10 See Dahlbäck Lutteman, *Astrid Sampe*.
11 Eero Saarinen to Astrid Sampe, correspondence, Astrid Sampe Archive, Nationalmuseum Library, Stockholm; Susanne Wasson-Tucker papers, Arkitekturmuseet, Stockholm.

Peter Seipelt

1   Peter Seipelt, email to the author, September, 30, 2010. This entry is based on this interview unless otherwise noted. Many thanks to Peter Siepelt for his kind assistance with this project. —AMT
2   "Peter Seipelt," in Jutta Beder, Lexikon der Textildesigner 1950 – 2000, online at www.bkm.uni-paderborn.de.
3   First introduced in 1963; *Quartet* had been discontinued in the United States by 1979.
4   Kristl Reinhardt Andrus, interview with Earl Martin and the author, September 16, 2010.
5   "Knoll's Curtain Call," *Designer's Journal* (April 1987): 6.
6   "Casements," in *Design Selection '89*, annual cat. Design Center Stuttgart (Baden-Württemberg: Haus Der Wirtschaft, 1989), 67.
7   J. Christophe Brünzli, telephone conversation with the author, January 19, 2011.
8   Ibid.
9   Catherine Murray, email to the author, September 15, 2010.

Hazel Siegel

1   "Curriculum Vitae: Hazel Siegel," ca. 1988, Hazel Siegel designer file, KnollTextiles Archive.
2   Ibid. Siegel left Designtex when it was purchased by Steelcase in 1988.
3   Merle Lindby-Young, email conversation with the author, September 13, 2010.
4   Hazel Siegel, telephone conversation with the author, November 15, 2010. Unless otherwise noted the information in this biography is derived from this interview. Many thanks to Hazel Siegel for her assistance with this project. —AMT
5   M. W., "The Derby Desk Line: Designing Out the Cost," *Interiors* (August 1990): 75.
6   E. D. Smith, "Hazel Siegel's First Collection for Knoll Reveals 33 Inspired Patterns Created in Just 10 Months," *Contract* (March 1990), reprint, Hazel Siegel designer file, Knoll Archives.
7   Ibid.
8   "Introduction: Hazel Siegel Collection," sales material, Hazel Siegel designer file, KnollTextiles Archive.
9   Ibid.
10 "Introduction: Hazel Siegel Collection."
11 See K. Hunt, *Bauhaus and Knoll Textiles* (Tokyo: Kashima Shuppankai, 1989).
12 Heidi Schwartz, "Textile Design Steeped in Tradition," *Business Interiors* (September/October 1990): 27.
13 "Introduction: Hazel Siegel Collection." Siegel was inspired by an Etruscan vase to create a design representative of ionic columns for *Etruscan Brocade*, while *Byzantium* used a weave from the Han dynasty and the design referenced Byzantine mosaics.
14 Leon Whiteson, "Eisenman Collection for KnollTextiles," Peter Eisenman designer file, Knoll Archives.
15 Justin Henderson, "Building Fabrics: Knoll Creates New Textiles for a Deconstructivist Hospital," *Interiors* (August 1992): 54.
16 Christa C. Thurman, "Ben Rose," in *Rooted in Chicago: Fifty Years of Textile Traditions* (Chicago: Art Institute of Chicago Museum Studies, 1997), 28.
17 Hazel Siegel résumé, 2010, mailed to the author, November 2010.

Peter Simpson

1   Peter Simpson, curriculum vitae, after 1987, Bute Fabrics Archive, Scotland. I would like to thank Catherine Murray, Design Director at Bute, for her assistance with this project. —AMT
2   Ibid.
3   Helen Douglas, "The Feel for Rugged Texture," in *Dissentangling Textiles*, ed. Mary Schoeser and Christine Boydell (London: Middlesex University Press, 2002), 177.
4   "How Donald Brothers Stay Small and Influence People," *Design* 254, (February 1970): 29.
5   Ibid. Simpson met Larsen while working at JOFA in New York and brokered the contract with Donald Brothers. His work with Jacobsen was mostly as a consultant for the textile designs for St. Catherine's College, Oxford.
6   Donald Brothers sample books 1950–61, University Archive, Records Management and Museum Service, Heriot-Watt University, Edinburgh.
7   Ibid.
8   Ibid.; and Knoll Textiles, "Wholesale Price List," January 15, 1962, KnollTextiles Archive.
9   For an illustration of *Woodlands*, see *Design* 75 (March 1955): 257; for *Kenya* see *Design* 109 (January 1958): 59.
10 "How Donald Brothers Stay Small."
11 Simpson, curriculum vitae, after 1987.
12 Amicia de Moubray, "Fabrics Weave their Way to the Executive Class," *Country Life* 192 (August 6, 1998): 42.
13 Ibid.
14 Ibid.
15 Peter Simpson, curriculum vitae, after 1987. From 1986 until his death in 1988 he served as a consultant to the company.
16 *Scotchwool*, *Berwick*, and *Fife* files, KnollTextiles Archive.
17 Peter Simpson, curriculum vitae, after 1976, University Archive, Records Management and Museum Service, Heriot-Watt University, Edinburgh.
18 Simpson, curriculum vitae, after 1987.
19 Ibid.

Stephen Sprouse

1   Patricia Morrisroe, "The Punk Rock Glamour God," *New York Magazine* (April 5, 2004): 36.
2   Ibid., 35.
3   John Duka, "The Rock Connection," *New York Times*, August 26, 1984, section 6, pt. 2, p. 190.
4   *Image by Design* was to promote the launch of the Polaroid SX-70 camera.
5   Roger Padilha and Mauricio Padhila, *The Stephen Sprouse Book* (New York: Rizzoli, 2009), 10.
6   Morrisroe, "Punk Rock," 38. Sprouse had been a long-time admirer of Andy Warhol. The two first met while Sprouse was working at Halston; Warhol was buried in a Stephen Sprouse suit.
7   Sprouse was allowed to use Warhol's artwork for other collections, a permission rarely granted by the Warhol Foundation.
8   The high cost was due in part to specifying custom-dyed cashmere by Agnona, a high-end Italian manufacturer, in order to get the Day-Glo he wanted. Padilha and Padilha, *Stephen Sprouse*, 11.
9   Lisa Lockwood, "What Really Happened at Sprouse," *WWD* 150 (1985): 1+, consulted online via *General OneFile* database, New York Public Library.
10 Woody Hochswender, "Patterns," *The New York Times*, October 25, 1988, B9.
11 In 2009, to coincide with the retrospective exhibition at Deitch Projects and the publication of *The Stephen Sprouse Book*, Louis Vuitton launched a capsule collection based on the initial Sprouse/Jacobs collaboration featuring the graffiti and cabbage rose designs.
12 Barbara Mayer, "Art for the People is Closer than You Think," *Athens Banner-Herald*, October 2003, F1.
13 Suzanne Tick, "Stephen Sprouse Journey" press release, ca. 2003, Stephen Sprouse designer file, KnollTextiles Archive.
14 "NeoCon: Making Themselves Right at Home," *Chicago Tribune*, June 15, 2003, section 15.
15 Chris Schmidt, "Fashion Comes Home," *New York Sun*, July 10, 2003, 17.
16 "Interior Design Asks Stephen Sprouse," *Interior Design*, Show Daily (2003), 8, clipping, Stephen Sprouse designer file, KnollTextiles Archive.
17 Suzanne Tick, interview with Ann Marguerite Tartsinis, February 7, 2011.
18 Jacob Bernstein, "Magic Marker," *WWD* 197, no. 10 (2009): 4, consulted online via *General OneFile* database, New York Public Library.

Gunta Stadler-Stölzl

1   For Stadler-Stölzl's career at the Bauhaus, see *Gunta Stölzl: Bauhaus Master*, ed. Monika Stadler and Yael Aloni (New York: Museum of Modern Art, 2009); Sigrid Wortmann Weltge, *Women's Work: Textile Art from the Bauhaus* (San Francisco: Chronicle Books, 1993); Leslie Jackson, "Gunta Stölzl," *Selvedge* 11 (2006): 56–57; Barry Bergdoll and Leah Dickerman, eds., *Bauhaus 1919–1933: Workshops for Modernity* (New York: MoMA, 2009).
2   Stadler-Stölzl lost her German citizenship in 1929 when she married Arieh Sharon, a Jewish architecture student from Palestine. The couple separated in 1932 and were divorced in 1936. See Stölzl, *Gunta Stölzl*, 117.
3   Ibid.
4   Monika Stadler, quoted in Matthew Bourne, "Interview with Monika Stadler," *Modern Carpets + Textiles* (Autumn 2005): 61.
5   See for example MoMA 477.1970.1, 477.1970.3, 477.1970.14, www.moma.org, and www.guntastolzl.org/Works.
6   Mary Roche, "Work of Noted Textile Designers Put on View at New Showroom," *New York Times*, February 27, 1947, 24.
7   Stadler-Stölzl had collaborated with Breuer on several important early furniture designs, including the 1921 *African Chair*, and actively corresponded with her former colleagues (including Gropius) during and after the war; see Stölzl, *Gunta Stölzl*, 63, 116, 118.
8   Ibid., 118.

Suzin Steerman

1   Mary Schoeser, ed., *International Textile Design* (New York: John Wiley & Sons, 1991), 185.
2   Hazel Siegel, interview with Ann Marguerite Tartsinis, November 15, 2010.
3   Ibid.; Schoeser, *International Textile Design*, 185.
4   KnollTextiles, "The Kabuki Collection," September 1994, introductions publicity material, KnollTextiles Archive.
5   Schoeser, *International Textile Design*, 185.

Marianne Strengell Hammerström

1   Birgit Lyngbye Pedersen, "A Matter of Taste: Cubist Printed Furnishing Fabrics from the 1950s, A Subjective and Aesthetic Perspective," *Scandinavian Journal of Design History* 11 (2001): 102. Pedersen defines Functionalism as "both an ideology and a style that from the start was a European-wide Social Democratic idea. It was aimed at the working classes as an improvement in the living conditions of the great majority of the population—the workers' own culture." For example, "the home was to be arranged expediently, beautifully and the basis of a financially rational philosophy."
2   Gustaf Strengell was a well-known progressive architect and designer, who was celebrated for his promotion of Functionalist theories.
3   Benedict Zilliacus, "Marianne Strengell: A Career Abroad," *Form Function Finland* 3 (1999): 48. Strengell said of her mother, "I don't know where she picked it up but she just had this beautiful inborn taste and sense of color and form." Marianne Strengell, Oral history interview by Robert F. Brown, January 8 and December 16, 1982, Archives of American Art, Smithsonian Institution.
4   Leslie Edwards, "Structure and Surface: Marianne Strengell and Woven Texture," *Modernism Magazine* (Winter 2007–8): 78.
5   Lise Osvald, "The Story of Kaj Dessau's BO, 1928–1941," *Scandinavian Journal of Design History* 3 (1993): 36.
6   Zilliacus, "Marianne Strengell," 48.

7   Osvald, "Story of Kaj Dessau's BO," 35; Marion Holden Bemis, "Marianne Strengell: Textile Consultant to Architects," *Handweaver and Craftsman* (Winter 1956–57): 9.
8   Brian Lutz, *Knoll: A Modernist Universe* (New York: Rizzoli, 2010), 107. Presumably Strengell met Kiljander when the two worked for Sirén on the interiors of the Helsinki Parliament House.
9   Quoted in Alice Adams, "Marianne Strengell," *Craft Horizons* (January/February 1963): 36; see also Ed Rossbach, "Marianne Strengell," *American Craft* 44 (April/May 1984): 9.
10   Ed Rossbach, "Marianne Strengell," *American Craft* 44 (April/May 1984): 18.
11   Edwards, "Structure and Surface," 80.
12   Mary Roche, "The Hand-Loomed Look," *New York Times*, September 4, 1949, 106.
13   "Fabric Forecast," *Interior Design* (April 1952): 106.
14   Manufactured by George Royle and exhibited at Strengell's Cranbrook exhibition in 1950.
15   "Fiberglas House: A Depression-born Industry," *Interiors* (October 1948): 115. Images in the article document the profusion of Knoll furniture in the interior. The fiberglas upholstery was mass-produced by Hess, Goldsmith, and Company; see "The House that Fiberglas Built," *Upholstering* (March 1948): 62.
16   See list of Knoll Planning Unit projects in Knoll Associates textile price list, November 1, 1948, Brooklyn Museum Library.
17   Strengell, Oral history interview.
18   Ibid.
19   "In Collection of Hand Prints," *Chicago Daily Tribune*, November 5, 1950.
20   "International Textile Exhibit Held at Knoll's," *New York Herald Tribune*, February 27, 1947, 18.
21   Knoll Associates textile price list," November 1, 1948, Brooklyn Museum Library.
22   "Petroff and Clarkson, New York," *Interiors* (August 1949): 100.
23   "House in the Museum Garden Features Modern Furniture," *Upholstering* (August 1949): 79.
24   Puli in "Parma Violet" was illustrated in *Interiors* (April 1952): 120.
25   "Eight Solutions to Merchandise Display," *Interiors* (October 1948): 111 (illus.); and "Knoll Webbings By-the-yard," *Interiors* (October 1949): 142. See also chap. 3 in this volume.
26   Bemis, "Marianne Strengell," 6. Swedish weaver Gerda Nyberg wove all the large rugs for the center's lobbies.
27   In 1940 Strengell married Sculptor Charles Yerkes Dusenbury; they had two children and were divorced in 1949. In August of the same year she married Hammarström; see *Interiors* (September 1949): 150.
28   Emile Gelé, "New Philippine Textiles," *Handweaver and Craftsman* 5 (Summer 1954): 15. For and in-depth look at Strengell's role in this project, see Megan Elisabeth Fiely, " ' Within a Framework of Limitations': Marianne Strengell's Work as an Educator, Weaver, and Designer," p. 89, MA thesis, Bowling Green State University, Ohio, 2006.
29   Gelé, "New Philippine Textiles," 14.
30   Ibid., 52.
31   Lysbeth Wallace, "Hand-Weaving in the Philippines,"

p. 59, report to the United Nations Technical Assistance Programme, 1953, Cranbrook Archives, Bloomfield Hills, Michigan. The report stated that "she has provided the project with some outstanding and unusual designs of upholstery, drapery and floor coverings. . . . The upholstery designed by Miss Strengell is to be used on furniture produced by Hans Knoll, NY. This furniture is now being manufactured by a local company, Rattan Art and Decorations, and the line will be called the Knoll International Line, and Manila will be the outlet for the whole far eastern area."
32   Christa C. Mayer Thurman, "Marianne Strengell," in *Design 1935–1965: What Modern Was, Selections from the Liliane and David M. Stewart Collection*, ed. Martin Eidelberg (New York: Harry Abrams, Inc., 1991), 205.
33   Edwards, "Structure and Surface," 84.
34   Zilliacus, "Marianne Strengell," 49; and Fiely, " 'Within a Framework',", 89. Fiely notes the rugs created for Tai Ping and accompanying drawings which are still in the Cranbrook Archives.
35   For examples see "Merchandise Cues," *Interiors* (April 1962): 140; "Merchandise Cues," *Interiors* (March 1963): 140.
36   Edwards, "Structure and Surface," 84. Wellfleet was home to several modernist architects and designers; see Christine Cipriani, "Bauhaus in the Breeze: Modernist Architecture on the Outer Cape," *Modernism Magazine* 12 (Winter 2009–10): 56–63.

Carol Summers

1   Carol Summers, interview with the author, March 10, 2011. Unless otherwise noted the information in this biography comes from this interview. Many thanks to Carol Summers for his assistance on this project. —SAT
2   "Chronology," in *Carol Summers Woodcuts: 50 Year Retrospective*, introductions by Charles Hilger and Matt Phillips, exh. cat. (New York: Woodstock Artists' Association; Santa Cruz, Calif., Museum of Art and History, and the artist, 1999), 58.
3   Carol Summers, email to the author, February 27, 2011.
4   Publicity release, June 21, 1954, Ringles design file, Knoll Archives.
5   See "Carol Summers," (artist page), Contemporary Prints Department, Davison Gallery Web site, www.davidsongalleries.com.
6   "Chronology," 58.

Angelo Testa

1   Angelo Testa, *Angelo Testa: Forty Years as a Designer / Painter / Weaver* (Chicago: The Gallery, University of Illinois at Chicago, 1983), 4.
2   June O. Goldberg, "The Brief Commercial Career of Angelo Testa," (MA thesis, Fashion Institute of Technology, New York, 2003) p. 29.
3   Ibid.
4   Ibid., 48–49.
5   Christa C. Mayer Thurman, *Rooted in Chicago: Fifty Years of Textile Design Traditions*, Museum Studies, vol. 23, no. 1 (Chicago: Art Institute of Chicago, 1997), 13.
6   Goldberg, "Brief Commercial Career," 93–94; Testa, *Angelo Testa*, 2.

7   For an illustration of Testa's *Indian Heads* described as "Angelo Testa for Knoll Associates," see "Fabrics," *Arts & Architecture* (March 1948): 32–36; for another credit of this Testa design to Knoll, see "The Good Word on Fabrics," *Interiors* (November 1947): 106–8. For mention of *Filo*, *Animal Forms*, and *Indian Heads*, on heavy cotton, and credited to Knoll, see Mary Roche, "Home: New Ideas and Inventions," *New York Times*, October 12, 1947, SM38. *Filo* by Knoll was honored as one the "Best of 1947" by AID; see Mary Roche, "Honors for Design," *New York Times*, February 15, 1948, SM38. An example of *Filo* (see fig. 1.14) was donated to the Cooper-Hewitt National Design Museum by Mae Festa who acquired it while working for Knoll (1948–52). By 1951 *Indian Heads* was being distributed by Knoll competitor Richards Morgenthau; see "High on a Mountain," *Interior Design and Decoration* (September 1951): 94.
8   Martha Kaihatsu, interview, ca. 1977, Knoll Archives. Kaihatsu worked for Testa for several years in the late 1940s before working for Knoll in New York where she ran the public relations department for a while in the 1950s.
9   Thurman, *Rooted in Chicago*, 13.
10   Ibid.
11   Ibid., 13–14.
12   For more complete client lists, see Goldberg, "Brief Commercial Career," 52–53; and Giles Kotcher and Daniel Czubak, "Angelo Testa: A Testament to the Bauhaus," *The Modernism Magazine* 3 (Spring 2000): 54.
13   Thurman, *Rooted in Chicago*, 17.
14   Peter Hall, "Angelo Testa," press release, September 30, 1982, University of Chicago.
15   Goldberg, "Brief Commercial Career," 2.
16   Testa, *Angelo Testa*, cover.

Suzanne Tick

1   Nelda Rodger, "What Makes Suzanne Tick?" *Azure* (September/October 2001): 93; and Suzanne Tick, telephone conversation with the author, February 7, 2011. Unless otherwise noted the information in this biography comes from this interview. Many thanks to Suzanne Tick for her kind assistance on this project. —AMT
2   Ibid.
3   Suzanne Tick, "A New New Day," memorandum, December 2004, Knoll Archives.
4   Ibid.; see chap. 6.
5   *Weave Three*, introduced the following year was also produced through this process; see "Suzanne Tick Designs Multicolor Line for KnollTextiles," press release, July 22, 1997, KnollTextiles Archive.
6   "Suzanne Tick is New Creative Director for KnollTextiles," press release, February 13, 1997, KnollTextiles Archive.
7   Rodger, "What Makes Suzanne Tick?", 94.
8   "KnollTextiles Introduces Sophisticated Upholstery Fabric" press release, May 7, 1999, KnollTextiles Archive.
9   Lois Lunin, "Playing with Light, Transforming Space," *Surface Design* (Fall 2001): 21.
10   "KnollTextiles Fabric Introduction," Winter 2001, KnollTextiles Archive.
11   See chap. 6 and designer biographies herein.

12   Museum of Arts and Design, "Studio Visit with Suzanne Tick," February 25, 2009, online video at *MadMuseum's Channel*, www.youtube.com/user/MADMuseum.
13   A selection of these lamps were featured in the 2006 Cooper-Hewitt National Design Triennial; see Barbara Bloemink, Brooke Hodge, Ellen Lupton, and Matilda McQuaid, "Suzanne Tick, Inc.," in *Design Life Now* (New York: Smithsonian, Cooper-Hewitt National Design Museum and Assouline Publications, 2006), 190.

Inge Toft

1   Arne Karlsen, *Modern Danish Textiles*, transl. Birthe Andersen (Copenhagen: Danish Society of Arts and Crafts and Industrial Design, 1959), 50; "Ingetoft, Inge," in *Kraks Blaa Bog* (Copenhagen: Krak, 1996), 534.
2   Birgit Lyngbye Pedersen, "A Matter of Taste: Cubist Printed Furnishing Fabrics from the 1950s, A Subjective and Aesthetic Perspective," *Scandinavian Journal of Design History* 11 (2001), 106–7.
3   Lesley Jackson, *Twentieth-Century Pattern Design: Textile and Wallpaper Pioneers* (New York: Princeton Architectural Press, 2002), 125.
4   Ibid., 125; Bodil Bødtker-Næss, "Textiles, Weaving and Printing," in *Danish Design*, ed. Svend Erik Møller, transl. Mogens Kay-Larsen (Copenhagen: Det Danske Selkab, 1974), 120.
5   Karlson, *Modern Danish Textiles*, 50.
6   For *Congo* illustration, see Jackson, *Twentieth-Century Pattern Design*, 127; for illustrations of Toft's textiles *Lahos*, *New Dehli* and *Tall Aas*, see "Stoffe Danesi," *Domus* (February 1957): 36.
7   Bødtker-Næss, "Textiles, Weaving and Printing," 116–21. Danish Women's Biographical Dictionary, online at www.kvinfo.dk/side/597/bio/675/origin/170/. Jackson (*Twentieth-Century Pattern Design*, 93) suggests that Helga Foght began running the firm in 1932.
8   Kirsten Toftegaard, curator, Danish Museum of Art and Design, email to the author, September 19, 2010. Many thanks to Kirsten Toftegaard for her assistance with this project.—AMT
9   Jackson, *Twentieth-Century Pattern Design*, 93. This suggests that Sampe would have known about or had a relationship with the firm. Alternatively, a Knoll representative may have seen designs by Ingetoft in the Danish Art Exhibitions circulating Europe and the U.S. at the time.
10   Knoll Textiles, "Price List," June 7, 1954, KnollTextiles Archive.
11   This was possibly for German distribution only. Dieter Gasse, Carl-Wolfgang Schümann, and Manfred Rusche, *Printed by Taunus Textildruck: 30 Jahre Textildruck in Deutschland am Beispiel einer Firma*, exh. cat. (Krefeld, Germany: Deutsches Textilmuseum, 1983), 5.
12   "Stoffe danesi," 36; Jackson, *Twentieth-Century Pattern Design*, 129.
13   *Kraks Blaa Bog*, 535.
14   Ibid.

2x4, Inc.

1   Knoll Textiles, "2x4 Fabric Introductions," 2004, KnollTextiles Archive.

2   Information on partners from 2×4 website, www.2x4.org.
3   Georgianna Stout, telephone conversation with Ann Marguerite Tartsinis, February 3, 2011.
4   2×4, Inc., *Field Theory* and *Chatter Collections* for KnollTextiles, brochure, 2004, Knoll Archives.
5   Alex Bagner, "All About Weave," *Wallpaper* (2004): 143–44.
6   For *Urban*, the motif was screen-printed on Knoll's upholstery fabric *Una*.

Nob and Non Utsumi

1   Parry Merkley, interview by Elizabeth St. George, January 27, 2011.
2   "Nob + Non Collection 1," n.d., Knoll Press Packet, Nob and Non Utsumi designer file, KnollTextiles Archive.
3   Ibid.; Suzanne Slesin, "Fabrics to Suit Urban Settings," *New York Times*, May 31, 1979.
4   Kristl Reinhardt Andrus, interview with Ann Marguerite Tartsinis and Earl Martin, September 16, 2010; Arthur Sager, interview with Earl Martin, October 3, 2010.
5   Andrus, inverview with Tartsinis and Martin.
6   "Knoll Unveils New Products at NEOCON," press release, June 12, 1979, Nob and Non Utsumi designer file, KnollTextiles Archive.
7   "Knoll International Fact Sheet," press release, n.d., Nob and Non Utsumi designer file, KnollTextiles Archive; Maureen D. Gries, "Knoll: Big Bucks for Design to Enter New Furniture Market," *ID: Industrial Design* 26 (November 1979), 29.
8   Knoll International, "Preisliste Textilien," January 14, 1982, private collection.
9   "Nob + Non Collection 1."
10 Ibid.
11 Ibid.; Karen Fawcett, "Nob + Non = Sophisticated + Tranquil Design," *Washington Star*, November 18, 1979.
12 First quote from "Knoll Unveils New Products at NEOCON"; second quote from Suzanne Slesin, "Fabrics to Suit Urban Settings," *New York Times*, May 31, 1979.
13 Sarah Booth Conroy, "Nob + Non = A Subtle Blend of Life and Design," *Washington Post*, March 9, 1980; Debra Piot, "Non, Nob Play Hob with Classic Design," *Christian Science Monitor*, n.d, clipping in Nob and Non Utsumi designer file, KnollTextileArchive; "Island Open on New York," *Abitare*, no. 185 (June 1980): 10–15.
14 Conroy, "Nob + Non."
15 There are varying opinions about the success of Collection 1. Kristl Reinhardt Andrus and Arthur Sager, general manager of Knoll Textiles, maintain that the collection was visually stunning but sold poorly. Peter Seipelt described the collection as an artistic and financial success, although this may relate more to the design's reception in Europe than to U.S. reaction. Andrus, interview with Tartsinis and Martin; Sager, interview with Martin; Peter Seipelt, interview with Ann Marguerite Tartsinis, September 30, 2010.
16 Gries, "Knoll: Big Bucks for Design to Enter New Furniture Market."
17 Paula Rice Jackson, "Japan Design," *Interiors* 147 (July 1988): 146.
18 "Nob + Non are People," press release, n.d., Nob and Non Utsumi designer file, KnollTextile Archive; "Question of Relativity," *Interiors* 144 (April 1985): 122–27.

Tim Van Campen

1   "Magic Carpets by Tim Van Campen," *Down East* (February 1993): 56; Jay Davis, "Tim Van Campen's Carpets," *Interior Design*, special market issue (September 1992). The published articles cited in this text were consulted as clippings in the Tim Van Campen designer file, KnollTextiles Archive.
2   Ibid. Sarah Medford, "Stepping onto the Future," *Metropolis* (September 1992); Van Campen curriculum vitae, Tim Van Campen designer file, KnollTextiles Archive.
3   Artist's statement, Van Campen Web site at www.vancampen.net.
4   Tim Van Campen email to Ann Marguerite Tartsinis, August 4, 2010.
5   Ibid.; Jean Godfrey-June, "All-American," *Contract Magazine* (May 1993), 84.
6   "The American Mosaic Collection," June 1993, introductions publicity material, KnollTextiles Archive; Godfrey-June, "All-American, 84; Artist's bio page, Van Campen Web site, www.vancampen.net.
7   Van Campen, email to Tartsinis.
8   See "Tim– Rugs/Designs," at Van Campen Web site, www.vancampen.net.

Robert Venturi
Denise Scott Brown

1   Kathryn B. Hiesinger, "Decorative Art and Interiors," in *Out of the Ordinary: Robert Venturi, Denise Scott Brown and Associates: Architecture, Urbanism, Design*, ed. David B. Brownlee, David G. DeLong, and Kathryn B. Hiesinger (Philadelphia: Philadelphia Museum of Art; New Haven: Yale University Press, 2001), 219–20; "Two-Way Stretch," *Interiors* (May 1984), 228–29, 258. Other architects tapped by Knoll included Richard Meier, Robert Siegel, Richard Sapper, Charles Gwathmey, and Niels Diffrient.
2   Diane L. Minnite, "Chronology," in *Out of the Ordinary*, 244–45; Stanislaus von Moos, *Venturi, Rauch, & Scott Brown: Buildings and Projects* (New York : Rizzoli, 1987), 328.
3   See, e.g., Robert Venturi, *Complexity and Contradiction in Architecture* (New York: Museum of Modern Art, 1966); and Robert Venturi, Scott Brown, and Stephen Izenour, *Learning from Las Vegas: The Forgotten Symbolism of Architectural Form* (Cambridge, Mass.: MIT Press 1972).
4   Venturi quoted in Hiesinger, "Decorative Art and Interiors," 201; first quote from Robert Venturi, Project statement, Furniture for Knoll, October 10, 1978, "PR/Press Info," Venturi Scott Brown Box 422, Venturi, Scott Brown, and Associates archive; second quote from Mary Nomecos for Robert Venturi to Nan Swid, October 10, 1978, "Correspondence," Venturi Scott Brown Box 421, Venturi, Scott Brown, and Associates archive.
5   Knoll International, "Robert Venturi Collection Price list," May 1984, Knoll Archives; Knoll press material, "Knoll Venturi Collection," Venturi folder, Knoll Archives. The debut of the *Venturi Collection* was extensively covered in design and architectural press. In addition to articles cited in other notes herein, see, e.g., "Venturi for Knoll," *Interior Design* 55 (May 1984), 181; "Robert Venturi: Venturi Collection of Knoll International," *Space Design* (Japan), no. 241 (October 1984): 41–60.
6   Venturi asked that credit for the project be extended to Scott Brown (design) and Frederic Swartz, Maurice Weintraub, and Paul Muller (project managers), among others; see "Profiles in History," *Architectural Record* 172 (June 1984); 170. Also, in addition to the creative contributions of Venturi and Scott Brown's firm and people at Knoll—Jeffrey Osborne, vice president of design, and Merle Lindby-Young, vice president of Knoll Textiles—the staff at the Fabric Workshop in Philadelphia, an experimental textile studio, helped to adapt the original hand-printed surface designs of *Grandmother* and *Tapestry* to plastic-laminate for the Knoll chairs. See Hiesinger, "Decorative Art and Interiors," 214; "Profiles in History," 170. For a discussion of problems with the attribution of Venturi and Scott Brown's work see Pat Kirkham and Yenna Chan, "Denise Scott Brown and Lela Vignelli," *Modern Women Artists at the Museum of Modern Art*, ed. Cornelia H. Butler and Alexandra Schwartz (New York: Museum of Modern Art: Distributed in the United States and Canada by Distributed Art Publishers, 2010), 267, 269.
7   "Profiles in History," 169; Hiesinger, "Decorative Art and Interiors," 213; Kirkham and Chan, "Denise Scott Brown and Lela Vignelli," 267–69; von Moos, *Venturi, Rauch, & Scott Brown*, 228–29.
8   Venturi quoted in Hiesinger, "Decorative Art and Interiors," 213; from Robert Venturi Project statement, "Grandmother pattern," July 19, 1990; "Canon: Contract & Coordination," Venturi Scott Brown Box 425, Venturi, Scott Brown, and Associates archives.
9   Hiesinger, "Decorative Art and Interiors," 214.
10 *Venturi Collection* file, KnollTextiles Archive.
11 Merle Lindby-Young to Mimi Taft and Jim Osborne, "Tapestry," memorandum, July 5, 1983, Venturi folder, Knoll Archives.
12 Hiesinger, "Decorative Art and Interiors," 219–20.
13 Ibid., 215. For reactions of some contemporary designers and architects see "Jury on Venturi," *Interiors* 144 (September 1984): 154–55.
14 Ibid., 197, 200. Venturi's showroom design also receive broad coverage in trade press; see Vincent Joseph Scully, "The Shape of Ourselves—Robert Venturi's Chairs," *Architectural Digest* 44 (April 1987), 62–63, 73; "New York Showroom designed by Venturi," *Architectural Record* 167 (March 1980), 97–102; "Complexity and Contradiction," *Interior Design* 51 (March 1980): 226–30; "Knoll International Showroom, New York, New York; Architects: Venturi, Rauch & Scott Brown, partner-in-charge: Robert Venturi," *Progressive Architecture* 61 (July 1980): 74–77.

Paule Vézelay

1   Ronald Alley, *Paule Vézelay* (London: Tate Gallery Publications Department, 1983), 9.
2   Germaine Greer, "Paule Vézelay [interview]," in Léonie Caldecott, *Women of Our Century* (London: British Broadcasting Corporation, 1984), 42. Vézelay said of the prewar British art scene that "English art then bored me almost to tears. . . . The English don't like originality very much in art."
3   Sarah Wilson, "Paule Vézelay," in *Dictionary of Women Artists* (London: Fitzroy Dearborn, 1997), online at www.courtauld.ac.uk/people/wilson-sarah/VEZELAY.pdf. Wilson ties the feminized masculine name "Paule" to the mode of the "liberated 'garçonne'" in Paris at this time. Her selected surname paid homage to the famous Romanesque cathedral at Vézelay in the Burgundy region of France.
4   Ibid.
5   Alley, *Paule Vézelay*, 11. Founders included Jean Arp, Auguste Herbin, and Jean Hélion among others.
6   "The Stream Revitalized," *Design* 124 (April 1959): 48.
7   Lesley Jackson, *Twentieth-Century Pattern Design: Textile and Wallpaper Pioneers* (New York: Princeton Architectural Press, 2002), 98.
8   See Bauret biography herein.
9   Knoll Textiles, "Price List," 1954, Knoll Archives.
10 "CBS Radio Executive Offices," *Interior Design* (January 1953): 53.
11 Petra Dupuits, *Sonia Delaunay: Metz est Venue* (Amsterdam: Reproduktieafdeling Stedelijk Museum Amsterdam, 1992), 19, 27. Vézelay came to Metz & Co. at the suggestion of her Abstraction Création (and later Groupe Espace) colleague Sonia Delaunay.
12 Alley, *Paule Vézelay*, 12.
13 Dupuits, *Sonia Delaunay*, 156.
14 Ibid., 157.
15 As the "London *délégué*" of the parent group she was responsible for recruiting British artists and architects; see Alan Fowler, "A Forgotten British Constructivist Group: The London Branch of Groupe Espace, 1953–59," *Burlington Magazine* 148 (March 2007): 173.
16 Ibid.; Excerpt from the Groupe Espace manifesto published in *Art d'Aujourd'hui* (October 1951).
17 Lesley Jackson, "Painterly Patterns: Artist Designed Textiles," *Selvedge* 9 (February 2006): 51. Vézelay's printed textiles for Heals included *Elegance* (ca. 1955); *Harmony, Modulation,* and *Crescents* (ca. 1956); *Pennons* (1958); and *Stanza* (1959).
18 Greer, "Paule Vézelay," 51.

Karl Vogelsang

1   Angela Oedekoven-Gerischer, ed. *Frauen in Design: Berufsbilder und Lebenswege siet 1900* (Stuttgart: Design Center Stuttgart, 1989), 186; Karin Vogelsang, email to the author, February 13, 2011. Unless otherwise noted the information in this biography is derived from this source. Many thanks to Karin Vogelsang, widow of Karl Vogelsang, for her kind assistance with this project. —CBPP
2   Hans Wichmann, *Von Morris bis Memphis: Textilien der Neuen Sammlung Ende 19. bis Ende 20. Jahrhundert,* (Basel: Birkhäuser, 1990), 180.
3   Karin Vogelsang, email.
4   Dieter Gasse, Carl-Wolfgang Schümann, and Manfred Rusche, *Printed by Taunus Textildruck: 30 Jahre Textildruck in Deutschland am Beispiel einer Firma*, exh. cat. (Krefeld, Germany: Deutsches Textilmuseum, 1983), 30, 34, 37, 45, 52, 57.

5 Ibid.
6 Ulrike Beer, "Heberlein Textil gibt auf," *Textilwirtschaft Online*. March 1, 2001.
7 Helga Baumann, *Deutsche Auswahl 1986: Ausstellung Gut Gestalteter Industrieprodukte* (Stuttgart: Landesgewerbeamt Baden-Württemberg, 1986), 60. Displayed in the "Furnishing Fabrics" installation of the 1989 exhibition; see *Design-Auswahl '89: gut gestaltete Industrieprodukte (Design Selection '89: Well-designed Industrial Products)*, exh. cat. (Stuttgart: Landesgewerbeamt Baden-Württemberg, Design Center Stuttgart, 1989), 66.

Margrete Warth

1 Margarete Warth, telephone interview with the author, April 15, 2011. Unless otherwise noted the information in this biography is derived from this interview. Many thanks to Margarete Warth for her kind assistance with this project. —CBPP
2 Martin Stumpf, Warth's colleague, telephone interview with the author, April 18, 2011; Advertisement for Knoll International, *MD Moebel Interior Design* (December 1972): 12. Knoll also exhibited some of the student designs at the Heimtextil fair; see the same advertisement; see also chap. 5 in this volume.
3 Student names handwritten below three separate textile entries: Friedrich Goth, Margarete Warth and Sybille Dobringer in Knoll Textiles, "Textile Price List 1973," April 1, 1973, pp. 22, 24–25, KnollTextiles Archive.

Henning Watterston

1 He was born Warren J. Watterston. The family was recorded as living in Appleton in 1920, and in Los Angeles (Burbank) in 1930. See U.S. Bureau of the Census, 14th census, population, 1920 and 15th census, population 1930, databases online at www.ancestry.com. He changed his name to Henning, which he thought would have the right sound for a designer, while he was studying in San Francisco (Clarissa Notley, personal communication with the author, March 3, 2011); I am grateful to Ms. Notley, Watterston's stepdaughter, for her assistance with this project. —SW
2 Eliot F. Noyes, *Organic Design in Home Furnishings* exh. cat. (New York: MoMA, 1941), 2. Rees also studied at the Rudolph Schaeffer School of Design; see ibid., 47.
3 Henning-Rees, "Texture Identity in Weaving," *Weaver* 6 (January–February 1941): 8–9; Anni Albers, "Handweaving Today: Textile Work at Black Mountain College," ibid., 3–7. For the ensuing debate, see Mary M. Atwater, "It's Pretty – but is it Art?," *Weaver* 6 (July–August 1941): 13–14, 26; Ed Rossbach, "Fiber in the Forties," *American Craft* 42 (October/November 1982): 15–19.
4 For the Pauson House see Henry Russel Hitchcock, *In the Nature of Materials, 1887-1941: The Buildings of Frank Lloyd Wright*, Reprint ed. (New York: Da Capo Press, 1973): 119; Looms were set up at Taliesin in 1941 at Watterston's direction; see Kathryn Smith, *Frank Lloyd Wright's Taliesin and Taliesin West* (New York: Harry N. Abrams, 1997), 135. From published sources, it is not clear when exactly Watterston and Rees went to Taliesin, or how long they remained, though one article reported that Watterston worked there for three years; see "Handweavers Design for the Power Loom," *Home Furnishings Merchandising* (June 1948): 49; Roger Friedland and Harold Zellman, *The Fellowship: The Untold Story of Frank Lloyd Wright and the Taliesin Fellowship* (New York: HarperCollins, 2006): 357, 369.
5 Watterston is listed with a San Francisco address in the exhibition checklist for *Modern Textile Design*, MoMA, 1945–46; MoMA Archives, CE II.1.83.1. His marriage to Rees was breaking up before they left Taliesin (Clarissa Notley, personal communication, February 28, 2011).
6 In 1947 Watterston gave his studio address as 135 Jackson St., San Francisco, "where all designing of woven fabrics for machine production is done, as well as a limited production of hand woven fabrics"; see *Interiors* (December 1947): 136.
7 "Handweavers Design for the Power Loom," 49; Menlo Textiles advertisement, *Interiors* (November 1947): 161; "The Good Word on Fabrics," ibid., 114, 164, 166; "A Review of the Fabric Market," *Interiors* (April 1948): 89.
8 Margaret Elizabeth Brinkman, "Some Selected Contemporary Textile Designers of the United States and their Contributions," p. 42, MA thesis, Oregon State College, 1949. Textiles designed by Watterston for Henod Textiles were shown at the Everyday Art Gallery at the Walker Art Center in 1949; see *Everyday Art Quarterly* 11 (Summer 1949): 5. They were also shown in the January 1950 edition of *Good Design*. The company's name (possibly derived from "Henning") suggests that it may have been owned or partly owned by Watterston. Henod Textiles was apparently no longer in business in 1951, when a letter sent to its New York address by the Cranbrook Academy of Art Museum was returned as undeliverable; see "exhibition invited" list, Cranbrook Academy of Art Museum curatorial exhibition files, Third Biennial Exhibition of Textiles and Ceramics, March 3–25, 1951.
9 Polly Weaver, "Jobs Looming," *Mademoiselle* (July 1950): 117; "Fabrics '51," *Interiors* (April 1951): 157, 189. Watterston's designs for Rodoma, Dunbar, Jack Valentine and Schumacher were shown in the Third and Fourth Biennial exhibitions at Cranbrook (1951 and 1953), and four of his textiles for Dunbar appeared in a 1951 exhibition in Baltimore; see *Living Up-to-Date*, exh. cat. (Baltimore Museum of Art, 1951): 18.
10 "Craftex Mills Adds Watterston to Design Staff," *Upholstering* (September 1952): 164.
11 For his work for Menlo see "A Review of the Fabric Market—in which we note the fruits of competition," *Interiors* (April 1948): 89. For the Koroseal fabric see Henning Watterston, "Technics and Techniques in Weaving," *Craft Horizons* 6 (August 1946): 23 (photographed by Imogen Cunningham); *Everyday Art Quarterly* 6 (Winter 1947–48): cover.
12 For first quote see Watterston, "Technics and Techniques in Weaving," 22; second quote see Watterston, in "Fabrics," *Arts & Architecture* (March 1948): 35.
13 John Leavitt, "Peter Pulman Leavitt— Literary Man and Artist—1913 to 2010," *Woodstock CT Café*, December 28, 2010, online (search "Peter Pulman Leavitt") at www.woodstockctcafe.com.
14 For a discussion of Watterston's work for Virginia Mills, along with several swatches of his designs, see "Maverick Mill: The Success Story of Virginia Mills," *American Fabrics* 62 (Fall/Winter 1963): 27–30.
15 According to John Flack, a designer for Leavitt, Watterston during the 1970s, clients looked to Watterston for color mixes and "scrambled" weave textures that were "special—not like you could get anywhere else"; John Flack, telephone interview with Susan Ward, February 25, 2011.
16 Clarissa Notley, personal communication.

Elizabeth Whelan

1 Elizabeth Whelan, telephone conversation with the author, January 1, 2011. Unless otherwise noted the information in this biography is derived from this interview. Many thanks to Elizabeth Whelan for her assistance with this project. —AMT
2 Peter Hall, "Function's Zen Master," *Metropolis* (July 2004), 100.
3 Craig Kellogg, "Down Mexico Way," *Interior Design* (July 2004), 160.
4 "KnollTextiles Presents Woodland Woven Paper Wall Covering," press release, ca. 2004, KnollTextiles Archive.
5 Ibid.
6 KnollTextiles, "Fabric Introductions," Winter 2004, KnollTextiles Archive.

Robin Whitten

1 "Knoll Salutes American Craftsmen with Series of Textile Collections," press release, January 28, 1987, Robin Whitten designer file, Knoll Archives.
2 Ayotte was a Rhode Island School of Design graduate. Robin Whitten, interview with Elizabeth St. George, January 29, 2011. Unless otherwise noted the information in this biography is derived from this interview. Many Thanks to Robin Whitten for her assistance with this project. —ES
3 Ibid.; Robin Whitten biography and artist's statement, ca. 1987, Robin Whitten designer file, Knoll Archives; "Linekin Bay Fabrics: Handweaving in a Maine Production Studio," *Fiberarts* 9 (January/February 1982), 39.
4 Ibid.
5 Quote from "Knoll Salutes American Craftsmen."
6 Merle Lindby-Young to Joyce Clark, memorandum, December 9, 1986, Robin Whitten designer file, Knoll Archives.
7 For a discussion of Whitten's studio and home in Maine, see Margaret Walch, "Linekin Bay Fabrics: The Down East Look," *American Fabrics and Fashion*, no. 111 (Fall/Winter 1977), 30.
8 Robin Whitten, interview with the author, January 29, 2011.
9 Ibid.; Whitten biography and artist's statement; Robert Janjigian, "Westweek Preview: Knoll Introduces a New Line of Textiles Saluting American Crafts," *Interiors* (February 1987): 91.

Leo and Gretl Wollner

1 Gretl Wollner has been known by a number of variations on her first name including Gretel, Grete, and Greta.
2 Leo Wollner and Inge Santner, *Leo Wollner textiliontwerper*, exh. cat. (Stedelijk Museum: Amsterdam, 1958); Jutta Beder, *Zwischen Blümchen und Picasso: Textildesign der fünfziger Jahre in Westdeutschland* (Münster: Lit Verlag, 2002), 213. Even today Austria requires its male citizens to serve either six months of military or nine months of civil service. From 1938 until 1945 Austria was occupied by Nazi Germany, as a result of this its citizens were required to serve in the Wermacht, or armed forces.
3 Wollner and Santner, *Leo Wollner textiliontwerper*, n.p.
4 Beder, *Zwischen Blümchen und Picasso*, 213.
5 Wollner and Santner, *Leo Wollner textiliontwerper*, n.p.
6 Hermann Berner and Werner Fifka, eds., *Das Bauhaus kam nach Mössingen: Geschichte, Architektur und Design der einstigen Textilfirma Pausa* (Mossingen: Talheimer, 2006), 35.
7 Ibid., 20, 36.
8 Wollner and Santner, *Leo Wollner textiliontwerper*, n.p.
9 "Michigan: Detroit Institute of Arts," *College Art Journal* 12 (Spring, 1953): 278.
10 Wollner and Santner, *Leo Wollner textiliontwerper*, n.p.
11 Beder, *Zwischen Blümchen und Picasso*, 227.
12 Berner and Fifka, *Bauhaus kam nach Mössingen*, 136.
13 "Preise der Stadt Wien 1959," April 30, 1959, Vienna Municipal Archive.
14 Quoted from Wollner and Santner, *Leo Wollner Textiliontwerper*, n.p. (transl. by the author). Gretl Wollner's involvement is uncertain, but she may be the woman behind an easel pictured in the frontispiece of the exhibition catalogue.
15 Grete Wollner and Leo Wollner, *Textilausstellung Grete und Leo Wollner im Österreichischen Museum für angewandte Kunst, Wien*, exh. cat. (Vienna: Österreichisches Museum für Angewandte Kunst: 1959), n.p.
16 "Neue Dekorationsstoffe, nach Entwürfen von Leo Wollner hergestellt," *Die Kunst und das schöne Heim* 57 (August 1959): 433.
17 "Miscellany," *Design Journal* 207 (March 1, 1966): 56.
18 "Knoll International," *Industrial Design* 19 (March 1972): 32–33.
19 "Sling, A Furnishing Fabric Designed by Gretl and Leo Wollner for Knoll International," *Industrial Design* 18 (June 1971): 53.
20 *Materials Monthly* (September 2007): 14.
21 Ibid.
22 "Transparente Fantasien," *MD Moebel Interior Design* (December 1972): 45–49.
23 Gabriele Braun (former student of Leo Wollner at the Academy of Fine Arts in Stuttgart (1969–76), currently conservator of the Pausa archival collection), email to the author, March 16, 2011. Many thanks to Gabriele Braun for her assistance with this project. —CBPP

Checklist of the Exhibition

Cat. 1 (see fig. 1.1)
Printed textile length
Noémi Raymond (American, born France, 1889–1980)
ca. 1941
Cotton; plain weave, screen-printed
102 × 48 in. (259.1 × 121.9 cm)
Raymond Collection, The Architectural Archives, University of Pennsylvania

Cat. 2 (see fig. B.100)
Printed textile length "Combination of Reeds and Horizontal Lines"
Noémi Raymond (American, born France, 1889–1980)
Probably made by Cold Spring Bleachery for Noémi Raymond
ca. 1941
Cotton; plain weave, screen-printed
99 × 50 in. (251.5 × 127 cm)
Raymond Collection, The Architectural Archives, University of Pennsylvania

Cat. 3 (see fig. 2.25)
Prototype for Knoll pattern *Isles*
Shirley Fletcher Rapson (later Nickerson; American, born 1923)
ca. 1945
Cotton; plain weave, screen-printed
34 × 30 in. (86.4 × 76.2 cm)
Shirley Fletcher Nickerson

Cat. 4
Pebble Weave webbing on *Model 657W* rocking chair
Webbing: attributed to Marianne Strengell Hammarström (American, born Finland, 1909–1998); chair: Ralph Rapson (American, 1914–2008)
Webbing made for Knoll Associates, Inc.; chair made by Knoll Associates, Inc.
ca. 1945
Webbing: cotton; plain weave; chair: birch
28 × 27 3/4 × 32 1/4 in. (71.1 × 70.5 × 81.9 cm)
Minneapolis Institute of Arts, Gift in memory of Mary Rapson, to commemorate her support of modern design, by Kenneth and Judy Dayton, Heino Engel (Germany), Dolly J. Fiterman, William and Jane Hession,

Philip W. Pillsbury, Jr., John P. Sheehy, Philip and Joanne Von Blon, and many other friends, 2000.164

Cat. 5 (see fig. 3.20)
Pebble Weave webbing samples
Attributed to Marianne Strengell Hammarström (American, born Finland, 1909–1998)
Made for Knoll Associates, Inc.
ca. 1945
Used for upholstery; cotton; plain weave
Each: 2 7/8 × 2 in. (7.3 × 5.1 cm)
KnollTextiles Archive

Cat. 6 (see page 85)
"Salt and pepper" webbing on *Model 50S* stool
Stool designed by Abel Sorensen (American, born Denmark, active 1940s–1960s)
Webbing made by Bridgeport Fabrics for Knoll Associates, Inc.; stool made by Knoll Associates, Inc.
Webbing introduced 1947; this example ca. 1947
Webbing: cotton; plain weave; stool: birch
17 3/4 × 24 3/4 × 19 in. (45.1 × 62.9 × 48.3 cm)
Knoll Museum, East Greenville, Penn.

Cat. 7
Webbing on *Model 652W* lounge chair with arms
Chair designed by Jens Risom (American, born Denmark, 1916)
Webbing made by Concordia-Gallia / Corporation for Knoll Associates, Inc.; chair made by Knoll Associates, Inc.
ca. 1950
Webbing: saran; plain weave; chair: maple
33 × 24 × 28 in. (83.8 × 61 × 71.1 cm)
Knoll Museum, East Greenville, Penn.

Cat. 8 (see fig. 3.5)
Pandanus ("Red Plaid" colorway)
Made in the Philippines for Knoll Associates, Inc.
Introduced 1947, this example ca. 1948
Wall covering, upholstery, and other uses; pandanus leaf fiber; plain weave
14 × 14 1/2 in. (35.5 × 37 cm)
The Museum of Modern Art, New York, P384

Cat. 9
Fishnet ("White" colorway)
Made by W. Auger for Knoll Associates Inc.
ca. 1947
Linen
58 1/2 × 18 in. (148.6 × 45.7 cm)
Richard and Trudy Schultz

Cat. 10 (see fig. 3.3)
Saran (P2, "Red and White Stripe" colorway), on *Model 666UAC* armchair
Chair: Jens Risom (American, born Denmark, 1916)
Upholstery made by Chicopee Manufacturing Corporation for Knoll Associates, Inc.; chair made by Knoll Associates, Inc.
ca. 1948
Upholstery: saran; twill variation; chair: maple, steel springs, cotton batting
31 × 20 1/2 × 20 in. (78.7 × 52.1 × 50.8 cm)
Private collection

Cat. 11 (see fig. 3.15)
Chinese Coins sample ("Yellow" colorway)
Noémi Raymond (American, born France, 1889–1980)

Made for Knoll Associates, Inc.
ca. 1948
Used for upholstery, drapery; cotton; plain weave, screen-printed
25 3/4 × 26 1/2 in. (65.4 × 67.3 cm)
The Museum of Modern Art, New York, P383

Cat. 12 (see fig. B.101)
Mosaic sample ("Persimmon on Sand" colorway), with smaller colorway swatches attached
Noémi Raymond (American, born France, 1889–1980)
Made for Knoll Associates, Inc.
ca. 1950
Used for drapery; rayon; plain weave, screen-printed
24 1/4 × 22 1/4 in. (61.6 × 56.5 cm)
KnollTextiles Archive

Cat. 13 (see fig. 3.16)
Mosaic ("Green on White" colorway)
Noémi Raymond (American, born France, 1889–1980)
Made for Knoll Associates, Inc.
ca. 1950
Used for drapery; rayon; plain weave, screen-printed
108 × 49 1/4 in. (274.3 × 125.1 cm)
Private collection

Cat. 14
Shooting Stars curtain
Marianne Strengell Hammarström (American, born Finland, 1909–1998)
Made for Knoll Associates, Inc.
Introduced 1947, this example ca. 1950
Used for drapery; rayon with cotton lining; plain weave, screen-printed
90 × 89 3/4 in. (228.6 × 228 cm); width at top: 42 1/2 in. (108 cm)
The Metropolitan Museum of Art, New York, Gift of Susan Lustig Peck, 1986, 1986.429.1

Cat. 15 (see fig. 3.14)
Campagna ("Green" colorway)
Angelo Testa (American, 1921–1984)
Made for Knoll Associates, Inc.
Introduced 1947, this example before 1950
Used for drapery; linen; plain weave, screen-printed
199 × 52 in. (505.5 × 132.1 cm)
Cooper-Hewitt, National Design Museum, Smithsonian Institution, Gift of Nicholas A. Pappas, FAIA, 2002-14-3

Cat. 16 (see fig. 1.14)
Filo
Angelo Testa (American, 1921–1984)
Made for Knoll Associates, Inc.
ca. 1948
Used for drapery; cotton; plain weave, screen-printed
31 1/2 × 24 3/4 in. (80 × 62.9 cm)
Cooper-Hewitt, National Design Museum, Smithsonian Institution, Gift of Mae Festa, 1991-157-8

Cat. 17 (see fig. 3.13)
Spines
Alexander Girard (American, 1907–1993)
Made for Alexander Girard
ca. 1948
Used for drapery; linen; plain weave, screen-printed
24 × 49 in. (61 × 124.5 cm)
Cooper-Hewitt, National Design Museum, Smithsonian Institution, Gift of Alexander H. Girard, 1969-165-15

Cat. 18 (see fig. B.88)
Markelius sample ("Blue" colorway)
Sven Markelius (Swedish, 1889–1972)
Made for Knoll Associates, Inc.
Designed ca. 1943, manufactured 1948–50
Used for drapery; linen, jute, cotton; plain weave, screen-printed
26 × 25 1/2 in. (66 × 64.8 cm)
The Museum of Modern Art, New York, P382

Cat. 19 (see fig. 3.9)
Textile related to *Sampe Stripe*
Astrid Sampe (Swedish, 1909–2002)
Made for Nordiska Kompaniet's Textilkammare, Stockholm
ca. 1948
Used for upholstery; cotton, fiberglass, wool; simple weave with twill variation
36 1/2 × 28 in. (92.7 × 71.1 cm)
The Museum of Modern Art, New York, Given anonymously, SC36.1975

Cat. 20 (see fig. 3.8)
Apples ("Red on Natural" colorway)
Stig Lindberg (Swedish, 1916–1982)
Made for Knoll Associates, Inc.
ca. 1948
Used for drapery; linen, jute, and cotton; plain weave, screen-printed
58 × 53 in. (147.3 × 134.6 cm)
Private collection

Cat. 21
Prestini data page with 6 colorway samples attached
Antoinette Lackner Webster (Toni Prestini) (American, 1909–1998)
Samples made by Louisville Textiles for Knoll Associates, Inc.
ca. 1950
Textile samples: cotton and rayon; plain weave; mounted on paper

11 × 8 1/2 in. (27.9 × 21.6 cm)
KnollTextiles Archive

Cat. 22
Prestini swatch ("Grey" colorway)
Antoinette Lackner Webster (Toni Prestini) (American, 1909–1998)
Made by Louisville Textiles for Knoll Associates, Inc.
ca. 1948
Used for upholstery; cotton and rayon; plain weave
3 1/2 × 2 3/4 in. (8.6 × 7.0 cm)
Private collection

Cat. 23 (see fig. B.77)
Prestini ("Orange-Yellow" colorway)
Antoinette Lackner Webster (Toni Prestini) (American, 1909–1998)
Made by Louisville Textiles for Knoll Textiles
This colorway ca. 1958
Used for upholstery; cotton; plain weave
48 × 23 in. (121.9 × 58.4 cm)
KnollTextiles Archive

Cat. 24
Prestini ("Red" colorway) on *Grasshopper* chair
Antoinette Lackner Webster (Toni Prestini) (American, 1909–1998); chair: Eero Saarinen (American, born Finland, 1910–1961)
Upholstery made by Louisville Textiles for Knoll Textiles; chair made by Knoll Associates, Inc.
ca. 1955
Upholstery: cotton; plain weave; chair: birch or maple, foam rubber
34 15/16 × 26 1/16 × 32 11/16 in. (88.8 × 66.35 × 83.15 cm)
Knoll Museum, East Greenville, Penn.

Cat. 25 (see fig. B.128)
Buster samples
Marianne Strengell Hammarström (American, born Finland, 1909–1998)
Made by Louisville Textiles for Knoll Associates, Inc.
Introduced 1949
Used for upholstery; cotton; plain weave
Each: 5 × 3 1/8 in. (12.7 × 7.9 cm)
KnollTextiles Archive

Cat. 26 (see fig. B.127)
Cartree samples
Marianne Strengell Hammarström (American, born Finland, 1909–1998)
Made by Louisville Textiles for Knoll Associates, Inc.
Introduced 1947
Used for upholstery; cotton; plain weave with alternating single and paired wefts
Each: 4 × 2 in. (10.2 × 5.1 cm)
KnollTextiles Archive

Cat. 27 (see fig. 3.17)
Devil samples
Marianne Strengell Hammarström (American, born Finland, 1909–1998)
Made by Original Textile Company for Knoll Associates, Inc.
Introduced 1947, these examples ca. 1950
Used for upholstery; wool, cotton; plain-weave–derived compound weave with supplemental wefts
Each: 5 × 3 1/8 in. (12.7 × 7.9 cm)
KnollTextiles Archive

Cat. 28
Scotch Linen sample ("Grey & White" colorway)
Franz Lorenz (Swiss, active ca. 1940–1960s)
Made by Donald Brothers for Knoll Textiles
Introduced 1950
Used for upholstery; linen; plain weave
8 3/4 × 9 1/4 in. (22.2 × 23.5 cm)
KnollTextiles Archive

Cat. 29
Scotch Linen sample ("TwoTone Orange" colorway)
Franz Lorenz (Swiss, active ca. 1940–1960s)
Made by Donald Brothers for Knoll Textiles
Introduced 1950
Used for upholstery; linen; plain weave
8 3/4 × 9 1/4 in. (22.2 × 23.5 cm)
Knoll Textiles Archive

Cat. 30
Scotch Linen sample ("TwoTone Red" colorway)
Franz Lorenz (Swiss, active ca. 1940–1960s)
Made by Donald Brothers for Knoll Textiles
Introduced 1950
Used for upholstery; linen; plain weave
8 3/4 × 9 1/4 in. (22.2 × 23.5 cm)
KnollTextiles Archive

Cat. 31
Scotch Linen sample ("Brown and White" colorway)
Franz Lorenz (Swiss, active ca. 1940–1960s)
Made by Donald Brothers for Knoll Textiles
Introduced 1950
Used for upholstery; linen; plain weave
8 3/4 × 9 1/4 in. (22.2 × 23.5 cm)
KnollTextiles Archive

Cat. 32
Scotch Linen sample ("Green, Yellow and Red" colorway)
Franz Lorenz (Swiss, active ca. 1940–1960s)
Made by Donald Brothers for Knoll Textiles
Introduced 1950
Used for upholstery; linen; plain weave
8 3/4 × 9 1/4 in. (22.2 × 23.5 cm)
KnollTextiles Archive

Cat. 33
Scotch Linen sample ("Green and Light Green" colorway)
Franz Lorenz (Swiss, active ca. 1940–1960s)
Made by Donald Brothers for Knoll Textiles
Introduced 1950
Used for upholstery; linen; plain weave
8 3/4 × 9 1/4 in. (22.2 × 23.5 cm)
KnollTextiles Archive

Cat. 34
Scotch Linen sample ("Red and Green" colorway)
Franz Lorenz (Swiss, active ca. 1940–1960s)
Made by Donald Brothers for Knoll Textiles
Introduced 1950
Used for upholstery; linen; plain weave
8 3/4 × 9 1/4 in. (22.2 × 23.5 cm)
KnollTextiles Archive

Cat. 35 (see fig. B.86)
Scotch Linen sample ("Black and White Plaid" colorway)
Franz Lorenz (Swiss, active ca. 1940–1960s)
Made by Donald Brothers for Knoll Textiles
Introduced 1950
Used for upholstery; linen; plain weave
8 3/4 × 9 1/4 in. (22.2 × 23.5 cm)
KnollTextiles Archive

Cat. 36
Scotch Linen sample ("Black and White" colorway)
Franz Lorenz (Swiss, active ca. 1940–1960s)
Made by Donald Brothers for Knoll Textiles
Introduced 1950
Used for upholstery; linen; plain weave
8 3/4 × 9 1/4 in. (22.2 × 23.5 cm)
KnollTextiles Archive

Cat. 37 (see fig. 4.40)
Sketch for Hans Knoll's office,
575 Madison Avenue, New York, N.Y.
Florence Knoll Bassett (American, born 1917)
ca. 1950
Pen, colored pencil, *Pandanus* (cabinet fronts), *Jhuri Silk* (curtains), and leather (chair seats) on paper

9 7/8 × 12 1/4 in. (25 × 31 cm)
Florence Knoll Bassett Papers, Archives of American Art, Smithsonian Institution

Cat. 38
Knoll Textile Kit
Eszter Haraszty (American, born Hungary, 1920–1994) and Ladislav Sutnar (Czech, 1897–1976)
Made for Knoll Textiles
ca. 1955
Cardboard, paper, textile samples, metal pins
Overall: 4 1/8 × 4 1/8 × 8 3/8 in. (10.5 × 10.5 × 21.3 cm)
The Museum of Modern Art, New York, Architecture & Design Study Center, SC156.2010.a-c

Cat. 39 (see fig. 3.28)
Chinese Coins sample ("Black on Red" colorway) with smaller colorway swatches attached
Noémi Raymond (American, born France, 1889–1980)
Made for Knoll Associates, Inc.
these colorways ca. 1950
Used for drapery; cotton; plain weave, screen-printed
27 × 25 1/2 in. (67.9 × 64.1 cm)
Private collection

Cat. 40
Apples sample ("Brown on Rust" colorway) with smaller colorway swatches attached
Stig Lindberg (Swedish, 1916–1982)
Made for Knoll Associates, Inc.
these colorways ca. 1950
Used for drapery and upholstery; linen, jute, and cotton; plain weave, screen-printed
26 × 24 in. (66 × 59.7 cm)
Private collection

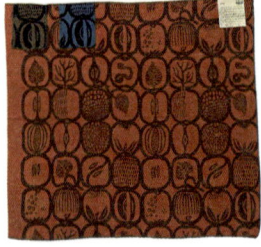

Cat. 41 (see fig. 3.30)
Ringles swatch ("Geranium Red" colorway)
Carol Summers (American, born 1925)
Made for Knoll Textiles
ca. 1954
Used for drapery; cotton; plain weave, screen-printed
6 1/2 × 5 in. (16.7 × 12.4 cm)
Private collection

Cat. 42 (see fig. B.80)
Shogi data page with nine colorway samples attached
Dennis Lennon (British, 1918–1991)
Made by American Art Textile Prints for Knoll Textiles
ca. 1954
Textile samples: linen; plain weave, screen-printed; mounted on paper
11 × 8 1/2 in. (27.9 × 21.6 cm)
KnollTextiles Archive

Cat. 43 (see page 6)
Knoll Stripes sample folder
Eszter Haraszty (American, born Hungary, 1920–1994)
Made for Knoll Associates, Inc.
ca. 1951
Textile samples: cotton; plain weave, screen-printed; mounted on paper
Open: 8 × 16 in. (20.3 × 40.6 cm)
KnollTextiles Archive

Cat. 44 (see fig. 3.32)
Knoll Stripes swatch ("Olive, Black, and Red" colorway)
Eszter Haraszty (American, born Hungary, 1920–1994)
Made for Knoll Associates, Inc.
ca. 1951
Used for drapery; cotton; plain weave, screen-printed
12 × 3 in. (30.5 × 7.7 cm)
Private collection

Cat. 45 (see fig. 3.50)
Nylon Transportation Cloth on *Womb* chair and ottoman
Upholstery: Eszter Haraszty (American, born Hungary, 1920–1994); chair: Eero Saarinen (American, born Finland, 1910–1961)
Made by Orinoka Mills for Knoll Textiles; chair and ottoman made by Knoll Associates
ca. 1965
Upholstery: rayon, nylon; plain weave; chair and ottoman: tubular steel, foam rubber over molded fiberglass platform
Chair: 35 1/2 × 38 1/2 × 29 in. (90.2 × 97.8 × 73.7 cm); ottoman: 15 × 25 × 21 in. (38.1 × 63.5 × 53.3 cm)
Cranbrook Art Museum, Bloomfield Hills, Mich., Gift of Glen Paulsen (CAM 1998.12)

Cat. 46 (see fig. 3.38)
Tracy ("White on White" sheer)
Eszter Haraszty (American, born Hungary, 1920–1994)
Made for Knoll Textiles
Introduced ca. 1952, manufactured ca. 1955
Used for drapery; silk gauze; plain weave, screen-printed
55 × 43 1/2 in. (139.7 × 110.5 cm)
The Museum of Modern Art, New York, Gift of Knoll Associates, SC30.1975

Cat. 47 (see fig. 3.37)
Tracy ("Black on White" colorway)
Eszter Haraszty (American, born Hungary, 1920–1994)
Made for Knoll Textiles
1952
Used for drapery; silk gauze; plain weave, screen-printed
107 × 49 in. (271.8 × 124.5 cm)
Cranbrook Art Museum, Bloomfield Hills, Mich., Museum Purchase, CAM 1953.3

Cat. 48 (see fig. 3.36)
Tracy ("Black and White on Yellow" colorway)
Eszter Haraszty (American, born Hungary, 1920–1994)
Made for Knoll Textiles
1952
Used for drapery; cotton, rayon; plain weave, screen-printed
108 1/4 × 51 3/16 in. (275 × 130 cm)
Cranbrook Art Museum, Bloomfield Hills, Mich., Museum Purchase, CAM 1953.4

Cat. 49 (see fig. 3.35)
Tracy ("Blue on White" colorway)
Eszter Haraszty (American, born Hungary, 1920–1994)
Made for Knoll International Bruxelles
Introduced 1952, this example ca. 1960
Used for drapery; cotton; plain weave, screen-printed
119 5/8 × 48 in. (303.85 × 121.92 cm)
Minneapolis Institute of Arts, Gift of funds from Richard L. Simmons, 2004.65.1

Cat. 50
Tracy on *Dobby* swatch and *Dobby* swatches Eszter Haraszty (American, born Hungary, 1920–1994)
Made for Knoll Textiles
ca. 1955
Used for drapery; cotton; plain weave with alternating single, paired, and tripled wefts, screen-printed
Tracy swatch: 5 3/4 × 6 1/2 in. (14.6 × 16.5 cm); *Dobby* swatches, each: 2 3/4 × 2 3/4 in. (7.0 × 7.0 cm)
Private collection

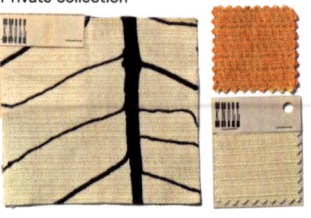

Cat. 51 (see fig. B.47)
Fibra sample ("Pink, Red, Cream on Orange" colorway)
Eszter Haraszty (American, born Hungary, 1920–1994)
Made by Printex for Knoll Textiles
Introduced 1953
Used for drapery; linen; plain weave, screen-printed
36 1/4 × 25 in. (92.1 × 63.5 cm)
Cooper-Hewitt, National Design Museum, Smithsonian Institution, Gift of Mae Festa, 1991-157-6-b

Cat. 52 (see page 307)
Fibra ("Navy, Turquoise, Emerald and Royal on White" colorway)
Eszter Haraszty (American, born Hungary, 1920–1994)
Made by Printex for Knoll Textiles
Introduced 1953
Used for drapery; linen; plain weave, screen-printed
164 × 51 in. (416.6 × 129.5 cm)
Andy Lin and Larry Weinberg

Cat. 53
Campagna sample ("White on Natural" colorway)
Angelo Testa (American, 1921–1984)
Made for Knoll Textiles
Introduced 1947, this example ca. 1958
Used for drapery; linen; plain weave, screen-printed
25 × 52 1/2 in. (63.5 × 133.4 cm)
KnollTextiles Archive, donated by Doreen Rose Stempien

Cat. 54 (see fig. B.29)
Dress in *Filigree* ("Black and White" colorway)
Dorothy Cole Ruddick (American, 1925–2010)
Made for Knoll Textiles
ca. 1950
Used for drapery; rayon; plain weave, screen-printed
The Estate of Dorothy Cole Ruddick

Cat. 55 (see fig. 3.43)
Sequence sample ("Yellow & Black" colorway), with small colorway swatches attached
Paule Vézelay (British, 1892–1984)
Made for Knoll Textiles
Introduced 1950, this example ca. 1951–55
Used for drapery; cotton; plain weave, screen-printed
25 1/4 × 49 in. (64.1 × 124.5 cm)
Private collection

Cat. 56 (see fig. 3.42)
Diamonds sample ("Yellow and Citron" colorway), with small colorway swatches attached
Albert Herbert (American, 1928–2007)
Made for Knoll Textiles
Introduced 1951, this example ca. 1954
Used for drapery; linen; plain weave, screen-printed
23 1/2 × 24 1/2 in. (59.7 × 62.2 cm)
Cooper-Hewitt, National Design Museum, Smithsonian Institution, Gift of Mae Festa, 1991-157-3-a

Cat. 57 (see fig. 3.45)
Lazy Lines ("Orange, Ochre, Yellow on White" colorway)
Astrid Sampe (Swedish, 1909–2002)
Made by Stonehenge Processing for Knoll Textiles
Introduced 1953, this example ca. 1955
Used for drapery; linen; plain weave, screen-printed
48 × 41 1/2 in. (121.9 × 105.4 cm)
The Museum of Modern Art, New York, Gift of Knoll Associates, SC18.1975

Cat. 58 (see fig. 3.46)
Pythagoras ("Spectrum Red" colorway)
Sven Markelius (Swedish, 1889–1972)
Made by Ljungbergs Textiltryck for Knoll Textiles
Introduced in the United States 1953, this example ca. 1956
Used for drapery; linen, cotton; plain weave, screen-printed

15 ft. 1 1/8 in. x 51 3/16 in. (460 x 130 cm)
Cooper-Hewitt, National Design Museum, Smithsonian Institution, 1956-123-1

Cat. 59 (see fig. B.28)
Sparklers sample ("Black and White on Grey" colorway)
Designed by Colcombet Fois or Buchet-Colcombet (Bucol)
Made by Knoll Textiles
ca. 1953
Used for drapery; silk gauze; plain weave, screen-printed
11 1/4 x 15 3/4 in. (28.6 x 40 cm)
Cranbrook Art Museum, Bloomfield Hills, Mich., T 2010.13.2

Cat. 60
Sparklers sample ("Black and White on Gold" colorway)
Designed by Colcombet Fois or Buchet-Colcombet (Bucol)
Made by Knoll Textiles
ca. 1953
Used for drapery; silk gauze; plain weave, screen-printed
8 3/4 x 15 in. (22.2 x 38.1 cm)
Cranbrook Art Museum, Bloomfield Hills, Mich.. T 2010.13.4

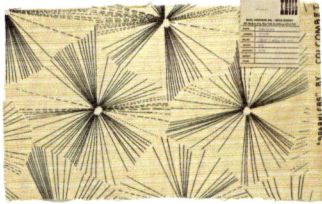

Cat. 61 (see fig. B.46)
Spruce sample ("Black and White on White" colorway)
Eszter Haraszty (American, born Hungary, 1920–1994)
Made for Knoll Textiles
ca. 1953
Used for drapery; silk gauze; plain weave, screen-printed
12 1/4 x 11 in. (31.1 x 27.9 cm)
Cranbrook Art Museum, Bloomfield Hills, Mich., T 2010.13.3

Cat. 62
Triad sample ("Black, Red, Pink, Persimmon on White" colorway)
Eszter Haraszty (American, born Hungary, 1920–1994)
Made by Printex for Knoll Textiles
Introduced 1954, this example ca. 1955
Used for drapery; cotton; plain weave, screen-printed
54 1/4 x 25 in. (138.7 x 63.5 cm)
Richard and Trudy Schultz

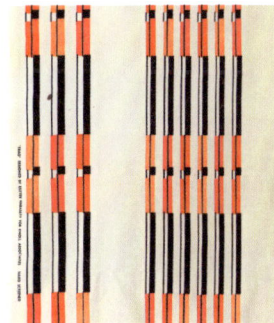

Cat. 63 (see fig. 3.44)
Kon-Tiki sample ("White on Bachelor Blue" colorway), with small colorway swatches attached
Inge Toft (Danish, 1929–1996)
Made by L. F. Foght for Knoll Textiles
ca. 1954
Used for drapery; cotton; plain weave, screen-printed
24 3/4 x 24 in. (62.9 x 61 cm)
Cooper-Hewitt, National Design Museum, Smithsonian Institution, Gift of Mae Festa, 1991-157-2-a

Cat. 64 (see fig. B.130)
Ringles
Carol Summers (American, born 1925)
Made for Knoll Textiles
ca. 1954
Used for drapery; cotton; plain weave, screen-printed
49 3/8 x 47 1/2 in. (125.4 x 120.7 cm)
Richard and Trudy Schultz

Cat. 65 (see fig. B.79)
Shogi sample ("Black on Natural" colorway), with small colorway swatches attached
Dennis Lennon (British, 1918–1991)
Made by American Art for Knoll Textiles
ca. 1954
Used for drapery; linen; plain weave, screen-printed
52 1/2 x 25 in. (133.4 x 63.5 cm)
Private collection

Cat. 66
Triad ("White, Black, Grey, Yellow on Light Grey" colorway)
Eszter Haraszty (American, born Hungary, 1920–1994)
Made by Printex for Knoll Textiles
Introduced 1954
Used for drapery; cotton; plain weave, screen-printed
21 1/4 x 12 3/4 in. (54 x 32.4 cm)
Richard and Trudy Schultz

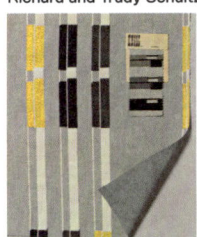

Cat. 67
Triad swatch ("Black, Charcoal, Slate and Stone on Off-white" colorway)
Eszter Haraszty (American, born Hungary, 1920–1994)
Made by Printex for Knoll Textiles
Introduced 1954
Used for drapery; cotton; plain weave, screen-printed
5 3/4 x 2 3/4 in. (8.6 x 4.2 cm)
Private collection

Cat. 68 (see also fig. 3.26)
Woman's jacket made from *Jhuri Silk* Textile handwoven in India by Sarabhal Agencies for Knoll Textiles
ca. 1955
Used for drapery; silk; twill weave.
Richard and Trudy Schultz

Cat. 69 (see fig. 4.47)
"Drum Beaters for Modern," featuring *Knoll Furniture and Textiles* at the Dallas Museum of Fine Arts
Page 72-73 from *Life* magazine
March 2, 1953
14 x 21 in. (35.6 x 53.3 cm)
Library, Bard Graduate Center: Decorative Arts, Design History, Material Culture; New York

Cat. 70 (see fig. B.50)
"The Knoll Handwovens" advertisement and AID invitation
Page from presentation volume made by Eszter Haraszty
ca. 1955
Samples of *Handwovens H900* and *H 930*, paper, printed paper, graphite, mounted on paper
18 1/4 x 26 1/4 in. (46.4 x 66.7 cm)
The Montreal Museum of Fine Arts, Liliane and David M. Stewart Collection, Gift of the American Friends of Canada through the generosity of Eszter Haraszty, D88.178.2.7

Cat. 71 (see fig. B.63)
"Perspective of Dallas exhibition," view 1
Page from presentation volume made by Eszter Haraszty
ca. 1953–55
Handwoven samples, paper, paint, cardboard and adhesive tape on paper
18 1/4 x 26 1/4 in. (46.4 x 66.7 cm)
The Montreal Museum of Fine Arts, Liliane and David M. Stewart Collection, Gift of the American Friends of Canada through the generosity of Eszter Haraszty, D88.178.1.10

Cat. 72
"Perspective of Dallas exhibition," view 2
Page from presentation volume made by Eszter Haraszty
ca. 1953–55
Handwoven samples, paper, paint,

cardboard and adhesive tape on paper
18 1/4 x 26 1/4 in. (46.4 x 66.7 cm)
The Montreal Museum of Fine Arts, Liliane and David M. Stewart Collection, Gift of the American Friends of Canada through the generosity of Eszter Haraszty, D88.178.1.11

Cat. 73 (see fig. B.62)
Handwoven used for edging on pillows, displayed at *Knoll Furniture and Textiles*, Dallas Museum of Art, 1952
Evelyn Hill Anselevicius (American, 1923–2003)
Made for Knoll Textiles
ca. 1952
Used for upholstery; wool, filament nylon
6 3/4 x 7 1/4 in. (17.1 x 18.4 cm)
Philadelphia Museum of Art, CTK1

Cat. 74 (see fig. B.61)
Handwoven panel
Evelyn Hill Anselevicius (American, 1923–2003)
Made for Knoll Textiles
ca. 1952
Used for upholstery; wool, viscose, rayon, synthetic raffia
104 x 35 in. (264.2 x 88.9 cm), including fringe
Philadelphia Museum of Art, Gift of Mr. and Mrs. George Anselevicius, 1983, 1983-42-2

Cat. 75 (see fig. 3.52)
Seven *Handwoven* samples, including *K51-H*, *K20-H*, *K3007-H*, *K3003-H*, on card
Evelyn Hill Anselevicius (American, 1923–2003)
Made for Knoll Textiles
ca. 1952
Used for upholstery; various materials including wool, gimp, plastic, and nylon
20 x 20 in. (50.8 x 50.8 cm)
Philadelphia Museum of Art, CTK 23

Cat. 76
Handwoven sample
Evelyn Hill Anselevicius (American, 1923–2003)
Made for Knoll Textiles
ca. 1952
Used for drapery; wool, plastic
5 x 4 in. (12.7 x 10.2 cm)
Philadelphia Museum of Art, CTK7

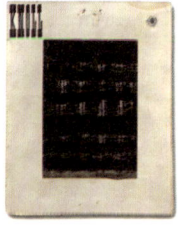

Cat. 77
Handwoven sample
Evelyn Hill Anselevicius (American, 1923–2003)
Made for Knoll Textiles
ca. 1952–60
Used for upholstery; wool
5 x 4 in. (12.7 x 10.2 cm)
Philadelphia Museum of Art, CTK8a

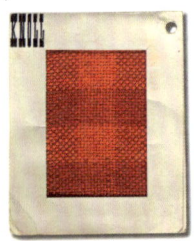

Cat. 78 (see page 103)
Handwoven sample
Evelyn Hill Anselevicius
(American, 1923–2003)
Made for Knoll Textiles
ca. 1952
Used for upholstery; wool
5 × 4 in. (12.7 × 10.2 cm)
Philadelphia Museum of Art, CTK12

Cat. 79 (see page 103)
Handwoven sample
Evelyn Hill Anselevicius
(American, 1923–2003)
Made for Knoll Textiles
ca. 1952–62
Used for upholstery; wool, gimp
5 × 4 in. (12.7 × 10.2 cm)
Philadelphia Museum of Art, CTK13

Cat. 80
Handwoven sample
Evelyn Hill Anselevicius
(American, 1923–2003)
Made for Knoll Textiles
1955–62
Used for upholstery; wool
5 × 4 in. (12.7 × 10.2 cm)
Philadelphia Museum of Art, CTK14a

Cat. 81
Handwoven sample
Evelyn Hill Anselevicius (American, 1923–2003)
Made for Knoll Textiles
1955–62
Used for upholstery; wool
5 × 4 in. (12.7 × 10.2 cm)
Philadelphia Museum of Art, CTK15

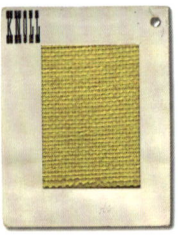

Cat. 82 (see page 103)
Handwoven, possible K24-H ("Black, Red, Shocking Pink" colorway)
Evelyn Hill Anselevicius
(American, 1923–2003)
Made for Knoll Textiles
ca. 1952
Used for upholstery; wool and nylon
5 × 4 in. (12.7 × 10.2 cm)
Philadelphia Museum of Art, 69-1983-15

Cat. 83
Handwoven sample
Evelyn Hill Anselevicius
(American, 1923–2003)
Made for Knoll Textiles
1955–62
Used for upholstery; wool
5 × 4 in. (12.7 × 10.2 cm)
Philadelphia Museum of Art, CTK8b

Cat. 84 (see fig. 3.55)
Handwoven H920 ("Black with Yellow" colorway)
Evelyn Hill Anselevicius
(American, 1923–2003)
Made by Rancocas Fabrics for Knoll Textiles
ca. 1952
Used for upholstery; wool, plastic; basket weave
Overall 32 1/2 × 49 in. (82.6 × 124.5 cm)
Richard and Trudy Schultz

Cat. 85 (see fig. 3.56)
Handwoven H910/1 ("Natural, White with Black" colorway)
Evelyn Hill Anselevicius
(American, 1923–2003)
Made by Rancocas Fabrics for Knoll Textiles
ca. 1952
Used for upholstery; wool, jute, plastic; plain weave with alternating single and paired wefts
78 × 5 1/4 in. (198.1 × 13.3 cm)
Richard and Trudy Schultz

Cat. 86 (see fig. 3.56)
Handwoven H910/2 ("Natural, Black with White" colorway)
Evelyn Hill Anselevicius
(American, 1923–2003)
Made by Rancocas Fabrics for Knoll Textiles
ca. 1952
Used for upholstery; wool, jute, plastic; plain weave with alternating single and paired wefts
30 × 26 in. (76.2 × 66 cm)
Richard and Trudy Schultz

Cat. 87
Handwoven H973 ("Royal, Cobalt Blue and Black Stripe" colorway)
Evelyn Hill Anselevicius
(American, 1923–2003)
Made by Rancocas Fabrics for Knoll Textiles
ca. 1955
Used for upholstery; wool; basket weave
12 1/2 × 45 in. (31.8 × 114.3 cm)
Richard and Trudy Schultz

Cat. 88 (see fig. 3.54)
Handwoven H971 ("Chinese Red, Persimmon and Shocking Pink Stripes" colorway)
Evelyn Hill Anselevicius
(American, 1923–2003)
Made by Rancocas Fabrics for Knoll Textiles
ca. 1955
Used for upholstery; wool; basket weave
6 × 48 1/4 in. (15.2 × 122.6 cm)
Richard and Trudy Schultz

Cat. 89
Handwoven H920, 4 samples on card
Evelyn Hill Anselevicius
(American, 1923–2003)
Made by Rancocas Fabrics for Knoll Textiles
1953–62
Used for upholstery; wool, plastic; basket weave; cardboard mount
Overall: 20 × 20 in. (50.8 × 50.8 cm)
Philadelphia Museum of Art, CTK25

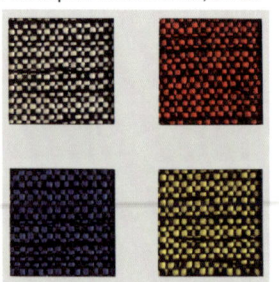

Cat. 90
Handwoven H966 ("Kelly Green and Aqua" colorway)
Evelyn Hill Anselevicius
(American, 1923–2003)
Made by Rancocas Fabrics for Knoll Textiles
1955–62
Used for upholstery; wool
5 × 4 in. (12.7 × 10.2 cm)
Philadelphia Museum of Art, CTK18

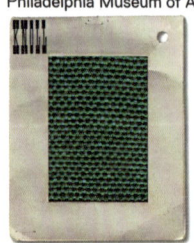

Cat. 91
Handwoven H967 ("Kelly Green, Aqua, and Turquoise Stripes" colorway)
Evelyn Hill Anselevicius
(American, 1923–2003)
Made by Rancocas Fabrics for Knoll Textiles
1955–62
Used for upholstery; wool
5 × 4 in. (12.7 × 10.2 cm)
Philadelphia Museum of Art, CTK19

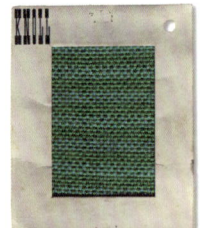

Cat. 92
Handwoven H900 ("Burnt Orange" colorway)
Evelyn Hill Anselevicius
(American, 1923–2003)
Made by Rancocas Fabrics for Knoll Textiles
ca. 1953
Used for upholstery; wool; plain weave
17 × 36 in. (43.2 × 91.4 cm)
Philadelphia Museum of Art, CTK4

Cat. 93 (see page 103)
Handwoven H940 ("Kelly Green, Royal Blue, and Turquoise" colorway)
Evelyn Hill Anselevicius
(American, 1923–2003)
Made by Rancocas Fabrics for Knoll Textiles
1955–62
Used for upholstery; wool, nylon, gimp and plastic; plain weave with alternating paired and tripled warps and paired wefts
5 × 4 in. (12.7 × 10.2 cm)
Philadelphia Museum of Art, CTK11a

Cat. 94
Handwoven, possibly H972 ("Royal & Cobalt Blue" colorway)
Evelyn Hill Anselevicius
(American, 1923–2003)
Made by Rancocas Fabrics for Knoll Textiles
1955–62
Used for upholstery; wool
5 × 4 in. (12.7 × 10.2 cm)
Philadelphia Museum of Art, CTK17a

Cat. 95
Handwoven, possibly H970 ("Chinese Red" colorway)
Evelyn Hill Anselevicius
(American, 1923–2003)
Made by Rancocas Fabrics for Knoll Textiles
1955–62
Used for upholstery; wool
5 × 4 in. (12.7 × 10.2 cm)
Philadelphia Museum of Art, CTK17e

Cat. 96
Handwoven H940 ("Beige, Tan, and Honey" colorway)
Evelyn Hill Anselevicius
(American, 1923–2003)
Made by Rancocas Fabrics for Knoll Textiles
1955–62
Used for upholstery; wool, nylon, gimp and plastic; plain weave with alternating paired and tripled warps and paired wefts
5 x 4 in. (12.7 x 10.2 cm)
Philadelphia Museum of Art, CTK11b

Cat. 97 (see fig. B.65)
Handwoven H900 ("Burnt Orange" colorway)
Evelyn Hill Anselevicius
(American, 1923–2003)
Made by Rancocas Fabrics for Knoll Textiles
ca. 1953
Used for upholstery; wool and nylon; plain weave
5 1/2 x 4 1/2 in. (14 x 11.4 cm)
Cranbrook Art Museum, Bloomfield Hills, Mich., T 2010.13.7

Cat. 98
Handwoven H900 ("Saffron Yellow" colorway)
Evelyn Hill Anselevicius
(American, 1923–2003)
Made by Rancocas Fabrics for Knoll Textiles
ca. 1953
Used for upholstery; wool and nylon; plain weave
6 x 5 1/4 in. (15.2 x 13.3 cm)
Cranbrook Art Museum, Bloomfield Hills, Mich., T 2010.13.8

Cat. 99
Handwoven H900 ("Turquoise" colorway)
Evelyn Hill Anselevicius
(American, 1923–2003)
Made by Rancocas Fabrics for Knoll Textiles
ca. 1953
Used for upholstery; wool and nylon; plain weave
5 7/8 x 4 1/8 in. (14.9 x 10.5 cm)
Cranbrook Art Museum, Bloomfield Hills, Mich., T 2010.13.6

Cat. 100
Handwoven H930 ("Turquoise and Black" colorway)
Evelyn Hill Anselevicius
(American, 1923–2003)
Made by Rancocas Fabrics for Knoll Textiles
ca. 1953
Used for upholstery; wool and rayon; basket weave
4 x 4 3/8 in. (10.2 x 11.1 cm)
Cranbrook Art Museum, Bloomfield Hills, Mich., T 2010.13.11

Cat. 101
Handwoven H930 ("Orange and Black" colorway)
Evelyn Hill Anselevicius
(American, 1923–2003)
Made by Rancocas Fabrics for Knoll Textiles
ca. 1953
Used for upholstery; wool and rayon; basket weave
4 5/8 x 4 1/4 in. (11.7 x 10.8 cm)
Cranbrook Art Museum, Bloomfield Hills, Mich., T 2010.13.9

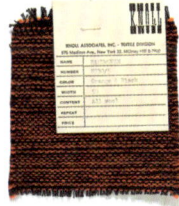

Cat. 102
Handwoven H930 ("Yellow and Black" colorway)
Evelyn Hill Anselevicius
(American, 1923–2003)
Made by Rancocas Fabrics for Knoll Textiles
ca. 1953
Used for upholstery; wool and rayon; basket weave
5 1/2 x 3 3/4 in. (14 x 9.5 cm)
Cranbrook Art Museum, Bloomfield Hills, Mich., T 2010.13.10

Cat. 103 (see fig. B.64)
Kerry Linen data page with 6 colorway samples attached
Evelyn Hill Anselevicius
(American, 1923–2003)
Samples made by Donald Brothers for Knoll Textiles
ca. 1953
Textile samples: linen, cotton; plain weave; mounted on paper
11 x 8 1/2 in. (27.9 x 21.6 cm)
KnollTextiles Archive

Cat. 104
Kerry Linen ("Black and White" colorway)
Evelyn Hill Anselevicius
(American, 1923–2003)
Made by Donald Brothers for Knoll Textiles
ca. 1953
Used for upholstery; linen, cotton; plain weave
21 1/4 x 25 1/2 in. (54 x 64.8 cm)
Philadelphia Museum of Art, CTK6

Cat. 105 (see fig. 3.19)
Puli swatches
Marianne Strengell Hammarström
(American, born Finland, 1909–1998)
Made for Knoll Textiles
ca. 1951
Used for upholstery; linen, jute, wool, rayon; plain-weave–derived simple weave.
Each: 2 7/8 x 2 7/8 in. (7.3 x 7.3 cm)
KnollTextiles Archive

Cat. 106
Puli ("Natural" colorway) on *Womb* chair and ottoman
Upholstery: Marianne Strengell Hammarström (American, born Finland, 1909–1998); chair and ottoman: Eero Saarinen (American, born Finland, 1910–1961)
Made for Knoll Textiles
ca. 1955
Upholstery: cotton, linen, jute, wool and rayon; plain-weave–derived simple weave; chair and ottoman: enameled tubular steel, latex foam rubber, over molded fiberglass platform
Chair: 35 1/2 x 38 1/2 x 29 in. (90.2 x 97.8 x 73.7 cm); ottoman: 15 x 25 x 21 in. (38.1 x 63.5 x 53.3 cm)
Yale University Art Gallery, Gift of Rosalie M. Berberian, M.P.H. 1967, M.Phil. 1980 (1992.64.1.1 and 2)

Cat. 107 (see fig. 3.58)
Rugby data page with 8 colorway samples attached
Astrid Sampe (Swedish, 1909–2002)
Samples made by Orinoka Mills for Knoll Textiles.
ca. 1955
Textile samples: cotton, wool, nylon; basket weave; mounted on paper
11 x 8 1/2 in. (27.9 x 21.6 cm)
KnollTextiles Archive

Cat. 108 (see fig. B.113)
Rugby ("Two-Tone Orange" colorway) on *Model 71* armchair
Upholstery: Astrid Sampe (Swedish, 1909–2002); chair: Eero Saarinen (American, born Finland, 1910–1961)
Upholstery made by Orinoka Mills for Knoll Textiles; chair made by Knoll Associates, Inc.
Chair introduced 1948, upholstery introduced 1954, this example ca. 1955
Upholstery: cotton, wool, nylon; basket weave; chair: wood legs, plastic shell, latex foam
31 1/2 x 27 x 23 1/2 in. (80 x 68.6 x 59.7 cm); seat height 17 in. (43.2 cm)
Private collection

Cat. 109 (see fig. 4.15)
Handwoven H950/2 ("Light Grey and White" colorway) on *Model 26* sofa from Deering Milliken & Company installation
Upholstery: Evelyn Hill Anselevicius (American, 1923–2003); sofa: Florence Knoll (American, born 1917)
Knoll Associates, Inc.
ca. 1958
Upholstery: wool; plain weave; sofa: wood frame, metal legs, batting
30 x 90 x 32 in. (76.2 x 228.6 x 81.3 cm)
Milliken & Company

Cat. 110 (see also fig. B.78)
Prestini ("Blue" colorway) on *Small Diamond* chair
Upholstery: Antoinette Lackner Webster (Toni Prestini) (American, 1909–1998); chair: Harry Bertoia (American, born Italy, 1915–1978)
Upholstery made by Louisville Textiles for Knoll Textiles; chair made by Knoll Associates, Inc.
ca. 1957
Upholstery: cotton; plain weave; chair: plastic-coated wire frame, foam rubber
Height at center of back 30 1/2 in. (77.5 cm), seat width 35 in. (89 cm)
Private collection

Cat. 111 (see also fig. 3.24)
Prestini ("Yellow" colorway) on *Small Diamond* chair
Upholstery: Antoinette Lackner Webster (Toni Prestini) (American, 1909–1998); chair: Harry Bertoia (American, born Italy, 1915–1978)

Upholstery made by Louisville Textiles for Knoll Textiles; chair made by Knoll Associates, Inc.
ca. 1957
Upholstery: cotton; plain weave; chair: plastic-coated wire frame, foam rubber
Height at center of back 30 1/2 in. (77.5 cm), seat width 35 in. (89 cm)
Private collection

Cat. 112
"Textiles" page featuring textile color wheels from Knoll catalogue mock-up Herbert Matter
ca. 1962
13 3/4 x 10 1/4 in. (34.9 x 26 cm)
Textiles mounted on paper
KnollTextiles Archive

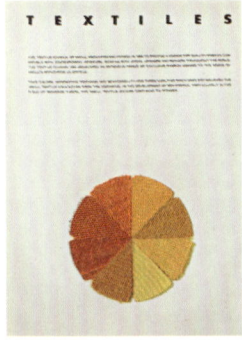

Cat. 113 (see fig. 3.63)
Spectra sample ("Turquoise and Green" colorway), with small colorway swatches attached
Eszter Haraszty (American, born Hungary, 1920–1994)
Made by Orinoka Mills for Knoll Textiles
Introduced 1955, this example ca. 1958
Used for upholstery; linen, cotton; twill variation
23 1/2 x 24 1/4 in. (59.7 x 61.6 cm)
KnollTextiles Archive, donated by Doreen Rose Stempien

Cat. 114
Spectra sample ("Orange" colorway)
Eszter Haraszty (American born Hungary, 1920–1994)
Made for Knoll Textiles / Interieur Forma S.A.
Introduced 1955, this example ca. 1970
Used for drapery; linen, cotton; twill variation
8 x 9 7/8 in. (20.3 x 25.4 cm)
KnollTextiles Archive

Cat. 115 (see fig. B.49)
Spectra Magna sample ("Blue and Green" colorway)
Eszter Haraszty (American, born Hungary, 1920–1994)
Made by Orinoka Mills for Knoll Textiles
Introduced 1955
Used for drapery; linen, cotton; twill variation
14 1/4 x 16 1/2 in. (36.2 x 41.9 cm)
Richard and Trudy Schultz

Cat. 116
Lana swatches
Eszter Haraszty (American born Hungary, 1920–1994)
Made by Orinoka Mills for Knoll Textiles
1956–78
Used for upholstery; wool, nylon; basket weave
3 1/2 x 2 3/4 in. (8.6 x 7.0 cm)
Private collection

 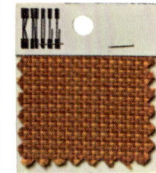

Cat. 117 (see fig. B.48)
Lana sample ("Persimmon" colorway)
Eszter Haraszty (American, born Hungary, 1920–1994)
Made by Orinoka Mills for Knoll Textiles
ca. 1960
Used for upholstery; wool, nylon; basket weave
25 x 17 in. (63.5 x 43.2 cm)
KnollTextiles Archive, donated by Doreen Rose Stempien

Cat. 118 (see fig. 3.59)
Lana ("Persimmon") on *Model 31* chair
Upholstery: Eszter Haraszty (American, born Hungary, 1920–1994); chair: Florence Knoll Bassett (American, born 1917)
Upholstery made by Orinoka Mills for Knoll Textiles; chair made by Knoll Associates
Chair made 1954–68, *Lana* introduced 1956, this example ca. 1956
Upholstery: wool, nylon; basket weave; chair: chrome-plated steel, foam rubber
28 3/4 x 23 3/4 in. (73 x 60.3 cm)
Brooklyn Museum, Gift of Liliane M. Stewart, 2002.70.1

Cat. 119
Lana Stripe ("Brown and Black" colorway) on *Model 72U* side chair
Upholstery: Eszter Haraszty (American, born Hungary, 1920–1994); chair: Eero Saarinen (American, born Finland, 1910–1961)
Upholstery made by Orinoka Mills for Knoll Textiles; chair made by Knoll Associates.
Introduced 1956, this example ca. 1962

Upholstery: wool, nylon; basket weave; chair: fiberglass shell, wooden legs, foam rubber 32 1/2 x 21 3/4 x 22 3/4 in. (82 x 55 x 58 cm)
Private collection

Cat. 120
Prisma ("Yellow" colorway)
Sven Markelius (Swedish, 1889–1972)
Made for Knoll Textiles
Introduced 1956, this example ca. 1970
Used for drapery; linen; plain weave, screen-printed
89 1/2 x 49 in. (227 x 124.5 cm)
University of Alberta Clothing and Textiles Collection, 1990.65.19a

Cat. 121 (see fig. 3.47)
Prisma ("Blue" colorway)
Sven Markelius (Swedish, 1889–1972)
Made by Ljungbergs Textiltryck for Knoll Textiles.
ca. 1956
Used for drapery; linen; plain weave, screen-printed
24 1/2 x 52 3/4 in. (62.2 x 134 cm)
Cooper-Hewitt, National Design Museum, Smithsonian Institution, Gift of Mae Festa, 1991-157-1-b

Cat. 122 (see fig. B.131)
Campagna ("White on White Sheer" colorway)
Angelo Testa (American, 1921–1984)
Made for Knoll Textiles
Introduced 1947, this colorway ca. 1958
Used for drapery; Dacron polyester and linen; plain weave, screen-printed
24 x 14 1/8 in. (61 x 35.9 cm)
Richard and Trudy Schultz

Cat. 123 (see fig. 3.65)
Shades and Tints
Emily Belding (American, 1903–1999)
Made for Habitat Associates
ca. 1954
Used for drapery; ramie; plain weave
69 x 41 1/2 in. (175.3 x 105.4 cm)
The Museum of Modern Art, New York, Gift of Habitat Associates, SC52.1975.1

Cat. 124 (see fig. 3.66)
Trellis ("White" colorway)
Ruben Eshkanian (American, born 1929)
Made in Belgium for Knoll Textiles
Introduced 1957, this example ca. 1960
Used for drapery; linen; plain-weave–derived simple weave
180 x 50 in. (457.2 x 127 cm)
Ruben Eshkanian

Cat. 125 (see fig. 3.70)
Scotch Mist ("Off-White" colorway)
Peter Simpson (Scottish, 1921–1988)
Made by Donald Brothers for Knoll Textiles
Introduced 1962, this example ca. 1970

Used for drapery; wool, linen; plain weave
70 7/8 x 49 in. (180.2 x 124.5 cm)
University of Alberta Clothing and Textiles Collection, 1990.65.23

Cat. 126 (see fig. 3.67)
Fiberglas Casement sample ("White" colorway)
Anni Albers (American, born Germany, 1899–1994)
Made by Original Textile Company for Knoll Textiles
ca. 1958
Used for drapery; fiberglass; plain gauze (leno) weave
16 1/2 x 14 1/2 in. (41.9 x 36.8 cm)
The Museum of Modern Art, New York, Gift of Josef Albers, 450.1970.90

Cat. 127 (see fig. B.4)
Prototype related to *Rail*
Anni Albers (American, born Germany, 1899–1994)
ca. 1959
Linen, paper tag; plain gauze (leno) weave
7 1/2 x 7 in. (19 x 17.8 cm)
The Museum of Modern Art, New York, Gift of Josef Albers, 450.1970.86

Cat. 128 (see fig. 3.69)
Rail ("Natural" colorway)
Anni Albers (American, born Germany, 1899–1994)
Made by Testori for Knoll Textiles
ca. 1962
Used for drapery; linen; plain gauze (leno) weave
39 x 45 1/2 in. (99.1 x 115.6 cm)
Richard and Trudy Schultz

Cat. 129 (see fig. B.5)
Track ("White" colorway)
Anni Albers (American, born Germany, 1899–1994)
Made by Testori for Knoll Textiles
Introduced 1965, this example ca. 1970
Used for drapery; linen; plain gauze (leno) weave
65 x 51 1/4 in. (165 x 130 cm)
University of Alberta Clothing and Textiles Collection, 1990.65.11

Cat. 130 (see fig. 3.68)
Lattice sample ("Oatmeal" colorway)
Anni Albers (American, born Germany, 1899–1994)
Made in Belgium for Knoll Textiles
Introduced 1959, this example ca. 1975
Used for drapery; linen; plain gauze (leno) weave
11 1/4 x 7 1/2 in. (28.6 x 19 cm)
KnollTextiles Archive

Cat. 131 (see fig. B.83)
Mira ("Red, Orange, and Persimmon" colorway)
Ross Littell (American, 1924–2000)
Made by Winston Prints for Knoll Textiles
Introduced 1958
Used for drapery; linen; plain weave, screen-printed
171 1/2 x 51 in. (435.6 x 129.5 cm)
Private collection

Cat. 132
Mira swatches
Ross Littell (American, 1924–2000)
Made by Winston Prints for Knoll Textiles

Introduced 1958, these examples ca. 1970
Used for drapery; linen; plain weave, screen-printed
Each: 5 × 5 in. (12.7 × 12.7cm)
KnollTextiles Archive

Cat. 133 (see fig. 3.71)
Spheres ("Black on Natural" and "Red and Orange on Persimmon" colorways)
Ross Littell (American, 1924–2000)
Made by Winston Prints for Knoll Textiles
Introduced 1959
Used for drapery; linen, cotton; plain weave, screen-printed
98 1/4 × 44 3/8 in. (249.6 × 112.7 cm)
The Montreal Museum of Fine Arts, Liliane and David M. Stewart Collection, Gift of the American Friends of Canada through the generosity of Ben Short, D87.236.1

Cat. 134
Criss-Cross ("Copper on White" colorway)
Ross Littell (American, 1924–2000)
Made by Winston Prints for Knoll Textiles
Introduced 1959
Used for drapery; linen; plain weave, screen-printed
15 3/4 × 15 3/4 in. (40 × 40 cm)
The family and friends of Ross Littell

Cat. 135
Criss-Cross ("Charcoal on White" colorway)
Ross Littell (American, 1924–2000)
Made by Winston Prints for Knoll Textiles
Introduced 1959
Used for drapery; linen; plain weave, screen-printed
15 3/4 × 15 3/4 in. (40 × 40 cm)
The family and friends of Ross Littell

Cat. 136
Chess ("Yellow on White" colorway)
Ross Littell (American, 1924–2000)
Made by Winston Prints for Knoll Textiles
Introduced 1959
Used for drapery; Dacron polyester, linen; plain weave, screen-printed
15 3/4 × 15 3/4 in. (40 × 40 cm)
The family and friends of Ross Littell

Cat. 137 (see fig. B.85)
Chess ("Tan on White" colorway)
Ross Littell (American, 1924–2000)
Made by Winston Prints for Knoll Textiles
Introduced 1959
Used for drapery; Dacron polyester, linen; plain weave, screen-printed
15 3/4 × 15 3/4 in. (40 × 40 cm)
The family and friends of Ross Littell

Cat. 138 (see fig. B.84)
Discs sample ("White on White" colorway)
Ross Littell (American, 1924–2000)
Made by Winston Prints for Knoll Textiles
Introduced 1959
Used for drapery; linen, cotton; plain weave, screen-printed
25 1/2 × 24 1/4 in (64.8 × 61.6 cm)
The family and friends of Ross Littell

Cat. 139 (see fig. B.68)
Linea sample ("Aqua/Turquoise/Reseda" colorway)
Suzanne Huguenin (Swiss, 1916–2008)
Made by Winston Prints for Knoll Textiles
1963–77
Used for drapery; linen; plain weave, screen-printed
17 × 50 in. (43.2 × 127 cm)
KnollTextiles Archive, donated by Doreen Rose Stempien

Cat. 140
Linea ("Lemon/Gold/Copper" colorway)
Suzanne Huguenin (Swiss, 1930s–2007)
Made by Winston Prints for Knoll Textiles
1963–77
Used for drapery; linen; plain weave, screen-printed
34 1/4 × 41 1/4 in. (87 × 104.7 cm)
The Montreal Museum of Fine Arts, Liliane and David M. Stewart Collection, Gift of the American Friends of Canada through the generosity of Ben Short, D87.122.1

Cat. 141 (see fig. 3.74)
Quartet curtain (Royal/Sapphire/Sky/Ice Blue colorway)
Suzanne Huguenin (Swiss, 1916–2008)
Made by Winston Prints for Knoll Textiles
1963–78
Used for drapery; Dacron polyester; plain weave; screen-printed
54 × 94 in. (137.2 × 238.8 cm)
Private collection

Cat. 142
Sarano swatches
Eszter Haraszty (American born Hungary, 1923–1994)
Made by Original Textile Company for Knoll Textiles
1956–60
Used for upholstery; saran; basket weave
Each: 3 1/2 × 2 3/4 in. (8.6 × 7.0 cm)
Private collection

 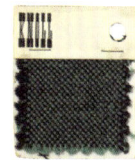

Cat. 143 (see fig. 3.75)
Nylon Homespun data page with 6 colorway samples attached
Suzanne Huguenin (Swiss, 1916–2008)
Samples made by Moss Rose Manufacturing Co. for Knoll Textiles
ca. 1958
Textile samples: nylon; plain weave; mounted on paper
11 × 8 1/2 in. (28 × 21.6 cm)
KnollTextiles Archive

Cat. 144
Knoll Nylon Homespun Two-Tone ("Fire Red and Copper" colorway) on *Model 92* chair
Upholstery: Suzanne Huguenin (Swiss, 1916–2008); chair: Pierre Jeanneret (Swiss, 1896–1967)
Upholstery made by Moss Rose Manufacturing Co. for Knoll Textiles; chair made by Knoll Associates
ca. 1960
Upholstery: nylon; plain weave; chair: wood, foam rubber, cotton webbing
29 × 22 × 31 in. (73.7 × 55.9 × 78.7 cm)
Knoll Museum, East Greenville, Penn.

Cat. 145 (see also fig. 3.77)
Knoll Nylon Homespun Two-Tone ("Black and White" colorway) on *Model 46* chair
Upholstery: Suzanne Huguenin (Swiss, 1916–2008); chair: Max Pearson (American, born 1933)
Upholstery made by Moss Rose Manufacturing Co. for Knoll Textiles; chair made by Knoll Associates
ca. 1965
Upholstery: nylon; plain weave; chair: cast aluminum, steel, plywood, plastic shell, latex foam rubber
35 3/4 × 18 × 18 1/2 in. (90.8 × 45.7 × 47 cm)
Private collection

Cat. 146
Knoll Nylon Homespun Stripe swatches
Suzanne Huguenin (Swiss, 1916–2008)
Made by Craftex Mills for Knoll Textiles
Introduced 1963, these examples ca. 1975
Used for upholstery; nylon; plain weave
Each: 2 3/4 × 3 in. (7 × 7.6 cm)
KnollTextiles Archive

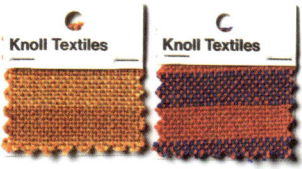

Cat. 147
Nylon Transportation Cloth ("Royal/Emerald" colorway) on *Model 428* barstool
Upholstery: Eszter Haraszty (American, born Hungary, 1920–1994); chair: Harry Bertoia, (American, born Italy, 1915–1978)
Made by Orinoka Mills for Knoll Textiles; chair made by Knoll Associates
ca. 1965
Upholstery: rayon, nylon; plain weave; chair: vinyl-coated metal, plastic shell, foam rubber
39 1/2 × 21 3/4 × 22 in. (100.3 × 55.2 × 55.9 cm)
Knoll Museum, East Greenville, Penn.

Cat. 148
Bangkok ("Electric Blue and Black" colorway)
Henning Watterston (American, 1916–2009)
Made by Craftex Mills for Knoll Textiles
Introduced 1961
Used for upholstery; nylon; plain weave with doubled warps, with backing
44 × 28 1/2 in. (111.8 × 72.4 cm)
Richard and Trudy Schultz

Cat. 149
Knoll Vinyl Cord swatches
Made in Germany for Knoll Textiles
ca. 1958
Used for upholstery; vinyl on cotton twill
Each: 3 1/2 × 2 3/4 in. (8.6 × 7.0 cm)
Private collection

Cat. 150
Striped Breathing Naugahyde swatches
Made for Knoll Textiles
ca. 1957
Used for upholstery; vinyl on cotton twill
Each: 3 1/2 x 2 3/4 in. (8.6 x 7.0 cm)
Private collection

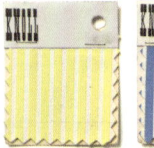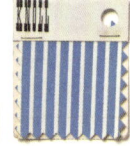

Cat. 151
Striped Breathing Naugahyde ("Lemon and White" colorway) on *Model 72P* side chair
Chair designed by Eero Saarinen (American, born Finland, 1910–1961)
Made for Knoll Textiles; chair made by Knoll Associates.
ca. 1960
Upholstery: vinyl on cotton twill; chair: plastic shell, wood legs, foam rubber
31 5/8 x 22 x 20 in. (80 x 55.9 x 50.8 cm)
Knoll Museum, East Greenville, Penn.

Cat. 152
Brigadoon memorandum with 6 samples attached
Suzanne Huguenin (Swiss, 1916–2008)
Made for Knoll Textiles
1960
Vinyl on cotton knit; mounted on paper
Overall: 11 x 8 1/2 in. (27.9 x 21.6 cm)
KnollTextiles Archive

Cat. 153 (see also fig. 3.61)
Brigadoon ("Black and White" colorway) on *Model 72P* side chair
Upholstery: Suzanne Huguenin (Swiss, 1916–2008); chair: Eero Saarinen (American, born Finland, 1910–1961)
Made by E. I. Du Pont de Nemours & Co. for Knoll Textiles; chair made by Knoll Associates
ca. 1965
Upholstery: vinyl on cotton knit; chair: fiberglass shell, metal legs, foam rubber
31 5/8 x 22 x 20 in. (80 x 55.9 x 50.8 cm)
Knoll Museum, East Greenville, Penn.

Cat. 154 (see fig. 3.79)
Skol sample ("Cerise" colorway)
Vibeke Bruun de Neergaard (Danish, active 1950s–1960s)
Made by C. Olesen for Knoll Textiles
Introduced 1960
Used for upholstery; wool, cotton; 3/1 twill weave
18 x 25 1/2 in. (45.7 x 64.8 cm)
Mae Festa

Cat. 155 (see fig. B.67)
Furrows swatches
Suzanne Huguenin (Swiss, 1916–2008)
Made in Belgium for Knoll Textiles
Introduced 1957, these examples ca. 1965
Used for upholstery; wool, cotton, rayon; plain weave
3 3/8 x 2 1/2 in. (8.6 x 6.4 cm)
Private collection

Cat. 156
Furrows ("Grey White" colorway) on *Model 72U* side chair
Upholstery: Suzanne Huguenin (Swiss, 1916–2008); chair: Eero Saarinen (American, born Finland, 1910–1961)
Made in Belgium for Knoll Textiles; chair: made by Knoll Associates
ca. 1965
Upholstery: wool, cotton, rayon; plain weave; chair: steel, plastic shell, foam rubber
31 5/8 x 22 x 20 in. (80.34 x 55.88 x 50.8 cm)
Dallas Museum of Art, General Operating Funds, 1988.70

Cat. 157 (see fig. 4.5)
Paste-up plan for H. J. Heinz Company executive suite, Pittsburgh, Penn.
Florence Knoll Bassett (American, born 1917), Knoll Planning Unit
ca. 1958
Pen, colored pencil, Knoll Handwoven textiles, and wood veneer on paper
10 1/4 x 7 7/8 in. (26 x 20 cm)
Florence Knoll Bassett Papers, Archives of American Art, Smithsonian Institution

Cat. 158 (see introduction)
Paste-up plan for Cowles Magazines executive office
Florence Knoll Bassett (American, born 1917), Knoll Planning Unit
ca. 1961
Cato and other textile samples, wood samples on paper
Overall: 14 3/4 x 10 1/4 in. (37.5 x 26 cm)
Knoll Archives

Cat. 159
Wulco ("Jade" colorway)
Handwoven in India for Knoll Textiles
Used for upholstery; wool and cotton; plain-weave–derived simple weave
ca. 1962
15 x 23 in. (38.1 x 58.4 cm)
KnollTextiles Archive, donated by Doreen Rose Stempien

Cat. 160
Apu ("Yellow and Red" colorway)
Made by Everest Fabrics in India for Knoll Textiles
ca. 1962
Used for upholstery; jute and cotton; plain weave
24 x 16 in. (61 x 40.6 cm)
KnollTextiles Archive, donated by Doreen Rose Stempien

Cat. 161
Mock-up for advertisement
Florence Knoll Bassett (American, born 1917)
ca. 1963
Cato and *Ebro* samples, pen, and colored pencil on paper
12 1/2 x 9 1/4 in. (31.7 x 23.5 cm)
KnollTextiles Archive

Cat. 162
Cato ("Sand" colorway) on *Model 63* sofa
Upholstery: Paul Maute (German, 1897–1982); sofa: Florence Knoll Bassett (American, born 1917)
Upholstery made by Paul Maute GmbH for Knoll Textiles; sofa made by Knoll Associates
ca. 1962
Upholstery: wool, viscose; plain weave with grouped warps and supplemental weft; sofa: steel and foam rubber
31 1/2 x 84 x 30 in. (80 x 213.4 x 76.2 cm)
Private collection

Cat. 163 (see fig. B.92)
Cato color or weave sample with manufacturer's tag
Paul Maute (German, 1897–1982)
Made by Paul Maute GmbH for Knoll Textiles
ca. 1965
Used for upholstery; wool, viscose; plain weave with grouped warps and supplemental weft
8 x 11 1/2 in. (20.3 x 29.2 cm)
KnollTextiles Archive

Cat. 164 (see fig. 5.1)
Cato ("Red" colorway) on *Model 72U* side chair
Upholstery: Paul Maute (German, 1897–1982); chair: Eero Saarinen (American, born Finland, 1910–1961)
Upholstery made by Paul Maute GmbH for Knoll Textiles; chair made by Knoll Associates
ca. 1965
Upholstery: wool, viscose; plain weave with grouped warps and supplemental weft; chair: fiberglass shell, wooden legs, foam rubber
31 5/8 x 22 x 20 in. (80 x 55.9 x 50.8 cm)
Knoll Museum, East Greenville, Penn.

Cat. 165
Sahara ("Gold" colorway)
Made by Orinoka Mills for Knoll Textiles
1959–72
Used for upholstery; wool and cotton; plain-weave–derived compound weave with paired warps
16 x 25 in. (40.6 x 63.5 cm)
KnollTextiles Archive, donated by Doreen Rose Stempien

Cat. 166 (see fig. B.55)
Inca, color or weave sample with manufacturer's tag
Sheila Hicks (American, born 1934)
Made by Paul Maute GmbH for Knoll Textiles
ca. 1966
Used for upholstery; wool; plain weave
4.5 × 9 in. (11.4 × 22.9 cm.)
Knoll Textiles Archive

Cat. 167
Inca color or weave sample with manufacturer's tag
Sheila Hicks (American, born 1934)
Made by Paul Maute GmbH for Knoll Textiles
ca. 1966
Used for upholstery; wool; plain-weave
9 × 5 1/2 in. (22.9 × 14 cm)
Knoll Textiles Archive

Cat. 168 (see fig. 5.7)
Inca color or weave sample with manufacturer's tag
Sheila Hicks (American, born 1934)
Made by Paul Maute GmbH for Knoll Textiles
ca. 1966
Used for upholstery; wool; plain weave
9 × 5 in. (22.9 × 12.7 cm)
KnollTextiles Archive

Cat. 169 (see fig. B.56)
Inca sample ("Red" colorway)
Sheila Hicks (American, born 1934)
Made by Paul Maute GmbH for Knoll Textiles
introduced 1966, this example ca. 1970
Used for upholstery; wool; plain weave
17 1/2 × 26 in. (44.5 × 66 cm)
Private collection

Cat. 170 (see fig. 5.8)
Inca ("Gold" colorway) on Stephens side chair
Upholstery: Sheila Hicks (American, born 1934); chair: William Stephens (American, 1932–2007)
Upholstery made by Paul Maute GmbH for Knoll Textiles; chair made by Knoll International
ca. 1973
Upholstery: wool; plain weave; chair: oak frame, plastic shell, foam rubber
32 × 19 × 22 1/2 in. (81.3 × 48.3 × 57.2 cm)
Knoll Museum, East Greenville, Penn.

Cat. 171 (see page 229)
Fence ("White" colorway)
Made in Germany for Knoll Textiles
Introduced 1964
Used for drapery; cotton; warp-twining with discontinuous wefts
66 3/4 × 37 3/4 in. (169.6 × 95.8 cm)
The Montreal Museum of Fine Arts, Liliane and David M. Stewart Collection, Gift of the American Friends of Canada through the generosity of Ben Short, D87.123.1

Cat. 172
Filigree sample ("White" colorway)
Made in Germany for Knoll Textiles
Introduced 1964
Used for drapery; polyester; linked and twisted set of elements
27 1/2 × 17 in. (70 × 43.2 cm)
KnollTextiles Archive

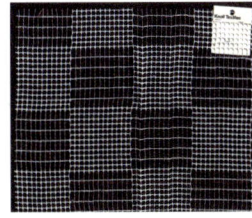

Cat. 173 (see fig. 5.3)
Horizons ("Off-white" colorway)
Paul Maute (German, 1897–1982)
Made by Paul Maute GmbH for Knoll Textiles
Introduced 1964, this example ca. 1970
Used for drapery; linen, wool, silk; plain weave with paired wefts and supplemental knots
68 × 46 1/2 in. (173 × 118 cm)
University of Alberta, Clothing & Textiles Collection, 1990.65.22

Cat. 174 (see fig. 5.10)
Jupiter sample ("Off White" colorway)
Julia Keiner Forchheimer (German, 1900–1992)
Made by Chicopee Mills for Knoll Textiles
ca. 1968
Used for drapery; Verel modacrylic, rayon, wool; plain-weave–derived simple weave with alternating warp twining
29 1/2 × 15 in. (74.9 × 38.1 cm)
KnollTextiles Archive

Cat. 175
York ("Olive/Blue" colorway) on *Model 152* (Pedestal) stool
Upholstery: Knoll Associates; stool: Eero Saarinen (American, born Finland, 1910–1961)
Upholstery made by C. Olesen for Knoll Textiles; stool made by Knoll Associates
ca. 1970
Upholstery: wool; basket weave; stool: vinyl-coated aluminum, latex foam rubber
16 × 15 in. (40.6 × 38.1 cm)
Private collection

Cat. 176 (see fig. 5.11)
Sample kit, "Handwoven Collection"
Lella and Massimo Vignelli (Lella: American, born Italy, 1934; Massimo: American, born Italy, 1931)
Made for Knoll Textiles
ca. 1967
Cardboard and paper, textile samples
Closed: 3 × 8 1/2 × 8 1/2 in. (7.6 × 21.6 × 21.6 cm)
Brooklyn Museum, X1188.3

Cat. 177
Sample kit, "Knoll Textile Collection 1"
Lella and Massimo Vignelli (Lella: American, born Italy 1934; Massimo: American, born Italy, 1931)
Made for Knoll Textiles
ca. 1967
Cardboard and paper, textile swatches
Closed: 4 × 11 1/2 × 9 3/4 in. (10.2 × 29.2 × 24.8 cm)
Brooklyn Museum, X1188.2

Cat. 178
Sample kit, "Knoll Textile Collection 2"
Lella and Massimo Vignelli (Lella: American, born Italy 1934; Massimo: American, born Italy, 1931)
Made for Knoll Textiles
ca. 1967
Cardboard and paper, textile swatches
4 × 11 1/2 × 9 3/4 in. (10.2 × 29.2 × 24.8 cm)
Brooklyn Museum, X1188.1

Cat. 179
Knoll Fabric Wheel
Made for Knoll Textiles
Introduced 1958, this example ca. 1970
Vinyl-coated metal, textile samples
Overall: 12 × 21 1/2 × 9 in. (30.5 × 54.6 × 22.9 cm)
Knoll Museum, East Greenville, Penn.

Cat. 180 (see fig. 5.26)
Nebula ("White" colorway)
Paul Maute (German, 1897–1982)
Made by Paul Maute GmbH for Knoll Textiles
ca. 1973
Used for drapery; wool, perlon, rayon; plain weave with alternating single and paired wefts
31 × 37 1/2 in. (78.7 × 95.3 cm)
KnollTextiles Archive

Cat. 181
Kamee, *Chord*, *Lasar* sample folder
Kamee and *Chord*: Paul Maute (German, 1897–1982)
Kamee and *Chord*: made by Paul Maute GmbH for Knoll Textiles; *Lasar*: made by McNutt Weaving
ca. 1980
Paper, textile swatches
16 1/2 × 11 3/4 in. open (41.9 × 29.9 cm)
KnollTextiles Archive

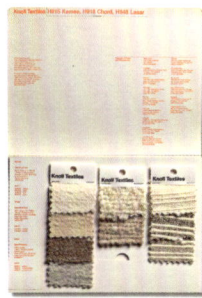

Cat. 182
Collage advertising scarf/panel
Wolf Bauer (German, 1938–90)
Made for Knoll Textiles
ca. 1970
Silk; satin weave, screen-printed
55 3/4 × 27 1/2 in. (191 × 69.9 cm)
Cora Ginsburg LLC

Cat. 183 (see fig. 5.13)
Mosaic ("Fuchsia" colorway)
Wolf Bauer (German, 1938–90)
Made in France for Knoll Textiles
Introduced 1968, this example ca. 1970
Used for upholstery; silk; plain-weave–derived compound weave
32 1/4 × 51 1/2 in. (81.7 × 130.5 cm)
University of Alberta Clothing and Textiles Collection, 1990.65.14b

Cat. 184 (see page 2)
Delta ("White/Orange" colorway)
Wolf Bauer (German, 1938–90)
Made by Pausa AG for Knoll Textiles
Introduced 1967, this example ca. 1975
Used for drapery; cotton velvet, screen-printed
46 × 55 in. (116.8 × 139.7 cm)
KnollTextiles Archive

Cat. 185 (see fig. 5.15)
Stones ("Pink/Red" colorway)
Wolf Bauer (German, 1938–90)
Made by Pausa AG for Knoll Textiles
Introduced 1967, this example ca. 1975
Used for drapery; cotton velvet; screen-printed
52 × 49 1/2 in. (132.1 × 125.7cm)
Cindia Reyes

Cat. 186 (see fig. 5.16)
Malitte seating system
Roberto Matta (Chilean, 1911–2002)
Upholstery made by Société Ariégeoise de Bonneterie; seating system made by Gavina division, Knoll International
Designed 1966, this example ca. 1971
Upholstery: nylon and vinyon; seating: polyurethane foam
Overall: 63 × 63 × 25 in.
(160 × 160 × 63.5 cm)
Brooklyn Museum, Gift of Knoll International, Inc., 78.128.1-5

Cat. 187 (see fig. B.105)
Slant ("Brown" colorway)
Ulrike Rhomberg (Austrian, born 1941)
Made by Pausa AG for Knoll Textiles
ca. 1971
Used for drapery; cotton velvet; screen-printed
93 1/2 × 46 in. (237.5 × 116.8 cm)
Private collection

Cat. 188 (see fig. 5.20)
Omahar ("Brown" colorway)
Francisca Reichardt Vietsch (German, born 1936)
Made by Pausa AG for Knoll Textiles
ca. 1971
Used for drapery; cotton; plain weave, screen-printed
90 × 48 in. (228.6 × 121.9 cm)
Carol Connell

Cat. 189
Omahar sample ("Purple/Ochre" colorway)
Francisca Reichardt Vietsch (German, born 1936)
Made by Pausa AG for Knoll Textiles
ca. 1971
Used for drapery; cotton; plain weave, screen-printed
8 3/4 × 48 in. (22.2 × 121.9 cm)
KnollTextiles Archive

Cat. 190 (see fig. B.102)
Omahar page from "Print Collection" binder
Francisca Reichardt Vietsch (German, born 1936)
Made by Pausa AG for Knoll Textiles
ca. 1977
Textile sample: cotton; plain weave, screen printed; mounted on paper
11 3/4 × 17 7/8 in. (29.9 × 45.4 cm)
KnollTextiles Archive

Cat. 191 (see fig. B.148)
Trails ("Flame/Orange" colorway)
Gretl and Leo Wollner (Austrian, Gretl: 1920–2006; Leo: 1925–1995)
Made by Pausa AG for Knoll Textiles
ca. 1972
Used for drapery, wall hanging; cotton; 4/1 satin weave, screen-printed
133 × 47 in. (337.8 × 119.4 cm)
KnollTextiles Archive

Cat. 192 (see fig. 5.19)
Sling ("White/White" sheer)
Gretl and Leo Wollner (Austrian, Gretl: 1920–2006; Leo: 1925–1995)
Made by Pausa AG for Knoll Textiles
ca. 1971
Used for drapery; cotton, polyester; compound plain weave with discontinuous wefts
32 × 58 in. (81.3 × 147.6 cm)
KnollTextiles Archive

Cat. 193 (see fig. B.147)
Sling ("Orange" colorway)
Gretl and Leo Wollner (Austrian, Gretl: 1920–2006; Leo: 1925–1995)
Made by Pausa AG for Knoll Textiles
ca. 1971
Used for drapery; cotton; plain weave, screen-printed
31 1/2 × 24 in. (78.7 × 61 cm)
KnollTextiles Archive

Cat. 194 (see page 14)
Rivers ("Purple/Brown" colorway)
Gretl and Leo Wollner (Austrian, Gretl: 1920–2006; Leo: 1925–1995)
Made by Pausa AG for Knoll Textiles
ca. 1972
Used for drapery, wall hanging; cotton velvet; screen-printed
103 × 46 1/2 in. (261.6 × 118.1 cm)
Cindia Reyes

Cat. 195 (see fig. B.34)
Caravel page from "Print Collection" binder
Lynne Crosbee (British, active ca. 1970s)
Textile sample made in France by Bianchini-Ferier for Knoll Textiles
ca. 1977
Textile sample: used for drapery; Clevyl; screen-printed; mounted on paper
11 3/4 × 17 7/8 in. (29.8 × 45.4 cm)
KnollTextiles Archive

Cat. 196 (see fig. B.57)
Dynamic swatches
Marga Hielle-Vatter (German, 1913–1997)
Made by rohi for Knoll Textiles
Introduced 1970, these examples ca. 1975
Used for upholstery; wool; plain-weave–derived compound weave
Each: 2 3/4 × 3 1/8 in. (7 × 8.6 cm)
KnollTextiles Archive

Cat. 197 (see also fig. 5.34)
Dynamic ("Fuchsia" colorway) on *Model 46* chair
Upholstery: Marga Hielle-Vatter (German, 1913–1997); chair: Max Pearson (American, born 1933)
Upholstery made by rohi for Knoll Textiles; chair made by Knoll International
ca. 1973
Wool; plain-weave–derived compound weave; chair: cast aluminum, steel, plywood, plastic shell, latex foam rubber
35 3/4 × 18 × 18 1/2 in. (90.8 × 45.7 × 47 cm)
Private collection

Cat. 198 (see fig. 5.35)
Tacoma color sample ("Red" colorway) with manufacturer's tag
Marga Hielle-Vatter (German, 1913–1997)
Made by rohi for Knoll Textiles
ca. 1977
Used for upholstery; wool; plain-weave–derived compound weave
10 1/4 × 7 3/4 in. (19.7 × 26 cm)
KnollTextiles Archive

Cat. 199 (see fig. 5.36)
Tournee ("Brown/Blue" colorway)
Marga Hielle-Vatter (German, 1913–1997)
Made by rohi for Knoll Textiles
ca. 1976
Used for upholstery; wool, cotton; plain-weave–derived simple weave
18 1/2 × 13 in. (47 × 33 cm), with cut out
KnollTextiles Archive

Cat. 200 (see fig. B.59)
Tournee color sample, ("Orange/Cinnamon" colorway) with manufacturer's tag
Marga Hielle-Vatter (German, 1913–1997)
Made by rohi for Knoll Textiles
ca. 1976
Used for upholstery; wool, cotton; plain-weave–derived simple weave
5 1/2 × 7 in. (14 × 17.8 cm)
KnollTextiles Archive

Cat. 201
Sequoia ("Greige" colorway)
Suzanne Huguenin (Swiss, 1916–2008)
Made by Weberei Eschen AG for Knoll Textiles
1974–82
Used for upholstery; wool, rayon; twill weave
13 1/2 × 10 in. (34.3 × 25.4 cm)
KnollTextiles Archive

Cat. 202 (see fig. B.70)
Sequoia ("Copper" colorway)
Suzanne Huguenin (Swiss, 1916–2008)
Made by Weberei Eschen AG for Knoll Textiles
1974–82
Used for upholstery; wool, rayon; twill weave
13 1/2 × 8 1/2 in. (34.3 × 21.6 cm)
KnollTextiles Archive

Cat. 203 (see fig. 5.33)
Sequoia ("Cerise" colorway)
Suzanne Huguenin (Swiss, 1916–2008)
Made by Weberei Eschen AG for Knoll Textiles
ca. 1980
Used for upholstery; wool, rayon; twill weave
11 1/4 × 17 1/2 in. (28.6 × 44.5 cm)
Cindia Reyes

Cat. 204
Knoll Textiles: The Upholstery Collection binder
Made for Knoll Textiles

Introduced ca. 1973; this example ca. 1978
Plastic, metal rings, textile swatches
Closed: 9 × 20 1/4 × 12 1/4 in. (22.9 × 51.4 × 31.1 cm)
KnollTextiles Archive

Cat. 205 (see fig. 5.32)
Cadet upholstery ("Red" colorway) on *Pedestal* armchair
Chair: Eero Saarinen (American, born Finland, 1910–1961)
Upholstery made by Homestead Fabrics for Knoll Textiles; chair made by Knoll International
ca. 1979
Upholstery: wool and nylon; plain weave; chair: plastic, steel, foam rubber
30 1/2 × 26 × 35 in. (77.47 × 66.04 × 88.9 cm)
Dallas Museum of Art, Gift of Knoll International, 1990.133

Cat. 206 (see fig. 5.25)
Serenade sample ("White" colorway)
Made by Paul Maute GmbH for Knoll Textiles
ca. 1972
Used for drapery; wool, Hostalen (polypropylene) strip, spun rayon, perlon; plain weave with supplemental weft pile
11 1/2 × 7 1/4 in. (29.2 × 18.4 cm)
KnollTextiles Archive

Cat. 207 (see fig. 5.24)
Durban sample ("Beige" colorway)
Jan-Paul Barnard (South African, born 1937)
Made by Barkor for Knoll Textiles
ca. 1973
Used for drapery; mohair, cotton; plain gauze (leno) weave
11 3/8 × 7 1/2 in. (28.9 × 19.1 cm)
KnollTextiles Archive

Cat. 208 (see fig. 5.22)
Puzzle sample ("Natural" colorway)
Margarete Warth (German, born 1951)
Made by Linotex for Knoll Textiles
ca. 1973
Used for drapery; acrylic, linen; warp twining with discontinuous wefts
11 5/8 × 7 1/2 in. (29.5 × 19.1 cm)
KnollTextiles Archive

Cat. 209
Cyclone ("Off-White" colorway)
Made by Linotex for Knoll Textiles
ca. 1973
Used for drapery; linen, polyester; warp twining with supplemental warp and discontinuous wefts
11 3/8 × 7 1/2 in. (28.9 × 19.1 cm)
KnollTextiles Archive

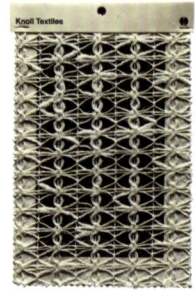

424

Cat. 210 (see fig. 5.23)
Comet swatches ("Natural" and "White" colorways)
Friedrich Goth (German, active 1970s)
Made by Krueger GmbH for Knoll Textiles
ca. 1973
Used for drapery; Dralon acrylic; warp-twining with discontinuous wefts
Each: 11 1/2 × 7 5/8 in. (29.2 × 19.4 cm)
KnollTextiles Archive

Cat. 211 (see fig. B.73)
Stratton ("Off-White" colorway)
Julia Keiner-Forchheimer (German, 1900–1992)
Made by Chicopee Mills for Knoll Textiles
ca. 1975
Used for drapery; Verel modacrylic, rayon and wool; plain gauze weave with supplemental warp
11 3/8 × 7 1/2 in. (28.9 × 19.1 cm)
KnollTextiles Archive

Cat. 212 (see fig. B.52)
Giro ("White on White" sheer)
Christa Häusler-Goltz (German, born 1943)
Made by Taunus Textildruck for Knoll Textiles
ca. 1978
Used for drapery; polyester and cotton; compound plain weave with discontinuous wefts
11 1/8 × 7 5/8 in. (28.3 × 19.4 cm)
KnollTextiles Archive

Cat. 213 (see fig. B.94)
Loop ("Natural" colorway)
Paul Maute (German, 1897–1982)
Made by Paul Maute GmbH for Knoll Textiles
ca. 1973
Used for drapery; wool and nylon; plain-weave–derived simple weave
11 1/2 × 7 1/2 in. (29.2 × 19.1 cm)
KnollTextiles Archive

Cat. 214
Eclat sample ("Curry-Beige" colorway)
Anni Albers (American, born Germany, 1899–1994)
Made by Pausa AG for Knoll Textiles
ca. 1977
Used for drapery; linen and cotton; plain weave, screen-printed
25 × 6 in. (63.5 × 15.2 cm)
KnollTextiles Archive

Cat. 215
Eclat ("Brown on Natural" colorway)
Anni Albers (American, born Germany, 1899–1994)
Made by New London Print Works for Knoll Textiles
ca. 1977
Used for drapery, upholstery; linen and cotton; plain weave, screen-printed
11 1/2 × 10 in. (22.9 × 25.4 cm)
KnollTextiles Archive

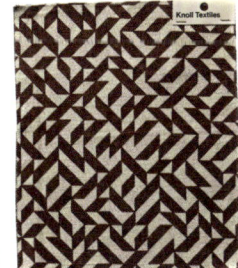

Cat. 216 (see fig. B.36)
Flair ("Blue and Beige" colorway)
Klaus Dombrowski (German, born 1938)
Made in Europe, possibly by Taunus Textildruck, for Knoll Textiles
1978
Used for drapery, upholstery; cotton; warp-faced compound weave (5/1 satin weave and 1/2 twill weave), screen-printed
11 1/8 × 7 7/8 in. (28.3 × 20 cm)
KnollTextiles Archive

Cat. 217
Flex ("Blue and Beige" colorway)
Klaus Dombrowski (German, born 1938)
Made in Europe, possibly by Taunus Textildruck, for Knoll Textiles
1978
Used for drapery, upholstery; cotton; warp-faced compound weave (5/1 satin weave and 1/2 twill weave), screen-printed
11 1/8 × 7 7/8 in. (28.3 × 20 cm)
KnollTextiles Archive

Cat. 218
Don ("Brown" colorway)
Christa Häusler-Goltz (German, born 1943)
Made in Europe, possibly by Taunus Textildruck, for Knoll Textiles
1978
Used for drapery and upholstery; cotton; warp-faced compound weave (4/1 satin weave and plain weave), screen-printed
11 1/8 × 7 7/8 in. (28.3 × 20 cm)
KnollTextiles Archive

Cat. 219 (see fig. B.53)
Domino ("Blue-Brown" colorway)
Christa Häusler-Goltz (German, born 1943)
Made in Europe, possibly by Taunus Textildruck, for Knoll Textiles
1978
Used for drapery and upholstery; cotton; warp-faced compound weave (4/1 satin weave and plain weave), screen-printed
11 1/8 × 7 7/8 in. (28.3 × 20 cm)
KnollTextiles Archive

Cat. 220 (see fig. B.51)
Aquarelle ("Gray/Gold" colorway)
Christa Häusler-Goltz (German, born 1943)
Made by Taunus Textildruck for Knoll Textiles
ca. 1977
Used for drapery; cotton; plain weave, screen-printed
56 1/2 × 51 1/2 in. (143.5 × 130.8 cm)
KnollTextiles Archive

Cat. 221 (see fig. 5.43)
Pyramid ("Violet/Purple" colorway)
Christa Häusler-Goltz (German, born 1943)
Made by Taunus Textildruck for Knoll Textiles
ca. 1977
Used for drapery; cotton; plain weave, screen-printed
110 × 52 in. (279.4 × 132.1 cm)
Cindia Reyes

Cat. 222 (not illustrated)
Pro sample ("White" colorway), with five small colorway swatches attached
Nob + Non (Japanese; Nob Utsumi, born 1945; Non Utsumi, born ca. 1944)
Made by New London Textile Print Works for Knoll Textiles
ca. 1979
Used for drapery; cotton; plain weave, screen-printed
27 × 24 1/4 in. (68.6 × 61.6 cm)
Private collection

Cat. 223 (see fig. B.140)
Pro ("White on Natural" colorway)
Nob + Non (Japanese; Nob Utsumi, born 1945; Non Utsumi, born ca. 1944)
Made by New London Textile Print Works for Knoll Textiles
1979
Used for drapery; cotton; plain weave, screen-printed
156 × 55 in. (396.2 × 139.9 cm)
The Metropolitan Museum of Art, New York, Gift of Knoll Textiles 1984, 1984.547.7

Cat. 224 (see fig. B.139)
Vision ("White" colorway)
Nob + Non (Japanese; Nob Utsumi, born 1945; Non Utsumi, born ca. 1944)
Made by New London Textile Print Works for Knoll Textiles
1979
Used for drapery; cotton; plain weave, screen-printed
144 × 55 in. (365.8 × 139.9 cm)
The Metropolitan Museum of Art, New York, Gift of Knoll Textiles 1986, 1986.41.1

Cat. 225 (see fig. 6.3)
Direction ("Rainbow/Stripe on White" colorway)
Nob + Non (Japanese; Nob Utsumi, born 1945; Non Utsumi, born ca. 1944)
Made by New London Textile Print Works for Knoll Textiles
1979
Used for drapery; cotton; plain weave, screen-printed
156 × 55 in. (396.2 × 139.9 cm)
The Metropolitan Museum of Art, New York, Gift of Knoll Textiles, 1984.547.10

Cat. 226 (see fig. 6.7)
Connection sample ("Spruce" colorway)
Adrian Parry (Adrian Pulfer, American, born Australia, 1950; Parry Merkley, American, born 1951)
Made by New London Textile Print Works for Knoll Textiles
1982
Used for drapery; cotton; plain weave, screen-printed, Teflon glaze
26 1/2 × 26 1/4 in. (67.3 × 67.6 cm)
KnollTextiles Archive

Cat. 227 (not illustrated)
Linea-T sample ("White" colorway)
Peter Seipelt (German, born 1937)
Made by Taunus Textildruck for Knoll Textiles
ca. 1982
Used for drapery; polyester, cotton; compound plain weave with discontinuous wefts
17 3/4 × 12 in. (45.1 × 30.5 cm)
Private collection

Cat. 228
Zigzag sample ("Silver/Beige" colorway)
Peter Seipelt (German, born 1937)
Made by Taunus Textildruck for Knoll Textiles
1982
Used for drapery; cotton; plain weave, screen-printed
25 3/4 × 25 3/4 in. (65.4 × 65.4 cm)
KnollTextiles Archive

Cat. 229 (see fig. B.115)
Basket sample ("Lilac" colorway)
Peter Seipelt (German, born 1937)
Made by Taunus Textildruck for Knoll Textiles
1982
Used for drapery; cotton; plain weave, screen-printed
16 × 25 1/4 in. (40.6 × 64.1 cm)
KnollTextiles Archive

Cat. 230 (see fig. 6.9)
Downtown
Alexandre Mimoglou (Greek, lives France, 1954)
Made by Taunus Textildruck Zimmer for Knoll Textiles
1982
Used for drapery; cotton; plain weave, screen-printed
48 × 52 in. (121.9 × 132.1 cm)
Cooper-Hewitt, National Design Museum, Smithsonian Institution, Gift of Taunus Textildruck Zimmer, 1983-19-5

Cat. 231 (see fig. 6.10)
Fortuna
Karl Vogelsang (German, born 1932)
Made by Heberlein Textildruck AG, for Knoll Textiles
1988
Used for drapery; cotton, plain weave, screen-printed
152 × 55 in. (386.1 × 139.7 cm)
Cooper-Hewitt, National Design Museum, Smithsonian Institution, Gift of Heberlein Textildruck, Switzerland, 1989-88-1-a

Cat. 232
Queen Anne side chair with cushion upholstered in *Grandmother*
Robert Venturi (American, born 1925) and Denise Scott Brown (American, born 1931)

Upholstery: made for Knoll International; chair: made by Knoll International
ca. 1984
Upholstery: cotton; plain weave, screen-printed; chair: maple plywood and plastic laminate
38 1/2 × 26 5/8 × 23 3/4 in. (97.8 × 67.6 × 60.3 cm), seat height 18 5/8 in. (47.4 cm)
The Museum of Modern Art, Gift of Knoll International, 302.1984

Cat. 233 (see fig. 6.11)
Grandmother
Robert Venturi (American, born 1925) and Denise Scott Brown (American, born 1931)
Made for Knoll International
1983
Used for upholstery and drapery; cotton; plain weave, screen-printed
155 × 55 in. (393.7 × 139.7 cm)
Joan H. and David E. Bright

Cat. 234
Sample kit
Takaaki Matsumoto (Japanese, born 1954)
Made for Knoll Textiles
ca. 1987
Colorless plastic, textile swatches, paper, metal
4 × 11 × 15 1/2 in. (10.2 × 27.9 × 39.8 cm)
Brooklyn Museum, Gift of Vera White Hollander, 2010.31a-b

Cat. 235 (see fig. 6.14)
Cobblestone sample ("Multi" colorway)
Jhane Barnes (American, born 1956)
Made by Franetta for Knoll Textiles
ca. 1983
Used for upholstery; wool, silk, cotton, and polyester; plain-weave–derived simple weave
10 3/4 × 17 1/4 in. (27.3 × 43.8 cm)
Cindia Reyes

Cat. 236 (see fig. B.12)
Melange, 4 samples
Jhane Barnes (American, born 1956)
Made by Franetta for Knoll Textiles
ca. 1983
Used for upholstery; wool, rayon, cotton, and silk; plain-weave–derived simple weave
Each: 11 1/2 × 17 in. (29.2 × 43.2 cm)
Cindia Reyes

Cat. 237 (see fig. 6.14)
Nuance, 8 samples
Jhane Barnes (American, born 1956)
Made by Franetta for Knoll Textiles
ca. 1983
Used for upholstery; wool, silk, cotton, and rayon; plain weave
Each: 11 1/2 × 17 in. (29.2 × 43.2 cm)
Cindia Reyes

Cat. 238
Rainbow Twill ("Russet" colorway)
Jhane Barnes (American, born 1956)
Made by Franetta for Knoll Textiles
ca. 1983
Used for upholstery; cotton, wool, rayon, and polyester; twill variation
168 3/4 × 57 3/4 in. (428.6 × 146.7 cm)
The Metropolitan Museum of Art, New York, Gift of Knoll Textiles, 1984.547.4

Cat. 239 (see fig. 6.13)
Rainbow Twill ("Navy" colorway) on *Stephens* armchair
Upholstery: Jhane Barnes (American, born 1956); chair: William Stephens (American, 1932–2007)
Made by Franetta for Knoll Textiles; chair: made by Knoll International
ca. 1985
Upholstery: cotton, wool, rayon, and polyester; twill variation; chair: oak frame, plastic shell, and foam
32 × 22 1/4 × 22 in. (81.3 × 56.5 × 55.9 cm)
Knoll Museum, East Greenville, Penn.

Cat. 240
Niji Net samples ("Desert" and "Sage" colorways)
Jhane Barnes (American, born 1956)
Made in Japan for Knoll Textiles
1986
Used for drapery; wool, polyester, and silk; plain gauze (leno) weave with paired wefts
10.75 × 16 in. (27.3 × 40.6 cm)
KnollTextiles Archive

Cat. 241 (see fig. B.13)
Fuji sample ("Natural" colorway)
Jhane Barnes (American, born 1956)
Made in Japan for Knoll Textiles
1986
Used for drapery; wool; plain weave with supplemental warp patterning
11 × 17 in. (27.9 × 43.2 cm)
KnollTextiles Archive

Cat. 242 (see fig. 6.24)
Sample package
Jhane Barnes (American, born 1956)
Made for KnollTextiles
1989
Case: of plastic, wool, polyester; Samples: machine knitted and woven samples of wool, cotton, polyester, nylon, rayon, and acrylic
Case: 19 1/2 × 13 3/4 in. (49.5 × 34.9 cm); samples, each: 11 3/4 × 18 in. (29.8 × 45.7 cm)
Cooper-Hewitt, National Design Museum, Smithsonian Institution, Gift of Knoll International, 1990-89-1-a/j

Cat. 243 (see fig. B.14)
Waves ("Ultramarine" colorway)
Jhane Barnes (American, born 1956)
Made in Japan for KnollTextiles
1989
Used for upholstery; wool and polyester; double-faced knit, piece-dyed
144 × 65 in. (365.8 × 165.1 cm)
Cooper-Hewitt, National Design Museum, Smithsonian Institution, Gift of Knoll Textiles, 1990-39-2

Cat. 244
Romanie ("Marine" colorway) on *Eastside* lounge chair
Upholstery: Jhane Barnes (American, born 1956); chair: Ettore Sottsass (Italian, 1917–2007)
Upholstery made in the United States for KnollTextiles; chair made by Knoll International
ca. 1990
Upholstery: wool and rayon; compound plain weave with supplemental warp; chair: steel frame, foam, and leather
34 × 32 × 31 in. (86.4 × 81.3 × 78.7 cm)
Knoll Museum, East Greenville, Penn.

Cat. 245
Transition ("Eucalyptus" colorway)
Jhane Barnes (American, born 1956)
Made in Japan for KnollTextiles
Introduced 1992, in production 2011
Used for panels and drapery; polyester; plain-weave–derived simple weave
Width 54 in. (137.2 cm)
KnollTextiles

Cat. 246 (see fig. B.17)
Gordian Knot sample ("Caladium" colorway)
Jhane Barnes (American, born 1956)
Made in the United States for KnollTextiles
1996
Used for upholstery; polyester; plain-weave–derived compound weave
12 × 9 in. (30.5 × 22.9 cm)
Private collection

Cat. 247 (see fig. 6.34)
Hilbert sample ("Teal" colorway)
Jhane Barnes (American, born 1956)
Made in the United States for KnollTextiles
1997
Used for upholstery; cotton; plain-weave–derived compound weave
12 × 9 in. (30.5 × 22.9 cm)
Private collection

Cat. 248
Fretwork ("Filigree" colorway)
Jhane Barnes (American, born 1956)
Made by Aramo for KnollTextiles
1992
Used for wallcovering; acrylic resin powder on paper backing
73 5/8 × 36 7/16 in. (187 × 92.5 cm)
Cooper-Hewitt, National Design Museum, Smithsonian Institution, Gift of Knoll Textiles, 1993-83-2

Cat. 249
Vertical Variations Jhane Barnes sample kit
Jhane Barnes (American, born 1956)
Made for KnollTextiles
ca. 1989
Textile samples, cardboard, paper
Closed: 10 1/2 × 6 5/8 in. (26.7 × 15.24 cm); open: 14 1/2 × 10 1/2 in. (359.4 × 26.7 cm)
KnollTextiles Archive

Cat. 250
Wallcovering Collection sample kit including patterns designed by Jhane Barnes
Made for KnollTextiles
ca. 1990
Various media
Closed: 7 3/4 × 10 1/2 in. (19.7 × 26.7 cm); open: 10 1/2 × 15 1/2 in. (26.7 × 39.4 cm)
KnollTextiles Archive

Cat. 251 (see fig. 6.20)
Tilt sample ("Teal" colorway)
Dana Romeis (American, born 1947)
Made by Craftex Mills for Knoll Textiles
Introduced 1985
Used for upholstery; wool, rayon, and nylon; plain-weave–derived compound weave
11 1/2 × 17 3/4 in. (29.2 × 45.1 cm)
Cindia Reyes

Cat. 252 (see fig. B.109)
Tilt ("Navy" colorway)
Dana Romeis (American, born 1947)
Made by Craftex Mills for Knoll Textiles
Introduced 1985
Used for upholstery; wool, rayon, and nylon;

plain-weave–derived compound weave
56 3/4 x 40 1/4 in. (144.4 x 102.2 cm)
Dana Romeis

Cat. 253
Flash sample ("Soldier" colorway)
Dana Romeis (American, born 1947)
Made by Craftex Mills for Knoll Textiles
Introduced 1985
Used for upholstery; wool, rayon, and nylon; double-cloth with plain-weave face and 2/1 twill back
11 1/4 x 17 1/2 in. (28.6 x 44.5 cm)
Dana Romeis

Cat. 254 (see fig. 6.21)
Slant sample ("Charcoal" colorway)
Dana Romeis (American, born 1947)
Made by Craftex Mills for Knoll Textiles
Introduced 1985
Used for upholstery; wool, rayon, plain-weave–derived compound weave
11 x 17 1/2 in. (27.9 x 44.5 cm)
Dana Romeis

Cat. 255 (see fig. B.110)
Pandora sample ("Blue" colorway)
Dana Romeis (American, born 1947)
Made by Craftex Mills for KnollTextiles
Introduced 1988
Used for upholstery; rayon; plain-weave–derived compound weave
11 1/2 x 17 1/4 in. (29.2 x 43.8 cm)
Dana Romeis

Cat. 256 (see fig. 6.23)
Zana Coordinate sample ("Slate" colorway)
Dana Romeis (American, born 1947)
Made by Callens Textielfabriek for KnollTextiles
Introduced 1988
Used for upholstery; cotton; plain-weave–derived compound weave
8 1/2 x 11 1/4 in. (21.6 x 28.6 cm)
KnollTextiles Archive

Cat. 257 (see fig. B.23)
Beaumont ("Ivory" colorway)
Anne Beetz (Belgian, born 1939)
Made in the United States for KnollTextiles
Introduced 1989
Used for upholstery; cotton and rayon; plain-weave–derived simple weave
37 x 57 3/4 in. (94 x 146.7 cm)
KnollTextiles

Cat. 258 (see fig. B.24)
Passerelle sample ("Lichen" colorway)
Anne Beetz (Belgian, born 1939)
Made in Belgium for KnollTextiles
Introduced 1989
Used for upholstery; cotton and linen; plain-weave–derived simple weave
18 x 11 1/2 in. (45.7 x 29.2 cm)
KnollTextiles Archive

Cat. 259 (see fig. 6.28)
Blue Night sample ("Burgundy" colorway)
Hazel Siegel (American, born 1942)
Made in Germany for KnollTextiles
Introduced 1990
Used for upholstery; cotton and rayon; compound plain weave with alternating weft and warp floats
16 1/2 x 11 1/2 in. (41.9 x 29.2 cm)
KnollTextiles Archive

Cat. 260 (see fig. 6.29)
Regal Brocade sample binder
Hazel Siegel (American, born 1942)
Made for KnollTextiles
ca. 1990
Textile samples (cotton, rayon, polyester), paper, cardboard
Open: 11 1/2 x 29 1/4 in. (29.2 x 74.3 cm)
KnollTextiles Archive

Cat. 261 (see fig. B.118)
Bauhaus Geometric sample ("Buff" colorway)
Hazel Siegel (American, born 1942)
Made in Germany for KnollTextiles
Introduced 1990
Used for upholstery; rayon, cotton, and polyester; plain-weave–derived compound weave
18 x 12 in. (45.7 x 30.5 cm)
KnollTextiles Archive

Cat. 262 (see fig. 6.30)
Diamond Back on *Model 180* armchair
Upholstery: Peter Eisenman (American, born 1932); chair: Enrico Franzolini (Italian, born 1952)
Upholstery made in the United Kingdom for KnollTextiles; chair made by Knoll International
ca. 1991
Upholstery: wool; plain-weave–derived compound weave; chair: beech and steel frame; foam rubber
30 3/4 x 19 1/4 x 22 in. (78.1 x 48.9 x 55.9 cm)
Knoll Museum, East Greenville, Penn.

Cat. 263 (see fig. 6.35)
A New Day sample kit
Suzanne Tick (American, born 1959)
Made for KnollTextiles
ca. 1996
Textile swatches, cardboard box, and various media
Box: 3 x 4 in. (7.6 x 10.7 cm); each swatch: 2 3/4 x 3 in. (7 x 7.6 cm)
KnollTextiles Archive

Cat. 264
Resolution ("Green Ribbon" colorway)
Suzanne Tick (American, born 1959)
Made in the United States for KnollTextiles
Introduced 1996, in production 2011
Used for panels; solution-dyed polyester; plain-weave–derived simple weave
Width 66 in. (167.6 cm)
KnollTextiles

Cat. 265 (see fig. B.134)
Silver Screen ("Gold" colorway)
Suzanne Tick (American, born 1959)
Made in Switzerland for KnollTextiles
Introduced 1998, in production 2011
Used for drapery; polyester and metallic backing; plain gauze (leno) weave
Width 57 in. (144.8 cm)
KnollTextiles

Cat. 266 (see fig. 6.38)
Heavy Metal ("Brass Rubbing" colorway)
Suzanne Tick (American, born 1959)
Made in the United States for Knoll Textiles
Introduced 2001, in production 2011
Used for panel and upholstery; recycled polyester and olefin; plain-weave–derived compound weave
Width 66 in. (167.6 cm)
KnollTextiles

Cat. 267 (see fig. B.135)
Macro ("Sheet Metal" colorway)
Suzanne Tick (American, born 1959)
Made in the United States for KnollTextiles
Introduced 2005, in production 2011
Used for panels; recycled polyester; plain-weave–derived simple weave
Width 66 in. (167.6 cm)
KnollTextiles

Cat. 268 (see fig. B.135)
Mezzo ("Oxide" colorway)
Suzanne Tick (American, born 1959)
Made in the United States for KnollTextiles
Introduced 2005, in production 2011
Used for panels; recycled polyester; plain-weave–derived simple weave
Width 66 in. (167.6 cm)
KnollTextiles

Cat. 269 (see fig. B.135)
Micro ("Silver" colorway)
Suzanne Tick (American, born 1959)
Made in the United States for KnollTextiles
Introduced 2005, in production 2011
Used for panels; recycled polyester; plain-weave–derived simple weave
Width 66 in. (167.6 cm)
KnollTextiles

Cat. 270
Imago Mirage ("Gold" colorway)
Suzanne Tick (American, born 1959)
Embedded textile (*Metallic Mesh*) made in Japan for KnollTextiles; *Imago* made in the United States for KnollTextiles
Imago introduced 2000, this version introduced 2001, in production 2011
Various uses; resin, embedded textile (polyester)
96 x 48 in. (243.8 x 121.9 cm)
KnollTextiles

Cat. 271 (see fig. B.136)
Hard Rock ("Patina" colorway)
Suzanne Tick (American, born 1959)
Made in the United States for KnollTextiles
Introduced 2006, in production 2011
Used for panels; recycled polyester and olefin; plain weave with paired wefts
Width 66 in. (167.6 cm)
KnollTextiles

Cat. 272 (see fig. 6.41)
Bandwidth ("Current" colorway)
Suzanne Tick (American, born 1959)
Made in the United States for KnollTextiles
Introduced 2008, in production 2011
Used for panels; Terratex™ recycled polyester; plain-weave–derived compound weave
Width 66 in. (167.6 cm)
KnollTextiles

Cat. 273 (see fig. 6.42)
Air Rights ("Satellite" colorway)
Suzanne Tick (American, born 1959)
Made in Japan for KnollTextiles
Introduced 2009, in production 2011
Used for drapery; polyester; compound plain weave with discontinuous wefts, screen-printed
Width 59 in. (149.9 cm)
KnollTextiles

Cat. 274 (see fig. 6.39)
Graffiti Camo ("Glo" colorway)
Stephen Sprouse (American, 1953–2004)
Made in the United States for KnollTextiles
ca. 2003
Used for upholstery and drapery; Trevira CS polyester velvet; digitally-printed
74 1/2 x 56 in. (189.2 x 139.7 cm)
KnollTextiles Archive

Cat. 275
Techno Tweed sample ("Optical Blue" colorway)
Stephen Sprouse (American, 1953–2004)
Made in the United States for KnollTextiles
ca. 2003
Used for upholstery; polyester and olefin; plain-weave–derived simple weave
9 x 9 in. (22.9 x 22.9 cm)
KnollTextiles Archive

Cat. 276 (see fig. B.145)
Paper Shift ("Mahogany" colorway)
Elizabeth Whelan (American, born 1961)
Made in Mexico for KnollTextiles
Introduced 2004
Used for wallcovering; paper; polypropylene backing; plain weave
24 x 24 in. (61 x 61 cm)
Elizabeth Whelan

Cat. 277 (see fig. B.145)
Shuffle ("Silver Pine" colorway)
Elizabeth Whelan (American, born 1961)
Made in Mexico for KnollTextiles
Introduced 2004
Used for wallcovering; paper; polypropylene backing; plain weave.
24 x 24 in. (61 x 61 cm)
Elizabeth Whelan

Cat. 278 (see fig. 6.40)
Pause ("Orange," "Grey," and "Blue" colorways)
2x4, Inc.

Made in the United States for KnollTextiles
Introduced 2004, in production 2011
Used for wallcovering; vinyl, nonwoven polyester-cellulose–blend backing
Width 54 in. (137.2 cm)
KnollTextiles

Cat. 279 (see fig. B.95)
Merge ("Viridian" colorway)
Abbott Miller (American, born 1963)
Made in the United States for KnollTextiles
Introduced 2006, in production 2011
Used for wallcovering; vinyl, cotton backing
Width 54 in. (137.2 cm)
KnollTextiles

Cat. 280 (see fig. B.87)
Margin ("Copper" colorway)
LTL Architects
Made in the United States for KnollTextiles
Introduced 2006, in production 2011
Used for wallcovering; vinyl, osnaburg backing
Width 54 in. (137.2 cm)
KnollTextiles

Cat. 281 (see fig. B.31)
Topography samples
Dorothy Cosonas (American, born 1961)
Made in Germany for KnollTextiles
Introduced 2006, in production 2011
Used for upholstery; polyester, cotton, acrylic, rayon; plain-weave–derived compound weave
Each: 9 x 9 in. (22.9 x 22.9 cm)
KnollTextiles

Cat. 282 (see fig. 6.46)
Harrison samples
Dorothy Cosonas (American, born 1961)
Made in the United Kingdom for KnollTextiles
Introduced 2007, in production 2011
Used for upholstery; wool, nylon; plain weave with quadrupled warps and wefts
Each: 8 1/2 x 8 1/2 in. (21.6 x 21.6 cm)
KnollTextiles

Cat. 283 (see fig. 6.45)
Rivington samples
Dorothy Cosonas (American, born 1961)
Made in Belgium for KnollTextiles
Introduced 2007, in production 2011
Used for upholstery; wool, cotton, acrylic, and polyester; plain-weave–derived simple weave
Each: 8 1/2 x 8 1/2 in. (21.6 x 21.6 cm)
KnollTextiles

Cat. 284 (not illustrated)
Rivington ("Sapphire" colorway) on *Model 71* armchair
Upholstery: Dorothy Cosonas (American, born 1961); chair: Eero Saarinen (American, born Finland, 1910-1961)
Upholstery made in Belgium for KnollTextiles; chair made by Knoll, Inc.
Upholstery introduced 2007; chair introduced ca. 1950, in production 2011
Upholstery: wool, cotton, acrylic, and polyester; plain-weave–derived simple weave; chair: polyurethane shell, plywood, oak legs, urethane foam
31 1/2 x 25 1/2 x 24 1/2 in. (80 x 64.8 x 62.2 cm)
KnollTextiles

Cat. 285 (see fig. B.32)
Gibson samples
Dorothy Cosonas (American, born 1961)
Made in Germany for KnollTextiles
Introduced 2007, in production 2011
Used for upholstery; cotton and polyester; plain-weave–derived compound weave with supplemental warp pile
Each: 8 1/2 x 8 1/2 in. (21.6 x 21.6 cm)
KnollTextiles

Cat. 286
Roundtrip samples
Dorothy Cosonas (American, born 1961)
Made in the United States for KnollTextile
Introduced 2010, in production 2011
Used for upholstery; solution-dyed nylon with Teflon coating; plain-weave–derived compound weave
Each: 8 1/2 x 8 1/2 in. (21.6 x 21.6 cm)
KnollTextiles Archive

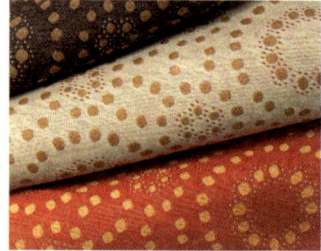

Cat. 287 (see fig. 6.47)
Courtship ("Windswept" colorway)
Dorothy Cosonas (American, born 1961)
Made in Germany for KnollTextiles
Introduced 2010, in production 2011
Used for drapery; Trevira polyester; plain weave
Width 72 in. (182.9 cm)
KnollTextiles

Cat. 288
Cato sample card
Paul Maute (German, 1897–1982)
Made in the United Kingdom for KnollTextiles
Introduced 1961, these colorways introduced 2007, in production 2011
Wool and rayon; plain weave with grouped warps and supplemental weft; mounted on paper
11 x 8 1/2 in. (27.9 x 21.6 cm)
KnollTextiles Archive

Cat. 289
Eclat Weave sample card
Original design: Anni Albers (American, born Germany, 1899–1994)
Made in the United States for KnollTextiles
Original design introduced ca. 1977, this version introduced 2007, in production 2011
Rayon, cotton, polyester; 3/1 compound twill; mounted on paper

11 x 8 1/2 in. (27.9 x 21.6 cm)
KnollTextiles Archive

Cat. 290
Mira Sheer ("Poppy" colorway)
Original Design: Ross Littell (American, 1924-2000)
Made in Japan for KnollTextiles
Original design introduced 1958, this version introduced 2007, in production 2011
Used for drapery; polyester; compound plain weave with discontinuous wefts, screen-printed
Width 60 in. (152.4 cm)
KnollTextiles

Cat. 291
Knoll Luxe sample box
The Moderns
Made for Knoll Luxe
2008
Acrylic, textile swatches
6 1/2 x 12 x 12 in. (16.5 x 30.5 x 30.5 cm)
KnollTextiles

Cat. 292 (see fig. B.33)
Bavaria ("Holly" colorway)
Dorothy Cosonas (American, born 1961)
Made in Austria for Knoll Luxe
Introduced 2008, in production 2011
Used for upholstery; acrylic, wool, cotton, cotton chenille, and polyester; plain-weave–derived simple weave
Width 54 in. (137.2 cm)
KnollTextiles

Cat. 293
Galloway ("Fortress" colorway)
Dorothy Cosonas (American, born 1961)
Introduced 2008, in production 2011
Made in the United Kingdom for Knoll Luxe
Used for upholstery; wool, cashmere; plain weave
Width 54 in. (137.2 cm)
KnollTextiles

Cat. 294 (see fig. B.98)
Mepal ("Willow" colorway)
Proenza Schouler (Jack McCollough and Lazaro Hernandez: both American, born 1978)
Introduced 2008, in production 2011
Made in the United States for Knoll Luxe
Used for upholstery; linen and silk; plain-weave–derived compound weave
Width 54 in. (137.2 cm)
KnollTextiles

Cat. 295 (see fig. 6.50)
Sandis ("Caramel" colorway)
Proenza Schouler (Jack McCollough and Lazaro Hernandez: both American, born 1978)
Made in the United States for Knoll Luxe
Introduced 2008, in production 2011
Used for upholstery; linen and cotton; plain-weave–derived compound weave
Width 54 in. (137.2 cm)
KnollTextiles

Cat. 296 (see fig. B.106)
Parker ("Tint" colorway)
Rodarte (Kate and Laura Mulleavy, American: Kate, born 1979; Laura, born 1980)
Made in Switzerland for Knoll Luxe
Introduced 2010, in production 2011
Used for drapery; polyester, viscose, linen, lurex, and cotton; plain weave face and back encapsulating laid vertical and horizontal elements
Width 59 in. (149.9 cm)
KnollTextiles

Cat. 297 (see page 269)
Auden ("Landscape" colorway)
Rodarte (Kate and Laura Mulleavy, American: Kate, born 1979; Laura, born 1980)
Made in Germany for Knoll Luxe
Introduced 2010, in production 2011
Used for drapery; ramie and polyester; plain gauze (leno) weave with supplemental weft
Width 58 in. (147.3 cm)
KnollTextiles

Cat. 298 (see fig. 6.51)
Cummings ("Shadow" colorway)
Rodarte (Kate and Laura Mulleavy, American: Kate, born 1979; Laura, born 1980)
Made in the United States for Knoll Luxe
Introduced 2010, in production 2011
Used for upholstery; cotton and silk; plain-weave–derived compound weave
Width 54 in. (137.2 cm)
KnollTextiles

Cat. 299 (not illustrated)
Cummings, ("Rain" colorway), on *Model 152* (Pedestal) stool
Upholstery: Rodarte (Kate and Laura Mulleavy, American: Kate, born 1979; Laura, born 1980); stool: Eero Saarinen (American, born Finland, 1910–1961)
Introduced 2010, in production 2011
Upholstery: made in the United States for Knoll Luxe; stool made by Knoll, Inc.
Upholstery: cotton and silk; plain-weave–derived compound weave; stool: vinyl-coated aluminum, urethane foam
16 1/2 x 15 1/2 in. (41.9 x 39.4 cm)
KnollTextiles

Cat. 293 *Galloway* ("Fortress" colorway) Dorothy Cosonas (American, born 1961) Introduced 2008, in production 2011, made in the United Kingdom for Knoll Luxe. Used for upholstery; wool, cashmere; plain weave. Width 54 in. (137.2 cm). KnollTextiles

- "A Humane Campus for the Study of Man." *Architectural Forum* (January 1955): 130–34.
- "A Knoll Extra." *Interiors* (June 1963): 14.
- "A New Home for Boris w." *Interiors* (December 1951): 115–18, 180–81.
- "A Review of the Fabric Market." *Interiors* (April 1948): 89.
- "A Survey of Furniture from 40-Odd Sources." *Interiors* (March 1948): 104–15.
- "A.I.D. Product Design Awards." *Interiors* (May 1955): 116.
- Aav, Marianne, and Jukka Savolinen, eds. *Essays on Finnish Modernism*. Helsinki: Designmuseo, 2010.
- Abercrombie, Stanley. *A Century of Interior Design, 1900–2000*. New York: Rizzoli, 2003.
- "Aerocor: New Potential for Owens Corning's Fiberglas." *Interiors* (February 1958): 126.
- Albers, Anni. "Handweaving Today–Textile Work at Black Mountain College." *The Weaver* 6, no. 1 (January/February 1941): 4.
- "ALCOA Complete." *Architectural Forum* (November 1953): 124–31.
- "Alice Crocker Lloyd Residence Hall." *Architectural Record* (April 1951): 112–17.
- "All That Glitters." *Industrial Design* (April 1972): 62–67.
- "American Fabrics Presents a Key to the Man-Made Fibers." *American Fabrics*, no. 26 (Spring 1953): 70–74.
- "An Old Food Company Builds a New Center for Research." *Architectural Record* (February 1959): 173–78.
- "Angelo Testa." *Arts & Architecture* (July 1946): 42–43.
- "Art Academy Has Power Loom." *Interiors* (December 1945): 122.
- Art Institute of Chicago. *Rooted in Chicago: Fifty Years of Textile Traditions*. Chicago: Art Institute of Chicago Museum Studies, 1997.
- "Art into Living: Integrated Fabrics." *Art News* (May 1947): 36, 60.
- "Arundell Clarke Textile Showroom." *Interiors* (October 1948): 150.
- "ATC International Air Terminal." *Architectural Forum* (March 1945): 97–105.
- "Available Now: The Best Furniture in Years." *Interiors* (March 1947): 78.
- Bach, Richard F. "American Industrial Art: An Exhibition of Contemporary Design." *Metropolitan Museum of Art Bulletin* 24, no. 2 (February 1929): 39–42.
- Baermann, Walter. "Post-War Upholstered Furniture." *Upholstering* (September 1944): 13–15, 42–43.
- Baltimore Museum of Art. *Living Up-to Date: An Exhibition of New Designs for the Home from September 25 to October 28, 1951*. Exh. cat. Baltimore: Baltimore Museum of Art, 1951.
- Barmash, Isadore. *The Self-Made Man*. New York: Macmillan, 1969.
- Bassett, Florence Knoll. "The Interiors at CBS." *Office Design* (May 1966).
- Bel Geddes, Norman. "Springless Furniture Suggests Design for Furniture of the Future." *Upholstering* (May 1943): 6–9.
- Berner, Hermann, and Werner Fifka, eds. *Pausa, Das Bauhaus kam nach Mössingen: Geschichte, Architektur und Design der einstigen Textilfirma Pausa*. Mössingen, Germany: Talheimer, 2006.
- "Best of the New Furniture." *Interiors* (October 1948): 92.
- Blaszczyk, Regina Lee. "Designing Synthetics, Promoting Brands: Dorothy Liebes, DuPont Fibres and Post-war American Interiors." *Journal of Design History* 21, no. 1 (March 2008): 75–99.
- Bourne, Matthew. "Form and Function." *Modern Carpets & Textiles* 1 (Autumn 2005): 61.
- "Breuer's Beautiful Plan for the Neumanns." *Interiors* (June 1956): 111.
- Brophyl, Gladys Rogers. "More Textiles Shown in 'Good Design' 1951." *Handweaver & Craftsman* 2, no. 2 (Spring 1951): 39.
- Brunetti, John. *Baldwin Kingrey: Midcentury Modern in Chicago, 1947–1957*. Chicago: Wright, 2004.
- Brunius, Jan, et al. *Svenska Textilier 1890 1990*. Trelleborg: Signum/Lund, 1994.
- Bryan, Dorothy. "Maria Kipp—Her Career as a Weaver." *Handweaver & Craftsman* 3, no. 1 (Winter 1951–52): 15–17, 59.
- Buffalo Fine Arts Academy. *Good Design is Your Business*. Buffalo, N.Y.: Buffalo Fine Arts Academy, 1947.
- "Building for Defense: A Trio of Modern Plants." *Architectural Forum* (November 1941): 331–34.
- *Bulletin of the Detroit Institute of Arts* 29, no. 2 (1949–50): 39.
- Byars, Mel. *The Design Encyclopedia*. New York: John Wiley & Sons, 1994.
- ———. *The Design Encyclopedia*. London: Laurence King, 2004.
- Caplan, Ralph. "Connecticut General: The Team Approach: A Round-Table Discussion Reveals How Connecticut General Got What It Wanted from Designers." *Industrial Design* (September 1958): 53.
- Caplan, Ralph. *The Design of Herman Miller*. New York: Whitney Library of Design, 1977.
- Carleton, J.R. "Furniture Webbing for Webbed Furniture." *Upholstering* (September 1945): 28–29, 60–61.
- "Carnegie Endowment for International Peace International Center, New York, N.Y." *Architectural Record* (January 1954): 121–31.
- Castillo, Greg. *Cold War on the Home Front*. Minneapolis: University of Minnesota Press, 2010.
- "CELA: Communications." *Progressive Architecture* (May 1956): 108–9.
- "Centre d'études et de recherches à Palo Alto." *Architecture d'aujourd'hui* (October 1956): 42–43.
- Clark, Robert Judson, et al. *Design in America: The Cranbrook Vision, 1925–1950*. New York: Harry N. Abrams, in association with the Detroit Institute of Arts and the Metropolitan Museum of Art, 1983.
- Cliff, Ursula. "Gallery 4: Florence Knoll." *Industrial Design* (April 1961): 66–71.
- "Come the New Fabrics." *Interiors* (March 1947): 82–83.
- "Communication, Electronics, Automation." *Progressive Architecture* (May 1956): 108–9.
- "Complexity and Contradiction." *Interior Design* (March 1980): 226–30.
- "Configurations in a Landscape." *Interiors* (March 1972): 76–91.
- Conran, Terence. *Printed Textile Design*. London: Studio Limited, 1957.
- Conway, Patricia L. "Design at CBS." *Industrial Design* (February 1966): 49–51.
- "Craftex Mills adds Watterston to Design Staff." *Upholstering* (September 1952): 164.
- Cranbrook Academy of Art Museum. *Fourth Biennial Exhibition of Textiles and Ceramics*. Exh. cat. Bloomfield Hills, Mich.: Cranbrook Academy of Art Museum, 1953.
- ———. *Marianne Strengell*. Exh. cat. Bloomfield Hills, Mich.: Cranbrook Academy of Art Museum, 1950.
- ———. *Second National Biennial Exhibition of Contemporary Textiles and Ceramics*. Bloomfield Hills, Mich.: Cranbrook Academy of Art Museum, 1949.
- *Current Biography Yearbook*. New York: H.W. Wilson Co., 1955, 334–36.
- "D&D Market Report." *Interiors* (October 1966): 160.
- *Davison's Textile Blue Book*. Ridgewood, N.J.: Davison Publishing Co., 1949.
- "Deft Remodeling Creates a Compact Sales Machine with a Billboard Front." *Architectural Forum* (June 1948): 88–91.
- "Design for New Textile Headquarters Deftly Handles Several Problems." *Architectural Record* (December 1958): 119–24.
- "Designers Cannot be Isolationists." *Upholstering* (October 1947): 32, 34.
- "Directions in Fabric and Fashion." *American Fabrics*, no. 63 (Winter/Spring 1964): 11.
- "Dorothy Liebes: California Craftsman Restates the Vocabulary of the Hand Loom in Terms of Modern Technique." *California Arts & Architecture* (February 1942): 20.
- "Dorothy Wright Liebes, First Lady of the Loom." *Interiors* (July 1947): 86–91, 134–36.
- "Down with the Overstuffed Chair." *Upholstering* (July 1948): 122.
- "Drake University: Dormitories and Dining Hall." *Progressive Architecture* (April 1955): 96–105.
- "Drum Beaters for Modern." *Life* (March 2, 1953): 72–76.
- Duckett, Margaret. "How Donald Brothers Stay Small and Influence People." *Design* 254 (June 1, 1970): 29.
- Dusenbury, Marianne Strengell. "Texture, Color and Quality." *California Arts & Architecture* (November 1942): 32–33.
- E. B. "Knoll Furniture." *Architectural Forum* (June 1948): 182, 186.
- Edwards, Leslie S. "Structure and Surface: Marianne Strengell and Woven Texture." *Modernism* 10, no. 4 (Winter 2007–8): 76–77, 84.
- Eidelberg, Martin, ed. *Design 1935–1965: What Modern Was*. Montréal: Musée des arts décoratifs de Montréal; New York: Abrams, 1991.
- "Eight Solutions to Merchandise Display: Fiberglas House." *Interiors* (October 1948): 112–17.
- "Eight Solutions to Merchandise Display: Knoll Associates Achieve Intimacy and Openness in Colorful Plan." *Interiors* (October 1948): 108–11.
- "Ein Mann will seine Umwelt mit den schönsten Farben schmücken." *Schöner Wohnen* (December 12, 1968): 162–63.
- "Emily Belding: Textile Designer." *Handweaver & Craftsman* 7, no. 1 (Winter 1955–56): 26.
- "Equipment for Living." *Arts & Architecture* (May 1945): 36–38.
- "Executive Offices for Knoll Associates." *Progressive Architecture* (October 1962): 176.
- "Fabric City." *Interiors* (June 1943): 11–14.
- "Fabrics and Papers Mix Happily with Nature in the Ossining Studio and Home of Designer Vera Neumann." *Interiors* (November 1951): 103.
- "Fabrics From Knoll . . . Swatches And All." *Interior Design* (April 1952): 19.
- "Fabrics from the New Spring Lines." *Interiors* (February 1943): 45.
- "Fabrics to the Fore in Homefurnishings." *Handweaver & Craftsman* 13, no. 3 (Summer 1962): 31.
- "Fabrics." *Arts & Architecture* (March 1948): 32–36.
- "Fabrics." *Arts & Architecture* (November 1954): 28.
- "Fabrics." *Everyday Art Quarterly*, no. 25 (1953): 10, 14–15.
- "Fall Fabric Report." *Interiors* (August 1966): 165.
- "Fall Fabrics 1950." *Interior Design* (October 1950): 60.
- "Felt but not Seen." *Interiors* (May 1949): 132–35.
- "Fiberglas House: A Depression-Born Industry Demonstrates Its Wares in a Remodeled Brownstone." *Interiors* (October 1948): 112–17.
- "Fibers and Colors Stripe Fabrics from Two Sources." *Interiors* (July 1957): 114.
- "For Office Flexibility." *Interiors* (June 1952): 140.
- "For Your Information." *Interiors* (December 1946): 14.
- "For Your Information." *Interiors* (February 1950): 142.
- Ford, James, and Katherine Morrow Ford. *Design of Modern Interiors*. New York: Architectural Publishing Co., 1942.
- "Forum of Events." *Architectural Forum* (May 1941): 76.
- "Forum of Events." *Architectural Forum* (July 1941): 56.
- "Forum of Events." *Architectural Forum* (October 1941): 106, 108.
- "Forum of Events." *Architectural Forum* (December 1941): 78.
- "Forum of Events." *Architectural Forum* (January 1945): 62.
- Foster, Norman, et al. *Walter Knoll: Design Reloaded*. Herrenberg: Neunplus 1, 2006.
- Frey, Berta. "American Handweaving—A Mid-Century Viewpoint." *Handweaver & Craftsman* 1, no. 1 (April 1950): 6.
- "From Knoll: Furniture and Fabrics for the Residential Market." *Interior Design* (October 1977): 120.
- "Furnishing the Dormitory." *Architectural Forum* (December 1951): 176–79.
- "Furnishings and Rooms in Baltimore Show." *Interiors* (December 1951): 16.
- "Furniture and Fabrics: Highlights from an Exhibition." *Everyday Art Quarterly*, no. 1 (Summer 1946): 9, 10.
- "Furniture Bid." *Business Week* (May 28, 1955): n.p.
- "Furniture Designs by Rado." *Interiors* (June 1955): 130.
- "Furniture Showroom." *Architectural Forum* (July 1949): 79–81.
- "Furniture Showrooms in New York." *Architectural Review* (December 1951): 383–87.
- Gasse, Dieter, Carl-Wolfgang Schümann, and Manfred Rusche. "*Printed by Taunus Textildruck": 30 Jahre Textildruck in Deutschland am Beispiel einer Firma*. Exh. cat. Krefeld, Germany: Deutsches Textilmuseum Krefeld, 1983.
- "Geladene Gäste." *MD Moebel Interior Design* (May 1974): 72–75.
- Ginsburg, Cora. *A Catalogue of Exquisite and Rare Works of Art Including 15th to 20th Century Costume Textiles and Needlework*. New York: Cora Ginsburg, 2003.
- ———. *A Catalogue of Exquisite and Rare Works of Art Including 17th to 20th Century Costume Textiles and Needlework*. New York: Cora Ginsburg, 2004.
- Girard, Alexander H., and W. D. Laurie Jr., with W. A. Bostick, eds. *An Exhibition for Modern Living*. Detroit: Detroit Institute of Arts, 1949.
- Goldberg, June O. "The Brief Commercial Career of Angelo Testa." MA thesis, Fashion Institute of Technology–State University of New York, 2003.

- Golden Gate International Exposition. *Decorative Arts: Official Catalog*. San Francisco: Department of Fine Arts Division of Decorative Arts, Golden Gate International Exposition, 1939.
- Gordon, Alistair. *Weekend Utopia: Modern Living in the Hamptons*. New York: Princeton Architectural Press, 2001.
- "Greater Beauty, Longer Service with Plastic Woven Fabrics." *Upholstering* (September 1948): 44–45.
- Gueft, Olga. "Florence Knoll and the Avant Garde." *Interiors* (July 1957): 59.
- Gueft, Olga. "Knoll Associates Move into the Big Time." *Interiors* (May 1951): 74–83, 152, 154, 156.
- Gueft, Olga. "Knoll au Louvre." *Interiors* (April 1972): 136–39, 160–61.
- Gueft, Olga. "Knoll without the Knolls." *Interiors* (August 1966): 15–151.
- Gueft, Olga. "Knoll—plus ça change." *Interiors* (May 1971): 122.
- Gueft, Olga. "Outpost in Dallas: Knoll Opens a Lone Star Branch." *Interiors* (June 1950): 90.
- Gueft, Olga. "Stage Setting by Gae Aulenti for the Greatest Modern Furniture Collection of Them All." *Interiors* (August 1970): 96.
- Gueft, Olga. "Swedish Carpentry Supports Swedish Textiles." *Interiors* (June 1958): 110–11.
- Gueft, Olga. "The Race to Design." *Interiors* (January 1955): 51.
- Gueft, Olga. "Three Judgments, Manufacturing the Prize Winners." *Interiors* (March 1950): 97.
- "Guide to Some Well Known Finishes and Finishing Terms." *American Fabrics*, no. 28 (Spring 1954): 80–83.
- "Hand-Screen Fabrics." *Interior Design and Decoration* (July 1949): 8.
- "Hand-Screened Moderns." *Interior Design and Decoration* (September 1949): 58.
- "Hans G. Knoll" (obituary). *Architectural Forum* (November 1955): 29.
- "Hans G. Knoll" (obituary). *Art News* (November 1955): 68.
- Harris, Mary Emma. *The Arts at Black Mountain College*. Cambridge, Mass.: MIT Press, 1987.
- "Havana Crash Kills Modern Furniture Pioneer" (obituary). *Interiors* (November 1955): 134, 136.
- Helfrich, Kurt G.F., and William Whitaker, eds. *Crafting a Modern World: The Architecture and Design of Antonin and Noémi Raymond*. New York: Princeton Architectural Press, 2006.
- Hession, Jane King, Rip Rapson, and Bruce N. Wright. *Ralph Rapson: Sixty Years of Modern Design*. Afton, Minn.: Afton Historical Society Press, 1999.
- Hiesinger, Kathryn B., and George H. Marcus, eds. *Design Since 1945*. Philadelphia: Philadelphia Museum of Art, 1983.
- "High on a Mountain." *Interior Design and Decoration* (September 1951): 94.
- Hogdal, Lis, ed. *Bruno Mathsson: Architect and Designer*. Malmö: Bökforlaget; New York: Bard Graduate Center for Studies in the Decorative Arts, Design, and Culture; London: Yale University Press, 2006.
- "Home/Contract Furnishing." *Industrial Design* (December 1969): 57.
- "How Livable is a Modern House?" *Life* (October 18, 1948): 105–8.
- "How One Space Became Four: Showroom and Offices for Scarves by Vera." *Architectural Record* 113 (February 1953): 159–64.
- "ID's 1969 Design Review." *Interiors* (January 1970): 106–9.
- "Insurance Sets a Pattern." *Architectural Forum* (September 1957): 112–27.
- "Integrated Fabrics." *Art News* (May 1947): 60.
- "Interior Design of C.B.S. Building, 51W52, New York." *Architect and Builder* 16 (July 1966): 12, 13.
- "Interiors for Interiors, or, A Stitch in Time." *Interiors* (September 1942): 20–23.
- "Interiors on the Horizontal in a Breuer House." *Interiors* (January 1957): 118.
- "Interiors Selection of 1942 Furniture." *Interiors* (February 1942): 38, 67.
- "International Textile Exhibition." *Upholstering* (April 1944): 17.
- Jackson, Lesley. *Twentieth-Century Pattern Design: Textile & Wallpaper Pioneers*. New York: Princeton Architectural Press, 2002.
- Kaihatsu, Martha, ed. Knoll Index of Contemporary Design. New York: Knoll Associates: 1954.
- Kardon, Janet, ed. *Craft in the Machine Age: The History of Twentieth-Century American Craft 1920–1945*. New York: Harry N. Abrams, with the American Craft Museum, 1995.
- Kassler, Elizabeth B. [Elizabeth Mock]. *If You Want to Build a House*. New York: Museum of Modern Art, 1946.
- Kirkham, Pat, ed. *Women Designers in the USA, 1900–2000: Diversity and Difference*. New York and New Haven: Bard Graduate Center and Yale University Press, 2000.
- "Knoll Associates Inc. Opens New Showroom in New York." *Upholstering* (June 1951): 86–87, 148.
- "Knoll Associates Introduce New Line of Office Planned Furniture." *Upholstering* (August 1952): 112–13.
- "Knoll Associates Introduces Textiles." *Upholstering* (April 1947): 92.
- "Knoll Associates, Bound and Covered." *Interiors* (December 1950): 126–27.
- "Knoll Associates Introduces Textiles." *Upholstering* (April 1947): 50, 92, 94.
- *Knoll Index of Contemporary Design*. New York: Knoll Associates, 1950.
- "Knoll International Makes a Residential Statement." *Residential Interiors* (July/August 1977): 20, 31.
- "Knoll Makes News." *Interiors* (September 1969): 158.
- "Knoll Textiles: A Flexible Element in Interiors." *Handweaver & Craftsman* 9, no. 3 (Summer 1958): 12–15.
- "Knoll Webbings By-the-yard." *Interiors* (October 1949): 142.
- "Knoll, Chicago: New Tune in the Same Key." *Interiors* (February 1954): 46–51.
- Knoll, Hans. "Reconversion Responsibility." *Upholstering* (July 1945): 28–30, 57.
- "Knoll's 'Leisure Collection.'" *Interiors* (March 1966): 32.
- "Knoll's Kaleidoscopic Knock-Down." *Interiors* (December 1952): 112–15, 175.
- "Knoll's Newest Showroom." *Interiors* (March 1961): 138–39.
- L.W. "Breuer's Beautiful Plan for the Neumanns." *Interiors* (June 1956): 108–11.
- L.W. "Furniture Flashes." *Interiors* (January 1955): 90–91.
- ———. "Furniture Report." *Interiors* (September 1955): 129.
- ———. "Knoll's Spare Parallel Bar System." *Interiors* (January 1956): 106–7.
- ———. "New Furniture: Part I of our Semi-Annual Survey." *Interiors* (July 1957): 98–99.
- ———. "The Complete Corporation on a 6' Module, Proven by Mockups." *Interiors* (January 1958): 76–85.
- "La France Fabric Design Contest." *Upholstering* (August 1947): 18–19.
- Larrabee, Eric, and Massimo Vignelli. *Knoll Design*. New York: Harry N. Abrams, 1981.
- Larsen, Jack Lenor, and Jeanne Weeks. *Fabrics for Interiors: A Guide for Architects, Designers, and Consumers*. New York: Van Nostrand Reinhold, 1975.
- Larsen, Jack Lenor. *A Weaver's Memoir*. New York: Harry N. Abrams, 1998.
- Le Corbusier. *Vers une architecture*. Paris: G. Crésetcie, 1924; trans. as *Towards a New Architecture*. New York: Payson and Clarke; London: Rodker, 1927.
- "Living Up-to-Date." *Arts & Architecture* (December 1951): 20–21.
- Lubell, Cecil. "Vera: Textile Designer for a Sophisticated Mass Market." *American Fabrics* 63 (Winter/Spring 1964): 87.
- Lustig, Alvin. "Modern Printed Fabrics." *American Fabrics* 20 (Winter 1951–52): 61–62, 72.
- Lutz, Brian. *Knoll: A Modernist Universe*. New York: Rizzoli, 2010.
- "Madison Room." *Architectural Record* (July 1947): 112–15.
- Makovsky, Paul. "Florence Knoll Bassett: The Conversation." *Metropolis* (July 2001): 97.
- "Marianne Strengell Writes about Designing Tomorrow's Fabrics." *Upholstering* (March 1947): 14.
- "Market Spotlight: For Office Efficiency." *Interior Design* (November 1971): 78.
- "Market Spotlight: Ten by Knoll." *Interior Design* (June 1957): 130.
- "Market: From Knoll Furniture and Fabrics for the Residential Market." *Interior Design* (October 1977): 120.
- "Market: Knoll is a Fabric House." *Interiors* (February 1974): 44.
- Marter, Joan, et al., ed. *Design in America: The Cranbrook Vision 1925–1950*. New York: Harry N. Abrams, 1983.
- Martinez, Katharine A., and Kenneth L. Ames, eds. *The Material Culture of Gender, the Gender of Material Culture*. Winterthur, Del.: Henry Francis du Pont Winterthur Museum, 1997.
- Mattson. Helena, and Sven-Olov Wallenstein, eds. *Swedish Modernism*. London: Black Dog, 2010.
- McCausland, Elizabeth. "Gallery of Everyday Art." *Arts & Architecture* (March 1946): 39.
- McFadden, David Revere, et al. *Jack Lenor Larsen: Creator and Collector*. London and New York: Merrell Publishers Limited, 2004.
- McQuade, Walter. "The Booming Office Planners." *Architectural Forum* (January 1962): 83.
- "Merchandise Cues." *Interiors* (August 1949): 134.
- "Merchandise Cues: Knoll's Casement Collection." *Interiors* (February 1964): 120.
- Miernyk, William H. "A Projection of Textile Production in the United States to 1970." Typescript, 1957, American Textile History Museum Library, Lowell, Mass.
- Miller, Frances. *Tanty: Encounters with the Past*. Sag Harbor, N.Y.: Sandbox Press, 1979.
- ———. *More About Tanty*. Sag Harbor, N.Y.: Sandbox Press, 1980.
- ———. *Tanty: The Daring Decades*. Sag Harbor, N.Y.: Sandbox Press, 1981.
- "Model of Office Planning." *Progressive Architecture* (March 1962): 151–57.
- "Modern Cherry Furniture Danish Designed." *Art News* 41 (April 1942): 35.
- "Modern Furniture Exhibition." *Interiors* (October 1951): 12.
- "Modern Furniture." *California Arts & Architecture* (January 1942): 21–23.
- Moholy-Nagy, László. "New Trends in Furniture." *Upholstering* (March 1943): 8–10, 28.
- Moholy-Nagy, Laszlo. *Vision in Motion*, 8th ed. Chicago: Paul Theobold and Company, 1969.
- Morse, John D. "The Story of Knoll Associates." *American Artist* (September 1951): 46–50.
- "Moss Rose Rewards Design Students." *Upholstering* (June 1947): 80–81, 102.
- Museum of Contemporary Crafts. *Dorothy Liebes: Retrospective Exhibition*. New York: Museum of Contemporary Crafts of the American Crafts Council, 1970.
- Museum of Modern Art. *Studies in Modern Art 4: The Museum of Modern Art at Mid-Century at Home and Abroad*. New York: Museum of Modern Art and Harry N. Abrams, 1994.
- ———. *Textiles USA*. New York: Museum of Modern Art, 1956.
- Musicant, Marlyn R. "Maria Kipp: Autobiography of a Hand Weaver." *Studies in the Decorative Arts* 8, no. 1 (Fall/Winter 2000–2001): 92–107.
- "Nelson and Eames Design New Pieces for Herman Miller." *Upholstering* (February 1951): 132.
- Nelson, George. *Display*. New York: Whitney Publications, Inc., 1953.
- Nelson, George, and Henry Wright. *Tomorrow's House: How to Plan Your Post-War Home Now*. New York: Simon and Schuster, 1945.
- "New Chairs." *Life* (May 20, 1946): 47.
- "New Color Philosophy at Knoll." *Interiors* (May 1959): 144.
- "New Furniture." *Arts & Architecture* (July 1948): 38–39.
- "New Furniture." *Life* (November 15, 1948): 115.
- "New Knoll Showroom: A Study in Space and Texture." *Interior Design and Decoration* (April 1951): 30.
- "New Nylons for Boris Kroll." *Interior Design* (August 1957): 116, 117.
- "New Patterns Feature in Plastic Webbing." *Upholstering* (January 1947): 50, 60, 74.
- "New Showroom for Knoll Associates, Inc." *Arts & Architecture* (November 1960): 14–15.
- "News: Commissions." *Interiors* (December 1967): 18.
- "News: Knoll International Bought by General Felt." *Interior Design* (October 1977): 27.
- "Newsreel." *Interiors* (February 1942): 56.
- "Newsreel." *Interiors* (June 1943): 62–63.
- "Newsreel." *Interiors* (July 1948): 124.
- "'Non-Objectionable' Modern." *Upholstering* (September 1947): 60.
- Noyes, Eliot F. *Organic Design in Home Furnishings*. New York: Museum of Modern Art, 1941.
- "Office Building—North American Life and Casualty Company Makes a Capital Investment in Minneapolis." *Architectural Forum* (January 1949): 75–81.
- "Office of Merit: CBS Offices by the Same Designer." *Architectural Forum* (January 1955): 134–39.
- "Offices on Both Coasts by Knoll." *Interiors* (January 1955): 60–63.
- Ólafsdóttir, Ásdís. *Le mobilier d'Alvar Aalto dans l'espace et dans le temps: la diffusion internationale du design 1920–1940*. Paris: Publications de la Sorbonne, 1998.
- Olivarez, Jennifer Komar. "Ralph Rapson and

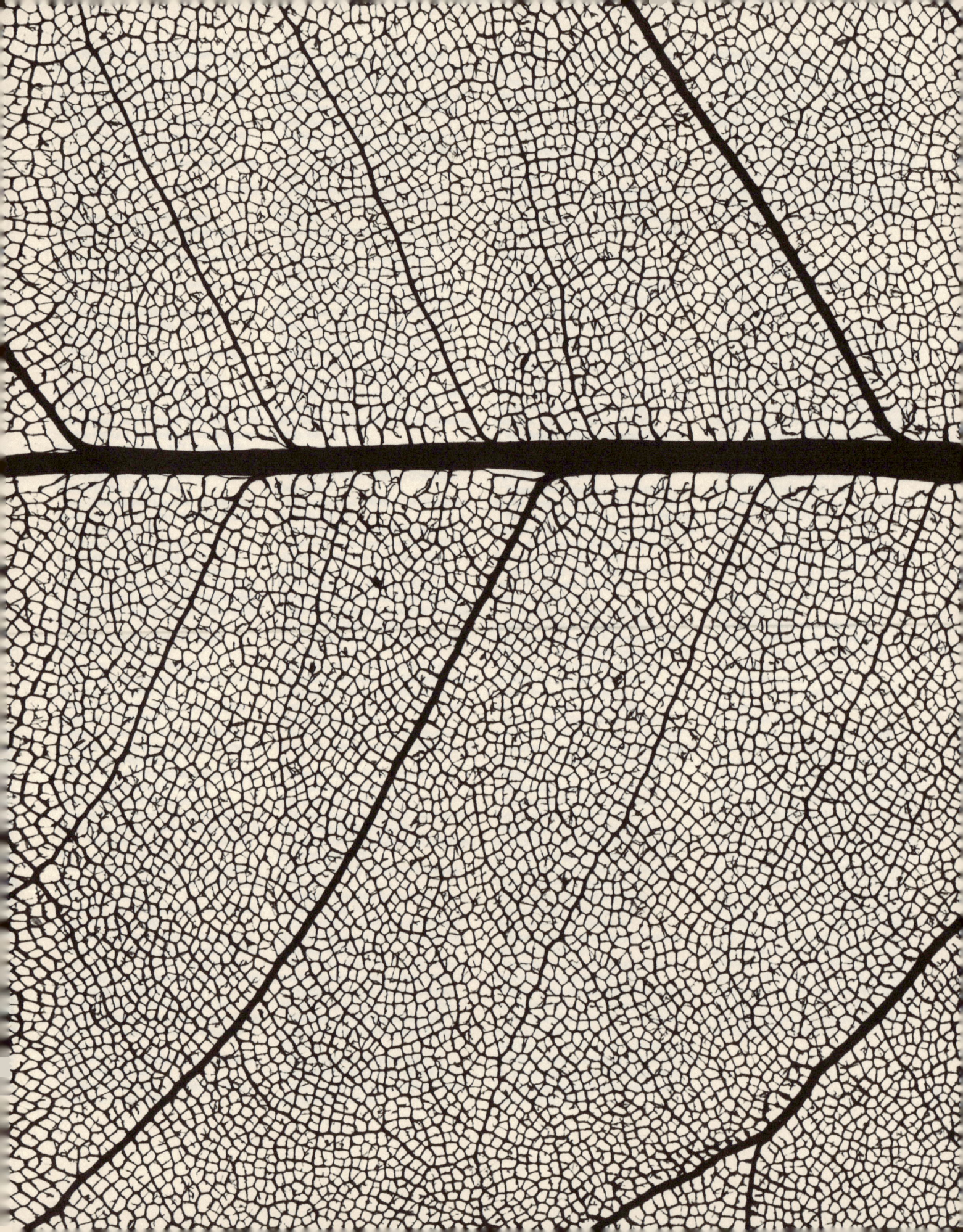